Hitler's Forgotten Ally

Hitler's Forgotten Ally

Ion Antonescu and His Regime, Romania 1940–44

Dennis Deletant

Professor of Romanian Studies, University College, London

First published 2006 by
PALGRAVE MACMILLAN
Houndmills, Basingstoke, Hampshire RG21 6XS and
175 Fifth Avenue, New York, N.Y. 10010
Companies and representatives throughout the world

PALGRAVE MACMILLAN is the global academic imprint of the Palgrave Macmillan division of St. Martin's Press, LLC and of Palgrave Macmillan Ltd. Macmillan® is a registered trademark in the United States, United Kingdom and other countries. Palgrave is a registered trademark in the European Union and other countries.

ISBN-13: 978–1–4039–9341–0 hardback
ISBN-10: 1–4039–9341–6 hardback

This book is printed on paper suitable for recycling and made from fully managed and sustained forest sources.

A catalogue record for this book is available from the British Library.

Library of Congress Cataloging-in-Publication Data
Deletant, Dennis, 1946–
    Hitler's forgotten ally : Ion Antonescu and his regime, Romania 1940–44 / Dennis Deletant.
        p.   cm.
    Includes bibliographical references and index.
    ISBN 1–4039–9341–6
    1. Antonescu, Ion, 1882–1946.   2. Romania—Politics and government—1914–1944.   3. World War, 1939–1945—Romania.   4. Romania—Foreign relations—Germany.   5. Germany—Foreign relations—Romania.   6. Heads of state—Romania—Biography.   7. Marshals—Romania—Biography.   I. Title.
    DR262.A5D45 2006
    949.8′02092—dc22
        [B]   2005056375

7   6   5   4   3   2   1
12 11 10 09 08 07 06

Printed and bound in Great Britain by
Antony Rowe Ltd, Chippenham and Eastbourne

Contents

Acknowledgements

Several institutions and persons have helped me to make this book what it is. Among the former, my greatest debt is to the Leverhulme Trust in the United Kingdom which awarded me a senior research fellowship, thereby allowing my college, University College, London, to release me from my teaching and administrative duties; and to the Center for Advanced Holocaust Studies at the United States Holocaust Memorial Museum in Washington, DC which granted me a William Rosenzweig Family Fellowship for the academic year 2000–1. I am especially grateful to Dr Paul Shapiro, Director of the Center, and to Dr Radu Ioanid, Head of the International Archival Programs Division, who both gave me warm encouragement in my research and expert navigation around the unique Romanian microfilm collection of the Center. That collection lies at the heart of this book.

In Washington, DC I was also fortunate to receive precious insights into the Antonescu era from my friends Mircea Răceanu and Dr Ernest Latham. Ernest has been a generous host during my visits to Washington, as has been Ruth Sulynn Taylor. To both go my heartfelt thanks.

In Romania Claudiu Secaşiu of the Council for the Study of the *Securitate* Archives (CNSAS) facilitated access to the Antonescu files while they were in the temporary custody of that body. Dr Şerban Papacostea, Professor Ioan Chiper and the library staff of the 'Nicolae Iorga' Institute of History helped me to identity and access secondary Romanian literature and relevant journal publications. I have drawn enormous benefit from the discussion of my research with Dr Papacostea and Professor Andrei Pippidi. Lya Benjamin and General Mihai Ionescu were generous with their time and their critical observations of existing scholarship – doubtless my own study will attract their incisive attention. Marius Oprea, Armand Goşu, Stejărel Olaru and Dragoş Petrescu of the Institute for Recent History were valuable sparring partners in analysing the Antonescu regime and its immediate aftermath.

My friends at the Babeş-Bolyai University in Cluj-Napoca created the conditions, both cerebral and culinary, in which I could reflect at length on the results of my work in the archives. Professor George Cipăianu was my anchor in Cluj, extending a warm welcome in his home and providing me with countless opportunities to review the progress of my study with him and his colleagues Dr Virgiliu Ţirău, Dr Liviu Ţârău, Ottmar Traşca, Ioan Ciupea, Dr Marius Bucur, Professor Gheorghe Mândrescu, Ştefan Matei, and Dr Toader Nicoară.

I owe my colleagues in the Department of East European Languages and Culture of SSEES, UCL, special thanks for taking over my share of administrative duties during my research leave, especially Dr Alex Drace-Francis who covered my teaching commitments, and Dr Rebecca Haynes who smoothed my path in dealing with Antonescu's uneasy alliance with the Iron Guard. My greatest debt is to Dr Maurice Pearton. Maurice read the manuscript of the book and gave it its final shape. His knowledge and understanding of twentieth-century economic and political history saved me from a number of critical errors. I record here with affection my gratitude for his unstinting assistance and guidance throughout the entire course of this project.

Abbreviations of Primary Sources

ANIC	Arhivele Naţionale Istorice Centrale (The Central Historical National Archives (formerly the State Archives) Bucharest)
ASRI	Archive of the Romanian Information Service [the Security Service]
CNSAS	Consiliul National pentru Studierea Arhivelor fostei Securităţi (National Council for the Study of the Archives of the former *Securitate*)
DGFP	*Documents on German Foreign Policy*, Series D: 1937–45, 14 vols, Washington, DC, London and Arlington, Virginia, 1949–76
MAE	Arhiva Ministerului Afacerilor Externe (Archive of the Ministry for Foreign Affairs, Bucharest)
MAN	Arhiva Ministerului Apărării Naţionale (Archive of the Ministry of National Defence, Piteşti)
PRO	formerly the Public Record Office, now the National Archives, London
USHMM	Archives of the United States Holocaust Memorial Museum

x

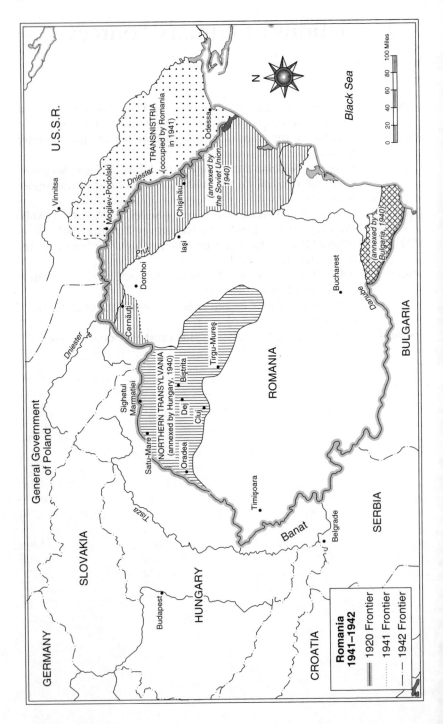

Introduction

Ion Antonescu was Romania's ruler from 6 September 1940 to 23 August 1944, the period of Romania's alliance with Nazi Germany and the consequent invasion of the Soviet Union. Romania retained her sovereignty throughout the period of the alliance. Respect for Romanian sovereignty was based on the identical interests which bound Hitler and Antonescu, and on the Führer's confidence in, and admiration for, the Romanian leader.[1] Both had seen service in the First World War, albeit on opposing sides, and the Führer respected Antonescu's experience as a military strategist. He also admired his qualities of leadership as Romania's ruler and his dedication to the Axis. Antonescu had, of course, his own country's interests uppermost in his mind, but in following Hitler, he served the Nazi cause. He was aware of the implications of the 'Final Solution' for the Jews in Nazi-occupied Europe, as his meeting with Hitler at Castle Klessheim in Salzburg on 13 April 1943 shows,[2] and made his own particular contribution to the solution of the 'Jewish problem' by deporting Jews from Bessarabia and Bukovina to Transnistria. Understanding of Antonescu's role and the policies of Romania under his direction has been impeded in English-speaking accounts by the lack of any systematic biography – the main available account stops at 1941. This book is designed to fill that gap. Antonescu, however, is not simply an interesting figure for historical enquiry. His ideas and policies are virulently contested topics in contemporary Romanian politics. Hence this account, in addition to establishing the details of his rule, also disentangles the various elements in the subsequent debate and the political aims which inspire it.

In the simple dichotomies of wartime and postwar evaluation, Antonescu counts as 'Fascist'. His was an authoritarian regime, which adopted some, but by no means all, of the trappings of Hitler's Germany and Mussolini's Italy. He had led a 'Fascist' government – a judgement which automatically assimilates the Iron Guard to the dominant parties in Germany and Italy. Above all, he had been an ally of those two states. Only in the 1960s did inquiry begin to discriminate between varieties of Fascism and raise questions hitherto ignored or dismissed as incompatible with the prevalent orthodoxy. But it was not until the mid-1970s that the complexity and inconsistency of his character was hinted at in Romania itself, and in the 1980s, and then outside Romania, that a discussion of Antonescu's departures from the dogmatic norm was initiated. These two approaches do more to explain his behaviour than the preceding orthodoxy.

For this reason, analysis has to begin by recognizing that Antonescu headed the third largest Axis army in the European war: 585,000 Romanian troops participated in the attack on the Soviet Union in June–October 1941;[3] that under his rule Romania contributed to the German war effort with oil and other raw materials, above all that he enjoyed Hitler's respect – all of which places Romania on a par with Italy as a principal ally of Germany and not in the category of minor Axis satellite. Antonescu was emphatically a complex and inconsistent figure. While he *inherited* the Axis alignment, this is not to say that he saw an alternative to it, and bore no responsibility for the internal political chaos he was called on to manage. This is the major paradox of his regime. There were others, however. He was a war criminal who sent tens of thousands of Jews to their death in Transnistria, and yet he refused to send other Romanian Jews to the death camps in Poland. He was an anti-Semite and yet, despite the deportations to Transnistria, more Jews survived under his rule than in any other country within Axis Europe. While up to 300,000 Jews were victims of Antonescu's policies, some 375,000 Jews are estimated to have survived, principally in Wallachia, Moldavia and southern Transylvania.[4] For five months he led a Fascist-style government, yet in January 1941 he removed that government after three days of street fighting and installed a military dictatorship. These inconsistencies were known, but could not be fully explored until the downfall of Communism in Romania opened the archives.

Without an appreciation of Romania's predicament in 1940, caught as it was between Hitler's Germany and Stalin's Russia, a realistic evaluation of Antonescu's foreign policy is impossible. Instead, Romania is neatly pigeonholed in the category of Axis states which attacked the Allies – in Antonescu's case, the Soviet Union – in order to expand territorially. In consequence of the Molotov–Ribbentrop Pact, the Soviet Union joined Germany in the invasion and partition of Poland, attacked Finland, entered the Baltic States, and took Bessarabia and northern Bukovina from Romania. These actions by Stalin conspired, in conjunction with those of Hitler, to destroy the interwar European order, replacing it with a new order in Central and Eastern Europe, one subject not to international deliberation and ratification, but to the interests Germany and the Soviet Union considered they had the right to claim and to impose.[5]

Fear of the Soviet Union drove Romania into alliance with Nazi Germany. 'Nothing could put Romania on Germany's side', remarked a member of the Romanian Foreign Ministry to the British Minister Sir Reginald Hoare in

March 1940, 'except the conviction that only Germany could keep the Soviets out of Romania'.[6] That conviction was quick to form after the collapse of France, the Soviet seizure of Bessarabia and northern Bukovina at the end of June 1940, and the loss of northern Transylvania to Hungary under the Vienna Award in late August 1940. One third of Romania's area was ceded in 1940 and with it Romania's population shrank from 19.9 million to 13.3 million.[7] The loss of the three territories led King Carol to accept Hitler's frontier guarantee, one he gave only after Carol's agreement to the Vienna Award. The same pragmatic considerations shaped the policy of Antonescu. Although Romania lost northern Transylvania at Germany's hands under the Award, it was only with German support that Antonescu could defend the country's territorial integrity and regain Bessarabia and northern Bukovina from the Soviet Union.[8]

The Soviet threat to Romania was catalogued in the Romanian government's reply to the British ultimatum of 29 November 1941.[9] Mention of it was suppressed during the period of Communist rule because of Soviet sensibilities and actions. Romanian and Western scholars were denied access to a significant part of the papers of Ion Antonescu, for they were removed from the Romanian archives by the Soviet authorities between 1944 and 1945 and never returned.[10] Copies of some of the files from Antonescu's office remained in Romania throughout the postwar period, but the Romanian authorities consistently denied access to scholars before 1989.[11] As a result the Soviet authorities were in a position to dictate an image of the Antonescu regime, one that was faithfully presented by Soviet historiography as 'criminal'.[12] It is not surprising that a class analysis of politics combined with censorship should lead one Soviet historian, I. Levitsky, to argue in an article published in 1985 that the reason behind Antonescu's participation in *Operation Barbarossa* was the result of 'the chauvinism of the Romanian ruling class'.[13] This is not to deny, of course, that the Antonescu regime was anti-Soviet.

Levitsky's condemnation of the Antonescu regime as 'criminal' echoed the charges levelled against the Marshal by the Soviet authorities at the end of the war. In Britain and the United States there was widespread sympathy for the Soviet Union, which had made the greatest land contribution to Hitler's defeat. This was reflected in the British press. Unfavourable comment in some British newspapers about Soviet behaviour in the countries it occupied at the close of the war was discouraged until the advent of the Cold War. Romania's military effort on the Allied side after the *coup* of 23 August 1944 went unnoticed. In a dispatch for *The Sunday Times* published on 7 January 1945 a special correspondent wrote:

> It is not generally recognized that of the nations fighting Germany today in Europe, Romania comes fourth in terms of mobilised men. She has 14 divisions fighting with the Russian armies, whereas France, for instance, has only seven in the field.[14]

This lack of recognition was attributable to the fact that until King Michael's *coup* against Antonescu, Romania had fought as an ally of Germany against the Soviet Union. In some quarters of the British Foreign Office the *coup* was seen as military opportunism and political expediency – joining the Allied side on the back of the Red Army in order to forestall Soviet occupation and to preserve the country's territorial integrity.[15] Had not the *coup* come only when the Red Army was on Romanian soil? some officials asked. In Britain especially at the end of the war, a war in which Britain had been the longest serving and, for almost two years, the sole combatant against Germany, there was little time for those who had been Hitler's associates. The Iron Curtain served to screen Antonescu and Romania's wartime experience from the consciousness of the Western public and the eyes of Western historians.

In Romania, political considerations after 1945 made the subject of Romania's alliance with Germany taboo. The Communist regime barred access to documents covering the years 1941–44. At the same time, the Romanian dead on the Eastern Front were denied official recognition and commemoration; the prospect of a pro-Soviet regime acknowledging casualties resulting from an attack on the Soviet Union – the Romanian soldiers who died in the Russian campaign between 1941 and 1944 – proved too embarrassing. The Military Museum in Bucharest underlined the point. Its exhibits defined the Romanian record in the Second World War by the years 1944–45. There was no mention of Romania's involvement in the German attack on the Soviet Union in 1941, and no memorabilia from the campaign.

The case of Antonescu is a clear example of the dictum that 'the past is more powerful than the present'. In twentieth-century Romanian history there is no figure more controversial. For most Western scholars, the Marshal is a war criminal, held responsible for the deaths of between 250,000 and 290,000 Jews and between 10,000 and 20,000 Romas. At the same time, his role in *saving* up to 375,000 Romanian Jews from deportation to the death camps in Poland is acknowledged.[16] For many Romanians, Antonescu is a national hero, a brave patriot who preserved Romania as a sovereign state during the war. In defending this sovereignty, Antonescu also saved many of Romania's Jews. Admirers of Antonescu prefer to overlook, or in some cases are ignorant of, Antonescu's excesses towards the Jews and Romas.[17] As Vladimir Tismăneanu has argued, a 'pseudo-sacred' aura surrounds him and calls to dispel it are seen by many in Romania as an effort to diminish their national dignity, to offend their sense of honour and blacken their past. 'In post-Communist societies, fantasies of persecution offer immense gratification to large strata of frustrated individuals.'[18] The political ground on which the Romanian view of Antonescu is advanced is nationalism, in the version vigorously promoted by Communist propaganda under Nicolae Ceauşescu. His regime added to the time-honoured symbols of the Romanian nation the figure of Ion Antonescu who was cultivated because of his anti-Soviet policy. In the eyes of the Romanian public Antonescu soon became the symbol of the struggle against Communism and the Soviet Union, as well as of the general aspiration for the recovery by Romania of Bessarabia and northern Bukovina.

Studies of Antonescu's rule in English have focused on his treatment of the Jews, and the present work draws on fresh material on the subject which I was able to consult during my tenure of a Leverhulme Research Award and a Rosenzweig Family Fellowship from the Center for Advanced Holocaust Studies of the United States Holocaust Memorial Museum.[19] Romania's military endeavour under Antonescu in the war against the Soviet Union has been comprehensively examined by Mark Axworthy.[20] Using Romanian sources, he offered a new perspective on the war against the Soviet Union, eschewing the sometimes one-sided German memoir accounts which seek to ascribe to the Romanians sole blame for defeat, and correcting Soviet accounts which often fail to distinguish Romanian actions from German ones. Less attention has been given to the dynamics of Antonescu's military dictatorship, the ambivalences and ambiguities in the nature of his regime, his tolerance of opposition, his attempts to secure satisfactory – in his judgement – armistice terms, and to his trial and execution in 1946. This book is an attempt to clarify these questions. In doing so, I seek to contribute to the historical evaluation of Antonescu. My purpose is not to engage directly in the politics of his memory, but inside Romania and also elsewhere any assessment of Antonescu is liable to be treated as a political issue. For this reason, some discussion of the politics of Antonescu's memory cannot be avoided.[21]

After the overthrow of Romania's Communist dictator, Nicolae Ceauşescu, in December 1989 the doors were opened to the archives and a deluge of books appeared in Romanian on Antonescu. It was understandable that, denied access to their past by the Communist regime, the postwar generations in Romania should want to see restored to history the figures they were led to regard as heroes, but this rehabilitation brought with it a danger of over-compensation in the other direction by creating myths which in turn deny the truth. Most of the authors of these works pass over the shameful aspects of his wartime record and create a myth, in his case of 'unjust treatment'. This myth was generated by his trial and conviction as a war criminal, and his execution on 1 June 1946. For many Romanians the fairness of the trial was compromised by its conduct by Communist authorities, and Antonescu's dignity before the firing squad – magnified by the erroneous belief that he himself gave the order to shoot – has earned him respect and sympathy.

Antonescu is seen as personifying, through his personal drama, the injustice endured by an entire nation.[22] The myth is enhanced by a reluctance on the part of many Romanians to recognize that there was a Holocaust of the Jews in parts of Romania and that Antonescu was responsible for it. The debate over Antonescu's role in the deaths of more than 250,000 Jews and between

10,000 and 20,000 Romas, and the issue of his rehabilitation, has become one of the most sensitive issues on the current political agenda in Romania. Corneliu Vadim Tudor, the leader of the Greater Romania Party, is a self-declared admirer of Antonescu and has been a fervent advocate of his rehabilitation.[23] The drive to rehabilitate Antonescu has brought together various interests of a political nature.[24] Tudor is seconded by anti-Communists, who regard anyone who was an opponent of Communism as *per se* worthy of admiration, irrespective of Antonescu's anti-democratic credentials, and by anti-monarchists, who exploit sympathy for Antonescu as a sentiment with which to condemn King Michael who, having ordered the Marshal's arrest on 23 August 1944 and his handover to the Soviets, is presented as the moral perpetrator of Antonescu's conviction and execution. However, Vadim Tudor appeared to have undergone a Damascene conversion in 2004, when he acknowledged the crimes perpetrated against the Jews by Romania's wartime regime.[25]

The degree of acceptance of Antonescu as a war criminal by Romanian historians, politicians and the public is the yardstick by which the country's willingness to face up to its record as an ally of Nazi Germany can be measured. On 22 October 2003, the President of Romania, Ion Iliescu, in response to international disquiet about tendentious official statements from Bucharest minimalizing or even, in some cases, denying Romanian responsibility for the persecution, deportation and physical destruction of Romanian Jews and other Jews under Romanian control between 1940 and 1944, and for the persecution and deportation of Romas between 1942 and 1944, grasped this particular nettle and announced the formation of the International Commission on the Holocaust in Romania, chaired by the Nobel laureate Elie Wiesel, and composed of recognized historians and public figures from France, Germany, Israel, Romania and the United States. In making his announcement, Iliescu committed the Romanian state for the first time to confronting its wartime record of the treatment of Jews and in the same breath provided public acknowledgement of a fact that had been evident since the overthrow of Communism in Romania – namely that the historical evaluation of Antonescu was not simply a matter for historians, but had become a political issue, both within and outside Romania.

The Commission issued its report in the middle of November 2004. Its executive summary was blunt:

> Of all Nazi Germany's allies Romania bears the responsibility for the greatest contribution to the extermination of the Jews, apart from Germany itself. The murders carried out at Iaşi, Odessa, Bogdanovka, Domanevka and Pecioara are amongst the most hideous crimes committed against the Jews during the Holocaust. Romania carried out genocide against the Jews. The survival of some Jews in certain parts of the country does not change this reality.[26]

The Commission concluded:

> The Romanian authorities bear the principal responsibility both for the planning as well as the implementation of the Holocaust. This includes the deportation and systematic extermination in Transnistria of the majority of Jews in Bessarabia and Bukovina, as well as of Jews in other parts of Romania; the mass murder of Romanian and local Jews in Transnistria; the mass executions of Jews during the pogrom in Iaşi; the discrimination and systematic degradation of all Romanian Jews during the Antonescu regime – including the confiscation of belongings, dismissal from employment, forced evacuation from rural areas and concentration in regional capitals and camps, and the wholesale use of Jewish males as forced labour under the same regime. The Jews were subject to degradation simply because they were Jews, they lost the protection of the state and became its victims. Part of the Roma population in Romania was similarly subjected to deportation and death in Transnistria.[27]

President Iliescu publicly endorsed the conclusions, but hardly had he done so than, on the expiry of his mandate in December, he decorated, among others, Tudor and Gheorghe Buzatu, an Antonescu apologist, historian and senior member of Tudor's Greater Romania Party, with the order of 'The Star of Romania'. The credit which Iliescu had gained from his endorsement of the Commission's report disappeared overnight. On 14 December, Wiesel returned his own medal with 'The Star of Romania' which Iliescu had conferred upon him in July 2002, expressing his

> sadness and disappointment that the man who set up the International Commission for the Study of the Holocaust in Romania had chosen to decorate two individuals whose hate-laden beliefs contradict the noble aims of the Commission. Corneliu Vadim Tudor and Gheorghe Buzatu are two known anti-Semites who deny the existence of the Holocaust.... I hope that you will understand that I cannot belong to any group of which Vadim Tudor is a member. It is therefore my decision to give up 'The Star of Romania' and to no longer wear the decoration.[28]

Treated as such, the issue of Antonescu and the Holocaust is one that cannot be resolved by scholarship. There are even those who do not want the issue resolved because a lack of resolution suits their purpose. Principal among the latter are nationalists who rely – in Arthur J. Schlesinger Jr.'s phrase – on 'exculpatory history'. Corruption of the truth and the distortion of the realities of the past are features of this history. Unacknowledged assumptions about ways of treating the past still rule and it would be rash to claim that attitudes have changed to the point where the link between historical enquiry and preferred political outcomes has been broken.

1

The Prelude to Antonescu's War

Romania's alliance with Germany between 1940 and 1944 was generated by the threat posed by the Soviet Union to Romania's territorial integrity, and by the disintegration of the European order established after the First World War. The war gave Romania a chance to gain the predominantly Romanian-populated province of Transylvania, then under Hungarian rule, and the region of Bukovina,[1] which Austria had acquired in 1775. The Allied Powers offered both territories to Romania in return for her entry into the war on the side of the Entente. This she did in August 1916, and it says much about the strength of character of King Ferdinand that he signed a declaration of war against his country of birth. Romania was duly rewarded at the Paris Peace Conference with Transylvania and Bukovina, despite her defection from the war in April 1918, when she was forced to sign a peace treaty with Germany. Two months earlier, Romanian troops, profiting from the disintegration of the Russian army in the wake of the Bolshevik revolution, had occupied the province of Bessarabia, which had been annexed by Russia in 1812. The union of Bessarabia with Romania, proclaimed by representatives of the Romanian majority in the province on 27 March 1918, was confirmed by the Paris Peace Treaties. It was not, however, accepted by the Soviet Union.

The enlarged Romanian state, *România Mare* (Great Romania), encompassed virtually all ethnic Romanians. It also included significant Slav, German, Hungarian and Bulgarian minorities. By the same token, Romania's leaders linked the integrity of her new borders to the maintenance of, and respect for, the new international order consecrated in the Peace Settlement. Defence of the European status quo thus became the cornerstone of interwar foreign policy pursued by all Romanian governments until the Munich Agreement of 1938. There were three bases to this policy: alliance with the other post-1919 states which shared a common interest with Romania in opposing frontier revision; collaboration with France, the strongest Western continental military power; and support for and participation in the League of Nations, which guaranteed the territorial integrity of its members.

These three features of Romanian foreign policy were harmonized by Nicolae Titulescu. In doing so he demonstrated that a small country's interests can be defended with accomplished diplomacy just as effectively as with military power. On being appointed Foreign Minister in October 1932, Titulescu's experience of, and faith in, the League guided his hand in his conduct of Romanian policy – he had been elected president of the 11th Ordinary Session of the League on 10 September 1930 and re-elected in 1931. Convinced that his country's security depended on maintaining international order, he sought to consolidate the Little Entente, formed in 1921 by Romania with Czechoslovakia and Yugoslavia as a deterrent against Hungarian revisionism. 'Revisionism means war' became a catchphrase of Titulescu, uttered with increasing frequency after the rise of Hitler, who advocated revision of the Versailles treaties. Hitler's challenge to the status quo encouraged Hungary to press her claims to Transylvania, and it was to counter the danger posed by Hitler to peace in Europe that Titulescu now took action. He advocated the creation of a system of collective security based on France, which had the largest army in Europe, and the Soviet Union, and it was he who helped to bring about the mutual assistance pact between Moscow and Paris in May 1935. Titulescu hoped that this agreement would form the nucleus of a large coalition of anti-revisionist states to hold Hitler in check and to this end he took Romania down the road to alliance with the Soviet Union.

The main stumbling block to such an alliance was the Bessarabian question. Soviet intransigence mollified sufficiently for Moscow to sign the Kellogg–Briand Pact in 1928, which outlawed war as an instrument of national policy. On the initiative of the Soviet government a supplementary protocol was signed in Moscow on 9 February 1929, by which the Soviet Union and its western neighbours, including Romania, agreed to put the Pact into effect immediately, without waiting for the other states to ratify it. In June 1934, an exchange of letters between Titulescu and Maxim Litvinov, Soviet Commissar for Foreign Relations, marked the resumption of diplomatic relations between the two countries and paved the way for Titulescu to seek a defensive alliance with the Soviet Union. Consequently, in September 1935, Titulescu began discussions with Litvinov over the conclusion of a Soviet–Romanian Treaty of Mutual Assistance. The international situation, however, turned against him. Titulescu's condemnation of the Italian invasion of Abyssinia in the autumn of 1935 and of the German occupation of the Rhineland in March 1936, as violations of the Covenant of the League of Nations, made him an enemy of both states, and led Mussolini to call for his dismissal. To add to Titulescu's problems, the Rhineland occupation exposed France's weakness. It denied French forces easy access to the Danube, which underwrote Romania's security, and caused Romanian politicians to question the wisdom of pursuing an alliance with the Soviet Union which, because of the feebleness of France, might bring Romania into dependence on her powerful eastern neighbour. Titulescu was himself aware of this danger and therefore, when he and Litvinov agreed, on 21 July 1936, to the general principles of the Soviet–Romanian pact, the question of its subordination to the Franco-Soviet alliance was the only article that divided the two ministers; Titulescu argued that the Pact should come into force only if France acted on the Franco-Soviet Treaty, but Litvinov disagreed. Titulescu was unable to extract from Litvinov *de jure* recognition of Romania's sovereignty over Bessarabia and, before he could proceed, he was dismissed by King Carol II, who shared his ministers' concern about a close association with the Soviet Union. Romanian foreign policy, with its principal pillar of France severely undermined and its architect of an accommodation with the Soviet Union removed, now sought to navigate its way between the competing interests of the Western allies and Germany.

The blows delivered by Mussolini and Hitler in 1936 to the prestige of the League of Nations, and to the principles of collective security and defence of the postwar territorial settlement, were only the first shocks to the European order on which Romania had based her interwar foreign policy. The event which shattered that order was the Munich Agreement of 30 September 1938, as a result of which Hitler succeeded in imposing his own revision of European frontiers. The occupation of Prague in March 1939 allowed Germany, through its takeover of all Czechoslovak commercial and foreign investments, to extend its economic dominance throughout south-eastern Europe, a dominance which it had achieved through the *Anschluss* via the Austrian banking system. Romania's contracts with the Skoda arms company made Germany, at a stroke, Romania's principal arms supplier. Furthermore, since these arms were supplied from German-controlled Czechoslovakia, there was no need for Hitler to divert output to the Romanian army from German factories.[2]

During Carol's state visit to London in November 1938, he tried unsuccessfully to counter German economic influence by putting forward proposals to the British for assistance to Romania based on credits and investments, but the British did not consider these economically sound. On his way back to Romania Carol visited Hitler in order to assure him of his country's equitable policy. The king wanted good commercial relations with Germany, but was concerned about Germany's position regarding Hungarian claims to Transylvania. Hitler, too, was anxious to extend trade between the two countries, but remained evasive about the Transylvanian question, realizing that German support on this issue gave him a vital lever of influence over both Hungary and Romania. Carol also discussed with Field Marshal Goering proposals for long-term economic collaboration between Germany and Romania and, in contrast to his failure with the British, found the Germans only too keen to take matters further.[3]

Romania thus found herself in a position of uncertainty after Munich. She was exposed to growing Hungarian pressure over Transylvania, was apprehensive of the Soviet Union's motives concerning Bessarabia and, given the weakness of France, could no longer rely on the security of the Little Entente. Defenceless against German pressure, King Carol sought to come to an accommodation with Hitler by making economic concessions. This shift in policy, discernible following the Munich Agreement, was confirmed by the appointment of Grigore Gafencu as Foreign Minister in December 1938. He was determined to pursue a German guarantee of Romania's territorial integrity in return for Romanian economic concessions.[4] Hence, in February 1939, Helmuth Wohlthat went to Bucharest to open negotiations on a German–Romanian economic agreement. In order to strengthen the Romania's bargaining position, Gafencu, using a decision made in February by the British government to follow up Carol's state visit by sending a limited economic mission to Romania, suggested to the Germans that Britain was a serious rival to them. On 10 March, Wohlthat submitted new, more stringent proposals which were tantamount to the subordination of Romanian industry and agriculture to the economic needs of Germany.[5] Alarmed by the hardening of the German position and by the entry of German troops into Prague on 15 March, Viorel Tilea, the Romanian minister to London, informed the British Foreign Secretary, Lord Halifax, on 17 March that his government had been asked to give Germany a monopoly of Romanian exports and to adapt industrial production in return for a guarantee of the country's borders. 'This', opined Tilea, 'seemed to the Romanian government something very much like an ultimatum'.[6] Fearing that Germany would seize Romania's oil, both Britain and France gave Romania guarantees on 13 April.[7] The Anglo-French guarantee was, as Carol and Gafencu had wished, a unilateral guarantee. It obliged the West to protect Romania against aggression, provided Romania defended herself in the event of attack, but the Romanians were not bound to help Britain or France if they were attacked.[8]

The Anglo-French move was primarily political. German preponderance in Romanian affairs was confirmed by the signature on 23 March of the German–Romanian economic treaty, which bound the Romanian economy more closely to that of Germany and under the terms of which the Germans undertook to supply the Romanian armed forces with arms and equipment and to provide assistance to Romania in cultivating foodstuffs and oilseeds, and in establishing new industries for processing agricultural products, all of which were of interest to the German economy. As far as possible, Romania 'struggled to keep the Reich from obtaining too favourable a rate of exchange and to retain as large a share as possible of its exports for the free world market'.[9] The agreement did not prevent Gafencu from professing his continued faith in a policy of neutrality or 'equilibrium', as he liked to term it, in a speech before the Chamber of Deputies in Bucharest on 29 June 1939:

It is a principle with us not to seek the support of one of the two great neighbouring Powers in turning against the other, in order to give no pretext for conflict on our frontiers or on our territory. This principle is of service to our interest, to those of our neighbours, and to the general interests of peace. A strong and independent Romania is, for the States that surround us, a guarantee of security.[10]

The maintenance of that 'equilibrium' rested on the tension between Nazi Germany and the Soviet Union, for the states of Eastern Europe represented a buffer-zone between the two great dictatorships, and the status quo of the area depended on Hitler and Stalin's mutual suspicion. That status quo, the underpinning of Romanian policy, was shattered by the signing of the Nazi–Soviet Pact of Non-Aggression, also known as the Molotov–Ribbentrop Pact after the names of the German and Soviet foreign ministers who signed it on 23 August 1939. Through the Pact Hitler claimed to have 'definitely sealed' the peace between the German Reich and the Soviet Union by establishing 'precisely and for all time' the respective zones of interest of the two powers. But hardly had the ink dried on the document before first Hitler, on 1 September, and then Stalin, 16 days later, attacked Poland and partitioned it. With Poland on its knees, the government and army command withdrew to Romania, where King Carol had given a promise of sanctuary. During the early hours of the following morning, Marshal Edward Smigly-Rydz, the head of the armed forces, crossed the Czeremosz bridge onto Romanian territory and was placed in confinement in Craiova.[11] President Ignacy Moscicki was sent to Bicaz and other members of the government to isolated localities such as Slanic and Băile Herculane.[12] There they were joined by some 45,000 Polish 'citizens', according to one source.[13]

The Soviet Union then entered the Baltic States, attacked Finland on 30 November, withdrew its support of the Balkan Entente, and forced Romania to cede Bessarabia and northern Bukovina in June 1940. These actions together conspired to destroy the European order and the nation-states established at the Paris Peace Conference in 1920. By the same token the Pact introduced a new order in Europe, one subject not to international deliberation and ratification, but to the interests the two partners considered they had the right to claim and impose.

The Soviet defeat of Finland in mid-March 1940 added further weight to those in the Romanian government who advocated still closer ties with Germany as a guarantee against attacks on their territorial integrity. At the same time, the provisions of the German–Romanian economic treaty of 23 March 1939 were beginning to be translated into action. Several German–Romanian companies for the exploitation of Romania's resources were founded.[14] Gafencu still sought equilibrium. He urged the government to 'save by all our means our political and economic neutrality, and in the same way as we have managed for many months, not weaken our positions whether by imprudent or provocative words and attitudes towards Germany, or by unfriendly words and postures towards the Western Powers, or by renunciation of any valuable element of our independence'.[15] But the reopening of the issue of Bessarabia by the Soviets and events in Scandinavia took the ground from under his feet.

When first Molotov, the Soviet Commissar for Foreign Relations, officially rekindled the Bessarabian question on 29 March 1940 by declaring before the Supreme Soviet that the Soviet government had never recognized the occupation of the province by Romania, and second, on 9 April, the Germans invaded Denmark and Norway, two neutral countries, which, like Romania, had tried to come to an understanding with Hitler, many Romanians felt that the writing was on the wall. King Carol's neutrality was becoming more precarious under the impact of German military success and Soviet pressure, and also because of Anglo-French efforts to disrupt oil supplies to Germany by acts of sabotage on the Danube which constituted an infringement of Romania's neutrality. The bungling of these attempts in April, made with the acquiescence of some members of the Romanian General Staff, compromised the Romanians in German eyes and exposed them to the risk of an invasion against which the British and French were powerless, in Romanian eyes, to provide help.[16] The French, nevertheless, did contemplate military aid. At the end of March, General Weygand, commander of French forces in the eastern Mediterranean, sent a representative to Bucharest to sound out the Romanians about the possibility of sending a French expeditionary air force. The project was vague and uncoordinated with the British. The French troops were in Syria and the Turkish government was reluctant to allow them to cross Turkey. The logistical problems were horrendous. The whole idea alarmed the Romanian General Staff who feared that the Germans would act pre-emptively against them. Gafencu responded by reassuring the Germans that he would resist all Anglo-French efforts to draw Romania into the war and that the Germans need not invade Romania to secure their supplies of oil.[17]

The German offensive in the West on 10 May 1940 against Holland and Belgium, in violation of their neutrality, radically changed King Carol's assessment of his position and marked the end of Romanian neutrality. The choice was no longer between Germany and the Western Powers. The rapid German victories in Holland, Belgium and France stunned the Romanians, who regarded every defeat for the Allies as an argument for closer association with Germany. From mid-May, Hungary and the Soviet Union began deploying troops along their borders with Romania and the Romanian High Command responded in kind. Bereft of any hope of Anglo-French help against his neighbours' territorial pretensions, King Carol turned decidedly towards Germany.

On 15 May, he told Wilhelm Fabricius, the German minister to Bucharest, that 'Romania's future depended solely upon Germany' and five days later

Prime Minister Gheorghe Tătărescu let Fabricius know that Romania was ready to align its foreign policy with Germany in return for an assurance against Russia.[18] On 24 May, Baron Manfred von Killinger, Hitler's special envoy to Bucharest, had a meeting with Colonel Mihai Moruzov, head of the Romanian Intelligence Service (SSI). Killinger's mission was to follow the activity of the British Secret Service in south-eastern Europe and Moruzov was a person with whom he felt he could collaborate.[19] The opinions expressed by Killinger to Moruzov were his own; no instructions had been given to him to bring them to the attention of the Romanian government. Yet, given his status, he must have known that they would be passed on to Carol. Killinger recognized that

> there is, on the one hand, a climate of opinion which is very favourable to Britain and France since the abiding conviction is that the creation of Greater Romania [Romania post-1918] is due exclusively to these countries and that, in the future, the fate of Romania will also be in the hands of the allies. On the other hand, there is an atmosphere which is unfavourable to close relations with Germany, either because of memories of the last war, or because of certain intentions which are attributed today to Germany.
>
> I am convinced, however, the reality is different. In the first place, although Britain and France perhaps contributed to the national claims of Romania, I see no possibility of their helping Romania today. On the contrary, by entering a war alongside the allies, Romania can only lose out. Romania is today surrounded by enemies: Hungary, Bulgaria and the Soviet Union. If it can deal with the first two on its own, there is no way it can cope with the Bolshevik torrent....
>
> Germany considers that there are two enemies. Enemy number 1: The allies who will attack the oil fields and installations from the air from bases in Greece or Turkey, from a distance of two or three hours' flying time. Enemy number 2: the Soviet Union which, in order to realize the pan-Slav idea, will attack Romania not only to retake Bessarabia, but in order to unite with the Slavs in the Balkan peninsula. In this scenario Romania will be devastated, including the oil fields, of course, if these have not already been destroyed by the Romanians. Obviously, in both cases, Romania will not be able to offer resistance for long. The only course is for the conclusion of an official bond with Germany which is both correct and certain, and which is the only one which can absolutely guarantee Romania's territorial integrity.[20]

On 28 May, Tătărescu informed Fabricius that friendly relations with Germany were 'based on active collaboration with Germany in all domains' and expressed 'the hope of the Romanian government that the framework of friendly collaboration with the government of the Reich would be extended'.[21] He drew the Reich's attention to the recent concentrations by its neighbours of troops on Romania's frontiers, which threatened the peace of the region. The German reply of 2 June was terrible blow. Instead of offering advice, Joachim von Ribbentrop, the German Foreign Minister, asked the Romanians whether they would be ready to make territorial concessions to their neighbours, particularly the Russians.[22] Carol was taken aback. While expressing willingness to enter into discussions with the Soviet Union over the conclusion of a pact of non-aggression, Carol was unwilling to consider the cession of Bessarabia and underlined this by stressing, through Tătărescu on 20 June, the importance for Germany of a strong Romanian state, guardian of the River Dniester and of the mouth of the Danube.[23]

What Carol did not know, of course, was that Germany had already recognized the Soviet claim to Bessarabia in the supplementary secret annex to the Nazi-Soviet Non-Aggression Pact. Article 3 of the annex read: 'With regard to South-Eastern Europe, the Soviet side emphasizes its interest in Bessarabia; the German side declares complete political *désintéressement* in these territories.'[24] Hitler's magnanimity in conceding the Soviet interest in Bessarabia was founded on an optimistic assessment of German power and Soviet weakness in south-eastern Europe, a view reflected in the prediction made by the German military attaché in Bucharest in December 1939 that 'the Russians will not occupy Bessarabia as long as Germany is strong enough. However, should we suffer a serious setback, or have all our forces engaged, Russia might take advantage of a rare opportunity which might not occur for a long time.'[25] The accuracy of the attaché's forecast was borne out by events. Shortly before midnight on 26 June, when German forces were completing their victorious sweep through France, Molotov summoned the Romanian minister in Moscow, Davidescu, to the Kremlin and presented an ultimatum demanding that Romania cede Bessarabia and northern Bukovina to the Soviet Union. The Soviet note called for a reply from the Romanian government within 24 hours. The Romanians appealed to the Germans for help, but Berlin responded by advising Bucharest to accept the conditions set by Moscow. Carol had before him the example of Poland, where war against either the Soviet Union or Germany might lead to the intervention of the other and to the partition of the country. Most of the king's advisers were against resistance and he acceded to the Soviet demands.

From the lost provinces, Bessarabia in particular, came tales of humiliation and injury inflicted on the retreating Romanians by the Russian population and especially by the Jews, who had scores to settle with their former masters over anti-Semitic legislation. In the summer of 1938, General Nicolae Ciupercă, commander of the Third Army, and as such responsible for law and order in Bessarabia, had forbidden the use of Russian in public in Chişinău on the spurious grounds that only the Jews used Russian.[26] In fact, there were nearly as many Russians in Chişinău eager to use their own language as Jews. The resentment Ciupercă and his kind had sown through their intolerance towards non-Romanians in Bessarabia – the Romanian mayor of Chişinău banned samovars from the teashops of the city in July 1938 – was now visited, indiscriminately and with interest, on Romanian troops, officials and civilians as they hastened to leave the province. Passions were stoked by the major Romanian dailies, which ran emotional eye-witness accounts of events in the Bessarabian capital. One example was the report carried by *Universul* on 1 July from its Bessarabian correspondent:

> Thursday [27 June], at 6 am I was at the headquarters of the Third Romanian army corps.... At 7 am it was announced officially 'Soviet troops will enter at 2 pm.'
>
> In the town, it was difficult to find any means of transport to the station, which was about four kilometres from the centre of town. Columns of refugees, each with a bundle of belongings in their hand, mothers carrying children in their arms and dragging others, their eyes clouded with tears, hastening their steps with a single objective in mind: the station...

The correspondent, Elefterie Negel, took the last train out of Chişinău, whose destination was Galaţi. His portrayal of the events *en route* was coloured with religious overtones redolent of a holy war between Christianity and Communism:

> Before entering the first station after Chişinău, thick columns of smoke rose in sacrifice towards the heavens.... We picked out the Mazarache church, with its Romanian heritage. It was thus that the Jewish Communists began their wicked deeds against the holy sites. In the compartment next door a woman is on her knees uttering prayers accompanied by curses against the pagans who had been cosseted for so long at the generous breast of the [Romanian] people.[27]

Emphasis was given in Romanian military bulletins to the actions of Jewish Communists as the Soviet army arrived in the two provinces. Romanian officers in Soroca were 'stripped of their insignia of rank by Jews while Soviet soldiers looked on'.[28] The commander of the frontier troops in Cernăuţi informed his superiors in Bucharest that as soon as the order for Romanian withdrawal was given, 'the Jews launched themselves into anti-Romanian protests, tearing and spitting on the *tricoleur* and climbing onto the monument to union with Romania where they hoisted the red flag'.[29] Other army reports came in of water and refuse being thrown at the departing Romanians, of Romanian officers being spat on, of having their epaulettes ripped off and in some cases being beaten by Jews. The head of the Soviet police in Chilia Nouă was 'the Jew Dr Rabinovici', the Soviet newspapers which appeared in Chişinău after the Soviet occupation were run by 'Jewish editors', at Ismail, 'the millers and bakers all Jews, refused to produce bread the day before the Soviet ultimatum, spreading the rumour immediately after the announcement of the ultimatum that the shortage of bread was due to the fact that the flour had been requisitioned by the [Romanian] army'. In Bukovina, the arms dump in Rădăuţi was attacked 'by a group of Jews', and at Gura Humorului, 'the Jews confiscated cars to prevent the Romanians from leaving'.[30]

Carol II reflected the reactions of many of his subjects as reports of the withdrawal reached Bucharest. In his diary entry for Friday, 28 June he wrote:

> The first items of news to reach us are very sad, the behaviour of the population in Bessarabia, especially that of the Jews, leaves much to be desired. The columns of refugees and trains were attacked by Communist hordes, which delayed even more the opportunity – ridiculously short as it was – for evacuation.[31]

Two days later he noted: 'The news from Bessarabia is still sad.... Many of the leaders of the Front for National Revival [Carol's Party] have shown themselves to be completely Bolshevized, being the first to have received the Soviet troops with red flags and flowers'.[32] That most of the local officials who turned Communist after the Soviet annexation were Romanian is borne out by Romanian army investigations which showed that before the Soviets began their campaign of deportations from the province, there were 505 Communist officials who were Romanian, and only 69 Jews.[33] Such evidence points to a broader range of sympathy for Communism in Bessarabia; it undoubtedly attracted support from among Jews, but it also found favour among the Russian, Ukrainian and even Romanian populations. In a number of towns the local minority populations were reported by the army to have joined in the humiliation of the Romanian troops:

> In Bolgrad, people gathered in groups at the appearance of Soviet aircraft and demonstrated their support. The same thing happened in other places in Bessarabia, the minority population being encouraged by the Russian motorized troops. The Bulgarian population in Bolgrad attacked the Romanians left in the town.[34]

These facts were completely overlooked in the Romanian press and in Romanian military reports, where it was solely the Jews who were blamed for the victimization of the Romanian army. Also ignored was the destruction by the Communists of shops in the two provinces which were owned by the predominantly the Jewish middle class. Instead, official opprobrium and popular hostility were heaped on Jews, irrespective of whether they had Communist sympathies or not. As a result, anti-Semitic feeling reached new heights, causing the General Staff to express its concern over 'reprisals' by Romanians against the Jews. In Bucharest, bars and cafés were closed early on government orders to avoid anti-Jewish 'excesses' by segments of the population. The potential for violence was recognized in a US legation telegram to the State Department of 12 July, which advised that 'Rumanians in general seem to wish to wreak their wrath either actively or passively on the Jews for the events which have taken place in Bessarabia'.[35]

It was in the ranks of the Romanian army itself that vengeance had first been wreaked on the Jews. Inflamed by the reports of the humiliation visited on the retreating troops, some Romanian soldiers exacted their revenge on Jews. On 1 July 1940, 52 Jews were shot in Dorohoi town by Romanian troops as they withdrew from the district of Herţa. An official investigation into the deaths revealed that the shootings took place during the burial of a Romanian officer in the local Christian cemetery and while a number of Jews were at their own cemetery burying a Jewish soldier. A salvo of shots was heard at the Christian cemetery, which the mourners assumed to be in honour of the fallen officer, but the gunfire increased in intensity creating panic, since those assembled thought the Russians had arrived. Everyone dispersed, leaving the coffin in the middle of the cemetery. In fact, the shots had been fired by soldiers from two regiments retreating from Herţa who, allegedly humiliated by Jews there, were out to exact their revenge by shooting at the Jewish mourners. The investigation surmised that the 'reprisals' had been planned because some soldiers went straight to the houses of Jews after the first shots were fired, while in the houses of Romanians icons had been placed in the windows or crucifixes painted on the walls in various colours as a signal to the soldiers not to fire on them. According to the report, 47 bodies had been identified; 15 were found in the Jewish cemetery, those of five Jewish soldiers were found nearby, while the rest were scattered throughout houses and in the streets.[36]

Isolated incidents of reprisals against Jews also occurred in Moldavia. On 30 June, a Jewish soldier was murdered by other soldiers. The following day, four Jews were shot by a gendarmerie officer in Şerbăuţi. On the same day, seven Jews were seen leaving Dolhasca station under escort of two soldiers and a junior officer. After entering a wood the Jews were shot. Several Jews were thrown from trains between Paşcani and Lespezi on 2 July. Four were killed and five badly injured. The perpetrators were not identified.[37] It was not only Jews who were the target of hostility: a Romanian soldier of Russian background was also cast out of a train.[38]

While most Jews in Bessarabia and northern Bukovina were doubtless pleased to seek the back of the Romanians, in the rest of Romania the Jewish population found itself saddled with a sense of guilt. The cession of the two provinces divided the Jewish population of Romania by placing it in two states hostile to each other. The shameful retreat from the two provinces inflamed anti-Semitic feeling in the country, forced the abdication of Carol and enabled the ascent to power of the Iron Guard. Shortly after the withdrawal, the leaders of the Jewish community strove to protect its members from an expected wave of violence by dissociating itself from the Jews of Bessarabia and northern Bukovina, and issuing fiery declarations of loyalty to the Romanian state. Horia Carp, the secretary general of the Jewish community, wrote in an editorial:

> We only know from rumours ugly deeds which allegedly occurred during the withdrawal from Bessarabia and northern Bukovina, deeds committed by some of the inhabitants of the evacuated territories, amongst whom there were also allegedly Jews. We do not know to what extent the rumours are true, nor to what degree the Jews of Bessarabia participated in the reprehensible events that were committed there. But whatever the truth, what blame do we bear for these acts of wild madness, perpetrated by people who were born and lived under a different rule, who did not have time to bind themselves spiritually to the [Romanian] people and the country, and with whom we do not have, and cannot have, any sympathy in deeds which are alien to our faith and to our historical tradition, in any time and in any place destiny has cast us?[39]

The official expression of the Jewish community's attitude regarding the loss of Bessarabia and northern Bukovina was signed by Wilhelm Filderman, President of the Jewish Federation, and by the Chief Rabbi, Alexander Şafran. It placed the accent on the Jews' sacrifices for and contribution to the creation of the Romanian nation-state:

> The Jews in the Old Kingdom – native Romanian Jews – born and raised in generations on the land of Romania, are and remain bound wholeheartedly to the Romanian soil, soil generously watered with the blood of their best sons, fallen in the War of Independence of 1877, in that of 1913, and in the Great War of 1916–1918. Their ideals have always meshed with those of all Romanians, and whatever may happen, and whatever they may endure, as always they are ready to be alongside the Romanian people, in understanding of their destiny which binds them inextricably to this land.[40]

True as these details were, they had little impact on the officers and men of the Romanian army of 1940. The whole anti-Semitic argument rested on a total denial of these facts. The army's experience in Bessarabia in late June completely undermined the efforts of the Jewish community in Romania proper to create a bond. Even before the territorial losses of summer 1940, the leaders of the community had launched a subscription campaign for the army, publishing in each issue of their newspapers *Curierul israelit* and *Tribuna evreiască* an appeal for money 'for equipping the army' and a series of observations critical of those who were slow to respond.[41] As a result of the hostility shown towards it during the withdrawal – hostility ascribed by the army solely to Jews – the army become totally infused with anti-Semitism. As if the supine surrender of the two provinces was not sufficient humiliation, the troops had to endure the insult and injury inflicted by Communist activists and sympathizers in the two provinces. Within a year, several in the ranks of the army were to seize the opportunity to play out their prejudices in murderous fashion.

The Soviet ultimatum of 26 June and its annexation of Romanian territory under the threat of the use of force amounted to international blackmail. The threat to use force was a threat to commit acts outlawed by the two conventions for the Definition of Aggression, signed on 3 and 4 July 1933, to which both the Soviet Union and Romania were signatories.[42] Romania acquiesced in the Soviet demands in an exchange of notes. The new status of Bessarabia and northern Bukovina, irrespective of all preceding legality, was therefore, from an international legal standpoint, based on a formal agreement contained in this exchange of notes, consenting to the retrocession of Bessarabia and the cession of northern Bukovina.[43] What was not consented to by Romania was the Soviet Union's annexation of the district of Herța in northern Moldavia, for it was not mentioned in the text of the ultimatum, or her occupation of four islands at the mouth of the Danube in autumn 1940.

Attached to the ultimatum was a small map on which the ceded territories were marked by a thick red line drawn in pencil. Not only did the thickness of the line cause confusion as to which localities fell on the Soviet side because it covered a seven-mile band on the map, but the roughness of the pencil stroke cut across the north-eastern corner of Moldavia and the town of Herța. Despite Romanian protests that this area was not mentioned in the ultimatum, the Soviet representatives on the Romanian–Soviet Commission established in Odessa to supervise its application insisted that the town was part of the ceded areas and Soviet troops occupied it.

The frontier imposed on Romania by the Soviet Union was by no means the ethnic line between Romanians and Ukrainians and the claim in the ultimatum that Bessarabia was principally peopled by Ukrainians was wildly inaccurate. Even the census taken in 1897 – while the province was under Russian rule – could not be adduced to bring the slightest support to the ultimatum's contention.[44] The Soviet claim to that part of Bukovina 'where the predominant majority of the population is connected with the Soviet Ukraine by common historical destinies' was less spurious, despite its formulation, which invited the charge of writing history backwards. Although Bukovina had never formed part of the Russian Empire, and its total population, according to the 1930 Romanian census, contained a majority of Romanians,[45] in the northern part demanded by the Soviet Union there was an absolute Ukrainian majority.[46]

The total area ceded by Romania to the Soviet Union covered 50,762 sq. km and contained a population of 3,776,000, of whom more than half, 2,020,000 were Romanian.[47] Romanian losses in men and equipment were communicated to London by the British military attaché, Lt.-Col. Geoffrey Macnab. He concluded that the 'withdrawal was in general very poorly executed and many units never received orders'. As a result, there had been 'about 75 courts-martial of officers for cowardice and inefficiency', the only details of which to emerge were the dismissal of the Commander of the 21st division, and the reduction to half-pay of Ilcuş, the Minister of Defence.[48] Fearful of what might befall them under Soviet rule, most of the Romanians took the painful decision to leave with the Romanian troops but, because of the short deadline given by the Soviets for the withdrawal of the Romanian army, they were forced to abandon their belongings. Even with the possessions they had, some of the Romanian refugees were attacked by armed groups of local Communists and robbed.

The first steps to aid the refugees were taken by the Romanian Red Cross. It instructed its local branches – there were 54 throughout the country – to set up canteens in the stations and on the routes along which the refugees were directed. Those from southern Bessarabia were placed in temporary encampments in the region of Topoloveni to the north-west of Bucharest, and in the county of Prahova, those from the northern part were quartered in the area of Târgu-Ocna and Bacău, while the refugees from Bukovina were sheltered in the region of Piatra Neamţ. A nationwide appeal was made for money, clothing and food to which private companies and institutions, as well as members of the public, contributed generously. On 6 July, the government set up a refugee committee to work under the auspices of the Ministry of Internal Affairs. Special offices were set up in prefectures and town halls to register refugees, to designate encampments for their shelter and to give them help in reaching them. The Ministry of Health was charged with ensuring adequate sanitation in the camps.[49]

In the meantime, the refugees were placed in schools, hostels, small hotels and rooms requisitioned from the public. Clothing and shoes were distributed by the Red Cross to the needy. Medical assistance and medicines were given free of charge. Some idea of the scale of assistance given can be gained from the work of the Red Cross office in Iaşi, which organized a canteen in the main railway station there. During the seven weeks from 25 June to 9 August it provided light meals for 6,577 refugees and gave first aid to over 2,000.[50] The plight of the refugees proved relatively short-lived. After the re-conquest of Bessarabia and northern Bukovina by the German and Romanian armies in July 1941, the great majority returned to their homes.

In the changed power configuration of 1940 the Soviet Union felt able to disregard the Romanian frontiers which had been decided by the Allies at the

Paris Peace settlement. Stalin looked to improve his defence position against Germany before Hitler made Romania a client state and advanced his defence line to the Prut. But the rapacious and cynical manner in which the Soviet Union exercised its claim to Bessarabia and northern Bukovina drove Romania into Germany's arms by leading King Carol to fear that Stalin might encroach further on Romanian soil. He therefore quickly declared Romania's solidarity with Germany before obtaining a guarantee from Hitler of his country's territorial integrity. On 1 July, the Romanian government renounced the Anglo-French guarantee, its membership of the Balkan Entente and of the League of Nations, and Carol informed Fabricius, the German minister in Bucharest, of his desire for a political agreement with the Reich, telling him that, without German protection, 'Romania is incapable of any action and is subject to Soviet Russian influence'.[51] The following day, the king requested that a German military mission be sent to Romania to help train the Romanian army and air force.[52] On 4 July 1940, Romania joined the Berlin–Rome Axis. Hitler now cleverly exploited his position. In a letter of 13 July, he reminded Carol of his acceptance of the Anglo-French guarantee and made German protection conditional on the settlement of the outstanding territorial disputes with Hungary and Bulgaria over Transylvania and Dobrogea, which the cession of Bessarabia and northern Bukovina had triggered.

At the height of the crisis over the Soviet ultimatum, Carol had called in the German minister, von Killinger, to protest at the pressure being placed upon him, not only by the Russians, but also by the Hungarians and Bulgarians:

> I fully realize that Germany can give me no support against Russia, but one thing she can do, and one act of friendship is worth another – for the oil has continued to flow without interruption precisely during your Western offensive – namely call off Hungary and Bulgaria.[53]

Hungary's revisionist ambitions were closely linked with those of the Third Reich. Like Hitler, Hungary's leaders had never accepted the 'injustices' of the Paris Peace Settlement and therefore Hitler's advocacy of revision of the Versailles Treaty encouraged Hungary to press her claims to her lost territories. The first success of Hungary's pro-German policy was gained in November 1938 when, under the terms of the First Vienna Award, Hungary acquired part of southern Slovakia from Czechoslovakia. In March 1939, she was awarded Carpatho-Ruthenia and then concentrated her attention on Transylvania. Hungarian strategy was to coordinate the claim to Transylvania with Soviet agitation over Bessarabia. A month after the issue of Bessarabia was raised in the Soviet press, the Hungarian chief of staff, General Henrik Werth, advised his government in a memorandum dated 12 December 1939 that in the event of a Soviet attack on Romania, Hungary should act to recover 'the whole of Transylvania'. He also instructed General Gabor Faragho, the Hungarian military attaché in Moscow, to discuss with the Soviet authorities the possibility of a coordinated attack against Romania.[54] Not content with its amputation of Romania by annexing Bessarabia and northern Bukovina in June 1940, the Soviet Union backed Hungary's claims to Transylvania. On 11 July, the Hungarian minister to Moscow sent a report to Budapest of a discussion he had had with Molotov, during which the Soviet Foreign Minister had made clear that the USSR considered Hungary's territorial demands on Romania to be justified, and offered its support for them should a conference be called to resolve them.[55]

Hitler's stance over Transylvania was dictated by his need for stability in preparing *Operation Barbarossa*, which was conceived with both Hungarian and Romanian participation. While warning the Hungarian prime minister on 10 July not to expect any help from Germany should Hungary attack Romania, Hitler was worried about a joint Russian–Hungarian move against Romania, which would threaten the oilfields and thus endanger his plans in Russia. He therefore offered his offices as mediator, and negotiations between Hungary and Romania began on 10 August at Turnu-Severin. After ten days' stalemate Hitler imposed a settlement. The German Foreign Minister, Joachim von Ribbentrop, and his Italian counterpart, Count Galeazzo Ciano, invited both sides to Vienna and told them to accept the result of their arbitration.

On the question of the future of Transylvania, Romanians were virtually unanimous that in political, cultural and economic terms it was more important to the cohesion of the Romanian state than Bessarabia, notwithstanding the painful consequences of the loss of the province. This view was conveyed by Ion Gigurtu, the Romanian prime minister, in a letter to Ribbentrop on 27 August 1940. Gigurtu explained that while Romanian public opinion had recognized the need to accept the Soviet ultimatum over Bessarabia and northern Bukovina, on German advice, in order to avoid war with the Soviet Union, the cession of part of Transylvania was a completely different matter. 'Transylvania', he wrote, 'was always considered by us as a fortress of Romanianism, in which our nation...developed'. The decision to cede Bessarabia had been taken, he argued, in order to deflect revisionist claims on Transylvania where the Romanians 'have lived for eighteen centuries'.[56]

Carol and his ministers were concerned that rejection of arbitration would lead to a Hungarian attack and German occupation of the oilfields, which might in turn provoke a Russian invasion of eastern Romania. The king convened a Crown Council in which members of the Iron Guard and other pro-German ministers were now present, and it voted 19 to 10 with one abstention for the acceptance of arbitration. Those against preferred defeat to disgrace; those in favour stressed the need to prevent the complete disintegration of Romania. Carol cast his vote with the latter.

Ribbentrop was instrumental in drawing up the terms of the Award and was driven by German strategic interests in doing so. By pushing the border of Hungary, which at this time was more closely linked to Germany than Romania, to the south-east Carpathian ridge, he gave the German army a natural defensive wall. At the same time, the new frontier ran only a few kilometres from the Romanian oilfields around Ploieşti, which were vital to Hitler's plan to attack the Soviet Union.[57] On the announcement of the Ribbentrop–Ciano adjudication on 30 August 1940, Mihail Manoilescu, the Romanian Foreign Minister, fainted on the table.[58] Under the terms of the Second Vienna Award, as it came to be known, Transylvania was virtually partitioned. Hungary received an area of roughly 43,000 sq. km in the north of the province representing roughly 40 per cent of its area and a population of 2.6 million.[59]

The partition triggered an exodus of Romanians from northern Transylvania. According to figures compiled by the official body set up to give assistance to these refugees, some 110,000 passed through its hands up to September 1943. Most were former employees of the Romanian state who overnight found themselves without jobs, including university and school teachers. Many were soon placed in the respective ministry and in the educational system; others were sent before local committees formed from the prefect, mayor and representatives of the Red Cross who were given the authority to requisition dwellings to house them. Every refugee was given a special identity card and assistance benefits until they found work. In order to qualify for continued receipt of the benefits after a period of 90 days, they were required to show that they had sought employment. Those who refused to take up a job offer were denied further assistance.[60] Unlike the refugees from Bessarabia and northern Bukovina, who were able to return to their homes in autumn 1941, those from northern Transylvania remained in exile until the return of the area to Romanian rule in spring 1945.[61] The plight of the peasant refugees was in many cases alleviated by the generosity of family and friends. This is not to say that they were forgotten by the Antonescu regime. In cabinet meetings measures addressing their problem were discussed and agreed, but they often proved ineffective. The situation of refugees in the county of Iaşi explains why. While the prefect managed to settle 1,719 out of 1,861 families of refugees in the period 1 July 1940–31 March 1941 (the vast majority from Bessarabia and northern Bukovina, but 110 from northern Transylvania), he was not able to rent out land to them. The land in question had been confiscated from Jews under the law. Of the 2,922 hectares involved, only 254 hectares were being farmed by refugee tenant farmers. The reason, the prefect explained, was the inability of the prospective tenants to raise the necessary funds, which was due in turn to the difficulties they faced in obtaining loans from the state.[62]

The Bulgarian claim was settled without controversy. Southern Dobrogea, an area of almost 7,000 sq. km where only about 25 per cent of the population was Romanian, was returned to Bulgaria under an agreement signed on 21 August and ratified by the treaty of Craiova on 7 September. The return was accompanied by an exchange of population: Romanian subjects of Bulgarian origin in the counties of Tulcea and Constanţa in northern Dobrogea were transferred to Durostor and Caliacra in southern Dobrogea, while the Romanians in the latter counties were moved in to take their place. Bulgaria also undertook to compensate the departing Romanians for their loss of property.[63] According to the figures of the joint Romanian–Bulgarian commission for the transfer, 103,711 Romanians were moved from southern Dobrogea and 62,278 Bulgarians settled from northern Dobrogea.[64]

In return for these territorial concessions Carol obtained Hitler's guarantee of protection, but it was for the Romania truncated at the behest of Hitler and it was too late to save his throne. One third of Romania's 1939 area was amputated in 1940 and with it Romania's population shrank from 19.9 million to 13.3 million.[65] In economic terms, the territorial losses were crippling: 37 per cent of the arable land, 44 per cent of the forest land, 27 per cent of the orchards and 37 per cent of the vineyards. Of the area given over to wheat (as of 1939) Romania lost 37 per cent, to maize 30 per cent, to sunflower 75 per cent, to hemp 43 per cent and to soya 86 per cent.[66] On a human scale, the loss of a population of whom half – some three million – were ethnically Romanian, was too much for most Romanians to stomach. Protests organized on 3 September by the anti-Semitic Iron Guard – which had never forgiven Carol for the assassination in November 1938 of its leader Corneliu Codreanu – led to the seizure of government buildings. Fearing a breakdown of order, Wilhelm Fabricius, the German minister in Bucharest, informed Berlin on 5 September that he had advised General Ion Antonescu, a former Minister of War, to demand dictatorial powers from the king.[67] However, we should not infer from this that the Antonescu regime was imposed by Germany. In fact, Antonescu's rise to power was brought about not by Fabricius, but by 'German-friendly' elements among the ministers and royal councillors who surrounded the king.[68]

Romanian–German economic relations and the importance of oil

In economic matters Antonescu, a soldier, was uncertain and cautious. While there was a huge gulf between Romania and Germany in economic output, in terms of resources Romania was of considerable importance to Hitler's war machine. At the time, she possessed significant exploitable reserves of oil. Before the First World War, Germany had been the principal investor in the Romanian oil industry, but after 1918 British, Dutch and American companies took over the bulk of drilling and refining for the international market.[69] Successive Romanian governments used oil to earn as much convertible Western currency as possible. There was a sharp rise in oil exports to Germany after 1935, but as late as 1937 Germany's share in Romania's foreign trade was no greater than it had been in 1929.[70] It was the change in the European political balance rather than direct economic penetration which enabled to be more comprehensibly realized what had already started: an increase in Germany's influence. The *Anschluss* with Austria in March 1938 started the ball rolling south-eastwards and paved the way for German dominance of Romania's economy.[71] This was sealed by the signature on 23 March 1939 of the Wohltat Agreement. This treaty and the oil agreement of May 1940 increased Germany's share of Romania's imports to 51 per cent and of her exports to 44 per cent in 1940.[72]

It was in order to deny Germany additional oil supplies that the British and French began to make advance purchases of Romanian oil on the open market. At the same time, in consultation with the Romanian authorities, they developed plans to destroy the oilfields and to interdict supply routes by the Danube and the rail network.[73] The purchases of oil, and winter ice on the Danube, together with the inability of the Germans to release the necessary rail tankers, combined to depress oil deliveries to Germany, but in March 1940 they began to recover. It was this point that the Royal Navy attempted sabotage on the Danube, which resulted in farcical failure. On 29 May, Romania signed the oil agreement with Germany and by August exports of Romanian oil had reached the agreed levels.[74] In 1940 and 1941, Romania supplied 94 per cent and 75 per cent of German oil imports respectively; in the assessment of one author, 'it is no exaggeration to state that the classic *blitzkrieg* campaigns of 1941–42 were fundamentally dependent on Romanian oil'.[75]

At the end of 1940, Dr Hermann Neubacher, the former mayor of Vienna, was named German Special Representative for Economic Problems to Romania. In this capacity Neubacher oversaw oil matters on behalf of the Ministry of the Economy of the Reich, and of the German Army, Navy and Air Force. All German requests for oil passed through Neubacher's office. This centralization of deliveries became necessary when some sections of the German army began to obtain fuel directly from Romanian companies. Such arrangements angered Antonescu, since he could not keep track of sales of oil at a time when the state budget was being drained by supporting the cost of the German military mission, as well by the provision of aid for refugees from the lost territories. Since the German military mission and the troops which were to provide instruction to the Romanian army (the 13th Motorized Division) had come to Romania at the invitation of the Romanian government, Romania was paying the sum of 100 million lei (2.5 million marks) a month for their maintenance. This sum increased over the following years in line with a slow devaluation of the leu.[76]

After Britain broke off diplomatic relations with Romania on 10 February 1941, and imposed a blockade on Romanian ships in ports under British control, Romania's trading links with countries overseas were cut and the country was thrown back on trade with continental Europe, in particular with Germany. In talks between Hermann Goering and Antonescu, as well as between the respective ministers of the economy, Walter Funk and Gheorghe Potopeanu, at the Belvedere Palace in Vienna, the conditions were established on 5 March 1941 for the integration of Romania into the German economic zone. Antonescu, speaking three days later, declared that Romania would give the fullest support to Germany in the war the latter was conducting, but control and management of the Romanian economy would remain firmly in the hands of the Romanian government. In practice, this meant that Romania would deliver to Germany only goods whose value could be covered by counter-deliveries made by Germany to Romania.[77]

The measures taken by the Germans to improve railways lines, to increase the numbers of rail locomotives and tankers, and to improve loading and unloading facilities along the route between Romania and Germany began to bear fruit in spring 1941, with the result that deliveries of oil to the Reich reached their height in 1941. After supplies had been interrupted by the freezing over of the Danube in the winter of 1940–41, and then again in April 1941, because of the destruction of bridges and the danger of mines, stocks of oil had reached record levels in Romania at Giurgiu on the Danube and Constanța on the Black Sea. From early summer, exports of oil on a prodigious scale were resumed. Between July and October, some 500,000 tons of fuel were delivered to Germany. During the whole year 3.9 million tons of petroleum products were exported by Romania, of which 2.9 million went to Germany and the German armies in Russia and in the Balkans. The rest was exported to Italy, Sweden, Switzerland and Turkey.[78]

Neubacher tried to persuade Antonescu to develop new oilfields, but the proposal for a new mining law, drawn up by a Romanian–German commission, was sabotaged by the bureaucracy, whose experience of feet-dragging was enormous. The new law was promulgated in July 1942, but the implementing legislation was not published until June 1943, and even then exploitation of the new deposits was slow. The Romanian government, realizing that it was exhausting the country's known oil reserves, stabilized production and reduced exports to Germany.[79] This was a further reason for Hitler to move against the Caucasian oilfields in summer 1942, an offensive which dragged the Romanian army to disastrous defeat alongside the Germans at Stalingrad. Although a huge increase in German synthetic production, and a growth in Austrian and Hungarian natural production, offset the fall in Romanian supplies of oil, the German army's voracious demands meant that Romanian oil remained crucial.[80] Thus the outcome in the main theatre of the war – in respect of armour – from the middle of 1942 to early 1944 was largely dependent on Romanian oil. It was in order to interrupt deliveries that the Allies attacked the Romanian oilfields in a series of air raids in 1943 and 1944.

Internal developments, 1918–40

Romania came out of the First World War with double its former population, territory and industrial capacity. The 7,300,000 Romanians had, by 1919, become 16,200,000, but they still lived mostly on the land. The country's economy, like that of its neighbours, was characterized by agricultural over-population and low productivity per hectare – about half that of Western Europe. The legacy of a different historical experience of the Romanians in the provinces which constituted the newly enlarged Romania, coupled with the diverse ethnic mix of the large minority Hungarian, German and Jewish populations which they contained, posed major problems of harmonization and consolidation which, in the brief interlude of the interwar period, the country's leaders had little time, capacity and will to address. The failure to solve them blighted the country's progress towards modernization and the exercise of genuine democratic rule.

There were contrasts in the pattern of economic development. Transylvania had benefited from Austrian and Hungarian investment until 1914, but the rest of the country remained underdeveloped. Although it possessed great natural wealth, with fertile soil and raw materials such as natural gas, lignite, oil, metals and forests, Romania lacked the industrial capacity to use these resources to the full. Industrial development was confined to an east–west axis from Timişoara to Braşov in Transylvania, and a north–south axis from Sighişoara in Transylvania to Ploieşti and Bucharest in Wallachia. This left the country predominantly agricultural, with great discrepancies between town and country. According to the 1930 census, almost 80 per cent of its working population lived on the land in villages that were poorly served by transport and communications. Its total population in 1939 was calculated to be 19,933,000.[81] Few villages had piped water or electricity, health services were primitive, especially in the more backward regions of Moldavia and Bessarabia, and in such conditions it is hardly surprising that at 17 per cent of live births, Romania had the highest infant mortality rate in Europe.[82] Only 13 per cent of the adult population were employed in industry, commerce and transport.[83] The 1930 census registered this as 947,739 persons.[84] The corresponding German figures were 42 per cent in industry and 26 per cent in agriculture (1930). In 1936, there were 440,000 persons in state employment in Romania compared with only 250,000 in Germany.[85] Whereas illiteracy in Germany had virtually disappeared by 1900, Romania's 1930 census registered an illiteracy rate of 43 per cent among those over the age of seven.[86]

These problems were of a complexity which would have taxed the most far-sighted government and the most thoroughgoing cadres of administration. In the interwar period, Romania had neither. The greatest discrepancy, from a western point of view, lay in the gulf between word and deed. Behind the façade of political institutions copied from the West the practice of government was subject to patronage and narrow sectional interests. Under the constitution of 1923 the king had the power to dissolve parliament and appoint a new government. The monarchy, which under King Carol I (1881–1914) and King Ferdinand (1914–27) had won the trust and affection of the Romanian population, soon lost much of its prestige through the antics of Carol II, who returned to the country from exile in 1930. Hugh Seton-Watson, a gifted young contemporary analyst, described Carol thus:

> Superficially brilliant and basically ignorant, gifted with enormous energy and unlimited lust for power, a lover of demagogy, melodrama and bombastic speeches, he was determined to be a Great Man, the Saviour and Regenerator of his country. His impressionistic mind was filled with admiration of Mussolini, then still the most picturesque figure on the European political stage, and he set himself to imitate him. In his untiring work, which lasted ten years, he combined a little of the terrorist methods of the Duce with much of the well-tried Balkan procedure of corruption and intrigue.[87]

Institutionalized corruption was matched by a personal variety. The exploitative rule of foreign princes in Wallachia and Moldavia in the eighteenth and early nineteenth centuries had helped to create a culture among the dominant elite in which rapacity was regarded as proof of dexterity and cunning, and therefore corruption of principles had become widespread. This culture had been assimilated by the small, bureaucratic middle class, who expected to rely on unofficial remuneration in the form of bribes to supplement their meagre salaries. There was no native economic middle class to act as a check on the elite, since commerce had fallen largely into the hands of the largely disenfranchised Jews, who were barred from public service.

Idealism was scorned and those who searched for it, the young, were driven to the sole parties which seemed to have any on offer, those of the Right. Although a radical land reform was introduced soon after the war, many peasants were unable to afford the loans necessary to buy agricultural machinery. The economic recession of the 1930s ushered in a decade of instability in which the xenophobia of the impoverished peasantry was exploited by right-wing movements, principally by the Iron Guard, and directed against the Jews. The latter's position as alcohol suppliers, moneylenders and middlemen in the timber trade made them disliked by the peasants and vulnerable to any force capable of mobilizing them. Disillusion with the failure of parliamentary government – represented principally by the National Liberal and National Peasant Parties – to solve economic problems fuelled support for the Guard, with its promise of spiritual regeneration and its programme of combating 'Jewish Bolshevism'.[88]

Combating 'Jewish Communism' was one of the slogans of the Iron Guard, a movement created and dominated, even after his death, by Corneliu Zelea Codreanu.[89] As one scholar has concluded, 'there can be no understanding of the Iron Guard without a thorough understanding of Codreanu', who was dubbed by his followers *Căpitanul* (The Captain).[90] It was Codreanu who inspired the Guard with his invectives against what he saw as 'the Judeo-Bolshevik' threat, against the drive for modernization through imitation of western political and economic institutions, and against a corrupt ruling elite.

Codreanu was born in 1899 in the northern Moldavia town of Huşi. His father, Ion Zelinski, had come to the town from Austrian Bukovina shortly before Corneliu's birth with his German wife, Elisabeth Brunner. Ion was engaged as a teacher at the local secondary school and in 1902 Romanian-ized his surname to Zelea and added a second one, Codreanu, in recognition of his forester lineage (*codru* means forest in Romanian). Between 1910 and 1916, Corneliu attended the military school at Mănăstirea Dealului in Wallachia, housed in a monastery, and it was in these surroundings that a respect for discipline and reverence for God were inculcated in him. At the end of the First World War he enrolled at Iaşi University, where he attended the lectures of Professor Alexandru Cuza, who presented Communism as a Jewish conspiracy against 'Christian' Europe. In 1923, Cuza founded the League of National Christian Defence (LANC)[91] with an anti-Semitic programme, the principal point of which was the application of a *numerus clausus* for the admission of Jews into the professions. But Codreanu, who aligned himself with Cuza, was not interested in pursuing this aim solely through the ballot box; it was to be imposed through violence, as events of 1923 were to show.

In October 1923, Codreanu organized a plot to shoot politicians who had supported an amendment to the Romanian constitution granting Jews the right to citizenship, but the plot was betrayed and Codreanu and a few of his friends were arrested, tried and acquitted. On leaving custody Ion Moţa, one of the conspirators, shot dead the man suspected of having betrayed them. A second event linked to the plot highlights another aspect of Codreanu's movement, namely its missionary role. In his autobiography Codreanu described how he received a vision of the Archangel Michael in the prison chapel which urged him to dedicate his life to God. After his release, Codreanu returned to Iaşi and set up the Brotherhood of the Cross (*Frăţia de Cruce*), an organization for young men designed to foster a national revival. He appointed Moţa head of the Brotherhood. The very name suggested a mystic communion among its members whose ritual required them to take a formal vow pledging their life to Codreanu and the Brotherhood. In this respect the Guard sits uneasily in a 'fascist' context, if only, as one scholar has put it, 'in that Codreanu's theories were derived from the Book of Revelation. He made a practice of going up into the mountains to pray. One does not hear that of Hitler or of Mussolini. The Guard was much more akin to the Russian *narodniki* than to any western model.'[92]

The first task they set themselves was to build a student centre, but Codreanu's notoriety led the local prefect, Constantin Manciu, to break up the student group with great violence, binding them with ropes and dragging them through the streets of the town. Codreanu took his revenge by shooting Manciu and two other officials in the Iaşi courtroom in October 1924. His personal popularity led the government to put him on trial far from Moldavia in Turnu-Severin, near the Yugoslav border. Nevertheless, the jury acquitted him, returning their verdict with LANC emblems in their lapels.

Cuza was becoming unnerved by Codreanu's violence and to avoid a rift in the LANC, Codreanu and a close friend, Ion Moţa, left for France. They returned in the spring of 1926 to contest the elections in which the LANC gained ten seats in parliament. Codreanu was not among the successful deputies and attacked the LANC for having sold out to the Jews. On 24 June 1927, he founded his own movement, the Legion of the Archangel Michael (*Legiunea Arhanghelului Mihail*), whose aim was to engender a spiritual regeneration amongst Romanians and to create 'a new type of man'.

The Legion began slowly, its first public meeting being held in December 1929.[93] In April 1930, Codreanu created a militant political wing of the Legion, which he named the Iron Guard (*Garda de Fier*), in order to combat 'Jewish Communism'.[94] Early in 1931, both the Guard and the Legion were banned by Iuliu Maniu's National Peasant government, but this did not prevent them from contesting the elections of that summer as the 'C. Z. Codreanu Group'. They failed to win a seat, but in a bye-election Codreanu was returned and his father won a second by-election in the following year. Outlawed again in 1932, they still contested general elections and in July won five seats.

A policy of propaganda by unpaid work was initiated by the Legion, but its value was often offset by the violence directed by some legionaries against their political opponents. The fear of unrest during an election campaign led I. G. Duca's Liberal government to dissolve the Guard yet again on 10 December 1933 and in the agitation that followed, several Guardists were killed and hundreds arrested. On 29 December, nine days after a fresh election victory, Duca was shot dead by three Guardists in Sinaia station. The assassins were sentenced to life imprisonment, but Codreanu was cleared of involvement and emerged from hiding to continue the Legion's communal work. In December 1934, Codreanu persuaded General Gheorghe Cantacuzino to found a new party, 'All for the Country' (*Totul Pentru Ţară*), which was based on the infrastructure of the Legion and which acknowledged Codreanu as its spiritual leader.[95] The Legion's increasing appeal to industrial workers was reflected in the foundation in

1936 of a Legionary Workers' Corps which attracted 6,000 members in Bucharest alone.[96]

Codreanu's autobiography appeared in the same year. Here he laid out the Legion's programme which, in part, was conceived like a monastic order. The Legion was endowed with a spiritual mission to change Romanians by creating 'the new man', one bent on social justice. There was no place for the bourgeoisie. His opposition to democracy was expressed in a virulent anti-Semitism. The Legion's articles of faith dictated a pathological hatred of Jews, whom Codreanu saw as the fount of Communism. Democracy was not good for the Romanians because it 'breaks the unity of the Romanian people, dividing it into parties, stirring it up and so, disunited, exposing it to face the united bloc of Jewish power in a difficult moment of history'. A multi-party system was, in Codreanu's view, incapable of ensuring continuity in development: 'It is as if', he wrote, 'on a farm the owners changed yearly, each coming with different plans, doing away with what the predecessors did'.[97]

The deaths of two legionary volunteers, Vasile Marin and Ion Moţa, in Spain at the beginning of 1937 provided an opportunity for the Guard to put on a display of strength in Bucharest. An appeal was made to students: 'The entire Romanian Christian body at the university, academies and senior schools in Bucharest regards it as a duty of honour regarding the sacrifice made by the two legionaries, former student leaders and heads of the generation of 1922, to be present on 11, 12 and 13 February for the funeral rites.' At the head of the cortège, which included the German minister Wilhelm Fabricius and his Italian colleague, marched several detachments of legionaries while the funeral service, held the following day, on 13 February, was conducted by four prelates of the Orthodox Church, metropolitan bishop Gurie of Bessarabia, Nicolae Bălan, metropolitan of Transylvania, Vartolomei, bishop of Ramnic, and Veniamin, the vicar of the patriarchate.[98] In his funeral blessing, Bălan gave thanks to the Lord

> that you have considered our people worthy enough to chose from their midst faithful warriors for your work, who from beyond the grave send us their mission and the confession of their faith, following the words of your great disciples from the earliest of times which rang out around the world: 'That is how I understood my life's duty. I loved Christ and I went happily to my death for him!'[99]

The December 1937 elections were a turning point for democracy in Romania. On the expiry of its term of office in November the Liberal government of Gheorghe Tătărescu resigned. King Carol invited Ion Mihalache to form a National Peasant government, but Mihalache objected to the inclusion of a political rival and refused. Carol therefore went back to Tătărescu. During the election campaign Maniu took over as head of the

National Peasant Party and, in order to overturn Tătărescu, made a pact with Codreanu and Gheorghe Brătianu, the leader of a dissident Liberal group. Maniu's action surprised friends of democracy in Romania and abroad.[100] Politically, he had nothing in common with the Guard; he merely wanted to use it to dissuade the Liberals from the use of intimidation during the campaign. No common lists of candidates were drawn up; the signatories simply agreed to support free elections.[101] Nevertheless, the Guard gained respectability from association with Maniu's name, while Maniu stifled the cause of democracy at a time when it was struggling for air, especially as the pact prevented his party from criticizing the Guard during the campaign. 'Above all', as Henry Roberts argued, 'it showed the National Peasants' own loss of confidence in themselves or their ideas, and was in the sharpest contrast to their refusals to make any deals on the road to power in 1927 and 1928'.[102]

The 'All for the Country' Party emerged with 66 seats (15.6 per cent of the vote), the third strongest party behind the Liberals (152 seats, 35.9 per cent) and the National Peasants (86 seats, 20.4 per cent). For the first time in the history of Romania a government had fallen in an election, for the Liberal Party failed to receive the 40 per cent of the votes that it required to stay in power.[103] Tătărescu resigned on 28 December and, the same day, Carol turned to the Transylvanian poet Octavian Goga, head of the National Christian Party, formed in 1935 from an alliance of Cuza's LANC with Goga's National Agrarian Party, to form a government, despite the fact that Goga's party had received less than 10 per cent of the vote (39 seats). By propelling the anti-Semitic National Christian Party to power Carol hoped to draw off support from the Guard.

Carol promoted anti-Semitism for political expediency. Under the Goga government anti-Semitism was raised to the level of state policy. One of Goga's first steps was to suppress, on 30 December 1937, the 'Jewish' newspapers *Dimineața, Adevărul* and *Lupta*, so-called because their editors or owners were Jewish, on the grounds of their 'destructive tendencies... which had ruined the country's moral health.[104] Newspapers in the major provincial towns were also closed 'because they were run by Jews'.[105] Goga cancelled licences to sell alcohol and tobacco held by Jews, and placed a ban on the employment of Jews and foreigners in cafés and restaurants, while the Bucharest bar association suspended its 1,540 registered Jewish lawyers from practising in Bucharest.[106] Istrate Micescu, the Foreign Minister who was responsible for leading the campaign to exclude Jewish lawyers from the Bucharest bar, while defending the anti-Semitic programme to the British and French ministers in Bucharest as necessary to avoid an Iron Guard government and promising moderation in its application, was at the same time telling the German minister that 'anti-Semitic measures would be intensified'.[107] This wave of discrimination culminated in a Decree on the Revision of Citizenship, promulgated on 21 January 1938, which targeted all Jews who had obtained Romanian naturalization, whether on the basis of their own declarations, or following a court decision. The Jews were required to submit documentary proof of their right to citizenship within 30 days, a condition that most could not meet since they could not obtain the necessary documents in time. As a result of the revision, completed on 15 September 1939, 225,222 Jews had their rights as Romanian citizens withdrawn.[108] The decree was intended to persuade Jews to emigrate, and demonstrated clearly what Carol had in mind for them when he gave an interview to A. L. Easterman, correspondent for the British *Daily Herald*, which was published on 10 January 1938.[109]

Public opinion in Britain was unnerved. The British minister in Bucharest, Sir Reginald Hoare, conveyed his government's concern to Goga over the anti-Semitic measures.[110] The French minister, Adrien Thierry, followed suit. Jewish and foreign business concerns ceased trading in protest against the government, thus threatening economic collapse. But anti-Semitism had become such a powerful card in Romania that no government could afford to ignore it. This was recognized by Franklin Mott Gunther, the US minister to Bucharest, in a prophetic cable to his Secretary of State dated 20 January:

> I regret to report my conviction that even if this [Goga-Cuza] Government should not survive the elections the issue of [anti-Semitism] itself is now so much to the fore that it will have to be espoused by any succeeding government or even dictatorship in response to a determined insistent public demand.[111]

New elections were called by Carol against a background of conflict between Cuza's supporters and those of Codreanu. At the urging of the Germans, who backed Goga, and of General Ion Antonescu, Minister of Defence in the Goga cabinet, Codreanu and Goga came to an understanding on 8 February 1938 whereby the former would run but not campaign. Carol clearly saw this arrangement between the ultra-nationalists as a threat to his power to manipulate and on 11 February he promptly dismissed Goga, whose final words in his farewell address to the nation were 'Israel, you have won!' On 20 February, Carol abolished the constitution and instituted a royal dictatorship.

A puppet government under the Patriarch Miron Cristea was sworn in, with Armand Călinescu, Codreanu's avowed enemy, as Minister of the Interior. Widespread arrests of Guardists were ordered in March, and in the following month Călinescu moved against Codreanu, ordering his arrest on 16 April on charges of insulting a minister in office. Codreanu had accused Nicolae Iorga, the historian and journalist, of 'spiritual dishonour' in denigrating the Guard's attempts to set up workers' canteens and Guardist-run shops. Codreanu was sentenced to six months' imprisonment and then hastily retried in May for conspiracy to take over the state. In a trial considered to be prejudiced against him, Codreanu was found guilty and condemned to ten years' hard labour. Călinescu then ordered the round-up of hundreds of Guardists, among them Codreanu's intended successor, Gheorghe Clima. Some of the other leaders went underground, including Horia Sima, a 31-year-old school teacher, and they organized squads to hit back at their opponents.[112] A Jewish lawyer was shot dead, Jewish shops were looted and synagogues set ablaze. Then, on 24 November, the Rector of Cluj University, a friend of Călinescu, was shot and wounded. Carol's patience with the Guard was finally exhausted. Codreanu, the three murderers of Duca, and ten other Guardist assassins, were taken from their prison and strangled in woods to the north of Bucharest on the night of 29–30 November. Their bodies were taken to the prison at Jilava and buried in the grounds. A communiqué of 1 December announced that they had been shot 'while trying to escape'.

News of the murders was met by the general public with disbelief and contempt. They were particularly disgusted by their cold-blooded nature and felt shame that their monarch could have been behind such a deed. Carl Clodius, the German economic specialist handling Germany's commercial relations with Romania, noted:

> The murder of Codreanu and his followers has changed the situation considerably. Condemnation of this murder is equally strong in almost all circles of the population. I encountered no Romanian politician who even attempted to defend the murder to me. Even members of the government have tried only hesitantly and with very weak arguments to motivate and explain the murder as a political necessity. The embitterment in the Iron Guard is tremendous.... The murder of Codreanu has shaken [Carol's] moral position in the country to such an extent that he will recover from it only very slowly, if at all.[113]

The violence of the measures taken by Carol against the Guard seems to have been driven by his fear of it as a tool of Hitler. The wave of arrests of Guardists had taken place soon after the *Anschluss* between Germany and Austria in March 1938, and the murder of Codreanu and 13 other Guardists occurred immediately after Carol's visit to Hitler, when the Führer had urged their release and the formation of a Guardist government.[114] The Guardists underground swore revenge. Horia Sima planned a *coup*, but the plot was uncovered and he fled the country on 8 February 1939 for Berlin.[115] Assassination teams were set up, but they were uncovered by the police. Eventually, on 21 September 1939, a group of six managed to ambush Călinescu, now prime minister, in Bucharest and shot him dead. Brutal reprisals were now taken against the Guard on Carol's order. Not only were the six Guardists responsible shot, and their bodies left on the spot where Călinescu fell for several days, but in each county prefects were ordered to select three members of the Guard for execution, while in the prison camps between 60 and 90 Guardists were shot. The British minister to Bucharest reported that some 400 Guardists were victims of Carol's revenge.[116]

Carol again appointed Tătărescu as prime minister in November 1939 in the hope of encouraging the National Liberals and National Peasants to join a national alliance, but both Brătianu and Maniu refused. D. J. Hall, a British propaganda representative, provided an acute analysis of the political situation in March 1940:

> The King has now gained such authority that his Ministers have no say whatsoever in the Government of the country. Many of them have, at one time or another, been engaged in questionable activities and the King's power is such that he is able to employ them as puppets. The Prime Minister, M. Tătărescu, is purely a mouthpiece for the King. The Foreign Minister, M. Gafencu, while sound enough in the theory of his foreign policy, and in his affection for the allied cause, has not the courage to withstand any demand made of him. M. Giurescu, the Minister of Propaganda, is pro-German in his inclinations, and all other members of the Government are dominated by fear. In fact, it may be said that if any explanation is ever required of any action of Romania, it can be found in that one word – 'fear'. Anyone who opposes the regime is a marked man. The secret police system has been developed to such an extent that there is no man of any importance, either in politics or commerce, who can do or say anything without being immediately observed. Many of the houses of these people have microphones fitted in them, and they are too frightened to have them removed.[117]

As German successes in the war alerted Carol of the advisability of German friendship, he became more conciliatory towards the Iron Guard. Carol had ordered the release of a number of Guardists from detention in January 1940. In May, Horia Sima, the Guard's new leader who had fled to Germany during the previous year, re-entered the country. On the fall of France in June, Carol established by decree the Party of the Nation (*Partidul Naţiunii*), a single party totally subservient to the king, and within days Sima issued a manifesto calling on the Guardists to join it. This outward sign of national unity proved irrelevant in the face of momentous events on the international stage.[118]

2
Antonescu's Path to Power

Ion Antonescu had the army in his blood. He was born on 2 June 1882 into a middle-class family in the southern Romanian town of Pitesti, and baptized into the Orthodox faith. His father, an army officer, wanted his son to follow in his footsteps and mapped out a military career for him, sending him to primary and secondary military schools in Craiova. On 1 July 1904, after two years at the Infantry and Cavalry School, he began service in the Romanian army with the rank of second lieutenant. Over the next two years he followed courses at the Advanced Cavalry School (*Şcoala Superioară de Cavalerie*) at Târgovişte. The peasant uprising of 1907 found him as head of a cavalry unit in Covurlui, in the south-east of the country, where his tact and conciliatory behaviour won him the admiration of King Carol I himself, who sent Crown Prince Ferdinand to Galaţi to congratulate him in front of the entire garrison.[1] On 10 May 1908, he was promoted to lieutenant and assigned to a cavalry brigade. Between 1911 and 1913 he attended the Advanced School of War (*Şcoala Superioară de Război*) in Bucharest, from where he emerged with the rank of captain. On the outbreak of the Second Balkan War in that year he served as a staff officer for operations in the First Cavalry Division. The experience gained in this post he was to put to good effect during the First World War.

On 15 August 1916, Romania entered the First World War on the side of Britain, France and Russia with a promise from the Allies that in the event of victory, Romania would gain Transylvania. The following day, Antonescu was appointed chief of operations to General Constantin Prezan, commander of the army of the north, and remained closely attached to the general throughout the war. In November, he was intimately involved in the unsuccessful military operations in defence of Bucharest; the capital was occupied by the Germans and the Romanian army began its retreat to Moldavia on 21 November. At the beginning of December, Prezan was appointed Chief of the General Staff and Antonescu, now with the rank of major, was transferred to become head of operations. It was in this role that he made a significant contribution to the tactics adopted during the battle of Mărăşeşti (25 July–21 August 1917), when the Romanian and Russian armies successfully resisted the German attempt to take Moldavia. On 1 September 1917, he was promoted to the rank of lieutenant-colonel. Antonescu lived alongside Prezan for the rest of the war, exerting a powerful influence on the general's morale.

The disintegration of the Tsarist army forced an armistice with the Central Powers (22 November 1917) and left the Romanian army open to attack from two sides – from southern Moldavia and from Ukraine, now occupied by German and Austro-Hungarian troops. In this situation the Romanian government decided to conclude a peace agreement with the Central Powers. Such an agreement, reluctantly accepted by the Allies, was in Antonescu's view 'the most rational solution'.[2] After the peace signed at Buftea near Bucharest in May 1918, Prezan went into retirement and Antonescu was given the command of a cavalry regiment. He returned to operations in November when Romania rejoined the war and Prezan was again made commander-in-chief. Antonescu's merits as an operations officer did not pass unnoticed. Ion Duca, a future prime minister, noted: 'The right arm of General Prezan was a young officer, Major Antonescu, a person of particular value who, through his intelligence, skill and activity, brought credit on himself and invaluable service to the country.'[3]

A more incisive appraisal of Antonescu was given by General Victor Pétin, France's military attaché in Bucharest. Antonescu was one of three officers proposed by the Romanian government in March 1920 for the post of military attaché in Paris and Pétin was asked by his own Minister of War to provide an assessment of each nomination. Petin pulled no punches in his characterization of Antonescu:

> Extremely industrious, of great military worth and well-suited from the Romanian point of view, to hold such positions with success. But Lt.-Col. Antonescu is extremely vain as regards his own person and his country, is chauvinistic, xenophobic and I am sure that we cannot count on him in any way to continue the policy of French–Romanian military *rapprochement* or to receive from him any sign of gratitude for the services made by France [to Romania].[4]

Needless to say, Antonescu was not the minister's choice and a Colonel Suţu was selected. However, two years later, Suţu had to leave Paris on extended leave and the Romanian government nominated Antonescu as his replacement. This time, the Minister of War in Paris felt obliged to accept the nomination, despite similar reservations about Antonescu in a report from General Pétin, dated 21 July 1922: 'A well-tried intelligence, brutal, duplicitous, very vain, a ferocious will to succeed – these are, together with an extreme xenophobia, the striking characteristics of this strange figure.' In an ambiguous yet prophetic sentence Petin added, 'Antonescu deserves a special place in the Romanian army.'[5]

On 1 January 1923, Antonescu was also accredited to London and Brussels. Judging from papers in the Ministry of War in Bucharest it seems that the decision to send him to Paris was taken in order to rescue him from 'a delicate situation' which had arisen in the Sibiu garrison, where he was commander of the cavalry school, due to the fact that 'he had grown accustomed only to command, while up to the rank he had, he had yet to learn how to listen'.[6] With accreditation in three capitals, it was not easy for Antonescu to make his presence felt in each, especially as he spent much of his time in Paris negotiating a credit for 100 millions francs for French arms. In London he not only worked alongside, but also became a personal friend of, the Romanian minister, Nicolae Titulescu.[7] In July 1926, Antonescu was released from his post and assigned to the cavalry training school in Sibiu. For a brief period in autumn 1928 he was secretary-general in the Ministry of War and in the same year married Maria Niculescu.[8] Three years later, he was promoted to brigadier-general and, on 12 December 1933, was appointed Chief of the General Staff. His priority was the modernization of the Romanian army, which he regarded as being incapable of meeting the country's defence needs. He considered its weapons and equipment to be outdated and to rectify these deficiencies he proposed to the cabinet the purchase of arms from abroad. Wrangling between Antonescu and the Minister of Defence, General Angelescu, about these purchases came to a head when the latter questioned the quality of small arms deliveries from Czechoslovakia, which Antonescu regarded as vital to his reforms. Exasperated and convinced of the futility of persevering with his plans he tendered his resignation to Prime Minister Tatarescu on 8 December 1934.[9]

The growing popular support for Corneliu Zelea Codreanu and the violence of his anti-Semitic Iron Guard, made it inevitable that it should attract Antonescu's attention. While Deputy Chief of the Army General Staff in 1933, Antonescu had ordered Military Intelligence to prepare a study of the Guard and its leader in order to evaluate its influence within the army. Antonescu's marginal notes on the report are revealing for his thoughts on the Guard at that time. To Codreanu's boast that 'in a single night anyone can make a [political] programme and it is not them for which the country feels a need, but for the men and the will to fulfil them', Antonescu added: 'Not serious. It is not possible to improvise the programme of the simplest family farm in a single night, let alone that of a body as vast as the modern state.'[10] Where Antonescu did have common ground with Codreanu was in seeing the Jews as a threat, but not – at this stage – in the method of dealing with it. When Codreanu described the Guard as 'defending Romania from the peril which is presented by the ever-growing invasion of the Jews', Antonescu remarked: 'Through the organization of the Romanian classes, and not through the brutal measures for which everyone clamours.'[11]

A shared distrust of King Carol and an intensive dislike of his mistress and confidante Elena Lupescu and fawning counsellor Ernest Urdăreanu led Antonescu to bow to the arguments of two of his friends, General Zizi Cantacuzino and an engineer Nicolae Mareş to meet Codreanu for the first time, in 1936. Antonescu found the Iron Guard leader arrogant – Antonescu was hardly noted for his humility – but committed to a purge of the political system.[12] On 24 July, Armand Călinescu, the Minister of Internal Affairs, noted: 'My informers tell me that a representative of Codreanu was received by General Ion Antonescu at Piteşti who greeted him with the words: "with all my achievements and symbols of rank, I cry out today: Long live the Captain".'[13]

The Guard's success, under the label 'All for the Country' Party, in the December 1937 elections – from which it emerged with 66 seats, the third strongest party behind the Liberals (152 seats) and the National Peasants (86 seats) – drove Carol to desperate measures. He ignored the election result and turned to the Transylvanian poet Octavian Goga to form a government, despite the fact that Goga's party had received less than 10 per cent of the vote (39 seats). Goga, however, who was a close friend of Antonescu, made his acceptance of the post conditional on the appointment of the Antonescu as Minister of Defence. Carol refused. Antonescu, too, turned down the offer from Goga, because, one of his admirer's explained, 'he believed Goga would direct our foreign policy towards Germany'.[14] Goga did not give up, arguing: 'My presence in the government will calm Germany, while your presence in national defence will provide a guarantee to France and England that our troops will never fight against them.'[15]

Antonescu was persuaded and accepted provisionally on 26 December. Carol was willing to have Antonescu as Minister of Communications but not at Defence. Armand Călinescu, the Minister of Interior designate, noted in his diary: 'I discussed with Ionel Antonescu. He would not enter [the cabinet] unless he received the army. With guarantees that we would not go with Germany.'[16] Given the king's opposition to his appointment as Defence Minister, Antonescu wrote to Goga rejecting his offer. In view of Goga's own condition of a role for Antonescu in his government, Carol was forced to discuss the matter directly with the General. He invited Antonescu to the Palace on 28 December and, with misplaced magnanimity, offered to forget everything that had divided them. Antonescu bluntly reminded Carol of the surveillance he had been placed under on Carol's orders when he was Chief of the General Staff in 1934 and the audience was quickly cut short. The next day, Carol recalled Antonescu and ordered him as an officer to accept the Communications portfolio. Antonescu's reply is instructive in two respects: it underlines both his sense of honour and his aversion to corruption:

> Your Majesty, in the presence of the order I submit. Your Majesty knows, however, that many irregularities occur in that ministry. If I were placed

in charge of it, I would not patronize the dishonour taking root there and thus, I could not accept the scandalous contracts, onerous for the country, that have been concluded there. I would be put, consequently, in a situation where I would be quickly relieved and thus my name would not bring benefit to the government, quite the contrary. I consider, therefore, that it would be better if I were appointed to the Ministry of National Defence, especially as I am a military man and I have many important tasks to fulfil for the Army.[17]

Carol cannot have been comfortable hearing these words. His regime had become a byword for corruption, and if we are to believe Constantin Argetoianu, one of Carol's ministers, the Communications Ministry had been 'persuaded' by Carol himself to give the industrialist Nicolae Malaxa, a member of the *camarilla* – the popular name for the king's inner circle – preference in the award of certain contracts.[18] The king accepted Antonescu's argument.

Antonescu moved quickly to reassure Codreanu. With Carol's approval he met the Iron Guard leader and told him that 'he was firmly resolved to maintain legality' and asked Interior Minister Armand Călinescu to adopt an unprovocative attitude towards the Guard. Codreanu, for his part, promised Antonescu to desist from any political violence. But it was not the Guard that posed the chief threat to public order. The paramilitary wing of Professor Alexandru Cuza's anti-Semitic, pro-Hitler League of National Christian Defence (LANC), known as the *lancieri*, was adopted by Carol in his attempt, like Mussolini, to have a fascist movement of his own. No more than an army of thugs, the *lancieri* rivalled, and in some cases exceeded, the Guard in their violence against Jews; indeed, the similarity of their uniforms – the only difference was the colour of the shirt: green for the Guard, blue for the *lancieri* – meant that often they were held responsible for each other's actions.[19] It was against this background that Antonescu clamped down on demonstrations by paramilitary groups, extending the provisions of martial law which had been admitted under the 1923 constitution.[20]

Antonescu's action did not prevent street brawls between the *lancieri* and Goga's supporters which occurred after a rift developed between Goga and Cuza over the intensity of the discriminatory policy in relation to the Jews. Faced with the collapse of public order, and mounting international condemnation of the Goga government, Carol attempted to set up a broad-based government which would include the National Peasant Party – but without Maniu – and Codreanu.[21] He asked Antonescu to act as an intermediary with Codreanu, but the latter refused Carol's overtures, telling Antonescu that he would go his own way. Carol was incensed and called on Călinescu to consider means of arresting Codreanu and suppressing the Guard. Antonescu was against the use of the army, arguing that only the law should be used. Carol called for new elections and as the campaign opened on 6 February, two Guardists were shot dead by *lancieri*.[22] Antonescu warned Codreanu against violent retaliation, a warning which Codreanu promised to heed on condition that Antonescu protect him if Carol moved against the Guard. Antonescu agreed. At the same time, Wilhelm Fabricius, the German minister in Bucharest, concerned at the drift into anarchy, called on Goga to come to an understanding with Codreanu. This resulted in an arrangement between the two on 8 February 1938 whereby Codreanu would run, but not campaign. Codreanu's decision was attributed by Sir Reginald Hoare, the British Minister, 'possibly... to the personal influence of General Antonescu over M. Codreanu'.[23] It was of no consequence. Carol was particularly indignant with Goga whom he dismissed on 11 February and three days later he formed a puppet government headed by the Orthodox Patriarch Miron Cristea. The new administration contained seven former prime ministers and three ministers from the previous government: Antonescu, Călinescu and Micescu. The retention of Călinescu, Codreanu's avowed enemy, at the Interior Ministry, was a signal that Carol meant business with the Guard.

Antonescu's sway over Codreanu brought him to the attention of the German minister Fabricius. In a dispatch of 10 February 1938 to the German Foreign Ministry, Fabricius reported:

> M. Antonescu served for a long time in London as Military Attaché and is a man of broad vision. On the other hand, he has no ties to Germany whatsoever. Since he is a man of determination who has his task of building up the striking power of the Romanian Army seriously at heart, we will have to try to develop further the contact which I have recently established with him.[24]

Ironically, Antonescu's desire to strengthen the Romanian army sprang from the threat to Romania's borders posed by German-supported Hungarian revisionism. He had recognized this threat in an analysis he made of the political situation shortly before being appointed Minister of Defence in which he predicted that there was more than

> a little probability of Russia concluding an alliance with one or both of the powers which had fallen under the sphere of influence of Germany and Italy, which would have the direct result for us of a war in the East concomitant with one in the West and South. Possibly, however, one can envision a war in the West concomitant only with one in the South, because our neighbours – Bulgaria and Hungary – are in the German–Italian sphere.[25]

As minister Antonescu, while not dismissing a Soviet threat, concentrated his attention on an attack on Romania's western frontier and, on 12 March

1938, he ordered the General Staff to prepare for 'a partial mobilization on the Western front'.[26] But it was the domestic scene that dominated his concerns. A month earlier, on 16 February, Antonescu saw Sir Reginald Hoare, the British minister, and assured him

> that the situation was much calmer now and that he had the army thoroughly in hand. I asked him if it was true that it was largely owing to his influence that M. Codreanu issued his statement...that he was giving up all electoral propaganda. He replied that it was true that he had given Codreanu advice on this score and had told him frankly that the country was drifting towards civil war and...[he] was fully resolved to use any measure of force necessary to prevent it.... He said that he had greatly disliked entering the Goga Government but as in the past he had been accused of conspiring against the King he felt that to refuse to do so would lend some colour to the charges of this nature...
>
> I told him that since leaving office the Liberals were inclined to tell me that the evidence was pouring in to the effect that the Codreanu organization and funds were derived from Germany. What did he think about it? He replied that when he had no evidence he was not prepared to make accusations, but he could tell me that he had warned Codreanu that these things were being said and had received from him a positive assurance that 'my hands are as clean as yours'. As for the Iron Guard movement, it was partly a revolt against the malpractices of party politicians and partly a mysticism. It could not be dealt with by force, but he hoped that as older and wiser men joined the movement it could be weaned from its more obnoxious aspects.[27]

Four days later, on 20 February, Carol abolished the 1923 constitution and instituted a royal dictatorship. It required the dissolution of all political parties. To Carol's surprise, Codreanu acquiesced without demur. The following day, Codreanu dissolved the 'All for the Country' Party and called on the Iron Guard to disband until 'the true king' – Carol's son Michael – ascended the throne. In his address to the movement and the public he gave his reasons:

> We do not wish to provoke force. We do not wish to attract violence. We have learned from our past experience when, contrary to our wishes, we were drawn down the path of violence. We will not respond to violence in any way, we will bear it.... We do not want a *coup d'état*...Our generation sees very well that the gauntlet has been thrown down. That gauntlet, however, will remain on the ground. We refuse to pick it up. The hour of our triumph has not come. It is still their hour.[28]

Lacking a motive for moving against the Guard, Călinescu, with Carol's agreement, invented one. Nicolae Iorga, the eminent historian and editor of *Neamul Românesc* (The Romanian People), ran a campaign attacking the Guard for its creation of workers' canteens and shops. Codreanu responded with a letter accusing him of 'spiritual dishonour'. Iorga demanded satisfaction over the insult.[29] At a cabinet meeting on 28 March, Călinescu recommended that Codreanu be tried for libel. Antonescu protested that such action was an abuse of power and resigned the next day.[30]

Călinescu was relentless in his pursuit of Codreanu. On 16 April, he ordered his arrest and in a lightning trial of three days Codreanu was convicted and sentenced to six months' imprisonment for libel. On 18 April, the first day of the trial, the press announced that Antonescu was to be pensioned off. One month later, on 17 May, charges of treason were brought against Codreanu. Călinescu invited Fabricius to his office to explain the 'evidence':

> The records of Codreanu have vanished and the material found was scanty. The prosecutor therefore insisted on using a document which was the Romanian draft of a letter that the accused had addressed to the Führer and Chancellor at the beginning of 1935.... The Minister of the Interior emphasized that he did not know whether the letter had reached its destination and had been answered.[31]

Both Antonescu and Maniu appeared as witnesses for the defence in Codreanu's second trial, before a military tribunal. A dramatic account of Antonescu's behaviour was given by an American journalist, Countess R. G. Waldeck:

> While the courtroom waited with baited breath, Antonescu was asked whether he considered Codreanu a traitor. Standing erect, the General marched over to the accused *Capitanu*,[32] held out his hand simply for Codreanu's and pressed it. 'Would General Antonescu give his hand to a traitor?' he demanded of the silent courtroom.[33]

In his statement to the court on behalf of Codreanu Antonescu declared:

> From the conversations that I had with Mr Codreanu I noted that he was not preoccupied with accession to power but by the country's affairs and he claimed to me that he was not yet prepared for government.... If I had noticed something suspicious in the accused in that he intended a revolt, I would not have talked to him. In respect of the arms, I told the accused to hand them over to the military authorities.... I cannot say whether the All for the Country Party is good or bad as I am a soldier. From the information that I had I cannot believe that the accused would be capable of treason.[34]

Hoare, too, was unconvinced by the evidence of Codreanu's treason but despite this, and the support of Antonescu and Maniu, the 'Captain' was convicted and sentenced to ten years' imprisonment. Antonescu was placed under house arrest in Predeal on Carol's orders, but when a French journalist managed to interview him, he was recalled to active service and assigned to the Third Army Corps in the Bessarabian capital Chişinău, well out of the way of foreign newspapermen and diplomats. In a memorandum to Carol, Antonescu gave an explanation for his behaviour towards Codreanu. Reminding him that he had negotiated with the king's knowledge with Codreanu to persuade him to withdraw from the electoral campaign at the beginning of February, Antonescu told Carol that he had given Codreanu his word that he would come to his aid 'should his fate be left to the total discretion of the authorities'. Codreanu had accepted that word.[35]

Carol's hostility towards Antonescu turned to vindictiveness. Antonescu's wife, Maria, had been married and divorced in France. In June 1938, with Carol's connivance, Maria's former husband was brought at state expense from Paris to bring an action of bigamy against Maria with the aim of discrediting Antonescu and putting an end to his career. The action collapsed when Antonescu's lawyer, Mihai Antonescu, produced the original French certificate of divorce.[36] Ion Antonescu's fury with Carol served only to widen the gulf between the two men. At the same time, his wife's victory confirmed Antonescu's reputation in the army as a man of honour and further tarnished Carol's own standing with his senior officers.

Events in Europe were a source of even greater concern to Antonescu. He was dismayed by the Anglo-French capitulation to Hitler over Czechoslavakia in September 1938. In recognizing in an interview with a French journalist that, after the Munich Agreement, 'an orientation towards the Axis was obligatory' for Romania,[37] he was expressing a view shared by the great majority of his countrymen. After the German occupation of the Sudetenland in October, the Romanian General Staff questioned the value of the degree to which Romania could rely on Britain and France.[38] The disillusionment of Francophile Romanians was reflected in a report sent by Fabricius to Berlin on 28 October:

> Gheorghe Brătianu is of the opinion, which by the way he has always held, that Romanian foreign policy must be oriented more strongly toward Germany.... For that reason he had turned to the Liberal Party – more specifically, the wing led by his uncle, Dinu Brătianu, although the latter had not wanted to hear anything of a pro-German policy.... As a result of the events of the last few weeks and under his influence, Dinu Brătianu had now come to realize that his previous attitude of 'everything with France' had been wrong. It was a bitter disillusionment over the fact that France had got Czechoslovakia into a difficult position and then left her in the lurch. 'The same might happen to Romania.' The old

friend of France had said, 'whereas, after all, before the war Rumania had obtained everything from Germany and had fared well in so doing; this would have to be the case again'.... At the same time the old Peasant Party leader, Maniu, has also reversed his position. In a memorandum which he submitted to the king, jointly with Dinu Brătianu, he too, demanded an alignment with Berlin...[39]

This radical change of sentiment among pro-Western Romanians was attributed by Dr Carl Clodius, Deputy Director of the German Foreign Ministry's Economic Policy Department, to

the collapse of France's political prestige, the growth of Germany's power in 1938, the realization that only Germany can provide effective protection against Russia, Romania's most dangerous enemy, and finally also to the consideration that Romania is economically dependent on Germany to an ever increasing degree.... Even pronounced opponents of Germany, who formerly never concealed their opposition in their conversations with me, now speak quite another language. There is no doubt that in most cases this change is due not to sympathy for Germany but solely to realistic political considerations, often even to fear of Germany.[40]

Antonescu remained in the shadows as Hitler quickly made himself master of much of continental Europe. An anonymous British observer of Romania was alert enough, however, to pick him out and noted prophetically in May 1940:

General Antonescu, a man of great integrity and a one-time Minister of War, has had most of his power taken from him. He is too independent a man for the King to control as he wishes.... Nevertheless, if the great crisis comes, it seems certain that General Antonescu will have to be called in, owing to the respect the army has for him.[41]

The crisis soon came. When news of the Soviet ultimatum demanding Bessarabia and northern Bukovina broke on 27 June, Antonescu asked for an audience with Carol and advised him to ask the Soviet Union for a longer period of grace in which to conduct an orderly withdrawal, both for the sake of army morale and in order to retrieve more equipment. He also called on the king to jettison his advisers. In a letter to Carol, formalizing his arguments, Antonescu urged:

The men and system must be changed immediately. If Your Majesty does not turn his ear to the suffering of the people in this last hour, total collapse, irreparable collapse...will follow.... Listen to me at least in this hour, Majesty. I was not an enemy of Your Majesty. I was a fanatic servant of this nation. I was removed through intrigue and calumny by those who have led this country to where it is now. Do not listen to them any longer, Majesty.[42]

The view that only Antonescu stood any chance of saving the nation was expressed by Britain's Minister Hoare who, nevertheless, feared that the situation was 'irretrievable'. With his usual flair for astute and succinct analysis, Hoare reported that 'the very competence that propelled Antonescu to the forefront in the crisis also made him the most threatening to Carol'.[43] Within days Hoare's prescience was confirmed; on 9 July, Carol ordered the arrest of Antonescu. Fear that he might be forced, as a result of the general's popularity, to bow to his call for change and relax his hold on power and on his monopoly of certain areas of the economy, drove Carol to this desperate step. It served only to remove any vestige of popular support that he might have retained. With Codreanu's fate in mind, a number of Antonescu's friends – among them Mihai Antonescu – appealed to German officials in Bucharest to intercede. Hermann Neubacher, the Reich's Special Representative for Economic Problems in Romania,[44] warned Ernest Urdăreanu, Carol's chief counsellor, that Antonescu's 'accidental death' would make 'a very bad impression in German quarters', while Fabricius told Prime Minister Ion Gigurtu that 'the arrest of Antonescu, who is rightly considered a man of the nation, could be very easily interpreted as a mistake, today, in the moment of *rapprochement* with Germany'.[45] It would be natural to interpret Fabricius's intervention as evidence that Germany regarded Antonescu as a man they could count on, but in fact Fabricius held quite the opposite view, as he warned Berlin:

> General Antonescu is close to the Guard. Up to the present, however, he has been on the side of France, where he attended War College; he has condemned the example of Munich and has reproached the French and English for not attacking the instigators. I am not convinced that he is a safe man.[46]

If Carol had any evil intent towards Antonescu, he was doubtless dissuaded from pursuing it by this German solicitude; he ordered the release of Antonescu on 11 July but had Mihail Moruzov, head of the Secret Service (SSI), intern Antonescu in the Bistriţa monastery in Vâlcea county on the grounds of his clandestine links to the Iron Guard.[47] On 12 July, Antonescu submitted his resignation to the army; this was accepted by the king.[48] Antonescu revealed later that throughout his internment he had kept in touch with the Germans through the intermediary of Mihai Antonescu, and had promised that he would not do anything to compromise the production of oil, coal and methane gas production.[49]

Carol's acceptance of the Vienna Award – which partitioned Transylvania – was the final straw for many Romanians. They took to the streets in Bucharest in their thousands in protests organized by the Iron Guard which called for the resignation of the government and the king. Guardists fired shots under the windows of the Royal Palace, and occupied Radio Bucharest and the Central Telephone Exchange. Other demonstrations and street fighting took place in Constanţa, Braşov and Timişoara.[50] Sensing that Carol would have to turn to Antonescu, Maniu had sent Princess Alice Sturdza to Bistriţa monastery to secure the general's release. Released from internment, Antonescu went to Predeal to stay with friends. On 1 September, Maniu, accompanied by his personal assistant Corneliu Coposu, and his secretary, Aurel Leucuţia, met Antonescu in Ploieşti, halfway between Bucharest and Predeal, where Maniu told him, to his disbelief, that the king would invite Antonescu to form a government. Both men agreed that Antonescu should accept on condition that Carol abdicated.

Horia Sima, the Iron Guard leader, buoyed by the success of the protests against the Vienna Award, tried to seize power himself. Fabricius reported to the German Foreign Ministry that an informant of the German Legation had had a discussion on 2 September with Sima, who asserted that 'Maniu had come to an agreement with the king whereby both of them would oppose implementation of the Award'. The Guard would now have to take power in the interest of German–Romanian collaboration.[51] Fabricius made enquiries and discovered that Sima had given false information: the Gigurtu government was willing to carry out the terms of the Award. A key figure in Antonescu's elevation to power was Valer Pop, a royal counsellor. Pop told the king that there were 'many voices' against him, including large sections of the army, and advised him on 2 September to turn to Antonescu.[52] Carol invited Antonescu to the Palace on 3 September, and in a tense meeting agreed to dispense with the *camarilla* and accept Antonescu's guidance, but he was unwilling to grant the General full powers. Antonescu honoured his understanding with Maniu by refusing the king's request to form a government.

Street protests designed by the Guard to force Carol to abdicate prompted Carol on 4 September to order, through Prime Minister Gigurtu, the execution of 15 Guardists in detention. Gigurtu, aware of the popular mood, refused and resigned. Carol again invited Antonescu to the Palace. This time, the latter decided to accept the mandate to form a government, but on condition that he confer on Antonescu 'all necessary power'. What this meant was to be agreed by the two men within 24 hours. Antonescu now addressed the task of forming a government. Both Maniu and Constantin (Dinu) Brătianu refused to commit respectively the National Peasant Party and the National Liberal Party until Carol abdicated. Horia Sima, in hiding in Braşov after his unsuccessful attempt to topple the king through street demonstrations, could not be found. It was Pop who kept Fabricius, the German minister in Bucharest, abreast of developments and seems to have been the first person to have alerted him to the idea of a government led by Antonescu. When asked by Fabricius about Antonescu's position over the Vienna Award and the proposed military mission, Pop was able to confirm Antonescu's pro-German stance and willingness to implement the Award.[53] Fabricius then stated that he had no objection to Antonescu's inclusion in a new government. It was with this conversation in mind that Fabricius advised Antonescu, at a meeting held early in the morning of 5 September, to assume dictatorial powers.[54] While Fabricius's support for Antonescu was important, it was not necessarily decisive since the General was the choice of several of Carol's ministers and counsellors.[55] Fabricius offered German support on condition that Antonescu implement the Vienna Award, receive a German military mission and strengthen economic ties with Germany, conditions which Antonescu accepted.[56] Fabricius's doubts about Antonescu's leanings evaporated and this change was reflected in his appraisal of the general as 'a man at the head of the Romanian government who is firmly resolved to carry out our important demands here'.[57]

Antonescu had been to see the king on the evening of 4 September to demand that he hand over power and on the following morning, after consulting his advisers, Carol accepted in the hope of restoring order and saving his throne. He issued decrees suspending the 1938 constitution, dissolving parliament and giving Antonescu full authority to govern.[58] Still the Iron Guard was not satisfied and demanded the king's abdication. It was joined by Iuliu Maniu and Constantin Brătianu, who refused to participate in any government under Carol. The Guard took to the streets of Bucharest again on 5 September, increasing the pressure on the king. At 9.30 pm Antonescu went to the Palace to deliver an ultimatum, explaining that he had failed to form a government because 'everyone is demanding Your Majesty's abdication', and warning that he was unwilling to put down the protests and cast 'the nation into a civil war and open the way to foreign occupation'.[59] By 'everyone' Antonescu meant not only Carol's senior ministers and counsellors, but also Maniu and Brătianu. Antonescu gave the king until 4 am to reply.

Carol called a meeting of his counsellors at which four of them voted for his abdication. Two generals, Paul Teodorescu and Gheorghe Mihail, backed the king who, according to one diplomatic report, devised a plan to withdraw the powers granted Antonescu the previous night and even to kill him. Word of the plan reached Antonescu who had not joined the calls for the king's abdication. This news caused him to change his mind. He dispatched a trusted aid to Carol with the demand that he abdicate no later than 6 am.[60] Before making his decision the king sought the advice of General Coroamă. Coroamă had Guardist sympathies and had just been appointed by Antonescu commander of the Second Corps – which covered all troops in Bucharest – on Horia Sima's recommendation.[61] In response to Carol's order to shoot on the crowd which had amassed outside the Palace calling for the king's abdication and which was spurred on by Guardist sympathizers, Coroamă told Carol that 'the army, which has left our territory to be invaded without firing a shot [a reference to Bessarabia]', would refuse. This, coupled with Fabricius's remark to Carol's envoy on the night of 5 September that 'the Reich places no value on [the king] remaining here, and I am studying train timetables for him',[62] removed any lingering doubts in the king's mind and, shortly after 6 am on 6 September, he signed the text of his abdication in favour of his 19-year-old son, Michael.[63] Carol and his entourage, including Elena Lupescu, fled the country the same day with a train-load of treasure under a hail of Iron Guard bullets.[64]

The argument has been made by some Romanian historians that Antonescu and the Iron Guard were brought to power under German pressure.[65] This is overstating the case. At no time did any German official call for Carol's abdication, even during the crucial events of 3–6 September.[66] The king's alignment with the Reich at the beginning of July had won him favour with Hitler, as pointed out by Neubacher in August to a Romanian military representative when he assured him that both the Führer and Foreign Minister Ribbentrop were adamant that Carol should remain king and lead the country, 'otherwise', as Neubacher put it, 'the country would be exposed to anarchy'.[67] Certainly, a withdrawal of German support was instrumental in persuading Carol to abdicate, but it was the mood of the Romanian population that proved decisive. The protests in response to Carol's supine surrender of territory during the summer, culminating in a huge demonstration of some 100,000 people in front of the Palace on the night of 5 September, left Fabricius in no doubt that the king had lost the confidence of the people and even made him fearful for Carol's safety.[68]

By the same token, there is no evidence that Hitler or any of his senior Nazi Party colleagues sought an exclusively Legionary government. They preferred a coalition of Carol, a disciplined legionary movement and other pro-German elements.[69] This approach was signalled by Hitler in late July when the Romanian minister in Berlin reported his comment that the German government would welcome greater participation in the Romanian government from 'nationalist' elements, such as the Iron Guard, and those who were friendly to the Reich, such as Gheorghe Brătianu. While there was a widespread belief in Romania at the time that the Guard had full German backing, research has shown that support from both the German state and the Nazi Party was minimal.[70] The Iron Guard was only one of the components which Hitler wished to see in the Romanian government, while Fabricius did not consider it ready for office at all.[71] Although the German legation in Bucharest and consulates in Romania received requests from the Guard to engineer Carol's abdication on 3 September, Fabricius received no authority from Berlin to act in this regard or to work for the installation of an Iron Guard government.[72]

In fact, after attempting to eradicate the Guard after the murder of Codreanu in November 1938, and again following the Guard's assassination of Prime Minister Armand Călinescu in September 1939, Carol had moved towards reconciliation with the Guard during the early months of 1940. He was attracted by their motto 'God, Nation and King', which he hoped to use to bolster his own position, but of greater importance to him were the military successes of Germany and its reputed backing of the Guard. On 26 May, Sima, freshly returned from Germany, saw Mihai Moruzov, head of the Romanian Intelligence Service, who told him of the king's wish to align Romania's policy with Germany's and for reconciliation with the Guard.[73] On 13 June, Sima gave his approval to complete cooperation between the Guard and Carol and, acting on this, proposed structural changes to the government party, the National Renaissance Front. The party was reconstituted as the Party of the Nation, into which the Guard was to be integrated. On 28 June, Sima joined the government in the improbable position of Under-Secretary of State at the Ministry of Education. On 4 July, he was appointed Minister of Cults and Arts in the cabinet of Ion Gigurtu but resigned three days later after his demand for a purely Guardist government had been rejected.[74] Two other Guardists joined the Gigurtu government: Vasile Noveanu as Minister of Public Wealth, and Augustin Bideanu as Under-Secretary of State at the Ministry of Finance. The Guard was, therefore, part of government before it came to power in September, but Carol's refusal to grant it a dominant role left Sima simmering with resentment. It was the public outcry over the Vienna Award which gave Sima the chance to convert his rage into action against the king. On 1 September, he called for Carol's abdication.

Whereas the Guard had ties – albeit somewhat tenuous – to Germany before September 1940, there is no reason to doubt Antonescu's claim, made at his trial in May 1946, that he had no close ties to the Reich before that date.[75] He came to power in a vacuum, inheriting a situation which was not of his own making. 'I went with Germany because I found the country committed to this policy, and no one then, whoever he might have been, could have given it a different direction without the risk of bringing ruin to the entire country.'[76] He went on to state that he maintained this policy for fear of Germany establishing a protectorate over Romania.[77] Indeed, he justified his continuation of Carol's pro-German orientation in a response in March 1941 to three letters from Constantin Brătianu[78] in which the latter expressed his concern at Romania's enmeshment with Germany:

An alignment with Britain would not only have brought us no effective support, but it would have exposed us to the danger of total collapse. Political alignment with Russia was a moral and factual impossibility. Being unable to count on Britain, and being unable to go alongside the Soviets, Germany remained the only force upon which we could rely both for economic and political support, as well as regards the possibility of creating real military power which we could use at the appropriate moment, in the manner most suited to our interests.[79]

3
Antonescu and the National Legionary State

Antonescu brought to office the mental hardware of a general, one which placed discipline at the head of his priorities. He was not intent on waging war to maintain power, but the threats to Romania were only too obvious and the options available to him extremely limited. As he himself put it, 'in today's circumstances a small country which is under threat, such as ours, does not do what it wishes, but what it can'.[1] King Carol had dismantled the existing political structure, so Antonescu did not have to do so himself. He had to put an end to internal disorder and try to establish what external security he could, with forces that were adequate to deal only with Balkan opponents. In essence, after 1940, *any* Romanian policy was going to be a military policy.[2]

Yet it is not easy to gauge the support that Antonescu had within the ranks of the army at the time of his assumption of power. It would be misleading to claim that he enjoyed the full backing of the army;[3] some senior officers were unhappy at his willingness to implement the Vienna Award, while Generals Mihail and Teodorescu, who had supported Carol in the abdication crisis, had even allegedly planned to kill Antonescu. As Antonescu admitted when he went to demand power from the king on 4 September, 'I did not have the whole army on my side', and he was accompanied by only one officer, Colonel Elefterescu.[4] The army was equally ambiguous towards the Iron Guard. According to Polish diplomatic reports, Guardist influence 'was significant' amongst middle- and lower-ranking officers, and young officers with Guardist sympathies had played a major role in organizing anti-Carol protests,[5] but Colonel George Magherescu, a member of Antonescu's military government set up in February 1941, claimed that 'if certain of the officers and a part of the troops had certain sympathy with the Guard, the great majority of the army was against the movement'. Indeed, he added that Antonescu's sympathy for Codreanu during his trial had antagonized some in the officer corps.[6] But it was the indiscipline and sheer lust for power of the Guard itself after September 1940 that was to alienate the army completely.

On 6 September, the new king, Michael, issued a decree granting Antonescu unlimited powers as Leader of the Romanian State (*Conducătorul Statului Român*), thereby relegating himself to the position of a ceremonial figure.[7] A further decree, signed by Michael two days later, defined Antonescu's powers. The *Conducător* had the authority to initiate and promulgate all laws and to modify those already in force; to appoint and dismiss ministers; and to conclude treaties, declare war and make peace.[8] The title of *Conducător* came to be identified with Antonescu, but it was not, in fact, new. Carol II had introduced it in February 1938 when he suspended the constitution and introduced a royal dictatorship proclaiming himself leader (*Conducător*) of the new state. Antonescu preferred to be addressed as 'General' and declared to the press that this term should be used in all communication with him.[9]

Although the monarchy's reputation had been deeply compromised by Carol, Antonescu, who himself had been a victim of the king's machinations, made every effort to strengthen the institution as a symbol of Romania's statehood. One of his first measures was to invite the Queen Mother, who had been driven from Romania by Carol to avoid further attention being drawn to his very public affair with Elena Lupescu, to Bucharest to be with her son. His concern for Michael was evident from the text of the invitation to Queen Helen, which requested her to take the first available train to be beside the king in order to complete his education, 'which he and our fatherland strongly desire'.[10] The task assigned by the General to the Royal Family was to be 'an example of morality, sobriety, of equidistance, of modesty, of civic consciousness and patriotic stance'.[11] While King Michael and his mother amply fulfilled this role, an overbearing attitude on the part of Antonescu towards them quickly developed, affronting their dignity, and relations between the couple and the general rapidly deteriorated.[12]

Antonescu's handling of the crisis facing the country after its territorial losses won the admiration of one diplomatic observer, Count Roger Raczynski, Polish ambassador to Romania:

> As a ruler of the country Antonescu has had to placate the Germans, whose apprehensions may be aroused by the independence of his character. In restless Transylvania the situation is particularly dangerous: there is in that area a serious threat of armed resistance to the entering Hungarian troops, or at least of organized sabotage.
>
> ...
>
> A most important achievement is the uneasy agreement he has reached with the Transylvanian leaders, by which they are refraining from resistance to the Vienna Arbitration; the general used the argument of the danger of German intervention.[13]

Antonescu's principal and most immediate foreign policy aims were to restore the *status quo ante* of the summer of 1940, which would see the return to Romania of all the territories annexed by foreign powers during 1940, that is, not only Bessarabia and northern Bukovina, but northern Transylvania as well. He made this clear in a cabinet meeting on 21 September 1940 when he called on the Romanian press not to 'abandon' all the matters 'in connection with our borders, our rights, and the aspirations of the Romanian people. This regards both the Romanians in Bessarabia and Bukovina, as well as those in Transylvania.' At the same time, he reaffirmed his commitment to Nazi Germany:

> As regards the Axis, I have told you: we will go 100 per cent to the death alongside the Axis. Either we triumph with the Axis, or we fall with it. If we fall with the Axis, we will not disappear from the map, just as neither Italy nor Germany will disappear, since a nation is a reality which cannot be suppressed. I wish, however, to overturn the Vienna Award – without saying as much, and I am preparing a campaign for world opinion.[14]

Antonescu's policies were purely pragmatic, dictated by Romania's interest and not by any sentiment of friendship he might have for Britain and France:[15]

> There are some newspapers, like *Porunca Vremii*[16] and others, which launch violent attacks. They are not worthy of a civilized state. From here on we must prove that, since we are a country with a government, that country is not governed by a crazy man, but by a civilized one, who realizes how the higher interests of the state must be defended. I am not sentimental when it comes to the interests of my people. I can be a very good friend of the British, but I am not going to go with them so as to bring down the state just out of friendship with them; I would go with my greatest personal enemy in order to save the country. But I have and have had nothing against the Germans. We fought in the war in 1916 and we got Transylvania. After that, however, we made the big mistake of not turning towards Berlin, for economic interest binds us to Germany. Now, where there are economic interests there are also political ones. We cannot disengage ourselves from this arrangement![17]

At the time of his appointment as Leader of the Romanian State, Antonescu was a man without a party. He himself recognized this. At his trial in May 1946, he recounted how after Carol's abdication on 5 September 1940, he said to Iuliu Maniu:

> Mr Maniu, my role will have to end here, I have no party, no political followers, I have no idea of whom to put in which position. Apart from

Mihai Antonescu and the military departments, I do not have the possibility of appointing anyone, I have not engaged in politics, although I am accused of doing so, with the visible result that I have no political followers. You wanted the abdication of the king, here, now take the leadership of the state. He answered me: We cannot take it, you are the one who must do it.[18]

Maniu regarded Antonescu as the right person to get the country out of the crisis. In his words, spoken at the Marshal's trial, 'It was my feeling that he had the moral authority, the support of the army and the disposition for state power.... For those reasons I said that Marshal Antonescu was, not the only choice, but the most suitable.'[19]

Antonescu had planned to form a national government, drawing on support from the two principal parties of democracy, the National Peasants and the National Liberals – who had supported him during the abdication crisis – as well as the Iron Guard. His desire to include the Liberals and National Peasants in a government of national unity should not be confused with any special sympathy on his part for democratic rule. His direct experience of government during the 1930s had soured his view of parliamentary rule, and he had nothing but scorn for the political parties, which he regarded as corrupt.[20] He was even more dismissive of the Iron Guard. He stated at his trial in May 1946 that he had met Sima only once, in July 1940, before the abdication crisis, and that he had formed a government with him because he 'represented the political base of the country at that time. The whole country had demonstrated its support for the Legionary regime.'[21] But he was soon made aware of the Guardists' character during his discussions with Sima and other Guardists over the composition of his cabinet on the night of 14–15 September, and came away with contempt for their naked lust for power and their total incompetence.

Sima's pretensions also unnerved Maniu. As the Polish ambassador reported:

The Iron Guard claimed at the outset all portfolios except those of Defence and Finance, and demanded the proclamation of Romania as a Legionary state and of the legionary movement as the only legally recognized political party. During the negotiations the Legionaries made considerable concessions, insisting only on the proclamation of the single-party character of the state. Maniu was the first to withdraw from the negotiations. The possibility of an understanding with the Liberals ... failed because the Party's leader, Dinu Brătianu, slated to head the Ministry of National Economy, could not countenance the proposed appointment to the cabinet of Atta Constantinescu, nominated by the Dissident Liberals ...[22]

In these circumstances Antonescu was thrown back on the Iron Guard, sympathy for which had grown considerably following the disasters of the summer, and whose political profile had been given a major boost when Carol included it in the Gigurtu government of 4 July.[23] A British assessment of Antonescu's predicament had its finger firmly on the pulse of Romanian feeling at the time:

> When called upon to form a government in September 1940, Antonescu made the King's abdication a condition, and having secured that, faced the task of governing the country in the face of a German menace of occupation with the people incensed at the loss of territory, with the new King only 18 years of age, and with the Iron Guard ready and anxious to make trouble.... As regards the German occupation, the only question was whether this should take place with or without consent. Although Antonescu had always been pro-British in sympathy, he decided that it would be better for the country not to be occupied by an openly hostile force. His decision has been severely criticized, but in view of the impossibility of obtaining help from the Allies, it is hard to see what else he could have done.[24]

Popular support for the Guard was recognized by the Polish ambassador:

> Following King Carol's abdication, the Iron Guard – despite the fact that the old political parties published a variety of proclamations – immediately emerged as the most active political force, and was able quickly to reconstitute its organization. On the day of Carol's abdication, Bucharest was covered with portraits of Codreanu. Legionary street demonstrations on 8 September drew over one hundred thousand participants; in Bucharest alone, eight thousand disciplined members took to the streets.[25]

While enjoying such a rapid expansion, the Guard lacked 'strong and experienced leadership'. The gaps left by the mass executions of Guardists under Carol 'were not and could not be filled'. There was 'an evident lack of unity both among the rank and file and within the leadership, and the latter will have difficulty in planning and carrying out its policies'.[26] While expressing sympathy for the Guard's 'sufferings' under Carol, Antonescu was careful to deliver a warning that it should not indulge in revengeful excesses. In an appeal to the nation on 11 September 1940, Antonescu singled out young legionaries:

> I have understood and understand your explosion of joy, because without being one of you, I have suffered terribly with you and for you. I suffered with you because I wanted what you wanted, my thoughts were your thoughts. I wanted Greater Romania to be a Great Romania.

I wanted to ensure, as did you, that justice reigned in this country, that only the law should be master, that only merit should count, and that not just one person but all should enjoy a comfortable life. I have suffered and you have suffered in the struggle for these same simple ideas. I have put this behind me. You should do the same. We cannot build with revenge, but with labour, not with disorder but with order.[27]

'Order and honesty' were, according to Fabricius, the principal points of Antonescu's programme.[28] The general placed great stress on rooting out corruption and his first steps in this direction were noble. All persons who had held senior offices in the state and government during the previous ten years were required, under decree laws published on 9 September, to declare the source and extent of their wealth, and that of their family, from the time they were appointed to office down to the present, and to reveal what proportion of that wealth had been sent abroad. He also set up commissions to investigate arms expenditure and the granting of mining and petroleum exploration rights over the previous twelve years. Yet little of substance was achieved. None of these measures had any real teeth and they signally failed to diminish, not to mention remove, the corruption which pervaded much of Romanian political and economic life. The Iron Guard was soon to make a mockery of Antonescu's attempts to 'cleanse' Romanian politics and to introduce a breath of fresh air into the conduct of power.

To maintain his grip at the helm of the country, while at the same time conceding the leading role of the Guard, Antonescu had the young king proclaim the country a National Legionary State by royal decree on 14 September, with Antonescu defined as 'the leader of the Legionary State and the head of the Legionary Regime'. He identified his association with the Guard by wearing its green shirt on several ceremonial occasions in the early autumn.[29] Sima was recommended as Vice-President to Antonescu by Hermann Neubacher, the Reich's special economic representative to Bucharest, to ensure that both the general and the Guard would accept Sima's leadership of the movement, since the latter had been only thirteenth on Codreanu's list of possible successors on his death in 1938.[30] Sima was proclaimed 'the leader of the Legionary Movement', which was 'the only movement recognized in the new state, having as its aim the moral and material enhancement of the Romanian people and the development of its creative powers'.[31] The direction in which these 'creative powers' were to be applied was not specified, although the Guard's behaviour was soon to make that clear. In the cabinet formed the following day, the Iron Guard was given posts which made it the dominant force in the government. Antonescu assumed the presidency of the Council of Ministers and appointed himself Minister of National Defence, while Sima was made Deputy Prime Minister. Five other ministries were given to Guard members, among them the Foreign Ministry (Prince Mihai Sturdza) and the Ministry of the Interior (Constantin Petrovicescu). Mihai Antonescu, the lawyer who had acted for the General's wife when she faced charges of bigamy two years earlier, became Minister of Justice. Ion Antonescu did enjoy respect amongst the Guard's members for having appeared as a character witness for Codreanu during his trial in May 1938. Touching on his relations with the Guard during his meeting with Hitler on 22 November 1940, he maintained that he had 'no political connection with the Iron Guard, but merely sympathized with it spiritually and supported it in its struggle for justice and international recognition'.[32]

The new government was burdened with internal conflicts, which derived from the duality of power between Antonescu and the Guard. Antonescu was reliant on the Guard because he lacked an organized base of public support. The Guard needed Antonescu because he was trusted by the army and the leaders of the democratic parties. But there was a disharmony inherent in the discipline Antonescu craved and the lust for power of an intemperate Guard. 'The Iron Guard's domination of the administrative system is of great importance in the competition with the General. The "Guardization" of the administration has been achieved in a single stroke, by the appointment of legionaries as prefects in all the fifty departments of the territorially-reduced country.'[33] With the extension of the Guard's power came an intensification of anti-Semitic propaganda, propagated in the pro-German newspaper *Porunca Vremii* (The Command of the Time)[34] and the Guard's own daily, *Buna Vestire* (The Annunciation).

After the proclamation of the 'National Legionary State', freedom of worship for the established confessions was recognized. Under a resolution of the Minister of Cults and Arts, Radu Budişteanu, of 9 September 1940, these were listed as the Romanian Orthodox, the Greek-Catholic, the Roman Catholic, the Armenian and Ukrainian Orthodox, the Calvinist, the Lutheran, Unitarian, Armenian-Gregorian churches and Islam. At the same time, the state recognized the '*de facto* existence of the Jewish confession, which must conduct itself according to ministerial laws to be issued later'. On the other hand, 'religious associations' – the term for neo-Protestant and other sects – were banned.[35]

Alarmed by the prospect of graver anti-Semitic measures in the new National Legionary state, Wilhelm Filderman, President of the Federation of Jewish Communities in Romania, expressed his concern to Antonescu, who assured him that he was not about to embark on a programme of persecution of the Jews. On 18 September, Filderman received a letter from the Secretary General of the Presidency of the Council of Ministers in which Antonescu was quoted as saying: 'Assure Dr Filderman . . . that if his co-religionists do not openly or secretly sabotage the regime, either politically or economically, the Jewish population will not suffer. General Antonescu keeps his word.'[36]

This prompted Filderman and other leaders of the Jewish community to send a message to Antonescu on 21 September assuring them of their good faith: 'Moved by the most sincere sentiments towards the throne and the country, the Jewish population of Romania wishes you a fruitful and peaceful rule and assures you that it will fulfil its duties faithfully and loyally.'[37] These sentiments were echoed in a more fulsome telegram sent by the Jewish community in Bucharest. Here the signatories 'addressed to the Almighty the fervent prayer that providence should watch over the success of your [Antonescu's] uplifting of the country'.[38]

On 5 October, Antonescu donned the green shirt of the Guard and addressed thousands of legionaries in Bucharest to mark 30 days since the installation of the National Legionary State. His speech was a rallying call to the Guard, but at the same time an appeal for reason:

> Legionaries, I have summoned you today from all corners of our ampu-tated country to honour the victory of 6 September. I have assembled you today, green shirts, whole and chaste souls.... I have summoned you to perform exemplary constructive deeds and to order you to put aside any thought of revenge or revolt.[39]

It was not long, however, before the Guard's lack of discipline and its penchant for violence sowed the seeds of discord between Antonescu and Sima, and exasperated the Germans. Their priority was economic efficiency, which the Guard disrupted. The consequences would be to increase their influence over the Romanian economy, apart from their holdings in it which, being inter-governmental, were longer term. On 5 October, a decree was passed providing for the appointment of 'commissars for Romanianiza-tion' to enforce compliance by companies with the directives of the Ministry of National Economy. Seven Guard commissioners were created for the oil industry and they addressed the task of 'Romanianizing' the oil companies by dismissing Jewish employees and foreign managers.[40] In the course of this campaign five British oil managers were seized by the Guard, tortured and forced to sign confessions admitting acts of sabotage.[41] Further anti-Semitic legislation was introduced expropriating real estate (5 October), forest land (12 November) and shipping (4 December) owned by Jews.

German hopes of taking advantage of the expropriations by buying the confiscated property were often frustrated by Guardists who resented what they saw as a new 'vassalage'. An article in *Buna Vestire* in early September exhorted that 'after being the vassals of Paris, the Romanians must not now become the vassals of Rome and Berlin'.[42] The property-owners were either coerced into selling their assets to the commissioner – usually a Guardist – or bureaucratic inertia delayed its sale to any buyer. The increasing power of the German minority, and the work of the SS *Volksdeutsche Mittelstelle* amongst them, coupled with the activity of the leader of the German minority, Andreas Schmidt, in promoting the rights of the ethnic Germans under the provisions of the Vienna Award, created anti-German resentment, even among the Guardists, some of whom were particularly irritated by the arrival of SD (*Sicherheitsdienst*) representatives on a mission to recreate the Guard on SS lines.[43] Their work resulted in the establishment of a Guardist police force (*poliția legionară*), which was used as an arbitrary tool of political and racial repression – in preference to the state police – on the orders of the Guardist Minister of the Interior, General Constantin Petrovicescu.

For their part, the Germans too were disillusioned with the Guard. Hermann Neubacher advised Dr Carl Clodius, Deputy Director of the Economic Policy Department at the Ministry, on 19 November that 'the time had come to put a stop to the anarchists and experimenters of the Guard'.[44] Neubacher was not alone in his annoyance. A demand from Sima in a letter to Antonescu in late October for a monopoly of power for the Guard and for the establishment of a new economic order elicited a terse reply, in which the general stated that he was unwilling to destroy the Romanian economy.[45] Even more of a threat to Antonescu's authority was the Guard's pledge to avenge its murdered leader, Codreanu. As a first step Mihai Moruzov, head of the Secret Service under Carol, had been arrested on 6 September. Changes were made at the Guard's insistence at the Ministry of the Interior. The Director General of Police appointed by Antonescu was ousted after a fortnight and replaced by Alexandru Ghica, a Guardist. A Criminal Investigation Committee was set up by the Guard to identify those responsible for the execution of Guardists under King Carol. The Commission ordered the arrest of 33 people, in addition to those already in custody in Jilava prison south of Bucharest. At the same time, exhumations and reburials of Guard dead took place with such frequency and macabre pomp that the new government earned the nickname of 'the regime of funeral processions'.[46] The culmination of these events was the reburial of Codreanu, scheduled for 30 November, for which a number of Guardists went to Jilava for his exhumation and for those of his 13 companions.

Two events combined to unleash the Guard's fury for revenge. The first was the decision of the Committee to transfer two senior officials, Gabriel Marinescu, a former Minister of the Interior, and Ion Bengliu, former head of the gendarmerie, held responsible by the Guard for the murder of their colleagues, to a sanatorium. The second was Antonescu's decision, made at the request of the Jilava prisoners who feared for their safety, to replace the team of Guardists working on the exhumations with a military guard. When the Guardists learned of these decisions they stormed into the cells of Jilava prison on the night of 26–27 November and massacred 64 ministers, and senior police officers whom they held guilty of murdering Guardists.[47] On the same night, eleven Jews were murdered by the Guard in Ploiești. The next day a group of Guardists shot dead Nicolae Iorga, Romania's eminent historian and elder statesman, and Virgil Madgearu, an ex-National Peasant Party Finance Minister.

It is not clear whether Sima knew of the Guards' plan to carry out the Jilava massacre. Antonescu, on the basis of information supplied to him by Eugen Cristescu, Moruzov's successor, suspected Constantin Petrovicescu, the Minister of the Interior, and his Guardist head of police, of at worst encouraging the killings and at best turning a blind eye. On the extent of Sima's complicity in the Jilava massacre hangs the answers to a number of questions surrounding the Guard's cohesion, discipline and fanaticism. Sima himself professed 'shock' at the murders, although Waldeck reported an Iron Guard source having told her that this reaction was contrived.[48]

This lawlessness dismayed Antonescu and disquieted Hitler, since Romania was of vital strategic importance in the Führer's plan to attack the Soviet Union. The military mission, requested by Antonescu on 5 September, had arrived in Bucharest on 14 October, with the secret task of preparing the Romanian army for the attack and of consolidating the air defences of the oilfields around Ploieşti.[49] But the failure of the Italian offensive against Greece, launched on 28 October from Albania, created an entirely new situation for Hitler. Britain had promised Greece all possible support, and on 31 October British forces moved into Crete. This afforded them, Hitler mistakenly believed, a base for air attacks on Ploieşti, which was only 500 km from Lemnos.[50] Romania now assumed an unforeseen importance because of the new front that was opening in the Balkans. In order to counter the threat, Hitler decided to use Romania as a springboard for an attack, through Bulgaria, on northern Greece; in this way he planned to deny the British the use of airfields in the region. On 4 November, he ordered the army to draw up plans for *Operation Marita*.

Neither Mussolini nor Antonescu was informed initially about Hitler's intentions, but in a letter to the *Duce* of 20 November, Hitler described the situation in the darkest terms: 'Since there is no effective defence of the oilfields, the situation, from the military point of view, is dangerous, while from the economic viewpoint, as far as the Romanian oilfields are concerned, it is truly terrifying.' The Führer's conclusion was that 'Hungary must agree to the passage of German units to Romania which will begin immediately. Romania will accept this increase in German armed forces as a strengthening of her own defence'.[51] Hitler's plans were embodied in Directive no. 18 of 12 November under which the German military mission in Romania was to be strengthened, and then preparations made for around ten divisions to enter southern Romania. At the same time, the German air mission was to be reinforced.

Antonescu was invited by Hitler on 21–24 November to Berlin to sign the Tripartite Pact of Germany, Italy and Japan, and for talks on military and economic cooperation. Hungary had signed the Pact on 20 November and Antonescu put his signature to it three days later.[52] When the Pact was originally signed – on 27 September 1940 – the adherence of smaller states had not been anticipated, but Hungary suggested this at the beginning of October.

Hitler promised Antonescu that now that Romania was an ally, 'he could assure him that Germany would support its ally in every respect, both politically and economically. Behind the existence of the Romanian state stood henceforth the whole of the German *Wehrmacht*.'[53] Yet the Pact did not affect the relations of the signatories with the Soviet Union, nor did it refer to the state of war that existed between Germany and Britain. It was invoked for the first time only on 12 December 1941 when Germany and Italy asked Romania to declare war on the United States. In this respect, it should be pointed out that there was no treaty binding Germany and Romania regarding a conflict between the Soviet Union and the two countries. The reason for this is probably that Hitler was anticipating a brief campaign in the East; Germany and Romania were engaged – from the point of view of international law – as were Germany and Finland, in a parallel war against the Soviet Union, while they were allies against the United States.[54]

This meeting was the first between Hitler and Antonescu, yet it was decisive for future relations between the two men. Far from being overawed by the Führer, Antonescu spoke his mind for two hours about the loss of northern Transylvania to Hungary, strongly criticizing the Vienna Award and expressing his determination to win back the area.[55] He tried to persuade Hitler to overturn the Award. Whether the Führer made such a promise – as indeed Antonescu said he did when he was being held in the Soviet Union – is doubtful. The German text of the interview makes it clear that Hitler did no more than hint that his postwar Europe would not necessarily have the same shape as in 1940; this by implication, if you wanted to draw one – and Antonescu certainly did – involved a revision of the Vienna Award. But Hitler was vague, never mentioned the Award, and made no promises.[56] Nevertheless, Antonescu's determination won Hitler's admiration and persuaded the Führer that Antonescu was a man he could trust.

The German offensive against Greece was laid out in directive no. 20 (*Operation Marita*), signed by Hitler on 13 December. The 16th Armoured Division was to join the German military mission, and seven divisions sent to the south of Romania. The arrival of the armoured division – via Hungary – was agreed on 23 November between Antonescu and General Erik Hansen, head of the military mission to Romania, but Hansen was ordered by Hitler not to mention the planned attack on Greece. Hansen and Fabricius met Antonescu on 21 December and informed him of the troop movements. The Romanian leader welcomed the reinforcements on condition that they be supplied from Germany for otherwise they would create food shortages in Romania. He realized that the arrival of the new forces was linked 'to an operation southwards', but Hansen refrained from commenting.[57]

Nevertheless, problems over the quartering of the troops, coupled with the growing tension between Antonescu and Horia Sima, prompted the former to request a second meeting with Hitler. Relations between

Antonescu and the Iron Guard had started on a downward spiral due to the murderous fanaticism of the Guard which was threatening anarchy. Murder was the solution favoured by the Guard to remove its opponents – as the Jilava massacres had shown – and the means of applying its anti-Semitism. Scores of complaints were lodged with the courts by Jews in several towns about the violence they had suffered at the hands of Guardists. In the period 15–28 November 1940, the Guardist police in Ploieşti arrested 58 Jews on the grounds that they were Communists. On 29 November, Sima, under pressure from Antonescu, dissolved this body in Ploieşti because of its lawlessness, and on the very same day the gendarmerie found the bullet-ridden bodies of five of those arrested.[58] In Constanţa, in an interval of just one week at the end of December, several Jews accused Guardists of using violence and intimidation in order to force them to hand over their shops to Romanians.[59]

On 13 December, Fabricius was recalled to Berlin and Manfred Baron von Killinger, German minister in Bratislava, designated his successor. This change of minister generated friction between Antonescu and his Foreign Minister, Mihai Sturdza, who confessed to Antonescu that he had suggested Fabricius's replacement during the visit to Berlin of 22 and 23 November. Antonescu promptly dismissed Sturdza and named the Romanian minister to Berlin, Constantin Greceanu, in his stead, but Antonescu effectively took control of the Foreign Ministry.[60] As von Killinger's arrival in Bucharest had not been fixed, Fabricius continued to run the German legation's affairs until von Killinger's arrival on 24 January 1941.[61]

In early January 1941, Sima complained to Antonescu about German acquisitions of Jewish properties in southern Transylvania on which the Guardists had designs, placing a further strain on relations between the two men.[62] Hitler's appreciation of the need for a stronger hand in dealing with the conflict may have been one of the reasons behind the recall of Fabricius; Fabricius himself believed the principal motive was Hitler's decision to take military action in south-eastern Europe. For the new tasks which this involved Fabricius felt that Hitler considered him to be 'a diplomat of the old school, a convinced pacifist and too soft'.[63]

It was Antonescu's concern about the Guard's activities that led him to request a meeting with Hitler around 10 January 1941. He added that Sima had already been invited by Baldur von Schirach, *Gauleiter* of Vienna, and State Secretary Ernst Bohle on the instructions of Hitler's deputy, Rudolf Hess, when they attended the reburial of the remains of Corneliu Codreanu on 30 November. On 12 January, invitations to both reached Bucharest. Initially, Antonescu rejected the idea of travelling with Sima, but changed his mind when he was informed that Hitler placed great value on their joint presence. Yet Sima, too, was unwilling to accompany Antonescu, believing that such a visit was a stratagem of both Ion and Mihai Antonescu by which he would be left out of the discussions, as had happened to the Guardist

Foreign Minister Mihai Sturdza during Antonescu's November visit. Despite the efforts of Fabricius to persuade him to the contrary, Sima announced on 13 January that he would not leave. Thus Antonescu travelled to Obersalzburg to meet the Führer on 14 January 1941, accompanied only by Fabricius.[64] Sima's absence meant that he had no chance to rebut the charges made by Antonescu against the Guard, nor did he give Hitler the opportunity to make a personal assessment of the Guard's leader.[65]

Antonescu, by contrast, had made an extremely favourable impression on Hitler during their November meeting, according to Paul Schmidt, Hitler's interpreter, despite his two-hour rant against the Vienna Award.[66] At the January meeting Antonescu was direct in his accusations against the Guard. Their first mistake, he argued, was to open their ranks to undesirable elements such as Communists. The second was the attempt to implement their revolutionary programme in one fell swoop, in spite of Antonescu's objections and those of the German legation. This had created confusion in those ministries under Guardist control, in particular in the Ministry of the Interior and of the National Economy. As a result public opinion, which had overwhelmingly supported the Guard, had now abandoned it. Antonescu asserted that he had been trying for some time to temper the Guard's zeal since 'he wished to retain the Legionnaire regime. He had to reorganize it, however, in order to be able to govern with it.'[67]

In reply, Hitler told the Romanian leader that he was the only person in Romania who could cope with any situation and that he accorded greater importance to his relations with Antonescu than to the relations between the Iron Guard and the Nazi Party. If Antonescu thought that breaking off relations between the Nazi Party and the Iron Guard would bring benefits, Germany would not regard this as a sacrifice. He was of the opinion, however, that it would be impossible to govern in Romania against the Iron Guard. Antonescu would ultimately have to become the leader of the Guard and the best thing would be if Antonescu put this proposal to the Guard himself.[68]

It is clear from the transcript of the meeting that Hitler did not, contrary to the assertions of several historians, 'give Antonescu a free hand to deal with the Guard', but he did feel sufficiently encouraged by the Führer's support for him to act against it.[69] The opportunity was provided by the murder of Major Doering, an officer attached to the German military mission, on 19 January outside its headquarters at the Hotel Ambassador in Bucharest.[70] Antonescu used the murder as a justification for the dismissal of the Guardist Minister of the Interior General Constantin Petrovicescu on the following day, declaring that 'the Minister of the Interior, nine hours after the assassination of a brave German officer in the centre of the capital, had not taken proper measures...nor had he ordered a guard to be placed around the military mission headquarters'.[71] At the same time, he removed the Guardist head of the police, Alexandru Ghika, the chief of the Bucharest police Radu Mironovici, and the chief of the *Siguranţa*, the security police, Constantin Maimuca. Ghika and Maimuca barricaded themselves in the *Siguranţa* headquarters, together with a group of about 50 Guardists, and opened fire on the troops who had been sent to eject them. The shots marked the beginning of the Iron Guard uprising.

A manifesto signed by Viorel Trifa, the head of the Romanian Christian Students' Union, was circulated shortly after Petrovicescu's dismissal. Together with a similar appeal by Dumitru Groza, the leader of the Legionary Workers' Union, it constituted a call for action and the institution of a legionary government:

> Romanians! A German major has been cowardly murdered on the orders of Britain on the streets of the capital by an agent of the Intelligence Service. The protectors and defenders of this assassin, a Greek by origin, are Eugen Cristescu, the head of the secret service, the former right-hand man of Armand Calinescu, and Alexandru Riosanu, the man of the Yids and Greeks. Instead of these satanic elements, the brave and upright General Petrovicescu has been forced to leave the government on the orders of the British government of freemasons. We ask General Antonescu to do right by Romanians. We demand the replacement of all masons and Yid-sympathizers in the government. We demand a legionary government. We demand the punishment of those guilty of the German major's murder. Romanian Christian students cannot accept the butchery of German soldiers on the streets of the capital by British agents.[72]

Guardist workers occupied the telephone exchange and some newspaper offices, where manifestos calling for the creation of a 'Legionary Romania' and appealing to the army not to 'unleash murder amongst brothers for the pleasure of . . . all the Jews and Jew-lovers' were printed.[73]

Both Antonescu and Sima sought German advice. Antonescu asked Fabricius to contact Obersalzberg on 21 January to elicit Hitler's views on the rebellion. Fabricius explained the situation to Ribbentrop. The reply from Hitler, who was standing behind his Foreign Minister, was: 'Since blood has flowed General Antonescu should intervene decisively and clean up. He should then reorganize the Guard under his own leadership.'[74] A request from a Guard delegation to Neubacher on the same afternoon for the German army to support them was turned down.[75] German neutrality in the uprising was confirmed by a note in the diary of General Franz Halder, Chief of the Army General Staff, who wrote that the military mission had been instructed not to intervene, but 'in case of necessity to support Antonescu with military force (upon a request being made to it)'.[76] Indeed, German efforts were directed towards mediation. The report of General Erik Hansen, head of the military mission, recorded that Fabricius had tried to mediate between Antonescu and Sima during the night of 21 January, but that his efforts had failed owing to the exaggerated pretensions of the Guard leader.[77]

The revolt was largely confined to Bucharest, but the Guardists did not limit themselves to defending their positions in public buildings. During the morning of 22 January, Guardists moved against defenceless Jews, looting and burning their homes, and cold-bloodedly murdering 120 of them.[78] That same afternoon Antonescu ordered the army to use tanks against the barricaded Guardists and by the evening they had occupied most of the buildings. Twenty-one soldiers were killed in the operations. Emissaries from the Guardists called on General Hansen, who told them that Antonescu had Hitler's support and that they should lay down their arms. Hermann Neubacher decided to intervene to put an end to the bloodshed. He told Sima that his uprising against Antonescu had no chance of success since the latter enjoyed the full support of the Führer. He advised the Iron Guard leader to withdraw his men from their positions, in which case their safety would be guaranteed. Sima accepted Neubacher's ceasefire terms to which Antonescu agreed.

Antonescu thanked Neubacher for his mediation. When, however, Antonescu told him that he would hang all the Guard leaders, Neubacher protested vehemently, making it clear that he would not have persuaded Sima to lay down arms had he known the general's intentions. The next day, 24 January, the new German minister von Killinger arrived in Bucharest. He carried with him clear instructions 'to support General Antonescu in any circumstances'.[79] In order to save the Guard leaders from the noose, members of the German secret service gave refuge in their homes to senior Guardists, from where they were smuggled to Germany. Sima, according to the Romanian Secret Service, was hidden in Neubacher's car and taken to the German legation in Sofia; he was then taken to Germany in an army lorry.[80] This was not the only instance of German assistance for the Guard: General Hansen, head of the German military mission, reported that many of the arms used by the Guardists had also been used at the beginning of September 1940 during the protests against Carol and had been brought from Germany.[81]

Thus ended a unique chapter in the history of Fascism in Europe. The Guard had been the only radical movement of the Right in Europe to come to power without the assistance of Germany or Italy, and the only one to be toppled during Nazi Germany's domination of continental Europe. During its period of rule, 'through its reach for total power, the excesses of the Legionary police, the utter mismanagement of the state administration and the economy by inexperienced youthful militants' it antagonized most middle-class Romanians and challenged Antonescu's own political authority.[82] Faced with the prospect of a complete breakdown in order in the country should the Guard seize control of the state, the officer corps stood firmly behind Antonescu and gave him its full support in his showdown with the Guard.

A ministerial meeting held over a year later, in December 1941, at which the part played by Orthodox priests in the Iron Guard rebellion was discussed, gave Antonescu the opportunity to reflect upon his alliance with the Guard:

> Now a new act of clemency [for those implicated in the rebellion] is being applied so that a new chance in life can be given to those who removed life, either by mistake or through ignorance, because they were drawn into a movement, either unconsciously – as many joined the legionary movement – or in the belief that they were supporting an action useful to the Romanian nation.
>
> I stood at the head of the latter. I had no alternative but to address myself to the nation through what was on offer from the nation at that juncture, namely through the Legionary movement, because all the other groups had either something wrong with them or had been dissolved. From the universities downwards the nation offered this Legionary movement. Everyone placed their hopes in it. I did not have 100 per cent faith in it, I told Mr Mihai Antonescu so. Later, this movement strayed onto a dangerous path instead of heading in a healthy direction. The Guardists won popularity through the use of terror and dynamism. People thought that if a hundred people got moving, if they fired guns, [then] that movement had vast numbers. The Legionary movement did not have vast numbers, it was merely dynamic; this was how it influenced people. Here we must add the mistakes made by former regimes, which caused people to look elsewhere for solutions.
>
> I brought down the Legionary movement. I, too, punished it. But the Legionary movement was brought about by the state, by the way in which it worked. The revolution in September [1940] was merely the explosion of a huge volcano, in which everyone cast embers, so that it would burn more fiercely and allow the country to rid itself of an evil man who had created an evil regime merely to keep himself in power.[83]

Despite their defeat the Guardists still had their supporters in eminent circles in the Reich.[84] In communicating his instructions to Fabricius's successor Killinger early in the morning of 25 January, Ribbentrop told him to advise Antonescu 'not to make the mistake of relying on the army to reconstruct the new state, but to consider exclusively the Legionary movement as the political basis of this new state'.[85] Antonescu did not heed this advice. Precisely the Guard's indiscipline, and its treachery, ruled it out as a partner. Although it is conceivable that Antonescu regarded the sympathy shown by some German officials towards the Guard as a ploy to create instability and provide the pretext for German intervention and the establishment of a protectorate, he knew that Hitler was against disorder. Once again, as he had done in the previous September, he approached the National Peasant Party leader Iuliu Maniu and the National Liberal head Constantin Brătianu to form a government of national unity, but they had no desire to be associated with a regime that had turned its back on parliamentary democracy and outlawed the activities of the democratic parties. Instead, they advised him to establish a military government.[86] The same advice had been given to him at the time of the Iron Guard rebellion, as he told Hitler at their meeting on 14 January 1941: 'He [Antonescu] had also received the advice to form a military government. That, too, he had rejected and termed unnecessary, for a purely military government was, in his opinion, the last card that a country could play.'[87]

He was soon to play that 'last card'.

4
Military Dictatorship and War

On 27 January 1941, Antonescu appointed a new cabinet formed almost entirely of officers. In doing so, he was introducing a military dictatorship.[1] His regime received the backing of the democratic parties. At a meeting of the National Liberal Party its leader, Constantin Brătianu, declared:

> Today we have a government of generals. It is the best solution possible in the current crisis...[Antonescu] is the only man who can govern in the country in the external and internal conditions of today. We owe him all of the support we can give him.[2]

Addressing the press on 1 February, and referring to himself, as was his wont, in the third person,[3] Antonescu laid out his programme:

> General Antonescu has not misled, is not misleading, and will never mislead [you]. I am not a tyrannical head of state, I have no clique to defend, and I have no interests or immoral life to hide. I will defend the country and its destiny against all sources of enmity and deviance.... After a complete return to work and discipline I will begin the political reorganization of the state.... This state will be a new state based on the primacy of what is Romanian in every domain and it will be founded on our agricultural and peasant structure.[4]

Antonescu was a soldier who saw the solution to problems in terms of *raison d'état*. He established a military regime under which senior officers took their orders only from him and usually disregarded any decisions taken by other ministers in the government. Thus in the deportation of Jews in the summer of 1941, which was entrusted to the army by the Antonescu, army officers ignored permits issued by the Ministry of the Interior allowing individual Jews exemption. This was the case with Jews who were US citizens.[5]

Antonescu openly admitted his regime's military character. On 19 November 1941, in a committee meeting, he confessed: 'I now want to declare before the world that this state is a militaristic one. That is the direction in which I am pushing it. I want to introduce a patriotic, heroic, military-type educa-tion, because economic education and all the others follow on from it.'[6] A few days later, he addressed the form of government in a cabinet meeting of 27 November 1941:

> I am by fate a dictator, because I cannot return to the old constitution, nor to parliament, nor to anything, and I can only solve these problems with the State Council and some experts around me, in order to harmonize all the problems.[7]

But unlike the dictatorships of Hitler and Mussolini, Antonescu's dictator-ship was not based on a mass political party or ideology. Antonescu's programme was a simple one: order within Romania and security for her frontiers.[8] They were to be provided by the police and the army. In his own words to Hitler in June 1941, he 'was neither a politician nor diplomat. He was born a soldier and wanted to die one'.[9] In a country unfamiliar with discipline, Antonescu tried to impose it, though his stric-tures sometimes extended to the ridiculous – a ban on walking the streets in shirtsleeves during the summer on pain of internment! While some transgressors were actually punished in this way, the moral and spiritual regeneration sought by Antonescu did not receive the public support he hoped for.[10] He was ultimately a lonely figure who found only two people – apart from his wife and mother – he felt he could trust: Veturia, the wife of the poet and former Prime Minister Octavian Goga, and Mihai Antonescu, whom he kept by his side even when Hitler asked for his dismissal in spring 1943.[11]

To what degree was Antonescu's Romania a totalitarian state?[12] As stated above, Antonescu did not seek to carry out a revolution based on a political ideology. His rule certainly intruded into the lives of Jews and Romas, but the vast majority of Romanians were subject only to the demands of a military policy, which any ruler of Romania after 1940 would have been forced to apply.

Antonescu's tolerance of the democratic opposition, the simple fact that he was prepared to engage in correspondence with its leaders – and also with Wilhelm Filderman, a senior figure in the Jewish community in the early months of the war – at once sets him apart from Hitler. By the draco-nian yardstick of the Nazi regime, Antonescu's dictatorship was less barba-rous for most of its subjects, although for tens of thousands of Jews it brought deportation, starvation and death. Freedom of worship was respected for most Christians and Moslems[13] and although on 17 September 1940, restrictions had been placed on the Jews' freedom to practise their faith, at the repeated request of Wilhelm Filderman, the president of the Federation of the Union of Jewish Communities (FUCE), Antonescu suspended their application.[14] Antonescu is perhaps best described as authoritarian rather than a totalitarian.

This brings us to the question of whether Antonescu was a fascist. His period as Romanian leader – strictly speaking King Michael was head of state – can be divided into two. From September 1940 to the end of January 1941 he led a government dominated by the Iron Guard which he then removed and replaced with his own military dictatorship. In the sense that the period of Iron Guard government and that of subsequent military rule were characterized by military alliance with Nazi Germany and by anti-Semitism, both the Guard and Antonescu were fascist. But an analysis of Romanian fascism requires a special study which is out of place here. Suffice it to say that if we define some of the characteristic features of fascism as a crisis of identity stemming from the traditional, often ethnic features of the community; an authoritarian, paramilitary type of organization; and a backward-looking stance, opposed to industrialization, then the most significant movement in Romania to which this definition could be applied was the Iron Guard. To these we can add in the Guard's case a strong anti-Semitism and a hatred of Marxism. As Henry Roberts rightly remarks, 'fascism is not generally anti-industrial. . . . But in the case of Rumania, with its particular position *vis-à-vis* industrial society, the fascist response in its most characteristic form involved this negation and an exaltation of the peasant.'[15]

There was no fascist party in power during Antonescu's dictatorship, but his rule was overtly anti-Semitic. Antonescu consolidated the anti-Semitic measures taken by King Carol's governments and by the National Legionary State under his own leadership.[16] Antonescu's first step in establishing order was a decree law introduced on 6 February, which outlawed all opposition to his regime. The penalty for unauthorized political organization, including marching and singing by political groups, was set at between 10 and 25 years' hard labour. The death penalty would apply to any person found in possession of arms without authorization. A series of other offences carrying the death penalty, such as espionage and treason, were added during the following months.[17] The National Legionary State was dissolved on 14 February and a massive operation was launched to round up those who had taken part in the uprising. More than 9,000 people had been arrested by the end of the month,[18] of whom significant proportion were Orthodox priests.[19] The Military Provost's office reported that 6,766 legionaries were sentenced to imprisonment during 1941.[20] Antonescu's measures were given the rubberstamp of approval in a popular plebiscite on 2–5 March when 99.9 per cent of the votes cast gave their approval.[21] Swift retribution was meted out to legionaries who murdered Jews after the rebellion. Two members of a so-called 'death squad' of the Iron Guard were arrested on 14 April 1941 for the murder of a Jewish bookseller, Max London, in Bucharest. On the following day, according to a newspaper report, they were sentenced to death and executed.[22] In May, a number of Guardists found guilty of the murder of Jews in Bucharest were also executed, while in July Sima and other Guard leaders were sentenced in their absence to forced labour for life.[23]

There was no role for parliament under Antonescu. In its stead a spurious assembly was invented – *Adunarea Obştească Plebiscitară a Naţiunii Române* (The General Plebiscitary Assembly of the Romanian Nation) – which was invoked only twice to cast votes and rubber-stamp Antonescu's policies.[24] There is no means of verifying the validity of these results, but in any case they could hardly be democratic because all public manifestations of opinion had been outlawed. The only formal body to meet on a regular basis was the Council of Ministers, chaired by Antonescu, which had no legislative or other statutory powers, but was simply a forum for the receipt of reports from ministers on the activity of their ministries.[25] The decisions reached were not collective, but those of Antonescu. This lack of wider accountability characterized the entire Antonescu administration.

At the head of local government sat the county prefects who were appointed either directly by the *Conducător* or, in the case of the provinces of Bessarabia, Bukovina and Transnistria, through the governor acting in Antonescu's name. They had complete authority over the administration and officials. Local councils were abolished and replaced with committees comprised of local administrative officials and representatives of the professions and of trade chosen by the prefect.

Antonescu's use of the decree epitomized the authoritarian nature of his rule. The decree of 6 February 1941, mentioned above, underpinned his system of repression. His instrument was the internment camp (*lagărul de internare*), to which those judged to be opponents of his regime or a threat to it could be sent, often simply on the recommendation of senior officials in the Ministry of the Interior. Recent research offers a total figure of 10,617 imprisoned under Antonescu, of whom just over 2,000 were Communists or sympathizers,[26] of whom 72 were executed out of a total of 313 sentenced to death between 1940 and 1944. Only Communists found guilty of acts of espionage or sabotage as Soviet agents were executed, while those who were shown to be members of the Communist Party of Romania had their death sentences commuted.[27]

Antonescu regarded Communism and the Iron Guard as one and the same in so far as they both presented the greatest threat to the Romanians and the Romanian state. 'Now there are no longer any Guardists; there are the Communists in green shirts; they took Codreanu's guard, they don green shirts and say that they are Guardists. In reality, they are Communists.'[28] In a meeting of the Council for Cultural and Religious Affairs held on 10 December 1941 he stated: 'I consider Communism to be the greatest enemy of the nation, it is a betrayal of the fatherland and I shall punish it with death, and all those who have donned the green shirt and have carried out criminal acts I shall punish in the same way.'[29]

Another target of Antonescu's anger were the neo-Protestant sects which advocated conscientious objection to military service. The sects had attracted a number of adherents among the peasantry from the Orthodox Church during the interwar years for reasons acknowledged by Antonescu:

> These sects have spread in our country because of the [Orthodox] priests, because of their lack of duty, or because they have not respected it as they should. They have taken advantage of the poorest. The peasants, through lack of money, have ceased to baptize their children or they have buried them without a priest, so that they have run to the first neo-Protestants they find who, in fact, do not have a spiritual agenda but only hidden political aims, undermining the state's authority...
>
> I am not minded to tolerate the neo-Protestants. I shall go to the limits to resolve this problem and to push back the waves of neo-protestants as far as I can. Even now they are to be found especially in the borderlands where, from the ethnic point of view, they have led us to lose certain positions. The struggle between us and the Slavs in northern Bukovina and, to a certain extent, in southern Bessarabia, has ended with losses because of this. The neo-protestants attack in the borderlands; this is a sign that certain political ends are on the agenda.[30]

The individual unauthorized sects, while counting their adherents in the hundreds rather than thousands, were still seen as significant enough by Antonescu to be singled out for attack in a Council of Ministers' meeting of 16 December 1941:

> What is happening with the 38 members of the Milenist sect?[31] All those who are active in illegal sects should be thrown into camps....If we allow citizens to be educated to refuse military service, then the Romanian people are doomed. You should shoot all those wretched sectarians. Marshal Antonescu orders you to shoot them. You just need to shoot one of them and [then] you will not find a single sectarian. [32]

Antonescu's hostility resulted in the deportation to Transnistria of some 2,000 neo-Protestants, members of the 'Inochentist' sect, in August 1942, a measure he acknowledged at his trial in May 1946:

> Many Romanians, unfortunately, joined these sects in order to escape the war.... What was the spiritual basis of these sects? To avoid taking up arms and fighting. So when we called them up, they refused to lay their hands on a weapon. There was a general revolt, and so I brought in a law introducing the death penalty. I did not apply it. And I succeeded in getting rid of these sects. The more recalcitrant ones I seized and deported.[33]

Within this statutory framework of dictatorship Antonescu did tolerate what might be termed dissent rather than opposition. It was expressed in the form of joint letters to Antonescu by Maniu and Brătianu which, while critical of his actions, regarded him as a necessary evil. Antonescu sent detailed replies, often with the offer to stand aside in favour of the two leaders, but on each occasion the offer was either declined or ignored. Typical of these exchanges was Antonescu's response in March 1941 to three letters from Constantin Brătianu[34] in which the latter expressed his concern at Romania's enmeshment with Germany:

> I have been reproached, not openly and to my face, of course for joining the Tripartite Pact. I did so out of a sense of foresight and self-preservation. Foresight because Hungary had joined *before me* [emphasis in the original]. In view of this situation I believed that, in the case of a German victory, Hungary could not be rewarded at our expense, while in the case of a German defeat we would share with Hungary the same responsibility before the victors. I also did it out of a sense of self-preservation. In today's circumstances a small country which is under threat, such as ours, does not do what it wishes, but what it can. The case of Yugoslavia, which does not have the Russians as neighbours and enemies, is obvious . . .
>
> In the political space which concerns us, we have a choice between Britain, Russia and the Axis powers. We cannot count on the support of Britain in the present political situation, a fact which you yourself recognize. An alignment with Britain would not only have brought us no effective support, but it would have exposed us to the danger of total collapse. Political alignment with Russia was a moral and factual impossibility. Being unable to count on Britain, and being unable to go alongside the Soviets, Germany remained the only force upon which we could rely both for economic and political support, as well as regards the possibility of creating real military power which we could use at the appropriate moment, in the manner most suited to our interests.'[35] If, however, both you and Messrs Maniu and Mihalache think that you can pursue a different policy I am ready to give way to you, to give you the power to better serve the country, that is to move from criticism to action. [36]

Antonescu repeated his offer to stand down in another reply to Brătianu of 10 May 1941 to which the Liberal leader responded: 'You know very well that such a change is impossible in today's situation and that, moreover, you are the only person who can inspire trust in the leaders of the two European dictatorships.'[37]

The backing Maniu and Brătianu gave Antonescu was driven by pragmatism, but this did not diminish their sympathy for the Western democracies, which they were convinced would emerge victorious from the war. In practical terms both were anxious to maintain the coherence of their parties with a view to returning to power at the end of the war. Antonescu, while scornful of the record of the parliamentary system in Romania, did nothing to frustrate their plans. He allowed Maniu and Brătianu to hold regular meetings with their parties to discuss their policy towards Antonescu, and these sometimes resulted in the issue of joint declarations attacking the Marshal, details of which were carried by the BBC in its broadcasts to Romania which were carefully monitored by the Romanian Intelligence Service (SSI) and digests supplied on a regular basis to Antonescu. In an attempt to ward off criticism from the Germans, Antonescu insisted that these meetings be called 'reunions'.[38] German anger at the long leash on which Antonescu held the opposition leaders was voiced during Antonescu's visit to Hitler between 12 and 14 April 1943 at Castle Klessheim in Salzburg. At the meeting with Hitler on 13 April at which the German Foreign Minister Joachim von Ribbentrop was present, the latter is reported in one source as describing Maniu's letters to the Marshal as treasonous: 'such a betrayal cannot be punished other than with death. In Germany, a man such as Maniu would have been hanged long ago.'[39] Antonescu explained that Maniu was regarded as an historic figure by the Romanian people, especially by the peasants, among whom he had particular influence, and who would become a martyr of any action was taken against him.[40] How much freedom Antonescu was prepared to extend to Maniu is shown by his indulgence towards the peace feelers put out to the Allies by the Peasant Party leader, among others, in 1943 and 1944.[41]

The Iron Guard rebellion and the subsequent imposition of a military dictatorship by Antonescu had no impact on the implementation of the *Marita* plan. On 20 January 1941, Hitler told Mussolini that the presence of German forces in Romania served three purposes: an attack on Greece; the defence of Bulgaria against the Soviet Union and Turkey; and the security of Romania.[42] On crossing the Danube Hitler expected an air attack on Ploieşti and he therefore ordered the strengthening of its air defences. At the same time, batteries were deployed along Romania's Black Sea coast to protect the port of Constanţa from a possible Soviet naval attack. The bulk of the German 12th Army assigned to the operation crossed into Bulgaria on 2 March. In the meantime, the British government drew the obvious conclusions from Antonescu's cooperation with Hitler and withdrew its minister, Sir Reginald Hoare, from Bucharest. The Romanian government responded by recalling its own minister, Viorel Tilea, from Bucharest on 23 February, and by halting oil deliveries to Turkey to prevent their resale to Britain.[43]

Initially, the *Marita* operation had little direct impact on Romania, but the situation changed with the *coup d'état* of 27 March in Belgrade in which Prince Paul, the Prince Regent, together with the Yugoslav government were overthrown by General Simovici just two days after its signature of the

Tripartite Pact. The *coup* was regarded by Hitler as a slap in the face and he decided the very same day to attack and dismember Yugoslavia.[44] While he planned to ask Italy and Hungary, and to a lesser degree, Bulgaria, to participate in the attack, Hitler had no intention of using Romanian forces, since 'Romania had to ensure primarily security against Russia'.[45] In fact, Antonescu was not told officially of the decision to invade Yugoslavia until 5 April when Neubacher, in the absence of von Killinger, informed him. Antonescu did not seem surprised and said that Romania had no pretensions regarding Yugoslavia with which it had always been on friendly terms. However, if Hungarian troops entered the Yugoslav Banat, he would order the Romanian army to drive them out.[46]

Antonescu's position changed, however, when he learned of the decision taken by Ribbentrop and Ciano at the Vienna Conference of 20–22 April to divide up Yugoslavia. On 23 April, he sent a memorandum to the German and Italian governments stating that, while Romania had not hitherto sought territorial expansion at the expense of Yugoslavia, the concessions made to Hungary and Bulgaria had changed the situation. He demanded the cession of the Yugoslav Banat to Romania and the creation of a free Macedonia with autonomy for the Romanians living in the Timok and Vardar valleys. But Hitler had other plans for these regions. While the western Banat had been promised to Hungary, the area around the Iron Gates defile of the Danube was to be the site of a huge hydroelectric power station – the brainchild of Dr Neubacher – which would provide electricity to the surrounding states which would control the site. Nothing came of the scheme at the time.[47] Although Hitler's promise to the Hungarians that they would receive the Serbian Banat was never withdrawn, the German Foreign Ministry's line in response to Romanian enquiries regarding the future of the region was that 'the fate of areas belonging to Yugoslavia will not be settled until the conclusion of peace'.[48]

Antonescu's greatest concern remained Soviet Russia. During his visit to Berlin in November 1940 he had drawn Hitler's attention to the danger of a Soviet invasion of Romania and as a result the head of the German military mission, General Erik Hansen, had received instructions on 26 November which stated that 'importance was not to be attached to frontier incidents; however, attacks by the Russians must be repelled by the German armed forces on land and in the air'. On 12 December, General Hansen announced his 'intention to use the German training troops in the case of military measures by Soviet Russia'. The Romanian plan in the event of a Soviet attack was to withdraw from Moldavia and occupy a line stretching from Brăila on the Danube to the Carpathians. In support of the Romanian army Hansen proposed to the Romanian General Staff that the German 13th Motorized Division be used. The 16th Armoured Division was to be held in reserve. Defence of the oilfields around Ploieşti was to be entrusted to units of the German air mission.[49]

A week earlier, Field Marshal Walther von Brauchitsch, commander-in-chief of the German Army, and General Franz Halder had reported to Hitler the details of the plan to invade the Soviet Union. On this occasion, Hitler expressed for the first time his belief that 'there is no doubt that Romania, and for that matter, Finland, will march alongside Germany in a campaign in the east'. Hitler's view was probably based on intelligence reports and on his meeting with Antonescu on 22 November, although on that occasion Hitler had not told the Romanian leader of his intention to attack the Russians.[50] Directive no. 21, codenamed *Barbarossa*, was signed by Hitler on 18 December, and envisaged the 'active participation' of Romania in 'the war against Soviet Russia'. Romania's role was to cover the attack made by the southern German flank and to operate alongside German forces advancing into Moldavia. These German forces were to comprise the German 12th Army which was to advance from Moldavia in a north-eastern direction while, in the south, auxiliary units were to force a crossing of the Prut and the Dniester. The exact roles to be played by Romania and Finland, and the subordination of their forces to the German command, were to be decided later.

On 3 February 1941, after further consultations within the German High Command about *Barbarossa*, Hitler declared that the most important task in Romania was 'defence of the oil region'; however, he gave no hint that he would share his plan with Antonescu at this stage. Indeed, the part assigned to Romanian forces in the attack depended on the German assessment of the preparedness and effectiveness of the Romanian army, and here opinions differed within the German High Command. At a meeting of General Headquarters of the German Army on 12 February, the view was put that the Romanian army 'could not be considered an army'.[51] In order to clarify what use might be made of it in *Barbarossa* Colonel Arthur Hauffe, Chief of Staff of the Army Mission in Romania, was instructed to draw up a report and his findings formed the substance of a letter of 24 February sent by General Halder, the Chief of the General Staff, to the commander of Army Group 'South', Field Marshal Gerd von Rundstedt, to whom the forces deployed in the attack on Ukraine were to be subordinated:

> According to the German Army mission in Romania, the Romanian Army, in the main, is not suited to independent warfare. Three infantry divisions (elite divisions) could probably be used for easier attacks in favourable conditions. The use of the motorized division within the German forces on the left flank seems possible for less difficult missions. Apart from these, we cannot establish precisely, at present, what forces can be counted upon. For defence operations, the maximum forces that can be taken into account are eight infantry divisions, four mountain brigades, and six cavalry brigades.[52]

The weakness of the Romanian army was probably the major reason for Hitler's decision, on 17 March, to modify the operational plan for Army Group 'South'. In a meeting with Field Marshal von Brauchitsch and General Franz Halder he gave instructions that 'only sufficient forces for the blocking of the enemy' should advance beyond the Prut, but they should be strong enough to prevent the Russians from advancing into Moldavia. Since the 12th Army was ordered to remain in Greece after the conclusion of *Operation Marita*, the southern flank in *Barbarossa* was assigned, on 25 March, to the 11th Army under General Eugen Ritter von Schobert. Five days later, Hitler explained to his commanders their mission under *Barbarossa*. The 11th Army had to provide 'the support necessary for the Romanian troops', who came in for harsh criticism from the Führer: 'No one should be under any illusion concerning the allies [of Germany]. Nothing can be done with the Romanians. Perhaps behind a very powerful obstacle (a river) they could ensure defence where there was no attack. Antonescu has enlarged his army, instead of reducing and improving it. The fate of large German units should not depend on the resistance of Romanian units.'[53]

Hitler was determined to keep Antonescu – along with the Finns and Hungarians – in the dark about the date of *Barborossa* until the last possible moment. On 23 May, Hitler gave the order that the commander of the 11th Army, General Eugen Ritter von Schobert, would be styled, on his arrival in Romania, 'commander-in-chief of German land troops in Romania'. Liaison between the commander, the German minister in Bucharest and the Romanian High Command was to be provided by the head of the German Army Mission to Romania. On the same day, von Killinger was instructed to inform Antonescu of the arrival of General Ritter von Schobert, and to tell him that 'an army to defend Romania against possible Soviet attacks had been been formed from divisions withdrawn from the south, as well as from other divisions'.[54] Von Schobert received express instructions from Hitler that he should avoid giving a direct reply to Antonescu should the latter ask him whether Germany was expecting a war or whether Germany would attack Russia should circumstances demand it.

As preparations for the attack gathered momentum, General Hansen was given command of the 54th Army Corps in Moldavia on 1 June and his place taken as head of the Army Military Mission by newly promoted General Hauffe; the command of the Military Mission as a whole was given to Lt.-Gen. Wilhelm Speidel, Head of the Air Mission.[55] During the following weeks the German 11th Army was deployed around Iaşi: the 54th Army Corps formed the right flank, the 30th Corps the centre, and the 11th Corps the left flank. Seven German divisions were to take part in the attack. Fifteen Romanian divisions were drawn up near the frontier with the Soviet Union; they were not subordinated to the German High Command because Romania had yet to be informed of *Barbarossa*. Nevertheless, on the advice of von

Schobert, the Romanian High Command had begun a partial mobilization 'in order to defend the frontier against a possible Soviet attack'.[56]

According to the calendar approved by Hitler for *Barbarossa*, the discussions with Antonescu about the attack were scheduled for 'around 12 June'. Antonescu was invited to Munich by Hitler and flew in on the afternoon of 11 June. He confided to the Romanian minister to Berlin, Raoul Bossy, that he knew from General Hansen about the imminent war between Germany and the Soviet Union, and that he could 'go as far eastwards as he wished'; the River Bug should be Romania's eastern frontier 'so that we can retrieve the Romanian population in the former Soviet Moldovan republic and gain the great port of Odessa. But once this area has been cleansed of Yids and Russians, a diplomatic campaign will be opened in order to regain Northern Transylvania'.[57]

On the following morning the Romanian leader was the first of the allies to be informed by Hitler of *Barbarossa*. 'Each ally will participate in the common glory,' the Führer proclaimed. Antonescu approved. Antonescu repeated his declaration, made on 21 September 1940 at a cabinet meeting, that the Romanian people were ready to march unto death alongside the Axis since they had absolute faith in the Führer's sense of justice. The Romanian people had bound its fate to that of Germany because the two peoples complemented each other economically and politically, and they had a common danger to confront. This was the Slav danger, which had to be ended once and for all. It was Antonescu's opinion that a postponement of the conflict with Russia would prejudice the chances of an Axis victory. The Romanian people, he continued, wanted the moment of reckoning with Russia to come as soon as possible so that they could take revenge for all that they had suffered at the hands of the Russians.

To Hitler's question as to whether, in the case of Romania's non-participation in the attack on Russia, the Russians might be more reserved regarding Romanian territory, Antonescu replied that he himself wanted to fight alongside the Germans from the very first instant. The Russians would bomb the Romanian oilfields and would never forgive the Romanians for standing aside and allowing the Germans to march against them.[58] A sense of that impatience had been evident from a letter written by Antonescu on 14 May 1941 to the German minister, von Killinger:

> It is preferable that the seizure of Bessarabia and northern Bukovina should continue to be characterized as an act of force and Romania has regarded it as such. We have no interest in legalizing this act, thereby giving the Soviets legal title for their occupation of these provinces.
>
> ...
>
> The Romanian government considers that this is not the moment to consecrate our frontiers with the Soviet Union precisely because of the

present unstable character of the situation and the possibility of further developments.[59]

The question of supreme command of the joint German–Romanian forces could now be settled by Hitler at the meeting with Antonescu. Romanian forces were assigned the task of protecting the right flank of Army Group 'South'.[60] These forces were integrated into a separate army group known as the 'General Antonescu' Army Group under the nominal command of Antonescu. This was made up of the German 11th Army and the Romanian 3rd and 4th Armies. In order to spare Antonescu's sensibilities Hitler told Antonescu that 'he intended to let him appear before the Romanian people as the supreme commander in this region'.[61] In effect, this group took its orders from the Commander of the German 11th Army, General Eugen von Schobert, as is clear from the guidelines for German–Romanian military cooperation laid down by Hitler in a letter to Antonescu of 18 June.[62] Here Hitler informed him that the 'daily incremental preparations by Russia to launch an attack would soon oblige him to use the German army to reduce this danger to Europe once and for all'. To this end, he would communicate his wishes to Antonescu regarding the role the Romanian army should play in this operation against Russia.[63] The Führer underlined the need for the direction of 'this overwhelming attack' to be concentrated 'in a single hand' and requested Antonescu's 'permission to send him from time to time those of his wishes which referred to the Romanian Army and whose execution, in the interests of a unified, coordinated direction of operations, must be considered absolutely necessary'.[64]

Within 70 hours, Antonescu got his chance to regain the lost eastern provinces of northern Bukovina and Bessarabia when *Operation Barbarossa* was launched on 22 June 1941. It was not preceded by a declaration of war. Two days later Romania's minister in Moscow, Grigore Gafencu, was summoned to the Kremlin by Molotov, the Soviet Foreign Minister. The latter requested an explanation for Romania's attitude. Gafencu told Molotov that he knew nothing. The Soviet minister made the following statement:

> Romania has no right to break the peace with the Soviet Union. She knew that after the settlement of the question of Bessarabia, we had no further demands. We have frequently stated, in categorical terms, that we desired a peaceful and independent Romania. Our desire, which has been proved by deeds, was to better the relations between us. When Germany gave you her so-called guarantee, we protested because we felt that that guarantee was destined to disturb the relations between the Soviet Union and Romania. The German guarantee meant the end of Romania's independence; you had entered into dependence upon Germany. Some months later, your country was occupied by German troops. You

were unable to offer any opposition. But you have no reason to associate yourselves with the German bandits against the Soviet Union. We are compelled to draw all the inferences implied by this aggression.

Gafencu countered these claims by expressing his 'profound regret' that the Soviet Union, by the policies it had lately pursued, had done nothing to avoid the situation that had arisen:

> By its brusque ultimatum of last year, when it demanded not only Bessarabia, but also the Bukovina and a corner of ancient Moldavia; by the subsequent violations of our territory; by the seizures made in the Lower Danube at the very moment when negotiations were in process to fix the new line of demarcation, the Soviet Union destroyed all feelings of confidence and security in Romania, and aroused the justified fear that the very existence of the Romanian state was in danger. Romania therefore sought support from another quarter.[65]

Antonescu's motive was not solely revenge. He saw the German attack as an ideological crusade against the infidel Communism and his participation in it as an act of Christian righteousness. In an order of the day Antonescu told his troops that the hour had arrived for the fight against the yoke of Bolshevism:

> Soldiers, I order you, cross the river Prut. Crush the enemy to the east and to the north. Free our enslaved brothers from the yoke of Bolshevism. Restore to the body of our country the ancestral earth of the Basarab[66] line, the princes' forests of Bukovina, your fields and pastures...
>
> You will fight shoulder to shoulder, spirit to spirit alongside the most glorious and powerful army in the world.
> ...
> Be worthy of the honour which history, the army of the great Reich and its unsurpassed commander Adolf Hitler has bestowed on you...[67]

Antonescu's sense of fulfilling a messianic mission is clearly expressed in his proclamation to the nation on the launch of *Operation Barbarossa*:

> Romanians, before the God of our ancestors, before history and Romanian eternity, I have today taken the responsibility of seizing with honour what was torn from us through enforced humiliation and treachery, with [my] decision to begin the sacred struggle for the re-conquest of the nation's rights...
>
> Our ancestors' coffins, our martyrs' crosses and the dues of our children command us to record our right to honour with our own blood, washing with that same blood the unjust page written last year in our

history, not by the Romanian people itself, but by its traitors.[68] In the name of our Christian faith, of Romanian rights and for our undaunted future Romanians, I summon you to battle, to the holy battle against the destroyers of civilization and of the church, of justice and of our own rights, to the holy battle for the nation and for the king, to the great and just battle alongside the great German nation, for the justice of mankind's future...[69]

With the same religious fervour, Mihai Antonescu, in a radio broadcast on the same day, opened with the words: 'Romanians, today our nation has begun a great holy war.'[70] King Michael was less altruistic; furious at not being informed by Antonescu in advance of the attack, he curbed his anger and in a telegram to Antonescu, expressed the popular mood:

At this moment when our troops are crossing the Prut and the forests of Bukovina to retrieve the sacred land of Moldavia of Stephen the Great, my thoughts go out to you, General Antonescu, and to our country's soldiers. I am grateful to you, General, that thanks solely to your work, steadfastness, and efforts, the entire nation and myself are living the joyful days of ancestral glory, while I wish our brave soldiers the health and power to consolidate for eternity the rightful frontiers of our people. May Romania live for ever. Long live our courageous army.[71]

The mood at the time in the capital is graphically conveyed by Gheorghe Barbul, secretary to Mihai Antonescu:

The streets of Bucharest were still empty and quiet. The radio suddenly burst into life through an open window. First of all, the Lord's Prayer, as usual, recited by a child. Then the announcer began to read the King's proclamation. Suddenly, people appeared at every window, their hair ruffled, and as though they had been freed from a feeling of suffocation, shouted: 'War. War with Russia'. In a few moments the street was full of a crowd which was running, as though from a fire, in one direction, towards the royal palace; the radio stations were playing at full blast; the whole city resounded to martial music. Then, suddenly, a deep silence: prayers; people had fallen to their knees. The moment they stood up they began to shout again: 'Long live the holy war! Victory to the crusade! Out with the Asiatic barbarians from Europe!' An old man climbed onto the palace railings. 'Forward', he shouted, 'may the Bolsheviks not celebrate a year's occupation of Bessarabia'. I did not dare look Mihai Antonescu in the eyes. He was overcome by emotion. Tears were streaming down his face.[72]

Mihai Antonescu went later that morning – 22 June – to the German legation to salute the crowd from the balcony. Alongside him stood von Killinger. It was, Barbul alleged, the first time that the Romanians had unreservedly shown support for Nazi Germany. As Barbul was leaving with Antonescu, von Killinger took the former by the arm and said: 'I have no illusions amidst this outburst of enthusiasm about the Romanians' secret wish. They want us to beat the Russians and then us to be beaten by the British.' Mihai Antonescu protested indignantly: 'such calumny on such a day'. And then, after Antonescu and Barbul had set off in their car, Antonescu settled back in the seat and added with a smile: 'At least von Killinger hasn't been taken in'.[73]

In the grand scheme of *Barbarossa* the part played by Romanian forces was a local, secondary one. To the Romanian public the operation was described by Antonescu as a 'holy war', undertaken to liberate Bessarabia and northern Bukovina, and its presentation in these terms was designed to motivate Romanian troops and mobilize Romanian public opinion. In reality, the attack in Bessarabia and northern Bukovina was directed by von Schobert, with German and Romanian forces fighting alongside each other. Territory freed by the German army from Soviet control was handed over to the Romanians, even though the Germans could have claimed the right of occupation. This consideration offers an additional explanation for Antonescu's determination to be involved in *Barbarossa*. If northern Bukovina and Bessarabia 'had been cleared solely by the German 11th Army, the Third Reich would have been the occupying power, under the rules of war, and as a result Romania's acts of sovereignty would have been merely mandates of the German state'.[74] As one historian has argued, given the fact that the effective command of the 'General Antonescu Army Group' was in the hands of von Schobert, Romania's position was that of 'a state which had accepted command of its troops by another state in order to liberate its own territory'.[75]

According to *The Times* correspondent Archibald Gibson, most Romanians were behind Antonescu when he joined Hitler's attack on the Soviet Union. However, it should hardly be a cause for surprise that there was no published dissent, given the regime's control of the press. On 2 July, the German 11th Army launched its attack from north of Iaşi. The Romanian 3rd Army, under General Petre Dumitrescu, conquered northern Bukovina, occupying its administrative centre Cernăuţi on 4 July.

Antonescu had recovered the lost provinces, as defined by their boundaries prior to the Soviet seizure in June 1940, by 27 July 1941 at a cost of 4,112 dead, 12,120 wounded and 5,506 missing.[76] On 23 July, he appointed General Gheorghe Voiculescu 'plenipotentiary of General Antonescu for the administration of Bessarabia'.[77] In recognition of the recovery of Bessarabia and northern Bukovina King Michael promoted Antonescu to the rank of Marshal on 22 August 1941.[78] Bessarabia and Bukovina were formally re-established as provinces of Romania by decree of Antonescu on 4 September 1941.[79]

The reconquest of Bessarabia and northern Bukovina confirmed Antonescu in his conviction of the righteousness of his cause. In an address to the people on 27 July 1941, the General pledged to

> carry the battle and the renewal forward, smashing to pieces everything which prevented our nation from affirming itself. Romanians will truly be masters in their country, while the peasants will indeed feel the joy of their labour and the fruit of their land. I will see to it until death that your rights be respected, that the new life which we are creating removes all memory of our past sins.[80]

While Britain and the United States refrained from condemning Antonescu outright, public opinion in Britain had already branded Romania an enemy state as a result of its alignment with Germany. Comparison with Finland's predicament in 1939 inevitably sprang to mind. But whereas Gustav Mannerheim, the army chief, and political leaders had resisted Soviet demands for territorial concessions in November, the Romanians in 1940 had supinely caved in. International sympathy for Finland's courageous response to its invasion by its mighty neighbour on 30 November 1939 earned it sympathy in the democratic West, which muted reaction to Finno-German cooperation. By contrast, there were no such considerations to temper judgement in the West of Romania's alliance with Germany. King Carol's lame acquiescence to Soviet demands in June 1940 served only to reinforce the disastrous image that he had projected since his imposition of a royal dictatorship in February 1938 of a self-serving unprincipled monarch at the head of a spineless nation. This was already clear before *Operation Barbarossa* was launched. As the American representative put it to Iuliu Maniu in June 1941, 'it was a pity' that Romanian sympathies for the Allies

> could not be made generally known in the United States, since public opinion there, as a result of Rumania's giving up everything to the Germans without a struggle, was putting Rumania in the same category as Hungary and Bulgaria, and it was already being hinted at in the American press that after the war Rumania together with those other two countries would not be represented at the Peace Conference table, as would Poland, Yugoslavia and Greece, which had at least made an effort to defend themselves.[81]

Antonescu was to reap the whirlwind of such disfavour. His participation with Hitler in the attack on the Soviet Union without a declaration of war obscured the fact that he was seeking to regain territory annexed under duress.

Most Romanian political leaders were content with the re-conquest and advised Antonescu against crossing the Dniester into the Soviet Union proper. Iuliu Maniu and Constantin Bratianu, respective leaders of the National Peasant and National Liberal Parties, urged the Marshal not to let Romanian troops go beyond Romania's historical frontiers. On 28 June, Maniu declared that 'the Romanian armies must not set foot on territories which have not belonged to us. A Romanian imperialism will be condemned by the whole world'.[82] In a letter to Antonescu of 18 July Maniu was even more forthright:

> We went into action to free Bessarabia, Bukovina and a corner of northern Moldavia.... The campaign of the Romanian army for their retrieval is not, therefore, aggression, with the intention of conquest, an intention which must be totally alien to us, but the consequence of an invasion which should have been repelled from the very first instant...
>
> It is unacceptable that we should present ourselves as aggressors against the Soviet Union, which is today an ally of Britain, which will probably be victorious, for any other objective than Bukovina and Bessarabia, in armed league with Hungary and the Axis which through an arbitrary decision, ratified by no one, tore away an important part of our country, sullying our territory and national pride and honour. [83]

Antonescu did not heed this advice. On the contrary, after the Soviets had been swept beyond Romania's pre-1939 borders, he affirmed his loyalty to Hitler's intentions in Russia on 31 July:

> I confirm that I will pursue operations in the east to the end against that great enemy of civilization, of Europe, and of my country: Russian bolshevism. Therefore, I have no conditions, and I will not be swayed by anyone not to extend this military cooperation into new territory.[84]

Despite the assertion that he had no conditions, Antonescu did add that he was convinced that the German leader would see that Romania's 'eternal and centuries-old rights' in the Carpathians were justly satisfied, an oblique reference to northern Transylvania.[85]

Antonescu's reasoning was strictly military, as one would expect. He recognized that Bessarabia was secure only as long as Germany defeated the Soviet Union. Of even more importance was his belief that the road to northern Transylvania lay through Russia and allegiance to Hitler.[86] After all, if the German leader had awarded northern Transylvania to Hungary, in large part to pre-empt a war between Bucharest and Budapest, and then guaranteed the new border of Romania to ward off a possible Soviet intervention that would have threatened Romanian oilfields, he might be amenable to changing his mind once the Soviet threat had been eliminated. Berlin was thus informed that Romania was 'participating in this war for the liberation of Romanian lands invaded without provocation'.[87] Antonescu's motives for continuing beyond the Dniester were

> Both in order to destroy the Russian fortifications in the Transnistrian region, and to reduce Russian military power.... We have requested and we continue to request a revision to the situation in 1940. The Romanian people is not a people of the steppe...In no case can this crossing of the Dniester, which is an occupation of a military character only, have any relation to Romania's rights in the West.[88]

The US government was similarly advised that:

> the aim of Romania was only to recover the territories seized by the USSR a year ago, namely the northern Bukovina and Bessarabia.... Romania had formulated no territorial claims and the occupation of certain areas was for reasons of strategic necessity...[The Romanian] government had formally notified the German government of its position, and specifically made it clear to the Germans that Romania would be unwilling to agree to any territorial expansion in the east in exchange for a renunciation of Romania's claims against Hungary in Transylvania, which will be maintained as a matter of prime national policy.[89]

Thus, on 3 August, the Romanian 4th Army began to cross the River Dniester and advance towards Odessa in an effort to cut off the Soviets retreating before the German 11th Army. The precise objectives of the Romanian advance were established by Hitler and Antonescu at their fourth meeting, held at Berdicev in Ukraine on 6 August. There Hitler also decorated Antonescu with the Knight's Cross of the Order of the Iron Cross, the first of 16 or 17 Romanian recipients – twice the number Hitler awarded to any other ally.[90]

Antonescu rationalized his march eastward in a meeting of the Council of Ministers on 6 September:

> History is written with the sword. Last year the Russians took Bukovina from us. We are now fighting to keep Bukovina under the rule of the Romanian nation. If we did not have powerful Allies, with whom we are united by common interests, we would lose it. We cannot resist before this threat, from the East. We had, therefore, throughout our history, to perform a continual balancing act. We lost what we lost because of King Carol's policy. If we had adapted ourselves to the political situation in Europe we would not have lost anything. But we did not adapt in time. We were sentimentalists in politics, even when it was a question of defending the Romanian nation. We have always been sentimentalists, because we are Francophiles – and we lost the frontiers of the Romanian

nation – because we were Anglophiles – and we lost the frontiers of our country! We, Francophiles! But the Romanian peasant does not know the meaning of the word. He has seen neither Frenchmen nor Englishmen, not even in paintings. We must be Romanian-philes and know how to defend our frontiers. In today's international circumstances whom could we rely on in our situation? On the Germans. If we do not rely on Germany, we will be ripped apart. Had we acted on time, we could have saved the Romanian state. And in the war which we are waging, could I, when the Germans were fighting the Russians, after we took Bessarabia, could I have stopped? Or could I have done as some say: waited, because the British might have given us Bessarabia in the peace settlement? Could I have stood with arms folded when the Germans were fighting with the Russians and have waited for Bessarabia to be given to us by the British? And once we had joined the war, without Germany we could not have taken Bessarabia. The bravery of the Romanian soldier? The skill of General Antonescu? Fancy talk. General Antonescu could have been a billion times more able and the Romanian soldier a million times braver, and still we would not have taken Bessarabia and Bukovina from the Russians. And after we had taken them with the help of the German Army, could I have stopped at the Dniester? Could I have said: I have taken what I wanted, I am stopping here? [91]

It might also have crossed Antonescu's mind that after their removal in January 1941, the leaders of the Iron Guard had found refuge in Germany and were conveniently waiting in the wings should Hitler deem it necessary to replace Antonescu.

Mihai Antonescu was carried away with success of the advance eastwards. In a speech to a group of visiting German journalists on 26 August 1941 he proclaimed:

National Socialism will give Europe a long epoch of peace, longer than the *Pax Romana*. The Führer and Germany have demolished the prejudices and the obstacles.... For 2,000 years we have been crushing every wave of invasion. For centuries the Slav masses could not reach the summit of the Romanian rock in their marauding waves.... It is my wish for the National Socialist future and for the great Führer that they can unite and elevate the whole of Europe with their grand creative and innovative ideas.[92]

The Romanian–German armies eventually captured Odessa on 16 October after fierce resistance from the Soviet forces had inflicted heavy Romanian losses. The creation of the province of Transnistria under Romanian administration was officially proclaimed. Soviet casualties were estimated at over 20,000. On the Romanian side, their losses since crossing the Dniester rose to over 98,000 (almost 19,000 dead, 68,000 wounded and more than 11,000 missing).[93] But the area was under Axis control.

Nevertheless, the lines of authority in Bessarabia, Bukovina and Transnistria were extremely blurred, causing inconsistency and confusion in the administration of these provinces and thereby leaving room for the exercise of individual discretion and the spread of corruption. The problem was exacerbated by a culture of bureaucracy which avoided risk-taking. This mentality encouraged inertia. The personality factor intervened to overcome inertia. Personal ties took precedence over legalized procedure. The ministries were treated as personal fiefdoms. These features of Romanian administration were regularly drawn to the surface by Antonescu, to his constant irritation, in his questioning of ministers during meetings of the Council of Ministers. Particularly telling in this regard is the meeting of 16 December 1941 during which the relationship between the provincial governors of Bessarabia and Bukovina and the ministries was discussed:

> *Mihai Antonescu*:...The Governor of the province is the supreme authority in the province. He represents the province and ensures its unity of action. He is appointed by the Leader of the State and is responsible to it for the efficient administration of the province. He is also responsible to the government for the application of the programme drawn up by it.
> ...
> The Governor is the head of the entire administrative personnel in the province and, in this capacity, he exercises control over all the administrative acts and bodies in the province, with the exception of those services which are reserved for the government and the central authorities in Bucharest.
> In his capacity as supreme authority in the province, he has the right to take decisions and to draw up ordinances and regulations which are applicable to the entire territory of the province.
> He is the head of the provincial police and responsible for the maintenance of public order. In this capacity he can give orders to the police and the security police and request the army's intervention in emergencies.

It could not be clearer than that.

> *General Constantin Voiculescu* [Governor of Bessarabia]: Nevertheless, we proceed differently. My Inspector of Police has left Chişinău and has been living for some time in Bucharest, and I do not know what he is doing.
> *Marshal Antonescu*: Dismiss him.
> *General Constantin Voiculescu*: It does not depend on me.
> *Marshal Antonescu*: What do you mean, it does not depend on you? You dismiss him and then you report to the Minister of the Interior:

I dismissed him for such and such reasons. You will dismiss him forth-with because, under the statute, you have the right to do so. Read the statute closely and keep it on your table.[94]

The dysfunctionality between the army and the civil authorities and institutions was a frequent refrain. In the same Council of Ministers' meeting Antonescu gave a concrete example:

Marshal Antonescu: Mr Mihai Antonescu has talked about communication. The transports of timber have come to a standstill because the army has laid hands on the wood required for the construction of a bridge and without this bridge the timber cannot be carried by rail. Similarly, there is the matter of the ploughs from Storojineț which have been seized by the territorial command.

General Cornel Calotescu [Governor of Bukovina]: As regards me, I have done exactly what Minister Mihai Antonescu had in mind. I intervened there at every point; that is I considered myself your representative. You, Marshal, are the leader and I am the administrator on your estate.

Marshal Antonescu: This incident has occurred. The army has seized the ploughs, which it considers war booty, although this is a matter of dispute. But let's say that this is the interpretation of a colonel in a recruiting centre: all the sky and everything on earth in Bukovina is his. When you see such a man, who blocks the general interest, you must intervene with all your energy to put a stop to such things.

General Cornel Calotescu: When the army entered Bukovina it considered everything war booty.

Marshal Antonescu: I gave you the latitude to decide what is necessary for the army and today I am told: We cannot bring timber to Cernăuți because the bridge is damaged and the material necessary for its repair is held by the army. Do you see what a farce we are in? Form upon form needs to be completed and thus all important operations are blocked. This is just like here, at the presidency, when I asked for certain construction work to be done and a certain gentleman got involved with all sorts of forms and the result is that six months have passed and nothing has been done, the price of the materials has increased by one hundred per cent and this loss will not be paid by that bureaucrat, but by the state and the taxpayers. The same thing happened with this colonel, who says that the ploughs or the timber are war booty.

General Cornel Calotescu: The directorate of fortifications has all kinds of materials, material for bridges, agricultural implements, cement in enormous quantities.

Marshal Antonescu: How is that possible? I had a collaboration meeting with the army, at the General Staff, and I gave an order that all perishable materials, cement, wood etc. should be sold or even given away to the civilian population, but nothing should perish. Last week I was given to understand that this operation had been carried out and now you come and tell me that huge cement stocks are held by the directorate of fortifications.

General Cornel Calotescu: Yes, they are at Suceava. I now need to contact a series of people so that I can obtain them. I summoned Colonel Gheorghiu and a second lieutenant there . . .

Marshal Antonescu: It is quite wrong of you, General Calotescu, to talk to them.[95]

That Antonescu should complain about the actions of the army of which he was the commander-in-chief says much about the weakness of his authority.

A chronic lack of communication created situations in which the left hand did not know what the right was doing. Referring to a prisoner's escape from jail, Antonescu told the Deputy Minister of the Internal Affairs:

Marshal Antonescu: Arrest his father and his whole family and keep them in jail until the fugitive is caught. Let us issue an order under which any escapee's entire family is arrested and detained until he is caught. Weren't the security police informed of this escape?

General Constantin Vasiliu: I spoke to the military prosecutor and he told me that he informed you people at the security police.

Ion Stănescu: We have received no word.

Marshal Antonescu: Just look at what disorganization there is in this country: the escape took place last night and neither the Ministry of Internal Affairs, nor the Security Police know anything.[96]

Until 3 August, when the Romanian army began crossing the River Dniester into the pre-1940 Soviet Union, Romania had been reconquering territory annexed under threat of war by Stalin. Indeed, the British government had not protested when Romanian forces crossed the Prut into Bessarabia and northern Bukovina at the end of June. But since August Romania had been conducting hostilities on pre-1940 Soviet soil. After the fall of Odessa in mid-October pressure began to build up from Moscow for Britain to declare war on Romania. Because Romania, alongside Finland and Hungary, was at war with the Soviet Union, Stalin urged Churchill to act. But Churchill was reluctant to do so and set out his reasons in a letter to Stalin dated 4 November:

These countries [Finland, Hungary and Romania] are full of our friends: they have been overpowered by Hitler and used as a cat's paw. But if fortune turns against that ruffian they might easily come back to our side.[97]

Stalin continued to press the matter as the Germans advanced towards Moscow and Churchill, realizing the need to give the Soviet leader a public gesture of support, finally acquiesced. On 29 November, the British government sent an ultimatum via the US legation to the Romanian government pointing out that for several months it had been conducting aggressive military operations on the territory of the USSR, an ally of Great Britain, in close collaboration with Germany, and warning that unless the Romanians ceased military operations in the USSR by 5 December the British government would have no option but to declare the existence of a state of war between the two countries.[98]

The Romanian government did not reply until the day after the expiry of the ultimatum. It offered a justification for Romania's military action against the USSR which, it was argued, was one of legitimate self-defence in the face of Soviet aggression which had begun in 1940 with the occupation of Bessarabia and northern Bukovina.[99] 'The Royal Romanian Government', the reply continued, 'is firmly convinced that its military action is the only way in which it can ensure its salvation against the visible Russian threat.'[100]

On 6 December, the US minister, Franklin Mott Gunther,[101] addressed the following message to Mihai Antonescu, the Foreign Minister:

> On 29 November, His Majesty's Government in the United Kingdom sent the Romanian Government through the US minister a message according to which if, by 5 December, the Romanian Government did not cease military operations and did not withdraw effectively from any active participation in the hostilities against the USSR, His Majesty's Government would have no option than to declare the existence of a state of war between the two countries. Since the Romanian Government has not responded to this message and since, according to the information available to His Majesty's Government there is no indication that the Romanian Government intends to accept the conditions mentioned above, a state of war will exist between the two countries from 12.01 Greenwich Mean Time on 7 December.[102]

After Britain declared war on Romania on 7 December, Antonescu, who had served as military attaché in London and had a great admiration for Britain, expressed regret in a radio broadcast that his people's centuries-old struggle to preserve its existence, liberty and unity had not been understood. Romania's present action was in continuation of that struggle:

> The declaration of war is without foundation. I regret that there has been so little understanding of the turmoil and tragedy which for centuries has enveloped the brave and ceaselessly tormented and unjustly-stricken Romanian people...

Romania accepts this challenge in the firm belief that, in the struggle against Communism, she serves not only the national belief, the right to preservation and honour of the Romanian people, but also serves, as in the past, through her struggle and her sacrifice, the very civilization to which Great Britain is bound.[103]

On 12 December, the day after Germany and Italy declared war on the United States, the ministers of Germany and Italy, von Killinger and Bova-Scoppa, went together to Mihai Antonescu and advised the Romanian government to consider itself at war with the United States under the terms of the Tripartite Pact. As a result, Gheorghe Davidescu, a senior official in the Foreign Ministry, handed Benton, the US chargé in Bucharest, the Romanian declaration of war.[104] A clear indication of where Antonescu's loyalties lay, despite these developments, can be gauged from his admission – made after the entry of the United States into the war following the Japanese attack on Pearl Harbor on 7 December – 'I am an ally of the Reich against Russia, I am neutral in the conflict between Great Britain and Germany. I am for America against the Japanese.'[105]

In order to placate its new ally, Britain was willing to recognize Soviet sovereignty over Bessarabia and northern Bukovina after the war. In an audience with Stalin on 16 December 1941, Stalin told the British Foreign Secretary Anthony Eden that he expected the western frontier of the Soviet Union to be the frontier of 1941, which included Bessarabia and northern Bukovina as part of the USSR, and that Romania should give special facilities for bases to the Soviet Union, receiving compensation from territory now occupied by Hungary. In a letter to Churchill who was in the United States, Eden predicted that 'if the Russians are victorious they will be able to establish these frontiers'.[106]

This escalation of Romania's part in the war prompted further misgivings, not only among political quarters but also among Antonescu's own senior commanders. In a series of memoranda, Antonescu's Chief of Staff, General Iosif Iacobici, fearing a surprise Hungarian attack from the West against southern Transylvania which was considered at risk because of the withdrawal of forces from there to support the campaign in the Soviet Union, urged the Marshal to limit his involvement east of the Dniester.[107] Iacobici was dismissed in January 1942 and replaced by General Ilie Șteflea, who endorsed his predecessor's views.[108]

Antonescu's binding of the Romanian past with a sense of faith, duty and sacrifice was given forceful expression in his order of the day to the Romanian army on New Year's Day 1942:

On 22 June [1941], by breasting the wall of fire, crime, shame, impiety and bestiality, you have entered history, truly brave and impressive, proud and avenging, as liberators of your brothers and of the Christian faith. Here is, eternally immortal, your great deed of glory, God will bless you for your services to the faith, while the brothers whom you have freed, who are forever indebted to us, will be, I am sure, always grateful to you.

. . .

The enemy has been defeated but he has not been crushed. Our duty is to carry the fight to the end. Do not listen to the propaganda of enemies and of the unprincipled, listen to the advice of your Marshal and the command of your people. Above all, listen to the sacred command which comes to us from beyond the grave, from the princely walls of Putna,[109] from the holy coffin at Dealu,[110] and from below the royal cripts at Argeș.[111]

Antonescu left Hitler in no doubt about his concern for northern Transylania, raising the matter on several occasions with Hitler, for example in the talks with the Führer held on 11 February 1942 when he told him that he did not regard the 1940 Vienna Award as definitive and that, whatever the German position, he would seek to reverse it.[112] Such was Antonescu's persistence on this subject that Hitler was moved to describe the Marshal as 'the most fanatic advocate of a people'.[113]

Iuliu Maniu and Constantin Brătianu kept up the pressure on Antonescu to withdraw Romanian forces from the Soviet Union, but he would not bow. A letter from Brătianu dated 24 September 1942 posing the following questions stung him into giving his reasons:

What will we have at the end of the war? What assurances can you have that Germany will restore to us Transylvania which she gave to Hungary in the Vienna Award? What will be our position if Germany does not win the war since we have done everything to make us enemies of Britain and the United States?

The war with Russia, which according to German propaganda should have ended at the end of 1941, then at the end of 1942, will go on into 1943.

I warned you on several occasions, in 1941 and 1942, that Romania should not send its troops into the heart of Russia, for it will place its very existence in jeopardy, for she risks being crushed in the armed conflict between two great powers and that, on the other hand, her economic situation becomes daily more critical.[114]

In a 125-page reply the Marshal wrote that to withdraw the Romanian Army from the Soviet Union would be a mistake because the front was 1,500 km away, winter was approaching, the stores and railways were in the hands of the Germans, and the *Luftwaffe* had the power to punish disloyalty. Antonescu asked Brătianu if he realized what would happen to the army, its soldiers and its equipment if Romania tried to abandon the front without the consent of the Germans. Not only would the army collapse, but the whole country with it, for the Germans would occupy Romania as they had done Serbia and Greece. Antonescu then gave vent to his anger, directing it at Brătianu:

> You want the defeat of the Bolsheviks, yet you protested when I signed the 'anti-communist pact'. . . . You are against alliance with Germany, yet you realize that we have no one else with whom to ally ourselves. . .
>
> Well, Mr Brătianu, when someone has been the head of a party which from top to bottom, from the village council to the minister's office, is responsible for administrative chaos, moral turpitude, the deliverance of the country into the hands of Jews and freemasons, venality, compromising the country's future and for bringing catastrophe to the country's frontiers, he no longer has the right to speak in the name of the Romanian community.[115]

In conclusion, the Marshal offered to hand over the government to Brătianu, and invited him to withdraw the army from the Soviet Union and come to terms with Britain. Brătianu, in his reply of 14 November, treated this offer as a 'joke'.[116] He might not have done so five days later when the major Soviet offensive at Stalingrad was launched.

The Romanian reinforcements which Antonescu had promised Hitler in a letter of 5 January 1942 arrived on the Eastern Front for the summer campaign. They were, however, under strength and lacking in heavy artillery. Without the industrial infrastructure necessary to be a significant producer of weapons, Romania had turned in the 1930s to the West for arms and armour. At the time she embarked on a rearmament programme in April 1935, her mechanized arsenal consisted of 76 light tanks acquired from France in 1919. In 1937, an order had been placed for 126 Skoda tanks from Czechoslovakia, whose delivery was honoured by the Germans after the occupation of that country, but these proved to be no match for the Soviet T-34s. Throughout the war Romanian artillery relied on older, lighter pieces than the Germans or Soviets and thus a Romanian infantry division was constantly outranged by a similarly sized German infantry division and the smaller Soviet one.[117] This deficiency in tanks and firepower meant that the Romanian Army was incapable of conducting or exploiting the major breakthroughs achieved by the German army in the campaign in Russia. Even in the advances of 1941–42, the Romanian army was given the role of performing frontal infantry actions, which inevitably resulted in heavy casualties even when they were successful.[118]

Seventy-five per cent of conscripts in the Romanian army were peasants and about half of these were illiterate. French and German advisers agreed that they were resilient and able to subsist on fewer rations than most French or German troops. They had good marching abilities and relied heavily on horsepower since the Romanian army had a little motorization.

Their unfamiliarity with motor vehicles – not to mention armour – made it difficult to prepare them against tank attack.[119] Field Marshal Friedrich von Paulus, Commander of the German 6th Army at Stalingrad, praised the qualities of the Romanian troops:

> In the summer campaign of 1942 the armies participating in the offensive were still far too weak, numerically, for the tasks allotted to them. To help fill the gap Supreme headquarters decided to bring the allied armies into the operations. The participation of allied troops was an issue which was to have grave repercussions in the future. In principle, the role envisaged for these troops was that of occupying and safeguarding the territories conquered by the German armies. Only the Romanians, who supplied the major contingent of allied troops, participated in large numbers in the actual offensive operations.
>
> In the circumstances, the fighting spirit and leadership displayed by the Romanian units in the Army under my command deserve special commendation [these were 20th Romanian Infantry Division and the 1st Romanian Cavalry Division, which were besieged with him in Stalingrad]. With the assistance of heavy weapons of the normal German type issued to them, and thanks to the determined leadership by their officers, these troops fought gallantly and showed great steadfastness in the face of all the hardships to which they were subjected.[120]

Other senior German commanders were less complimentary. In Field Marshal von Rundstedt's opinion, the Romanian officers and NCOs were 'beyond description', although he did have words of praise for the Romanian mountain troops.[121] Germans of lower rank were also critical of the way in which Romanian officers treated their men. An Austrian count, Lieutenant Graf Stolberg, reported: 'Above all the officers were no good … they did not take any interest in their men.' A pioneer corporal from the 305th Infantry Division noticed that the Romanian field kitchens prepared three sets of meals – 'one for officers, one for NCOs and one for the men, who got only a little to eat'.[122]

From 28 June 1942, the new German summer offensive – *Operation Blue* – rolled steadily forward. The major objective was the pincer move on, and capture of, Stalingrad, the great industrial metropolis of south Russia, with its armament factories and its important river docks on the Volga, and the conquest of the Caucasian oilfields. On 23 July, Hitler issued directive no. 45. The 17th Army, the 3rd Romanian Army and the 1st and 4th German Panzer Armies, concentrated under the command of Army Group A, were ordered to advance to the conquest of the Caucasus via Rostov, where Hitler proposed to surround and defeat the enemy. The 6th Army, under the command of von Paulus (Army Group B), was ordered to capture Stalingrad and throw a cordon between the Don and the Volga. Because of his Romanian family contacts (he was married to a Romanian) Paulus was selected for the post of Deputy Commander-in-Chief of a new Romanian–German Army Group Don, which was to be formed from the 3rd and 4th Romanian Armies, the 6th German Army and the 4th Panzer Army, and placed under the command of Marshal Antonescu after the capture of Stalingrad.

Early in the autumn, the 3rd and 4th Romanian Armies were brought up to protect the right and left flanks respectively of the 6th Army. The 3rd Romanian Army, under General Petre Dumitrescu, was placed to the north of Stalingrad, while the 4th Romanian Army, under General Constantin Constantinescu, was positioned to the south. Each of their divisions, only seven battalions strong, had to cover a front of 20 km. Both Romanian formations were very inadequately armed, having no heavy artillery and few effective anti-tank weapons. They had only some horse-drawn 37 mm Pak anti-tank guns, which the Russians had nicknamed the 'door-knocker' because its shells could not penetrate the armour of the T-34 tank.[123] Without effective anti-tank defences the Romanian infantry were often gripped, according to General Hermann Hoth's chief of staff, by 'panzer fright' and threw down their weapons. The Romanian prisoners were rounded up into columns, but before they were marched off to camps, many were shot down by Red Army soldiers on their own account.[124]

The German troops suffered heavy losses as they clawed their way into Stalingrad. Paulus begged for reinforcements and for better arms for the Romanians. He tried to enlist the cooperation of General Dumitrescu in the hope that, through Antonescu, help might be extended to the Romanians and to his own Army. Hitler ignored these requests. In the middle of November, he sent Paulus a signal saying that he now expected one final, supreme effort by the 6th Army to wipe out the Russian forces in Stalingrad. On 19 November, the 21st Soviet Army and the 5th Soviet Tank Army broke through the front of the Third Romanian Army on the Don. The German neighbours of the 20th Romanian Infantry Division watched 'masses of Soviet tanks and waves of infantry, in quantities never seen before, advancing against the Romanians'. Major Bruno Gebele, commander of a German infantry battalion, learned from the commander of the adjoining Romanian regiment, that the latter's men had only a single 3.7 cm horse-drawn Pak for the whole of their sector, but the Romanian soldiers fought bravely. The next day, 20 November, the 51st and 57th Soviet Armies, with strong armoured support, broke through the front of the 4th Panzer Army and 4th Romanian Army to the south of Stalingrad. Despite stubborn Romanian and German resistance, the Soviet 65th Army cut off a path of retreat to the west from a bend in the Don, and it was in this area to the south-west of Raspopinskaia that five Romanian infantry divisions under General Mihail Lascăr, belonging to the Romanian 3rd Army, were forced to surrender on 24 November after their ammunition ran out. The Soviet forces took more than 30,000 Romanian prisoners and all of their equipment.

On 24 November, Hitler ordered his forces to hold Stalingrad. On 12 December, the 4th Panzer Army and the Romanian 4th Army tried to battle its way to the encircled forces but was stopped some 40 km short of its objective. On 24 December, the Soviet Armies counterattacked and virtually destroyed the 4th Panzer Army and the Romanian 4th Army. Of the latter's three divisions only two battalions survived. By early January, von Paulus's supplies were nearly exhausted. German attempts to relieve him by air were thwarted by bad weather and by the Soviet air force. On 8 January, the Soviet command sent von Paulus an ultimatum to surrender but it was rejected under Hitler's orders. The Soviet Armies went over to the offensive and split the German resistance. On 31 January, the southern group under von Paulus, who had just been promoted to Field Marshal by Hitler, surrendered and two days later the remnants of the northern group also capitulated. The Russians took more than 90,000 prisoners.

In the course of the Soviet counter-offensive at Stalingrad two German armies, two Romanian armies and one Italian army were decimated. The Romanian losses in the 3rd and 4th Armies in the period from 19 November 1942 to 7 January 1943 were put at 155,010 dead, wounded or missing, most of the latter being taken prisoner.[125] This represented over half of Romania's 31 active field divisions[126] and a quarter of all Romanian troops engaged on the Eastern Front.[127] In a telegram addressed to his Chief of Staff, General Ion Șteflea, on 30 December 1942, Antonescu praised the courage of the Romanian troops while accepting responsibility for not doing more to prevent the defeat:

> I bear the responsibility before history because I did not do more than I did to avert the massacre of the armies which was due to the cavalier attitude of the German command, the total lack of foresight and passiveness with which it received the alarm signals and the [news of the] preparations, known in advance, of the enemy.

Blame for the disaster lay, in Antonescu's view, squarely with General Hauffe, who he claimed left the Romanian forces with insufficient anti-tank weapons, without air cover and without the support of reserves when they ran out of ammunition.[128]

Hauffe was received by Hitler in his *Wolfsschanze* headquarters on 21 December 1942. The Führer, who on principle refused to apportion 'blame', ordered Hauffe to tell Antonescu that 'what was important at the present juncture was the front'.[129] This he did a week later in Predeal. On 10 January 1943, Antonescu visited Hitler. Their discussions lasted two days. At the centre of their talks lay the defeat of the Romanian armies and the re-formation and equipping of the Romanian divisions in Russia. It was agreed that the first step should be the re-armament with German weap-onry of the six divisions on the Caucasus front, followed by that of the two divisions in the Crimea, the two on the coast based around Mariupol, and six new divisions. The First Romanian Tank Division, which had been destroyed, was also to be re-created. Altogether, 19 Romanian divisions were to be completely re-armed; the cost would be covered by a credit given by Germany. Until this was achieved, Romania's contribution to the war was to be limited to the 8th division in the Caucasus and the two divisions in the Crimea.[130]

During the talks the crisis that had emerged in the personal relations between Antonescu and the German command over Stalingrad was resolved. On the orders of Antonescu, General Şteflea, Chief of the Romanian General Staff, asked for Hauffe's recall during the visit to Hitler's headquarters. As a result Hauffe was replaced as head of the German military mission to Romania and representative to the Romanian army command by General Erik Hansen on 28 January 1943.[131]

The Axis defeat at Stalingrad marked a turning point in the war in Europe; the German Army lost the initiative in the war against the Soviet Union. By failing to bring the oilfields of the Caucasus under his control, Hitler lost the ability to conduct a prolonged war against the Anglo-American naval powers. After Stalingrad, he no longer knew how to win the war.[132] Yet Antonescu remained optimistic. A week after von Paulus's surrender at Stalingrad, the Romanian leader was telling his minister in Berlin, who had expressed serious doubts about a final German victory: 'you do not know about the secret weapons which Hitler showed me at our last meeting, nor his war plans, nor the masses of soldiers which he will throw against the Russians in the summer. There is no doubt that the Germans summer offensive will crush the Russian army.'[133] At the same time it was becoming increasingly clear that Antonescu had shown considerable wisdom in accepting General Şteflea's advice that he should not commit all of his forces to the campaigns in the Soviet Union, holding half of them in reserve to protect his country's sovereignty. It now seemed that he might have to use them for this purpose.

There were no major public outbursts of anger at the Stalingrad catastrophe, and even private protest appears to have been muted. Only a handful of volumes of such letters could be mustered in preparation for Antonescu's trial in 1946.[134] Questioned in an interview in March 1943 about his reasons for driving the Romanian army to Stalingrad, Antonescu explained to his interlocutor, the writer Ion Brătescu-Voineşti, that in the opinion of some people 'with responsibility for the past, but who do not wish to take responsibility for the future except by giving advice' – a reference to Iuliu Maniu and Constantin Brătianu – he should have stopped the Romanian advance at the Dniester. Had he done this, he would have left the enemy in Odessa on Romania's flank, thus giving him the opportunity to invade again, 'to tear from us what we have won back with such a painful sacrifice, and to conquer our entire country'.[135]

The strain of events at Stalingrad surfaced in his reply to a letter criticizing his leadership from an erstwhile friend, Nicolae Mareş, of 22 December 1942:[136]

> I have received your letter. All I can tell you is that you are a completely irresponsible person... Others might tell you that you should be locked away but I think that given your state of agitation your madness knows no bonds... You continually assert things which you cannot prove. Everything you hear on the street from Yids, gossips, wretches and bastards you take seriously.
> ...
>   But I know the truth and I am dismayed by so many bastards and bare-faced lies.... I ask you now, is it intelligent, is it human, is it patriotic to harass a man who is striving in the face of so much pressure to save everyone... Are you an idiot, or of bad faith, I ask myself.[137]

After the Stalingrad disaster Romanian forces on the Eastern front totalled eight divisions, of which six had been integrated into the German 17th Army at the Kuban bridgehead in the Caucasus. The other two divisions were defending the coast on the Crimea. On 10 September 1943, the Soviet army moved against the bridgehead, pushing the Germans and Romanians back to the Crimea. All six divisions, totalling 50,139 men, were evacuated to the Crimea by 2 October, and the remaining Germans escaped on 8 October.[138] The defence of the Crimea now fell to the 17th Army under General Erwin Jaenecke, while the remains of the Romanian 3rd Army were moved to defend Transnistria and the Black Sea coast to the west of the Dnieper. Antonescu was sceptical about the ability of the Axis forces to hold the Crimea but Hitler was determined to defend it and on 29 November he wrote to Antonescu saying so.

Defeat at Stalingrad strained even further the tense relations between Antonescu and King Michael and his mother, Queen Helen. The king often complained that Antonescu treated him like an inexperienced youth – Michael was almost 40 years his junior – and that he had little regard for his mother. A note of an interview on 26 November 1943 between King Michael and a British intelligence officer made by Henry Spitzmuller, a French diplomat who remained in Romania after the fall of France, gives a clear picture of Michael's feelings:

> 'Did you know', the King told Mr House, 'that Marshal Antonescu declared war without even forewarning me, and that I learned about this deed from the radio and the newspapers?' Then the King and Queen Mother described the scene that they had had with the Marshal who had been incredibly insolent towards them...
>   Returning to the subject of our conversation, the King said: 'I needed a great deal of self-control to put up with what I have since Marshal

Antonescu took over the government, violating the Constitution. I have withstood the greatest insults and have done so out of duty to the country. Be assured that I do not lack courage, nor the sense of sacrifice. I have often drawn up plans with my faithful colleagues to overthrow this odious regime which is currently oppressing the country. But what would be the point of a *putsch* when we lack the means to take it to its logical conclusion? Such a move would merely play into the hands of Antonescu and the Germans. As regards the Marshal, any chance of compromise is out of the question. You might say', the king added, 'that he is mad in the medical sense of the term and that he considers himself greater than Mussolini at the height of his power.'

The Queen Mother then remarked that she and Marshal Antonescu were at daggers drawn and said that he considered her to be the evil genius behind the King.[139]

Defeat at Stalingrad left a deep impact on Mihai Antonescu. He began to temper his anti-Semitic zeal and sought to present a more favourable image of himself to the Western Allies, seeking to distance himself from the genocidal measures for which he was partly responsible in the summer of 1941. Aware that a reckoning with the Allies was ever more likely, he was anxious to show himself as a saviour of the Jews. The eagerness with which he asked Romanian diplomats in neutral states to present him to the British and Americans as sympathetic to the Jews, the solicitude with which he treated pleas from the International Committee of the Red Cross and the Vatican to improve the conditions of the deportees in Transnistria, and his readiness to assist Jewish emigration all led him to believe that he would emerge from the war with clean hands. An example of his special pleading with the Allies is the cable sent to Alexandru Cretzianu, the Romanian minister at Ankara, on 14 March 1944:

> I should be grateful if you would let Mr Steinhardt[140] know that it is not only now, but always, that I have been in favour of emigration. In 1940, as Minister of Justice, I prevented massacres and abuses of property, ordering the arrest of those guilty.

He went on to claim that in March 1941 he had informed Himmler that the Romanian government was 'against any physical solution or harsh individual measures of constraint, since the Romanian people are a tolerant people and do not accept crimes as a political method', and that all Jews who wanted to do so would be able to leave Romania. When the Germans made a formal request to take exclusive charge of matters relating to the Jews in 1941, he had refused. In 1942, when the British government had asked him through the Swiss embassy in Bucharest whether Romania would allow Jews to leave, he had replied that it would. As a final point to be transmitted to the US ambassador, he committed the Romanian government to permit the emigration of children from Transnistria.[141]

The Axis retreat before the advancing Soviet armies injected a dose of foreboding into Antonescu's New Year's Day address of 1944. Gone was the triumphalism of the previous years, now it was the preservation of national unity and the very defence of European 'civilization' in the face of the Soviet threat that were paramount. The Marshal turned yet again to God for justice:

> For you, Romanians, at this beginning of the year, I express my unwavering belief in God's justice and in our rights...
>
> I direct my thoughts towards the just Lord, our protector, not only to ask for the protection of our faithful nation, but also to offer him my prayer as a man who waits to see humanity, justice and peace return to the peoples of the world...
>
> Only in unity will we be able to ensure justice for our nation and the unity of its lands.... only in unity will we be able to ensure the freedom, honour, prosperity and rights of every person, without which life is a trial.[142]

In waiting to 'see humanity, justice and peace' return to the world, Antonescu was admitting, perhaps unconsciously, that the Romania over which he presided at the beginning of 1944 had made its own significant contribution to the inhumanity, injustice and war of the previous three years.

5

Antonescu and the Jews

Jews had been in the lands composing Romania since the fifteenth century.[1] Sephardi Jewish merchants from the Ottoman Empire were reported to have been caught up in one of the campaigns of Prince Stephen the Great of Moldavia (1457–1504) against the Turks.[2] Jewish merchants made their first appearance in Wallachia in the middle of the sixteenth century when the presence of two Sephardi Jewish shopkeepers in Bucharest is recorded.[3] It was towards the end of the century that the first organized Jewish community was established in Transylvania, in Gyulafehervar (Alba Iulia), the seat of the prince. It was composed of Turkish Sephardi Jews who were involved in trade with the Ottoman Empire, but their legal residence was restricted to this town alone. Their numbers were soon swelled by Ashkenazi Jews who came from Poland.

A dearth of statistical data makes exact calculation of the numbers of Jews in Moldavia and Wallachia before 1800 difficult. Jewish immigration into the principalities turned from a trickle into a torrent in the middle of the century as a result of persecution in eastern Europe. Pogroms in Russia and Russian Poland drove thousands of Yiddish-speaking Ashkenazi Jews into Moldavia in the 1830s and 1840s and within a generation they formed a majority of the population in such towns as Iaşi, Botoşani, Dorohoi, and Fălticeni. The construction of synagogues followed. These Jewish communities were centred on the traditional settlement (*shtetl*), in contrast to the largely Sephardi communities in Wallachia, which were more assimilated into Romanian society.[4] Although restrictions were placed on the entry of Jews into Moldavia, the authority of the principality was too weak to ensure their enforcement. Barred, and barring themselves, from assimilation, these Jews were denied the right to naturalization until the Romanian government was forced by the Great Powers to accord it in 1879. But the right was hedged with such restrictions that fewer than 2,000 had succeeded by 1920.

Anti-Semitism was widespread and respectable among most Romanians. The peasants' dislike stemmed from the Jews' position as alcohol suppliers, moneylenders and middlemen in the timber trade, while the upper classes looked on them with suspicion. Additionally, arrivals from Russia during the nineteenth century, even though in flight from pogroms, were regarded as Russians and therefore particularly unreliable. In Bessarabia the Jews remained a community apart from the Romanian peasant majority. Of the 206,958 Jews in Bessarabia in 1930, some 201,278 declared Yiddish to be their native language, while their second language was invariably Russian rather than Romanian. Anti-Semitic feeling among the newly arrived Romanian officials was exacerbated by their suspicion of the Jews as Bolshevik agents, following the influx of Jewish refugees into Bessarabia in the wake of the Russian civil war. Antonescu's career developed squarely in this milieu.

King Carol's abandonment of neutrality at the end of May 1940 coincided on the domestic front with his reconciliation with the anti-Semitic pro-German Iron Guard. As Romania aligned herself more closely to Germany, so the position of the Jews became more precarious. The pro-German cabinet of Ion Gigurtu introduced a decree on 9 August which, by changing the legal status of Jews and denying them civil and political rights, was a replica of Hitler's Nuremberg laws. Jews were divided into three categories: the first comprised those who had settled in Romania after 30 December 1918; the second, Jews naturalized before 30 December 1918 and those who had fought in the Romanian army, including their children; and the third, the rest. Under this decree all Jews were barred from being career officers in the army – although Jews in the second category could be soldiers – and those in the first and third categories could not be lawyers, notaries, public servants or purveyors of alcohol, nor could they conduct trade in rural areas. They were banned from running or letting cinemas, editing books, Romanian newspapers and journals, participation or membership of national sporting associations, or from doing menial jobs in public institutions.[5] Instead of military service, Jews in the first and third categories were to pay a special tax or perform community labour (*munca de interes obştesc*). Under a separate decree of the same date, marriages between Romanians and Jews were forbidden.[6]

A letter of 26 August 1940 from a manager of Astra Română, the subsidiary of the Royal Dutch Shell company in Romania, to his superior in London, gives details of additional arbitrary measures directed against Jewish youth:

> One of the side-issues of the present anti-Jewish movement has been to exclude all but Christian Romanian citizens from the *Straja ţării* (Guardians of the Country) movement, which is a cross between the Boy Scout/ Girl Guide and *Hitlerjugend* movements.[7] This was not done by law but by a decision of the leader himself, and for the time being his word is as good as law. As all children have to wear the uniform of the movement to school, the outward result will be to brand the unfortunate Jewish children – with, perhaps the intention of making their lives so miserable that they will prefer not to frequent Romanian schools.

The *Straja Țării* was also in charge of all sport throughout the country, and it was hardly possible to raise a racket or throw a ball without the stepmotherly intervention of the movement or of one of its many subordinate federations. It has now been decreed by the *Straja Țării* that no one but members of the new National Party can be on the committee of a sports organization, and that no one but a Christian Romanian citizen can be a member of a sports club.

The Astra Română Sports Club has therefore had to bring itself formally into line with this fiat, with the result that no Jews or foreigners are now members. This means that they cannot contribute to the funds of the Club and would not be allowed to compete in any competitions organized by the Club.

As regards the use of the Snagov premises, as well as the various tennis courts and swimming pools which have been provided at Astra's various administrations, these do not in any way belong to the Sports Club but have been provided and are maintained by Astra Română. Astra have done this for the benefit of their employees in order to provide them with recreation, not with sport, and they are at the disposal of all employees without discrimination. It remains to be seen whether this attitude will be allowed to pass unchallenged by the powers that be, or whether it will be considered as a defiance of the 'national' policy of the Romanian state.[8]

With the accession of Antonescu and the Iron Guard to power and the proclamation of a National Legionary state on 14 September 1940, new anti-Semitic measures were taken. These prompted Wilhelm Filderman, the president of the Federation of the Union of Jewish Communities (FUCE), to write to Antonescu on 15 September expressing his concern. Antonescu replied – adopting as was his wont the third person – through his cabinet secretary as follows:

Mr Filderman is requested to be understanding and to make those of his same faith throughout the whole country understand that General Antonescu cannot perform miracles. He found the country in a state of anarchy and in chaos in all respects and at all levels. There was also a week of romantic enthusiasm. A generation which had been tormented, attacked, kept under surveillance and murdered had the right to explode when it was unshackled. In ten days' time it will calm down and as each day passes it will respect the discipline of the laws of the land. I assure Mr Filderman of this and I also assure him that if his co-religionists neither sabotage the regime openly nor behind the scenes, nor politically nor economically, the Jewish population will have nothing to suffer.

The word of General Antonescu is his bond. But the Jewish population must renounce – and I make this point seriously without making any threats – the methods which it has employed to date – because that was the nature of the political regimes – of economic enslavement, of political and moral enfeeblement of our national resistance, and of exploitation of our poverty.[9]

On 17 September, restrictions were placed on the Jews' freedom to practise their faith but, at the repeated request of Filderman, Antonescu suspended their application. Similarly, the Ministry of Cults and Arts rescinded on 26 September its original decision of 12 September to ban Jews from performing on the stage, although it qualified this by allowing them to appear only in Jewish theatres and stipulating that their plays should be advertised as 'Jewish theatre'.[10] On 5 October, a decree law was passed providing for the appointment of commissars, who had to be Romanian, to enforce compliance by companies with the directives of the Ministry of National Economy.[11] This decree ushered in what was known at the time as 'the policy of Romanianization'.

On 3 October, Jews had been barred from renting pharmacies – most pharmacies were either rented or owned by Jews – and on 5 October, rural real estate was expropriated from Jews, as were forest land, mills, distilleries and cereal stocks on 12 November, and shipping on 4 December.[12] The right of Jews to plead at the bar was limited by law to representation of their co-religionists as private persons (17 October), while Jewish doctors were allowed to treat Jewish patients only (15 November). According to data held by the FUCE 1,577 doctors out of a total of 1,877 were victims of this measure. The needs of the state, however, soon produced a change of policy. In February 1941, the Ministry of National Defence decided that Jewish doctors, pharmacists and veterinary surgeons who were called up should be paid according to their qualifications. Similarly, Jewesses were employed as doctors or nurses in time of war behind the front lines.[13] Under a decree of 16 November 1940, industry, private business and non-profit organizations were required to replace their Jewish employees with Romanians by 31 December 1941. However, many Jews were kept on through 'individual dispensations' which were 'purchased' from the 'Romanianization' inspectors.[14] Official statistics showed that of 28,225 Jews employed in business on the eve of the decree, 17,134 were still in work under the dispensations on 31 December 1941.[15]

A voice raised in harmony with these measures was that of the demographer Sabin Manuilă, responsible in the state statistical office for computing and assessing the population movements provoked by the territorial losses of summer 1940. In his opinion, the Jewish danger was predominantly economic and in a paper published in October 1940, he advocated greater control of the Jews' wealth in order to channel these resources for the benefit of the country at large.[16]

On the authorities' own admission the process of Romanianization was carried out from the very outset in a chaotic fashion. Instead of being phased in, in stages involving the identification of companies, the listing of their assets and then their nationalization, it was recognized that 'the system used was a random one, founded on rumour, denunciation and in particular information which hid a personal interest to become a Romanianization commissioner or inspector, or to force Romanianization on a company for which there was a buyer in early discussions'.[17]

The frequent abuses committed by the commissioners, who were almost exclusively Iron Guardists, so angered Antonescu that he took steps to curb the excesses. At a Council of Ministers' meeting on 13 December 1940, he proposed that regional inspectors be appointed to supervise the activity of the commissioners and that those who objected to his policy should be dismissed. A few weeks later, on 19 January 1941, he went even further by abolishing the posts of commissioners and replacing them with a commission in the Ministry of National Economy to manage the respective companies.

However, there was no respite in the application of anti-Semitic legislation after the Iron Guard's removal; the policy of Romanianization continued apace. Under Antonescu's dictatorship the anti-Semitic measures were extended. It was on his orders that the Foreign Ministry advised the passport office on 7 March 1941 that henceforth passports issued to Romanian citizens of Jewish origin should bear the inscription 'Jew or Jewess' in the top left-hand corner of the first page. The criteria for applying this specification were those laid down in the law of 8 August 1940 regarding the legal status of Jews.[18] A series of measures was introduced to prevent Jewish craftsmen and tradesmen from practising. On 28 March 1941, the Ministry of Labour, Health and Social Protection instructed prefectures to cancel the contracts of Jews apprenticed not only to Christian employers, but to Jewish ones as well, and to stop the issue of new ones.[19] On the same date, urban property owned by Jews was nationalized. In an effort to rationalize Romanianization of Jewish property the government created on 3 May 1941 the National Centre for Romanianization (*Centrul Naţional de Românizare*).[20] It was charged with administering the assets nationalized from the Jews, with 'Romanianizing economic life' and with paying the former Jewish owners compensation totalling eight times their gross income, as established by the taxes they paid. Much of the property confiscated from Jews was let out to Romanians. Although Mihai Antonescu claimed in March 1944 that to that date 'not a single Jewish asset among those expropriated from the Jews in 1940 and 1941 has been sold',[21] there are reports in the Romanian press of the time of Jewish possessions being sold by auction.

Expressions of the ideological rationale of Romanianization were presented in various official publications. Romanianization represented 'not only the cleansing from the realms of property and from economic activity of the dominant and acquisitive Jewish and foreign elements, but even more than that, and consecutively, a creative measure designed to give a thorough guarantee of a pure, healthy, durable Romanian control of property and of economic activity'.[22] Arguments were invoked to justify the policy. The nationalization of Jewish assets was posited 'morally on the idea of national need, while its legal basis was the state's right to expropriate any asset in exchange for a normal indemnity'.

Antonescu's government undertook to underwrite the process of nationalization by providing credit through a special bank, the *Credit Românesc*, which was set up on 29 April 1941, but its disbursement, according to government statistics, was sluggish. Antonescu himself recognized that given the volume of Jewish capital in the Romanian economy, it would have been impossible to remove it without provoking a major economic crisis:

> We stand with certain industries of ours at the total discretion of others. They cannot function, therefore, due to a lack of capital. Figures have been produced on my orders from which you will see how the proportion of Romanian capital is dwarfed by foreign and Yid capital. You will see that the solution to the problem is not so easy, it has to be resolved methodically, in stages, since this capital, which has been infiltrated over twenty years since the war, cannot be removed in a day. We ought to replace it but we do not have the means. This has been the major problem of the Romanian nation. If we remove the Jews, this enormous void is created in the Romanian economy, which will produce a general, irreparable catastrophe for our state and its recovery will be impossible.[23]

In Bessarabia and northern Bukovina the expropriation of Jews took place after their reconquest, on 4 September 1941, as part of the legislation applied to these provinces. That legislation included the same anti-Semitic measures adopted in Romania since the loss of these territories on 28 June 1940. Thus the Romanian state now nationalized all property and assets owned by Jews. In contrast to the situation in the Old Kingdom (Wallachia and Moldavia) and southern Transylvania, Jewish commercial and industrial property was included. The only exceptions were synagogues and cemeteries in use at the time of the nationalization laws introduced in autumn 1940.[24]

As a consequence of the expropriation of Jewish property in the Old Kingdom and southern Transylvania alone, the following assets had been nationalized by September 1942: 52,527 hectares of land, 113 sawmills, 343 industrial properties, 152 vessels and 30,691 urban dwellings.[25] But these figures disguised the ambivalence of the whole process of Romanianization. A report of the Iaşi chamber of commerce of 26 January 1942 disclosed the reality of the situation in that county:

no distinction has been or is made between Romanian and Jewish commerce; the latter continues to exist and is active, either under the cover of Romanian names, or openly and legally (greengrocers and grocers, sausage sellers, booksellers, stationery, perfumes and clothing).... The lack of energy of those authorities called upon to contribute to Romanianization, the fiscal requirements, taxes and stamps ... the severity of the law of sabotage which hovers like a permanent and terrifying threat over any enterprise, have led many to withdrew in horror from business and to consider it not as a fine and to a certain degree fruitful occupation, but on the contrary, a dangerous and expensive adventure ... [26]

Similar contradictions emerge from comparisons of national and local statistics regarding the number of Jews employed by companies following the introduction of the discriminatory measures in this field on 16 November 1940. Official figures show a decrease in their number from 28,225 in November 1940 to 16,292 in February 1942, and to 6,506 in February 1943.[27] Yet the Labour inspectorate in Iaşi reported not a decrease but an increase, from 1,745 to 1,886, in the number of company-employed Jews in the county over the period November 1940–December 1943, stressing that 'the Romanianization campaign had not achieved its objectives'.[28] This gives credibility to secret reports which estimated the number of Jewish employees at over 21,000 in the spring of 1943.[29] They remained in place for a variety of reasons, the main one being that they were crucial to the running of their companies. As the Labour secretariat pointed out in April 1942, some companies discouraged Romanian employees from developing the skills required from the Jewish employees they were intended to replace; in other cases the Jews themselves refused to pass on the necessary knowledge; while in a number of instances Romanians were too lazy to acquire the expertise from Jewish employees.[30] In other sectors of the economy, too, the progress of Romanianization seems to have been chequered. The number of commercial enterprises owned by Jews and foreigners fell from 53,919 (38.3 per cent) in September 1940 to 41,640 (28.1 per cent) as of 1 June 1943.[31]

The military status of the Jews and compulsory labour

As the prospect of Romania's entry into the war grew with her membership of the Tripartite Pact in November 1940, so clarification of the military status of the Jews became more pressing. A decree on their status was introduced on 5 December 1940 which exempted Jews from military service but obliged them to pay military taxes and to perform community labour (*munca de interes obştesc*) at the discretion of the state. Similar labour obligations were required under a decree of 15 May 1941 of Romanians between the ages of 20 and 57 who were unemployed, except married women or those with children.[32] After the German–Romanian attack on the Soviet Union of 22 June 1941, a further decree of 14 July 1941 stipulated that Jewish males aged between 18 and 50 could be used only by the army general staff individually or in groups for community labour designated by the army or by other state institutions. The maximum period of labour ranged, according to the age of the person drafted, from 60 to 180 days a year, but in a period of prolonged mobilization or war it could be unlimited. Those summoned for work on certain projects in groups were to be formed into labour battalions (*detaşamente de lucru*) under army command and fed and quartered. Doctors, pharmacists, veterinary surgeons, engineers, architects, active or retired officers were exempted from manual labour, but could be drafted to perform their professions if required and to receive a salary. Other Jews who did community labour had the right to the same food, maintenance and pay as ordinary soldiers if they worked under army command. If they were placed in the charge of the other institutions, they would receive only army pay.

In all cases the Jews would be dressed as civilians, being obliged to present themselves for work with suitable seasonal clothing and two changes of underwear. On their left arm they wore a yellow armband with the name of the recruitment centre. Former officers and lower ranks were required to wear respectively, on the yellow armband, a yellow or white six-pointed metal star. When they worked locally the Jews were to live at home; otherwise they had to provide bedding and eating utensils.[33]

Throughout the time Romania was at war under Antonescu the Jews were required to perform community (later known as forced) labour.[34] There was considerable confusion over the implementation of the compulsory labour provisions owing to the numerous and sometimes conflicting orders in this respect issued by the Ministry of Internal Affairs and the army, the latter being responsible for the compulsory labour 'recruitment' centres. After the decision was taken to press able-bodied Jews between the age of 20 and 50 into compulsory labour on the railways, all prefects were ordered by the Ministry of Internal Affairs on 1 August 1941 to request lists of these Jews from the recruitment centres set up by the army for this purpose.[35] The prefects were charged with the selection of Jews who were then to be examined by a doctor before being sent to the respective place of work. Those declared fit were allowed to take clothing and other belongings that were strictly necessary. The journey to their assigned place of work was to be made under an escort of policemen and gendarmes. For their labour the Jews were to be paid 90 lei a day, the railway board being responsible for their food and shelter.[36] On 2 August, the Interior Ministry informed prefects by telegram that Jews engaged in compulsory labour were to be paid 25 lei a day plus 10 lei for their upkeep.

Food was not always provided by the railways, as the board itself admitted. In a number of cases it was left to local Jewish committees to provide food for the labourers, but they 'encountered great difficulties since they were not allowed to enter the villages to buy food'.[37] The director of the railways board, Colonel T. C. Orezeanu, advised the Interior Ministry of this situation, pointing out that traders throughout the country 'refuse to sell essential foodstuffs (bread and meat, etc.) which are rationed', and asked the Ministry to instruct prefects and mayors 'to facilitate the procurement of food necessary for feeding Jews in work detachments on the railways'. The Ministry sent out such an instruction on 19 August.[38] On 4 August, the army informed the prefect of Brăila that Antonescu had 'given several orders that Jews should be used for work on the roads and for general duties in the towns in return for food and tobacco, yet the order had not been carried out'. The prefect was 'kindly requested' to ensure that the order was implemented.[39]

Some army officers were moved to intervene on behalf of Jews in compulsory labour detachments. Their motives are unclear but their action prompted the Defence Minister to issue an order on 29 July banning 'requests for favours for Jews in the detachments. These shameful interventions show the mentality of some officers who disregard the national imperative and diminish the prestige of the army.'[40]

The question of community labour (*munca de folos obştesc*) was raised by Antonescu at the first meeting on 19 November 1941 of a coordinating council set up to review economic affairs.[41] It was the prerogative of the government alone, Antonescu said, to decide what kind of labour should be performed; as regards young people, he continued, the work would be organized by the extramural secretariat of the Ministry of Culture; as regards the elderly, it was a matter of wait and see. Mihai Antonescu then told the Marshal that the Minister of the Economy, Ion Marinescu – who was present – wanted to raise the question of 'Jewish labour':

> *Marshal Antonescu*: The problem is being studied and is almost completed. We will oblige them to make a financial contribution.
>
> *Colonel R. Davidescu*: The question is being examined by the General Staff.
>
> *General N. Stoenescu*: It is a matter of all Jewish taxpayers being obliged to pay a fixed tax of 30,000 lei plus 3 per cent of their income.
>
> *Marshal Antonescu*: Do not fix it at 30,000 lei, because not all will be able to pay this sum. You should assess the fixed contribution in relation to the taxes paid to the tax office.
>
> *General N. Stoenescu*: We have set this tax at 30,000 lei because some of them have low incomes, while 3 per cent of income will be added for the wealthy to pay.
>
> *Marshal Antonescu*: How can a poor Jew pay 30,000 lei?
>
> *General N. Stoenescu*: Then he will have to perform community labour.
>
> *Marshal Antonescu*: I do not want community labour [from them], I want every Jew to pay.

Mihai Antonescu: A solution can be found: an application in principle with exceptions.

Marshal Antonescu: It must be a correct solution, so that everyone should pay in relation to their possibilities and their income. What is the method for applying this just principle, so that the Yids pay in relation to their means?

Mihai Antonescu: I think that the Finance Minister is right when he says that to consider the tax register is not enough. But it means that we privilege the Jews, because it is the Jew in particular who has always had the possibility of having his income entered in the tax register at a very low level. A rate can be fixed, however, a minimal individual tax, apart from the rate for incomes, and the Ministry of Finance can reduce this rate for special cases if it thinks it necessary.

Marshal Antonescu: No. We will create abuses. We must apply a solution which will not allow a dishonest official to extort the Jews.

M. Vulcănescu: The problem must be seen in this light: there are Jews who have money, who are involved in business. These people can pay. But there are others, who have been removed from business and they cannot pay. The labour must be organized...

Marshal Antonescu: Those who cannot pay will perform community labour. And if they cannot perform it, the [Jewish] community will pay for them. The community will pay for those who cannot work through illness.

M. Vulcănescu: The Germans have a well-organized system in this regard: they have put them [the Jews] in ghettos and they work as shoemakers and tailors, etc., fulfilling in this way even the Germans' needs.

Marshal Antonescu: They do the same work here as well, as tailors or something else. They have produced an income for us at Târgu-Jiu [internment camp] of two million [lei].

M. Vulcănescu: This work can be set against the sums they owe.

Marshal Antonescu: But I note that we have moved away from the subject. Here, in Romania, community labour has not produced results because the Yids have got round it and our crooks have played along. The Yids were given unskilled labour to do, labour which was not in line with their abilities and training. I want us to get out of this situation. I want them to make a contribution for the Romanian nation. The Jews: they shed no blood for this nation, they use its roads, they make a very small contribution given its hardships. So we must force them to pay a tax. This problem must be studied, so that we can see how to make them pay, so that we avoid their being fleeced and so that the obligatory payment is just, in line with the ability to pay of every Jew. Those who have been removed from business will be forced to carry out community labour. If someone cannot do it, he will pay. He who cannot pay will be paid for by the community. If not, he will expelled [deported] from the country, because we do not keep parasites here. First of all, he will be kept in a camp and then expelled [deported], if the community does not pay.

...

30,000 lei is too much.

Mihai Antonescu: But there is a difference between between 10,000 and 30,000.

M. Vulcănescu: It represents 3 billion lei.

General I. Sichitiu: It represents two billion or more.

Marshal Antonescu: But supposing a Jew has a family of seven?

Mihai Antonescu: Women and children do not pay.

General N. Stoenescu: With 30,000 lei as the minimum rate, we have two billion a year.

M. Vulcănescu: The [Jewish] community has that money. It has the means to pay it.

Marshal Antonescu: Can it?

M. Vulcănescu: Yes.

Marshal Antonescu: Good. Do it. Then what we have decided now in this regard must appear in a communiqué.[42]

Community labour was carried out by Jews on the basis of requests made to the army by public institutions. The Jews were summoned to recruitment centres, where they were assigned their tasks. Those assembled in camps and ghettos, as was the case in Bessarabia and northern Bukovina before deportation to Transnistria, were placed under an army or gendarmerie guard. Here, too, work was assigned by the camp or ghetto commandant. In Constanţa the assignment was made by the prefect's office, and in Bucharest by the town hall. The most common duties were road and bridge repairs, cleaning of streets and public spaces, the clearing of snow, or agricultural labour. Professionals and skilled workers were usually used in their areas of specialization.

It was the poor who were used for manual labour; the wealthier were either retained at their place of work as specialists, or they simply paid large bribes to be exempted from forced labour. According to one source, of the 84,042 Jews eligible in 1941, only 47,354 persons were actually called upon, the rest being exempted for various reasons.[43] In the following year, only 53 per cent of eligible Jews (15,015 of 28,650) presented themselves for work in the labour battalions on railways and roads. Under pressure from companies and institutions almost 17,000 Jews who were employees were spared forced labour. In 1943, of 101,641 such persons registered, 42,397 carried out manual work in labour battalions, the remainder being used in industry (24,218), exempted or failing to appear for work in the battalions.[44] Between 1 January and 23 August 1944, 10,024 Jews were mobilized in 19 labour battalions for forced labour.

Jewish productivity in forced labour gave results below the expectations of the Romanian authorities. This is not surprising since in many cases the Jews were obliged to undertake work for which they had no experience or were physically ill-suited. In some areas the police reported that Jews had to be ordered by the Jewish Union FUCE to work slowly in order to force the state to pay them a wage.[45] Breaking the forced labour regulations attracted harsh punishment, although to what degree it was applied is unclear. An order of 19 July 1941 issued by Antonescu, relayed by the General Directorate of Police to all regional inspectorates, decreed that Jews in labour camps should perform hard labour and that, if anyone fled, one in ten of the detainees should be shot in reprisal. On the same subject of indiscipline one scholar cites a police report which states that on 22 December 1942 in the whole of Transnistria only 330 Jews had been deported for avoiding the forced labour requirements.[46] How reliable this report is can be judged from a table drawn up by the Golta gendarmerie – most probably in February 1943 – which gives the number of inmates of the labour camp in that town alone, who had been sentenced by a military court for forced labour offences (mainly failure to report for duty), as 303![47] Since there were many similar labour camps in Transnistria, the number of such deportees must have been considerably higher.[48]

Jews were also required to hand over articles of clothing 'for the social good'. A decree to this effect was introduced by Antonescu on 20 October 1941 and supplemented by a further decree on 17 January 1942 which allowed Jews to make a cash payment instead of providing the required clothing.[49] On 6 April 1943, Radu Lecca, the government plenipotentiary for Jewish affairs, wrote to Mihai Antonescu informing him that a large number of Jews – 20,000 – did not have the means to comply with the decrees. These Jews had been prosecuted and in some cases sentenced to jail. To avoid the overcrowding of jails with 'these 20,000 paupers', the committee responsible for Jewish affairs, under Lecca's chairmanship, had decided in a meeting of 19 January 1943 to instruct the Central Jewish Office to collect the sum of 100 million lei to be handed over to the Social Service Council, and in return the prosecution of the impoverished Jews would be dropped.[50]

The Star of David

There is confusion in the minds of several historians about Ion Antonescu's instructions regarding the compulsory wearing of the Star of David. It was Mihai Antonescu who gave the order on 8 August 1941 that all Jews in Romania 'wear a distinctive sign', one which translated into the Star of David. Its introduction was postponed, after consultation with the Ministry of Finance, until Jews had paid their contribution to the fund for the assimilation of the re-conquered provinces of Bessarabia and northern Bukovina (*împrumutul reîntregirii*).[51] This did not stop some prefects from enforcing the measure on their own initiative. Their move prompted the Ministry of Internal Affairs to telegraph all prefects on 31 July 1941 a request that they ensure that no Jew 'wear a distinct sign that he is Jewish, because such distinguishing signs can lead to undesired reactions'.[52]

This advice was overturned by Marshal Antonescu on 3 September in an order that Jews wear the Star of David. His decision chimed with the rantings of the pro-Nazi newspaper *Porunca Vremii* (Command of the Times), which insisted in its issue of 6 September 1941 on the wearing of distinctive sign by the Jews so that they could be easily identified: 'A single armband would be good enough, on which the single word "Yid" should be printed.'[53] Within five days Antonescu had changed his mind. The reason was a memorandum from Wilhelm Filderman in which he complained that the order for Jews to wear the star 'marked a return to the Middle Ages'. During an audience with Filderman on 8 September, the Marshal told Mihai Antonescu, who was also present, to issue instructions 'for the removal of [the obligation to wear] the sign throughout the whole country'.[54]

There is a strong temptation to believe that this order had validity for all Jews under Romanian jurisdiction. The words *throughout the whole country* are important in this regard. While Jews in the Old Kingdom, southern Transylvania and the Banat were spared, those remaining in Bessarabia and Bukovina, and others in Transnistria were obliged by local decrees issued under Antonescu's authority by the governors and prefects to wear the Star. The regulations for the ghetto in Cernăuţi are typical. [55] In Rădăuţi, also in the province of Bukovina, the director of a local distillery was asking the prefect several months later, on 20 January 1942, for his Jewish employees to be exempted from wearing the Star whilst at work 'as is the practice in Cernăuţi'. The prefect gave his approval, but ordered that the Star still be worn in the town.[56]

The distinction made by Antonescu between Jews from the Old Kingdom, southern Transylvania and the Banat and those from the territories formerly part of the Soviet Union is also evident from the intervention made by the Romanian government on behalf of the Romanian Jews in Germany and in occupied countries in which the wearing of the Star was an issue. A report of the German legation in Paris, dated 12 June 1942, is explicit on this subject. It pointed out that the Romanian Consul-General in Paris had informed it that the Romanian government did not agree to the application of special measures regarding the Romanian Jews in countries under German occupation and had expressed the wish that the Romanian Jews be treated in the same manner as the Swiss and Hungarian Jews. The Consul-General therefore requested that the Romanian Jews be exempted from wearing the Star of David, that interned Jews be released and that the confiscated goods of Romanian Jews be returned. The German legation went on to report that the Romanian Consul-General had also argued that since the Romanian

Jews were not obliged to wear the Star by the Romanian government, then neither should the Romanian Jews in Germany wear it. According to the German Security Service in Paris, the report said, the Romanian and German governments had agreed that Romanian Jews be treated no differently from German Jews, but the Consul-General denied this.[57]

The internment of Jews

Security considerations were invoked not only to justify deportation but also internment of Jews. Ion Antonescu, on being informed on 18 July 1941 that 1,165 young Jews had been rounded up in Ploieşti and interned in the Teiş camp in Dâmboviţa, ordered that they should be made to perform hard labour and that if any of them escaped, 'one in ten should be shot'; if they did not work satisfactorily, they should be denied food. He added that this order be applied 'to all camps with Jews and prisoners'.[58] In fact, several of the Jews in Teiş camp were not only veterans of the First World War, but being between the age of 50 and 60 were exempt under the law from the requirement to perform compulsory labour. Thirteen such veterans petitioned the Minister of the Interior on 18 August for their release on this basis and their request was granted a week later.[59] Further releases were ordered after a commission from the Ministry examined the status of the Jews and recommended that 1,225 internees be released 'on condition that they did not return to the oil region [of Ploieşti], but should settle elsewhere, since their presence in the region presented a danger to security owing to their obvious anglophile sentiments.' The Army General Staff decided to close the camp on 18 November, but ordered that some 200 of the Jews be sent to another camp at Găieşti for compulsory labour, while a further 235, who were unfit for labour, should be allowed to settle in a county capital, other than Bucharest or the oil region.[60]

Ion Antonescu's order to intern the Jews was soon shown to be ill-considered and intemperate. On 23 July 1941, the Ministry of Defence asked the Ministry of Internal Affairs to provide details of how many Jewish cobblers and tailors were being held in internment camps; they were needed, in addition to the Jews already working in the army's workshops under the compulsory labour scheme in order to increase the output of boots and uniforms for the army.[61] In the western county of Bihor the prefect complained to the Ministry of Health that among the Jews deported to the town of Beiuş were three village pharmacists; as a consequence, these villages were left without a pharmacy. The prefect asked that the Ministry either to send Christian chemists to replace them or to let the Jewish pharmacists return as a matter of urgency.[62]

Food shortages and lack of medical assistance for the Jews who were sick meant that many of the Jews were too weak to work. Even the military authorities were sympathetic to their complaints. The garrison commander in Slatina, Colonel Angelescu, forwarded a memorandum from Felix Sechter in the name of the Jews from Moldavia who had been interned in a camp on Slatina in the south-west of the country. In his covering note, the commander confirmed that the criticism of the lack of food and medical care were justified and 'demand an urgent resolution'.[63]

On 20 February 1942, the Ministry of the Interior received Antonescu's order that all Jews who were Communist activists, especially those in Bucharest, the oil well region of Ploieşti, and in the ports of Constanţa and Giurgiu, together with all Jews who had settled clandestinely in Bucharest during the preceding two years, should be interned and deported to Transnistria in the spring. The order emphasized that the operation should not be conducted 'in a wild manner'. No measures were to be taken against non-Communist Jews. Antonescu's order went on to state:

> I have guaranteed the life and liberty of native Jews in my declarations. I must keep my word. If, however, the Jews commit acts against the public order, security and our interests, measures must be taken against the guilty parties and possibly against the community. In this regard they must be warned by the Ministry of the Interior through their communities.[64]

Ion Antonescu's anti-Semitism

How far Antonescu was driven by personal feelings of anti-Semitism? One scholar has argued that 'although an anti-Semite, anti-Semitism was not one of his defining characteristics'.[65] Yet in his correspondence and in cabinet meetings he often expressed himself in caustic anti-Semitic terms, ones which clearly drove his discriminatory measures. Angered by the heavy losses suffered by the Romanian army in the advance eastwards, which he attributed entirely to 'the Jewish commissars' in the Red Army, Antonescu erupted into a paroxysm of rage against the Jews in a directive sent to Mihai Antonescu from the front on 5 September 1941. Returning to his refrain of 'purification', he predicted that victory would allow the Axis to 'cleanse' the world of Jews:

> The soldiers at the front run the great risk of being wounded or killed because of the Jewish commissars, who with a diabolical perseverance drive the Russians from behind with revolvers and keep them in their positions until they die to the last man. I have found out about this and am disgusted.

He urged Mihai to re-intern the Jews from Moldavia – some of whom had been released after the advance across the Dniester – in preparation for deportation:

All the Jews should be re-interned in camps, preferably in those in Bessarabia, because I will drive them from there into Transnistria once I free myself of the present problems. Everyone should understand that it is not a matter of a struggle with the Slavs, but with the Jews. It is a struggle of life and death.... For us to be victorious we must be resolute. Everyone should know this. It is not economics which are paramount at this time but the will of the nation itself. That will does not depend on the thriving affairs of certain people, but on the victory of everyone against Satan. And the war in general and the battle for Odessa in particular have offered abundant proof that Satan is the Jew. [66]

Referring again to the commissars Antonescu ranted: 'He, and only he, leads the slaves like a herd of cattle and causes their death by firing the last bullet. Hence our great losses. Had the Jewish commissars not been around, we would have reached Odessa long ago.'[67]

In his 125-page reply of 29 October 1942 to successive letters from Dinu Brătianu complaining about his conduct of the war, the Marshal gave vent to his anti-Semitism in frequent references to the 'Yids' (*jidani*):[68]

There were shortages [of food and goods] last winter as well. There were also shortages in certain regions when times were normal; proof of this is in the protests of the *Motzi* [Romanians living in the Apuseni mountains in Transylvania], of the workers and miners in the Jiu Valley and from other industrial regions, which a memory perhaps deliberately fatigued causes you to forget. Now they have quietened down, to your regret and that of the Yid in London...[69]

You know that I came to power in times that were most difficult and dangerous for the state and its leader; and, above all, you know that I ran and run the country without a party and party supporters, without any banking organizations, assisted only by one person, Mr Mihai Antonescu, and undermined by all the Yids, all the profiteers of the old regime and the whole of finance and industry, under the patronage, both open and occult, given by you...[70]

Do not forget that during the twenty-two years of democratic regimes, the great majority of credits given by the government through the National Bank and the banks supported by the National Bank went to the Yids and foreigners...[71]

The command of our forces, reinforced by a German army, will be shortly assumed by me. The honour is not mine, but it is for you all.... It is something which cannot be understood by some of the former politicians in Romania who blinded by passion, envy and self-interest – hang around street corners and with circumspection criticize pointlessly or pointedly any action good or bad, and who comment upon and spread any rumour put about by Yids and perfidiously and surreptitiously stir up things.[72]

We will have, Mr Brătianu, if we win the war, what you lost, we will have, if God helps me and if the people continue to listen to me and follow me, a Romania greater than that which the democracies massacred. And even if fate decrees that we should have nothing, the question is whether I could have avoided going to war in 1941 to liberate Bessarabia and Bukovina when the opportunity arose. The Yids, the businessmen and you could have avoided it, the people and I could never have done so.[73]

The depth of Antonescu's anti-Semitism comes to the surface in the virulence of the language which he uses to describe them. He sees them as a 'disease', 'parasites' to be cleansed from the body of Romania. An example of this discourse is the interview given to the novelist Ion Brătescu-Voineşti on 5 March 1943. Justifying his alliance with Germany, he launches into a diatribe against the country's 'enemies':

The Germans helped us to re-conquer Bessarabia and Bukovina, they helped us to arm ourselves, to begin delousing the country of its internal enemies, the Jews, enemies whom I consider to be more poisonous than the external ones, because the latter can lead to amputation of the country's limbs, but internal enemies can poison and corrupt the soul of our people.[74]

As the possibility of an Axis defeat loomed larger, the Marshal became more concerned about a reckoning at the hands of the victorious Allies for his actions against the Jews. In a meeting with finance officials on 20 April 1943, Antonescu was told that the shortage of money in circulation was because those Jews who had been 'removed from normal economic life were trading, as before, without paying tax and without penalty, like Romanian traders. For this reason a large part of the money was in the hands of the Jews.' The Marshal proposed an answer to this problem:

One [solution] would the most radical: to take all the Jews and send them across the border. But we are a small country, not a big country, like Germany. I am fighting to win the war, but the democracies may happen to win it. And we know what democracy means; it means Judeocracy. So, why should I expose the future generations of the nation to punishment for such a measure of mine decision to expel the Jews.[75]

Troubled about the introduction of premium payable by Jews for their bread ration in October 1943, he asked an official from the Ministry of Supply about an ordinance to this effect which had been posted up in the Danubian port of Galaţi. To the answer that it was only a local measure – which was untrue – the Marshal retorted:

Generalities are made of local things. A foreigner comes along, sees this ordinance, takes it straight to Geneva, from where it immediately reaches London and Washington. You realize what damage just these little things can do to the country. We can do anything, but we should not legislate for it.... Only the stupid murder and pillage on the basis of written orders. It can be done without giving an order.[76]

But he could not keep his innate anti-Semitism repressed for long. In a meeting of the Council of Ministers of 22 April 1944, he declared angrily:

I have seen Jews with spectacles perched on their noses who pretend innocence on the street and who are undoubtedly making a mental note of everything they see and then note in down on paper. There are certainly many amongst them who are in the service of the enemy and have radio transmitters which they use to pass information on to the British and the Russians...

These wretches will pay very dearly. Furthermore, all the guides who lead the Russians through the mountains are Jews from Târgu-Neamț and the whole region. You see what an evil race [the Jews] are and how they bring destruction upon themselves...

One solution is for us to remove them from these towns and take them to others, if there are many of them. We should settle them as we did in Buhuşi, in one or two market towns, move out all the Romanians, and let them live amongst themselves...

The second solution is to gather them in ghettos in each town, to say to them: 'this is the area where you live, do not leave it. We will bring you food, do what you want, we will not kill you, we will not harm you.'...

The third solution is for us to take them from there [Bessarabia?] and bring them back. But this is the most dangerous solution and the most catastrophic for the Romanian race. I cannot bring them back. Many have escaped and I cannot bring the others as well, because I am sure that they would stone me...

One of these solutions must be applied.

Constantin Vasiliu, the Under-Secretary at the Ministry of Internal Affairs, favoured the ghettoization 'solution', on the grounds that it was the simplest and that moving the Jews to a new area would be difficult and time-consuming.

The Marshal's anger against the Jews continued unabated:

While the Romanian soldier heads for Moldavia with his knapsack on his back (and the Marshal imitated a man in this position), the Red Cross lorries of Dr Costinescu[77] with tarted-up ladies in fine dresses come to Moldavia to take the children of Yids to safety.... The army knows this and the day of reckoning will come.... That's what happened in Transnistria as well. There too the Red Cross came and enquired about the Yids, but it never asked: how is the Romanian soldier, has he got enough food, etc.?[78]

The children referred to were orphans who had lost their parents during their period of deportation to Transnistria.

Oblivious, it seems, of the consequences of his own anti-Semitic measures, Antonescu launched into another diatribe against the Jews at a Council of Ministers' meeting on 6 May 1944:

> I know one thing which I saw. All the Jews over fifteen do nothing except talk and criticize. The streets in Bacău, Iaşi, Roman and Vaslui are full of Jews, while the Romanians are digging, reaping and working on the roads. I gave an order two weeks ago in this respect, when I summoned the army chief and told him to do this, not to expect the villager to do everything while letting the Yid stand around talking and doing nothing. I am not a devourer of Yids, but do you not consider it an enormous injustice to the Romanian people that the Jew, who lives here sheltered from battle, should do business and live as well as possible, while the Romanian is dying at the front and performing all the labours behind the front?[79]

The Jews were 'sheltered from battle' because they were barred from serving in the army under the law introduced in December 1940. On the other hand, statistics compiled by the Central Jewish Office in April 1944 showed that there were about 50,000 Jews mobilized in compulsory labour battalions.[80]

Yet on rare occasion Antonescu was also capable of contrition. Informed about the murders of Jews in Chişinău, he revealed in a meeting of the Council of Ministers on 4 December 1941 that 'It was the greatest disappointment, I can say, in my career, that there could took place what took place under my regime, and that my regime could be stained by such bastards, like other regimes. The matter is all the more painful since many soldiers are involved.'[81]

The Central Jewish Office

Despite the anti-Semitic measures taken after Antonescu came to power, Jewish political organizations were still allowed to operate – but at a price. Harassment by central and local government officials took the form of extortion, yet Zionist organizations continued their activity, closely monitored by the security police, the *Siguranţa*. The most representative of the Jewish bodies was the Federation of Jewish Communities in Romania (FJCR), led by Wilhelm Filderman, and he was regarded as the prominent figure in Jewish public life. Filderman kept a vigilant eye on the impact of Antonescu's actions against the Jews, sending protests to the Marshal regularly and frequently obtaining audiences with him. The very fact that Antonescu was willing to receive Filderman, coupled with the lack of institutionalized regulation of Jewish affairs in Romania, irritated SS *Hauptsturmführer* Gustav Richter, the Counsellor for Jewish Problems at the German legation in Bucharest, who pressed Mihai Antonescu to set up a government-controlled body to remedy this situation. Initially, Richter wanted a free hand in setting up the new Central Jewish Office (CJO) and Mihai Antonescu was inclined to accede to his wish, but the Marshal saw this as an infringement of Romanian sovereignty and objected. Disagreement over the role of the CJO between the German legation and the representatives of the Marshal delayed the creation of the Office, and so while the decree ushering in its existence was published on 17 December 1941 – the autonomous FJCR had been disbanded the previous day – details of the regulations governing its activity appeared only on 31 January 1942, and it began to operate two weeks later.[82]

The German preference was for the establishment of a Jewish body in Romania similar to the *Judenräte* in Poland which would implement German plans for the 'de-Jewification' of the country, the deportation of the Jews and their eventual eradication. The Romanian view was less draconian and was tempered to some degree by Jewish intervention. Essentially, it saw the CJO as an instrument of economic extortion and exploitation of the Jews, in both financial and material terms. This latter approach prevailed and was evident in the regulations published in the Official Bulletin, the register of government legislation.[83]

The Central Jewish Office (*Centrala Evreilor*) was a national body with a central committee in Bucharest and local ones in the provinces. It was charged, among other things, with the exclusive representation of the interests of Romanian Jewry, with the organization of Jewish 'work projects' and other forms of forced labour, and with the creation and updating of files on all Romanian Jews, including the issue of photo identity cards that Jews had to carry. The central committee became synonymous with the Central Jewish Office (CJO) itself and was directly subordinate to Radu Lecca, who had been appointed by Mihai Antonescu on 30 October 1941 on the recommendation of Gustav Richter, 'Plenipotentiary of the Government for the Preparation of Matters Regarding the Reglementation of the Regime for Jews in Romania'.[84] This committee comprised a president and secretary-general, and the heads of eight departments: culture and education, emigration, finance, press and publishing, professional retraining, religious affairs, statistics and welfare.

In essence, Antonescu's treatment of the 'Jewish problem' after the deportation of the Jews from Bessarabia and Bukovina in the autumn of 1941 reflected his determination to affirm Romanian sovereignty against Nazi Germany, hence his resistance to German efforts to dictate the policy of the CJO and to counsels to deport the Jews of the *Regat* to Poland in summer 1942. The CJO itself has been best described as combination of 'servility, collaboration, and assistance...reflecting the special ambivalence of Romanian political reality'.[85]

While there was no formal link between the German legation and the CJO, the Germans, through the person of Richter, did lean heavily on Lecca, who often supported his demands. Lecca accepted Richter's recommendation of Dr Nandor Gingold, a young doctor, for the key position of secretary-general. Gingold had been introduced to Richter by a colleague in the legation whom the doctor was treating.[86] He was not a public figure. Married to a Christian, Gingold converted to Roman Catholicism at the time of the creation of the CJO in December 1941. Lecca chose H. Streitman, a journalist who enjoyed the respect of the major political parties in the pre-Antonescu era, as president of the central committee. He, too, was a convert, but had reverted to Judaism. Streitman was on amicable terms with Veturia Goga, the widow of Octavian Goga, leader of the government which introduced the first anti-Semitic measures in 1938, and it was she who probably recommended him to Lecca. Streitman did not disappoint; he proved to be an obedient servant of the regime and encouraged other Jews to do the same in the articles he wrote for the *Jewish Gazette* (*Gazeta Evreiască*), the official weekly of the CJO. He was doubtless driven by considerations of pragmatism: collaboration was preferable to extinction. His role as president was purely symbolic; Gingold was the effective head of the committee, a position which was formalized when he took over the CJO in 1943 and in which he stayed until his resignation in April 1944.[87]

Gingold was often summoned to German legation to receive 'advice' from Richter and his colleagues. He was told from the outset of his appointment to marginalize Filderman, to put a halt to Jewish emigration to Palestine, and to remove Jews from commerce and business. For all their attempts to persuade Berlin that the CJO was under the complete control of the legation, German diplomats were forced to admit that the demands put to Gingold had not been met. In summer 1942, reports from staff at the legation complained to Berlin that the Romanian government still tolerated Jewish emigration and that Filderman still had the ear of the Marshal.[88] Gingold justified his acceptance of his role at the first meeting of the central committee: 'If we do not agree to assume the task of leading the Centre, the government will appoint its own officials and thus there will be no further opportunity for rescue or procrastination, and in this case everything will collapse.' [89] Procrastination was necessary, in his opinion, because he believed that Hitler planned first, to concentrate the Jews of Europe – including Romanian Jews – in Poland, and then, after the war, to deport them to a land of their own outside Europe.

More forthright in his views was A. Willman, editor of the *Jewish Gazette* and head of the press and publishing department of the central committee.

A former Zionist, he openly supported the idea of the resettlement of the Jews, although he was vague about their destination, toying with the 'eastern territories', including Transnistria. That said, neither Gingold nor Willman was involved in the deportations of Jews to Transnistria, although Gingold, a staunch anti-Communist, did not raise any objections to the deportation of Jewish Communists from Romania in summer 1942. Willman's ideas soon led to a deep rift with Gingold, who accused him of being a German agent and managed to remove him from the committee.

Gingold's action showed that he was no mere servant of the German legation; contrary to instructions from German diplomats, he consulted Filderman and Zionists, even, in the case of the latter, persuading Dr Theodor Loewenstein-Lavi, a Zionist of the *Ichud* wing, to join the central committee as head of the Department of Education and Culture in spring 1942 with the agreement of his colleagues. The rationale in favour of this move was put by Moritz Geiger:

> We are now in a prisoner-of-war camp; we [the Jewish leaders] are the officers among the prisoners in the camp; our duty is to assure the best conditions for the rank and file; in order to fulfil this aim, it is inevitable that contact should be made with the commanders of the camp, namely the Germans; through negotiations and attempts at convincing them [to modify their attitude] we must try to assure the best possible conditions.[90]

This approach did not find favour with all leading Jews. Many spoke out against any cooperation with the CJO, among them the Zionist leader Avram Leiba Zissu, and the writers Ury Benador, Chaim Rabinson and Ion Calugaru.

The initial tasks carried out by the CJO were statistical surveys, the mobilization of Jewish forced labour for the army, the mandatory collection of money and materials for various state institutions, and provision of welfare for Jews. On 20 August 1942, Lecca told Antonescu of his proposal that the CJO collect the sum of 1.2 billion lei from the 16,000 Jews who had been kept on in their jobs through 'individual dispensations', which they had 'purchased' from the Romanianization inspectors. The money would allegedly be used to help the families of those who were performing community labour. After government scrutiny of the scheme, the sum proposed was increased to two billion lei, half of which was to be collected immediately and half by the end of the year. In the event, according to Lecca, little more than half the sum was raised, of which 400 million lei was handed over to the Patronage Council, a charitable organization for social works headed by Antonescu's wife, Maria.[91] Further government levies on the Jews continued. On 11 May 1943, Lecca informed the CJO that the government

> bearing in mind that, while Romanian soldiers are sacrificing themselves at the front, the great majority of the Jewish population continues to

enjoy the freedom to conduct trade and to live sheltered from the dangers of war, has resolved that this population should contribute the sum of four billion lei to the financial needs of the country.

Half the sum was backdated for payment for 1942; the other half represented the contribution for 1943. Failure to pay the levy established by the commissions due to be established by the government would result in deportation to Transnistria.[92] Filderman protested vigorously to Antonescu about the amount of money expected from the Jewish community and the Marshal, exasperated, gave the order for Filderman's deportation, despite the latter's poor health. The order was carried out 30 May when the Jewish leader was taken to Moghilev.[93] He remained there for two months before pressure from Queen Helen, the papal nuncio, Andrea Cassulo, the International Commission of the Red Cross, Iuliu Maniu, and leading members of the Liberal Party led Antonescu to allow Filderman's return to Bucharest in August.[94] On 30 August 1943, Lecca revealed that 15 per cent of the levy would be administered by the CJO and used according to his instructions. Consequently, he informed Gingold on 11 November that in response to the latter's verbal request, he had given his approval that half of this percentage would be used to equip Jews in labour battalions and the other half paid to the aid committee for Jews deported to Transnistria (see below).[95]

The special position of the Jews in Romania – with the exception of those in Bessarabia and northern Bukovina – compared with those in German-occupied countries explains why the CJO's activity differed so much from that of the *Judenräte* elsewhere. There were no ghettos in Romania proper (Wallachia, Moldavia, southern Transylvania and Banat). It is true that in some provinces, especially in Moldavia and southern Transylvania, the Jews were obliged to move to towns, but they were not obliged to wear the Star of David – although they were in northern Bukovina, Bessarabia and Transnistria. No activity more graphically illustrated the ambiguous relationship between the CJO and the leading Jewish personalities than the delivery of aid to the Jews deported to Transnistria.

The Jewish Aid Committee

No greater attempt to alleviate the living conditions of the Jewish deportees in Transnistria was made than by the Romanian Jews themselves. This was done through an Aid Committee (*Comisiunea de Ajutorare*), which was established in February 1942 to distribute food and clothing to the Jews.[96] The Committee operated within the Central Jewish Office in Romania (*Centrala Evreilor din România*) and was offered – but did not always accept – advice given by the leading Jews in Romania, most notably Filderman, Mişu Benvenisti, a leading Zionist, and the Chief Rabbi, Alexandru Şafran.

The existence of the Aid Committee was unusual. The idea that it could function under a regime that was bent on removing unwanted Jews seems fantastic, not to mention the fact that the committee was in inspiration and action Jewish; furthermore, the acceptance by Antonescu of direct personal communication with Filderman, albeit only while he was head of the FJCR (they exchanged letters and held meetings to discuss the plight of the Jews), suggests a small measure of ambivalence on the part of Antonescu towards the Jews.

When news of the ordeals experienced by the Jews from Bessarabia and Bukovina reached Filderman, he appealed to Antonescu to change his mind. His plea fell on deaf ears. Subsequent representations from Filderman and others to allow the dispatch of aid and money to the deportees by the Jewish community in Romania were more successful. On 10 December 1941, Antonescu's decision to allow the FJCR to send money and medicines to the deportees in Transnistria was relayed to the relevant government bodies. But it took several months for Alexianu and the Central Jewish Office to come up with a solution as to the means by which the aid should be sent. It was agreed in March 1942 that the monies could be sent through the National Bank in Bucharest in the account of the Transnistrian government and that the medicines be sent to the prefect's office in Moghilev, from where they would be distributed by the province's drug administration.[97] Initially, sums were deposited individually by relatives and friends of the deportees, but this practice caused such confusion that Antonescu subsequently ordered that all monies should be channelled through the aid committee.

Unfortunately for the deportees, they often failed to receive the money, or were short-changed. A similar fate occurred with money sent through (illegal) couriers, most of whom were Romanian officials or gendarmerie personnel stationed in Transnistria. Several of the latter were court-martialled for acting as go-betweens and sentenced to short terms of imprisonment. But it was not only Romanian officials who were found guilty of corruption. The aid committee received complaints that a number of ghetto heads sold the food and clothing which had been sent in their care to Jews in the ghetto, or in some cases embezzled the funds transmitted through the Central Jewish Office.[98]

A significant change took place in the method of distributing aid in 1943. Acting on the recommendations of a delegation of Romanian Jews, headed by Fred Şaraga, which visited several ghettos and camps in Transnistria between 1 and 14 January 1943, the Aid Committee targeted their assistance at specific ghetto heads who enjoyed the trust of their communities.[99] As a result, there was a significant increase in the amounts of money and goods that reached their intended recipients. The Romanian Intelligence Service (SSI) reported on 2 December 1943 that the CJO had managed to send clothing through the Aid Committee to four times the number of Jews in the course of that year than in 1942.[100] That said, it should be borne in mind that the local Ukrainian Jews, with few exceptions, received no such assistance. Many of them watched enviously as those from Bukovina and Bessarabia were given the means of making their lives just a little more bearable.

6
Antonescu and the Holocaust

The Jews were the principal victims of Ion Antonescu's regime. As Romania's largest ethnic minority, their deportation constituted the principal means for Antonescu to satisfy his desire to 'purify' and 'homogenize' Romania's population. But deportation was not the only fate of the Jews. Romania is part of the geography of the Holocaust because on its territory, and in lands under Romanian control, Antonescu was responsible for the systematic murder of Jews.

The Holocaust in Romania was unlike that in other parts of Europe and the Soviet Union.[1] In the first place, the mass murder was carried out by the Romanian authorities under Antonescu's military dictatorship, and Romania was a sovereign German ally. Second, the deaths of Jews at the hands of the Romanians were the result not only of systematic killing, but also of deportation and its consequences. The Romanian and German armies shot 12,000–20,000 Jews in Bessarabia and Bukovina during July and August 1941.[2] Romanian forces themselves put to death an estimated 15,000–20,000 Jews in Odessa in a similar manner in October 1941. Of the 147,000 Jews who were deported from Bukovina and Bessarabia to Transnistria between 1941 and 1943, at least 90,000 died, the majority from typhus and starvation.[3] During the same period, 130,000–170,000 local Ukrainian Jews are estimated to have perished in the same province.[4] These figures – almost 300,000 Jews in all – give the Antonescu regime the sinister distinction of being responsible for the largest number of deaths of Jews after Hitler's Germany – the deportation of 500,000 Jews from Hungary, including 151,000 from the formerly Romanian territory of northern Transylvania, to the death camps in Poland was carried out after the German occupation of that country on 19 March 1944.[5] Third, Romania's 'Jewish policy' was independent of Germany's in the sense that Antonescu acted of his own volition, but in a context established by Nazi domination of continental Europe. For example, in the summer of 1942 Antonescu changed his mind about acceding to German requests that the remaining Jewish population of Romania, from the Banat, southern Transylvania, Wallachia and Moldavia, be deported to the death camps in Poland.

It was not by chance that the word 'purification' came most frequently from the lips of Ion and Mihai Antonescu when referring to the need for deportation of the Jews; this connotation underlines the racial character of their policy towards the Jews. When examining the regime's minority policies, it should be borne in mind that the legislation regarding the Jews in the period 1941–44, like that in the years immediately preceding, was directed against the Jews as a race, and the Jews in Romania were the only minority population to suffer such racial discrimination. The deportation of the Jews, while representing the fundamental objective of Antonescu's minority policy, was accompanied by a less draconian project to remove Romania's other minorities and to bring in Romanians who lived outside her borders.[6]

Antonescu himself indicated that the fate of the *ost-Juden* (lit. eastern Jews) had been raised at his meeting with Hitler in Munich on 12 June 1941.[7] This emerges from a complaint made by Antonescu in August to von Killinger, the German Minister in Bucharest, that the German army had begun, on 7 August, to send back from the Ukraine the Jews from Bessarabia and Bukovina whom the Romanian gendarmes had driven across the Dniester as part of the plan to 'cleanse' the two provinces of Jews. Antonescu claimed that the return of these Jews was 'contrary to the guidelines which the *Führer* had set forth to him in Munich regarding the treatment of the *eastern* [my emphasis] Jews'.[8] For Hitler and Antonescu 'eastern' connoted Jews who had come under the influence of Soviet Communism and this reading would explain the different policy adopted by Antonescu towards the Jews of Bessarabia and Bukovina compared with that towards the Jews in the provinces of Romania which had not been under Soviet rule.[9] What exactly these guidelines were is not a matter of record, although it is not difficult to imagine, given the massacres of Jews carried out subsequently by the SS *Einsatzgruppe D* and the Romanian army in Bessarabia and beyond the Dniester.

Antonescu's obsession with the Bolshevik menace was the principal driving force behind his policy to remove the Jews from territories taken by the Romanians in summer 1941. The vast majority of the Jews in the provinces bordering on, and occupied by, the Soviet Union between 1940 and 1941 – Bessarabia and Bukovina – were deported to Transnistria and more than 60 per cent of them were murdered or died as a result of disease or starvation. Among Transnistrian Jews, more than 80 per cent are estimated to have perished. On the other hand, the Jews in the Old Kingdom of Romania – the provinces of Wallachia and Moldavia – and in southern Transylvania, which remained in Romanian hands after the Vienna Award of August 1940 gave the northern half to Hungary, were more assimilated, were deemed by Antonescu to be less Communist in their propensities and were, therefore, largely spared.

To ascribe the deportation of Jews solely to fear of Bolshevism would be a gross simplification. It was also inspired by Antonescu's innate anti-Semitism, a sentiment shared by Mihai Antonescu and the leading figures of the regime. Antonescu's intention to expel the Jews from Romania when conditions permitted is evident from a cabinet meeting held on 7 February 1941:

> If times were normal, I would proceed in a normal manner with the removal *en masse* of the Jews, that is, with their expulsion over the frontier. But today I cannot do that.... And so I see the problem from a totally specific angle, in line with the current international situation.
>
> I want to create a purely Jewish quarter in the capital, whose limits will be established later, but whose axes will be drawn by the Yids... and within two years everything Jew in the capital must go into this Yid citadel, and everything that is Romanian must leave. Then the Yids can live in their own environment, with their trade, their synagogues etc., until the time of peace will come when we can cast them over the frontier, into areas which will be established later...
>
> As for Moldavia... the towns where there are many Jews must be looked at, like Focşani, Iaşi, Galaţi, Bacău, Roman, Fălticeni etc. In time, Yids might be brought from the towns and concentrated into certain centres.[10]

It is important to note that Antonescu is referring here not merely to the Jews of Bessarabia and Bukovina but to those in the capital Bucharest and in the core Romanian province of Moldavia. Notes made in the margin of a letter from the Federation of Jewish Communities by Antonescu on 27 May 1941 confirm his prejudice towards Romanian Jews in general. To complaints from the Federation that Jewish traders were unable to get edible oil or flour Antonescu responded, 'that's good'; advised that Jewish bakers in the Moldavian town of Piatra Neamţ could not get flour, Antonescu commented, 'because they are crooks and sell only to Jews'. On the other hand, he did accept the argument that there were more Christian speculators than Jewish ones with the words, 'that is true'. While admitting that accusations in disparaging terms against Jewish merchants were carried in official publications and noting 'that they should cease',[11] Antonescu took no steps to prohibit them.

Expulsion of the Jews from Romania was the tool for implementing Antonescu's policy of 'ethnic and political purification'. Mihai Antonescu made this clear at a cabinet meeting over which he presided on 17 June, only a few days before the German–Romanian attack on the Soviet Union:

> We must use this hour to carry out the purification of the population. For this reason, Bessarabia and Bukovina will experience Titus's[12] policy with regard to certain ethnic groups – and I assure you, not only in respect of the Jews, but of all nationalities; we will implement a policy of total and violent expulsion of foreign elements.

Mihai already had in mind territorial expansion as far as the River Bug as an instrument for removing unwanted peoples:

> Gentlemen, I think that we must use this moment – although when we were discussing this problem a few months ago.... General Antonescu called me a megalomaniac – to extend our frontier to the Bug and to reaffirm our old historical settlements; let us use this moment to pursue the great fight against the Slavs.[13]

Eight days later, at another ministers' meeting, Mihai revealed that Antonescu had already taken the decision to round up the Jews in preparation for deportation: 'General Antonescu has taken the decision – whilst he is in Moldavia – to remove the Jews from this very moment from all the villages in Moldavia, Bessarabia and Bukovina. This measure is already being applied in Moldavia.'[14]

The immediate purpose was to clear the area behind the Romanian and German lines of Jews on security grounds. Antonescu felt that they represented a threat to the army. On 19 June, Antonescu ordered General Ilie Steflea, Chief of the General Staff, 'to identify all Yids and Communist agents and sympathizers in the region. The Ministry of Internal Affairs must know them and must forbid their movement and be ready to do whatever I order with them at the appropriate moment.'[15] Two days later, the Army General Staff relayed the General's order to the gendarmerie that all able-bodied Jews between the ages of 18 and 60 should be moved immediately from the villages in the frontier area between the Siret and the Prut to the camp in Târgu-Jiu and to the surrounding villages. The remaining Jews from the area, as well as Jews from other villages in Moldavia, were to be deported with their necessary belongings within 48 hours to towns in the respective counties. Jews in the rest of the country were to be moved to towns within four days. In an effort to prevent abuses, those caught ransacking Jews' homes or stealing their harvest would face the death sentence.[16] It was in this atmosphere of feverish anticipation of the attack on the Soviet Union, of trepidation and unease over its outcome, of obsessive security and distrust of the Jews, a distrust cultivated by Antonescu himself, that the events of 28–30 June in the Moldavian capital of Iași, which have come to be known as the Iași pogrom, took place.

The Iași pogrom

Reconstructing these events, in which an estimated 1,500 Jews were massacred in Iași and a further 2,713 died during deportation by train southward is no simple matter. The numbers themselves of those shot in the city are the subject of dispute.[17] The self-serving nature of official reports – some of which contradict each other in essential details – and the absence of an accurate record of the number of victims are impediments to providing a clear account of the murderous behaviour of, principally, German forces and of the criminal incompetence of the Romanian military authorities. There is also a suspicion of involvement in the murders of Jews in Iaşi of officers of the Romanian Secret Service (SSI) who are known to have despatched there by its director Eugen Cristescu, just before the massacre.[18] However, the relevant SSI records were destroyed, probably in November 1944.[19]

Iaşi itself was a tinderbox at the end of June 1941. Jews represented approximately half of Iaşi's population of 100,000 at the outbreak of war.[20] Stationed in the town were German troops who regarded Jews as spies and saboteurs who should be shot on sight. There were indeed a number of Communists as well as Soviet agents who had been parachuted into the area during the previous month and also in the days leading up to the beginning of hostilities. Around the German Military Command were clusters of Gestapo, *Sicherheitsdienst* (SD) and *Geheime Feldpolizei* (SS police), aided by Iron Guard collaborators and informers. To add to this explosive mix there were Romanians from Bessarabia, displaced by the Soviet annexation of the previous summer, and Jews deported from the rest of Moldavia on 21 June and brought, by a grave error of judgement by the Romanian General Staff, to Iaşi.[21]

In preparation for the attack on the Soviet Union on 22 June 1941 the three armies in the 'General Antonescu Army Group' each took up a position along the Prut. The city of Iaşi came within the area of deployment of the German 11th Army, and consequently Antonescu declared it a German military zone, on the understanding that it would continued to be administered by the Romanian civil authorities. On 21 June 1941, General Hans von Salmuth, commander of the German 30th Corps, issued an order establishing his command over all the Romanian forces in Iaşi. German patrols took to the streets, thereby in effect establishing a rival authority to that of the Romanian police. At the same time, Antonescu, at the request of the Romanian 4th Army, took steps to secure the Prut and the area behind it.

The Jews in Moldavia were the target of these measures, since the army harboured strong doubts about their loyalty to the Romanian state. The Jews may have been forgiven for a lack of enthusiasm for Romanian rule, in view of the string of anti-Semitic measures that had been taken since the beginning of 1938 under the Goga–Cuza government and which had gained in intensity since Antonescu had come to power in September 1940, but not by the General Staff. Senior generals regarded the Jewish communities in the province as riddled with Communist infiltrators of Jewish origin, and fear of sabotage and espionage by these elements led them to urge Antonescu to remove the Jews. He needed little persuasion.

No thought had been given by the General Staff to the logistics of deportation or to its economic consequences. Not surprisingly, given its scale and scope, and the imminence of war, the operation could not be completed in the time envisaged. Roads were choked with troops and transport was unavailable. The impracticality of deportation was compounded by an order from the Ministry of Internal Affairs, of 3 July 1941, under which Jews from *towns* in Moldavia were to be moved to county capitals. Only partial evacuations took place and the numbers of Jews affected is not clear, but official figures indicate that from the towns of Darabani, Mihăileni and Săveni in Dorohoi county 3,289 Jews had been sent to Târgu-Jiu by 28 June, and that a total of 2,052 had been moved from Iaşi county by 2 August.[22] Among the latter were a number of Jews who were victims of the two 'death trains' which left Iaşi on 30 June with Jewish deportees bound for Călăraşi in the south.

Antonescu, at his trial in May 1946, justified the deportations from the war zone on humanitarian as well as military grounds:

> *Antonescu*: ... It is a military principle: along the front and in proximity to it the civilian population must be moved. Had you gone along the front in September 1940 ... in June 1941, when we entered the war ...
> *President* [of the court]: The reasons were military ones ... ?
> *Antonescu*: Military ones.
> *President*: The excesses which were committed ...
> *Antonescu*: It was a measure taken for the political security of the state, a question of military security and of military operations and even a matter of saving their lives. Mr President, had I left them [the Jews] there where they were, not one of them would be alive today.

It is debatable whether, at the time, humanitarian considerations were uppermost in Antonescu's mind.[23] If so, it is ironical that, without Antonescu's order for the deportation, Jews from rural areas in Moldavia would not have been brought to Iaşi where some of them ended up as the human cargo of the two 'death trains'.

Tension increased as a result of two Soviet air raids on the city on 25 and 26 June. Several buildings were hit but there was no major damage. However, the result was a veritable paranoia about target spotters who allegedly signalled to the aircraft by radio, torch or by hanging out red fabrics. Jews were accused and a number were arrested, some of whom proved their innocence. Nevertheless, as a precautionary measure the army ordered the confiscation of all radios from Jews. The bombings also led many people – Jews and Christians – to seek permission from the Romanian authorities, since it was in a military zone, to leave the city and to this end they gathered at the police headquarters, the *chestura*.

It was against this background of anti-Semitic feelings that the bloody events in Iaşi took place. The first murders occurred on 26 June when Sergeant Mircea Manoliu, a former member of the Iron Guard, escorted three Jews – Iosub Cojocaru, Leon Schachter and Herşcu Wolf – who were already under arrest to the garrison's target practice range and shot them. Cojocaru was killed, Wolf was badly wounded, while Schachter managed to escape.[24] On the same day, the military command instructed the police to mark the location of any unexploded bombs from the Soviet air raids. Although there was a unit of bomb specialists in the town, the police selected five (six according to some sources) Jews to locate bombs, probably out of spite. The five were taken to the courtyard of a regimental headquarters to mark unexploded bombs with whitewash but they were arrested on the order of the regimental commander on suspicion that they were signalling, using the whitewash, to Soviet bombers. On the following evening, 27 June, the five were placed under an escort under the command of the same Sergeant Manoliu to be taken to the headquarters of the 14th Division, but Manoliu stopped at the target range where all the Jews were shot dead. The murder was committed 'in the absence of any order from above', according to the Prefect of Iaşi county, Colonel Dumitru Captaru, who asked the 14th Division commander on 29 June to take measures against Manoliu.[25]

Manoliu, in the meantime, continued to vent his anti-Semitic spleen. He did so on the basis of an order issued by the prefect and the head of Iaşi police on the afternoon of 26 June to carry out house searches for radio transmitters and Communist propaganda.[26] On the morning of 28 June, Manoliu and a group of 30 soldiers robbed and assaulted a number of Jews on the pretext that they were searching for radio transmitters. The police intervened to stop these abuses, but Manoliu appealed to a passing German unit for help, claiming that the Jews in the district were concealing radios. The Germans assisted in the searches during which, according to a police report, Romanian soldiers from the 13th Infantry regiment maltreated the Jews.[27] On learning of this Captaru organized Manoliu's arrest, but he was released shortly afterwards by the legal officer (*pretor*) of the 14th Division. The officer concerned was sentenced by his superior, General Ion Topor, to ten days' incarceration.[28]

Reports came into the police in the evening of 28 June that gunfire could be heard in Iaşi and that it 'probably came from Communists and Yids'. Others reports of a similar nature followed.[29] It seems, however, that the firing started at the signal of a flare fired by a German plane. Although a Romanian column came under heavy fire there were no casualties and although searches were made of the buildings from which the shots were believed to have originated, no snipers or weapons were found. The German command, however, claimed that it had 'about twenty dead and wounded', but refused to let Romanian officers verify their claim. Instead, German patrols were ordered to round up thousands of Jews and march them in columns to the grounds of the police headquarters. The patrols murdered some Jews *en route*. The Jews, some of them women and children, ran the gauntlet of a motley mass of Romanian and German troops and members of the Todt organization, Romanian gendarmes and civilians, who spat, jeered and threw stones at them. By 1.00 pm there were 'about 3,500 suspects, most of them Jews, in the courtyard of the police HQ'.[30]

An inspection of the Jews was made by the police, who released a number of them – the figures range from 200 to 2,000 – but as these left other columns arrived. What happened next is not disputed, but the identity of the perpetrators is. Around 2 pm the Jews assembled in the courtyard of the police headquarters were subjected to a hail of gunfire, as a result of which several hundred were shot dead.[31] The massacre continued throughout the afternoon until 6 pm, with an interruption while General Stavrescu, the commander of the Romanian 14th division, tried to persuade the Germans to stop.[32] Some scholars – invoking the reports on the events by Romanian officials – have concluded that it was the Germans alone who fired on the Jews, others that Romanian soldiers were also involved, although Stavrescu's unsuccessful intervention suggests that in their participation the Romanian troops had not been acting under orders.[33]

Some 2,500 Jews survived the massacre. General Stavrescu, following Antonescu's orders to remove the Jews from Iasi, organized their evacuation by train and they were marched under escort of police and gendarmes to the station.[34] Some of the Jews, horrified by what they had been through and terrified by what might await them, broke out of the columns and were shot by German troops. At the station the Jews were herded into freight cars, which were crammed to capacity and then locked in to prevent escape. Some were clubbed with rifle butts as they were pushed into each wagon by German soldiers and Romanian police.[35] Further columns of Jews followed on to the station, many of them preferring an uncertain fate by evacuation to what they regarded as certain death by remaining in Iaşi.

Two trains left the city.[36] The first left between 3.30 and 4.15 am, bound for an internment camp in Călăraşi. Before it did so, wooden planks were nailed over the larger air vents to prevent escape. It consisted of almost 40 freight cars and carried between 2,430 and 2,530 Jews. Its route was erratic since contradictory orders for its itinerary were given by the army command and the Ministry of the Interior. Travelling at a snail's pace it covered barely 40 km in 17 hours. As the day wore on, the temperature inside the wagons became unbearable in the midsummer heat and the over-crowding prevented the Jews from moving. No concern was shown by the escort, commanded by a police detachment under sergeant Ion Leucea, to give the occupants water. According to the testimony of a survivor, some drank their own urine, many fainted and some went mad. At Sabaoani station some of the evacuees managed to dislodge the planks to get air and escape. They were fired on by the guards.[37]

At Târgu Frumos the train stopped and four wagons were opened. About 200 Jews were allowed off, dazed and dehydrated, and were ordered by the local police chief Ion Botez to go to the synagogue. On the way, one survivor recalled, they were beaten by Botez. On 1 July, at daybreak, a lorry load of gendarmes arrived at the station from Iaşi under the command of Second Lieutenant Aurel Triandaf who took over command of the train and ordered that the remaining wagons be unlocked. In a statement made in August 1945 for a war crimes tribunal the former mayor of the town described the scene:

> The wagons were opened for the removal of the bodies and the more bodies there were the more cramped the people had been so that in some wagons there were as many as 140–145 people, of whom about 80–90 were dead. We tried to get the bodies out with the help of those still alive, but this was impossible because of their weak condition and because of the stench from the bodies. I ordered the police to get some gypsies to perform this task. The gypsies, tempted by the possibility of finding shoes and clothing, agreed and this helped to save those who were still alive. There were a very large number of bodies, some wagons were half full with them, so that it was very difficult to complete the unloading in the roughly two hours that the train was scheduled to stop in the station. The station master, on his own initiative, delayed the departure of the train for half an hour, but he was continually being called by the army general staff officer in Iaşi, who kept on telling him to despatch the train because it was blocking the line for the military train. After a while the station master told me that there had been an accident on the line at Ruginoasa and that the train would not be able to leave for a few hours. Heaps of bodies had been piled up in the station and it was difficult to shift them. Water and bread was provided for each wagon after the bodies were removed from them. When we tried to give water to [those in] the first wagons, which were in a siding, we were prevented by German and Romanian soldiers who were in the station in large numbers but after about an hour we succeeded in giving the water. This was because of a moving scene when a man in one of the wagons on the fourth siding tied together strips torn from his dirty shirt and dangled them from the wagon into a puddle from which he sucked the water. I pointed this out and was able to improve things. When we wanted to leave the doors of the wagons open, those inside asked us to close them because they were being hit by stones thrown by the soldiers in the station. About 5 pm the line was cleared and orders were given for the train to leave immediately. There were still wagons from which the bodies had not been removed.[38]

The train reached Mirceşti, some 40 km from Târgu-Frumos, the following morning. Three hundred more corpses were unloaded from the train. On 3 July, it arrived in Sabaoani, 10 km further down the track. From there it went on to the town of Roman, but because of the stench the train was not allowed into the station. It was therefore sent back to Sabaoani where another 300 bodies were taken off before being shuttled back to Roman. There some of the evacuees were bathed and deloused. Particular care was given to the Jews by the local Romanian Red Cross led by Victoria Agarici. The survivors were moved to another train which set out for the original destination – Călăraşi – passing through Mărăşeşti, where the bodies of ten more victims were unloaded, Inoteşti, where 40 more corpses were removed, and Ploieşti, where the Jews were given drinking water and bread. On the afternoon of 6 July the train finally arrived at Călăraşi.

The 1,011 survivors had been transported a distance of some 500 km in six and a half days, in searing heat and without water for the initial part of the journey. More than 1,400 Jews died on this first 'death' train. Those who survived were interned on the parade ground of a regimental garrison and were given food and water. Assistance was also given by the Bucharest Jewish Community through a representative. At the end of August they were released and allowed to return to their homes.

The fate of the Jews in the second 'death' train was equally harrowing, although their ordeal was shorter. On 30 June, at about 6 am, 1,902 Jews were bundled into a train made up of 18 wagons. It took eight hours to cover the distance of 20 kilometres to the village of Podul Iloaei. Once again, the overcrowding, heat and lack of water struck down the evacuees. 1,194 Jews died and were buried in the village cemetery.

Many relatives were unaware for days of the fate of their loved ones. Rebeca Joseph Hirsch wrote a postcard on 11 July to the American minister asking for his help in locating her husband, who had disappeared on 29 June, leaving her with two teenage daughters and no support. On 21 July, a letter went out from the Legation to the prefect in Iaşi pointing out that Hirsch was an American citizen and requesting help in locating him. The folder on her case in the State Department archives contains a postcard by his daughters dated 9 August indicating that someone had seen him in Buzău doing road work and another card from Rebeca Hirsch to the consulate confirming that she still has no news, stating that she is ill, the daughters have no support and asking that Legation officers undertake an investigation in Iaşi, a request she repeated two weeks later in another postcard. Other cards followed with continuing appeals for help in getting herself and her daughters to the United States. Finally, on 5 September, she was able to share with the Legation in a letter a detailed account of her husband's death. It seemed that on 29 June he had been loaded onto a sealed freight car with some 100 other Jews and suffocated on one of the 'death trains'. His corpse was removed from the train on 2 July at Mirceşti.[39]

The total number of victims of the Iaşi pogrom, including those on the two 'death' trains, is difficult to establish with certainty.[40] While the deaths claimed by the trains have been computed with relative accuracy – between 2,700 and 2,800 – and some 1,000 are estimated, with good reason, to have been gunned down in the police courtyard, it is not at all clear how many Jews were murdered elsewhere in the city between 26 and 30 June. German diplomats in Bucharest put the total figure of dead in Iaşi at *at least* 4,000, which seems the best summary we can offer, but figures as high as 8,000, 10,000 and 12,000 have also been advanced.[41]

Documents point to the involvement of the Romanian Secret Service (*Serviciul Secret de Informaţii*) alongside units of the Romanian and German armies. In testimony given to the public prosecutor on 12 November 1945, Traian Borcescu, the former head of the SSI administrative office, stated:

> As regards the preparation and staging of the massacres in Iaşi, I suspect that they were the work of the First Operative Squadron [of the SSI] since Eugen Cristescu [head of the SSI] said to me on his return from Moldavia to Bucharest: 'The great deeds which I carried out in Moldavia I carried out in concert with the section II of the General Headquarters, and namely with Colonel Radu Dinulescu and Lt.-Col. Gheorghe Petrescu. In addition, I know from [SSI agent] Grigore Petrovici that a major role in the preparation of the pogrom was played by Junius Lecca, SSI head of counter-espionage in Iaşi who provided all the information on the Jewish quarters and congregations in the city and who passed this information on to Eugen Cristescu, who together with section II of the General Head-quarters and the German command worked out the plans for the massacre in Iaşi.[42]

From Borcescu's testimony it appears that the SSI may have played only a preparatory role in the pogrom, but he went on to declare:

> In respect of the massacre, although the echelon did not receive orders to participate, nevertheless the following teams drawn from the echelon did take part: a team led by Grigore Petrovici and Captain Gheorghe Balotescu, another one led by Major Tulbure, another under the command of Gheorghe Cristescu-Gică, Eugen Cristescu's brother. I only know of these, but there may have been others. These teams worked under the command of Florin Becescu-Georgescu.[43]

Ion Antonescu's responsibility for the Iaşi pogrom is a matter of vigorous debate. The first reports to reach Antonescu in his train explained the events in Iaşi as a response by the Germans to the actions of Communist agents, parachuted in to make contact with the Jews in order to carry out sabotage behind the German–Romanian lines, and it was under the influence of such reports that he issued a retaliatory order which was relayed to units in Iaşi by the chief of the General HQ, General Ioaniţiu, late in the night of 30 June: 'General Antonescu ordered that all the Jewish Communists in Iaşi, and all those found with red flags and firearms, are to be executed tonight. Report the execution [of the order] to Ialomiţa [the place of Antonescu's quarters in the train *Patria*].'[44] Whether any executions were carried out that night is not known. However, in an attempt to justify the massacre at the police headquarters, Mihai Antonescu, acting on behalf of Ion Antonescu in Bucharest, authorized the publication of a communiqué on 2 July which read:

> The Soviets are seeking by all means to carry out acts of sabotage, disorder and aggression behind the front. To this end they have been parachuting in spies and terrorist agents, who are making contact with agents resident in the country and with the Judeo-Communist population in order to organize acts of aggression. Some of these agents have been captured, while the attempted acts of aggression have been punished. In Iaşi 500 Judeo-Communists, who fired on German and Romanian troops from their houses have been executed.[45]

Yet the day before, Ion Antonescu had ordered an immediate investigation into the violence perpetrated by General Emanoil Leoveanu, the Chief of Police. Instead, however, of dealing with one report, the historian is faced with an extraordinary situation: the existence of two reports, written and signed by the same person – Leoveanu – bearing the same date and number, but with a different content.[46] One of the reports argues that the pogrom was a response to provocation by Jews, who fired on German and Romanian troops and exculpates the Romanian authorities of any wrongdoing; the other makes no mention of Jewish provocation and lays the blame for the attacks on Iron Guardists and shows that the German commandant claimed falsely to have had suffered casualties among his men. In this report, too, the Romanian authorities are praised for carrying out their duty. An analysis of the reports indicates that the latter was written shortly after the former on the instruction of Antonescu, who was angered by the German behaviour.

After the pogrom Antonescu ordered the removal of Jews from Iaşi to camps in the south of the country. This was done, Mihai Antonescu explained to Franklin Mott Gunther, the American minister to Bucharest, in order to 'save them', but in the execution of this order, as he himself admittted, 'grave mistakes had been made or excesses committed'.[47] What Mihai Antonescu apparently did not add was that Ion Antonescu had justified this decision for fear of sabotage and espionage by the Jews behind the front line, the very same fear that provided one of the reasons for the deportations of Jews from Bessarabia and Bukovina.[48]

That Antonescu was well aware of the random murder of Jews in Iaşi by Romanian soldiers is evident from an order of his which was transmitted on 4 July by the Minister of the Interior, General Dumitru Popescu, to the police and gendarmes:

> The disorder which occurred a few days ago in Iaşi has placed the army and the authorities in a completely unfavourable light. The withdrawal from Bessarabia was a veritable dishonour for the army when it allowed itself to be insulted and attacked by Jews and Communists without

reacting. The shame is even greater when soldiers, on their own initiative and often solely in order to rob or mistreat, attack Jews and kill them at random, as was the case in Iaşi. The Jewish race has drained, impoverished, speculated and stopped the development of the Romanian people for several centuries. The need to rid ourselves of this blot on Romanianism is beyond dispute, but only the government has the right to take the necessary measures. These measures are being applied and will be continued according to norms which I shall decide. It is unacceptable, however, for each citizen or each soldier to assume the role himself of solving the Jewish problem by robberies and massacres. By such behaviour we show the world that we are an undisciplined and uncivilized people and we place the authority and prestige of the Romanian state in a totally unpleasant light. I completely forbid, then, any action taken on individual initiative and hold the military and civilian authorities responsible for the precise execution of this order . . .[49]

An attempt to gauge popular Romanian reaction to the excesses perpetrated against the Jews was made by Cloyce K. Huston, Second Secretary at the US Legation in a memorandum forwarded by Gunther to Washington on 19 August:

The Rumanians have heretofore insisted upon being known as a tolerant people, and I do not doubt that the majority of them learn of the massacres and other atrocities with, possibly, a slight feeling of satisfaction, mixed with a stronger sense of surprise, shock and misgiving . . .

I [Gunther] have already reported by telegram (no. 716 of 1 August 1941, 9 am) the suggestion that General Antonescu was 'sick at heart' because he had not been able to curb the bloody excesses committed against the Jews. *The fact remains, however, that he issued the first order.* (my emphasis)

While recognizing that Iuliu Maniu, the National Peasant Party leader, and 'certain officials' in the Foreign Ministry had 'openly deplored the extreme violence and drastic measures that have been employed against the country's Jewish population', the memorandum pointed out that 'there has been no popular uprising or movement against all these cruelties'. It suggested as an explanation that

the ethical sense of the Rumanian people has been somewhat dulled by recent miseries and disasters, the loss of Bessarabia, then of Transylvania and the Dobrodja, the dethronement of a King, a catastrophic earthquake,[50] a bloody revolution, and, in this part of the world, war in all its most hideous aspects, including the reported butchery of prisoners and even of elements of the local Rumanian population suspected or popularly accused of Communist sympathies, with the result that they are not fully conscious of the horrors of the Jewish phase.[51]

The Jews of Romania certainly were, and it was Ion Antonescu who gave the order for the next phase in the torment of the Jews to begin: the 'forced migration' of the Jews in Bessarabia and Bukovina.

The deportations – the preferred term in Romanian official parlance was 'evacuation' – were carried out by the Romanian army and gendarmerie and were in retaliation for the hostility which Antonescu alleged was shown by Jews towards the Romanian army during its withdrawal from these provinces in June 1940, and the subsequent behaviour of Jews towards the Romanian population in these territories during the period of Soviet rule from June 1940 until July 1941. Antonescu also invoked security grounds, namely that he did not want Jews on whom he felt he could not rely behind the Romanian lines.[52] The clearest insight into Ion Antonescu's motives for deporting the Jews is provided by his response to two petitions sent to him in October 1941 by Wilhelm Filderman protesting at the deportations.[53] Antonescu's reply, dated 19 October, was published in the national and local press – Filderman's petitions were not – at the end of the month and reignited a vigorous anti-Semitic campaign.

Mr Filderman, no one can be more sensitive than I am to the suffering of the humble and defenceless. I understand your pain but all of you should, and especially should have, understood mine at the time, which was the pain of an entire nation. Do you think, did you think, of what we were going through last year during the evacuation of Bessarabia and what is happening today, when day by day and hour by hour, we are paying generously and in blood, in a great deal of blood, for the hatred with which your co-religionists in Bessarabia treated us during the withdrawal from Bessarabia, how they received us upon our return, and how they treated us from the Dniester up to Odessa and in the area around the Sea of Azov?

But as is traditional, you want to turn yourselves on this occasion as well from the accused into the accusers, pretending to forget the reasons behind the situation which you complain about. Allow me to ask you, and through you to ask all your co-religionists who, the greater our sufferings and blows received by us, the more frenetically their applause.

What did you do last year when you heard of the Jews' behaviour in Bessarabia and Bukovina towards our withdrawing troops who up to then had protected the peace and wealth of those Jews? I shall remind you.

Even before that appearance of the Soviet troops the Jews of Bessarabia and Bukovina, whom you defend, spat on our officers, ripped off their epaulettes, tore their uniforms, and when they could they beat our soldiers to death in a cowardly fashion. We have proof.

These same wretches welcomed the Soviet troops with flowers and celebrated their arrival with wild enthusiasm. We have photographs as proof.

During the Soviet occupation, those for whom you showed concern today betrayed the good Romanians, denounced them to face the wrath of the Communists, and brought tears and mourning to many Romanian families.

Every day the horribly mutilated bodies of our martyrs are brought out of the cellars of Chişinău. This is their reward for having laid a a friendly table for twenty years for these ungrateful beasts.

These are facts which are known, which you, too, certainly know, and which you can find out about any time in detail.

Did you ask yourself why the Jews burned their houses before withdrawing? Can you explain why, during our advance, we found young Jews of fourteen and fifteen with grenades in their pockets? Did you ask how many of our people fell, murdered in a cowardly manner by your co-religionists?, and how many were buried alive. If want proof of this, you will have it.

These are acts of hatred, bordering on madness, which your Jews have displayed towards our tolerant and hospitable people who are today worthy and conscious of their rights.

In response to the generosity with which they were received in our midst and treated, your Jews, who have today become Soviet commissars, are driving the Soviet troops in the region of Odessa using unprecedented terror – corroborated by Russian prisoners – to a useless massacre, in order solely to cause us losses.

In the area of the Sea of Azov our troops made a temporary withdrawal and left behind several wounded officers and soldiers. When they resumed their advance they found the wounded terribly mutilated. People who could have been saved drew their last breath in terrible torment. Their eyes had been plucked out, their tongues, noses and ears cut off. Can you imagine, Mr Filderman, the scene? Are you horrified? Are you not moved?

You ask yourself why such hatred is shown by Russian Jews with whom we have never had a quarrel? But their hatred is a general hatred, it is your hatred.

Do not be moved, if you really have souls, by things that are not worth it, be moved by what is worth it. Weep with the mothers who have lost their children who were tortured in this fashion, or with those who have brought such evil upon themselves and do so to you as well.[54]

Reliable accounts of the behaviour of the minority population towards the departing Romanians are lacking. Although there was allegedly some photographic evidence of such behaviour by Jews during the withdrawal of June 1940, and there were several reports of such incidents from the Romanian troops withdrawn from the two provinces,[55] even the latter reports suggest that it was not only Jews who welcomed the arrival of Soviet troops and ridiculed the departing Romanians. Russians and Ukrainians living in Bessarabia were glad to see the back of the Romanian administration and made no secret of their feelings. That Jews should express relief at the prospect of release from crude anti-Semitic policies, and do so in a demonstrable manner, is hardly surprising. Yet other Jews, the more wealthy among them, fearing for their fortunes at the hands of a Communist regime, were apprehensive at the prospect of Soviet rule and showed their concern by withdrawing with the Romanian forces. Finally, if retaliation against the Jews for their treatment of the withdrawing Romanian forces from the provinces in June 1940 was one of the motive invoked by Antonescu for deportation, then it made no sense to include the Jews from southern Bukovina and Dorohoi county in northern Moldavia which were not annexed by the Soviet Union in June 1940 and had remained part of Romania.[56]

Concentration of the Jews in towns was a prelude to their deportation. This, at the least, can be inferred from Mihai Antonescu's speech delivered on 3 July at the Ministry of Internal Affairs:

> Ethnic and Political Purification. We find ourselves at the broadest and most favourable moment for a complete ethnic unshackling, for a national revision and for the cleansing of our people of all those elements alien to its spirit, which have grown like mistletoe to darken its future. To avoid losing this unique opportunity, we must be implacable.... The action of purification would be carried out by concentrating or isolating all the Jews – as well as the other foreigners whose attitude is doubtful – in places where they could not exercise their baneful influence.[57]

Five days later, he was more explicit. At another meeting of the cabinet over which he presided in the absence of Ion Antonescu, he declared:

> At the risk of not being understood by some traditionalists who may still be among you, I am for the forced migration of the whole Jewish population in Bessarabia and Bukovina, which must be expelled *over the frontier* [my emphasis]. Similarly, I am for the forced migration of the Ukrainian population which has no place here at this time.... I do not care. The Roman Empire carried out a series of barbarous deeds against others yet it was still the grandest and most extensive political entity.
>
> I do not know how many centuries will elapse before the Romanian people will have a greater freedom of action to carry out the ethnic purification and national revision.... there is no moment in our history more favourable...for a complete ethnic unshackling, for a national revision and purification of our people...

So let us use this historic moment to cleanse the Romanian land and our nation of all the misfortunes which have befallen it down the centuries, in which we could not be our own masters.... If we have to, we should use the machine-gun.[58]

It is also worth noting that Mihai Antonescu spoke here of *the whole Jewish population in Bessarabia and Bukovina*.

Two stages emerged in the deportation process. Originally, Antonescu saw the expulsion as a one-step operation, a corollary to the German–Romanian advance through Bessarabia and Bukovina, which would sweep all the Jews before it and drive them into Russia. The Romanian leader admitted as much in a cabinet meeting of 6 September 1941:

Our aim must be that the state of Galicia be founded to provide a link between us and the Germans, while this Galicia should be cleansed of Yids and Slavs, just as I am fighting now to cleanse Bessarabia and Bukovina of Yids and Slavs.... we have tens of thousands of Jews whom I intend to cast into Russia...[59]

But the German refusal to accept the influx of Jews on territory under their control forced Antonescu to modify his timetable and conduct a holding operation, leaving the Jews on the Bessarabian bank of the Dniester in makeshift camps. His enthusiasm to rid Romania of her Jews got the better of his military judgement, as the German High Command was quick to demonstrate. Pushing tens of thousands of Jews into battle-zones created problems of logistics and security, which the German Army had no time or inclination to address.

Yet several thousand Jews did not survive the German-Romanian invasion of the Soviet Union to be expelled across the Dniester.[60] From the earliest days of the attack, the mass killing of Jews was a feature of the combined Axis advance through northern Bukovina and Bessarabia.[61] The ground for such action had been prepared by General Constantin Vasiliu, head of the gendarmerie in the Ministry of the Interior, who, on 17 June, relayed to gendarmerie units that would be deployed in Bessarabia Antonescu's idea for 'cleansing the terrain' of Jews.[62] This policy was described as 'the extermination on the spot of all Jews in rural areas, enclosing them in ghettos in urban areas, and the arrest of all those suspected of being Communist party members or of having held important functions under Soviet rule'.[63] Vasiliu's orders to the gendarmerie were explicit:

The Jewish minority is to be pursued with the utmost vigour, since it is known that the Jews, almost in their entirety, collaborated with Communism and perpetrated acts of the greatest hostility against the Romanian army, authorities and population. As regards this population, one should exercise the greatest vigilance, so that not a single guilty individual escapes the retribution he deserves.[64]

These orders were a reflection of measures ordered by Hitler, more specifically the 'special tasks' assigned to the head of the SS, Heinrich Himmler, by Hitler on 13 March 1941 in *Operation Barbarossa*, the attack on the Soviet Union. Defined in the 'Guidelines for *Führer* Directive 21 Regarding Special Areas', these 'special tasks' involved the preparation of 'political administration within the operational area of the army' and were to be carried out by mobile commandos of security police under the command of Himmler. These commando units, known individually as *Einsatzkommandos*, and collectively as *Einsatzgruppen*, were set up and integrated into the army's operational structure in April 1941.[65]

In war zones, assessing 'guilt' was an arbitrary exercise which resulted in the murder of many innocent Jews in the two provinces. On 27 June, at Sculeni, on the border between Romania and Soviet-occupied Bessarabia, fierce fighting took place between Romanian–German and Soviet forces. The Romanian troops involved came from the 6th mountain regiment commanded by Colonel Ermil Matieş which had been garrisoned at Bălţi in Bessarabia until the Romanian withdrawal from the province during the previous summer and which had been allegedly humiliated by Jews during its departure in 1940. During the fighting at Sculeni, officers from the regiment claimed that they had been attacked by local Jews with grenades and fired on. After the occupation of the village, the German commander of the sector, Colonel Buck, ordered the evacuation of the civilian population, which was taken to another village Stânca Roznovanu, where it was screened under the supervision of Captain Ion Stihi, Second Lieutenant Eugen Mihăilescu, and the former Guardist mayor Gheorghe Cimpoeşu, being divided into Jews and Christians. The latter were taken to two others villagers while the Jews were held. Mihăilescu, an Orthodox theology student and former Guardist, and Captain Stihi forced 40 Jews to dig graves and then gathered in some tent canvas the gold, jewels and other valuables the Jews had. Following this, the three men, together with Sergeant Vasile Mihailov, shot 311 Jews with machine-pistols. Cimpoeşu and another person, Parashiva Barloanschi Moroşeanu, then took the valuables and clothes of the murdered Jews for themselves.

These events were confirmed by the testimony of Romanian officers in the regiment in a report compiled on 20 July by the commander, Colonel Matieş, who accused the Jews of having attacked the regiment and admitted 'giving Captain Stihi the order to arrest and execute all the suspect Jews in Sculeni'.[66] Ten days later, in response to a query from divisional headquarters about the incident, Matieş noted 'his surprise that this matter is raised again when the soldiers of this regiment at Sculeni have suffered a great deal at the hands of all the Yids who remained in this village. That is why they were executed according to orders from above'. Matieş confirmed in another report the next day that 'the regiment was following orders from above' in executing the Jews.[67] In a statement given shortly after the massacre, Lieutenant Andronic Prepeliţă, adjutant to Captain Stihi, stated that women and children were among those shot.[68] Similarly, Matieş reported, a company from the same regiment had been surrounded in the village of Mărculeşti by Soviet troops and 'about 300 armed Jewish civilians who caused painful losses to this company'. When Mărculeşti was taken by the Romanian army, a group of 400 Jewish men and women were caught, of whom about 80 were wounded, 'a fact', Matieş stated, 'that proves that they fought against us, in civilian clothes. On this occasion, too, I ordered their execution *en masse*.'[69]

On 3 July, troops of the 16th Infantry Regiment occupied the village of Ciudei in Bukovina. Under the command of Colonel Valeriu Carp, these soldiers shot almost the entire Jewish population. The number of victims was between 450 and 572. On 4 July, Romanian troops occupied the town of Storojineţ. Here, too, a large number of Jews were murdered – according to reports some 200, among them women and children. Some 4,000 Jews were placed in a ghetto before being sent to the transit camp at Edineţi for deportation to Transnistria. Exemptions were given to doctors, specialists in the distilling of alcohol and workers in the timber trade. Some Romanians were singled out by local Jews for their decent treatment, among them the local gendarmerie commander Bârzescu and the mayor's secretary, Isidor Palade. Jewish children were among those shot by Romanian soldiers in the nearby village of Ropcea while at Iordăneşti the local inhabitants themselves murdered four Jews, including two children.

On 5 July, murders of Jews took place in all the villages in Storojineţ county in Bukovina, some of them committed by locals.[70] The latter were responsible for the deaths of 15 Jews at Bănila on the River Siret. In Cernăuţi (Chernivtsi), more than 2,000 Jews were killed within 24 hours of the entry of Romanian troops on 6 July, according to one source.[71] On 7 July, 400 others, including the Chief Rabbi Dr Mark, were murdered by German SS troops.[72] During the reconquest of northern Bukovina at least 4,000 Jews are believed to have been murdered by Romanian and German troops and by Romanian and Ukrainian villagers.[73]

In Bessarabia, it is estimated that more than 12,000 Jews were shot by German and Romanian forces by the end of the summer; about half of these are ascribed by some scholars to the mobile German death squads of SS Colonel Otto Ohlendorff's *Einsatzgruppe D* operating with the support of the German and Romanian armies in Bessarabia and northern Bukovina.[74] At Noua Suliţă, between 8 and 10 July, the 9th battalion Romanian mountain troops, under the command of Colonel Cârlan, was reported to have shot 800 Jews on the streets of the town and in their homes, and at least 100 Jews were murdered on the orders of Second Lieutenant Savin Popescu from the

37th infantry. The 7th police company 'executed at least 227 other Jews at Noua Suliţă' during this same period.[75] On 11 July, ten Jews were shot in the garden of the Jewish community centre in Bălţi by German soldiers on the orders of Colonel Koller and Captain Prast.[76]

Pride in the efficiency with which *Einsatzgruppe D* meted out death prompted it to record its dissatisfaction with the arbitrary fashion in which Romanian troops carried out their murders. In a report dated 31 July 1941, an *Einsatzgruppe* commander complained: 'The Romanians act against the Jews without any idea of a plan. No one would object to the numerous executions of Jews if the technical aspect of their preparation, as well as the manner in which they are carried out, were not wanting. The Romanians leave the executed where they fall, without burial. The *Einsatzkommando* has urged the Romanian police to proceed with more order from this point of view.'[77] A similar complaint was relayed to his superiors by SS Major Gmeiner on 16 July:

> The General Staff Officer for Intelligence has tried to see whether anything appropriate could be done about the unrealistic and sadistic executions carried out by the Romanians and whether they can be prevented. He would be particularly pleased if objects and belongings could be secured against pillage.[78]

In tandem with the massacres of Jews throughout Bessarabia during July, the policy of 'cleansing the terrain' was applied with vigour.[79] On 8 July, an order was given to the second bureau (intelligence) of the General Staff to draw up a plan for the expulsion of Jews from Bessarabia. The result was a scheme to select small teams of Romanians from areas already freed from Soviet occupation to travel to villages in Bessarabia in advance of the Romanian army 'to create an atmosphere hostile to the Jewish elements, so that the local population itself will seek to remove the Jews by means they find most appropriate under local circumstances'. Those chosen would already have Soviet identity documents, and their families could be held as hostages to ensure compliance with instructions. Teams were assembled to move to villages along the line of advance to Chişinău and they were activated within a few days.[80] On the same day, Colonel Teodor Meculescu, the newly appointed head of the Chişinău Inspectorate of Gendarmes, issued his first general order, which was 'to identify and arrest all Jews of both sexes and any age still found in rural areas'.[81] Within 24 hours gendarmerie units were reporting to the Military Governor of the province, General Gheorghe Voiculescu, that the 'cleansing of the terrain' was already under way in Bălţi, north of Chişinău.[82]

The Jews expelled from rural areas around Bălţi were assembled in places where no preparations had been made to shelter, feed or guard them. The same situation prevailed throughout Bessarabia. In his inspection of a number of these sites near Bălţi, General Ion Topor, the senior judicial officer in the army, complained on 14 July about the conditions and recommended a solution: either deportation of the Jews across the Dniester, or their transfer to the interior of Romania to perform compulsory labour. Ten days later, Governor Voiculescu ordered the setting-up of camps into which the expelled Jews were to be concentrated; Jews in cities were to register in three days for employment in forced labour. On the same day, 24 July, Voiculescu gave another order for the 'acceleration of the operation to establish a ghetto' in Chişinău in furtherance of a previous command to this effect.[83]

This 'acceleration' entailed not just the issue of eviction notices to Jews, but in some cases their forcible removal from their homes without warning by police. They were driven on foot to a southern district of the city called Visterniceni, where many of the buildings had been damaged during the hostilities. The round-up of Jews was arbitrary, with former government officials who were Jews, Jews married to Christians and Jews who had converted to Christianity all being swept along since no clear instructions had been given about their treatment. No complete record of the names of the Jews enclosed in the ghetto was made, a fact which was to make detection of the fate of individuals difficult. Administration of the ghetto was entrusted initially to Colonel D. Tudose, head of the Chişinău garrison, who reported not to Voiculescu but to the commander of the Romanian 4th Army, but it passed subsequently through five different military and police units. The ghetto itself was placed under a subordinate military command, under Captain Besuţiu. These alternative lines of command, issuing from Ion Antonescu to Governor Voiculescu on the one hand, and from Antonescu to the military command on the other, allowed Voiculescu later to deflect criticism from Antonescu of how the ghetto was run.[84]

By the end of the month, more than 10,000 Jews had been crammed into the ghetto under police and military guard.[85] Figures given by Besuţiu to Tudose in mid-August indicated that there were 10,578 Jews in the ghetto, of whom 3,117 were men, 5,261 women and 2,200 children (aged under 16) almost equally divided between the sexes. On 21 August, Tudose forwarded another set of figures, also received from Besuţiu, which matched the earlier report except for a reduced number of men – 594. The disproportion of men to women resulted from the Soviet draft of men of military age as well as the flight of able-bodied males in the face of the Romanian–German advance. The reduction in the number of men had a more sinister explanation: their murder in the village of Ghidighici, which is described below.[86] Ghetto numbers increased during late August with the internment of Jews from areas outside Chişinău; Jews found hiding in Lăpuşna county were sent to the ghetto, as were others who had broken Antonescu's ban on travel without permission. As a result, the ghetto population had increased by the end of the month to 11,328, close to the maximum of 11,525 recorded in late September by the Romanian authorities.[87]

A Jewish ghetto committee, composed of 22 'intellectuals', was set up and its leader, Guttman Landau, treated with Tudose over the running of the ghetto. Landau secured the commander's agreement to the operation of a bakery, supplied with flour from the garrison; a ten-bed clinic was also improvised, with medicines provided by the army. The committee was instructed to assemble Jews for forced labour duties, a duty it performed obediently although it did intervene successfully with the commander for their suspension on Rosh Hashana (22–23 September) and Yom Kippur (1 October). By this time, conditions in the ghetto had deteriorated markedly. The flour supply allowed the baking of 100 g of bread for each Jew only, and just 200 families could be fed by the communal kitchen, which offered soup and polenta. Soon the authorities were reporting 10–15 deaths per day.[88]

Jews fit for work were expected to clothe and feed themselves from the payment they received for their labour. A message dated 4 August from General Palangeanu, chief of staff of the Romanian 4th Army, to the authorities in Bessarabia carried Antonescu's order that all Jews be used for road repairs and other labour duties, while a few days earlier, an instruction from the Ministry of the Interior stipulated that the Jews be paid:

If the work merits 120 or 150 lei a day, this is what should be paid.... The employers should not keep the difference between what it would be appropriate to pay the Jews and what they actually pay them. This difference should belong to the Jew, from which he must clothe himself, get shoes, and survive the winter, when there will no longer be work to do.[89]

In fact, a uniform daily rate of 25 lei in food and 10 lei 'living expenses' was fixed, but even this was not paid as the employing institutions were often either unable or unwilling to pay the Jews. In the words of a local police inspector writing to Governor Voiculescu:

Jews...were supposed to be paid twenty-five lei a day, which they did not receive, because the authorities for which they worked had no funds. Today, the authorities, knowing that Jewish labour must be paid, no longer ask for them, depriving the Jews of the single possibility they had to secure their own existence. The material situation of the Jews becomes worse with each day that passes, and the...danger of exanthematic typhus is imminent.[90]

While police headquarters in Chişinău stated that the Jews were receiving 'thirty-five lei a day plus food from the German authorities' and from 'the other authorities' food plus ten lei per day, the Jews were becoming desperate because they had 'no food, no clothes and no money'. As a consequence, the death rate among them had risen 'to an average of fourteen a day'.[91]

Death on a larger and more violent scale had occurred among the Jews of the ghetto at the beginning of August.[92] On 1 August, a German officer of the *Einsatzkommando 11a* ordered the ghetto committee to provide 250 men and 200 women for labour outside Chişinău at Visterniceni. Shortly after the selection of the Jews, a Soviet air-raid took place and the *Einsatzkommando 11a* shot all but 39 of them.[93] According to one of these survivors, he and the others were forced by the Germans to bury the victims in anti-tank ditches left by the Red Army and were told by a German officer to warn the ghetto inhabitants that they would share the same fate 'if they did not stop signalling with lights to the incoming Russian planes'. A week later, a Romanian road inspector took 500 men and 25 women from the ghetto to carry out road repairs in the village of Ghidighici. Only 200 of the Jews returned. The others were mown down by a machine-gun company under the command of Captain Radu Ionescu. Ionescu admitted during his trial in October 1950 that the Jews had been killed 'on the army's orders' for 'rebellion and attacking Romanian troops'.[94]

Similar atrocities took place elsewhere in Bessarabia. At the end of July 1941, Romanian troops reached Cetatea Albă (Akkerman). On the orders of the gendarme commander of the town, Major Mircea Georgescu, around 360 Jews were sent from the village of Bairamcea in a convoy guarded by gendarmes to Cetatea Albă and locked in one of the synagogues. In another synagogue the gendarmes assembled more than 2,500 Jews from the town. Eye-witnesses testified after the war that most of these were shot near a stone quarry on the outskirts of the town by execution squads under the command of Captain Alexandru Ochişor on the orders of Colonel Marcel Petală, military prosecutor of the 8th Army, Major Virgil Drăgan, and Horia Olteanu of the SSI (Romanian Intelligence Service).[95] Just a few days later, on 9 August, SS *Untersturmführer* Heinrich Fröhlich and gendarmerie captain Ioan Gheorghe Vetu sent in a joint report from the same area of Cetatea Albă that Fröhlich had gone to the village of Tătăreşti

> where there was a camp with 451 Jews under the command of gendarmerie captain Ioan Gheorghe Vetu of the Legion of Gendarmes in Chilia Nouă, to whom I transmitted General Antonescu's order to execute them immediately. The undersigned, Captain Vetu, being informed of the order, told the Legion commander who ordered me to carry out this order and to report back. This is the reason why we drew up this present report.[96]

Confirmation that the massacre took place comes from a note from the head of the Bessarabian gendarmerie, Colonel Teodor Meculescu, of 17 December 1941, in which he informed a commission of enquiry, set up on Antonescu's orders, to investigate abuses against the Jews during deportation, that Captain Vetu had 'appropriated' various objects of value from the murdered Jews. In the preface to the note Meculescu refers to 'the 'attached copy of the report' of Fröhlich and Vetu regarding the execution of Jews in the commune of Tătăreşti.[97]

7
Deportation

In continuance of the policy of 'cleansing the terrain', Romanian gendarmes drove columns of Jews on foot from Bukovina and Bessarabia towards the north of the latter province and over the Dniester into what was at the time German-controlled territory. The mass character of the deportation – children, women, the aged and infirm included – shows clearly that Antonescu's intention was to ethnically cleanse the two provinces of Jews. Those that had the opportunity took with them clothes, food, money and jewellery. The Germans were unwilling to accept large numbers of Jews and sent them back.[1] On 31 July, General Eugen von Schobert, commander of the German 11th Army, informed the Romanian general staff that the 'movement of large masses of Jews in the army rear can pose a serious threat to troop supply and is thus intolerable'. He gave a warning that any further 'deportation of Jews or Russians eastward over the Dniester' would be prevented by German troops.[2] The threat was ignored. Romanian gendarmes began to drive the Jews across the river further north. In some cases Romanian army engineers erected pontoon bridges, which were immediately dismantled after the expulsion of the Jews.[3] Romanian gendarmes in Soroca, in northern Bessarabia, reported that on 5 August the Germans had sent 3,000 Jews back across the Dniester to Atachi 'from the 12,000 that had been sent across the Dniester' by the Romanians at Moghilev (Mohyliv Podil's'kyi).[4] On the same day, the Romanian army telegraphed General Ioan Topor that there were there were about 20,000 Jews from the county seats of Hotin (Khotyn) and Storojineţ (Storozhynets') on the road to Atachi whom the Germans had refused to accept. Three days later, the gendarme inspectorate in Cernăuţi telegraphed that 20,000 from the county of Hotin had been driven across the Dniester but that the Germans had begun, on 7 August, to send back from the Ukraine everyone from Bessarabia and northern Bukovina, irrespective of their ethnic background.[5] In the words of a German SD report, the Jews were 'chased back and forth until they dropped.... Old men and women lay along the road at short distances from each other...'[6]

On 16 August, Antonescu challenged von Schobert's decision to return expelled Jews to the Bessarabian side of the Dniester. He complained to von Killinger, the German minister in Bucharest, that German units near Soroca were sending back Bessarabian Jews who, according to Antonescu, had been taken with them by retreating Soviet troops. Antonescu claimed that the return of these Jews was 'contrary to the guidelines which the Führer had set forth to him in Munich regarding the treatment of the eastern Jews'.[7] Antonescu's complaint was referred by von Killinger to Berlin, after which an official of the Foreign Ministry contacted the General Headquarters of the *Wehrmacht* about it, explaining:

I have been unable to discover anything at the Foreign Ministry regarding guidelines which the Führer gave General Antonescu with respect to the treatment of the eastern Jews. The official record of the conversation between the Führer and Antonescu in the Führer's apartments in Munich does not contain anything on this subject. However, as the Führer talked to Antonescu in Munich also on other occasions, it is entirely possible that the question of the eastern Jews was also discussed there. In any case, there is no reason to doubt the accuracy of General Antonescu's assertion. I therefore recommend that General Antonescu's wish be given consideration and that the German military authorities concerned be instructed not to move the Jews back to Bessarabia.[8]

Such instructions do not appear to have reached Colonel Otto Ohlendorf, head of *Einsatzgruppe D* who decided to drive all Jews in Moghilev back into Bessarabia; they were to be brought to Yampol and sent back across the Dniester. On 20 August, 200 'old and sick' Jews who might slow the march to Yampol were segregated from the rest and shot by *Sonderkommando 10b*. Ohlendorf's plan was to trick the Romanians by sending the Jews across rapidly during the night. On reaching the bridge, a further 300–400 Jews who were considered 'slow-moving' were murdered by *Sonderkommando 10b* and *Einsatzkommando 12*. As the Germans trained their machine-guns on the Romanian bridge guards, the columns of Jews were driven across. *Einsatzkommando* troops reported hearing gunfire on the Romanian side and there is little doubt as to who the targets were. By 29 August, *Einsatzgruppe D* was able to conclude:

Romanians had driven thousands of specially selected persons, those infirm and unable to work, along with children, from Bessarabia and Bukovina into German-controlled territory. A total of some 27,500 Jews [were] forced back into Romanian territory at Svanitsa-Moghilev-Podolsk and Yampol, and 1,265, some of them younger adults, shot.[9]

Other columns of Jews, many of whom had been deported by the Romanians from Bukovina, were assembled at Kamenets-Podolsk. The problem of what to do with them was solved by the offer to the military governor of the area from Friedrich Jeckeln, responsible for the rear lines of communication in Army Area South and the Reichkomissariat Ukraine, to 'liquidate' the Jews by 1 September. A massive bloodbath ensued. Between 27 and 29 August, some 23,000 Jews were murdered, each by a shot to the nape of the neck in huge bomb craters outside the town.[10]

With nowhere to send the Jews on the Romanian side of the Dniester, the Romanian gendarmerie set up transit camps in Bukovina at Secureni and Edineţi, and in Bessarabia at Vertujeni and Mărculeşti, into which more than 50,000 Jews were herded.[11] In a report of the security police (*Siguranţa*), drawn up in reply to a 'request by telephone made on 10 September 1941' (from whom is not stated) the sites of concentration of the Jews in Bessarabia were listed: Chişinău ghetto 11,328 Jews; Tighina camp 65; Cahul camp 524; Ismail ghetto 69; Chilia Nouă 281; Orhei 334; Răşcani 3,072; Limbenii Noi 2,634; Răuţel 3,235; Vertujeni 22,964; Vâlcov 35.[12] The living conditions were appalling. Poor sanitation, a shortage of water and a lack of food quickly led to the outbreak of disease. The mortality rate soared. In a review of the situation in Secureni and Edineţ submitted on 11 September to the provincial administration, Colonel Ion Mănecuţă, head of the gendarmerie in Bukovina, pointed out that the majority of the Jews

> have no clothing and nothing to cover themselves with. Since most were sent to the Ukraine and then forced back by the Germans, they have either lost or had taken from them in the Ukraine everything they had. They have nothing available to prepare food, each person cooks in the house where they are staying. There is a shortage of medicines.[13]

Antonescu and his senior officials had never regarded the camps and ghetto in Chişinău as anything more than a way-station.[14] The initial thrust to deport the Jews had been frustrated by objections from the Germans in command of the area between the Dniester and the Bug, but once Antonescu had been given control of ithe region under the Tighina Agreement of 30 August – creating in the process Transnistria – the second stage of the deportations began. Romanian rule of Transnistria gave Antonescu a 'dumping ground' for the Bessarabian and Bukovinan Jews, but this was envisaged by Antonescu as a temporary location; deportation across the Bug was to be the eventual destination of the Jews as the Agreement specified.[15] Antonescu's longer-term aim was to colonize Transnistria with Romanians living not only beyond the Bug but also to the west of the Dniester, as he made clear in December 1941:

> We will give some compensation to those who have lost land in Transnistria but we will seek to drive them beyond Transnistria, because

Transnistria is destined to be colonized with Romanians of ours, Romanians whom we shall bring from beyond the Bug and even from this side [i.e. the Romanian side] of the Dniester.[16]

It was at Tighina that Antonescu convened the governors[17] of Bessarabia, Bukovina and Transnistria late in August 1941 and gave them the order for the deportation of Jews across the Dniester to recommence. General Cornel Calotescu, Governor-designate of Bukovina, General Gheorghe Voiculescu, Governor-designate of Bessarabia, and Gheorghe Alexianu, Governor-designate of Transnistria, were given details as to how the Jews were to be sent across the Bug.[18] In an undated memorandum to Antonescu, written at the end of the year, Voiculescu wrote that the governors had received 'precise instructions' on the way in which the deportation of the Jews to the Bug was to be carried out.[19] Antonescu himself referred to his plans in this respect at a cabinet meeting of 4 December 1941:

I warned you – you, General Voiculescu, and you too, Alexianu – that it was my intention to take the Jews to the Bug. Instead of eating the bread of the land of Romania, let them eat the bread there. I told you to take steps so that the execution of the plan should be flawless. The operation began in November. From August to November we had three months, and we organized it as we did. The same thing is valid for Bukovina.[20]

General Ioan Topor, who held the senior legal position in the Romanian Army known as *Marele Pretor*, was charged orally by Antonescu and in writing by Colonel Petrescu, head of counterintelligence of the Romanian Army, with coordination of deportation.[21] He issued orders on 7 September to the Inspector of Gendarmes in Bessarabia, Colonel Teodor Meculescu, to proceed with the deportations on 12 September, starting with the camp at Vertujeni, and laid down guidelines for their implementation;[22] these guidelines were applied at other camps and in the Chişinău ghetto.[23] The commandant of the Vertujeni camp, which held 22,969 Jews according to a gendarmerie statistic of early September,[24] was instructed by Topor through Meculescu to form the Jews into convoys of 1,600 and to send them across the Dniester at a rate of 800 per day; between 40 and 50 wagons were to be provided for each convoy of 1,600 Jews to carry the old, the sick and children; the convoys were to leave Vertujeni every other day; and gendarmes along the designated routes were to assist local inhabitants in burying the dead.[25] The punishment for those Jews who did not conform to these procedures was disguised as the codeword 'Alexianu', the name of the Governor of Transnistria; it meant 'execution on the spot'.[26]

The use of the codeword is confirmed in testimony to a gendarmerie commission of Lt. Augustin Roşca, who accompanied one such convoy on 8 October. His orders, received from a General Staff officer, included the use of a codeword, as the commission report reveals:

This special codeword was relayed to him [Roşca] by the commander of the Hotin legion, Major Drăgulescu, who told him that on the orders of the Army General HQ, Jews who could not keep up with the convoys, either through incapacity, or through illness, should be executed. To this end he ordered him [Roşca] to send a man ahead, two days before the departure of each convoy, to dig pits with the help of the local gendarmes every ten kilometres which could take around 100 bodies – those who had fallen behind and had been shot . . .

Lt. Roşca carried out these orders to the letter, which resulted in the shooting of about 500 Jews amongst those deported along the route Secureni-Cosăuţi. The same procedure was applied to the convoys between Edineţ and Cosăuţi, where the deportations were carried out by Lt. Popovici from the same unit, under the orders of Lt. Augustin Roşca.

Because of the steps taken to dig the pits in preparation for the burials, the peasants in the villages along the routes learned of what was to occur. They therefore waited at the edge of the route, hiding in maize-fields or other places, for the executions to take place in order to throw themselves onto the bodies to rob them.

From the verbal declaration of Lt. Augustin Roşca, it emerges that the preparations for, and especially the carrying out of, the executions produced such moments of drama that the participants would bear for a long time the impression of those events.[27]

It took several day of consultation involving Topor and the Governor of Bessarabia, Gheorghe Voiculescu, before Meculescu issued the deportation order for Vertujeni. In the event, its execution added to the misery of the Jews. Witnesses at the trial of the camp commandant as a war criminal, which opened in Bucharest on 14 May 1945, testified that never at any time were more than 6–8 wagons supplied for the convoys of 1,600 persons. A gendarmerie officer escorting the convoys stated that the deportees were not given food on departure and that there were insufficient wagons for the elderly, infirm and children. Only a light guard accompanied the Jews, which made them easy prey for civilians who attacked and robbed them en route. 'The road between Vertujeni and Cosăuţi [at the Dniester]', the officer went on, 'was dotted with those who did not have the energy even to get to the crossing-point'.[28]

At the Mărculeşti camp officials of the Romanian National Bank was sent to buy up the valuables of the Jews in exchange for *Reichskassenkreditschein* (RKKS), the currency introduced by the German authorities in occupied Ukraine and in circulation in Transnistria. According to witnesses at the Bucharest war crimes trials of 1945, this official, Ioan Mihăescu, after initially purchasing jewels and gold objects from some Jews at knock-down prices, simply confiscated these valuables from others. Mihăescu himself painted a harrowing picture of the camp: 'mice swarmed in their thousands down the dirt-alleys and through the houses, the flies, in a totally inordinate number, were extremely tiresome. Because of this, sleep was impossible. Many of the officials' belongings were gnawed by rats.... We were all dirty and there were no washing facilities.... The Jews give a watch or two in exchange for a loaf of bread.' A colleague of Mihăescu described the scene on his arrival at the camp: 'I found there thousands of deportees who were living in a state of indescribable misery. The corpses of the deportees were laying everywhere, in cellars, in ditches, in courtyards.'[29] Antonescu himself recognized the scale of Jewish dead. Reacting to a claim in November from one of his ministers that all the Jews had left Iaşi, the Marshal retorted: 'The Yids have not yet left Iaşi. I have enough problems with those I drove to the river Bug. Only I know how many died en route.'[30]

Antonescu's responsibility for the deportations and their consequences is evident from his remarks at a meeting of the Council for Supply on 6 October 1941:

As regards the Jews, I have taken measures to remove them entirely and once and for all from these regions [Bessarabia and Bukovina]. The measure is being applied. I still have in Bessarabia approximately 40,000 Jews, who in a few days will be driven across the Dniester, and, if circumstances permit, *they will be driven beyond the Urals*. (my emphasis)[31]

Deportation, he emphasized yet again, was the instrument of ethnic purification:

As regards commerce, it is beyond dispute that we must start from the beginning, because I have excluded the Yids and slowly, slowly I am driving out the other foreigners as well, apart from those who have long had business there. But my tendency is to carry out a policy of purification of the Romanian race, and I will not give way before any obstacle in achieving this historical goal of our nation. If we do not take advantage of the situation which presents itself today on the international and European level in order to purify the Romanian nation, we shall miss the last chance that history offers us. And I do not wish to miss it, because if I do so future generations will blame me. I can get back Bessarabia and Transylvania, but if I do not purify the Romanian nation then I have achieved nothing, for it is not frontiers that consolidate a nation, but the homogeneity and purity of its race. And that is my principal goal.[32]

At the local level in Bessarabia, Meculescu, after dealing with Vertujeni, turned his attention to the deportation of Jews from the Chişinău ghetto and the other ghettos in southern Bessarabia, submitting his proposals to Topor and Voiculescu for approval. On 10 October, he issued orders to the gendarmerie. The crossing points for the Chişinău ghetto were Rezina to

Râbnița to the north, and Tighina to Tiraspol to the south. Once over the Dniester, the Jews would become the responsibility of the Transnistrian gendarmerie.

In Bukovina the Governor, General Cornel Calotescu, acted on orders received through Topor's delegate, Lt.-Col. Petrescu. In a subsequent report on the deportations for Antonescu, Calotescu pointed out that he did not see a copy of the deportation order even though he requested one, but that he had merely been informed by Topor's delegate that 'on the Marshal's orders all Jews in Bukovina would be evacuated to Transnistria in ten days'. The deportations began in the south of the province (in Suceava, Campulung and Radauti) between 10 and 15 October. A programme was drawn up by Calotescu for the Jews in the provincial capital Cernăuți to be assembled in a ghetto on 11 October, prior to deportation.[33] This operation involved the herding of about 50,000 Jews into a small area of the town which, according to its mayor Traian Popovici, could house a maximum of 15,000 persons. Popovici recorded in a memorandum the details of the deportations, which commenced on 13 October. Between this date and 15 November, when the deportations were suspended because of the bad weather and, it appears, a shortage of freight cars, 28,391 Jews were deported to Transnistria in 14 trains supervised by the gendarmerie. In addition, 395 Jews identified as Communists or considered undesirable were deported.[34]

According to Popovici, Calotescu ordered that before deportation the Jews should go through a screening process; between 15,000 and 20,000 were to be selected 'for their usefulness to the Romanian state'. Mihai Antonescu had been advised of the damage that the deportation of the Jews was causing to the economy and so he laid down guidelines for the exemption of those vital to the national interest. Calotescu charged the army and the mayor's office with setting up a selection committee to issue permits to those chosen to remain in Cernăuți. Initially, they were given four days in which to carry out this complicated procedure 'for fear', Popovici wrote, 'that the trains, provided for the evacuation of the Jews to Transnistria, might be given another purpose and therefore we would be placed in the situation of not being able to proceed with the evacuation of the Jews'. An ad hoc committee of Jews was set up on Popovici's orders to provide a list of all the Jews remaining in the ghetto according to their skills, and this list was submitted to Calotescu who, in discussion with Popovici and the military commander of Cernăuți, General C. Ionescu, decided on the percentage of each professional category of Jews who should remain. In fact, many Jews entered their names under more than one category as a hedge against deportation, and consequently received multiple permits, which then found their way into the hands of those with similar names. Faced with this situation, the committee set about verifying whether the recipients of permits were entitled to them, an exercise which took 18 days. As a result, 16,569 Jews received authorization to remain in Cernăuți.[35]

Details of the manner in which the deportation was carried out in Dorohoi were provided by a lawyer, Constantin Muşat, who was commissioned by the Federation of Jewish Communities under Filderman, to carry out an enquiry.[36] By placing Muşat's report alongside the official account, given by the county prefect, Colonel Ion Bărcan, a comprehensive picture of events can be drawn.[37] On 5 November, the prefect had been handed a deportation order from Calotescu, issued on 28 October, by Lt.-Col. Petrescu. The order set out the conditions under which the deportations were to take place, with guidelines as to who was to be exempted. These guidelines had been drawn up by Mihai Antonescu, who ordered that 'property owners, industrialists, traders, craftsmen and intellectuals vital to the national economy as well as public officials and public service pensioners should not be deported'.[38] The pensioners included war veterans and their families. A selection committee was set up to determine who would be deported according to these guidelines, but the guidelines were not respected.[39]

As the prefect admitted, 'in spite of the rigour of the selection, exceptions to the norm which we followed crept in ... we could not exempt all those who had fought in the war of 1916–1918 (there were none from 1877), since these together with their families represented more than two-thirds of the total number of Jews and thus the deportation would have been rendered almost pointless'.[40] Muşat presented a different story; the selection was far from rigorous, on the contrary it was done 'in a completely arbitrary fashion, with no objective criterion ... because certain people had a decisive influence with the committee and paid sums ranging from 200,000 to one million lei, or gave valuables such as astrakhan coats and jewels in order to obtain a provisional authorization [for exemption], which was cancelled within twenty-four hours'.[41] The sick, the old, invalids, young children, war veterans and war widows were swept up in the operation, which began on 7 November.

The first Jews deported were those who had gathered in the town of Dorohoi from Darabani and Rădăuţi. They hired carts to take them and their belongings to the station where they were searched by gendarmes and had fabrics and leather goods they were carrying confiscated. The prefect confirmed the search, but denied claims that clothing was confiscated; 'the only food confiscated was that considered to be surplus and considered to be hoarded'.[42] Carpets, cushions and mattresses were also confiscated on the grounds that, on arrival at Atachi on the River Dniester, the deportees would be taken from the train and driven in columns on foot to Transnistria. On previous occasions when other deportees reached the Dniester, they had had heavy baggage with them, which had to be left in the station at Atachi and Mărculeşti.[43]

The Jews were herded into freight cars. 'No more than fifty were put in each car', the prefect wrote, 'since there was no space for any more, while the doors to the cars were locked on only one side of the train, the doors on the other side being left unlocked so that the guard escort could inspect the cars more easily when the trains stopped in stations'.[44] In the second train, which left on 8 November, were Jews from Săveni and Mihaileni. Four days later, the deportation of the local Jews from Dorohoi itself began. Their houses were sealed by officials from the town hall with a notice that read: 'state property, whoever disturbs it will be shot on sight'.[45] On 14 November, the last third of the Jews in Dorohoi town were ordered to the station but were sent back to their homes after being told that an order suspending their deportation had been given 'due to a lack of freight cars'.[46] Some 6,000 Jews were deported from Darabani, Rădăuţi, Săveni and Mihaileni, and about 3,000 from Dorohoi town. At the time of his enquiry – the end of November – Muşat stated that 2,500 Jews were left in Dorohoi.[47]

The Israeli writer Aharon Appelfeld recalled his experience of deportation from Bukovina at this time in a memoir of a journey in 1998, which took him back to the places of his childhood:

From Czernowitz we travelled to the great cemetery of the Jews in Bukovina – a cemetery that extends along the Dniester and Bug rivers and is called Transnistria. Here, during the war, the Jews of Bukovina and Bessarabia were brought in trains and on forced marches. They were dispersed across this broad plain – some to labor camps, some to ghettos, and some to extermination camps. In 1941, death was not yet industrialized, and any means of killing was used. My father and I were on a forced march that began with two hundred people and ended with thirty. I tried to describe that march in one of my journals: For days now we have been trudging through roads of deep mud, a long convoy, surrounded by Romanian soldiers and Ukrainian irregulars who slash us with whips and shoot. Father holds my hand very tightly. My short legs don't touch the ground any more. The chill of the mud cuts my hips. Darkness is all around, except for Father's hand. I don't feel anything, actually, not even his hand. My hand is already partly paralyzed. I know only a slight movement, and I'll drown. Not even Father can save me. Many children have already drowned that way.

At night, when the convoy stops, Father fishes me out of the mud and wipes my feet with his coat. I lost my shoes long ago, and I sink my frozen feet in the lining of his coat for a moment. The tiny bit of heat hurts so much that I quickly withdraw my feet. That rapid movement, for some reason, makes Father angry, and I burst into tears. Father consoles me and says that now we mustn't indulge ourselves. Mother used to use the word 'indulge' a lot, but now it sounds strange, as though Father or I were mistaken. I don't let go of his hand and fall asleep. Not for long.

While the sky is still dark, the soldiers wake up the convoy with whips and shots. Father carries me on his shoulders, and when the whip strikes him, he sets me on my feet and drags me. The mud is deep, and I can't feel solid ground. It hurts me, I cry. Father responds immediately: make things easier for me, easier. I have heard those words more than once here. After those words a fall was heard, a cry, a vain effort to save the drowning child. Not only children drown. Even tall people fall to their knees and drown. In the autumn the water rises, and the road is a deep bog. Father can no longer carry his rucksack and drag me along at the same time. He opens the rucksack and throws some of the clothes into the mud. Now his hand holds me very tightly. At night when the convoy halts, he rubs and massages my arms and legs and dries them with the lining of his coat. For a moment it seems to me that not only Father is with me but also Mother, whom I loved so much.[48]

To add to the misery of the deportation, women were deported from the county of Dorohoi whose husbands – about 1,000 in number – had been pressed by the army into labour battalions in August 1941 and were away performing compulsory labour in other parts of Romania.[49] The women were told that their husbands would follow them and had therefore left with their children, albeit with great reluctance. Without support from the husbands, these families found it difficult to survive starvation and disease. For this reason, the death rate among all Jews deported to Transnistria was highest among those removed from Dorohoi. On their return from labour duties at the beginning of December, the men found their families deported and their houses sealed. They petitioned Marshal Antonescu to bring their families back, and some of them even asked for permission to be sent to Transnistria in order to support their women and children. The Marshal passed on their requests to Radu Lecca, the man appointed to deal with Jewish affairs in Mihai Antonescu's office, and Lecca raised the matter with Mihai. Mihai said that the repatriation of the Jews from Dorohoi was impossible since the area in the meantime had been incorporated administratively into Bukovina whose governor, General Cornel Calotescu, having deported most of the Jews of the province, was opposed to repatriation.[50] Furthermore, the army, in its need for labour, refused to allow the men to move to Transnistria and in many cases the suspension of deportation meant that they had to remain in Dorohoi.[51]

Cases of American citizens who were victims of violence or deportation came to the US Legation's attention.[52] On 3 November, the Legation received a telegram from Jacob Hernes (Harnis) in Moghilev. He was an American citizen who, with his non-American wife and American son, had been evacuated from Vascăuţi, Bucovina. He was already well known in the Legation because he was a paralytic invalid and had had a lengthy correspondence with the Legation earlier in the year because during the Soviet occupation of Bukovina he had sent his American passport to the American Embassy in Moscow. With the outbreak of the war he had contacted the American

Legation in Bucharest requesting that they issue him the appropriate documents. A note was prepared the following day, 4 November, urging the Foreign Ministry to effect his immediate return in view of his status as an American citizen and his precarious health. Shortly thereafter a third family with American citizens was identified as being in Transnistria. A registered letter dated 17 October from the Legation had been sent to the Goth family in Cernăuţi; the mother, Ida Goth, and her daughter, Sofie, were both American citizens. The letter was subsequently returned to the Legation with a note to the effect that the addressee was in a ghetto and could not be found.[53]

One can only speculate how such frustrations may have contributed to the premature death on 22 December 1941, of the American minister in Bucharest Franklin Mott Gunther. He was 56 and had been suffering from acute leukaemia.[54] He had consistently drawn his Secretary of State's attention to the measures taken against the Jews prior to and after the outbreak of war on the Eastern Front and had vigorously conveyed his government's concern and horror to Romanian officials. Gunther had made this clear in a memorandum of 15 November to Cordell Hull:

> As you know, I have constantly and persistently held before the attention of the highest Rumanian officials the inevitable reaction of my Government and the American people to such inhuman treatment and even outright slaughter, of innocent and defenseless people, citing at length the atrocities committed against the Jews of Romania.[55]

On 10 December 1941, Antonescu's office informed the governors of Bessarabia, Bukovina and Bessarabia of his decision to call a temporary halt to the deportations until the spring.[56] On the same day, Antonescu gave his permission for aid in the form of money and medicines – and later, clothing – to be sent to the deportees in Transnistria.[57] A commission set up by Antonescu to investigate the conduct of deportations from Bukovina found that at the end of January 1942 there were 21,626 Jews left in Cernăuţi, of whom 16,391 had permits, 235 were Communist suspects awaiting deportation and around 5,000 had remained illegally.[58] At the end of March 1942, Antonescu approved a request from Governor Voiculescu of Bessarabia that 425 Jews who were left in ghettos in the province or had been left free 'according to orders from above' be sent to Transnistria by train.[59] Shortly afterwards, Antonescu ordered the resumption of deportation from Bukovina. Governor Calotescu submitted progress reports to the Marshal. One, dated 12 June, gave the number of Jews 'evacuated' from the city of Cernăuţi on 8 June as 1,705 (619 males, 691 females and 395 children) and those from Dorohoi on 11 June as 308 (176 males, 70 females and 62 children). The criteria for deportation from Cernăuţi was that 'undesirables', 'suspect persons' and 'those that had had authorizations with a stripe' (i.e. authorizations issued by Popovici's commission) should be the first to be removed. Two hundred and fifty deportation teams were constituted, made up of a government official, a junior gendarme and a police officer, who took the Jews to an assembly point set up by the army from which they were taken to a deportation zone codenamed 'Macabi'. The operation began at 4 am and at 9.30 am all the deported Jews were in the zone. There the Romanian currency they had was changed into *Reichskreditkassenschein*, the currency in circulation in Transnistria, at the rate of 60 lei to one RKKS. At the same time, the Jews were obliged to cash in their valuables for RKKS. A body search of the Jews then followed, and any lei or valuables found were confiscated. Calotescu's report stated that every Jew from Cernăuți was given bread sufficient for three days and then put in a train for Moghilev.[60]

A balance sheet of the progress of deportation, provided at Antonescu's request by Governor Voiculescu on 21 August 1942, reported that 55,867 Jews from Bessarabia had been deported to Transnistria, and 45,867 Jews from Bukovina, via Bessarabia. Following the resumption of deportation in May 1942, a total of 231 Jews had been deported from Bessarabia.[61] On the same day, Governor Calotescu informed Antonescu's office that during July 4,094 Jews had been deported from Bukovina and that a further 19,475 remained to be deported. He proposed to deport all of the latter, except those assigned to compulsory labour and those exempt under orders given previously. This left 6,234 Jews to be deported from Cernăuți, and 592 from the town of Dorohoi. Their deportation was planned for October.[62]

The mechanism of deportation had involved Traian Popovici, the mayor of Cernăuți. His role in the selection committee racked his conscience. While more than 28,000 Jews were deported from Cernăuți in October and November 1941, his committee issued permits for more 16,000 to remain, according to the criteria communicated to him by Governer Calotescu. When the deportations of Jews resumed in May 1942 after their suspension in mid-November, Popovici was deeply troubled. More than 4,000 Jews were sent to Transnistria in July. At the height of these fresh deportations Popovici wrote a memorandum dated 14 July 1942 in which he criticized the reasoning behind them and the manner in which they were conducted. The references in the memorandum to the Marshal in the third person indicate that it was addressed not to him but perhaps to Mihai Antonescu. It is not clear, however, whether it reached either man.

Popovici could not rely on philo-Semitic arguments, even if he wanted to. He had to appeal to the Antonescu regime in its own rhetoric. Hence he did not deny the existence of 'the Jewish problem', but focused entirely on the method of dealing with it:

> With profound regret, however, the operations for deportation which have been carried out since then, namely those of last autumn and those of June of this year, which have not come to an end even now, have been conducted in the most profoundly negative and arbitrary manner

possible. For example, all the Jews without exception have been deported from southern Bukovina, that is, from a territory which had not been occupied [by the Soviets] and in which, therefore, the Jews could not have shown hostility towards our armies in retreat. Not one craftsman or self-employed person has been left in the towns of Suceava, Câmpulung, Vatra Dornei, Gura Humorului, Solca and Rădăuţi, with the result that in the meantime it was necessary to bring back some of these Jewish craftsmen. In northern Bukovina the deportations were carried out in such an arbitrary and negative manner that...they catered foremost to the insatiable appetite for enrichment of the those carrying them out and their intermediaries, without any consideration for the catastrophic consequences and incalculable repercussions which such methods can have on our national, economic and moral interests [while provoking] in the hearts of the Romanian population in Bukovina the most profound pain and inexplicable sorrow.

Through these methods, unfamiliar in civilized countries, and totally alien to the spiritual structure of the Romanian people in this province, which has been brought up over the last 150 years to respect the law and in the most profound public morality...the Romanians have been condemned to witness how hundreds and thousands of Jews, most of them personal acquaintances alongside whom they had lived their whole lives, were led through the streets of Cernăuţi on Sunday mornings, while the church bells were ringing the summons to the holy mass, in convoys flanked by armed police and soldiers, carrying on their backs their entire fortune, calling out and shouting in their pitiful desperation...

...

All this [misery] could have been avoided, and in addition an incomparably more respectable result from all points of view achieved – even a complete solution by now to the entire Jewish problem – if European methods had been applied.

What is important for us Romanians as regards the solution of this problem is our prising ourselves away from the economic claws of the Jews, and if there is a way of meeting this objective in a more perfect manner by legal, civilized means, [then] it is not in our national interest to show to the world that we are opposed in principle to applying methods in keeping with the level of culture of more civilized countries.

He then attacked the abuses and the irrationality of the deportations:

The profoundly reprehensible methods described above have completely stripped the entire Jewish population of their fortunes valued in millions. Although this money was supposed to enter the state's coffers, almost all of it has been plundered by those involved in the deportations. The Jews have been insulted because as a result of these methods, useful, irre-proachable persons, well known for their loyalty, have been deported, old women over seventy, the sick and the disabled, pregnant women and the mentally ill. On the other hand, enemies of the state, proven Communists and other dangerous persons, have been kept here because fabulous sums were paid, up to one million lei for every Jew to be spared deportation...

Romania's international reputation and its 'national dignity 'had suffered enormous damage' because

those deported, once they had reached their destination, had been exposed to the most unimaginable torments and in some cases, since not even the most rudimentary shelter had been prepared for them, had been left in the middle of winter, up until 20 December, under the open sky. This had happened in Bershad in Balta county. On average between 60 per cent and 70 per cent of the deportees had perished because of this – in Balta even 85 per cent – and along with them, our importance as a civilizing factor in South-Eastern Europe, had perished as well in an extremely painful manner.

Those carrying out the deportations had been driven by 'principles of the cruellest barbarity':

Owing to all these principles by which the executors of the Marshal's order had been guided, the solution to the Jewish problem in Romania, this great act of historical importance, the most important act of govern-ment of the present regime, this act, which was destined to be the basis of the revival our entire life as a state, this act, which could stand for centuries as an act of permanent national pride, has turned out to be an act of the basest wickedness, an act of eternal shame, which has all the ingredients to expose us, perhaps for ever, to the contempt and hatred of the whole of mankind.

Popovici was certain that Antonescu was unaware of the enormities being committed in his name:

It is an extremely grave matter, a matter of such enormous gravity that it cannot fail to be brought to the knowledge of the Marshal who, quite apart from the fact that he would undoubtedly disapprove, given the force of his personality, in the most resolute way of the use of these Asiatic methods, will certainly strive by immediate and categorical means to make certain amends and to remove, at least in part, the horrible stain of shame and decadence which a handful of irresponsible and criminal figures have applied to the cheeks of our entire nation.

Although Popovici had requested an audience with the Marshal in October 1941 to bring these abuses to his attention, he had not been received. Undeterred, he had drawn up a memorandum for Antonescu detailing the conduct of the deportations from Cernăuți, but this, too, had not had any effect since, Popovici concluded, such memoranda 'were destined not to always reach his excellency [the Marshal]'.

> The application of the above-mentioned measures, and especially those of a purely Bolshevik character, which are an affront to our religious sentiment, have already created an intolerable atmosphere in Bukovina, a spiritual environment most hostile to the maintenance of public order. I personally have witnessed at least twenty times acts of wild aggression perpetrated in broad daylight, in the centre of Cernăuți, by people on the street against innocent, educated Jews, former senior magistrates, doctors, lawyers. Steps must be taken with the utmost urgency, since the present situation in Bukovina differs in no degree from that in the Soviet Union and therefore completely undermines the point of our present war which we are conducting alongside our allies, the point of 'The Holy War' against the heathen Bolsheviks.

Popovici's anger was roused not against deportation *per se*, but against the inhuman manner in which it was carried out and the damage that it was causing the economy:

> By reducing the number of Jews through arbitrary deportation *over the limit imposed by our economic needs* [my emphasis] we put at risk any chance of economic recovery for this sorely-tried province.

Antonescu had been made aware by the army general staff at the end of November 1941 of the massive disruption to commerce and light industry caused by the deportations in Bessarabia and Bukovina. To rectify the situation he approved the granting of state credits to Romanians who wanted to go into business in these provinces, and the setting-up of cooperatives in villages, but at the same time he made it clear that members of minority ethnic groups should be prevented 'from infiltrating themselves into the economy of the villages and the re-conquered provinces'. This last measure was to be 'applied with complete discretion, but also with great determination'.[63]

Popovici, too, pointed to the economic damage caused by the deportation of the Jews but proposed a different solution: the return of some of the deportees 'in order to reinvigorate' the economy. He concluded his petition by calling for the respect of the pension rights of Jews who had been in public service and of Jewish war veterans; for the 'severest punishment' of public bodies who had made a profit out of the deportations; for the removal of those in illegal occupation of the homes and apartments of deported Jews who were paying 'derisory' rents for them to the town hall; and finally, rather insensitively, for the sale through public auction of possessions handed over by the Jews in order to raise money for Romanian refugees who had lost their belongings during the Soviet occupation of Bukovina.[64]

Three months after Popovici's July 1942 petition, the Marshal reversed his decision on deportation.[65]

8

Transnistria: The Fate of the Jews and Romas

Transnistria was set up in consequence of successful military operations beyond the Dniester in summer 1941 and lost when it became untenable in early 1944. Between those dates Romanian officials administered the area and were responsible for the native Ukrainian Jews and the Romanian Jews deported there.[1]

Aware of Antonescu's wishes regarding the return of northern Transylvania, on 27 July 1941 Hitler first dangled the prospect of Ukrainian territory southwest of the Bug before the Romanian leader, inviting him to assume responsibility for the region to the south-west of the Bug. As Romanian troops marched on Odessa, Hitler wrote again to Antonescu on 14 August, proposing that the Romanian leader take over the entire area between the Dniester and the Dnieper. Three days later, Antonescu explained that, since he lacked 'the means and trained staff', he could assume responsibility for the administration of the territory between the Dniester and the Bug only; for the remaining area – between the Bug and the Dnieper – he would be willing to supply troops for security. At the same time, Antonescu asked Hitler to specify the rights and duties of a Romanian administration in what would become Transnistria.[2]

Following this correspondence, Romanian and German commands signed an agreement at Tiraspol on 19 August which allowed Antonescu to establish a Romanian occupation government 'in the occupied territory between the Dniester and the Bug, with the exception of the region of Odessa'.[3] The agreement was consolidated by a convention signed on 30 August at Tighina, Bessarabia, giving the Germans control of the main railway lines and the port facilities of Odessa which were vital to supplying their armies in the east, but leaving almost everything else to the Romanians. Hitler acceded to Antonescu's request that the northern border of Transnistria, which had not been stipulated in the convention, be drawn to include the towns of Moghilev, Zhmerinka and Tulcin. The borders were recognized in a German order of 4 September establishing a boundary separating Transnistria from the German Army Group South Rear, and stipulating what persons and goods were to be permitted across in either direction.[4] On 17 October, the day after the fall of Odessa, Antonescu officially decreed the creation of Transnistria with Odessa as its capital.[5]

The new territorial entity created in these agreements encompassed a swathe of territory beginning on the eastern shore of the Dniester and extending to the Bug, which emptied just across from Mykolaiv. It was bounded in the south by the Black Sea and in the north by the River Liadova and covered some 40,000 sq. km. Unlike Bukovina or Bessarabia, Transnistria, which means 'beyond the Dniester', had no historical pedigree as a separate administrative entity;[6] it had never been ruled by Romanians and in the population, put at two and a half millions in the Soviet census of 1926, the Romanian element amounted to just over 10 per cent (290,000).[7] The majority of its inhabitants were Ukrainians and Russians, but among the Slavic majority, there also lived 125,000 Germans, and 300,000 Jews.[8]

It should be emphasized that no mention was made in the Tighina convention of annexing or incorporating Transnistria into Romania, despite periodic exhortations from Hitler to Antonescu to do so.[9] Antonescu's principal reason for not wishing to annex Transnistria also stemmed from a desire to restore the *status quo ante* the summer of 1940, which would see the return to Romania of all the territories annexed by foreign powers during 1940 – not only Bessarabia and northern Bukovina, but northern Transylvania as well. He made this clear in talks with Hitler held on 11 February 1942 when he told the German leader that he did not regard the 1940 Vienna Award as definitive and that, whatever the German position, he would seek to reverse it.[10] A second reason for Antonescu's unwillingness to annex Transnistria derived from his view of the anti-Soviet war as a defensive war, one undertaken in order to neutralize the threat of Soviet Bolshevism to Romania. In Antonescu's view, annexing Transnistria would have only served to rub salt into the wounds of the Russians and intensify Russia's undying enmity.[11]

Antonescu's decree of 19 August established the government of Transnistria and set the tasks of the administration.[12] These were to supervise the resumption of economic activity, particularly agriculture and the transportation system; to set up a local police force under the supervision of the Romanian gendarmerie; and to open schools and churches. To run Transnistria, Antonescu appointed Governor Gheorghe Alexianu, a professor of administrative law at Cernăuți University and a close friend of Mihai Antonescu, who as Romanian Foreign Minister and Vice Premier was second only to Marshal Antonescu in authority in Romania.[13] Alexianu held the office until 27 January 1944.[14] Described in some sources as a 'Western-type intellectual', Alexianu had in fact been the sponsor of the anti-Semitic measures adopted by the government of Octavian Goga between December 1937 and February 1938.[15] Until December 1942, Alexianu maintained his headquarters in Tiraspol.[16] Afterwards, he moved to Odessa, where the renovated Vorontsov Palace was used both as residence and seat of government. The governor's staff consisted of a series of Directorates, responsible for the various fields of administration, agriculture, industry, education, finance and transportation. A large number of Russian-speaking Bessarabians were brought into the government to improve communication with the local population, as well as young Romanians, lured by exemption from the military draft and a salary double that of a similar post in Romania plus a subsistence allowance commensurate with the basic salary.[17]

Transnistria was divided into 13 districts, each called *judeţ* as in Romania, which were headed by a prefect who had to be Romanian and was typically an army officer. The sub-prefect was a local. The districts in turn were divided into rayons (*raioane*), as under the Soviets. Each of the 64 rayons was run by a praetor, appointed by the prefect, who was a Romanian civil servant or an officer. They were assisted by former Soviet officials. The chief civil officer in the town was the mayor (*primar*) who, except in the case of Odessa and Tiraspol, was responsible to the praetor. The mayors of the two principal towns were directly responsible to the governor. The professional competence of these officials is a matter of dispute. A German officer who accompanied Marshal Antonescu on an inspection trip through Transnistria in 1942 commented: 'Most of the prefects are meritorious colonels and make a good impression. Most of the praetors seem to be usable. The overwhelming majority of mayors, especially in the small localities, on the other hand, are indolent, inexperienced Ukrainians of limited intelligence.'[18]

The status of the 130,000 ethnic Germans in Transnistria was regulated by an agreement negotiation by Mihai Antonescu and Manfred von Killinger, the German minister to Romania, on 14 and 15 November 1941. Under its terms, the German villages – 228 in number – were placed under the authority of the *Volksdeutsche Mittelstelle* (Ethnic German Liaison Office) whose head was SS *Oberführer* (Colonel) Horst Hoffmeyer. It was Hoffmeyer who nominated the heads of the German settlements subject to their approval by the respective Romanian prefect.[19]

At the time of the establishment of Romanian rule, Antonescu set up 'The Romanian Orthodox Mission in Transnistria' (*Misiunea Ortodoxă Română*) with the express purpose of restoring organized worship in the Orthodox faith to the area.[20] The first head of the mission was archimandrite Iuliu Scriban, who was appointed on 15 August 1941.[21] Many of the majority Ukrainian population, denied the possibility of practising their Orthodox faith under Soviet rule, appear to have welcomed this initiative. Some 250 Romanian priests were sent to Transnistria to assist 219 local priests. By 1943, several hundred churches had been reopened and religious education reintroduced into schools. Two seminaries were opened, one at Dubăsari and the other at Odessa, where a cantors' school was also established.[22] These achievements were short-lived because of the precariousness of the military situation at the close of 1943. Metropolitan Visarion Puiu, the head of the mission, sent a request to the Marshal on 1 December to be allowed to return to the monastery of Neamţ on the grounds that the evacuation of the province was being prepared, that there was a shortage of trained clergy and that there was a lack of funds. In his candid letter to the Marshal the metropolitan complained that he had waited six months to receive a printing press and expressed his 'profound disgust at the chicanery and delays faced by the mission in attempting to acquire the necessary paper'.[23] His request was granted.[24]

The Romanian administration of the new province was marked by corruption, capriciousness and incompetence. This Romanian laxity contrasted sharply with the industry and organization of the Germans and their thoroughgoing methods in the *Reichskommissariat* Ukraine. But the bribery and speculation that Romanian laxity engendered gave the region's inhabitants a measure of private enterprise and personal initiative. If the first period of occupation, extending from October 1941 to the spring of 1942, was distinguished by chaos; the second, lasting from spring 1942 until the winter of 1943, saw a period of relative calm and stability in which the economic life of the province was partially restored and, according to one study, brought an improvement in living conditions for the population in comparison with the privations of Soviet rule.[25] As a result, Romanian occupation came to have contradictory meanings to the local population.

For non-Jews, Romanian rule seemed less draconian and considerably more benevolent than German rule in other parts of Soviet territory, or Russian rule. This relative improvement in the standard of living for the non-Jews – greater abundance of food and the lower unemployment – came at the price of the eradication of the local Jews. After the winter of 1943, this sense of well-being was punctured as the Romanians began to prepare for withdrawal in the face the Soviet army's advance westward.

Whilst unwilling to consider annexation of the territory Antonescu did give some idea of his thinking on the future of Transnistria under Romanian rule in December 1941. At a Council of Ministers' meeting attended by Alexianu, he questioned the governor on the situation there:

> *Prof. G. Alexianu*: The situation in Transnistria is very good. Order there is perfect. We, Marshal, are there in the idea that we will rule this province for ever.
>
> *Marshal Antonescu*: That is, the Romanian nation will keep it.
>
> *Prof. G. Alexianu*: That depends solely on you.
>
> *Marshal Antonescu*: It does not depend just on me, but on the whole of Romania. You should work there as though Romania had installed itself in those territories for two million years. What might happen afterwards we shall see!
>
> *Prof. G. Alexianu*: That is just what I wanted to hear from you.
>
> *Marshal Antonescu*: I told you that I can make no political declaration regarding Transnistria.

Prof. G. Alexianu: Everyone knows that they have to work as though everything was permanent between the Bug and the Dniester.

Marshal Antonescu: For the time being you should what is necessary on the Dniester, you should work there as though you were working for millions of years. Do not expect us to make declarations in this regard, because we should not have to make them.

Prof. G. Alexianu: We are discussing it here.

Marshal Antonescu: If I tell you that very many people come and raise the question of permanency [in Transnistria].

Prof. G. Alexianu: That is also the general feeling of the local population.

Marshal Antonescu: Do you think that people who have made history have discussed it with people on the street when making it? History is not made on the streets. The people on the streets are the beneficiaries and we need not be influenced by what they say.

Prof. G. Alexianu: I want to assure you that, as regards agriculture, every effort possible is being made. The agronomists who have arrived here are working flat out. We are, it is true, rather backward as regards agriculture, but we continue to sow seed even now and to produce beetroot of good quality.

Marshal Antonescu: But is the population helping with the work on the land?

Prof. G. Alexianu: I am not happy with their assistance. This population was used to being forced to work under the whip. The moment they saw that they were not driven away and that they had sufficient food, they did not turn up for work. We realized that we too were in the same situation and that we had to force them to work. We forced them and now they have begun to work because we need them. I asked you in a report allow us to amend the administration in Transnistria as regards the gendarmerie. We really need the gendarmerie and the army to force the population to work.[26] When you took the decision in August the army was tied up at Odessa. Now we have troops in Transnistria who are there for no reason. I am in complete agreement with the army and there exists the closest harmony between us.[27]

For the Jews and Romas, however, Transnistria was for much of the period of Romanian rule synonymous with terror and death. Even before the area was placed under Romanian administration, an unknown number of Jews there had been murdered by troops of the *Einsatzgruppe D*. In compliance with the terms of the Tighina convention, most of *Einsatzgruppe D* soon moved beyond Transnistria, with the *Einsatzgruppe* units, *Sonderkommando 11a* and *Einsatzkommando 12* taking up their murderous activity in Mykolaiv on 14 September. *Sonderkommando 11b* remained, laying in wait outside of Odessa in anticipation of the city's fall. The exact number of Jews murdered in the province by the commandos remains unknown, but it certainly ran into many thousands.[28] Calculations based on reports of the gendarmerie and other official Romanian documents indicate that approximately 45,000 Jews survived the first wave of slaughter by *Einsatzgruppe D* in the northern and central districts of Transnistria, a further 45,000 in the districts of southern Transnistria, and almost 100,000 in Odessa.[29]

Under Antonescu, Transnistria was the graveyard of an estimated figure of 220,000–260,000 Jews, and up to 20,000 Romas.[30] Most of these deaths resulted from inhumane treatment and a callous disregard for life rather than from industrialized killing. The forced marches of Jewish deportees – including young, old and sick – to the eastern extremity of Transnistria with the intention of driving them across the Bug into German hands, the murder by Romanian and Ukrainian guards of those unable to keep up with the columns, the massacre by the Germans of those who did cross, the eventual refusal in late summer 1941 by the Germans to accept any more for fear of spreading typhus, the consequent herding of Jews into makeshift camps without adequate food or health care, these actions resulted in the initial wave of deaths through malnutrition and disease in the autumn and winter of 1941. The toll increased dramatically with the murder by shooting of thousands of Jews in Transnistria in December 1941 and January 1942 on the orders of the Romanian authorities there. Later, several thousand Jews were shot in 1942 and 1943, largely by SS units in south-eastern part of the province who were aided by the German minority there.

The massacres in Odessa, October 1941

On 18 October 1941, two days after the fall of Odessa, General Constantin Trestioreanu, deputy commander of the city, issued the order for the creation of a provisional ghetto for the city's Jews in preparation for their deportation to the east.[31] The central point of the ghetto was Odessa prison. Within ten days a total of 16,258 Jews of all ages had been interned in the area around the jail.[32] For Antonescu urgency in completing the operation was given by the destruction of the Romanian headquarters in the city. On the evening of 22 October 1941, the former NKVD headquarters in Odessa on Engels Street, where General Ioan Glogojanu, the Romanian military commander of the city had set up his base, was blown up by Soviet agents. Romanian records show that there were 61 victims, including General Glogojanu, 16 officers, 35 soldiers and 9 civilians. Four German naval officers and two interpreters were also among the dead. No trial of the suspects was considered; Antonescu went straight ahead and ordered swift and indiscriminate reprisals:

a) For every Romanian and German officer killed in the explosion, 200 communists were to be hanged; for every soldier, 100 communists; the executions will take place today; b) all the Communists in Odessa will be taken hostage; similarly, one member of each family of Jews. They will be informed of the reprisals ordered as a result of the act of terrorism and will be warned, they and their families, that if a second similar act takes place they will all be executed.[33]

The order was transmitted to the military authorities in Odessa during the early morning of 23 October, and over the next 48 hours several hundred Jews and Communists – one source puts the number at 417[34] – were hanged or shot.[35] In addition, many thousands of Jews were force-marched to Dalnyk, a few kilometres outside the city. On the intervention of Odessa's mayor, Gherman Pântea, and the acting military commander, General Nicolae Macici, the column was sent back to Odessa, but not before those Jews at the head of the column were herded into four large sheds and machine-gunned to death, after which the sheds were set on fire. How many Jews were killed in this way is not known, but a figure of 20,000 was mentioned at Macici's trial in May 1945. This is close to the figure in a German officer's report that 'on the morning of the 23 October, about 19,000 Jews were shot on a square in the port, surrounded by a wooden fence. Their corpses were doused with gasoline and burned.'[36]

Those in authority in Odessa at the time the reprisals were carried out were tried as war criminals in Bucharest in May 1945. Each tried to pin the blame for the massacres on the other.[37] Despite the evidence presented that Macici had been sent to Odessa by his superior, General Ion Iacobici, commander of the Romanian 4th Army, immediately after Iacobici had received Antonescu's order for reprisals, Macici denied that he was responsible for carrying it out, pointing out that it was General Constantin Trestioreanu, deputy commander of Odessa, who had reported to Antonescu that the order to take reprisals had been implemented. In answer to the charge that he had done nothing to stop the massacres, Macici replied that General Iacobici had been aware of what was happening in the city and had issued no orders to stop the reprisals. On 22 May 1945, Macici and Trestioreanu were among a group of 29 officers sentenced to death for war crimes; a further eight were sentenced to various terms of imprisonment.[38]

It was only in a Council of Ministers meeting of 13 November that Antonescu referred to these events in Odessa. Addressing Alexianu, the governor of Transnistria, he asked:

Antonescu: Was the repression severe enough?

Alexianu: It was, Marshal.

Antonescu: What do you understand by 'severe enough'? You are rather soft on others but not on the Romanian nation.

Alexianu: It was very severe, Marshal.

Antonescu: I said that 200 Jews should be shot for every person killed and 100 Jews for every person wounded. Was that what was done?

Alexianu: They were both shot and hanged on the streets of Odessa.

Antonescu: That's how you should act, because I am responsible before the country and history. Let the Jews come from America and hold me responsible! I will not allow, however, the confiscation of the Jews' wealth. The Jews should not be handled with kid gloves because they, if they could, would not treat us in that way, nor you, nor the others present here. My point of departure was the idea that, if no Romanian would kill me, no one will kill me. That's why I am not letting up on the Jews. Don't think that they will not exact revenge when they can. But, so they that they have no one to take revenge, I'll finish with them first. And I am not doing that for personal reasons, but for the people of this country.[39]

In a declaration made by Alexianu on 29 April 1946 in preparation for his trial, he stated that he had 'absolutely no role in the executions which took place in Odessa. I found out about these executions in a totally secret manner from Colonel Broşteanu, the head of the gendarmerie in Transnistria, and later from General Macici, the commander of the army in Transnistria.'[40]

Antonescu himself, in response to a question from the public prosecutor in a pre-trial examination as to who bore the responsibility for the Odessa massacre, admitted that he gave the order for reprisals for the blowing-up of the Romanian headquarters in the city, but not for massacres. He explained:

In July or June 1944 General Pantazi came to my office and told me: 'Marshal, sir, I have given orders that the bodies of those massacred in Odessa be disposed of.' I immediately replied: 'What is all this about? You have never spoken to me about this before', to which he responded: 'I, too, knew nothing about it, I have just found out about it from a brochure which appeared in Stockholm in which it is alleged that 27,000 people were massacred at Odessa.' It was the second surprise for me, because no one had mentioned this brochure to me till then. I said to him right then: 'It cannot possibly be true, you realize what it means and how long you need to gather 27,000 persons and the means necessary to kill them at the same time?'

Nevertheless, I was so disturbed in fact that I summoned Mr Alexianu straightaway and asked him: 'What's all this about? How far is it true? Why didn't you ever inform me about what happened? Mr Alexianu replied, I quote, 'It isn't true, Marshal sir.' I asked him: 'Then how many were killed exactly?' He answered: 'At most, six hundred.' To which I said: 'Well, then, Mr Alexianu, even if it was 600, why didn't you tell me at the time?' Of course, whatever the truth of the matter, Mr Alexianu can only be held responsible for keeping the matter from me. Although he was governor at that time, he had not moved to Odessa and had not taken over control of the southern area [as] military operations had only ceased a few days earlier. While I was being held in Moscow I was handed a protocol and I was forced in conditions which are beneath my dignity, that of the Romanian people, and even of the Russian people, to sign it and record for posterity the allegation – among other things – that 225,000 people had been massacred at Odessa. Because it was such an exaggeration – I will not use another term – I signed, because the document had no value, absolutely none, since when we entered Odessa, there were, on the basis of the census, only about 300,000 people. That means that the whole of the population of Odessa had been murdered in a few hours, which was untrue and was impossible. Since the beginning of man it has not been possible for anyone to assemble 200,000 people and, in particular, to kill them. To do this you would need a huge area, endless means to murder them, and days on end to carry it out...

...

Another fact which shows how false this accusation was is that a few months later another protocol was presented to me by the Russians in the same circumstances. This time, it claimed that, amongst other things, that 100,000 people were massacred at Odessa. I signed this too, pointing out to them that I was doing so under pressure. And so, the Stockholm brochure spoke of 27,000 persons, the first protocol of 225,000, and the second of 100,000. What is the truth in this matter? Even today I do not know, and probably it will never be known exactly.[41]

That the exact number will never be known is in large measure due to Antonescu himself. He seems to have made little effort to discover the full extent of the reprisals he had ordered, and it is difficult to believe his assertion that he learned of the massacres in Dalnyk only in summer 1944 when the figure of 19,000 victims was being reported by a German officer in Bucharest to Berlin in November 1941.

This gruesome retaliation was succeeded by an order, published on 7 November 1941, requiring all male Jews aged between 18 and 50 years to report to Odessa's jail within 48 hours. Four days later, Alexianu issued decree no. 23 providing for the establishment of ghettoes and concentration camps.[42] Tens of thousands of Odessan Jews were despatched to Bogdanovka (Bohdanivka) in the county of Golta.

Alexianu placed his hopes for solving the Jewish problem into transferring the Jews across the Bug. In a report to Antonescu dated 12 November 1941, Alexianu declared:

For the purpose of solving the Jewish problem in Transnistria we are currently conducting negotiations with the German authorities for their [the Jews'] transfer across the Bug. At several points, such as Golta, some of the Jews have already begun to cross the Bug. We will not have quiet in Transnistria until we carry out the decision in the Tighina convention regarding the transfer of Jews across the Bug.[43]

At the same time Alexianu intended to follow Antonescu's lead in bringing Romanians living beyond the Bug to Transnistria:

> *Alexianu*: I plan to bring everything beyond the Bug to Transnistria. The villages between the Bug and the Dniester must be settled in Transnistria. I need, however, the data of Mr Manuilă.[44]
> *Antonescu*: Don't you have them?
> *Alexianu*: No. I have sent a commission over the Bug to inspect the villages.[45]

The spread of typhus was a paramount concern to both the Romanian authorities in Transnistria and to the Germans beyond. Typhus proliferated in conditions of poor sanitation and a lack of fresh water and medical supplies. The deported Jews were particularly susceptible to its ravages and fear that they would pass on the infection to Romanian and German troops drove Alexianu and his subordinates to a monstrous solution. He was encouraged in this by Antonescu's cruelty and indifference towards the Jews.

The typhus problem reared its head in the Council of Ministers' meeting of 13 November. General Constantin Voiculescu, the Governor of Bessarabia, reported the presence of typhus in Soroca county:

> *Marshal Antonescu*: Are the trains for washing and delousing working?
> *Dr P. Tomescu*: We have sent a larger number there than to other areas. We have 200 and more.
> *Marshal Antonescu*: Probably the delousing ovens are not working.
> *Dr P. Tomescu*: They are, but there are few of them. We have sent 115 new ones.
> *Marshal Antonescu*: Cannot the army provide some?
> *General C. Pantazi*: Yes.
> *Marshal Antonescu*: Then take a note that we will come in with major assistance with the army's delousing ovens.
> *General C. Pantazi*: This matter has reached me, [with a request] that I should give delousing ovens.
> *Marshal Antonescu*: You have got to intervene quickly. Otherwise the disease will spread in Moldavia. So, the army's delousing ovens are to be sent in massive numbers to that region.
> *Prof. Gh. Alexianu*: You have give approval that several ovens should be given to me in Transnistria.
> *Marshal Antonescu*: Let those people there [Jews] continue to die.
> *Prof. Gh. Alexianu*: The troops are dying.
> *Marshal Antonescu*: The troops have delousing ovens.
> *Prof. Gh. Alexianu*: They have only a few.
> *Marshal Antonescu*: Where are they being used?
> *Prof Gh. Alexianu*: In the villages where the Jews have arrived. I have 85,000 Jews. I must delouse them, otherwise they will infect everyone.

Marshal Antonescu: Let this matter be studied and let us see what we can provide in Transnistria. Rudimentary ovens should be made. I am not sending the army's material there. I'll send it to Bessarabia because I can retrieve it.

General C. Voiculescu: I have provided a model of a fixed oven which can be made in every village.

Marshal Antonescu: This is what I have to say, Mr Alexianu. In my experience exanthematic typhus breaks out in February. We must organize ourselves by then. We must limit the area of the disease, send bath and delousing trains, because otherwise we will have a wide-scale epidemic in February. So take measures now, Mr Tomescu. The disaster will come in February, when a person is weakened by the winter, because he has not fed himself properly and has not left his house.[46]

The fate of the Jews of Odessa and southern Transnistria was discussed at a meeting of the Council of Ministers attended by Alexianu on 16 December 1941. There, Antonescu told Alexianu 'to remove the Yids immediately from Odessa because, due to the resistance at Sevastopol, we can even expect a [Soviet] landing at Odessa'. When Alexianu asked the Marshal to provide a ship for the Jews' evacuation, Antonescu inquired: 'So that you can send them to the bottom?' Alexianu answered: 'So that I can take them to Oceakov.' Antonescu continued with his questions:

Marshal Antonescu: As regards the Yids, how much time do we need to solve the problem? How many Yids have you got at Odessa?

Gh. Alexianu: Almost a hundred thousand. I decided to take them to the naval barracks, but there I haven't any food to give them and there is only room for 10,000. If they move through the villages, they will spread typhoid. I'll take 10,000 to Alexandrovskaia [near Odessa] and the rest to the Bug or we'll even send them across. But the Germans refuse to take them.

Marshal Antonescu: This matter is being discussed in Berlin. The Germans want to take all the Yids from Europe to Russia and settle them in a particular area, but it will take some time for this plan to be carried out. What are we to do in the meantime with them? Are we to wait for a decision to be taken in Berlin? Are we to wait for a decision that concerns us all? We have got to take care of them. Pack them into the catacombs, throw them into the Black Sea, but get them out of Odessa. I don't want to know. A hundred can die, a thousand can die, all of them can die, but I don't want a single Romanian official or officer to die.... Remove the Yids, then, from Odessa. I am afraid that, on account of these Yids, a catastrophe might occur in the event of a Russian landing at Odessa or in the neighbouring region.[47]

Alexianu did precisely that. On 2 January 1942, he issued order no. 35 giving instructions for the deportation of Odessa's remaining Jews – estimated to number 40,000 – to the northern part of Oceakov county and to the southern part of Berezovka county. The first deportations were scheduled for 10 January 1942. On the same day, a further order of Alexianu required all Jews to hand over all gold, jewels and valuables to posts in the centre and suburbs of Odessa which were staffed by civil and military officials. For deportation, Jews were restricted to a baggage allowance of 20 kg. Under the terms of the same order (no. 7) a ghetto in the Slobodka district of Odessa was set up to which all Jews within Odessa and its suburbs were required to report within 48 hours.[48] An intelligence report of the Romanian 4th Army, dated 10 January 1942, noted that 'the order for the ghettoization of the Jews in Odessa produced particular satisfaction amongst the local population'.[49]

The deportations began on 11 January. Jews were marched daily from the ghetto to Odessa railway station in columns of about 1,500 men, women and children, including the old and sick. One notable voice was raised in Odessa in opposition, that of the mayor of Odessa, Gherman Pântea, who appealed to Alexianu to exempt teachers, artisans and Karaites (Jews of Turkish descent who practised the Mosaic law) from the process, but it fell on deaf ears. In a report of 15 February, Colonel Emil Broşteanu, Inspector of Gendarmes in Transnistria, informed Bucharest that 28,574 Jews had been deported from Odessa to Berezovka.[50]

Antonescu never secured German agreement to let the Transnistrian Jews into *Reichskommissariat* Ukraine, but despite this, the Romanians still managed to push several thousand Jews across the river. In February 1942, the German Foreign Ministry was notified that 10,000 or so Jews had been sent across the Bug 'illegally' in the area of Voznesensk. Berlin promptly asked the transfer to be stopped, if only because of the risk of starting a typhus epidemic. Indeed, by December 1941, hundreds of Jews had been dying daily at Bogdanovka (Bohdanivka) from typhus, malnutrition and exposure to the extreme cold. Adolf Eichmann, the SS Jewish affairs expert, informed the German Foreign Ministry in April 1942 that, while Berlin approved of the Romanian effort to get rid of the Jews, this particular operation was dangerous, chaotic and uncoordinated. If the Romanians failed to stop the transfer, the SD would be free to shoot the Jews.[51] The Romanians eventually complied.

The massacres at Bogdanovka, Golta county

The original areas for concentrating the Jews on the Bug, in preparation for their expulsion into the German-controlled area of Ukraine, were listed as Mitkin, Pechora and Rogozna in northern Transnistria, the town of Obodovka and the village of Balanovka in the county of Balta, Bobrick, Krivoye Ozero and Bogdanovka, a large state farm in the county of Golta.[52] However, the large numbers of deportees involved created huge logistical problems for the Romanian authorities, who had made no plans for feeding or caring for the Jews either *en route* or at their destination. A typhus epidemic among the Jews led the Transnistrian government to divert all Jewish convoys in southern Transnistria to the county of Golta. The prefect, Modest Isopescu, a lieutenant-colonel in the gendarmerie, was ordered to concentrate the convoys around the Bogdanovka state farm and, by November 1941, some 28,000 Jews had been assembled. On 13 November, Isopescu sent a confidential report to Alexianu describing the situation in his county:

When I took over the county I found several camps of kikes (*jidani* in Romanian), some of whom had been assembled in the towns here, while the great majority had been sent from across the Dniester. Approximately 15,000 had gathered in the village of Vazdovca in the district of Liubashevka, a Romanian commune, while there were about 1,500 each in Krivoye Ozero and Bogdanovka. Those in Vazdovka were stricken with typhus and about 8,000 died, including those who died of starvation. The mayor of the commune appealed in despair for permission to move them because of the continual danger of infection. I ordered the 20th Infantry Regiment, which was quartered there, to place a guard on them so that the civilian population did not come into contact with them, and to transport them to Bogdanovka, a village on the banks of the Bug, with the intention of sending them across the Bug. Those from Krivoye Ozero were sent to Bogdanovka as well, and were placed in the pig sties of the state farm.

Before the convoy of *jidani* from Vazdovka arrived, 9,000 kikes were sent from Odessa, so that today, with those who were already there and those who arrived in the meantime, there are 11,000 *jidani* in pig sties which could not hold 7,000 pigs. The mayor of the village and the manager of the state farm came to me today in despair because they were told that there were 40,000 more *jidani* on the way from Odessa.

Since the state farm cannot hold them all, and those outside the sties kill those inside in order to take their places, and the police and gendarmes cannot keep pace with the burials, and since the waters of the Bug are being used as drinking water, an epidemic will soon spread over the entire area.

They are not fit for labour, for of the 300 brought to Golta for construction work almost 200 have died, while another 50 are dying despite being relatively well cared for. The majority have tuberculosis, and suffer from dysentery and typhus.

To avoid contamination of the region we beg you to give the order immediately that no more *jidani* should be sent to this area. I hope to be able to soon send those already here across the Bug, so that we will soon have the air completely clean. I ask, however, that we should not be infected again by new convoys of *jidani*.[53]

It goes without saying that the herding of Jews into pig sties was the ultimate debasement of their dignity.

Isopescu, like Governor Alexianu, was under the impression that it would be possible to send the Jews across the Bug into the hands of the Germans. In his report of 19 November, Isopescu noted: 'There are still Jews hiding out in the villages. I ordered searches so that they could be brought to Bogdanovka where we could concentrate them in one place before transferring them over the Bug, and we are negotiating with the Germans to this end.'[54] By the end of November the situation at Bogdanovka, and at the other improvised camps at Domanovka and Akmecetka, had reached crisis point through overcrowding and the spread of typhus, which had reached endemic proportions among the inmates. At Bogdanovka there were about 48,000 Jews, most of them from Odessa, and around 7,000 from southern Bessarabia, Domanovka held around 18,000 Jews, gathered from three districts in the south of Transnistria, while the Akmecetka camp, located on an abandoned pig farm halfway between the other two camps, had some 4,000 sick, elderly and women, described by the gendarmes as unfit for labour.[55] Still, the convoys of Jews continued to arrive, despite Isopescu's pleas to Governor Alexianu that the population of Golta itself was in danger of infection. Contact between the Jews and the local Ukrainian inhabitants, who went to Bogdanovka to sell food, the Ukrainian militia and the Romanian gendarmes who guarded the camp, had spread the disease, while at Domanovka the able-bodied Jews were sent out to work the land.

By the middle of December, Isopescu's nightmare had become reality. He estimated the number of Jews in Bogdanovka at 52,000; some were crammed into the 40-odd cowsheds, while others were out in the open, scattered over an area of 3 km on the west bank of the Bug, 35 km south of the town of Golta. Overcrowding, typhus and temperatures of −30 degrees C all contributed to a sudden rise in the death rate; in the cowsheds the living and dead lay alongside each other. According to the gendarmerie commander based in the camp, Sergeant-Major Nicolae Melinescu, the death rate jumped from between 50 and 100 Jews a day, to 500 a day.[56]

An added torment for the Jews was Governor Alexianu's order to Isopescu, issued by telegram at the beginning of November, to 'collect' valuables from the Jews, i.e. the money, gold rings and jewellery which they had taken with them to trade for their survival. These belongings were to be transferred to the Romanian National Bank. On 19 November, Isopescu reported to Alexianu that some of the Jews

> had items on them of great value in gold and jewels. The guard over them at the state farm is weak owing to a shortage of men.... I found that even the local [Ukrainian] police who had been summoned to assist with the guard had robbed them and then killed them. All these policemen have been arrested.[57]

Yet according to statements made by survivors at his trial in 1945, Isopescu, in concert with his deputy, Aristide Pădure, Melinescu and the praetor of Golta, Gheorghe Bobei, grossly abused their positions by keeping many of the valuables collected from the Jews, instead of handing them over to the National Bank.[58] On occasions, the Jews were robbed of their possessions by policemen.[59] As the food shortage in Bogdanovka took its toll, so Bobei set up a bakery with the help of a Jewish inmate called Izu Landau. Its capacity was 500 loaves a day for a population which stood at about 48,000 at the end of November. Bobei and Landau offered the bread to deportees at 5 gold roubles a loaf. This lasted only a few days since most of the Jews did not have such sums and the bakery ran out of flour.[60]

Isopescu's description of the Jews' plight at Bogdanovka and his pleas that no more columns should be sent to his camp prompted Alexianu to take drastic measures. A complete paper trail leading directly to the massacre of Jews in Bogdanovka cannot be established – although this should not surprise us given that similar portentous orders were never communicated in writing by Antonescu or by Alexianu. The records available relating to events at Bogdanovka indicate that an order from Alexianu was delivered verbally and in person to Isopescu by a special envoy that the Jews in the camp should be shot. Isopescu passed the order on to Pădure, who, seeing nothing criminal in it, committed it to paper and sent it to Vasile Mănescu, the praetor of Domanevka.[61] The latter, in turn, passed the order to Nicolae Melinescu, the senior gendarmerie officer at Bogdanovka. At this point, as the indictment against those involved in the massacre relates,

> Melinescu showed a spark of humanity. He knew how to rob the Jews, he knew how to torture them, he knew how to shoot them from time to time, or to beat them, but the extermination of those 48,000 persons was something he told [Mănescu] that he did not understand and could not carry out. He could not.[62]

In the face of this refusal either Isopescu or Pădure, or perhaps both, decided to use the local Ukrainian police to carry out the mass murders. Seventy police were assembled at Golta and placed under the command of Afanasie Andrushin, a 51-year-old Ukrainian policeman born in Chișinău. His knowledge of Romanian was fragmentary – he could not read or write the language. Before leaving for Bogdanovka, according to Melinescu, he received a written order dated 13 December from Pădure to shoot all the Jews left in Golta, with the exception of a number of 'specialists', including doctors. This was Pădure's solution to the problem of typhus. There were no survivors of this operation; the only information about it comes from declarations made during the 1945 trial.[63]

After the Golta Jews had been murdered, Andrushin received a written order, signed by Pădure, to shoot all the Jews in Bogdanovka camp.

He presented this order to Mănescu, the official (*pretor*) responsible for the camp. Mănescu kept the order and in its stead gave Andrushin a signed piece of paper on which he had copied the original. Andrushin reached Bogdanovka on the morning of 20 December and told Sergeant-Major Melinescu that he had written orders to shoot all the Jews. Melinescu asked to see it but Andrushin, who could not read Romanian, was unable to identify it among his papers and left them all on Melinescu's desk. Melinescu found the order, summoned two of his men, showed it to them and, contrary to instructions, kept the piece of paper until 1943, when he showed it to a court martial investigating abuses committed by civilian staff in Golta and by members of the gendarmerie. The paper, signed by Mănescu, was quoted during the 1945 trial:

> Gendarmerie post Bogdanovka:
> Mr Andrushin from Golta will report to you with 70 policemen who will execute the Jews in the ghetto. The gendarmes will not take part. The valuables will be collected by me. Tear up this piece of paper.
> Vasile Mănescu, 20 December 1941[64]

The massacre began the following morning. According to the prosecutor's statement at the postwar trial, the intended victims were split into two groups. The first were the sick, elderly and infirm, who were crammed into stables. Hay was scattered on the stable roofs, doused with petrol and then torched. It was estimated that between 4,000 and 5,000 perished in the inferno. The remaining 43,000 Jews were driven in groups to a nearby forest, stripped of their belongings, made to kneel at the edge of a ravine and shot in the nape of the neck. The murders took place over several days. On the orders of Isopescu the bodies were cremated. Such was the number of dead that the cremations continued throughout January and February 1942.[65]

Mănescu was also found guilty at his trial in 1945 of ordering the murder of 18,000 detainees at Domanevka. Many of the Jews were suffering from typhus, and again fear of the disease spreading seems to have driven the massacre. Once again, the executioners were local Ukrainian policemen, under the command of Mihail Cazachievici, a Ukrainian-born Romanian. The shootings began on about 10 January 1942 and continued until 18 March.[66]

Several thousand Jews are estimated to have perished as a result of disease and hunger in the camp at Akmecetka – the numbers range from 4,000 to 14,000. From May 1942, Isopescu began sending the sick and emaciated from all the camps in Domanovka district to die a slow death in Akmecetka. The camp was a former state pig farm, 'Akmecetka Ponds', 12 km from the village of Akmecetka. The Jews lived there in dilapidated barracks, with neither doors nor windows, surrounded by deep ditches and guards. The camp served as a giant sickness centre, in which infirm and sick Jews were concentrated. Isopescu allowed the patients to die from hunger, providing them with only the most meagre of supplies. These were principally made up of corn meal, which the inmates were unable to cook, and hence ate raw. According to depositions made at his trial, Isopescu often showed up drunk at the camp and took photographs.[67]

The record of bestiality shown by the Romanian authorities at Bogdanovka, Domanovka and Akmecetka ranks alongside the most horrific acts of mass butchery carried out during the war. This was a solely Romanian affair. The part played by the Germans was largely that of spectators. They may well have put pressure on Alexianu to give the initial orders to Isopescu, fearing as they did a typhus epidemic that would spread across the Bug into their own area of Ukraine, but the evidence suggests that they did not participate directly in these murders. Through his initial decision to deport the Jews from Bessarabia and Bukovina, and the later one regarding those from Odessa, Ion Antonescu bears the responsibility for the deaths from typhus and starvation, and for the mass shooting of the Jews.

If a report, dated 12 February 1942, by Alexianu to Antonescu on the state of agriculture in the province is to be believed, then the starvation of the Jews was an act of extreme callousness. Far from painting a picture of food shortages in Transnistria, Alexianu wrote that measures had been taken to buy pigs and cattle which were surplus to requirements from local peasants and place them in the existing state farms; seven sugar factories out of 19 had been reopened as well as four distilleries processing alcohol from molasses. Soap factories using the residue of sunflower oil had resumed operation. Alexianu reported difficulties in canning vegetables due to a shortage of tin. A bumper fruit harvest was expected, with much of the fruit being pulped and made into jam – there were factories at Odessa, Spicov, Berşad and Moghilev – and juice for export to Germany. Chicken batteries at Berezovka and Ciclenic produced 500,000 and 300,000 eggs respectively – over what period was not specified. At Golta there was a refrigeration plant and a poultry farm, where it was planned to raise over 500,000 chickens.[68] In a second report, dated the following day, Alexianu admitted that there were transport problems in Transnistria because of congestion on the railways, caused by German troop and munitions movements. Road transport was impossible in winter, he wrote, because of the snow and the long distances.[69] In these circumstances, food supplies to remote areas were bound to be affected. And yet, cognizant of this, Alexianu continued to deport the Jews of Odessa eastwards.

The refugees were directed through the ethnic German-inhabited area of Transnistria which was under the control of the Special *Kommando R* of the Ethnic German Liaison Office (*Volksdeutsche Mittelstelle; Vomi*), and the Ethnic German Self-Defence Corps (*Volksdeutsche Selbstschutz*) under the command of SS Colonel Horst Hoffmeyer. It was Hoffmeyer who nominated the heads of the German settlements subject to their approval by the respective Romanian prefect. By the middle of January 1942, the columns of Jews reached the district of Worms, one of the ethnic German towns in Transnistria. Alarmed by their numbers and their condition, the local commander, SS Lieutenant Streit travelled to the Special Kommando Headquarters in Landau to report that tens of thousands of Odessa Jews, under the supervision of the Romanian rural police, were being driven across his area towards the Bug. Streit was given orders to prevent the Jews, if necessary by force, from entering the German villages. Weak and helpless Jews were to be 'liquidated, with the help of the *Volksdeutsche Selbstschutz*'.[70]

Streit followed these orders, reporting to Landau that 3,000 Jews had been shot and their bodies burned on pyres. The survivors were now sent north-east and halted near Vossenensk, on the bank of the Bug at a section where the river was at its widest. Still in the ethnic German area they were at the mercy of the local *Selbstschutz* heads in Lichtenfeld and Rastatt. Their commander, Hoffmeyer, did not wish to assume responsibility for the fate of the Jews and so went to Berlin in January for advice. He was informed that Himmler had issued an order that Jews in his area should be eradicated and that the *Special Kommando* and the *Selbstschutz* be used for the task.[71] Hoffmeyer informed his local commanders of his orders on his return to Landau and they decided to move the Jews from Vossenensk to Berezovka, under guard of the Romanian rural police, where they were murdered by the *Selbstschutz*.[72]

A series of war crimes tribunals held in Bucharest in 1945 established the responsibility of a number of senior Romanian gendarmerie officers in Transnistria in handing over Jews to the German authorities.[73] In May 1942, about 20,000 Jews deported from Odessa to Berezovka, some 75 km to the north-east, were marched into the countryside and shot by *Selbstschutz*. Their numbers were swollen by Jews from smaller towns and villages. Other mass murders were carried out by the *Selbstschutz* in Mostovoi A member of the German Foreign Ministry gave a total figure; he wrote that about 28,000 Jews had been handed over to the local ethnic Germans in Transnistria. 'Meanwhile, they have been liquidated' (*Inzwischen wurden sie liquidiert*).[74]

It was not only in the south of Transnistria that the Romanian and German authorities acted in concert. On the afternoon of 3 July 1942, Colonel Irimescu, the commander of the 1st Watch Division, informed the Romanian Fourth Army headquarters that it had handed over 247 Jews to the Germans at Brailov on Transnistria's northern border, and that the Jews had been 'executed' at 18.30 hours 'east of the Bug'. On 18 July, the 4th Army asked the 1st Watch to report urgently who handed the Jews over, where the Jews were from, and why. The reply came back that the Jews had fled from Brailov on German territory, 10 km to the north of Zhmerinka, onto Romanian territory, and that the handover had been made on orders given on 3 July by the gendarmerie in Moghilev.[75] We have an eye-witness account of the murder of this column of Jews by an SS unit. It was seen by George Tomaziu, a Romanian artist who had been sent to Transnistria to provide set designs for the Odessa opera in 1942.[76] He combined his artistic talents with noting the movements of German units for British intelligence.[77]

The establishment of ghettos in Transnistria[78]

The conditions under which all Jews – both deportees and locals – were to live were initially laid down by the Romanian prefects, once they had established themselves in the newly designated county seats of Transnistria. They instructed the local Jews in certain towns to declare themselves to the authorities, to leave their houses and to move into ghettos. On 3 September 1941, Colonel Vasile Nica, the prefect of Balta county, ordered all the Jews – or 'kikes' (*jidani*) as he termed them in the ordinance – in the town to move into the ghetto, in an area restricted to four streets, within three days. He appointed the Jewish elder Pribluda Şloimu Abramovici head of the ghetto, allowing him to select colleagues to assist him in administration. A bakery, pharmacy and a hospital staffed solely by Jews were to be established independently by the Jews, and flour for the bakery to be provided by the town of Balta against payment. A market was to be set up in the ghetto where the inhabitants could buy and sell produce between 9 am and 12 am. The head of the ghetto was authorized to set up a Jewish police force to protect the lives and belongings of the residents. Entry to and exit from the ghetto between 11 am and 4 pm were allowed for those with a permit issued by the ghetto commandant – a gendarmerie officer. All Jews of both sexes between the ages of 14 and 60 were required to present themselves daily at 7 am at the ghetto centre in order to be allocated work by the ghetto commandant. For monitoring the movements and activities of the Jews, all ghetto residents were to be issued with identity cards, signed by the ghetto head and countersigned by the commandant, and a number, which they would sew on their clothing next to the Star of David. Without this number no Jew could go out into the town. All the Jews were to be entered into a register for census purposes, and those that failed to register were to be denied bread, even on payment. All other Jews, be it from elsewhere in the town, the county or others who arrived in the district, were to be sent to the ghetto. Any act of insubordination, revolt or 'terrorism' on the part of a Jew would lead to his punishment by death and that of 20 other Jews.[79]

Nica's order also provided for the establishment of ghettos in other towns in Balta county. It was followed by similar decrees in other areas of Transnistria. Thus Colonel Ion Lazăr, the prefect of Tulcin county, who reached his seat somewhat later owing to its distance from Odessa, ordered the setting up of ghettos in the towns of Tulcin, Spicov and Bratslav. His order was even more draconian than Nica's, warning that 100 Jews in the ghetto would face execution alongside the party deemed guilty of any transgression.[80] These severe punishments were threatened in an army ordinance of General Hugo

Schwab, a Romanian of German background, which was posted on the streets of the province in Romanian, German and Russian:

> The Jews will live in ghettos, colonies and labour camps. All Jews at present in Transnistria who do not report to the authorities within ten days from the posting of this present order for the purpose of the fixing of their place of residence will be executed. The Jews are forbidden to leave the ghettos, labour camps and convoys without the approval of the authorities. Those who do not respect this order will be punished by death.... Every Jew brought to Transnistria who tries to cross, or has crossed, into Romania without the approval of the authorities will be executed. Anyone who gives shelter to the Jews...will be sent to prison for a period of between 3 and 12 years and fined between 100 and 200 marks.[81]

The gendarmerie was charged with the rounding up of the Jews throughout Transnistria. According to gendarmerie order no. 1, issued on 8 September 1941, they were charged with checking the number of Jews in each town and village, verifying the setting-up of ghettos and driving Jews deported to Transnistria 'into ghettos in the garrison towns of companies or squads under tight security so that they did not trickle back across the Dniester', into Bessarabia.[82] By the middle of October, Colonel Emil Broşteanu, the head of the gendarmerie in Transnistria, reported to Governor Alexianu that the concentration of the local Jews in ghettos had been completed.[83] This was, however, an over-simplification. In Golta county, for example, the establishment of ghettos does not appear to have been completed until summer 1942.

Living conditions in the ghettos

The official determination of living conditions for all Jews in Transnistria – deported and local – was set out in decree no. 23 issued by Gheorghe Alexianu, Governor of Transnistria, on 11 November 1941.[84] Here, the term colony (*colonie*) was introduced to describe those communities of Jews living in towns and villages. Later, in the language of official reports, as we shall see in respect of Golta county, 'ghetto' and 'colony' were sometimes interchangeable – the ghetto comprising no more than three or four houses – while the distinction between 'colony' and 'labour camp' (*lagăr de muncă*) was occasionally blurred, the term 'labour colony' (*colonie de muncă*) being employed. Alexianu's decree also performed linguistic acrobatics, avoiding use of the word 'deported' and its derivatives, and preferring instead the euphemistic 'evacuated'. The decree provided a regulatory framework for the Romanian Jews who had survived deportation and the local Transnistrian Jews who escaped murder by the invading German and Romanian armies. Ghettos were set up in both towns and villages. There were approximately

200 camps and ghettos in Transnistria and they had several things in common: they were cold, crowded, the food supply was meagre and in many cases at starvation level, they were ravaged by typhus, and the death rate, particularly in the period between October 1941 and the spring of 1942, was calamitous. In the 30 months of their existence the camps and ghettos witnessed the deaths of tens of thousands of Jews. Moghilev county, which had 35,826 deportees from Bukovina, Bessarabia, Dorohoi and the Old Kingdom (Wallachia and Moldavia) in November 1943 according to a gendarmerie report, was the most densely populated, with 53 ghettos and one camp. In 26 of the ghettos there were fewer than 150 detainees. Fifteen ghettos housed 150–300 people, five ghettos 300–500, and two ghettos between 500 and 1,000. Only five ghettos had more than 1,000 Jews, the largest being Shargorod with a population in September 1943 of 2,971 Jews. In a report dated 24 December 1941, the Romanian Intelligence Service stated that in Moghilev county there were approximately 70,000 Jews, of whom 56,000 had been brought from Bessarabia and Bukovina, and between 13,000 and 14,000 were local. In the town of Moghilev itself there were 8,000–9,000 Jews from the two provinces and 4,000–5,000 local Jews.[85] In September 1943, Moghilev town sheltered more than 13,000 deportees, but many of these lived outside the ghetto.[86]

For thousands of Jews in Transnistria it was the camp rather than the ghetto that circumscribed their existence. There were basically two kinds of camp: concentration and labour. Concentration camps, into which many of the deported and local Jews were herded in the autumn of 1941, were usually set up in former Soviet state farms – abandoned barns or pig sties – in the vicinity of villages or towns. Labour camps were places of punishment where Jews were gathered to carry out particular tasks: road, bridge or building construction. The labourers were deported Jewish Communists or Jews from historical Romania – Wallachia, Moldavia, southern Transylvania and the Banat – who had avoided compulsory forced labour duties.

Alexianu's decree provides a misleading outline of the living conditions of the Jews. It should be borne in mind that Antonescu's original intention for the Jews was to cast them beyond Transnistria into Russia. The Germans' refusal to allow this caught Antonescu and, by extension, his governor of Transnistria, Alexianu, completely off guard. The ghetto experience in Transnistria, therefore, was unlike that in German-occupied Europe. There, Jews were concentrated in Jewish communities which had a social infrastructure to assist them. As has been pointed out, the fate of the Jews in Warsaw, where tens of thousands of Jews were amassed, was appalling, but even under such dreadful conditions the death toll was 12–15 per cent; in Transnistria, it reached 30–50 per cent during the winter of 1941.[87] When the Jews arrived in Transnistria, they found the area ravaged by war. Many of the towns and villages in which ghettos were established bore the marks of bombardment, and often Jews were placed in half-destroyed houses, open to the elements and without sanitation. Ragged, dirty and hungry, and having spent what money they had to buy food in order to survive the ordeal of deportation, they presented a woeful spectacle to the local population. Their weak physical condition made them even more vulnerable to endemic typhus. Survivors' accounts relate the appalling conditions against which they struggled for survival. Adults were often only half-dressed, while children wore rags since they had sold their clothing for bread.[88]

Deportation of the Romas

A second group targeted for deportation to Transnistria by Antonescu were the Romas. They were joined by a third group, the Inochentists, a small religious sect of some 2,000 Romanians, who were sent there on Antonescu's orders because of their conscientious objection to military service. More than 25,000 of a total of 208,700 Romas – the estimated size of the Roma population in Romania in 1942 – that is 12 per cent, were deported.[89]

As in the case of the Jews, deportation of the Romas was selective.[90] But here the parallel ends. Legislation was introduced in the period 1938–44 against the Jews as a race. The same was not true of the Romas. No measures were placed on the statute book during this period which affected all Romas. Most of the Romas were of no interest to Antonescu and were unaffected by the persecution directed against certain of their number. The majority of Romas retained the same rights under the law as did other Romanian citizens, though whether those rights were always respected remains an open question. Unlike the Jews, the Romas did not lose their rights as citizens, and their property was not 'Romanianized'. This did not mean that they did not harbour fears about their future. The spectre of deportation hung over them as well and it became especially vivid in the threats made against them by local officials infected with racism.

Deportation of the Romas was, in conception and in practice, the work of the Antonescu regime.[91] Nothing in the experience of the Romas in Romania could have prepared them for the action taken by Antonescu against some of their people. That is not to deny that anti-Roma sentiment and even racist ideas existed about them. The demographer Sabin Manuilă, who was the Director of the Central Institute of Statistics, which was subordinated to Ion Antonescu, saw the Romas in a sinister light. In his view, the Romas insinuated themselves into the sound body of the Romanian nation, thereby reducing its eugenic potential.[92] In an article published in November 1940, Manuilă revealed a darker side when addressing the status of the Romas:

The Gypsy problem is the most important and acute racial problem in Romania.... The anthropological Gypsy type must be defined as an undesirable one which must not influence our racial constitution....

The types who have reached leadership positions and have committed political crimes, completely foreign to the mental and moral structure of the Romanian soul, are obviously of Gypsy origin.... The Gypsy mix in the Romanian blood is most dysgenic influence that affects our race.[93]

In an approach redolent of Nazi ideology, Manuilă sought scapegoats for the woes of the Romanian people in the Roma. This warped approach to Romania's political and social problems found an echo in the work of Simion Mehedinţi. Writing in 1942, he declared: 'The time has come to put an end to this anarchy.... Not only the race hygiene of all European countries demands the expulsion of Jews, Gypsies, and all other sartoide elements...'[94]

Anti-Roma measures were first proposed by Antonescu at the beginning of 1941. At a meeting of the Council of Ministers on 7 February, Antonescu suggested the removal of Romas from Bucharest and their settlement in compact villages in Bărăgan, a low-lying area to the east of the capital. He envisaged the construction of a handful of villages, each housing 5,000–6,000 families:

All the Gypsies in Bucharest must be moved. But before moving them, we must consider where we are going to put them and what we are going to do with them. The solution would be to wait until the marshes in the Danube are cleaned up, so that we can build villages for them there and give them fishing to live on. But that is some way off. Another solution is to enter discussions with the major landowners. There has always been a shortage of labour in Bărăgan. Let us build temporary, not permanent, villages, some houses and huts, drains, shops, pubs, etc. Let us take a census of their numbers and move them *en masse* to those villages. We'll build three or four villages, each with 5,000–6,000 families, and put security guards around them so that they cannot leave. They will live their life and work there.[95]

This proposal was never implemented, but it does indicate the lines along which Antonescu's mind was working: removal of the Romas away from urban centres. The acquisition of Transnistria gave him an area beyond Romania's historical borders to which he could despatch undesirable peoples: first, the Jews in autumn 1941, and then the Romas in 1942.

Antonescu took his decision to deport Romas in May 1942, but not all Romas were to be targeted. On 22 May, the Marshal's orders were communicated to the Ministry of Internal Affairs to deport certain categories of Romas who were considered to be 'a problem'. A census was made by the police and gendarmerie three days later to determine which Romas fell into this category.[96] Those included were nomadic Romas and their families, and among sedentary Romas those who had a criminal record, re-offenders and the unemployed. A total of 40,909 Romas were recorded, of whom 9,471 were nomadic and 31,438 in the aforementioned categories of sedentary Romas.[97] The 25,000 or so Romas who were deported to Transnistria were, with few exceptions, those who figured on these lists.

The groups of Romas targeted by the census reveal the basis for selection of those to be deported. Official documents speak of the need to 'cleanse' the towns and villages of needy and destitute Romas who had no means of supporting themselves or their families, and of those who lived by begging and stealing. At his trial in May 1946, Antonescu justified deportation on the grounds of the thefts committed by Romas during the blackout in Bucharest and in other towns:

> Because of the blackout in Bucharest and in other towns, there were thefts and murders which led the public to call upon me to take protective measures.... After intensive investigations it was discovered that those responsible were Gypsies, some of them armed with weapons. Amongst all those Gypsies deported were some who had seventeen convictions. So I said, since Mr Alexianu needed manpower in Transnistria, take them to Transnistria. I deported them to Transnistria. It was my order and I take responsibility for it.[98]

It would seem, therefore, that social and public order considerations were behind Antonescu's decision to deport these Romas. Yet the offences committed by the Romas in the towns were a spurious justification since the majority of Romas lived in villages. Equally, social considerations do not provide a convincing reason for deportation; for that to be the case, all the needy and destitute should have been deported, irrespective of their ethnic background. But in this respect, only the Romas were singled out.[99] Dismissing a racial motive is less easy. It is true that there is no mention in official reports of the racial 'inferiority' of the Romas, but they do contain frequent references to the Romas as 'dangerous', 'undesirable' and 'parasitic'. We should bear in mind, moreover, that characterizations of the Romas as 'racially inferior' had been expressed by influential minds, among them Sabin Manuilă and Simion Mehedinți, who had not merely subscribed to Antonescu's ethnic policies but had promoted them.[100]

It is temping to see Antonescu's deportation of the Romas as being racially motivated, and driven by the desire to 'homogenize' Romania's population by removing the minorities and bringing in Romanians who lived outside her borders. The argument that the Antonescu's deportation of the Romas was driven purely by ethnic prejudice is vitiated by the fact that not all Romas were 'transferred unilaterally' to Transnistria. Only those who led a nomadic existence and could not be assimilated into the settled life of the bulk of the population of Romania, and those who were regarded as a threat to the calm of established society, were singled out for deportation.

The other Romas – the great majority – whose way of life conformed largely to accepted norms, were spared. Why that was so is not clear; neither Antonescu nor any of his officials gave a direct answer. From the measures taken against the Romas we can conclude that a combination of social and ethnic considerations was the motivation. In Antonescu's eyes, the lifestyle of one particular category of Romas – the nomads – marked them out as 'alien' and beyond assimilation, therefore 'undesirable'. 'Undesirability' also categorized those settled Romas with a criminal record, but they were singled out because of their ethnic identity.

Deportation of the Romas was carried out in two stages. The first to be rounded up were the nomadics, who from 1 June 1942 were assembled by the gendarmerie in county towns and then taken to Transnistria. The order for deportation was given by Ion Antonescu.[101] The nomadic Romas travelled on foot with their wagons, from one gendarmerie post to another, so that their journey lasted several weeks. This particular operation was brought to a close on 15 August. Those Romas who at the time of deportation were at the front or were called up in the army and stationed in Romania were removed from army records and sent to join their families in Transnistria. In this category of nomadic Romas, a total of 11,441 (2,352 men, 2,375 women, and 6,714 children) were deported.[102]

As regards the settled Romas identified in May 1942, the gendarmerie was ordered to screen them. The first group chosen for deportation were Romas considered 'dangerous and undesirable', together with their families, who numbered 12,497. The other 18,941 were to be moved later. The families of Romas who had been called up into the army, or who were eligible for call-up, were left *in situ*, even if they were part of the group considered dangerous. At the time when the deportation of the nomadic Romas was under way, the Ministry of Internal Affairs did not have a plan for dealing with the removal of the sedentary Romas. They were either to be sent to Transnistria or interned in camps in Romania proper. Eventually, a decision was taken in favour of the first option. The initial plan envisaged the transport of Romas in July by boat, first down the Danube, and then across the Black Sea. It was prepared down to the last detail, but was abandoned in favour of transport by rail which was judged to be far easier to implement. The starting date of the operation was fixed by Antonescu for 1 August but, due to the change of plan, did not get under way until 12 September. Over a period of eight days, nine special trains from various towns in the country converged on Transnistria with the settled Romas.[103]

Gendarmerie records show that 13,176 such Romas considered to be a threat were deported in September 1942. Their number included Romas not slated for deportation. This was a result of absconding by some and their replacement with Romas who actually wanted to go to Transnistria, in the mistaken belief that they would be given land there. These turned up at the stations and having no identity papers, were swept up in the haste of departure.

Other Romas took the train independently to Tighina in Bessarabia, and mingled with the deported Romas on arrival. The bureaucratic muddle characteristic of the Antonescu regime led to numerous abuses. Caught up in the deportation were families of Romas serving in the army, Romanians, Turks and Hungarians who were rounded up in error, male Romas married to Romanians, and Romas in employment or with means of support. These cases were raised in the numerous protests and even greater number of requests for repatriation addressed to the authorities. Furthermore, Romas were taken from their homes without being allowed to take personal belongings or household effects; their houses and other belongings were taken over by the National Centre for Romanianization.[104]

When the screening of the other 18,941 sedentary Romas listed in the May 1942 census was carried out by the gendarmerie, the intention was that those called up into the army, or eligible for service, should be interned in camps in Romania. It was then decided that they should be deported as well, but the operation never took place since Antonescu took the decision to suspend deportations of Romas and Jews on 13 October 1942. On the following day, the Ministry of Internal Affairs ordered a halt to the deportation of nomadic Romas and those with a criminal record; only those Romas 'who through their presence represent a danger to public order' should still be deported.[105]

Nevertheless, Romas not in this category continued to be deported. Romas who had either avoided the two major deportation operations, had been released from prison, or who had been placed at a later date on the list of 'undesirables', in total several hundred Romas, were sent to Transnistria after October 1942. The last deportation took place in December 1943 when a transport of 56 Romas from the town of Piteşti and the county of Argeş crossed the Dniester; of these 20 were described as 're-deported'. This transport took the number of Romas deported to Transnistria between June 1942 and December 1943 to over 25,000. At the beginning of October 1942, when the two major waves of deportation had been completed, there were 24,686 Romas in Transnistria, of whom 11,441 were nomads, 13,176 sedentary and another 69 who had been deported after being released from jail.[106]

No sooner had the major deportations been concluded in September 1942 than scores of protests reached Antonescu about the arbitrary manner in which the selection of Romas had been made. Village mayors and local gendarmerie commanders echoed the complaints of the deported, their relatives and their male relatives at the front. Some Romanian political and cultural personalities also lent their voices, among them the Liberal Party leader Constantin Brătianu, who sent a note to Antonescu asking what the 'wretched' Romas had done to deserve this treatment and why there was so much 'hatred' against them. In December 1942, the Ministry of Internal Affairs investigated the complaints of settled Romas who had been swept up and dumped in Transnistria. As a result 311 heads of family (1,261 persons) were given permission to return home, although not all were repatriated.

Particularly poignant were the protests of deported Romas who had fought in the Romanian army during the First World War and of Roma conscripts; as the Ministry of Internal Affairs pointed out, 'while doing their duty to their country, in positions of the greatest honour, their families were rounded-up and evacuated to Transnistria'[107] Antonescu's office and the Army General Staff demanded that in such case the families be repatriated and in most case they were.

Once in Transnistria the Romas were settled in villages in the south-east of the territory, on the banks of the Bug, in the counties of Balta, Berezovka, Golta and Oceakov. Most of the nomadic Romas were placed in Golta, and almost all of the sedentary ones in Oceakov. For some their dwellings were *bordeie*, hovels dug out of the earth with a cover of reeds or maize stalks. The more fortunate were given houses. To make room for them, the local Ukrainians had to 'double up' in neighbours' homes. Several villages on the Bug were completely evacuated to this end and the Ukrainian population moved inland. These villages were termed *colonii* ('colonies') by the Transnistrian authorities and contained several hundred people. They were neither camps nor ghettos, as in the Jewish experience, even though Romanian documents also use these terms, but areas reserved for Romas in the centre or on the periphery of a village. The deportees were under the guard of gendarmes, but were allowed to move within the village or commune in order to earn their living.

The Romas' existence in Transnistria was regulated by resolution no. 3149 of the Transnistrian government dated 18 December 1942. Among its stipulations were the settlement of Romas in villages in groups of 150–350, according to labour requirements, the employment of skilled Romas in existing workshops and in others which were to be created, and the use of the unskilled in agricultural labour, timber-felling, the gathering and processing of animal skins, and the collection of metals and rags. Through these measures the Romas were expected to eke out a living, at least on paper, but the reality was cruel. Only few Romas were given the chance to work. Only a small number were used on the farms, whose directors preferred to use local Ukrainian labour, while only a handful of workshops were set up. Living conditions were extremely harsh. As in the case of the deported Jews, insufficient food was provided and the Romas could not obtain their own supplies. The ration laid down by the government was not respected, and sometimes was not distributed for weeks. Often, no wood was made available for heating and cooking. Clothing, too, was a major problem, especially since the Romas had not been allowed to take a change of clothing with them or personal effects. The deportees lacked cutlery and cooking utensils. Medical assistance was virtually nonexistent, as were medicines. Those who had items of gold, Romanian money or other valuables sold them in order to survive.

A description by a police agent of the Romas' plight in Oceakov county, dated 5 December 1942, is indicative of the appalling conditions in which lived at that time:

> During the time that they stayed in the barracks at Alexandrudar, the Romas lived in an indescribable misery. They were not given enough food; only 400 g of bread for those fit for work, and 200 g for the elderly and children. They also received a few potatoes and, very occasionally, salted fish, but this in only small quantities. Because of the poor diet some Romas – and these formed the majority – grew so thin that they became merely skeletons. Ten to fifteen of them died by the day – especially recently. They were covered in lice. They were given no medical care and there was a complete absence of medicines. They have no clothing and go about naked, lacking entirely underwear and shoes. There are some women whose lower regions are completely uncovered. Soap has not been supplied to them since they arrived, and as a result they have been able to wash neither themselves nor the single shirt that they have.
>
> Generally speaking, the Romas situation is awful, almost unimaginable. Because of their misery many of them have become shadows and almost wild. This state of theirs is due to the poor housing and food, and to the cold. Because of the starvation to which they are subjected, they have frightened the Ukrainians with their thieving. If at home in Romania some Romas were always stealing, they did it out of habit, while there in the camp, even the honest Roma took to theft, because they were driven to this shameful act by hunger. Because of their bad treatment, 309 Romas had died up to 25 November of this year. Bodies of Romas were found on the highway between Oceakov and Alexandrudar. They had died of hunger and cold.
>
> Although the Romas in the barracks at Alexandrudar have been given more decent quarters in the villages mentioned above, the problem of the Romas in Oceakov county has not been resolved. To a certain degree their situation has improved, since they are less exposed to the cold and have been deloused. But if they are not given wood and other fuel, the Romas will be tempted to do what they did to the barracks, that is to make them uninhabitable.[108] And the cold will drive them to this, without their realizing that they are making things worse for themselves and that the danger of death from cold is even greater. Similarly, if they are not given more decent food, medical care and medicines, as well as clothing for some of them, the deaths among the Romas will not fall, but will increase daily as it gets colder. Similarly, the thefts from the Russian population will grow. In fact, the local population is outraged and their morale is very low because they have been moved from their homes in winter to make way for the Romas whom they cannot stand.[109]

By spring 1943, thousands of Romas had perished. In fact, most of the deaths among the Romas in Transnistria occurred in the winter of 1942. The scale of death can be gauged from a report sent by the authorities in Landau district to the prefect's office in Berezovka county in connection with a typhus epidemic which broke out in the middle of December 1942 in the Romas' 'colonies' there: the disease had reduced the number of Romas from about 7,500 to somewhere between 1,800 and 2,400.[110]

Following this tragedy, there was a modest improvement in the lot of the survivors. Most of the colonies were broken up and the Romas were scattered across villages. There they were given work on public projects, farms or in workshops where they could ply their trade and earn a living. They were used on road building, track repairs and tree-felling. As this labour was paid, the Romas were able to buy food for their families. Some were hired out by the prefect to the Todt organization for work on military projects such as bridge-building in Nikolaev region across the Bug in German-controlled Ukraine.[111] Others found a niche in the local Transnistrian economy by offering their traditional skills. Such was the case of the comb-makers. In February 1944, there were 1,800 in Berezovka county As the Roma mayor on the farm at Suhaia Balka wrote in a petition to the prefect of Berezovka dated 11 March 1944:

> For four months we have received nothing from the farm or the state, but we live only from our labour and from the income which we get from the sale of combs. From the latter we have been able this winter to clothe ourselves and to feed ourselves in a decent manner.[112]

Agriculture also offered a means of existence for the Romas. In summer 1943, the Romas in Balta county were moved from villages to hovels (*bordeie*)[113] and given land to work in order to feed themselves. Proposals were even submitted for the creation of Roma agricultural colonies, with their own land and tools. But such possibilities varied from county to county. In some areas the Romas still faced death from starvation and cold in 1943. The situation was especially stark in Golta, where the head of the local gendarmerie described what was effectively a regime of murder applied to Jews and Romas:

> From verified sources, the Jews in the county of Golta have not been given food for months. Similarly, neither have the Romas nor has the labour camp in Golta, where there are 40 persons. All of the above work and they are required to work, even though they keel over through hunger.[114]

A handwritten, unsigned message from the Golta prefecture to the Inspectorate of Gendarmes bearing the same date hints at a food shortage for the Roma: 'The Jews and prisoners [of the labour camp] are given sufficient hot food while the Gypsies are given only what food we have available.'[115] In this same county Ion Stancu, the mayor of the Romas in Kamina Balka, also bemoaned about the lack of food: 'During the day we work on the collective farm, while at night we mount patrols. We are given very little food, 300 g of flour, 500 g of potatoes and 10 g of salt per person, and nothing else.'[116]

The Romas' circumstances varied from county to county, and even from farm to farm. They depended on the efficiency of Romanian officials and the willingness or ability of local communities to supply food. The local Ukrainians saw the Romas as a burden, and the Romanian authorities often had to intervene with the Ukrainian communes and villages to give them food in line with the orders of Gheorghe Alexianu, the Governor of Transnistria. Romanian administrators often complained that the Romas shirked work or performed it half-heartedly, stating that they preferred to roam the villages and beg. In order to acquire food, some Romas stole, forming themselves into bands. Gendarmerie posts reported on the fear these bands inspired in the Ukrainian population. These same reports tell of the regular flight of Romas from their 'colonies' on the Bug where conditions were especially grim; to escape the hunger and disease Romas independently, or in groups, tried to get back to Romania, often by following railway tracks, but in most cases they were caught. In autumn 1943, when the level of those apprehended topped 2,000, a makeshift camp was set up in Golta town to intern 475 Romas.

Many of the deported Romas died in Transnistria from hunger and illness, but there were no organized executions, as was the case with the Jews. There were, however, instances of Romas being shot by the gendarmerie, as happened at Trihati in Oceakov county, where a report from May 1943 states that gendarmes killed a number of Romas who had arrived in search of work.[117] The total number of Roma who died in Transnistria is unknown. A gendarmerie assessment in May 1944 of the numbers who made their way back to Romania after the abandonment of the territory two months earlier found only 6,000 persons, but this census was made at a time of upheaval; areas of eastern Romania were already occupied by Soviet troops at a time when Romas were still drifting back and were no longer available for the census. Some Romas who lived in tolerable conditions may well have remained in Transnistria. It is unlikely, then, that as many as 19,000 of the 25,000 Romas deported to Transnistria died, but it is almost certain that more than half did.

Most of the Romas who did return accompanied the Romanian troops and officials retreating before the Soviet advance. They did not wait for any authorization but simply crossed the Dniester back into Bessarabia. In some cases, they were assisted by units of the Romanian and German armies, and by railway workers. On 19 April 1944, the head of the gendarmerie issued an order that Romas who had fled from Transnistria should be apprehended and put to work on local farms. The order was repeated on 17 May. Provisional shelter was arranged, but many Romas refused to perform labour on the grounds that they lacked the necessary experience. As a result, many risked dying of hunger. The authorities gave in and the Romas were allowed to return to their native villages. Antonescu's overthrow removed the spectre of further discriminatory measures against them. On 13 September, the new police authority instructed the gendarmerie to allow all the Romas who had returned from Transnistria to be left in peace and to be given assistance in finding suitable employment.[118]

The deportation of the Romas to Transnistria was a Romanian affair. Ion Antonescu was responsible for it; it was he who gave the order for deportation. There is no evidence that Hitler put pressure on Antonescu to follow his own genocidal policies towards the Romas under German rule. In Romania, the operation was carried out by the Ministry of Internal Affairs, in conjunction with the gendarmerie and the police. The Transnistrian government was also involved, most directly at the level of its local public administration. Lack of planning, incompetence and indifference to the fate of the Romas, not just on the part of the Romanian authorities, but in some cases on that of the local Ukrainian population, left the Romas in some counties without adequate food and shelter in an inclement climate. In other areas, the documents point to a concerted effort by the local authorities to ensure the Romas' survival. As with the Jews of Bessarabia and Bukovina, the question remains whether deportation to harsh, desolate regions of Transnistria, where the soil was poor, was tantamount, in the mind of Antonescu, to sending the Romas to their death.

Further deportations of Jews

On 22 May 1942, the Ministry of Internal Affairs sent out a circular to the police and gendarmerie relaying an order from Marshal Antonescu which it had received from his office. All active Communists, as well as those who had gone underground in the capital, were to be deported to Transnistria. Police figures put the number of those active at 746; other Communists were held in internment in Târgu-Jiu or in prison serving sentences handed down by the courts.[119] The Ministry proposed to the Army General Staff that the activists be interned in Vapniarka camp, situated in Jugastru county, Transnistria, 'in order to keep them isolated and to forestall any attempt to disturb order behind the front'.[120] It also recommended that the *Jewish* Communists in Târgu-Jiu and those that had been imprisoned for their activity should be sent to the same camp.[121]

Other offences were added to the list of those who incurred deportation. On 17 July 1942, Antonescu ordered that all Jews who had broken the law regarding price ceilings and restrictions on the sale of certain products – as was the case of Jews in Galati with the sale of thread, and those in Bucharest with footwear – be sent to Transnistria. This order affected Jews from the Old Kingdom, Banat and southern Transylvania. The official Romanian line, expressed in a report compiled for Antonescu by his office, was that this 'measure, like others taken by the Marshal involving the deportation of Jews to Transnistria – Jewish Communists, Jews who had adopted another religion, Jews who avoided compulsory labour – was designed to combat non-compliance with the law and to free up the towns crowded with Judaic parasitical elements who live by breaking the economic laws and those on internal security'.[122] On 31 July 1942, the Ministry of Internal Affairs informed the gendarmerie that, in accordance with the Marshal's order, 'Jewish Communists who were at liberty in Romania, Jews who had requested repatriation to the Soviet Union after the invasion of Bessarabia and Bukovina in June 1940, and Jews held in Târgu-Jiu camp on suspicion of being Communists' should be deported to Transnistria.[123]

On 8 September 1942, the deportation began of almost all the Jews – 407 – among the Communists interned in Târgu-Jiu to Vapniarka.[124] They arrived on 16 September. They were joined by some 80 Jews from Jilava prison near Bucharest, and 600 Jewish Communist activists who came from all corners of Romania. The other inmates of the camp were 140 Ukrainians, Russians and Romanians, most of them local offenders. The callous disregard for the well-being of the detainees which typified the behaviour of most of the camp commandants in Transnistria soon became evident in Vapniarka. A month before the Jews' arrival, one of the inmates showed signs of paralysis of the lower limbs. Within weeks, many of the other internees fell victim to the same condition. Jewish doctors among the inmates examined the invalids and concluded that the diet was to blame. They discovered that the commandant, Lt.-Col. Ion Murgescu, had sanctioned the feeding of the prisoners with of a type of pea used for feeding cattle, and that this had caused the paralysis in humans. They called for an immediate halt to its use.[125] According to a report of the Ministry of the Interior at the time, 23 detainees died in the camp between 17 September 1942 and 15 December 1943.[126] However, the doctors in Vapniarka submitted their own findings to the Romanian authorities in two memoranda, the first dated 20 January 1943, the second, 8 March. By the first date, 66 prisoners had paralysis of their lower limbs, and more than 400 showed 'signs of advanced paralysis'.[127] On receiving the first memorandum, the doctor responsible for the Vapniarka, Lt.-Col. Gheorghe Tataranu, gave orders that the peas should cease to be fed to the internees, but it was too late to to stop or reverse the progress of the paralysis in those already affected. By 1 March, the camp doctors counted 139 cases of paralysis.[128]

For the Communist Jews in Vapniarka death by paralysis was not the only fate that awaited them.[129] As the Red Army pushed westwards, about 70 Communists – those considered most dangerous – were transferred to a prison in Râbniţa in October 1943. The other prisoners were sent to Grosulovo camp near Tiraspol.[130] Many of the prisoners in Râbniţa were murdered by retreating German forces on 18 March 1944.[131]

It is important to point out here that punishment by deportation to Transnistria as an administrative measure and not by sentence of the courts was applied only to Jews. Thus the Communists interned in the Târgu-Jiu camp who were Christians, were not sent, as their Jewish fellow comrades were, in September 1942, to Transnistria.[132] If a Christian common-law criminal or speculator was deported to Transnistria, it was the exception, not the rule.

The Roman Catholic Church and the deportations to Transnistria

After the creation of Transnistria, the papal nuncio in Romania, Andrea Cassulo, requested permission from Foreign Minister Mihai Antonescu to send a Catholic mission to serve the spiritual needs of Catholics in the territory. Monsignor Marcu Glaser was appointed head of this mission, which had its headquarters in Odessa, in July 1942, and in the following June he was given the title of Bishop of Cesaropolis. At the end of March 1944, he left Odessa in the face of the Soviet advance. Before his withdrawal, the Holy See sent two other missionaries, Father Pietro Leoni, a Jesuit, and Father Jean Nicholas, an Assumptionist, who were to minister to the Catholic faithful after the re-imposition of Soviet rule. In April 1945, they were both arrested by the NKVD and subsequently jailed.[133]

It was the Vatican's view that a Jew ceased to be a Jew on conversion to Christianity. It was on this basis that Cassulo intervened on numerous occasions to protect Jews in those cases where his prerogatives under the Concordat of 12 June 1929 between the Vatican and the Romanian state entitled him to defend the rights of Catholics.[134] He informed Rome on 8 January 1941 of the difficulties faced by Jews who had converted to Catholicism in practising their faith.[135] These Jews were not allowed to attend Catholic schools. Cassulo had taken up the matter with Ion Antonescu two months earlier and had received an assurance that the law would be modified. On 16 February, the nuncio wrote asking him to expedite this matter:

> I can tell you that every day the representative of the Holy See receives letters, entreaties from parents who find themselves in a very grave situation. Their children are, on the one hand, rejected by the Jewish schools and at the same time, under the law, they cannot attend the Catholic schools, for the only reason that their parents are of Jewish origin.[136]

On 21 February he was able to tell the Vatican that Antonescu had signed a decree on 19 February which allowed all Christian children to attend Christian schools, irrespective of their ethnic background.[137] During the following month, however, the Romanian press announced that the government had forbidden Jews, under pain of the harshest sanctions, to change their religion.

This was a reference to Antonescu's decree no. 711 of 21 March 1941, which forbade the conversion of Jews to any other faith, and which drew a rebuke from the Orthodox Metropolitan of Transylvania, Nicolae Bălan. On 2 April, the latter sent a letter of protest to General Radu Rosetti, the Minister of Education and Religious Cults, affirming that the state had no right to intervene in matters of dogma:

> In principle no one on earth can prevent the Gospels and the redeeming grace of our Lord Jesus Christ from being imparted to any man. The Son of God came down to earth and suffered death on the cross for the salvation of all people who want to believe in him.
>
> Even less so is this interdiction [regarding conversion] in the power of the state. It cannot make itself master over what it does not possess, over the grace and will for salvation of the Lord.
>
> The state could do something else: stop the immixture of Jewish blood and Romanian blood by forbidding mixed marriages, irrespective of whether the Jews are baptized or not. It cannot go any further, involving itself in matters of dogma.
>
> . . .
>
> We ask you, therefore, Minister, to kindly withdraw the decree since it is contrary to church dogma. If you do not do so, we are obliged to tell you that we will consider this decree as void for the Church which I tend.

The Metropolitan's objections were passed on to Antonescu by Rosetti with the observation, 'I cannot believe that the Church refuses to carry out the teaching of the Saviour to give unto Caesar what is Caesar's.' Antonescu was more prosaic: 'The Metropolitan of Transylvania has begun to exaggerate. The Minister of Justice is asked to examine whether the laws of the state allow the head of the church to adopt an official stance and to threaten not to carry out the law...I will take a decision afterwards.'[138]

In response to a telegram from the Vatican for details, Cassulo replied on 31 March that the Romanian Foreign Ministry had assured him that it had no part in this measure. The nuncio protested that the right to freedom of worship should be respected. On 12 May, Cardinal Maglione in the Vatican telegraphed Cassulo to find out whether he had received such an assurance and on 15 May the nuncio replied that he had. This was not, however, the end of the matter. Converted Jews still encountered obstacles, placed by officials of the regime, in practising their new faith, so much so that Cassulo was moved to draw Mihai Antonescu's attention to them in a letter of 4 December 1941.[139]

The admission to baptism of the Jews was viewed with resentment by the Romanian government. The number of Jews requesting it grew, especially as word got round that the Holy See, in the light of the danger in which Jews had been placed, had given orders that they be baptized in large numbers.[140]

As a result, the Romanian minister to the Vatican complained to Cardinal Maglione on 18 April 1942 that the number of conversions was excessive and suggested, in the name of his government, that the Pope suspend them, a suggestion that was firmly rejected.[141]

If Cassulo had every right to intervene on behalf of Catholic Jews, he showed no hesitation in going beyond strictly confessional bounds in striving to help the entire Jewish community. He wrote to Maglione on 7 August 1941, after the attack on the Soviet Union, referring to the 'great severity of the measures taken against the Jews and the apparently excessive repression'. He was using all his influence in favour of the victims, but the situation, he confessed, was difficult.[142]

On 5 December Cassulo explained to his superiors that the government had taken harsh measures against the Jews on the grounds that they were Communist sympathizers:

> In the absence of any authority which could help them, [the Jewish families] turned to the representative of the Holy Father in the conviction that only this moral authority could help them in this matter. I thus found myself in a very delicate and difficult position. On the one hand I thought it my duty to concern myself with these poor families, on the other I had to proceed with discretion with the government to avoid exceeding the agreed limits of my mission by interfering in the country's internal affairs.[143]

The nuncio nevertheless found a way of helping the non-Catholic Jews: 'At the invitation of the government, I presented lists of those persons who, on the basis of formal declarations given to me, presented no risk to the authorities.'[144]

He remained steadfast in his determination to show his concern in demonstrable ways to the government. In July 1942, there was discussion in Jewish circles of the news that the nuncio had instructed Catholic parishes to hold a special service on Wednesdays for Jews deported to Transnistria.[145] In September, President Roosevelt sent a special representative, Miron Taylor, to tell the Pope at first hand of his concern at the physical destruction of the Jews by the Nazis. News of the visit was reported to Antonescu. On 23 September, Cardinal Maglione telegraphed Cassulo with a request to intervene on behalf of the 3,000–4,000 Catholic Jews in Transylvania, mostly in the diocese of Timişoara, who were threatened with deportation under 'a decree of the [Romanian] government according to which all Jews in southern Transylvania were to be deported to Transnistria'.[146]

To show that Romania had nothing to hide, Mihai Antonescu authorized a visit by Cassulo to Transnistria. At the beginning of April 1943 Cassulo went first to Odessa, from where he travelled to Chişinău. In both cities only a few Jews had survived murder and escaped deportation. He then went on to Cernăuti and thence to Moghilev, visiting the Jewish ghetto and camps for Russian prisoners of war.[147] He returned to Bucharest at the beginning of May. On 18 May, Cassulo wrote to Mihai Antonescu to draw his attention to the special cases. Among the Jews deported to Transnistria were 8,000 orphans, of whom 5,000 had lost both parents. Would it not be possible, he asked, to bring them back to Romania for possible emigration to Palestine? In the meantime, they could be placed with Jewish families. This was the Filderman plan. Before his visit to Transnistria, Cassulo had been alerted to the situation of the orphans by the Chief Rabbi, Alexander Safran. On his return, he asked to see Radu Lecca, the Commissioner for Jewish Affairs. Cassulo laid out before him the proposals made by the Jewish leaders. One of the most important was the transfer to the western part of Transnistria of the Jews in camps and ghettos in the eastern part of the province. The Jews there were often sent in labour detachments across the Bug to work for the Germans and on completion of their task were murdered by the local German police. Lecca gave the impression to Cassulo of being sympathetic to these ideas, even assuring him 'that a good number of orphans would be sent to Palestine'.[148]

By late summer nothing had been done for the orphans. On 6 September, the nuncio took up the matter with Mihai Antonescu, informing him of Lecca's assurance about passage to Palestine. He injected a note of condescension: 'I believe, Mr Minister, that a single word from you would solve the matter and give these poor little ones a less troubled future.' Antonescu replied on 25 September that 'the information that Your Excellency has been given is not correct, for up to now no one has submitted to the government concrete proposals for the organization of transport of Jewish children in Transnistria'. Three days later, Cassulo forwarded Filderman's proposals with the nuncio's own covering note requesting that Antonescu, having examined it, tell him 'if the conditions meet in substance those which the Romanian government wishes so that the transport [of the orphans] has the desired guarantees'.[149]

Not every Catholic bishop displayed such Christian charity towards the Jews. In early summer 1943, the nuncio had to deal with a storm in a teacup regarding the use made by Jews of the Vatican Information Service to pass on messages to their families, from abroad and from within Romania. The Service was open to all internees and deported persons, be they soldiers or civilians. On 21 July, Cassulo reported to Cardinal Maglione that 'the majority of the messages sent to this nunciature through the information service are addressed to persons of the Jewish race', For this reason the Bishop of Timişoara, Augustin Pacha, had seen fit to write to him that 'most of my faithful are of German origin and are truly indignant ... at this transmission of letters to the Jews, making the open and public accusation that the Jews, enemies of the German people, are being especially favoured'. As a consequence, Cassulo asked the cardinal whether he ought to suspend the service in Timişoara.[150]

Maglione, in his reply of 20 August, underlined the impartiality of the Church's action in conveying these family messages. The Holy See, he wrote,

> in its charitable work for the relief of the suffering produced by the war, makes no distinction in religion or nationality. If the demands for the information service in Romania come in large part from the Jews, that is not of course because of any preference shown towards the Jews, but because of the simple fact that the Jews residing on Romanian soil are very numerous and their parents, who live in different parts of the world, wish to have news of them.

The Cardinal suggested that Cassulo continue to send messages to Timişoara without recourse to the assistance of the Episcopal secretariat there.[151]

During this same period, Cassulo had his own problem to deal with, that of defending baptized Jews. Many of them had also been deported to Transnistria. In the case of the Catholics, the nuncio could use the concordat as a basis for his intervention. On 14 January 1943, Cardinal Maglione had instructed Cassulo to remind the Romanian government about its promises to allow baptized Jews freedom of worship. Despite the receipt of assurances from Mihai Antonescu, Cassulo find himself obliged to complain yet again on this subject on 20 May: in Cernăuţi the local authorities were refusing to recognize the rights of baptized Jews, accepted by the government, to be received into the Catholic Church. Five days later, Cassulo sent a circular to Catholics bishops in Romania informing them that despite what Romanian officials might say, they were entitled to receive into the Church Jews who had following the necessary instruction and who made a daily profession of the faith.[152] Impediments still remained in Cernăuţi, as Cassulo reminded Mihai Antonescu on 7 September.

They seemed to have been removed when, three months later, on 7 December, the nuncio transmitted to the Vatican a 'clear and categorical assurance' given in a cabinet meeting that the Church could 'freely enjoy the rights which had long been recognized'.[153] Once again, this 'assurance' proved worthless. Difficulties persisted in Cernauti for baptized Jews, as Cassulo complained to Mihai Antonescu on 18 February 1944. Although instructions had been issued by the Ministry of Internal Affairs that the police should recognize the acceptance of Jews into the Catholic faith, they were being ignored in Cernăuţi:

> Today, that is three months after the publication of the aforementioned instructions, Catholics of Jewish race are taken to the police who wish to confiscate their identity card bearing the word Catholic and force them to apply for a card which states that they are of the Mosaic faith.... It is disgraceful for me to have to insist yet again that it is question here not

only of a matter regulated by the Concordat, but also of a point on which the last assurances of the Royal Romanian Government are too explicit for them to continue not to be applied.[154]

The same problem emerged yet again a little later, but in a different form. This time it involved the schools. Baptized Jewish children found themselves barred from attending Christian schools. Cassulo wrote to Mihai Antonescu on 14 July to complain yet again about this situation, explaining that only children who were already baptized at the time Antonescu issued his instructions in December 1943, and only those in the Old Kingdom, were being allowed to attend Catholic confessional schools.[155] His intervention became immaterial within a month with the overthrow of Antonescu. The new government announced shortly after King Michael's *coup* that all measures taken against the Jews would be abrogated.

In pleading the cause of the Catholics of Jewish origin, Cassulo had a justification based on the Concordat and on the assurances of goodwill given by the government to the Vatican. His interventions on behalf of the Jewish community, on the other hand, required particular tact, for such action ran the risk of being vehemently rejected as interference in Romania's internal affairs. Even so, the nuncio had the example before him of the Holy Father when giving aid to the deported Jews. Pope Pius XII was moved by the plight of the Jews in Transnistria to make a donation of 1,353,000 lei at the beginning of 1944 to assist them. The money was sent via Cassulo and remitted to the head of the Central Jewish Office by the Romanian Foreign Ministry on 5 February 1944.[156]

Two weeks earlier, Cassulo received a memorandum, probably from the Chief Rabbi, Dr Safran, describing the position of the orphans in Transnistria. Given the high rate of mortality there, there numbers were high, put at 'about 4,000 children between two and sixteen'. Only a small number of them were living in improvised orphanages, the others being exposed to the elements with barely any shelter.[157] 'The state of physical misery and want of these poor little children is indescribable, since the deportees do not have the means to support their own children, not to speak of the orphans.' On 22 January, Safran paid a visit to Cassulo to tell him that the government had given its approval for orphans up to the age of 12 to be brought back to Romania and asked the nuncio to intervene to get this age limit raised to 16.[158] In response, Cassulo addressed an appeal to Mihai Antonescu on 26 January calling for 'his charitable intervention' to raise the age limit to 16 and 'to accelerate the return of the orphans to more normal conditions'.[159] Shortly afterwards, on 2 February, he again approached the Foreign Minister on behalf of the Jews who had been delivered by the Romanian authorities in Transnistria into the hands of the Germans. He forwarded an anonymous plea for help for the Jews in Tulcin county who had been sent across the Bug to work for the Germans. Cassulo added his own voice: 'the case is serious and urgent. A feeling of Christian humanity drives me to commend it to your attention.'[160]

While the case of the 4,000 orphans received the highest profile at this point, the fate of the bulk of the deported Jews was not forgotten. On 28 February, a telegram from Monseigneur Roncalli, the apostolic delegate to Istanbul, reached the Vatican. The Grand Rabbi of Jerusalem, Isaac Herzog, had been to the delegation to thank the Holy Father for his good work over the previous months and asked the Holy See to intervene urgently on behalf of the 55,000 Jews in Transnistria.[161] On 2 March, the Vatican passed the message on to Cassulo, with instructions to do everything he could. The nuncio, fully aware of the situation, replied two weeks later that there was no point in adding to the appeals already made at the request of Dr Şafran; the Romanian government was leaning towards conciliation and it would be better if it did not fear the reaction of those who were the implacable enemies of the Jews: the Germans. The nuncio added some news of significance: the civil administration of Transnistria had been withdrawn and most of the Jews had been evacuated to Bessarabia, beyond the reach of the retreating Germans.[162]

9
Suspension of Deportation, Repatriation and Emigration of Jews

In the summer of 1942, Antonescu made a fundamental change to his policy towards the Jews, a shift that underlined a basic difference in approach to what both Hitler and Antonescu termed 'the Jewish problem'. The change involved two momentous decisions. The first was Antonescu's refusal to participate in the Final Solution, the second his reversal of the policy of deportation to Transnistria. Not only did he decide against acceding to German requests that the remaining Jewish population of Romania – from the Banat, southern Transylvania, Wallachia and Moldavia – be sent to the death camps in Poland, but he also suspended the deportations to Transnistria.

The broad details of the application of the systematic liquidation of the Jews as a goal of state policy – Hitler's Final Solution – had been elaborated at the Wansee Conference on 20 January 1942. Pressure was exerted by SS *Hauptsturmführer* Gustav Richter, the Counsellor for Jewish Problems at the German legation in Bucharest, for Romania to impose the policy on its own Jews, and on 22 July 1942 he reported to Berlin that Mihai Antonescu had given his government's agreement to the deportation of Romanian Jews to the death camps in Poland.[1] On 26 July, Heinrich Himmler, head of the SS, was informed that preparations for the deportations were under way and that the first of a number of trains would leave 'around 10 September' for the district of Lublin, 'where those fit for labour would be put to work, while the rest would be subjected to the special treatment' – i.e. liquidation.[2]

Indeed, on 10 July 1942, Colonel R. Davidescu, the head of Antonescu's office, had instructed the Ministry of Internal Affairs to compile figures for the number of Jews in Transylvania and to study the feasibility of sending 'to the Bug all the Jews in Transylvania except the intellectuals essential for our needs (doctors, engineers, etc.) and the industrialists necessary for the management of different enterprises in order to make room for the shelter of the Romanian refugees from the ceded part of Transylvania'.[3]

Rumours of a plan to deport Jews from southern Transylvania and Banat startled Jewish leaders, particularly those in the regions targeted. In fact, a group of Romanian intellectuals in the Banat, alarmed by German press reports in late 1941 of the deportation of Jews from southern Transylvania and Banat, sent a protest to the Romanian authorities – it is not clear to whom – in which they wrote:

> Whatever our view of the Jews, we are Christians and human beings . . . and we shudder at the idea that the innocent citizens of a state could be stripped of all their wealth and driven from the land of their birth, land in which the bones of their parents, grandparents and ancestors have lain for centuries. Marshal Antonescu has explained that the deportation of Jews in Bessarabia and Bukovina was carried out because of the criminal activities which they allegedly committed against the army and Romanian population . . . . Not only can such an accusation not be levelled at the Jews of Transylvania Banat, but on the contrary, we must recognize that both on the occasion of the cession of part of Transylvania and after that, both the Jews in the ceded territories, as well as those that remained, behaved impeccably.[4]

The Romanian Intelligence Service reported that Baron Franz von Neumann, the owner of textile and chemical factories in Arad, travelled to Bucharest 'around 20 August' in an effort to get the deportations postponed until the following spring, 'when the conditions for transport would be better'.[5] His efforts included his promise of a 100 million lei contribution by the Jewish communities of Banat and southern Transylvania – scheduled to be the first to be deported – for the construction of the 'Palace of the Handicapped,' whose project director, Dr Stoenescu, was Antonescu's personal doctor.[6]

The leaders of the democratic parties raised their voices in protest, much to the annoyance of the Marshal. On 10 August, he wrote on a report giving statistics of the urban Jewish population: 'I shall ignore everyone and every difficulty in cleansing this nation totally of this blight. I shall castigate in due course all those who have come – the most recent being Mr Maniu – and will come to stop me from responding to the wishes of the vast majority of this nation.'[7] On 20 August 1942, the Romanian Intelligence Service noted that a memorandum, signed by 'a group of Romanian intellectuals (university professors, writers and schoolteachers)' had been sent to the Palace.[8] The memorandum condemned the 'unjust treatment handed out to the Jews in recent years in Romania' and the 'organized horrors' involving the deportation of the Jews:

> It is a proven fact that the deportations are organized in such atrocious conditions that the so-called moving of Jews to the eastern territories is being transformed, in fact, into a methodical and persistent act of extermination. For two years we have been at the forefront of the states which

persecute the Jews. In an atmosphere of the wildest persecution, through endless falsifications of the truth, through the cultivation of enmity and hatred, through the exasperation of antagonisms, we have made the Jewish question the only problem of state in Romania.

The Jews have been excluded from the community. Their wealth and property have been expropriated, the elementary right to work and to existence has been taken from them. They struggle between the restrictions and the oppression which we feel extending to the smallest preoccupations of life. We have established an anti-Jewish regime which even the *Bukarester Tageblatt*, the official paper of the German legation, calls the most drastic in the whole of south-eastern Europe.

The signatories pointed out the consequences of these measures and the danger that they posed to the Romanian national interest:

On the domestic front we have promoted a sort of anarchic fanaticism, which openly proclaims the right to kill, steal and demean; we have thus created, through the means of state authority, a current of social disintegration, endangering the principle of legality and of security of the citizen...

We can expect the Jewish problem to be resolved, in general, at the peace conference which will determine the fate of all states. There, the situation of the Jews in Romania will be established and there, too, will be decided the fate of Romania itself. Until then, we must bring ourselves in line with international law and guarantee the right to life and legal protection of every Jews in the territories which we claim, because no where have territories been awarded, nor are they awarded except with the populations which live in them. Our national interests must be defended in time through a policy of foresight by which not one principle upon which our rights could be based could be attacked or disturbed.

Romania was singled out for the harshness of its anti-Semitic policies:

Romania cannot remain the only state to carry out in full a plan for the extermination of the Jews, conceived by interests hostile to our country, when in Germany, which runs the anti-Semitic policy in Europe, and where the National Socialist regime has been in power since 1933, the measures taken against the Jews have not reached the level of gravity which they have in our country.... Only in the occupied countries, in countries which cannot save themselves, the Jewish population – but only a small part – has been deported.

By their actions the Romanians were placing at risk their national interest, and jeopardizing the chances at the end of the war of regaining northern

Transylvania. This was clear from the public messages addressed by Churchill and Roosevelt to the Jewish Congress in New York, that 'the punishment of countries which had persecuted the Jews represented one of the aims of the war', from the declarations of Molotov, the Soviet Foreign Minister, that 'the Allies reserved the right to demand reprisals and compensation for the atrocities committed in Bessarabia and Bukovina'. A time of reckoning awaited Romania:

> We imagine too easily that within our frontiers we can resort to injustice and violence, to the demeaning and decimation of the coinhabiting populations, without having to give account to the states which once consecrated our just cause [the creation of greater Romania in 1918], the same states who tomorrow, whatever the outcome of the war, will have the same decisive word.[9]

On 12 September, Iuliu Maniu, the Peasant Party leader, stated that the Jewish question was becoming of matter of great international importance in the wake of Roosevelt's message and Churchill's declaration, which announced that those who deported Jews would be subject to punishments without precedent in history. Two days later, Ion Mihalache, Maniu's deputy, voiced his disapproval of the deportation, adding that according to his information these measures had been taken at the suggestion of foreign circles 'alien to the humanitarian traditions of our people.' On 16 September, Maniu declared: 'I have said it once and will go on saying it: we will pay dearly for the maltreatment of the Jews. I have been told, for example, that important wealthy Jewish families have also been removed from Arad and Timişoara. Why wealthy families? I do not understand.' Constantin Brătianu, the liberal leader, was even more forthright. Speaking on 25 September he expressed his outrage: 'The deportation of the Jews is continuing under different pretexts which discover new guilty persons who are despatched. These horrors, which represent a slap on the country's face, are all the more revolting because in their innocence, the old, women and children are being sent to their death.'[10]

On 23 September, the Director General of Romanian Railways, General T. C. Orezeanu, wrote to Radu Lecca, Plenipotentiary for Jewish Affairs in Romania,[11] informing him that the head of the German Railways 'Ost-Berlin' had convened a conference for 26–28 September to draw up a timetable for special trains carrying Jews from Romania to the General Government (German-occupied Poland), and requesting details so that the Romanian delegates to the conference could come to a decision in the matter.[12] In his reply sent the following day, Lecca confirmed that Marshal Antonescu had 'given orders that the evacuation[13] of the Jews from Romania be prepared in the smallest detail by the Ministry of Internal Affairs, on the basis of instructions given by Mr Mihai Antonescu'.[14] At the same time, however, Franz

Rademacher, the head of the Jewish Department of the *Abteilung Deutschland* (the German Foreign Ministry body responsible for the Jewish question) relayed to Berlin the information from 'two sources in Romania, Dr Emil Hoffman (the press attaché at the German legation in Bucharest and an adviser to the Romanian government, and a member of the Iron Guard), that [Marshal] Antonescu in fact had no intention of deporting the Romanian Jews'.[15]

Antonescu's real intentions on this subject are a puzzle. Certainly, Lecca's reply to the Director General of Romanian Railways bears out Richter's report of Mihai Antonescu's assent to deportation. If Lecca is to be believed, Mihai was telling Richter the truth when he said that his government had agreed to deportation. The Marshal then changed his mind.[16] Whatever the explanation, steps to implement the deportation of Romanian Jews to Poland were never taken. Romanian railway representatives failed to attend the meeting in Berlin organized by Adolf Eichmann on 26 September at which they were expected to discuss the transport of Jews from Romania 'by "special trains" every other day, each carrying 2,000 Jews to Belzec. A German railway expert was sent to Bucharest to make arrangements, but no deportations took place'.[17] Antonescu may well have considered capitulation to German pressure as an affront to Romanian sovereignty since the German plan not only targeted Jews from the Regat, the Banat and southern Transylvania, but proposed their deportation to a foreign territory.[18]

When rumours spread of the plan for deportation of the Jews to Poland, Mihai Antonescu recognized that he and the Marshal had considered the matter. At a Council of Ministers meeting of 29 September 1942 he declared:

> Rumour factories are being organized which have an ingenious and diabolical machine for launching rumours which are designed to paralyse the moral effects of an action of ours and to replace them with other elements of unease or even to create elements of unease. My conviction is that the principal organizer of this machine is the Yid. And if this system continues, be certain that we will adopt the most severe measures. I have checked this against one fact. At a certain point, the issue of sending some Jews from our country elsewhere was discussed. Nobody except the Marshal, me, and a person liaising with the government of the Reich knew about this. Only three lines were written, very vague, and the only one to know about this problem was somebody in the German SS. Well then, exactly five days after this conversation, the whole of Transylvania was invaded by the news that the Romanian government was expelling the entire Yid population from Transylvania in order to create room for 20,000 or 100,000 German families from towns bombed by the British. [19]

The decision to suspend the deportation of the Jews to Transnistria was conveyed by Mihai Antonescu to a meeting of the Council of Ministers on

13 October from which the Marshal was absent. Since the beginning of July rumours had been circulating in Bucharest about Ion Antonescu's health. Throughout the summer he had been laid low by a mysterious ailment which had severely limited his public appearances.[20] Mihai prefaced his announcement by referring, albeit obliquely, to the international concern expressed at his regime's treatment of its Jews:

> Recently, a great deal of dissatisfaction and in particular an unfavourable attitude has been created in connection with the treatment of the Jews. There is no point in my telling you that I, who signed the law on expropriation of Jewish property, am not a philo-semite, and I take no honour in considering – however much I might be driven by the universal laws for the protection of man – that it is a duty for us to look after these elements, as we would look after Romanians. I consider, however, that because of the international situation and because of the fact that in other countries the treatment of the Jews is different from that in Romania, we must avoid creating – given that the Romanian soldier, through his genuine heroism, is raising our history to new levels and is building around the Romanian people an atmosphere of civilization and national consciousness – we must avoid creating a situation in which it appears that, through administrative measures or our own omissions, we do not care if, at the level of degrees of civilization, the Romanian government is not contributing to this prestige created by the army, or, on the contrary, is working against it...

The prestige of the government was at stake over its handling of the Jewish 'problem':

> The main reason why I have convened you here is this problem of the Jews which also threatens the government. If you want to know the truth, I can tell you that recently I have received a whole series of details on this subject even from German circles from whom I was informed last year about such matters. It was pointed out to me that people attribute these measures [against the Jews] to German initiative and influence when the Germans have nothing to do with them.

Mihai Antonescu underlined his point when turning to the 'Romanianization' of commerce which involved the 'removal of Jews from the important positions in the national economy':

> I am not carrying out anti-Semitic reform for the Germans and under the doctrine of Dr Rosenberg,[21] however powerful and healthy it is, and however great the danger that Jewish Communism or simply the Judaic ideology might represent. What interests me is to make Romanian

nationalism and to take from Dr Rosenberg's reform and the German experience the wise decisions and not any measure which does not suit our country.... We must make our anti-Semitic reform a creative reform, not a demagogic one, to prevent damage to ourselves and remaining fixed in the positions we create. This is our situation.

These words brought Antonescu to the heart of the business of the meeting. As was customary in the parlance of the Antonescu regime, the word 'deportation' was avoided:

For the time being all transports of Jews across the Dniester are suspended.[22] The transports will be henceforth organized by a joint body, which will be set up by the General Staff, the Ministry of Internal Affairs, the Ministry of Finance and the Presidency of the Council of Ministers.... The General Staff give the orders, the Ministry of the Interior must carry them out, the prefecture of police begins the manhunt in Bucharest in order to catch those [Jews] on the list.... We hold to the principle that all Jews who are dangerous because of their subversive or Communist activity will be subjected to all rigours and the harshest measures will be applied to them, including the death penalty, to avoid agitation over this measure.[23]

This suspension of deportation also affected those Jews currently in custody for shirking compulsory labour. While Mihai Antonescu's words made it clear that the deportation of Jews was to be *suspended*, it was equally plain that a resumption was envisaged once the new body he had referred to was set up.

The Marshal never explained his decision; it was probably influenced by a conjunction of factors rather than by one specific consideration. He was aware that the deportations had exacerbated Romania's already negative image in Washington – this was underlined by a call to the Romanian government by the US Secretary of State Cordell Hull in September 1942 for a halt to the deportations to Transnistria on pain of measures being taken against Romanians living in the United States. On top of this, vigorous protests had been made at the plan for the deportations of Romanian Jews by the Swiss *chargé d'affaires* René de Veck, the Apostolic Nuncio Andrea Cassulo,[24] and the Metropolitan of Transylvania, Nicolae Bălan, in which it was pointed out that deportation, the institution of ghettos and the wearing of the Star of David had been measures taken only in satellite and occupied countries such as Croatia and Poland, and not in other sovereign Axis members such as Italy and Hungary.[25]

A particular impact on the Marshal was made, according to a declaration of the Chief Rabbi of Romania, Alexander Şafran, by the Metropolitan of Transylania Nicolae Bălan, who recalled in 1961 that the interventions which we attempted to make with the government and with Romanian persons of influence had been unsuccessful. There was a last chance: an approach to the Metropolitan of Transylvania, Monseigneur Bălan. The latter, in reply to my personal request, came from Sibiu, the bishop's residence, to Bucharest, to talk to me. My meeting with the prelate took place in the house of General Vaitoianu. It was dramatic. After only a few hours, Metropolitan Bălan informed me that he had persuaded the Marshal to cancel the decision to deport the Jewish population of Transylvania.[26]

A crucial influence on Antonescu's decision was Helen, the Queen Mother. The queen was identified in Nazi circles as the leading opponent of the measures taken against the Jews in Romania.[27] A report from SS *Hauptsturmführer* Gustav Richter, Counsellor for Jewish Affairs at the German legation in Bucharest, dated 30 October 1942, is eloquent in this respect:

A Swiss journalist reports the following: 'On the occasion of the last[28] transport of Jews to Transnistria, the philogist Barbu Lăzăreanu (Lazarovici) was also due to be arrested and deported. The police commissioner, however, gave him a breathing-space of "two days" to arrange his situation. Lăzăreanu, therefore, contacted a friend, the well-known doctor Victor Gomoiu, who is well regarded by Helen the Queen Mother. Gomoiu, a man so nice that he could not imagine that the Jews are so persecuted, went in person to Strada Sfântul Ion Nou [a building in which the Jews were assembled for deportation] to see for himself the pitiful state of these unfortunate persons.

As a result Dr Gomoiu immediately got in touch with the Queen Mother, and the latter with King Michael. The Queen Mother told the King that what was happening to people in this country was a disgrace and that she could not bear it any longer, all the more so because the king – her son – and her name would be permanently associated in Romanian history with the crimes committed against the Jews, while she would be known as the mother of 'Michael the Wicked'. She is said to have warned the king that, if the deportations were not immediately halted, she would leave the country. As a result the king immediately telephoned the Prime Minister Mihai Antonescu and, as a consequence, a meeting of the Council of Ministers took place following which not only those arrested were released, but a communiqué of the Presidency [Marshal Antonescu] was released. Amongst the Jews deported recently, several hundred were shot, some by the Germans, others by the Romanians.[29]

Antonescu's about-turn on deportation may be seen as opportunism but it was an opportunism that saved the remaining Jews of Romania from death camps in Poland. Had the Iron Guard under Horia Sima still been in power in Romania, there is no doubt that it would have acceded to the German request to implement the Final Solution.

One can only speculate on whether the slowdown in the German advance before Stalingrad in October 1942 was also a factor in Antonescu's decision to reverse the deportations, but the Marshal was astute enough to realize that a short war against the Soviet Union offered the best chance of a victory and he may well have had an eye on the eventual peace settlement when considering the consequences of his reversal of policy on deportation.[30] Instead, Antonescu turned to emigration to Palestine as a solution to the 'Jewish problem'.

Emigration certainly found favour with Mihai Antonescu. On 2 July 1942, he had declared:

> I am in agreement if the Romanian state can undertake an emigration policy that would remove from the country as many foreign elements as possible. It is all the same to me if these elements are taken beyond the Bug, in Transnistria, or beyond the Mediterranean to Palestine; the essential thing is that these elements leave our territory.[31]

On 9 October 1942, Filderman was invited to meet Alfred Tester, the representative in Bucharest of a Greek shipowner Yanos Pandelis, and Constantin Bursan both of whom, according to Radu Lecca, the Plenipotentiary for Jewish Affairs in Romania, were double agents of British and German intelligence.[32] They proposed that he finance an operation for the transport of Jews from Romania by sea which they, with their connections in shipping, would organize. Filderman's priority was to save the surviving Jews in Transnistria; the first step in their emigration would have to be, Filderman insisted, their return to Romania. He also demanded that the emigrants be given safe conduct, a step which implied German acquiescence in the plan. Tester and Bursan told Filderman that they would relay Filderman's views to the authorities and get back to him.[33]

Pandelis was no stranger to the business of facilitating Jewish emigration from Romania.[34] He had been responsible for the passage of the ill-fated *Struma*, a small vessel which had sailed from Constanta on 12 December 1941 for Palestine with 769 passengers.[35] It soon became clear that figures in government were closely associated with the emigration proposal. Radu Lecca raised the matter with the Central Jewish Office. Figures were attached to the scheme: 70,000 Jews deported to Transnistria were to be allowed to emigrate against payment of 200,000 lei (about $350) per person. Although Lecca hinted that the Germans had given their approval to the plan, the first report of the proposal to Berlin, from the Bucharest legation, dates from 12 December 1942, that is, some two months after it was first put to Filderman. In a letter to Berlin, Killinger acknowledged his source as Lecca when providing the details and the information that both Marshal Antonescu and Mihai Antonescu supported the plan. The destination of the Jews, Kill-inger stated, was Palestine and Syria. Lecca, he wrote, had received instruc-tions from the Marshal to organize 'the emigration of 75,000 to 80,000 Jews to Palestine and Syria'. The only condition for emigration was the 200,000 lei fee.[36] Killinger's interpretation of the plan was that the Marshal, while still anxious to solve the 'Jewish problem', preferred emigration to deportation. This shift in policy required a reaction from Berlin.

The Foreign Ministry replied on 9 January 1943 to von Killinger, stating that Lecca's plan 'represented a partial resolution unacceptable within the framework of the fundamental lines followed by the German government for a European solution to the Jewish problem'. Emigration, it was argued, would place a great strain on Germany's relations with its friends in the Middle East and would also deliver 80,000 Jews to its enemies, who would have no impediment in acting against the Axis.[37] Killinger was instructed to take every step to prevent the plan's implementation; in Germany's view, the significance of the plan was not as a means to save the Jews deported to Transnistria, but as a signal to the Allies that Romania was not a subservient lackey of Germany.

The German High Command informed the Foreign Ministry, on 15 January 1943, that five ships had already sailed and that permits for ten more had been granted.[38] German objections were to no avail. They were reflected in a report sent to Eichmann in early March 1943 which stated that Romanian ships carrying many hundreds of Jew were leaving for Palestine from the ports of Constanța, Brăila and Galați. Some of the vessels sailed under the Romanian flag to Turkey where they offloaded their passengers who trav-elled on to Palestine. The German legation in Bucharest had been instructed to tell the Romanian government that the ships involved were 'absolutely necessary' for the Axis war effort and that this traffic should be halted. Moreover, the emigration of Jews was 'not desirable, not only because of our [German] general policies towards the Jews, which it seems are disadvan-taged by this practice, but also because of their influence on our policies toward Turkey and the Arab countries'.[39]

Hitler himself attempted to bring Antonescu round to his way of thinking over the 'Jewish problem'. At their meeting at Castle Klessheim in Salzburg on 13 April 1943, Hitler

> explained that in this problem – he did not want it to appear as a criticism – he had a different view to that of the Marshal and Admiral Horthy. The Führer then pointed out the measures used to remove the Jews both from the economy and from cultural life, as result of which there had been a veritable flourishment. In other countries, in which the Jewish problem had not been clarified, like, for example, Hungary, the situation was much more complicated. The Jews were the natural allies of Bolshevism and the candidates for the opposition which had been taken over by

Bolshevism. The Führer was therefore of the opinion, different to that of the Marshal, that it was all the better to take radical action against the Jews....In Germany, in the wake of the eradication of the Jewish problem, there was now a united people, without any opposition. There were no impediments in the economy, neither was there any turning back on the road already taken.

Antonescu replied that he would love to remove the Jews from Romania but he was not very clear as to where to take them. He reminded [Hitler] of the difficulties he had in transporting the Jews from Romania, through Bulgaria and the attitude of the Bulgarians was the result of German influence...[40]

At a meeting on the following day with German Foreign Minister von Ribbentrop, also at Castle Klessheim, Antonescu, in response to a question from von Ribbentrop as to whether the Romanian Jews could not be sent to Russia,

> spoke of 100,000 Jews whom he would like to move to the Crimea to use them there in the mining industry...
>
> He [Antonescu] requests, however, that they should not be murdered, since on a previous occasion he found himself forced to stop the deportation of Jews to Russia when it was revealed that they had been purely and simply murdered there.[41]

German opposition did block a proposal put by Filderman to Bursan on 2 January 1943 that 5,000 orphans be repatriated from Transnistria to Romania while onward emigration plans were explored. Richter, the counsellor for Jewish affairs at the Bucharest legation, received word of the idea and told Lecca that the Romanian government should reject it. At the same time, he reported Filderman's proposal to Eichmann. Filderman's request was made in the knowledge that the British were prepared to admit 4,500 children and 500 adult escorts to Palestine, a move that was confirmed by a statement on 3 February by Oliver Stanley, the British Colonial Secretary, regarding the designation of 29,000 entry certificates still available under the 1939 White Paper.[42] Startled that this would spur moves in Romania to facilitate emigration, Eberhard von Thadden, the deputy official in the German Foreign Ministry responsible for Jewish Affairs, wrote to Killinger on the following day with orders that he demand that Bucharest revoke any decision allowing the emigration of Jews. Eichmann himself told the German Foreign Ministry on 3 March that he had learned of discussions carried out by Jewish officials in Romania to secure transit visas from the Turks for a group of 1,000 Jewish children and 100 accompanying adults to travel by train to Turkey *en route* to Palestine. He asked the Ministry to 'prevent the planned emigration'.[43]

Antonescu was not impervious to entreaties from Filderman. Filderman persuaded the Marshal in January 1943 to allow Jewish children from Hungary to cross Romania on their way to Palestine. On 10 February, the Romanian border police at Curtici, on the frontier with Hungary, reported the arrival of 72 children, who were then escorted to Giurgiu, on the Danube.[44] The New Zionist Organization took advantage of Antonescu's acquiescence in the emigration of Jewish children by arranging for a small group of Jewish children, some of them Polish nationals, to travel overland via Bulgaria to Turkey. They left by train on 14 March 1943, only to be met by German officials at the Bulgarian frontier point with Turkey who singled out the Polish children and sent them to the German-occupied Poland. On 4 April, Killinger warned the counsellor for Jewish matters at the German legation in Sofia, SS *Hauptsturmführer* Danecker, that a further transport of 74 Jewish children was being arranged from Bucharest by the Romanian state transport agency *Romania*. He advised that

> The agency *Romania* has been informed that [the transport] would not be in the interest of the Reich, since it would be an emigration not only from Romania, but also from Europe, at a particular time when efforts were being made for the resolution of the Jewish problem in Europe.[45]

He asked that if the transport began, the counsellor should give orders that its onward journey from Bulgaria be halted. Two days later, Killinger told Lecca to inform Nandor Gingold, secretary-general of the Central Jewish Office (CJO), that Jewish refugees discovered in Bulgaria would be arrested. This information prompted the Zionists to suspend such departures.

On top of this, conflicts with the New Zionist Movements vitiated the cooperation necessary for the organization of new transports. Frustrated by the constant bickering amongs Zionist factions in Romania, the Mossad (Hebrew for 'institute') decided to set up its own emigration operation from its offices in Istanbul.[46] Shaul Avigur was sent to the city in October 1943 to coordinate the work; at the same time, he sent a strongly worded message to the Jewish leaders in Romania demanding greater unity.[47] Ze'ev Shind, a senior Mossad activist, turned to Yanos Pandelis, the Greek agent. The latter's part in the *Struma* disaster made him an unwelcome partner to the Zionists whom Shind was endeavouring to involve in the revival of emigration by sea, but Shind was certain that one successful voyage would bring them into line. To this end he set up a cover transport agency in December 1943, the Oficiul Roman, Agentie de Transporturi (ORAT).[48] ORAT was staffed by Jewish youth movement members who worked closely with the Palestine office of the Jewish Agency in Instanbul. Pandelis's role was to obtain exit visas. Shind's faith in Pandelis was vindicated when one of two boats – the *Maritsa* – purchased by the Agency in Varna for the transport of refugees from Constanta was confiscated in January 1944 by German patrol boats on its way to the Romanian port. By using his extensive network of contacts in Bucharest and Constanta, Pandelis was able to buy its release.

The German action demonstrated their continued determination to frustrate Jewish emigration. They were well aware of the contacts between Mossad's centre of operations in Geneva[49] and its representatives in Bucharest and Istanbul from copies of correspondence between these offices which they had been given by Hans Volti, an agent for Swiss intelligence who acted as a courier between Geneva and Bucharest.[50] The German Foreign Ministry passed this information on to the Romanian authorities as evidence of 'hostile' activities carried out by the Zionists against the Romanian government and in January 1944 the leaders of the New Zionist Movement and Jewish youth movements were arrested, among them Misu Benvenisti. They were charged with helping refugees enter Romania illegally with forged identity papers, but most of the senior figures were released in mid-March; the youth members were detained for several months.

ORAT continued its transport of Jews by sea to Istanbul throughout the spring. From there the refugees travelled overland to Palestine, within the quota of permits issued by the British. Turkish visas for the passengers and Red Cross protection for the vessels was obtained through the offices of Charles Kolb, the representative of the International Committee of the Red Cross (ICRC) in Romania who had arrived in Romania in October 1943. Kolb had visited Transnistria and was deeply moved by the plight of the deportees, especially the orphans. To his mind, emigration offered their best hope of salvation. In mid-May 1944, Kolb was asked by Jewish organizations in Romania to issue certificates to Jews who wished to emigrate and by the end of the month some 1,400 Jews had left by boat. His action produced a warning from the ICRC on 29 June to respect ICRC's principle of strict political neutrality:

> You must avoid undertaking actions that could be seen as more political than humanitarian. We feel that your action with regard to the special permits that are required for Jews and foreigners who wish to leave Romania is a step too far.[51]

In his reply of 25 July, Kolb pointed out that

> M. de Weck, the Swiss Minister [to Romania], had at the start of the anti-Semitic legislation obtained that the Swiss Jews should not be subject to the clauses of the various special laws, since Switzerland did not allow the differentiation of its nationals according to race and religion. M. de Weck managed to have this exemption extended to the Jews of nations for whom Switzerland acts as a Protecting Power. The same is true for foreign Jews under the aegis of the legations of Sweden and Spain. Thus all the Jews who come from neutral and enemy countries are not subject to this

special legislation and need not be mentioned. I cannot concern myself with Jews who are nationals of the Axis powers since their respective governments would certainly allow no such intervention.[52]

German opposition to these departures had little effect on Marshal Antonescu. He had given his approval in mid-December 1943 for two Bulgarian-registered vessels, the *Maritsa* and the *Milka*, to enter Romanian ports, chartered by ORAT to carry refugees, to Turkey, and at the same time he granted a request from the Romanian Red Cross for a transport of 150 Jewish children from Transnistria to leave on a Bulgarian-registered vessel, the *Bellacitta*, which it had chartered in Varna.[53] In the case of adult refugees Antonescu could be less sympathetic; on 7 March 1944, he rejected a proposal of the authorities in Bukovina to bring 2,000 adult Jews from Cernăuţi to the port of Constanta for emigration.[54]

On 3 August 1944, three Turkish vessels, the *Mefkure*, the *Morina* and the *Bulbul*, which had been chartered in May by ORAT, finally left Constanţa for Istanbul with Mossad approval with more than 1,000 emigrants. Although Turkey had broken diplomatic relations with Germany two days earlier, and there was hesitation about sending the boats in the new circumstances – Mihai Antonescu advised against sailing – the vessels displayed the Red Cross and there was no indication to suggest that the German navy would attack them. Indeed the German navy had provided an escort around a minefield outside Constanţa harbour. Early on the morning of 5 August, the *Mefkure*, the last of the boats to sail, was attacked by a submarine in the Black Sea and sank, with the loss of 277 lives.[55] Conflicting accounts of the disaster given by survivors did not allow the identity of the submarine to be established; investigations pointed to either an accidental attack by a Soviet submarine or a deliberate attack by a German one.[56] The other two boats escaped and reached Turkey from where their passengers were taken overland to Palestine.

The disaster did not dissuade Mossad from pressing ahead with further transports. The Jews in Palestine were desperate to capitalize on Admiral Horthy's decision of 19 July to stop the deportation of Hungarian Jews and to allow those with immigration permits for Palestine to leave. Their determination was expressed in letters sent by Mossad to Zionist representatives in Romania on 14 August: 'The reasons [that force us to continue] are the facts rooted in the situation itself, which has not changed because of the disaster. Saving Jews, especially those from Hungary, is imperative, and building Palestine through immigration is also imperative. Under present conditions, we have no alternative but sea transports.'[57] Mossad considered that passage through Constanţa for these survivors was the most efficient means of getting them out of Europe since Mihai Antonescu had expressed his willingness to allow Hungarian Jews to transit Romania and leave by sea.[58] On 23 August, the Antonescu regime was overthrown; preparations for sailings went on and a number of vessels with Hungarian refugees and children from Transnistria left in the autumn.

Emigration was not an option for the Jews surviving in Transnistria. Return to Romania was expressly forbidden unless a case for wrongful deportation could be made. A decree law of 22 September 1942 instituted the death penalty for Jews of both sexes above the age of 15 who had been deported to Transnistria and who returned 'in a fraudulent manner to Romania'. Those who abetted this 'crime' through instigation, complicity or failure to report it were liable to a term of forced labour of between 5 and 25 years.[59] Jews therefore resigned themselves to life in the ghettos and the camps. Even those Jews who had been deported on suspicion of being Communists and proved not to have been were not allowed to return to Romania.[60]

By summer 1943, pressure from two fronts was beginning to have an effect on Romanian policy towards the deported Jews. The first was the Eastern Front, where Soviet advances reminded the Romanian dictator and his closest associates of the precariousness of their position and a probable reckoning with the Allies. The second was Wilhelm Filderman, Chairman of the disbanded Romanian Jewish Federation, who bombarded Antonescu and General Constantin Vasiliu, the head of the gendarmerie, with memoranda demanding the repatriation of *all* Jews from Transnistria.[61] Some progress was made in this respect when, on 30 September, the Romanian Council of Order (*Consiliul de Ordine*), a new state body for repatriation, ordered the gendarmerie in Transnistria to repatriate all Jews sentenced for contraventions of the forced labour requirements who had completed their terms of punishment. Upon arrival in their places of origin, the Jews concerned were to report to the local police.[62]

A security police report from Chişinău of 2 November stated that

> on 17 October 1943 thirty-four Jews passed through Ungheni [on the border of Bessarabia and Romania] by train, of whom nine, originally from Cernăuţi, have been released from the labour camp in Golta, Transnistria, and twenty-five, originally from Bucharest, from the labour camp in Ananiev, Transnistria.[63]

On 12 October 1943, Filderman addressed a memorandum to the Romanian government proposing that the deported Jews be brought back to their places of domicile in Romania.[64] On 13 November 1943, Mihai Antonescu sent a copy to General Vasiliu, the Minister of the Interior, of a memorandum, also dated 12 October, on the feasibility of repatriating the Jews deported to Transnistria with a request that the two men discuss the matter. The memorandum offers a statistical summary of the situation of the Jews in Transnistria at the time:

> in 1940 there lived in Bessarabia, Bukovina and the county of Dorohoi about 300,000 Jews of whom 275,419 resided in the territory occupied by the Soviet Union (*Analele Institutului Statistic al Romaniei*, 1942, vol. 1, pp. 340–1) while today there remain only 16,000 Jews in Bukovina

(*Bukarester Tagblatt* of 8 August 1942) and 3,000–4,000 in Dorohoi. Therefore, 280,000 Jews no longer live in these areas. The *Bukarester Tagblatt* of 8 August 1942 claims that 185,000 Jews were deported, to which figure, if we add the deportations after 8 August 1942, we would have about 190,000 to 200,000 Jews deported. As regards the remainder up to 300,000, there is official data. It is known, however, that a number of Jews were deported under Soviet rule [from Bessarabia and northern Bukovina], while a number of Jews were taken when the Soviet troops withdrew [from Bessarabia and northern Bukovina] or they followed these troops.... Today only about 78,000 deported Jews are still alive in Transnistria, so that 122,000, that is 61% have died in two years.[65]

These 78,000, the memorandum continued, were made up of 25,000 men, the majority over 50 years of age, 33,000 women and 20,000 children of both sexes, under the age of 18. The larger number of women was explained by the fact that women had been deported from the county of Dorohoi whose husbands were working in other counties in the kingdom. The women had been told that their husbands would follow them. The women had, therefore, 'taken their children by the hand and left with only the clothes they had on them'. For this reason, the death rate had been highest amongst those deported from Dorohoi. On their return from labour duties, the husbands had stayed in Dorohoi 'while their wives and children are still in Transnistria'.[66]

The memorandum is forthright in its explanation of the inconsistencies in the application of the orders for deportation. The reasons for the deportations, it stated, were the behaviour of the Jews towards the Romanian army when it withdrew from Bessarabia and northern Bukovina, and their behaviour towards the Romanians during the Soviet occupation of these provinces:

> During the deportations the Vice-President of the Council of Ministers [Mihai Antonescu] decided that property owners, industrialists, traders, craftsmen and intellectuals vital to the national economy as well as public officials and public service pensioners should not be deported. The order, however, was not carried out in Bessarabia, or in Bukovina, or in Dorohoi, only in Cernăuţi where through its application about 16,000 Jews stayed behind.[67]

From an examination of the reasons for deportation it had emerged that various categories of Jews had been deported 'contrary to the government's intentions'. These were first, the Jews living in the county of Dorohoi and in southern Bukovina. 'Since these lands had never been occupied by the Soviet Union, their inhabitants could not be considered guilty of the aforementioned accusations.' War veterans, widows and war orphans from the First World War, descendants of veterans of the War of Independence

(1877–78), women and children whose husbands were still doing compulsory labour in Romania, had all been victims. In this category were Jews who, on the outbreak of war, had been sent to Wallachia from the area of the front in Bukovina and Dorohoi but who, on the intervention of the Ministry of Finance, had been sent back to their homes in the autumn of 1941 in order to subscribe to the war loan to which Jews were required to do by law. After subscribing, the order for deportation came and they were deported. Had they remained in Wallachia they would have been safe.

A second group of Jews who had been deported 'contrary to the government's intentions' were those from Wallachia, Transylvania and the Banat who happened to be on family visits or on business in Bessarabia. Other groups deported were active and retired public servants from Bessarabia and northern Bukovina who had been deported before Mihai Antonescu's order they these Jews should be exempt – among these was the president of the appeal court in Cernăuți and his counsellors – and the wives and children of Jews deemed useful to the economy.

It was natural, the memorandum argued, that the Jews in the above categories should be repatriated but it went on to propose that all other Jews should be included:

> We believe and we ask that the others be brought back, both because, as has been seen, the deportation was carried out in a general fashion, without an examination of individual culpability, and on human grounds. Indeed, even if all the Jews are considered guilty, any punishment has a term and even those sentenced to hard labour for life are amnestied or pardoned for general or special reasons.

Making the case for repatriation in terms similar to those used by Filderman in his petitions to the Marshal, the memorandum became more graphic:

> When two thirds of the deported have died within two years, when there are families with ten members of whom only one or two survive, when there are children whose parents have died in exile, when thousands of the deportees, barefoot and hungry, can only find as daily sustenance a cup of boiling water in which 30 to 40 grams of maize float around, and thus the third of the Jews who survive are threatened with death, their suffering merits, we believe, forgiveness, especially as the majority of survivors are women and young children.[68]

Reinforcing the case for repatriation, the memorandum turned to the Marshal's own words in an address to schoolchildren in Odessa, reported on 1 June 1943, when he said that children's hearts 'should be sown with the love of one's fellow being and brother, to prepare them to understand later that man must be regarded, treated and governed like a human being, whatever his language, faith, merits or sins'. If the deported Jews had sinned, it declared, they had suffered enough to be forgiven.[69]

In conclusion, as a home for the deported Jews, the memorandum proposed that they be returned to Bessarabia, Bukovina and Dorohoi since of the original 'approximately 300,000 Jews and 125,655 Germans who lived there, the Germans had been repatriated to Germany and only 78,000 Jews survived in Transnistria, so that their return will pass unnoticed'. If a 'solution' involving concentration was preferred, then the Jews could either be grouped, according to origin, in towns in Bessarabia, Bukovina, Dorohoi and in the kingdom, or in ghettos 'similar to those in Transnistria'.[70]

After consultations between Mihai Antonescu, Vasiliu and the Marshal, the order was given on 8 December for the repatriation of the Jews from Dorohoi who had been deported to Transnistria, of those formerly interned at Vapniarka, and of the 16 survivors of the group of 568 Jews deported for having requested repatriation to the Soviet Union after the loss of Bessarabia and northern Bukovina.[71] The first group of Jews from Dorohoi, numbering around 1,500, returned to Romania on 20 December. At the same time, another 70 deportees were repatriated, among them the 16 survivors mentioned above. Between 20 and 25 December, 6,107 Jews, mostly from Dorohoi, were moved from Transnistria to Moldavia.

At a meeting on internal security chaired by Mihai Antonescu on 21 January 1944, the latter made it clear that any mass withdrawal of civilians from Transnistria, Bessarabia, Bukovina and Moldova in the face of the Soviet advance would cause major political problems since it would empty these territories of their Romanian population. Any suggestion that the state might play a part in such an evacuation was to be dismissed. He was even more opposed to the evacuation of the Jews from Transnistria, apart from those from Dorohoi. Jews from Bukovina who had settled in Bucharest would be forced to move to the provinces or to return to their place of origin. Turning to Jews of foreign nationality, he ordered the following measures:

> The Jews who have come from Spain will be treated as Spanish citizens. Those Romanian Jews who have taken out Chilean, Spanish or Swiss nationality, etc. in order to avoid obligations [compulsory labour] cannot be treated as such. They will either be treated as the Romanian Jews, or expelled.[72]

Five days later, the Marshal spelled out his reasons for his opposition to the repatriation of Jews from Transnistria:

> I cannot agree to have any Jews return to Romania from anywhere on earth when I cannot receive Romanians. We will evacuate only Romanians [from Transnistria] . . . . But if there is space, I would give some thought to

them [the Jews], not to settle them permanently, but for them to be sent over our borders in a very short space of time. But for us to let in all the Jews from Transnistria, as the Jewish Community has brazenly requested, when I cannot bring the Transnistrians [Romanians], would mean committing the greatest crime in the history of the nation. If I cannot bring Transnistrians, then I cannot bring a single Jew, for we would cause chaos. All the more reason why I cannot bring Jews or Ukrainians. No Ukrainian from Bukovina has any business in Romania. We will only evacuate Romanians.[73]

In a letter written on 4 February 1944 in response to the architect Herman Clejan's criticism of the slow rate at which Jews were being repatriated from Transnistria, Antonescu explained:

Do not forget that we have over 200,000 Romanians in Transnistria as well as more over the Bug river who, as the Front approaches our borders, must come to Free Romania. The situation of our brothers raises for the Romanian nation one of the greatest problems of conscience and I am profoundly worried for these hundred thousands of Romanians, whom we cannot shelter in the country. Understand that in these conditions it is morally and politically impossible for me to agree to bring back the Jews from Transnistria. About this there can be no question. I have commanded, however, that the Jews from immediately near the front are to be brought into southern Transnistria, from whence they could be trans-ported out of the country by the Jewish Community, through the connec-tions which it has abroad. From among the Jews in Transnistria I have repatriated only those who were deported there by mistake, thus approx-imately 7,000 Jews from Dorohoi and 4,500 orphaned children . . . [74]

Antonescu's concern for the plight of the 200,000 Romanians in Transnistria, while understandable, omits to recognize that they, unlike the Jews, had not been deported by Antonescu but had settled there of their own volition.

On 10 February 1944, General C. Z. Vasiliu, the head of the gendarmerie, informed the Central Jewish Office that the Council of Order had given its approval a week earlier, on Antonescu's recommendation, for the transfer of all Jews deported to Transnistria to be moved to the port of Odessa, or to the counties of Odessa and Oceacov in order to facilitate their emigration. Vasiliu asked the CJO to make the necessary arrangements since it was responsible for the transport, subsistence and housing of the Jews. The CJO pointed out that it would be impossible to move 'move than 40,000 people', and in any case, the emigration of such a number 'was out of the question'. With this in mind the CJO requested that the Jewish deportees in the coun-ties of Ananiev, Berezovka, Oceacov, Balta, Golta and Tulcin – totalling approximately 10,000 persons – be moved to other counties, in particular

Moghilev, Dubăsari, Tiraspol and Râbnița, since the distances involved were shorter and space had been created there as a result of the repatriation of some 7,000 Jews to Dorohoi, the Regat, and Transylvania, and of Jewish orphans.[75] On 6 March 1944, 1,846 orphans under the age of 15 were repatriated and later in the month 2,518 deportees returned with the help of Jewish aid committees in Bucharest. Most of the latter were allowed to return to their homes, with the exception of 563 Communists interned at Vapniarka who were sent under escort to Târgu-Jiu.[76]

Time was of the essence for the survival of the Jews in Transnistria. As the Soviet forces threw the Germans back, Antonescu prepared to withdraw from the area and, on 15 February, it was announced that the 'government of Transnistria' had been abolished and replaced by 'The Military Administration of the Territory between the Dniester and the Bug'. This was merely one step away from the cession of the whole area to the retreating Germans. Within a month the Romanian authorities had handed over control; on 13 March, Antonescu resolved that the Romanian administration be withdrawn from Transnistria and that all Jews there should be brought for their own safety to Bessarabia and Bukovina.[77] As Romanian officials left Odessa, they plundered the Jewish cemetery, removing marble tombstones and sending them by rail to various masons in Bucharest for sale as building material. News of this vandalism reached Antonescu, who condemned the desecration as 'an odious and thoughtless act which could have consequences for the whole nation'. He ordered the return of the stones at the expense of those responsible on pain of internment and commensurate confiscation of their wealth.[78] Whether such sanctions were taken again the plunderers is unclear, but certainly restitution became impractical in the face of the advancing Red Army.

Antonescu was equally anxious to hide from the Russians evidence that he had removed property from Transnistria. At a meeting of the economic council on 19 February 1943, he explained why he had not signed a decree for the transfer of assets from the province:

> Why didn't I sign the decree? Here is the real season: nothing must appear in the Official Bulletin, not one document which shows what we brought from Transnistria.... We might lose the war and then the Russians would come and hold us to account for this, referring to the very documents we drew up. But if they find no trace, what will they do? I shall not declare what I took from Transnistria. But if they find evidence in our documents, then they can say: this is what you took.[79]

On 16 March, General Constantin Vasiliu, the head of the gendarmerie, informed Romanian Army Chief of Staff, that Antonescu had given orders for the repatriation of all Jews deported to Transnistria. Those deported from Bessarabia would be settled in Bălți and Hotin counties, those from

Bukovina in the city of Cernăuţi and in the districts of Cernăuţi and Storojineţ. Those from the Regat would be returned to their homes and the Jews interned in Grosulovo camp and those imprisoned in Râbniţa jail would be transferred to the Târgu-Jiu camp.[80] Most of the Communists among the prisoners in Râbniţa never saw Romania again.[81] Although the Ministry of Internal Affairs gave the order on 16 March to the gendarmerie in Râbniţa to evacuate the jail, the telegram never arrived because the post office in the town had been closed. On the evening of 18 March, some 60 of the prisoners – apparently common law offenders – were removed from the prison under escort on the order of the local gendarmerie commander. Shortly afterwards, some of the partisans were also led away. The chief jailer, Văluţă Pintilie, in the absence of the prison governor who was on sick leave, handed over control of the prison and its inmates – 215 in number according to the transfer document – to a German officer named Uresan Zozi.[82] The officer, identified as a captain in some witness statements, told Pintilie to identify the principal Communists and the two of them, accompanied by a Kalmuk soldier, went from cell to cell as the soldier shot each prisoner in the back of the neck.[83] Fifty-two prisoners were murdered, among them the female partisans.[84]

Charles Kolb, the delegate of the International Committee of the Red Cross, complained to Antonescu on 30 March 1944 of the delay in implementing his order for repatriation. He advised the Marshal that there was no knowledge of the order in Shargorod, Murafa and Jmerinca. Massacres of Jews by German troops had been reported in Balta, Moghilev and Cernăuţi, but he had been unable to verify the information. He therefore suggested that the Jews in these areas be placed under the protection of Romanian troops, a step which given the rapid withdrawal of Romanian forces from Transnistria was virtually impossible to implement. [85]

Romania's attitude to the Jews of Hungary

As a result of the German occupation of Hungary on 19 March 1944, Hungarian Jews were targeted under the Final Solution programme. Romania, as a consequence – and Slovakia for a brief period – became a place of refuge. The Germans were aware of this and, on 30 March, alerted their officials to take steps to prevent the 'illegal flight' of Hungarian Jews.[86] Killinger was instructed to put pressure on the Antonescu regime to cooperate, and on 29 May a harsh law was introduced imposing the death penalty on Jews entering the country illegally and on those who assisted them.[87] In practice, this law was never applied,[88] although some of those who were caught by the Romanian border police were sent back to northern Transylvania and subsequently deported to Auschwitz. As in other aspects of Romania's relations with Nazi Germany, there were two sides to the coin of this apparent compliance with German wishes: despite the enactment of the law, Mihai Antonescu was willing to allow Hungarian Jews to cross Romania and leave by sea. He had given an undertaking to this effect to Charles Kolb, the representative of the International Red Cross, at a meeting with him in Bucharest on 1 June 1944.[89] Indeed, according to a report sent on 17 June by Leland Harrison, the American minister in Berne, to the US Secretary of State, confidential instructions had been issued to Romanian border authorities to facilitate the admission of Jews from Hungary.[90]

How far the Marshal was aware of Mihai Antonescu's assurances is unclear. Radu Lecca, in his memoirs written after his release from jail in 1963, but published only after the revolution, opined that 'if the Marshal had known about the presence of such [Jewish] refugees from Hungary, he would have given the order to shoot them (in accordance with the law then in effect) in order to prevent other Hungarian Jews from trying their luck in Romania'.[91] But Lecca, as a key instrument of the regime's anti-Jewish measures, knew full well that this law, introduced on 29 May 1944, was never applied.[92] An order to shoot Jews who crossed into Romania illegally and their accomplices had been issued long before the enactment of the above law, as emerges from a document from a court martial in Cernăuți on 20 January 1943 in which the president of the tribunal resolved that 'the order of Marshal Antonescu for the border guards to shoot Jews who try to cross the frontier on the spot be applied, and if they are caught in the act with accomplices the same punishment should be applied to the latter. This is the only way that we can solve the problem.'[93] First-hand evidence of Antonescu's draconian policy in this regard can be found six months later in the Marshal's response to reports from his intelligence service of attempts by Jews from Sofia who had been moved to the Bulgarian capital to enter Romania clandestinely: 'Those caught in the act of crossing secretly should be shot on sight. Those who succeeded in crossing should be sent to Transnistria.'[94] Now, it appears, the scale of entry of Hungarian Jews into Romania was kept from him. Pecuniary gain derived from the escapees drove some officials in the Ministry of the Interior to cover up the extent of the activity, a simple task since the influx of Hungarian Jews was in the form of a trickle rather than a stream. Humanitarian considerations influenced others. General Constantin Vasiliu in the Ministry of the Interior ordered the police not to give visas to Hungarian Jews who had entered illegally or with false papers 'since according to orders from above their entry into Romania is banned'. Informing the Romanian Foreign Ministry of this order on 4 May, he requested Mihai Antonescu to instruct Romanian consular officials abroad to do the same.[95] Within the police General Nicolae Diaconescu is said by Lecca to have protected Hungarian Jews,[96] while in one notable case, that of Ernest Marton, the former editor of *Uj Kelet* (New East), the Jewish daily of Cluj, a Romanian diplomat helped him to flee to Bucharest where he became head of the Committee for the Aid of

Jewish Refugees from northern Transylvania which operated under the aegis of the Zionist emigration office.[97]

One credible account of the number of Hungarian Jews who crossed clandestinely from Hungary into Romania during 1944 puts the figure at approximately 1,500.[98] This modest number seems all the more striking given the fact that some of the largest ghettos, set up in northern Transylvania in April and the beginning of May 1944, such as those of Oradea, Cluj and Târgu-Mureş, were close to the Romanian border.[99] A number of reasons explain why only a small number of Hungarian Jews took the opportunity to escape. First, most of the able-bodied Jews had been enrolled into compulsory labour service units and their families were unwilling to leave without them, especially as there would be little or no means of supporting young, old and infirm members. Second, families in this position were afraid to make the illegal border crossing. Third, and most relevant in explaining the lack of urgency with which the Jews treated escape, most of them were unaware of the terrible implications of the German occupation of Hungary and remained in ignorance even though senior figures in the Jewish community in northern Transylvania had been alerted about the death camps in Poland. A number of them decided to escape to Romania immediately.

Those Jews who escaped did so largely on their own initiative. Some used local Romanian guides, to whom they paid a fee, others crossed on their own and bribed Romanian border guides, still others did both. Members of the Romanian National Peasant Party in Cluj sheltered Jews and arranged to smuggle them across the frontier, the most prominent being Aurel Socor, a lawyer, who was eventually arrested together with twelve Jewish refugees from Poland and taken to a Gestapo prison in Budapest.[100] Raoul Şorban, a Cluj artist, acted as a link with Ernest Marton and the Committee for the Aid of Refugees from northern Transylvania.[101] In Oradea, Alexandru Pap helped a number of Jews to flee from the ghetto, Janos Szakadati and his wife Juliana, and Ioan and Margareta Pârvulescu gave shelter to Jews, and Gheorghe Mangra, a caretaker, and Emil Maxim, a teacher at the Greek-Catholic seminary, hid Jewish children in the school.[102]

A number of escapees were helped by Zionist networks,[103] or even by individual Hungarian officials. Police sources in Turda, the nearest town to Cluj in southern Transylvania and the first resting place for escapees from the region, reported on 25 May that the head of Hungarian counter-espionage in Cluj had been accused by the Gestapo of aiding the escape of Jews across the frontier as had a gypsy, who worked as a Hungarian agent. Even German officers were involved. A note of the Romanian Intelligence Service (SSI) recorded that the German legation in Bucharest, while expressing satisfaction with the measures taken by the Romanian authorities to prevent a mass influx of Jews from Hungary, drew attention to the fact that 'the passage of Jewish refugees from Hungary to Romania had been strongly assisted to date by the Romanian border authorities and by the Romanian population in

Transylvania'. The legation had also been alerted to the fact that 'numerous Jews from Hungary had been brought directly to Bucharest with the help of elements of the German army and of some members of the Romanian Intelligence service who had been corrupted by the large sums given by the respective Jews or by their relatives in Romania'.[104]

Not all who crossed into Romania managed to evade the border guards. Those who were caught were in some cases sent back across the frontier into northern Transylvania. An army report dated 8 July describes the handling by frontier guards in Beiuş near Timişoara of a group of 15 Jews who had entered Romania illegally. The Jews were allowed to join local Jews for communal meals, a single NCO was assigned to escort the Jews back to the border, one of the refugees escaped from under escort, and no list of the names of the Jews handed back was compiled.[105] These Jews were subsequently deported to Auschwitz.[106] Beiuş was one of the principal crossing points into Romania, together with Arad, Braşov, Sighişoara, Timişoara and Turda. Arad and Turda saw the largest numbers of refugees. In Turda, a local relief team was set up under Arnold Finkelstein, a community leader, who was assisted by Arieh Hirsch, Carol Moscovits and Eszter Goro (Frankel). Hirsh supplied escapees with new identity papers and travel documents for onward journeys. Among the many escapees to pass through the team's hands were Ernest Marton and Moses Carmilly-Weinberger, chief rabbi of the Neolog community of Cluj.[107]

On 18 July 1944, Admiral Horthy stopped the deportation of Hungarian Jews and authorized those with immigration permits for Palestine to leave. Horthy's decision was relayed to the Romanian legation in Budapest by the Swiss legation. The majority, the Swiss advised, were to be transported on Swiss Red Cross vessels from Constanţa, while others – about 100 persons every day – would travel through Bulgaria and Turkey. The Swiss asked the Romanian government to issue transit visas on collective passports for the routes between Curtici-Constanţa, and Curtici-Giurgiu. It further requested the Romanian railways to provide about 120 passenger carriages for the journey from the Hungarian frontier – the Hungarian authorities had undertaken to supply the same number up to Curtici. Mihai Antonescu cabled the Romanian legation in Berne on the same day: 'I have authorized the transit of all those who have entered Romania up to now. Figures have not been established and have not been put to us.'[108] He informed the Hungarian government that he would give his permission for the transit of Hungarian Jews on condition that they embarked immediately from Romanian ports.[109]

The Germans were alarmed by the Romanians' indulgence. Five days before Horthy's decision, Horst Wagner, a senior official in the German Foreign Ministry, had asked Killinger about the Romanian government's toleration of the emigration of Hungarian Jews to Palestine and on 26 July, Killinger confirmed that this was happening with the consent of Marshal Antonescu. On 8 August, Wagner proposed to Ribbentrop that he request

Antonescu to apply the anti-Jewish laws on the statutes in Romania rigorously, but the request, although forwarded through Killinger, was overtaken by Antonescu's overthrow.

The Jews in Palestine were desperate to capitalize on Horthy's decision. Their determination was expressed in letters sent by Mossad to Zissu and others in Romania on 14 August: 'The reasons [that force us to continue] are the facts rooted in the situation itself, which has not changed because of the disaster. Saving Jews, especially those from Hungary, is imperative, and building Palestine through immigration is also imperative. Under present conditions, we have no alternative but sea transports.'[110]

Romanian Jews in Germany

The situation of Jews who were Romanian citizens in Germany and in German-occupied countries was regulated by a convention signed between Germany and Romania on 23 March 1935.[111] Under its terms, Romanian citizens in Germany enjoyed the protection of the Romanian state, and vice versa for German citizens in Romania. However, the application of the convention created numerous problems. The German authorities treated Romanian Jews like German ones, subjecting them to deportation, expropriation and forced labour. Mihai Antonescu, as Romanian Foreign Minister and a specialist in international law, was especially angered by this breach of Romanian sovereignty and instructed his diplomats in Berlin, Paris and Vienna to protest vigorously and on several occasions he was successful in protecting Romanian Jews. Particularly active in this respect was Constantin Karadja, the director of the political department in the Foreign Ministry, Gheorghe Lecca, the general secretary, Dinu Hiott, the minister to Vichy, Ion Gheorghe, his counterpart in Berlin, and Emil Pavelescu, the consul in Paris. Although 'several dozen'[112] Romanian Jews returned to Romania in 1943 and 1944 from Germany, it is calculated that more than 3,300 Romanian Jews were deported from France by the Germans, of whom fewer than 100 were saved.[113]

10
The *Coup* of 23 August 1944

As the military situation steadily deteriorated after the Soviet victory at Stalingrad in January 1943, Marshal Antonescu's mind began to turn to consideration of an understanding with the Allies. His thoughts were shared by Mihai Antonescu, Vice-President of the Council of Ministers, who took the lead in taking soundings of the Italians. The Marshal tolerated such peace feelers from within his own government and from the opposition leader, Maniu. Mihai Antonescu gave some indication of his own change of heart in January 1943 to Bova-Scopp, the Italian minister in Bucharest. Bova-Scoppa went to Rome to present a report of his conversation with Antonescu to Galeazzo Ciano, the Italian Foreign Minister, who had already anticipated the new mood of the Romanian leaders. In his diary entry for 10 January Ciano noted:

> I think the Germans would do well to watch the Romanians. I see an about-face in the attitude and words of Mihai Antonescu. The sudden will for conciliation with Hungary is suspicious to me. If the Russian offensive had not been so successful I doubt that all this would have taken place.[1]

Mihai Antonescu's proposal elicited some sympathy from Ciano who recorded on 19 January:

> Bova-Scoppa has made a report on his long conference with young Antonescu who has returned from German headquarters. The latter was very explicit about the tragic condition of Germany and foresees the need for Romania and Italy to contact the Allies in order to establish a defence against the bolshevization of Europe. I shall take the report to the Duce and shall make it the subject of a conversation which I have been planning for some time. Let us not bandage our heads before they are broken, but let us look at the situation realistically and remember that charity begins at home.[2]

Mussolini, however, was not swayed by Ciano's argument:

> Taking my cue from Bova's report I told the Duce what I thought. The Duce began by replying that 'he was sure that the Germans would hold tenaciously'. Then he listened to me attentively. He naturally refused Antonescu's offer, saying that 'the Danube is not the way we must follow'. But he did not react when at a certain point I said openly that we too should try to make some direct contact.[3]

The *Duce* reiterated his view the following day, 21 January:

> As I anticipated Mussolini wanted to reread the Bova report. He described Antonescu's language as oversubtle and he reaffirmed in terms much stronger than those of yesterday his decision to march with Germany to the end.[4]

This rebuff prompted Mihai Antonescu to attempt direct contact with the diplomatic representatives of the Allies in neutral countries with a view to concluding a separate peace. He himself raised the matter with Andrea Cassulo, the papal nuncio in Bucharest, while the Romanian minister in Berne was instructed to make contact with the papal nuncio there. In March, the Romanian minister in Madrid asked his Portuguese and Argentinian counterparts to let the American ambassador, Carlton Hayes, know of Romania's desire to conclude a peace with the Allies. Similarly, Victor Cadere, the Romanian minister in Lisbon, took soundings in October of President Salazar and of the British Ambassador. In December, the Romanian chargé in Stockholm, George Duca, contacted the British and American ministers in the name of Maniu and Brătianu. All these efforts foundered on the Anglo-American insistence on 'unconditional surrender', proposed by Roosevelt and accepted by Churchill at the Casablanca Conference in January 1943, which could not be reconciled with Antonescu's desire to guarantee Romania's postwar independence from the Soviet Union.

When questioned by the writer Alexandru Brătescu-Voineşti, in an interview published on 5 March 1943 in the pro-regime *Porunca Vremii* (The Command of the Times) as to why, having sided with the Axis, he did not maintain links with the Allies in case they emerged victorious, Antonescu retorted, 'How, in the first instance, could such a stance be hidden from our own allies? And then, our major virtue, admired without reservation by our own great allies, is, alongside the bravery of our army, our loyalty, sincerity and lack of duplicity. This loyalty will represent one of the most precious possessions when peace is concluded.'[5]

These peace feelers were not unknown to Hitler. At their meeting at Klessheim castle in Salzburg on 12 April 1943 the Führer confronted Antonescu with the information he had from German intelligence about the approaches made in Madrid and asked him 'to analyse them' from the point of view of their impact on the international community. 'He did not expect an immediate answer from Antonescu' to this unexpected problem. 'He would fully understand, even if Antonescu did not give him a reply.' Antonescu replied on the spot: 'He could assure Hitler that the entire Romanian nation supported him now, more than ever, and that he would not allow anyone to carry out a policy other than that which he [Antonescu] considered the best one, in the interests of Romania and of Europe.' He promised the Führer that 'Romania would continue alongside Germany until the end of the war .... The policy of the opposition, especially Maniu, did not count.... However, he [Antonescu] could not touch Maniu, since he [Antonescu] knew his people and did not want, through measures taken against Maniu, to make a martyr of this man who was advanced in years and who had negative ideas, thereby granting him what he had long wished to obtain.' He told Hitler that he would never take an initiative without informing him and undertook to investigate the action of the Romanian minister in Madrid. At the same time he defended Mihai Antonescu: 'It was inconceivable that Mihai would have tried to conclude peace or to request assistance from the Americans or other states, since he [the Marshal] would not have anyone alongside him who would be disloyal to Germany.' Hitler accepted this declaration of loyalty.[6]

Nevertheless, Hitler returned to the subject the next day. He was concerned that the approaches made in March by the Romanian minister in Madrid gave the impression to the foreign (Portuguese and Argentinian) diplomats that Romania and Germany were ready to conclude a peace with the Allies. The Führer stated that 'the important problem was that the main enemies of the Axis had formed a completely erroneous impression about the position of Germany and Italy and that was due solely to the action of Mihai Antonescu'. He asked the Marshal to ensure that such a thing would never happened again. The latter replied that he was grateful that they had discussed this problem, 'but the truth was totally the reverse of what Germany knew'.[7]

Antonescu was being less than honest with the Führer in this matter. He was aware of the approaches made by his Foreign Minister and did nothing to stop further soundings of all three allies made by Mihai Antonescu and Maniu through different channels over the following twelve months. In their turn, the Western Allies, led by the British, sought to maintain regular contact with King Michael. In autumn 1943, a British intelligence officer, using the cover of a journalist, met the king and Queen Helen at the Palace in Bucharest in order to gain a first-hand account of the political situation in Romania and Michael's own position. A note of the interview, made by Henry Spitzmuller, a French diplomat who remained in Romania after the fall of France to serve the Allied interest,[8] offers a rare, contemporary, first-hand account of Michael's predicament and his relations with Antonescu, which shows them to have been severely strained. The king told the officer, a Mr House, not to

> forget to explain that consideration for my country's future does not blind me to the fact that the Allies' policy is based on cooperation between the three Powers and I therefore understand that Russia and Romania must come to some kind of agreement.

Mr House then remarked that the Allies had repeated most recently that unconditional surrender remained the essential condition of any armistice. 'I know', the king replied, 'but it is not because of this formula that I would refuse to negotiate if the occasion arose. Without underestimating its importance, I consider and hope that even the framework of this formula would permit interpretations which would allow me to accept it.'

The conversation then concentrated on the possibility of a *putsch* linked to an approach by the king to the Allies. The king and all those present explained to Mr House that such a move would result in the complete and immediate occupation of the country by the Germans, who would then have all the resources of Romania at their disposal. The king and his counsellors again explained to Mr House that the situation in Romania at that moment was unique in the sense that Marshal Antonescu's government represented only a tiny minority which, having taken power and maintained it with the support of the Germans, had imposed and continued to impose on the country a policy which was contrary to its wishes and its interests. A new government which would truly represent the people's wishes could only come to power through a *putsch*, which was impossible at the present moment with close cooperation with the Allies.

'If the Allies made a landing in the Balkans', the king said, 'everything would be simpler. The peninsula is practically undefended, but if Romania were to be occupied by the Germans the situation would immediately become less favourable.'[9]

The acceptance of unconditional surrender by the Romanians, whether Maniu or Antonescu, was the stumbling-block in all subsequent negotiations held between Maniu's representatives and the Allies in Cairo in the spring of 1944.[10] Yet approaches made in December 1943 by Soviet officials to Romanian diplomats in Stockholm suggested that their government wished to set up independent contacts with Antonescu and Maniu and was prepared to accept less than unconditional surrender. A curious situation thus emerged in which both the Romanian government and opposition were seeking to obtain the best possible terms for an armistice in parallel negotiations, one in Cairo with the Allies collectively and the other in Stockholm with the Russians separately. Not surprisingly, both Antonescu and Maniu believed that they were in a position to bargain over unconditional surrender – hence the misunderstanding that arose between the Allies and Maniu, and the increasing British irritation with the latter. Maniu wanted some assurance as to what conditions he could get before making any plans to overthrow Antonescu, and was particularly anxious to prevent Soviet occupation of Romania. The Russians, on the other hand, doubtless took the pragmatic view that it was more realistic to treat with Antonescu since he controlled the army and an about-turn by the latter against the Germans would preclude the need for a coup by the opposition which the Communists did not control.

Antonescu's own position on the desirability of an armistice is evident from a memorandum of what appears to have been a meeting between the Marshal and Iuliu Maniu dated 21 January 1944.[11] Antonescu argued that it was very difficult for Romania to withdraw from the war, given the importance of Romania's oil to Germany. Maniu said that 'realistic solutions should be found to change our military and diplomatic position.' The memorandum continued:

> What are these solutions? Marshal Antonescu asked that they should be put to him in practical terms, but you [Maniu] were unable to do this. Mr Maniu thinks, however, that Marshal Antonescu has a mission and that he can take the country out of the war immediately. What would this mission be ? Mr Maniu must be explicit. Over the last three years he has been floating the same theoretical ideas, which seem deceptive.
>
> But Mr Maniu avoids and hestitates to ask himself, and in particular, to show how Romania's withdrawal from the war could be carried out in practical terms – a withdrawal which is the wish of the Marshal and of the entire population – [and] whether the allies and the Germans would guarantee our borders and future. Yet neither side is giving us these guarantees, nor will they, or – what is more to the point – can they give them, guarantees which we have been seeking for three years. In these circumstances, who can attempt capitulation or a laying down of arms especially when – in either case – Romania will be forced, like Italy, to tolerate fighting on its own territory by both sides?[12]

Hitler was made aware of the continuing Romanian overtures to the Allies and ordered plans to be drawn up for the occupation of the country. Similar plans had already been prepared for the occupation in March 1944 of Hungary, whose reliance as an ally had been long shown to be wanting. Before taking action against the Marshal, the Führer decided to give him one last chance. The two leaders met at Klessheim on 23–24 March 1944, where Hitler railed against the duplicity of the Hungarians, declaring to Antonescu that he had irrefutable evidence of their intention to withdraw from the war.[13] Unaware that his future hung in the balance, Antonescu pledged continued loyalty to Hitler. Not for the first time, Hitler was impressed by Antonescu's sincerity and decided not to remove his friend.[14] His faith in his Romanian ally was borne out by Antonescu's obstinate refusal to turn against Germany by accepting armistice conditions laid down by the Allies.

We can only speculate on the consequences of a decision by Hitler to occupy Romania; there is no doubt that King Michael would have had the support of most of his generals in ordering his army – half of which was held in reserve in Romania to defend the country – to take up arms against the Germans, and that the ensuing hostilities, by crippling German resistance, would have accelerated the Soviet advance westwards in Moldavia. Of one thing, however, we can be certain: German occupation would have the same monstrous impact on Romania's surviving Jews of Wallachia, Moldavia and Wallachia as it did on the Jews of Hungary. After the German occupation of that country on 19 March 1944, Jews were rounded up in ghettos with the collaboration of the Hungarian gendarmerie and sent to Auschwitz.

Antonescu, aware of the fragility of Romania's territorial integrity in the face of the Soviet advance, continued to hold out for armistice terms which would guarantee Romania's independence of Soviet authority. Yet the more he delayed, the closer the Red Army moved and the greater the threat of occupation. On 29 March, the Red Army took Cernăuţi in northern Bukovina. Odessa, the Crimea's main port, fell on 10 April, bringing Romania's occupation of Transnistria effectively at an end, while the evacuation of the Crimea was completed on 13 May. Only King Michael and his advisers seemed to grasp the fact that Stalin would be tempted to withold his assent to armistice conditions if he manoeuvred himself into a position to impose them through military might. Antonescu refused to accept what he considered to be unsatisfactory terms from the Allies; furthermore, he was adamant about not abandoning his German ally, who was now on the defensive. At a Council of Ministers' meeting on 6 May 1944, the Marshal made his position clear:

> So, gentlemen, [we should have] a perfectly correct attitude in our relations with the Germans: in 1940 we bent down before them, are we now to hit them when they are beaten and faced with destruction? We cannot do that, gentlemen. I was not a Germanophile and will never be. I told Hitler so. You cannot ask the Romanian people to love the German people. When we lost all [those] territories as a result of the political and military actions of the Germans, you cannot ask the Romanian people to love you. The Romanian people marches alongside the German people out of self-interest, and when you are in a position to help it [the Romanian people] win its rights, it will show its gratitude to you. We must behave correctly towards the Germans.[15]

Antonescu gave these same reasons for remaining loyal to his German ally at his trial in May 1946. When questioned about his meeting with Hitler on 6 August (it took place, in fact, on 5 August), Antonescu replied:

> Before 6 August I wanted to go to Germany on my own initiative – I had never been before on my own initiative, but now in 1944 I wanted to – to raise the matter of the Romanian army's withdrawal from the war. As a soldier, I have been throughout my life a man of honour and loyal, and I did not want to break with Germany, because Germany was and can be a great power, and Romania, being a small power, must think of that. And so, I wanted to break with Germany in a decent way and to warn her: you did not keep your word to guarantee Romania's frontiers, there are not sufficient forces to meet a concerted Russian attack, and so Romania runs the risk of being totally overrun and destroyed, therefore I am withdrawing from the war. I was advised not to do this by everyone; they were all terrified of what would happen in Romania if I told Hitler and gave him advance warning. Think of it, a war between us and the Germans on our territory, which would cause the damage that it did, and besides that, I was not a partisan, I could not and would not, even if I lived a million years, stab a comrade who had been alongside me in an action in the back.[16]

This stubbornness determined the king, in concert with the opposition leaders, to plot his overthrow.[17]

Following the disaster to Romanian troops at Stalingrad, King Michael, in his 1943 New Year broadcast to his people, called for peace and for Romania to discontinue the war alongside Hitler. Marshal Antonescu was furious, as was the German minister in Bucharest, who protested violently. Irritated by what he considered to be the indecisiveness of the opposition led by Maniu and Brătianu, the young king declared later that he had been ready to take Romania out of the war against the Allies in February 1944, but that 'whenever plans appeared to be maturing he was prevented from taking action by objections raised by the opposition'.[18] The king's impatience was doubtless a sign of his youth (he was only 22), and the elderly Maniu advised more prudently against a *coup* at that time on the grounds that there were too many German troops in the country. Nevertheless, the king could turn to the wise counsels of his mother, Queen Helen, of General Sănătescu, the head of the military household, and of Grigore Niculescu-Buzeşti, the head of the cipher and communication section of the Foreign Ministry.

At this time Maniu was in regular radio contact with the British via a radio operator called Nicolae Ţurcanu (codenamed 'Reginald') who had been sent into Romania in June 1943 by the Special Operations Executive.[19] At the end of October 1943, Maniu had expressed a desire to leave Romania in order to contact the Russians with British assistance. In response, the

Foreign Office told Maniu that any approaches from Romania, be they from individuals or from the government, should be addressed to all three Allies and that they should take the form of an offer by a duly authorized emissary to sign an unconditional surrender to the three principal Allies.[20] The Foreign Office told the Soviet government about Maniu's request. At the end of December 1943, the Romanian Counsellor in Stockholm, George Duca, contacted the British and American ministers in the name of Maniu about peace terms, unaware that his own minister, Frederick Nanu, had been approached, on 26 December, by what Nanu took to be an NKVD officer, with an offer to deal with the Romanian government.[21] Clandestine contact was maintained for several months. Nanu was told that the Russians would keep the Western Allies informed and that strict secrecy should be maintained. On 13 April 1944, armistice terms agreed by the representatives of the American, British and Soviet governments in Cairo were transmitted to the Marshal and to Maniu. They called for a Romanian *volte-face* against the Germans, the payment of reparations to the Russians, the confirmation of Bessarabia and northern Bukovina as Soviet territory, the restoration of northern Transylvania to Romania, and the granting to Soviet troops of unrestricted movement, although not occupation, throughout Romania during the period of the armistice.[22]

The receipt of the terms seems to have caused a breach to open up between the Marshal and Maniu. In a letter he wrote in mid-April, Maniu stated that Antonescu 'wished to continue the war at the side of the Germans', while Maniu accepted the terms and said that once he was certain that Antonescu could not be moved, he would act in conjunction with the king.[23] An appeal to Antonescu to cease hostilities against the Allies was submitted under the signature of 69 university teachers in April. Overtly pro-Soviet in sentiment, it reflected political reality as regards the key role that the Soviet Union would play in determining Romania's fate, accepting at face value the promises of the Kremlin:

> At this crucial time for the existence of the Romanian people, the Soviet Government, in agreement with the governments of Great Britain and the United States, states before the whole world that it does not intend to destroy the Romanian state, nor to annex territories beyond the frontiers of 1941, nor to change the existing social system of the country . . .
>
> The Romanian people, exhausted by a war too long for its resources, cannot fight any longer. Step out into the streets and ask the passers-by, go into the villages and towns, listen to the voice of the people. Everywhere you will see despair in their eyes and [hear] the same reply: NO.
>
> Why should we continue to fight? The vital interests of the state and of our people require the immediate cessation of war, however difficult this step might be. The sacrifices which Romania should make will be incomparably smaller and less painful than the continuation of the war.[24]

On 5 May 1944, Anthony Eden, the Foreign Secretary, saw the Soviet ambassador to London, Feodor Gusev, and 'casually' mentioned the possibility of some sort of understanding on the problems of Greece and Romania, as Eden put it later, 'agreeing between ourselves as a practical matter that Rumanian affairs would be in the main the concern of the Soviet government while Greek affairs would be in the main our concern, each government giving the other help in the respective countries'.[25] The suspicion that the Western Allies, and in particular Britain, had abandoned Romania to the Russians troubled Maniu, who used the Romanian emissary to Cairo, Constantin Vişoianu, to voice these concerns to Christopher Steel, the British representative, at the end of May. This provoked Eden to instruct Steel to tell Vişoianu that there was no use in his trying to obtain assurances about British policy 'as distinct from that of the Soviet government'.[26] But there was no rebuke from Eden when Steel, in answer to a further question from Vişoianu as to whether Maniu should form 'a democratic coalition embracing the Romanian Communist Party', replied that in his own view a broad national union of this kind would be 'warmly welcomed by Allied public opinion'.[27]

This cautious advice probably confirmed Maniu in his view that it would be good politics to bring the Communists into a coalition, and when Vişoianu asked Daniel Semionovici Selod, the assistant to Nikolai Novikov, the Soviet representative in Cairo, to suggest a name, Selod replied 'Lucreţiu Pătrăşcanu'.[28] Although held under house arrest throughout 1943 and early 1944 at a mountain village called Poiana Ţapului near Sinaia, the king's summer residence, Pătrăşcanu was kept informed of plans to take Romania out of the war by his brother-in-law Colonel Octav Ulea, Master of Ceremonies at the Palace.[29] In April 1944, Pătrăşcanu negotiated an agreement with Titel Petrescu, the leader of the Social Democrats, to set up a United Workers' Front, thus giving the Communist Party greater authority. Both men took part in the secret preparations for the *coup* under the king's chairmanship. Pătrăşcanu was brought into meetings of a sub-committee under Colonel Dumitru Dămăceanu, which prepared plans for the defence of Bucharest and at the beginning of June he suggested that the Communist Party's military representative, Emil Bodnăraş (codenamed Engineer Ceauşu), should attend since he could organize small bands of armed workers who could assist in a *volte-face*.

Bodnăraş was no ordinary official of the Communist Party; he was also an NKVD officer whose role in the preparations for the coup remains shadowy and has consequently fomented speculation, including the suggestion that he was used by Marshal Antonescu as a clandestine conduit to the Soviet authorities.[30] After the Axis defeat at Stalingrad, it was clear to the Antonescu that it would be prudent to establish closer links with the Russians and Bodnăraş was an obvious channel. Unlike his colleagues Dej, Apostol, Chişinevski and Georgescu, he had been exempted from internment at the Târgu-Jiu prison camp, after being released from Caransebeş prison in December 1942, on the grounds of having been an officer in the Romanian army. Bodnăraş made his first appearance at one of the meetings to prepare the *coup* at a house on Calea Moşilor on the night of 13 June.[31] Even members of the king's circle were impressed by Bodnăraş's dedication and the latter, in his turn, was sufficiently convinced by the thoroughness of the plans to be able to satisfy his Communist colleagues that the Romanian Communist Party only stood to enhance its position by joining the National Peasant, National Liberal, and Social Democratic parties in the formation of the National Democratic Bloc (NDB) on 20 June 1944.[32]

A week later, the Allied representatives in Cairo received the plan drawn up by the king and the NDB for the *coup*. To be successful, Maniu argued, the *coup* had to be accompanied by three Allied actions. First, there should be a major Soviet offensive on the Romanian front within 24 hours of the *volte-face*; second, three airborne brigades, either Anglo-American or Soviet, with an additional 2,000 parachute troops, should be dropped at the time of the *coup*; third, there should be a heavy bombardment of communications with Hungary and Bulgaria. The plan met a favourable response from both the British and American representatives, yet when the American suggested a tripartite meeting to discuss it, the Soviet representative, Nikolai Novikov, said that this would be premature.

Novikov waited in vain for instructions from Moscow. The Russians had nothing to lose by pinning their hopes on a bilateral deal with Marshal Antonescu; this had the double advantage for them of dealing directly with Romania's military leader, thereby obviating the need to negotiate with Maniu, and of giving them time, in view of the Marshal's hesitancy, to prepare for their military occupation of Romania. Indeed, at the beginning of June, Madame Alexandra Kollontay, a veteran revolutionary and the Soviet minister in Stockholm, had offered improved armistice conditions to Nanu which, in addition to an unconditional promise to return Transylvania, pledged to allow 'free areas' where the Romanian government would be sovereign and where no foreign troops would be allowed to enter, to show leniency over reparations, and to allow 15 days between the signing of an armistice and a Romanian declaration of war on Germany.[33]

At the Marshal's request Hitler received him at his headquarters at Rastenburg in East Prussia on 5 August. The Führer, according to a Romanian officer present, used the meeting, lasting some six hours, to deliver a rant against all who had betrayed him, especially the German people, who had showed no gratitude for the heights to which he had raised them.[34] To Antonescu's complete surprise, Hitler posed the leading question as to whether Romania intended to fight on; the Marshal temporized by saying that this depended on Germany's commitment to assist Romania in stemming the Russian advance and on the attitude of Hungary and Bulgaria.[35] He returned to Bucharest in deep depression and did nothing about the

Soviet terms. In the meantime, Maniu was desperately seeking a reply from Cairo to the *coup* plan sent on 27 June. On 7 July, the king and his advisers, including the opposition leaders, fixed 15 August as the date for action, hoping to synchronize their action with a Soviet offensive. The longer the *coup* was delayed, the greater the chance that the Red Army would push forward, occupying more Romanian territory and giving Moscow a reason for preferring a straightforward military conquest of the country without any help from the king and the opposition. Moreover, the increasingly frequent Anglo-American air raids on the oilfields around Ploieşti and on Bucharest were a reminder to the Romanians of the cost of the alliance with Germany.[36] Still Maniu heard nothing from Cairo, and the *coup* was postponed. Finally, on 20 August, the long-awaited Soviet offensive came, prompting Maniu to inform Cairo that the king and his group had decided to take action.

On that date the Soviet generals Malinovsky and Tolbukhin successfully launched a massive assault confided to two armies of almost one million troops and 1,500 tanks against the combined German and Romanian forces straddling the Prut. The northern offensive, aimed at Focşani, Bucharest and Turnu Severin, breached the front south of Iaşi and the king rushed from Sinaia to Bucharest to consult his advisers.[37] The representatives of the political parties could not be located. The king asked Colonel Dămăceanu how long he needed to get his part of the plan, namely to seize the telephone exhange and the radio station, ready, and was told five days. The *coup* was therefore fixed for 26 August at 1 pm. The Marshal and Mihai Antonescu would be invited to lunch, after which there would be an audience to discuss the course to be adopted. If the Marshal refused negotiation with the Allies, the king would dismiss him and appoint a new government to be drawn from the opposition parties. This government would invite the Germans to evacuate Romania and empower its emissaries in Cairo, Barbu Ştirbey and Constantin Vişoianu, to sign an armistice.

On the following evening, 21 August, the plans agreed by the king and his advisers the day before were approved by the members of the NDB at their last full meeting before the *coup*. It was attended by the king, Maniu, Brătianu, Pătrăşcanu, Titel Petrescu, Grigore Niculescu-Buzeşti, the head of Foreign Ministry communications, Ion Mocsony-Styrcea, the Marshal of the King's Household,[38] General Constantin Sănătescu, and Mircea Ionniţiu, the king's private secretary.[39] Pătrăşcanu came with a draft proclamation for the king's approval and argued, with Petrescu's backing, for a government of national unity led by Maniu. Maniu refused and pressed for a government of technicians, headed by a soldier, to handle the armistice conditions and the presence of the Red Army. The matter was left in the hands of Maniu and Pătrăşcanu, who were to draw up a list of ministers by 23 August. It was agreed that the politicians should disperse until the projected day of action, 26 August.

Yet once again, unforeseen circumstances intervened in the timing of the *coup*. Antonescu, dismayed by the rapid advance of the Soviet forces, was moving back and forth between the front in southern Moldavia and Bucharest and decided to return to the front on 23 August. This meant that he would be absent from the capital on the day fixed for the *coup*. The news, which had been picked up fortuitously by Styrcea while he was at the Marshal's villa in Snagov,[40] was quickly transmitted to the king, who was able to get word to Maniu that the *coup* should be brought forward to 23 August. Mihai Antonescu, the prime minister, was unnerved by the deteriorating military situation and decided, on his own initiative, to negotiate an armistice with the Allies. He told the Marshal on the evening of 22 August and the latter raised no objections. That same evening the Marshal told the German minister Clodius that he would make one last effort to halt the Russians, and that in the event of failure, he reserved the right to act as he saw fit. After the meeting with Clodius, Mihai Antonescu sent a courier to Stockholm instructing Nanu to tell Madame Kollontay of the Romanian government's willingness to conclude an armistice. In the event the courier arrived on 24 August, the day after the *coup*.[41]

Early in the morning of 23 August, Mihai Antonescu and Madame Antonescu tried to persuade the Marshal to see the king and agree to an armistice. Although the Marshal refused to commit himself, Mihai telephoned the king's office and spoke to Ionniţiu who woke the king. Michael agreed to see them both at 3 pm. In a last-ditch effort to get the Marshal to conclude an armistice, Maniu and Constantin Brătianu asked the historian Gheorghe Brătianu, the Liberal leader's nephew, to use the respect he enjoyed with the Romanian leader to persuade him to see the king that afternoon. The Marshal listened to Brătianu's arguments and apparently agreed to go to the Palace, but on condition that Maniu and Gheorghe Brătianu send him a letter by 3 pm confirming that they stood behind him in signing an armistice.[42]

The king now convened his advisers and decided that the showdown with the Marshal should take place at his audience that afternoon. Niculescu-Buzeşti and Styrcea left the Palace to warn Maniu and Pătrăşcanu respectively, but Maniu was not at home and Pătrăşcanu's contact said that Pătrăşcanu and Titel Petrescu would come to the Palace, but only after nightfall. Similarly, Gheorghe Brătianu could find neither his uncle nor Maniu and was therefore unable to meet the Marshal's condition that he should bring a letter from both by 3 pm. When Gheorghe Brătianu turned up to see the Marshal empty-handed the latter was furious and said that Mihai Antonescu could go to the Palace alone and pass on the Marshal's apologies to the king.[43]

Mihai Antonescu arrived for his audience at the appointed time and was received by the king and General Sănătescu. He offered Marshal Antonescu's apologies, at which point Sănătescu left the room and telephoned the Marshal, saying that there was no point in snubbing the king at this critical time. The Marshal relented and agreed to come. He was escorted into the drawing room to meet the king who was with Mihai Antonescu and Sănătescu. The Marshal proceeded to give a detailed account of the situation at the front and said that he would only conclude an armistice after warning Hitler. The king replied that the military situation would brook no further delay; since Soviet troops were already in occupation of part of the country an armistice should be signed immediately. Asked by the king whether he would stand aside for someone who would contact the Allies, the Marshal replied, 'Never'. After withdrawing briefly to his study to inform his advisers – Styrcea, Buzeşti, Ionniţiu and General Aurel Aldea – that the moment had now come for the Marshal's arrest, the king returned to the drawing room and told the Marshal that, in accordance with the wishes of the Romanian people as expressed through the four democratic parties, he was taking the country out of the war to save it from disaster. If the Marshal refused to implement the king's wish that an armistice be concluded, then he should consider himself dismissed.[44]

When the Marshal retorted he took orders from no one, the king replied that, in that case, he was dismissed and he left the room. As he did so he signalled to his aide, Colonel Emilian Ionescu, to arrest the Marshal and Mihai Antonescu. Ionescu summoned the four-man guard that had been prepared for such an eventuality and amid the protests of the Marshal, the two Antonescus were escorted upstairs and locked in the King's strong room.

Back in his study the king consulted his advisers as to the immediate steps to be taken. The leaders of the political parties had to be informed of the arrests, the Allies had to be notified, the military plan for the *coup* had to be executed, but most important of all, a prime minister had to be named to replace Mihai Antonescu. In the absence of Maniu, it was decided to appoint General Sănătescu, who enjoyed the respect of the army. Ionniţiu typed out a decree to this effect, the king signed it and the new prime minister set out for army headquarters to transmit the order for Romanian troops under Colonel Dămăceanu to take up positions at strategic points in Bucharest and to cease hostilities against the Soviet forces at the front. Proof that the army placed their loyalty to their supreme commander, the king, above that to Marshal Antonescu, was the fact that not a single senior officer disobeyed Sănătescu's orders and not one of them defected to the Marshal.

Since Maniu and Pătrăşcanu had failed to agree on a list of ministers, and neither was at the Palace, the new government had to be formed on the spot from among the king's advisers. Niculescu-Buzeşti, a counsellor in the Foreign Ministry, was elevated to Foreign Minister and General Aldea became Minister of the Interior, while the representatives of the four parties in the DNF – Maniu, Brătianu, Petrescu and Pătrăşcanu – were appointed Ministers of State without Portfolio. Ionniţiu was doubtless not alone in feeling at the time that the politicians had, at this crucial moment, shown themselves to be 'a pathetic bunch'.[45]

The first of them to appear at the Palace was Pătrășcanu, who arrived shortly after 8 pm. He brought with him the king's proclamation, which was approved after amendments by Buzești and Sănătescu, and the texts of two decrees, previously agreed at meetings of the NDB, granting an amnesty to political prisoners and abolishing the internment camps in which many Communists and other political detainees had been held. At the same time, Pătrășcanu asked the king for the post of Minister of Justice. Since none of the other political leaders had cabinet seats, the king did not want to risk an accusation of partiality, but given Pătrășcanu's legal background, his diligence in producing the draft proclamation and the decrees and that he was the first member of the NDB to appear at the Palace, the king offered him a compromise, Minister of Justice ad interim. The fact that Pătrășcanu, alone among the political representatives, secured this temporary position gave rise in accounts about the formation of this new government to the supposition that he was acting on orders from the Communist Party and this, in turn, helped to cement the fiction in Communist historiography of the dominant role of the Party in the *coup*. In the circumstances, it was the most immediately plausible appointment for Pătrășcanu, given the speed of events on the afternoon of 23 August and the lack of time in which to contact the leaders of the Communist Party.[46]

Pătrășcanu was followed shortly afterwards by Titel Petrescu and then, an hour or so later, by Emil Bodnăraș who was presented to the king under the name of 'Engineer Ceaușu' and head of a group of Communist-trained armed civilians known as the 'Patriotic Guards'. About an hour after the recording of the king's proclamation to the country announcing the *coup* and the immediate cessation of hostilities with the Allies was broadcast, Marshal Antonescu, who was still locked in the palace strong room, asked for paper and made his will. Another hour passed before Bodnăraș and a group of armed workers took charge of the two Antonescus and drove them to a safe house in the Bucharest district of Vatra Luminoasă.[47]

A few hours later, Antonescu's fellow ministers, General Constantin Pantazi, Minister of Defence, General Constantin Vasiliu, Under-secretary of State at the Interior Ministry, and Colonel Mircea Elefterescu, head of Bucharest Police, were taken into custody.[48] On 31 August, shortly after Soviet troops entered Bucharest, Lt.-Gen. Tevcenkov, political chief of the Second Ukrainian Front, acting on Stalin's orders, went to the head of the Bucharest garrison, Iosif Teodorescu, to take Antonescu into Soviet custody.[49] Teodorescu invited General Aurel Aldea, the Minister of the Interior, and General Victor Dombrovski, mayor of Bucharest, to the garrison and they informed Tevcenkov that they were unaware of Antonescu's whereabouts. Tevcenkov insisted on finding out, whereupon Teodorescu phoned the government and after a while a man in civilian clothes arrived. He introduced himself as Bodnăraș, a member of the Central Committee of the Romanian Communist Party. Asked by

Tevcenkov for information about Antonescu, Bodnăraş replied that he was being held by the Communists.

Tevcenkov and General Nikolai Burenin, the commander of Soviet forces in Bucharest, accompanied by some 40 Soviet officers and men, were then taken by Bodnăraş to the two-storey house where Antonescu and his colleagues were being held. The Marshal occupied a room on the second floor, while Mihai Antonescu, Pantazi, Vasiliu and Elefterescu were kept on the ground floor. They were guarded inside the house by ten armed civilians. There was no guard on the outside. Tevcenkov told Bodnăraş that because of the poor security he proposed to take the prisoners into Soviet custody. Bodnăraş preferred to keep the captives where they were, but under a guard reinforced by Soviet soldiers. Tevcenkov rejected this proposal, accepting instead the continued presence of some of the armed Romanian civilians around the prisoners. Bodnăraş added that 'the [Romanian] government did not want Antonescu to end up in Moscow'. At 5 pm on the same day – 31 August – Antonescu and the others were taken to the headquarters of the Soviet 53rd Army.[50]

On the following day, the group was visited by General Aldea and then taken by lorry to Urziceni. On 2 September, they continued by road to a station on the Soviet side of the frontier, where they were put in a train for Moscow. After a three-day journey they reached the Soviet capital, from where they were driven 'in comfortable vehicles' to a castle some 60 km away. According to an account written by Pantazi's son, they were well treated.[51] Each member of the group had his own room and was allowed to walk in the park. Nevertheless, on 8 November, the Marshal tried to hang himself with a noose made from strips torn from his bedsheet, but was discovered in time by Vasiliu. Subsequently, a Soviet officer was billeted with the prisoners.

11
The Trial of Ion Antonescu

Romania's external position immediately after the *coup* was that of an independent state waging war against its former allies on the side of its former enemies, with whom its relationships were covered by the Armistice Agreement between the Allies and Romania signed in Moscow on 12 September 1944.[1] As part of the armistice agreement the British suggested to the Soviet Foreign Minister Veaceslav Molotov that an Allied Control Commission be set up to oversee the implementation of the terms, but the Soviet determination to have the main say in this matter was carried through in their armistice draft of 31 August, which stated that the terms would be implemented 'under the control of the Soviet High Command, hereinafter called Allied (Soviet) High Command, acting on behalf of the Allied powers'. Stalin used the Armistice Agreement to subvert the effects of the 23 August *coup* which had threatened to wrest the initiative in Romanian affairs from him. In order to regain the initiative the Soviet leader fashioned from the armistice a legal framework for securing a dominant political and economic interest in Romania. Since the Soviet Union had a monopoly of its interpretation, the Armistice Agreement became the mechanism for the takeover of Romania.[2] Articles 13 and 14 provided for the arrest of war criminals and the dissolution of 'Fascist-type' organizations. Antonescu's detention in Russia was now placed on a legal footing.

These articles, in practice, provided the basis for the transformation of Romania into a Communist state. With the entry of the Red Army, the advance units of which arrived in Bucharest on 30 August, the country came under Russian control. The Allied authority set up to supervise the execution of the Agreement was *de facto* Russian. Soviet policy in Romania was designed to exact retribution for the Romanian invasion of the Soviet Union and to provide for permanent military security – a notion implying not merely disarmament and treaty guarantees but also the abrogation of the political power of those who had launched the invasion.[3]

British and American diplomats did not consider the conditions unduly harsh, although Averell Harriman had serious doubts about Soviet intentions and predicted that the terms would 'give the Soviet command unlimited control of Romania's economic life' and, more ominously, 'police power for the period of the armistice'.[4] Both the British and US governments endorsed the agreement without demur; indeed, their acceptance of Moscow as the place of signature was a tacit admission that their eastern partner, as the principal belligerent ally in Eastern Europe, had earned the right as victor to dictate terms to the Romanians. That the Soviet Union should adopt this position was accepted as inevitable by Churchill in a speech to the House of Commons delivered on 26 September 1944. The Prime Minister admitted that:

> the armistice terms agreed upon for Finland and Romania bear, naturally, the imprint of the Soviet will – and here I must draw attention to the restraint which has characterized the Soviet treatment of these two countries, both of which marched blithely behind Hitler in his attempted destruction of Russia, and both of which added their quota of injuries to the immense volume of suffering which the Russian people have endured, have survived, and have triumphantly surmounted.[5]

Against Churchill's statement, made when the Red Army was still fighting its way across Eastern Europe, must be set the belief of King Michael and his ministers that his *coup* against Antonescu and the *volte-face* against the Germans had earned Romania the right to be treated not as a defeated enemy, but as a new co-belligerent. Such a view received no sympathy from Stalin, who was unwilling to forgive Romania for its contribution to *Operation Barbarossa*. Yet ironically, by facilitating the Red Army's advance in the Balkans, King Michael's action was to seal his country's consignment to the Soviet sphere of influence and Stalin's domination. With Soviet troops pouring into Romania and Bulgaria, Churchill was determined to save Greece – and possibly Italy – from a Communist takeover, a spectre that was to haunt Churchill's policy towards Romania.

By the time that Churchill decided to divide up responsibility in the Balkans with Stalin by talking to him personally, Britain had few cards to play. The Russians were already in occupation of much of Romania and Bulgaria and so, when Churchill flew to Moscow at the beginning of October 1944, he got straight down to business and proposed the now notorious 'percentages agreement', struck on the evening of 9 October.[6] Although Churchill maintained in his memoirs that 'only immediate wartime arrangements' were under discussion, he knew that Stalin could not be dislodged by force from the position of influence which he had gained. Thus in proposing the deal, Churchill was merely being pragmatic, recognizing Soviet preponderance in the Balkans, one which was restricted only by the Red Army's own operational problems.[7] Stalin interpreted the 'percentages agreement' as he chose, and the absence of any Western forces, not just in Romania, but in the whole of Eastern Europe, ensured that the exercise of Soviet authority in the area remained unrestricted.

This became abundantly evident in the case of Ion Antonescu. On 10 May 1945, just two days after the Soviet ratification in Berlin of the German surrender in Europe, the conditions in which he and his colleagues were held in Russia changed radically. They were taken from the relatively calm atmosphere of the castle and its surroundings to the Liubyanka jail in Moscow. Here they were placed in cells with numerous other prisoners. The Marshal was interrogated by Lavrenti Beria's deputy, Abakumov, and, according to the memoir he submitted to the court during his trial, he was forced to sign a number of declarations, among them one in June that 225,000 Russians had been murdered at Odessa in 1941.[8] Extracts from these declarations, relating to his meetings with Hitler, were quoted by Colonel R. Rudenko, the principal Soviet prosecutor at the Nuremberg trials.[9]

A clear sign that the Communist authorities were determined to ensure a 'guilty' verdict was their reaction to the publication of any facts which were inconvenient. A note of the Romanian Intelligence Service (SSI), dated 20 April 1945, stated that 'the journalist Horia Tăriceanu (a Jew) claims that the *Israelite Courier* has been suspended on the grounds that it published an article from which it emerged that the Jews in the capital did not wear the Star of David thanks to ex-Marshal Antonescu who was opposed to this Fascist measure taken by the Germans'. The note went on:

> According to the journalist, although the Jews are to some degree grateful to the former leader Antonescu, they cannot come to his defence because the Communist Party and the Soviets will not allow any form of defence of Antonescu.[10]

When and by whom was the decision taken to send the Marshal and his fellow detainees back to Romania? We find the answer in a telegram of 13 May 1946 from the State Department to Burton Berry, the US political representative in Bucharest. The 14 articles of the armistice agreement, concluded between the Allies and Romania in Moscow on 12 September 1944, required the Romanian government 'to collaborate with the Allied (Soviet) High Command in the apprehension and trail of persons accused of war crimes'.[11] In this respect the agreement was no different from that agreed with other co-belligerents of Germany who had fought against the Soviet Union such as Finland, but the articles' formulation made it clear that in its implementation the interpretation of what constituted a war crime rested with the Soviet authorities. The summary given by Juho

Paasikivi, President of Finland, on 8 July 1945 of the Soviet position regarding his country could have been applied to that *vis-à-vis* Romania:

> The Russians consider Finland's war crime and guilt to be that Finland waged war alongside Germany against the Soviet Union, and those Finns who led Finland into the war bear war guilt.... In the Russians' opinion just as Hitler and his men must be punished for starting the world war, so must the Finns who were guilty of starting the war be punished.[12]

The desire to take back what Stalin had seized from Romania in June 1940 was not an acceptable defence to the Russians. For most Romanians, matters were made worse by the fact that under the constitution no crime had been committed with which Antonescu could be charged; nor was there any provision for the establishment of special tribunals, such as the People's Tribunal, which judged war criminals.

A retroactive law 'to pursue and punish those guilty of the disaster brought on the country or of war crimes' received the royal assent on 21 April and was published in the official bulletin on 24 April 1945.[13] Article 1 defined those 'guilty of the disaster brought on the country' as a) persons who had backed Hitler or espoused fascism and who bore the political responsibility for allowing German troops to enter Romania; and b) persons who had given their support to the above deeds, either in speech, writing or by any other means. Article 2 proclaimed those 'guilty of the disaster brought on the country through the commission of war crimes' as persons who had taken the decision to declare war on the Soviet Union and the United Nations, who had treated prisoners in an inhuman manner, who had ordered or carried out acts of terror or cruelty against the population in the war zones, who had taken repressive measures against civilians out of racial or political motives, and who had ordered forced labour or the deportation of people.[14] Conviction under article 1 carried imprisonment for a term of between five years and life, while that under article 2 attracted forced labour for life or the death penalty.[15]

People's Tribunals were to be set up to try those charged with the above crimes.[16] A time-limit of 1 September 1945 was chosen for the completion of the trials but the lengthy procedure of interviewing and compiling witness statements rendered the date unrealistic. As a consequence, it was extended to 1 June 1946. This explains the haste with which the two sets of appeals in the Antonescu trial were heard, these being adjudicated in only six days – between 25 and 31 May 1946 – so that the process could be completed by the due date.[17]

The first trials took place in May 1945. In answer to the charge that he had done nothing to stop the Odessa massacres, General Nicolae Macici replied that General Iacobici had been aware of what was happening in the city and had issued no orders to stop the reprisals. On 22 May 1945, General Constantin Trestioreanu and General Macici, accused of the reprisals against the Jews in Odessa in October 1941, were among a group of 29 officers sentenced to death for war crimes; a further eight were sentenced to various terms of imprisonment.[18]

Antonescu was tried because Stalin wanted it. On 4 April 1946, the Soviet ambassador informed the Romanian government that it had agreed to its request to hand over the two Antonescus, Constantin Pantazi and Constantin Vasiliu for trial in Romania.[19] The US administration was informed by the Soviet embassy in Washington in a note dated 5 April that the Soviet government proposed to hand over to the Romanian government Eugen Cristescu, Radu Lecca, Gheorghe Alexianu and Mircea Elefterescu 'in addition to those named in the embassy's note of 26 February'. The persons mentioned in the earlier note are not named, but they doubtless included the two Antonescus, Pantazi and Vasiliu. The State Department replied to the Soviet embassy on 3 May that it had 'no objection to the surrender of these persons to the Rumanian government; also that the Chief US Prosecutor at Nuremberg foresaw no possibility of using any of them'.[20]

Ion Antonescu was already in Romanian hands on 14 April, as the transcript of his interrogation by Avram Bunaciu, a public prosecutor, at 21.30 hours on that day shows. Asked how he was feeling, Antonescu replied:

> It is this dampness, this cement, the iron bars, the absence of sun and light. In Russia we were taken out to walk for thirty minutes in the sun, not only us, but all the prisoners. We stayed in special rooms. . . . [Here] the soldiers on the corridor load and unload their rifles, seemingly in an ostentatious manner. There are two ladies in the cell next to me. The Russians did not do that. And this in country which I served for forty-five years. I do not think that it is very nice.

To a question about his food, he revealed: 'I do not eat meat, I am a vegetarian. But I have no special requests for food.'[21]

Political considerations determined the date of the trial. Stalin clearly felt confident that the Groza government could bring Antonescu to trial without arousing displays of anger in Romania which might have caused public unrest and possibly threatened Soviet control of the country and the delivery of reparations. But more importantly, there was electoral capital to be gained. Burton Berry, the US political representative in Bucharest, in a telegram to Washington sent at 9 am on 3 May, informed the State Department that 'Marshal Antonescu, General Pantazi, General Vasiliu, Eugene Criste u, George Alesseanu and Radu Lecca have been brought to Bucharest from ssia and will be placed on trial before People's Court May 6th accus responsible for country's disaster or guilty war crimes. Some

18 additional persons present or in absentia will also be tried.'[22] In a second telegram, dispatched barely nine hours later, he reported:

> The war criminal trials of Marshal Antonescu and other ministers scheduled to open May 6 (My tel. 466 of May 3) are reliably reported as being organized to aid a future governmental electoral ticket by seeking to discredit National Peasant and National Liberal leaders Maniu and Bratianu in the course of the testimony. It is even reported that Molotov at Paris has requested a selected dossier on the two men to be used in the present sessions of Foreign Ministers and that the Marshal and Mihail Antonescu have been promised certain clemencies if they implicate Maniu and Bratianu during the trials. For political purposes the Government seeks to compromise other personalities in addition to the Papal Nuncio (My tel 467) including Jewish leaders and political deputies of Bratianu and Maniu.[23]

Ion Antonescu, alongside 23 others, was brought from the cells in the basement of the Ministry of the Interior to stand trial on 6 May 1946 for 'bringing disaster upon the country' and 'the crime of war'.[24] It was a key moment in Romania's contemporary history. The protagonists of one dictatorship faced judgement passed down by what many Romanians regarded as another. Reuben Markham, the correspondent of the *Christian Science Monitor* and one of barely a handful of non-Romanians present at the trial, described the popular mood:

> The Romanian nation felt he [Antonescu] was being tried by Russia, whose army was occupying the country. They saw that the judges were dupes of Russia and that the two [*sic*] Communist prosecutors were fanatical agents of Russia. A large proportion of the journalists in the court room, most of whom were non-Romanians, were militantly in the service of Russia and ostentatiously hostile to the helpless Marshal. They vociferously cheered when he was condemned to death by the Communist-led court responsible to Communist Minister Lucretsiu Patrascanu. Most Romanians at that moment felt they were in the Russian trap, along with the Marshal, and that it was they who were being tried, derided, condemned.[25]

The trial began at 8 am on 6 May 1946 in an ordinary court building on Ştirbei-Vodă no. 108 in Bucharest. The street was cordoned off by gendarmes and access to the courtroom was by invitation only. Those admitted to the gallery were carefully selected by the Communist authorities to guarantee the smooth stage-management of the trial. The tribunal was made up of Alexandru Voitinovici, its president, assisted by Constantin Balcu and seven 'people's judges', all Communists. The prosecution team was the same, headed by Vasile Stoican, seconded by Constantin Dobrian, a procurator at the appeal court in Timisoara, and Dumitru Saracu, a public prosecutor. Antonescu's defence counsel were two local lawyers appointed by the court, Constantin Paraschivescu-Bălăceanu and Titus Stoica, who were allowed contact with him only the day before. Their arguments could only be in mitigation. Also present in the courtroom were representatives of the Allied Control Commission, local and foreign pressmen, photographers and newsreel cameramen.[26]

The examination of the accused lasted two days. A sensitive analysis of Antonescu's deportment during the trial was given in a series of articles by the novelist, George Călinescu, who in his capacity as director of the daily *Naţiunea* (Nation), attended the proceedings:

> Let us begin with the Marshal. He is unchanged. Seen from close up, he shows a certain physical tiredness due to his age; from a distance he has the same unchanged countenance. The impression of many has been that his bearing is impassive, which is not true. He is a man of placid, yet solid nerve, of a military education, without particular intellectual complications. His uniformly ruddy complexion helps him to hide his reflexes. Within these limits, his bearing betrays an imperceptible nervousness and a care-laden soul. His hands and jaws tremble discreetly, and he purses his lips to stifle an intermittent sigh. At the outset he seeks a natural, defensive pose, he looks around the room without focusing on anything, he draws his hand across his forehead, he places it under his chin, he discreetly relaxes his bones which have become tired with sitting, he covers his hands in front of the cameras. But when the light is switched on for filming, he suddenly assumes an authoritarian, statuesque profile and maintains it determinedly while the camera is running.[27]

Under questioning from the president of the tribunal, Antonescu sought to justify his actions. Asked about the discriminatory measures against the Jews, codified in the laws on Romanianization, he replied:

> These laws on Romanianization were imposed by the people on the street and by the Iron Guard. These laws...the demands of the Guard were much greater. We had to fight very hard to reduce these demands and, seeing that I could not convince the Guard, I summoned Mr Filderman, whom I have proposed as a witness to come here to confirm or deny this. And I said to him the following: 'Mr Filderman, this is what the street wants. We have two solutions: to let the people on the street take all your property and kill you, or to procede like sensible people, and we in the government act in such a way that you too can live and so we should take part of your belongings.'...I agreed then with Mr Filderman, the proposal was mine, that we should take from the rich Jews their houses and assets in the countryside, where Jewish workers were not employed and could not be employed, and leave them everything that

was productive – commercial and industrial assets – so that they could take in there all the Jews who had been dismissed, because neither the state or other institutions would accept them. And in this way they could continue to live.[28]

Challenged about the pogrom at his trial in May 1946, Antonescu told the court that at the time he was at the front in southern Moldavia:

I went to Iaşi and I spoke to the German commander because Iaşi was at that time in the German military zone, German troops were operating there and it was also a front-line zone, with the city occupied by German troops due to cross the Prut. And so I went to Iaşi and spoke to the German general and told him, 'if there is a repeat of this, I shall sent a telegram to the Führer and renounce command of the front.' And then the German general said to me, 'I assure you, general, that it will not happen again.'

Asked about the numbers of victims of the pogrom, Antonescu said that he never knew the actual figure:

I do not remember, however, I was told of 2,000 and because of these 2,000 I went personally to Iaşi. I even came under attack from enemy aircraft in Nicolina station . . . . I gave the order for an enquiry to be set up to find out who was responsible, and I found out straightaway that the German Gestapo there and the Iron Guardists, and I found only one Iron Guardist.[29] I gave the order – just one – that he should be tried. I followed this matter personally and saw that he was acquitted. That shows you what the mood was then – I had to keep on eye on it – they acquitted him. I sent him for trial a second time and I enquired what had happened to him and was told: He was sent to the front and he died there.

To this the public prosecutor retorted, 'You were so well informed that I can tell you that this man is presently under arrest by the People's Tribunal. [30]

Antonescu accepted full responsibility for the reprisals he ordered to be taken at Odessa:

When in October 1941 there happened what happened, that is the blowing up of the entire military command of the Odessa sector, I was asked to approve the taking of reprisals. There is provision for reprisals in international law when the enemy adopts measures unacceptable under the normal rules of war. I gave my approval for reprisals to be taken. I also stipulated the figure. I accept the entire responsibility for this. I have spent my whole on the basis that the leader, when he wins, has all the glory, even when the merit is not his, and when he loses, he accepts the entire responsibility, even if he is not guilty and others are. He is therefore responsible.... Although I gave the order, I have never been in favour of massacres. And you will never find a signal from me for the massacre, not of thousands of people, but of a single person. On the contrary, I shall be able to prove to this esteemed tribunal how many serious punishments I have handed down to those who committed much more serious abuses.

Pressed by the public prosecutor to state who signed the order for the murder of 200 Soviet citizens for every officer killed, and 100 for each soldier, Antonescu admitted he had:

And I ordered it because I also gave an order in Romania[31] at the beginning of the war, and I executed no one. And I also introduced many repressive laws, which are adopted by every state in time of war, which were not, however, applied. No child aged fifteen was executed, although there was a law... not one Jew who came to Romania was executed, although there was a law that they should be executed.[32]

The Romanian administration of Transnistria was also raised by the president, who asked Antonescu whether in justifying the 'plundering' of Transnistria he did so out of ignorance or with the full knowledge of what had occurred. The Marshal denied that Transnistria had been plundered:

We had the occupying power's right. In every war, from Ghenghis Khan to the present, the occupying power lives in occupied territory and where it carries out operations. We had a right. Apart from that, we created an administration in Transnistria of which we are proud. And later on the documents will appear. Abuses were also committed, this has happened down the ages, because a head of state or the head of a body cannot be everywhere. Abuses occur. I punished them severely. And I shall produce concrete cases of extremely grave punishment. But not only did we not pillage Transnistria, Mr President, but we gave the local population better conditions than they had had previously. I shall prove this, and Mr Alexianu will also be able to prove this.[33]

He went on to explain that fear, in the case of a Germany victory, of being caught in a German pincer convinced him of the need to hold on to Transnistria:

Germany had long posed the question of 'Drang nach Osten'. And so it wanted to advance through Salonica. There is a ribbon of ethnic Germans which starts with the Sudetens and carries on through Hungary, Slovakia, through Hungary, our Banat and on to Salonica. Therefore an arm which stretches down to our southwest. If Germany had been victorious in Russia, it would have extended another arm, through another ribbon of ethnic German states, towards Odessa. Romania, therefore, would have found itself, in the case of a German victory, caught in these two German arms, which would have been ... have led to the assimilation of the Romanian people. In order to have a card in our hand in the case of a German victory, to prevent the Germans laying their hands on Odessa and thus catching us in the two arms which I have just mentioned, I decided that I would not give up Transnistria, because I did not want to enter this German pincer.[34]

In response to the public prosecutor's question of what strategic and national necessities required the deportations of '26,000 gypsies, Innochentists, religious sects and anti-Fascists fighters', Antonescu declared:

> *Antonescu*: There are three problems here, Mr President: the problem of the gypsies, the problem of the sects, and the problem of the anti-Fascists fighters of whom the public prosecutor speaks. The problem of the sects: Mr President, many Romanians, unfortunately, went over to these sects in order to get out of fighting. What was the spiritual message of these sects? Not to lay hands on a weapon, in other words, not to fight. And then we would recruit a person, enrol him in the army and he would refuse to use a weapon. There was a general revolt, and so I introduced a law establishing the death penalty. I did not apply it. And I succeeded in abolishing these sects and I took some of those who were more recalcitrant and deported them.... Had we let the matter drop they would have spread rapidly throughout the whole country. Everyone was going over to these sects, to avoid military service. I had to take very drastic measures. But I did not execute anyone.... The Gypsy problem. Because of the blackout there were murders and thefts in Bucharest and in other towns, and therefore public opinion demanded protection from me, because they could not defend themselves. People broke in at night. After many enquiries it was discovered that gypsies, some of them armed with weapons of war, were carrying out these attacks. All these gypsies who were deported, some had seventeen convictions. And so I said, since Mr Alexianu needs manual labour in Transnistria, because they were short of it, I said: have them and take them to Transnistria. I deported them to Transnistria. It was my order and I take the responsibility for it. And I can justify why I did it. As for the anti-Fascists, I did not send one to Transnistria.
>
> *President of the Court*: Yet you sent the anti-Fascists from Târgu-Jiu camp.
> ...
> *Antonescu*: Several hundred Communists. I said, they are Communists, the Communists are coming, let them be where there are Communists. I sent them there for reasons of security.

Asked by the president of the Tribunal why he had marched alongside Hitler as far as Stalingrad if he had, as he had claimed, no intention of occupying territories in the Soviet Union, Antonescu replied:

> When a country commits itself to a war, the country's army must go to the ends of the earth to destroy the enemy's forces and to win the war. It is a military principal of paramount strategic importance and has been applied from the time of the Romans to the present. Look at history and you will see that no one stopped at the frontier, but they pursued and destroyed armies. When Hannibal was defeated in Italy, Scipio followed him to Africa and Spain. He defeated him at Zama and destroyed Carthage. Napoleon reached Moscow, Alexander I of Russia got as far as Paris. The Russians have been so many times to . . . (*cut short by the President*).[35]

After a trial lasting ten days Antonescu and his associates were found guilty. Hundreds of telegrams from all over the country – many from Communist-backed trade union groups – demanding the death penalty for Antonescu and his 'clique' were received by the People's Tribunal.[36] On 17 May, he was sentenced to death, together with Mihai Antonescu, Constantin Vasiliu, Gheorghe Alexianu, Constantin Pantazi, Radu Lecca and Eugen Cristescu; the other ten were given terms of imprisonment. Although Antonescu had said during his trial that he would not appeal against his sentence, he gave a power of attorney to his lawyers – Constantin Paraschivescu-Bălăceanu and Titus Stoica – to launch one.[37] He was joined by 11 of the others sentenced. The appeal was based on the claim that the law of 24 April 1945 was unconstitutional; war crimes were a concept of international law and the judgement of them was the province, under the Armistice Convention of September 1944, solely of all the signatory powers not just of one of them; the Romanian constitution did not provide for the setting up of special courts such as People's Tribunals; the constitution did not allow the death sentence in peacetime. These arguments were rejected on 31 May by the court of appeal, which reaffirmed the constitutionality of the law setting up the People's Tribunal. [38]

On 15 May, two days before the sentences were handed down, Burton Y. Berry, the US political representative in Bucharest, reported on the probable outcome of the trial and the king's plan of action to the State Department:

> Sometime tomorrow special court is expected to return death sentences for Ion and Mihai Antonescu and several other principal persons charged with war crimes. After announcement of verdict anyone convicted may beg the King's clemency, in which case he must confirm or commute sentence.
>
> Whereas year or more ago country would have solidly favored execution of all 16 defendants, temperament of people has changed in favour of leniency. Moreover, much publicized Maniu handshake (REMYTEL 496,

May 14)[39] instead of acting to his discredit has confirmed people's opinion that Antonescus are not so bad after all.

Nevertheless, in view of record, it seems unlikely that King will commute any sentences upon his own responsibility. Therefore they are likely to be carried out unless, as in early series of trials, Soviet Government speaking through voice of Communist Rumanian Minister of Justice indicates they should be commuted.

According to present plan King, when government presents for signature decree for execution or clemency, will suggest to Prime Minister that he inform 3 principal Allies of decision of the court and intention to carry out that decision at the time prescribed unless, before the hour to carry it out arrives, three Allies make other recommendations.

King told me at private luncheon today that his purpose was to give three great Allies an opportunity to ask for custody of Rumanian war criminals if we think they can be of any service at Nürnberg or elsewhere, to protect Monarch from criticism at home and abroad in confirming verdict of court and to place upon Groza Government responsibility for informing American, British and Soviet authorities of intended action without placing those authorities in position where normal course of events is retarded by failure on their part to take action.

Of course Groza may not inform British and American authorities, knowing in advance desires of Russian authorities, but in any event responsibility is clearly his. I see no American advantage in retarding normal process of justice in these trials but should it be to the interest of our Government the opportunity may exist if immediate action is taken.[40]

King Michael's intention to offer the Antonescus to the Nuremberg Tribunal was a means of postponing the execution of the probable death sentence and, perhaps, even of saving their lives, but his plan had been overtaken by events. As we have seen, the State Department had already informed the Soviet authorities that its representative at Nuremberg saw no purpose in summoning the Antonescus.

After the pronouncement of the sentence, pressure was placed on the king by the Soviet representatives on the Control Commission and the government of Petru Groza, 'to make a gesture in favour of Groza to make up for the hostility shown towards the government and the Russians during the independence day parade of 10 May'. In return, Groza and Gheorghe Tătărescu, the Foreign Minister, promised to 'persuade the Russians to cancel any carrying out of the death sentence'.[41] At the parade several Romanians had shouted support for the king; they were promptly arrested. Marshal Tolbukhin, the President of the Allied Control Commission, General Susaikov, his deputy, and Major Skoda, Susaikov's adjutant, urged the king to decorate Groza, stating that 'they would acccept nothing less to alleviate their anger at the events of 10 May'.[42] When the king rejected these overtures,

Tătărescu and Lucrețiu Pătrășcanu, the Minister of Justice, in an audience with Michael, insinuated that the legislation regarding war crimes could be extended in time and the wave of arrests enlarged in order to include the leaders of the opposition.

On 27 May, the king gave in to this blackmail; at an elaborate official ceremony in Constanța, he decorated Groza with a citation said to be composed by Tătărescu 'appreciating the achievements of the government presided over by Dr Groza'. As Burton Berry reported:

Local observers believe explanation for above events can be found in government's electoral plans. A Palace source stated last evening that the King under government pressure agreed at last moment to unprecedented citation with award to Groza in return for promised alleviation in campaign for trials of war criminals and those responsible for country's disaster.[43]

The king's hope, expressed in words to the French representative in Bucharest Jean-Paul Boncour – 'I prefer to risk unpopularity rather than to shed blood' – proved illusory.[44] On the same day as Groza's decoration, 27 May, sentences varying from a few months to three years were announced for those arrested on 10 May and simultaneously a wave of arrests struck the capital involving members of the National Peasant and National Liberal parties as well as local employees of the US and British military and political missions.[45]

Following the rejection of Antonescu's appeal on 31 May, pleas for clemency were entered on Antonescu's behalf to King Michael on the same day: one by his mother, Lița Baranga, and a second by his lawyer, Constantin Paraschivescu-Bălăceanu.[46] The other six who had received the death sentence also lodged appeals to the king. The constitution of 28 March 1923, which was reactivated on 1 September 1944, gave the king 'the right to pardon or reduce punishments for crimes' (article 88). At the same time, 'no act of the king was valid unless it was countersigned by a minister, who through the countersignature becomes responsible for that act' (article 87).[47] Pleas for clemency were forwarded to the king, together with a recommendation from the Minister of Justice. It was therefore the Minister of Justice, and thus the government, not the monarch, who was responsible for any decision taken.

On the morning of 31 May, the king gave separate audiences to Groza and Tătărescu. They probably told him of the government's decision on the convicted men for, that afternoon, in a telephone conversation with Berry, the king told him of the government's intention to carry out the death sentences on Antonescu and the three principal associates, and to commute the sentences of the three others. The king asked Groza to present their recommendation in writing and to seek the opinion of the Allied Control Commission. According to his authorized biography, the king asked that the sentences be commuted on the grounds that the constitution did not allow the death sentence in peacetime, but his reasoning failed because the deeds of the accused had been committed during the war.[48] Groza is also said to have invoked in support of the government's decision the 'inter-allied policy regarding war criminals'.[49] Suspecting that Groza meant 'Soviet' by 'inter-allied', the king sought the view of the Western Allies in this matter, but in vain. Berry himself was reported to have been embarrassed when the king asked him what the 'inter-allied' view on Antonescu's sentence was since he had received no instructions from Washington on this matter. Nor, it appears, did his British counterpart, Ian Le Rougetel, receive any from London.[50]

On the following day, 1 June, the day of the executions, the king received Lucreţiu Pătrăşcanu, Minister of Justice, at 10.30 am, who presented him 'a communiqué in vague terms'. The king refused to sign it. Groza arrived at 11 am and half an hour later he, Pătrăşcanu and Tătărescu had an audience with the king in which they submitted a text 'accepting the government's responsibility for the decision to be taken and alluding, at the same time, to the manner in which the Soviet head of the Allied Control Commission was pressing for execution'.[51] The text, bearing the date 31 May 1946, and signed by Pătrăşcanu, hinted at the political considerations behind Antonescu's sentence:

> In the name of and at the behest of the government I have the honour to propose to Your Majesty the rejection, for major interests of state, of the appeals for clemency made by Ion Antonescu, Mihai Antonescu, C. Vasiliu and Gh. Alexianu, and the commutation of the death sentence given to C. Pantazi, Radu Lecca and Eugen Cristescu to forced labour for life. The government permits itself to request Your Majesty to approve in its entirety this recommendation, bearing in mind the need to satisfy the major interests of our country.[52]

What these 'major interests' were is not clear.

The king finally gave in to the wishes of the government as he was required to do under the constitution. He issued a decree commuting the sentences of Cristescu, Lecca and Pantazi.[53] There was no mention in the decree of a rejection of the pleas for clemency of the two Antonescus, Vasiliu and Alexianu.[54] The decree was published in the Official Bulletin; Pătrăşcanu's recommendation of execution was not.

The government lost no time in carrying out the death sentences. On the same day, 1 June, Pătrăşcanu set the legal procedures in motion.[55] Two procurators were instructed to go to Jilava prison where the condemned men were being held. They arrived there at 4.15 pm and made arrangements for the executions with the prison commandant, a representative of the Ministry of Internal Affairs, a doctor and the prison chaplain, an Orthodox priest.[56] They set the time of execution for 6 pm. They then visited each of the condemned men in their cells. A detachment of 30 policemen was brought to the prison to form the execution squad at 3 pm. Between 5 and 5.30 pm family members were allowed to take their leave of the condemned men in their cells. Ion Antonescu received his wife with a bunch of red roses and gave a rose to each of the other visitors, the Marshal's mother, Mrs Nicolescu (the Marshal's mother-in-law) and a niece. After the departure of the family, the procurator entered the cell accompanied by the priest. Antonescu asked that he should not be blindfolded nor his hands tied. He was marched out of the prison block at the head of the other three condemned men in single file flanked by a firing squad and led to open ground some 300 metres away known as 'The Valley of the Peach Trees'. The four men were each stood before a wooden post; only Vasiliu did not refuse a blindfold. Shortly after 6 pm, as the firing squad took aim, Ion Antonescu raised his trilby hat in salute and then fell, like his colleagues, under a volley of fire. The officer commanding the firing squad then administered shots to the head of each of the victims.

When news of the execution spread, embellishments were added which created a legendary version. Reuben Markham, the correspondent of the *Christian Science Monitor*, gave eloquent currency to the myth in the English-speaking world:

> And the Marshal himself gave the command to the squad of executioners to fire. They proved more nervous than he. For years Antonescu had been the most outstanding soldier in the land. He had a commanding mien and imperious gaze; he was known to be wilful, hard, stern. As the boys, standing a few feet in front of him with their fingers on the triggers of their guns, looked into his flashing eyes they trembled a little. As they fired the General fell, but was neither killed nor unconscious. Partially rising on all fours, he stretched out his right hand toward the executioners and shouted, 'Shoot again, boys, shoot!' Well, they shot again and again and an officer finished him off with a revolver.[57]

This version diluted Antonescu's crimes in pity and cast him as a hero in the popular mind.[58] It was revived publicly after 1990. Yet a film of the execution, released after 1990, does not support this version of events; it shows him lying motionless on the ground as the *coup de grâce* is given. In an ironic testimony of Antonescu's own obsession with 'Judeo-bolshevism', and in an effort to add vitriol to claims that Antonescu was 'victimized' by the Communists and Jews – and to emphasize that the army had no involvement in the execution of its former commander[59] – apologists of the Marshal regularly maintain that the firing squad was made up of 'police officers, many of them Jews'.[60]

Such aberrations obscure the dignified manner in which the Marshal faced his end. His own words, in a final letter to his wife, written after he had been sentenced to death, show that he regretted nothing, that he regarded his actions as justified by a sense of duty towards his country and that the verdict of his contemporaries meant nothing to him; the only judgement acceptable to him was that of posterity:

My dear Rica,

I have stood with my head held high before the court, just as I stand before the supreme judgement.

No one in this country has served the ordinary people with as much love and interest as I have done.

I gave them everything, from my own toil to our joint labours, from my soul to our life together, without asking anything, and we ask nothing now. Their subjective judgement today does not demean us and does not affect us, it is only tomorrow's judgement that will be the right one and it will extol us. I am prepared to die, just as I was prepared to suffer.

As you know my life, especially those four years in power, was a Calvary. So was your life, but it was uplifting and will be immortal.

Circumstances and people did not permit us to do the good which together we wanted to do so fervently for our country.

The Supreme Will decided thus.

I have been a failure.

Others, too, have been. Many others.

After the correct judgement of history has assigned them their place, so it will determine ours.

Peoples everywhere throughout history have been ungrateful.

I regret nothing and you should regret nothing.

Let us respond to hate with love, to blows with kindness, to injustice with forgiveness.

My final wish is that you should continue to live. Withdraw to a monastery. There you will find the peace necessary for the soul and the piece of bread which today you cannot afford. I shall ask to be buried alongside those who were my ancestors and guides. There at Iancu Nou I shall be amongst those with whom I shared joy and hardship in my childhood. Circumstances drew me apart from them in life, but my soul has never forgotten them. Perhaps you will consider that there too, beside me, should be your final resting place.

As we are lowered into the earth, me today and you tomorrow, we will be uplifted, I am sure. It will be the only just reward.

I hold you close in my arms with great warmth and embrace you lovingly.

Not one tear.

Ion[61]

Despite the procedural flaws in Antonescu's trial, it is hard to escape the conclusion that a court set up by the Western allies would have found him guilty of war crimes on the evidence available at the time. The complaint of many Romanians, both then and now, is that the Marshal was tried by a court in the pocket of a totalitarian power – a traditional adversary of the Romanians – and that he was convicted because he had attacked that power. To supporters of the Western democracies, the trial was a travesty of the very principles of justice which the Western allies claimed to represent and underlined to them the reality that the United States and Britain were simply spectators of the imposition of Soviet power in their country. Against this view must be placed the fact of Antonescu's orders to murder innocent civilians in Odessa in October 1941 and his responsibility for the deportations of tens of thousands of Jews – men, women and children, the old and the infirm – without ensuring or even considering the means for their survival.

An indication that the Soviet authorities had settled their account with Antonescu was the winding-up of the People's Tribunal by decree on 28 June 1946.[62] It had been in existence for less than 18 months.

12
Conclusion

Under Communist rule the image of the past was manipulated to suit the regime's ends. Ion Antonescu's name was, for the early part of the period, largely taboo. Romanian historians were directed to adopt various 'coping strategies'[1] to deal with Romania's war record. One strategy was justification, used to explain the conquest and occupation of Transnistria between 1941 and 1944. The occupation was justified by contrasting the Romanian regime in Transnistria with the more draconian German rule of other former Soviet territories. A second strategy was evasion. This involved, in particular, inflating the role of the Romanian Communist Party in the *coup* of 23 August, and emphasizing Romania's contribution to the war against Germany. A third strategy was the quest for scapegoats. Romania was a victim of Nazi Germany which imposed its political and military will upon the country. The Soviet Union, Hungary and Bulgaria shared their part of the 'guilt' as revisionist states which had pounced upon a politically isolated Romania. Britain and France were blamed for failing to provide a counterweight to the Soviet Union and Germany. Antonescu's fault was to lead Romania single-handedly into a calamitous war.[2]

With the imposition of Communist rule, Romania was forced to turn its back on the West and face eastwards. The first steps in the new cultural direction were taken under the cover of the Paris Peace Treaty of February 1947. One of its provisions required Romania to undertake to outlaw all Fascist organizations on Romanian territory and 'all other bodies engaged in anti-Soviet propaganda'. In furtherance of this commitment, the Romanian authorities argued that 'the struggle against those who sought to prevent the democratization of the country could not be pursued without banning all publications which propagated Fascist ideas and without a general effort *to purge all publications in general*' (my emphasis). In appealing to the Peace Treaty the Romanian Communist regime sought to ban all literature which did not suit its ideological mission, that of communizing Romanian society. To this end the Ministry of the Interior issued a circular to all libraries and bookshops in spring 1948 forbidding them to provide or sell 15 categories of works, among them all school textbooks published before 1947, all books relating to Russia, France, Britain, the British Empire and the United States before 1944, all books favourable to a regime or government other than the Soviet one, and all books showing Western cultural influence in general, in Romania's past.[3]

In May 1948, the Ministry of Information published a list of 8,000 titles which were to be withdrawn from circulation. Many Romanians must have been amazed to find the names of Winston Churchill and Charles de Gaulle, the Soviets' wartime allies, included among them.[4] Books on Antonescu, the Iron Guard, the Romanian royal family, Bessarabia and the Romanian occupation of Transnistria were removed from libraries. As well as the purge of politically incorrect titles, the activities of journalists, writers, artists and musicians were brought under the Agitation and Propaganda (Agitprop) section of the Central Committee of the Party. Nothing could be published or performed without approval. Education was similarly treated. In August 1948, the Law for Educational Reform closed down all foreign schools, including those run by religious orders. A purge was conducted of the teaching profession and university students. Eminent professors were removed from the faculties of history and philosophy and their places taken by Stalinist indoctrinators, the most notorious of whom in the history field was the Agitprop activist Mihai Roller.

During the 1950s and early 1960s, the interpretation of the Second World War by Romania's historians was straightforward and dictated by the precepts of Marxism-Leninism. The war was defined as a 'class struggle', and the attack on the Soviet Union was denounced as the work of 'imperialists'. The blame for the attack was placed squarely on Nazi Germany, the Romanian 'capitalists' and 'fascists', and Antonescu. This approach allowed the Romanian regime conveniently to overlook those aspects of the prelude to Romania's war with the Soviet Union which did not fit the Marxist-Leninist thesis and might revive anti-Russian sentiment: the Soviet Union's ultimatum to Romania in late June 1940 and Romania's re-conquest of Bessarabia and northern Bukovina the following year; Romania's deployment of a largely peasant conscript army against a fellow army of the 'popular masses'; and the Romanians' capture of Odessa in October 1941 which dented the Red Army's image of invincibility. Such aspects were avoided not only by historians in Bucharest, but also by those in Moscow and in Chişinău, the capital of the successor Soviet republic to Bessarabia, the Moldavian Soviet Socialist Republic.[5]

The officially sanctioned view of Romania's role in the war was presented in Roller's textbook *Istoria RPR* (History of the Romanian People's Republic) in a chapter entitled 'The participation of bourgeois-landlord Romania in the criminal anti-Soviet war'.[6] There was no mention of the Soviet ultimatum of 26 June 1940; the Russian occupation of Bessarabia and northern Bukovina was presented as the result of an 'understanding':

On 27 June 1940, following an understanding between the Soviet Union and the Romanian Government, Bessarabia and northern Bukovina are liberated, and thus is liquidated the territorial conflict which existed between the two governments, a conflict which was reborn following the counter-revolutionary intervention of the Romanian army against the Soviets in 1918.[7]

The heads of the National Peasant and National Liberal Parties, respectively Iuliu Maniu and Constantin Brătianu, are said to have turned their backs on the 'patriotic and democratic forces' and supported Antonescu. On 22 June 1941, Antonescu, with the support of King Michael and these two leaders, forced Romania into the 'criminal, anti-Soviet war' started by Hitler's Germany with the collusion of the American and British imperialists. All the scapegoats are neatly bundled into one paragraph.[8] Maniu and Brătianu are presented as accomplices of Antonescu in the 'Fascistization' of Romania, while their protests to Antonescu, and those of Romanian military commanders such as General Ilie Şteflea, against carrying the war beyond the Dniester are not recorded – all for the reason that any mention of such protests would highlight the Romanian claim to Bessarabia – and hence a justification for the hostilities against the Soviet Union – and would vitiate the class perspective of the textbook.[9]

Under Ceauşescu the principal figures of Romania's past were restored to their respected place in history. Contemporary Romanian historiography assumed a vision of preordained history which portrayed the Socialist Republic of Romania as the natural continuation of the pre-war national unitary state, and in this context the Iron Guard and Antonescu were, broadly speaking, seen as 'aberrations' from the natural course of Romanian history. The association between Antonescu and the Iron Guard was played up, as was the part of Nazi Germany in the accession of both to power. The Guard was presented as a threat to the independence of the Romanian state from Hitler and held solely responsible for xenophobic actions against the Jewish, Hungarian and Slav minorities.[10] Yet the mass support the Guard enjoyed amongst the Romanian population was neither acknowledged nor explained. With the Guard's removal from power by Antonescu in January 1941, Antonescu was left to shoulder the blame exclusively for Romania's war against the Soviet Union:[11]

On June 22, 1941, when the German aggression against the Soviet Union began, Ion Antonescu decided to enter the war as Adolf Hitler's ally. The moment the anti-Hitlerite coalition (the USSR, Great Britain and the USA) was set up, Romania was officially at war with Great Britain and the United States (December 7 and 12, 1941). Acting contrary to the Romanian public opinion and the democratic and progressive forces and regardless of the attitude of the military leaders, of the officers and soldiers who didn't want to fight far off the country's boundaries, Ion Antonescu during an interview with Hitler (August 6, 1941) agreed that the Romanian army should continue the military operations on the territory of the USSR.[12]

As Ceauşescu developed the policy of *rapprochement* with the West, the earlier thesis of collusion between the Western Allies and Germany against the Soviet Union was discarded. Appeasement was adduced as the explanation for Romania's abandonment by Britain and France; implicit in this was the accusation that the West bore some responsibility for Romania's alignment with Germany.[13] At the same time, Antonescu's part in the war against the Soviet Union was played down. Instead, the importance of the period 1941–44 was measured in terms of the preparation for the *coup* of 23 August 1944, described variously in the Ceauşescu years as an 'anti-Fascist armed uprising' and a 'national revolution'.

The *coup* – King Michael's arrest of Ion Antonescu – had a crucial impact on the course charted by Stalin for the Romanian Communist Party. It was also responsible for bringing Gheorghiu-Dej to the forefront of political events, thereby launching him on the road to power. Since Gheorghiu-Dej emerged first as the leader of that wing of the Party which was most closely involved in the *coup*, and he then went on to secure his domination of the entire Party, the *coup* was accorded a sacred place in Party history. Even before Gheorghiu-Dej achieved supremacy within the Party and was able to control its historiography, his Communist colleagues sought to deny the credit gained by the king and the major democratic parties for the coup by assuming it exclusively for themselves, thereby claiming legitimacy for their rule. To this end, the role of the Romanian Communists in the *coup* was deliberately exaggerated by the Party. King Michael was relegated to the position of a mere spectator. In this endeavour, Communist apologists were abetted by the suppression by the Communist authorities of any accounts of the *coup* which did not fit into their scenario of the events. Therefore the accounts of key participants in the events, that is, of the king and of members of his entourage who escaped to the West, describing the king's crucial act in ordering the arrest of Marshal Antonescu on 23 August 1944, were largely unknown in Romania before the overthrow of the Communist regime.[14]

Under Ceauşescu the 23 August *coup* became the major event of Romania's war. First, it was presented as the culmination of the allegedly Communist-led anti-Fascist resistance to Antonescu. Second, it marked the *volte-face* against Germany and the beginning of Romania's part in the defeat of Hitler. Third, it provided legitimacy for the autonomous course initiated by Gheorghiu-Dej and continued by Ceauşescu.[15] Emphasis on Romania's contribution to the defeat of Germany was given especially by military historians working under the direction of Lt.-Gen. Dr Ilie Ceausescu, a brother of the President and Deputy Minister of the Armed Forces. Such was their insistence on the importance of the 23 August *coup* and the Romanian reversal of arms that they advanced the extraordinary claim that Romania's effort in the war against Germany – of less than one year – had shortened hostilities by 200 days. No mention was made of Romania's three-year campaign alongside Nazi Germany between 1941 and 1944.[16]

In the mid-1960s, a new element hovered over the presentation of Antonescu's war record: Ceaușescu's claim to Bessarabia and northern Bukovina. His speech of 7 May 1966 on the occasion of the forty-fifth anniversary of the foundation of the Romanian Communist Party constituted the strongest and most authoritative claim that Communist Romania made to Bessarabia. He criticized resolutions of the third, fourth, and fifth Romanian Party congresses, held in 1924, 1928 and 1932, in which 'Romania was mistakenly called 'a typical multinational state' formed from 'the occupation of certain foreign territories'. He added:

> The indications given to the party to fight for the severance from Romania of some territories which were overwhelmingly inhabited by Romanians did not pay heed to the concrete conditions in Romania – a unitary state. They were deeply erroneous; they actually called for the dismemberment of the national state and the Romanian people's disintegration. Marxist-Leninist teaching proclaims the right of the peoples to self-determination not with a view to the disintegration of the established national states, but, on the contrary, with a view to the liberation of the oppressed peoples and their constitution into sovereign national states in conformity with the will and decision of the mass of the people. [17]

The Romanian Party's mistaken stance over the territories acquired at the end of the First World War was a

> consequence of the practices of the Comintern which laid down directives that ignored the concrete realities of our country, gave tactical orientations and indications which did not comply with the economic, social-political and national conditions prevailing in Romania.[18]

Whilst pointing to the injustice of the Molotov–Ribbentrop Pact, on the basis of which the Soviet Union annexed both territories, Ceaușescu did not go as far as to say that Antonescu was justified in recovering these territories in summer 1941; Ceaușescu left this to be implied by his historians, who did so in the 1970s by defining the starting-point of Antonescu's war as his advance across the Dniester, i.e after the re-conquest of Bessarabia and northern Bukovina. This approach allowed those leaders of Romania's democratic parties who had protested against the continued advance across the Dniester to be rehabilitated as Romanian patriots. Iuliu Maniu and Constantin Bratianu, respective leaders of the National Peasant and National Liberal Parties, had urged Antonescu not to let Romanian troops go beyond Romania's historical frontiers.[19] On 28 June 1941, Maniu declared that 'the Romanian armies must not set foot on territories which have not belonged to us. A Romanian imperialism will be condemned by the whole world.'[20] Yet the restoration of the 'bourgeois' democratic parties to the pantheon of Romanian history, significant though it was, paled before a reassessment of Ion Antonescu himself which took place in the mid-1970s.

The degree to which Ceaușescu succeeded in mobilizing support for his regime from intellectuals was one of the features of his rule.[21] Broadly speaking, Ceaușescu achieved that success by using the 'nation' as his constant point of reference in defining his policies. The appeal of such a definition drew its vigour from the fact that national identity had been central to Romanian culture and politics long before the imposition of Communist rule in Romania and Ceaușescu's promotion of it enabled him to project himself as the latest in a line of Romanian heroes who were seen as defenders of the Romanian nation. It was in this context that the young Ceaușescu was written in 1975 into the novel *Delirul* by Marin Preda in which Ion Antonescu is introduced as a central figure.[22] By a quirky twist of fate – which Preda could not have foreseen – Ceaușescu was to share the fate of his fellow character Antonescu in front of a firing squad.[23]

At the time of *Delirul*'s publication, Preda enjoyed both critical and official appreciation.[24] At the beginning of March 1974, Preda had been elected a corresponding member of the Romanian Academy of the Socialist Republic of Romania. This accolade conferred authority for his treatment of a subject which until the appearance of *Delirul* had been strictly taboo in official discourse. It is generally believed that Preda spent a good deal of time researching the career of Antonescu and that he enjoyed privileged access to materials in the Romanian archives.[25] But it was not only in *Delirul* that the Marshal reappeared in the public domain in 1975. He was also reintroduced in another novel, *Incognito*,[26] whose author Eugen Barbu had been elected a corresponding member of the Academy at the same time as Preda.[27] Their presentations of Antonescu were, however, quite different. Barbu's figure was the object of character assassination at the hands of an author who selectively used official material to pass judgement on the dictator – his access to this material also suggested the official sanction given to his novel. Antonescu's trial is fictitiously recreated and provides the author with an opportunity to attack the corruption of Romanian politics with an acerbity that exceeds the condemnation of it in the trial itself.

This one-sided treatment of the Marshal contrasted with his sympathetic portrayal in *Delirul*. Preda's novel effectively rehabilitated the wartime leader and was said to have been validated by the ideological committee of the Central Committee.[28] Naturally, there were limits to what the Central Committee would accept. Antonescu is frequently described as 'the dictator', and his decisions are largely presented without comment by Preda. The main character of the novel, Ştefan, is employed by a Bucharest newspaper to cover events on the Eastern Front. On his return to the capital, he discovers that his despatches have been censored to disguise the heavy Romanian casualties. His condemnation of this censorship is contrasted with Antonescu's persistent misleading of the nation over the cost of the campaign in the Soviet Union. Preda, on the one hand, presents Antonescu as saviour of the nation from the Iron Guard through his crushing of the rebellion in January 1941, but on the other, regards him as leading the nation to disaster by invading Russian territory beyond Dniester. Neither he nor Barbu says anything, however, about the fate of the Jews in the re-conquered territories, or in Transnistria.

What was unique about Preda's portrayal of Antonescu is the human dimension he gave to it. The self-centred, conceited and unfeeling dictator of Barbu's novel is unrecognizable in the tragic figure of the Marshal in *Delirul*. 'In his dressing-gown and slippers, the leader Antonescu reviews – through the hand of Preda the writer – all the stages of his rise, from 1917 until September 1940....A reminiscence and analysis of Romania's situation in 1941 in which his mother becomes no only confessor but also coun-sellor.'[29] In a lengthy conversation with his mother, Antonescu explains that he came to power to save the country. Warned by his mother of the dangers of joining the Axis Powers and of applying Nazi-inspired policies against the Jews, Antonescu reaffirms his determination to retrieve Bessarabia, and here Preda doubtless struck a powerful note of sympathy with his readers.[30] Not surprisingly, this partial apologia of Antonescu provoked sharp criticism in the Soviet *Literaturnaia gazeta*, which prompted the Romanian authorities to instruct Preda to produce a revised edition. The changes made were largely cosmetic.[31]

Antonescu was not the only Romanian leader to appear in *Delirul*. What intrigued readers were the allusions to Ceauşescu and his wife, Elena. Chapter 11 introduces a young Communist, held in jail on Christmas Eve 1940, who can easily be identified from his attempts in 1933 to gather signatures on a petition in support of railway workers arrested for their part in organizing strikes. The 15-year old boy is handed over to the police to be taken back to his native village and is none other than the young Nicolae Ceauşescu. His presence in the novel is doubtless the price paid by Preda for having the privilege of making a best-seller out of the Marshal.[32]

Ceauşescu's historians began in the 1980s to argue that the Soviet annex-ation of Bessarabia and northern Bukovina had opened the doors to the installation of the pro-German government of Ion Gigurtu on 4 July 1941, and the participation of the Iron Guard in it. By this reckoning, Antonescu's alliance with Hitler was in part the fault of Moscow, but a direct link between the Soviet ultimatum and Antonescu's reconquest of the territories was studiously avoided.[33] If references to the re-conquest by Antonescu of Bessarabia and northern Bukovina were muted during the Ceauşescu years, there was absolute silence regarding the Romanian campaign beyond the Dniester, the Romanian administration of Transnistria, and the operations in southern Russia and the defeat at Stalingrad. Antonescu's deportation of the Jews and their fate in Transnistria was completely ignored. A major volume on *The Great Battles Fought by the Romanians*, published in 1982, omitted any mention of Romania's participation in the German attack on the Soviet Union on 22 June 1941, or of the hostilities in the Soviet Union in which the Romanian army was involved.[34] Its coverage of Romania's part in the Second World War focused entirely on the period after 23 August 1944.[35]

If fear of upsetting Soviet sensibilities deterred the Romanian authorities from taking Antonescu's rehabilitation further, outside Romania, émigrés had no such inhibitions. In a partnership which buried differences in political ideology, documents and memoirs were channelled to émigré publishers from Bucharest to promote Antonescu's rehabilitation. Iosif Constantin Drăgan, a frequent visitor to Ceaușescu, sponsored the publication of four huge volumes of documents by his publishing house *Nagard* in Milan, which represented a beatification of Antonescu.[36] The provenance of many of these documents was not indicated, making it difficult for scholars to test their reliability.

One of the most pernicious consequences of the Communist regime was the perverted image of the past that it left. Yet manipulation of the past for political ends did not end with the collapse of Communism. Since the overthrow of Ceaușescu the case of Antonescu has become in the first instance a political matter and only at a secondary level an historical one.[37] Exaltation of Antonescu and exaggeration of his political merits, combined with a minimalization of his responsibility for the death of more than 250,000 Jews, have been used as a weapon of propaganda by those who invoke patriotism in the name of ultra-nationalism against both constitutional monarchy and democratic forces in general.[38] Ultra-nationalist politicians such as Corneliu Vadim Tudor have striven to exploit sympathy for Antonescu as a weapon again King Michael, who was accused of having ordered the Marshal's arrest and handover to the Soviets, thereby becoming the moral perpetrator of Antonescu's convinction and execution.

Romanian historians are agreed on certain facets of Antonescu. All recognize his devotion to Romania, and the word 'patriot' is commonly used to describe him. Yet, the use of this word is, in Antonescu's case, inappropriate. Patriotism, as John Lukacs has pointed out, is often confused with nationalism – or in my definition, ultra-nationalism, in the mind of the same person. You can be a patriot and, at least culturally speaking, cosmopolitan. Antonescu was not cosmopolitan; he had little time for Romania's minorities. Patriotism is not necessarily racist, as ultra-nationalism has to be. A patriot will not exclude a person of a different race from the community in which they have lived together and whom he has known for years; but an ultra-nationalist will always harbour suspicions towards someone who seems not to belong to the same community as he or she does, or rather, does not think in the same way as he or she does. This was the mind-set of Antonescu.[39] Even so, being an ultra-nationalist (or 'patriot') does not excuse war crimes; being a 'patriotic' war criminal hardly constitutes grounds for entry into the gallery of a nation's heroes.

A second quality attributed by Romanian historians to Antonescu was his sense of 'honour'. Few students of Romania would dispute this appreciation. And yet Antonescu's sense of honour made him inflexible and rigid. Romania under Antonescu was led into a war on the basis of his word of honour to Hitler and was expected to stay in the war – in the view advanced by Antonescu in his last meeting with King Michael on 23 August 1944 – as long as honour required it.[40]

It is as an example of patriotism and honour that Antonescu is advanced by some ultra-nationalists as a model for Romanian society today. And yet, the example even in those two respects is flawed. He has no credentials as a model for a democratic Romania and while it was not he who introduced the policy of ethnic intolerance and persecution into Romania, it was he who extended it. Romanian ultra-nationalists deny this and seek to whitewash their country's record under Antonescu's rule.[41] In 1991, on the eve of the anniversary of Antonescu's execution as a war criminal on 1 June 1946, the Romanian parliament stood for one minute in silent tribute. The reaction of the Romanian authorities to the invitation launched by nine Romanian foundations and societies to King Michael to attend a fiftieth anniversary symposium, held in Bucharest on 8–9 October 1994 to mark the 50th anniversary of King Michael's *coup* and his arrest of Antonescu on 23 August 1944, said much about their values. Whilst granting Antonescu's *chef de cabinet* a visa to participate in the anniversary symposium, President Iliescu saw fit to deny one to King Michael, the author of the *coup* against Antonescu.

Iliescu's contradictory response to this episode in Romania's war record merely highlights the political delicacy in which the Romanian president and government found themselves whenever the names of Marshal Antonescu and the king were raised. To celebrate the event of 23 August 1944 meant to recognize the decisive role played by King Michael in Romania's recent history. At the same time, a celebration of 23 August ran the risk of upsetting those nationalists in the Romanian governmental coalition who idolized the Marshal and who considered the *volte-face* against the Germans to be an act of national betrayal. In the face of this predicament, the Romanian authorities buried their heads in the sand and hoped the problem would go away.

One of the most persistent apologists of Antonescu is Gheorghe Buzatu, formerly a member of the 'A. D. Xenopol' Institute of History in Iaşi and a senator in Vadim Tudor's Greater Romania Party in the 2000–4 parliament. After 1990, Buzatu initiated a series of collections of documents on the Antonescu era which were decidedly selective and designed to promote a positive image of the Romanian leader. A feature of Buzatu's studies has been his sympathy for Antonescu and the collective depiction of Jews as supporters of the Communist regime in Romania.[42] More ambiguous in his approach to the atrocities carried out under Antonescu is Ion Calafeteanu, an historical researcher who, after 1989, became a senior official in the Romanian Foreign Ministry. On the occasion of President Iliescu's presence at the inauguration of the United States Holocaust Memorial Museum in Washington in April 1993, Calafeteanu published two articles in the Romanian press. In the second, he employed a particular kind of sophistry by writing that 'the only country in Nazi-dominated Europe where the Final Solution was not applied was Romania inside its January 1941 borders'. As Victor Eskenasy has pointed out, by adding *inside its January 1941 borders* Calafeteanu sought to exculpate Antonescu for the atrocities committed in northern Bukovina and Bessarabia by the Romanian authorities *after* they were regained by Romania in the summer and autumn of 1941.[43]

One of the most extreme of Antonescu apologists was Radu Theodoru, a former leading figure in Vadim Tudor's Greater Romania Party and president of the Marshal Antonescu Foundation. Theodoru's writings were characterized by a virulent anti-Semitism, exemplified in *România ca o pradă* [Romania as a Prey][44] and *Nazismul Sionist* [Zionist Nazism].[45] In the first Theodoru claimed that Romania was a safe haven for Jewish refugees during the war and contrasted the 'humanitarian' spirit shown by the Romanians with the 'great harm' which the Jews caused Romania down the centuries. The true Holocaust, he argued, was that experienced by the Romanians under Communism:

> I affirm with all responsibility that the Judaic minority of Romania constituted and continues to constitute one of the long-term noxious factors responsible for a long series of crimes against the Romanian people beginning with the Holocaust in the [Communist][46] extermination camps and ending with the cultural Holocaust.[47]

There were, nevertheless, some encouraging signs with regard to Holocaust-denial in Romania. President Emil Constantinescu, in a message addressed to the Federation of Jewish Communities in Romania on 4 May 1997 to commemorate Holocaust Day, acknowledged for the first time Romania's collective responsibility for its part in the Holocaust. Without mentioning Antonescu by name, Constantinescu pointed out that

> Romania's wartime authorities more than once attempted to oppose the Nazi demand for the complete liquidation of the Jewish population, organized the immigration of groups of Jews to Palestine, even openly protected some personalities of the Jewish community in Romania. But the same authorities organized deportations and issued racial legislation.

Today we accept responsibility for this dramatic inconsistency. The sacrifice of thousands of Jews from all over Romania weighs heavy on our hearts, on those of all Romanians.[48]

Romanian textbooks also began to include Antonescu. Although in the Ministry of Education-sponsored *History of the Romanians from 1821 to 1989* for 18-year-olds published in 1995[49] there was no mention in the section on Romania during the Second World War of Antonescu's treatment of the Jews, nor of his trial in May 1946, it was covered in a refreshingly objective 'alternative'[50] manual for the same age-group written by group of young historians led by Sorin Mitu and published in 1999.[51] Lya Benjamin offered an invitation to discussion of Antonescu's anti-Semitic measures in a richly annotated study entitled *Prigoana si rezistență în istoria evreilor din România, 1940–1944* [Persecution and Resistance in the History of the Jews in Romania, 1940–1944],[52] while Dinu Giurescu revisited some of the most controversial aspects of the Marshal's record in his *România în al doilea război mondial (1939–1945)* [Romania in the Second World War].[53] In providing a balanced account of Antonescu's part in the German attack on the Soviet Union in the summer of 1941, and the consequences of it for the local Jewish population, Giurescu performed a valuable service to Romanian readers, fed hitherto on a diet of half-truths. Yet he often struck a polemical note which deflected him from recognizing Antonescu's part in the deaths of Jews in Transnistria. Stung by what he regarded as the collective incrimination – in a number of recent studies on Transnistria which have appeared abroad – of the Romanians, Giurescu blurred the issue of Antonescu's culpability by submerging it within 'the Jewish holocaust in the Second World War and the Communist genocide between 1945 and 1989' and by taking this equivalence further in stating that 'the Nazi regime, like the Communist regimes of East-Central and South-East Europe, as well as the Soviet one, used the power of the state in the name of an ideology in order to eliminate physically, socially, and culturally entire categories [of persons] who had been declared *a priori* enemies who had at all costs to be liquidated'.[54]

President Constantinescu's candour over the Holocaust in Romania was not shared by his successor, Ion Iliescu. In line with his previous obtuseness regarding Romania's treatment of Jews under its jurisdiction during the war, Iliescu stated in an interview published on 25 July 2003 in the internet version of the Israeli daily *Ha'aretz* that 'the Holocaust did not only affect the Jews in Europe. Many others, including Poles, died in the same way.' Iliescu continued, 'During the Nazi period in Romania Jews and Communists were treated in the same way. My father was a Communist activist and was sent to a camp. He died at the age of forty-four, less than a year after he returned.' The president did recognize that 'the massacres in Bucharest and Iași in 1941, and the deportation of Jews to concentration camps in Transnistria did take place in Romania, but the leaders of the time are responsible for those events...and it is not possible that the Romanian people and society be accused of this'. The Israeli Minister of Justice Yosef Lapid, described Iliescu's remarks in an Israeli radio interview as 'insensitive'.[55]

Iliescu's interview came at a time of tension in Romanian–Israeli relations, a tension generated by a communiqué issued by the Romanian government on 13 June 2003 following the signing of a cooperation agreement between the Romanian National Archives and the United States Holocaust Memorial Museum. The communiqué 'stated categorically that within the borders of Romania there was no Holocaust in the period 1940–45'.[56] This phraseology was similar to that used in 1993 by the Romanian historian Ion Calafeteanu.[57] David Peleg, a senior official in the Israeli Foreign Ministry, summoned the Romanian ambassador to inform her that Israel was concerned about the Romanian government's position since it was not 'consonant with the historical truth'.[58]

Several studies on Antonescu's record in respect of the Jews have been published in Romania since 1990, notably those of Jean Ancel, the Romanian-born Israeli scholar whose principal works have also appeared in English and Hebrew.[59] In contrast to Ancel, Alex Mihai Stoenescu gives a sympathetic and sometimes partisan view of the Marshal's intentions and motives in his *Armata, Mareşalul şi Evrei. Cazurile Dorohoi, Bucureşti, Iaşi, Odessa.*[60] A major source of Romanian documents on the subject is Matatias Carp's three-volume *Cartea Neagră.*[61] One of the more important English-language titles on Transnistria is Alexander Dallin's *Odessa, 1941–1944: A Case Study of Soviet Territory under Foreign Rule.*[62] As pioneering as he was at the time, Dallin did not enjoy the cooperation of the Soviet or Romanian authorities, nor was he able to consult the hundreds of thousands of pages of Romanian and Soviet documentation now available in the United States Holocaust Memorial Museum's archives. The latter museum's collection of Romanian records formed the basis of Radu Ioanid's recent history, *The Holocaust in Romania. The Destruction of Jews and Gypsies under Antonescu Regime, 1940–1944.*[63] Ioanid provides a path-breaking synthesis, cataloguing and describing Antonescu's systematic measures to expel and eliminate the Jews and Gypsies from Romania. In addition to Ioanid, other scholars such as Lya Benjamin, Randolph Braham and Paul Shapiro have edited mulit-authored volumes, document collections, or taken a regional approach to Romania's Holocaust history by focusing on the fate of Jews from Bessarabia.[64]

While improved access to archival sources has generated the studies mentioned above, a complete biography of Antonescu in any language is still lacking. The most comprehensive and best-documented study of Ion Antonescu's military and political career is the monograph of Larry L. Watts which covers the period from 1916 to 1941.[65] The book, then, does not tackle the Antonescu dictatorship, which is only presented in an epilogue of some 50 pages. In his introduction, Watts addresses the dilemmas thrown up by any consideration of Antonescu and his use as a political football by interested parties. Yet where Watts' discussion is most relevant is in relation to the period 1941 to 1944, the most controversial years of the Marshal's rule, precisely the years not covered in detail by the author. Watts raises questions in his introduction such as the degree to which Antonescu could or could not be considered a war criminal, suggesting that Antonescu's 'war crimes' (Watts' style) guilt was based on 'rotten foundations', and arguing that the trial of Antonescu had 'more in common with sheer political expediency than accepted legal principles' (pp. 4–5). Watts adduces little evidence to support these statements. For those interested in how the historical reconstruction of Antonescu has become a political one, Watts himself offers valuable evidence from his own statements.

This is not to say that Watts' work does not have considerable merits. Its strengths are its examination of the Marshal's military career, his relationship with the Iron Guard leader Corneliu Codreanu, with King Carol II, and his period at the head of the National Legionary State (1940–41). Admirably and extensively researched, it offers one of the most penetrating views in English of interwar Romanian politics. Watts is particularly convincing when he argues that the legacy bequeathed by Carol II was one that only Antonescu appeared able, or willing to confront in September 1940 and it was a measure of Antonescu that he accepted the task of leading Romania in the absence of an almost total lack of support from Romania's politicians.[66]

Watts has sympathy, like most biographers, for his subject, but it sometimes takes him into the realms of the apologist. Most historians would find it difficult to agree with Watts' contention that 'Antonescu shared the values for which they [the Allies] struggled'.[67] In his desire to emphasize the positive aspects of the Marshal's rule, Watts makes the claim that the living standards of the average Romanian in terms of food supply and energy consumption in 1944 were higher than in the years 1990–93.[68] It would be interesting to see the respective data and source. Antonescu's aim when accepting power in September 1940 was, as Watts claims, to try to keep his country from sliding further into the abyss.[69] If the abyss is defined by war, loss of life and eventual occupation by a totalitarian power, then Antonescu patently failed his fellow Romanians. Whether any other Romanian leader could have done better in the political configuration of Europe in 1940 is open to doubt; that another leader might have done worse is more than probable. Finally, Watts does not appear willing to accept Antonescu's responsibility for the deportations of Jews from Bukovina and Bessarabia to Transnistria. Only this conclusion can explain why Watts should consider the Marshal to have been, relatively speaking, 'a good man'.[70]

Given the importance of Romania to Hitler's war machine, the neglect of Antonescu by anglophone historians is even more puzzling. One might be tempted to ascribe it to the language barrier. But this would be equally valid in respect of the Finnish military leader, Marshal Carl Gustav Emil

Mannerheim, about whom several books in English have appeared,[71] and of Hungary's wartime leader, Admiral Miklos Horthy.[72] Our avoidance of Antonescu stems, I suggest, from the difficulty of understanding the ambiguities and ambivalences of Romania's record during the war, which in turn make the task of assessing Antonescu's role appear daunting.

Antonescu inherited from King Carol a poisoned chalice; Romania's predicament on the eve of the war was that of a state determined to preserve not only its identity but also its existence between significantly more powerful neighbours. Romania was in the circumstances of 1940 driven into the arms of Germany following the Soviet annexation of Bessarabia and northern Bukovina. Had Romania defied the Soviet Union in June 1940 she would probably have gained, like Finland a year earlier, widespread sympathy, but little else. Germany could not help her since her hands were tied by the Molotov–Ribbentrop Pact. When Romania did go to war against the Soviet Union in the following year she did so as Germany's ally and thus incurred the enmity of Britain. Her alliance with Germany was not embodied in any treaty, merely signified by adherence to the Tripartite Pact. She was not a totally voluntary partner, as the opposition of Maniu and Brătianu demonstrated, but she was a partner and not vassal, and remained under the control of a Romanian ruler.[73]

Antonescu remained the ultimate arbiter of Romanian policy. Although he remained master of his own country, any attempt to withdraw from the war invited German occupation before 1944. By 1944, the attrition of German forces deprived Hitler of the force necessary to punish Romania for doing just that. As long as Romania was able to preserve her internal cohesion and some military might, she was able to preserve her freedom of action. This she did until the invasion of the Red Army.

Antonescu's treatment of the Jews was ambivalent; for the Jews of Bukovina and Bessarabia, Antonescu was a cruel anti-Semite; for those of Moldavia, Wallachia and southern Transylvania, he was a providential anti-Semite.[74] Even his inhuman and shameful behaviour towards the Jews of Bukovina and Bessarabia admits a distinction to be drawn between Romanian and German action. While German and Romanian forces joined in mass executions of Jews in Bessarabia and Bukovina in the summer of 1941, after that date Romanian treatment of the Jews broadly speaking followed a separate course. If, as in the German case, discrimination was followed by deportation, deportation, in the Romanian case, did not lead to the gas-chamber. Tens of thousands of Jews from Bessarabia, Bukovina and Transnistria were indeed shot in the period from winter 1941 until early spring 1942 on Romanian orders in Golta county, but subsequently the plight of the Jews in Transnistria was characterized by degradation and callous neglect. Jews residing in Ukraine beyond Transnistria were likely to suffer a quick death by shooting at the hands of the Germans, but in Transnistria Jews often faced a slow death by typhus or starvation. The contrast between German and Romanian actions is illustrated by the fact that the largest proportion of Jews to survive Axis rule during the Second World War in the Soviet Union was in Transnistria.

The question remains as to whether deportation of the Jews and Romas to harsh, desolate parts of Transnistria, with an inadequate supply of food, virtually no medical care, little shelter against the extremes of summer and winter, and no sanitation, was not tantamount, in the mind of Antonescu, to sending the Jews and Romas to their death? Leaving aside speculation, the blunt truth is that Antonescu's action led to the death of tens of thousands of Jews and Romas. Antonescu's letter of 4 February 1944 to the architect Herman Clejan is striking for its use of impersonal language in that section where he alludes to the suffering of the Jews. His discourse is that of a person seeking to absolve himself of any responsibility for the fate of the Jews in Transnistria:

> In the current war, which covers the entire globe, the Jews have not been excused from the sufferings and miseries which all of humanity must endure. If in this period of food shortages and unsanitary living conditions the lives of Jews were also lost, this only indicates that the merciless rules of war – which we have not provoked – have also imposed upon the Jews the imperative of paying a blood tribute. The other Romanians who fight on the front lines die daily by the thousands. However, as a man of European formation I have never supported the murders of anyone and can never do so. I have taken measures and will take further measures ensuring that murders will not be committed against the Jews, wherever they are found.[75]

His self-description as 'a man of European formation' is a chilling reminder that in his case, as in that of many other anti-Semites, the values of Western civilization were only a veneer and that, if scratched, would reveal a darker core in which base instincts festered. He was impusive in his judgements. The first reports to reach Antonescu in his train of the Iaşi pogrom in June 1941 explained the events in Iaşi as a response by the Germans to the actions of Communist agents, parachuted in to make contact with the Jews in order to carry out sabotage behind the German–Romanian lines, and it was under the influence of such reports that he issued a retaliatory order which was relayed to units in Iaşi by the chief of the General HQ, General Ioaniţiu late in the night of 30 June: 'General Antonescu ordered that all the Jewish Communists in Iaşi, and all those found with red flags and firearms are to be executed tonight. Report the execution [of the order] to Ialomiţa [the place of Antonescu's quarters in the train Patria].'[76] Whether any executions were carried out that night is not known.

Antonescu's claim at his trial that he had 'never supported the murders of anyone' is contradicted by his order to carry out mass reprisals against

'Judeo-Communists' in Odessa for the mining of the Romanian headquarters in October 1941. Yet he did not deny responsibility for his actions. Antonescu delegated authority to the governors of Bessarabia, Bukovina and Transnistria but he made it clear at a meeting of the Council of Ministers on 6 September 1941 that he accepted responsibility for their actions with his words, 'The responsibility is mine before the judgement of history.'[77]

That judgement can now be given.

In 1941, Romania entered the war against the Soviet Union to restore her territorial integrity; in 1944, she turned her forces against Germany to preserve it. The moment that the Red Army entered Romania the alliance with Germany lost its *raison d'être*. After the 23 August *coup* Romania contributed more than 16 divisions and suffered a further 170,000 casualties in the final Soviet campaigns against Hitler.[78] In terms of troops engaged in the European theatre of war at that time Romania's participation was the fourth largest after the Soviet Union, the United States, and Great Britain. Her military endeavour on both sides, from 1941 to 1944, and from 1944 to 1945, was a remarkable contrast to the supine surrenders of territory in 1940.[79]

By astutely co-opting Romanian forces in the thrust westwards Stalin effectively placed Romania's fate at the mercy of his troops, large units of which were stationed in the country for 'recuperation'. It was a 'recuperation' which lasted until 1958. In March 1945, when Stalin ordered the demobilization of Romanian forces, unchallenged Soviet military occupation of Romania provided the underpinning for the communization of the country. That process ceased on 22 December 1989. On that same day the Second World War also finally came to an end for Romania.

Annex

The Supreme Commander of the Army the Department of the Civil Government of Transnistria Ordinance no. 23

We, ION ANTONESCU, Marshal of Romania, Commander-in-Chief of the Army:
  Through Professor G. ALEXIANU, Civil Governor;
With regard to the fact that there is a large Jewish population on the territory of
  Transnistria which has been evacuated from various battle-zones, in order to
  protect the rear of the front;
With regard to the need to organize communal living for this evacuated population;
Seeing that this population must find a means of existence on its own account and
  through labour;
By virtue of the full powers accorded by Decree no. 1 of 19 August 1941, issued at Tighina;

We command:

Article 1 All Jews who have come from the battle-front in Transnistria, as well as
Jews from Transnistria, who for the same reasons were moved into various centres, or
those who remain to be moved, are subject to the rules of life established by this
present ordinance.

Article 2 The Inspectorate of Gendarmes in Transnistria determines the localities
where the Jews can be housed. The Jews will be housed with regard to the size of their
family in the dwellings abandoned by the Russian or Jewish refugees. Each family of
Jews who receive a dwelling will be obliged to tidy it up forthwith and to keep it clean.
If there are not enough of these dwellings, the Jews will also be housed in private
homes, which will be allocated to them, for which they will pay the determined rent.

Article 3 All the Jews in a commune will be listed into a special register, in which will
be entered:

1. Their name and first name;
2. Their nationality;
3. Their religion;
4. Their age;
5. Their profession;
6. The locality from which they come.

Each Jew will be issued with an identity card with all the above details.

Article 4 A Jew can only leave the commune in which his domicile has been fixed if
he has the authorization of the county prefect.

Article 5 All the Jews in a commune form a colony, which is administered by a head
of the colony appointed by the district pretor.

The colony head is assisted by group leaders.

Each colony head will appoint a group leader for every twenty Jews, and he will be responsible for the whereabouts of all group members, for the well-being of the group, and will bring to the notice of the authorities any transgression by a member of the group. The colony head and the leaders of the group are personally responsible for the whereabouts of all the Jews in the colony and for the executions of all the orders handed down by the administration and by the gendarmerie.

Article 6 The head of the colony is obliged to make a list of all the professional persons, the craftsmen and all able-bodied people in the colony.

On the basis of the lists submitted by the colony head, the mayor of the commune will organize labour in the colony and in the commune in the following manner: Craftsmen will be obliged to perform any service according to their skills that is required.

Professional persons will make themselves available to the commune authorities and will be used whenever the need arises.

Manual labourers will make themselves available to the town-hall and will perform any labour required of them for the benefit of the colony and the commune, or public service tasks;

They will be used for agricultural labour, for road or bridge repairs, for wood-cutting in the forests, quarrying stone or any other materials. In return for labour duly performed the labourer will receive meal coupons to the value of one-day's labour, one-day's labour being valued at one mark a day for manual labourers, and two marks a day for qualified professionals.

The gendarmerie will continuously inspect and control the Jewish colonies, and will report their findings to the higher authorities.

Article 7 The use of Jews from one commune for labour in another, will be made with the approval of the county prefect.

The movement of specialists from one county to another in order to perform work will only be permitted with the approval of the Director of Administration and Labour of the [Transnistrian] government.

Article 8 Any Jew found in a place other than that in which his residence is fixed without the approval of the authorities, will be considered a spy and immediately punished according to military law in time of war.

Article 9 Jewish specialists may be used with government approval on all projects necessary for the reconstruction of industrial plants destroyed by war, for the reopening of factories, or for any other uses that may be deemed necessary.

Article 10 County prefects and the Inspector of Gendarmerie are charged with the implementation of the present ordinance.

Issued in our office, today, 11 November 1941[1]

Notes

Introduction

1. Antonescu and Hitler met ten times, on 23 November 1940, 14 January 1941, 12 June 1941, 6 August 1941, 11 February 1942, 10–12 January 1943, 12 April 1943, 2–3 September 1943, 23–24 March 1944 and 5 August 1944. Mark Axworthy terms their meeting at Rastenburg on 2–3 September 1943 as 'unscheduled'. Mark Axworthy, Cornel Scafeş and Cristian Craciunoiu, *Third Axis, Fourth Ally. Romanian Armed Forces in the European War, 1941–1945* (London: Arms and Armour, 1995), p. 121; see also Andreas Hillgruber, *Hitler, König Carol und Marschall Antonescu. Die Deutsch-Rumänischen Beziehungen, 1938–1944* (Wiesbaden: Franz Steiner Verlag, 1965), p. 173. The Romanian leader was 'the first foreigner to be awarded the Knight's Cross of the Iron Cross, the only one to be solicited for military advice, and probably the only person – German or foreign – permitted to out-talk and contradict the Führer'. Joseph Rothschild, *East–Central Europe between the Two World Wars* (Washington: Washington University Press, 1975), p. 317.
2. As does that with von Ribbentrop on the following day; see chapter 5.
3. Axworthy, Scafeş and Craciunoiu, *Third Axis, Fourth Ally*, p. 216. After Italy signed an armistice with the Allies on 8 September 1943, Romania became the second Axis power in Europe.
4. Radu Ioanid, *The Holocaust in Romania. The Destruction of Jews and Gypsies under Antonescu Regime, 1940–1944* (Chicago: Ivan R. Dee, 2000. Published in association with the United States Holocaust Memorial Museum), p. 289.
5. Dennis Deletant, 'The Molotov–Ribbentrop Pact and its Consequences for Bessarabia: Some Considerations on the Human Rights Implications', *Revue Roumaine d'Histoire*, vol. XXX, nos 3–4 (1991), pp. 221–2.
6. Maurice Pearton, 'British Policy towards Romania 1938–1941', *Anuarul Institutului de Istorie 'A. D. Xenopol'*, vol. 23, no. 2 (1986), p. 551.
7. By contrast, Hungary's population grew from about 9 million in 1939 to an estimated 14.7 million in 1941, including almost 1 million Romanians. Axworthy, Scafeş and Craciunoiu, *Third Axis, Fourth Ally*, p. 17.
8. Antonescu's pragmatism is noted by Franklin Mott Gunther, the American minister in Bucharest. In a report to the US Secretary of State of 25 February 1941 he wrote: 'It has always been my impression – one which has recently been confirmed – that the General's pro-German as well as his anti-British feelings are not dictated by sentiment but solely by what he considered to be national interest and dates from Russia's invasion into Rumania and the collapse of France.' Larry Watts, *Romanian Cassandra. Ion Antonescu and the Struggle for Reform, 1916–1941* (Boulder, CO: East European Monographs, 1993), p. 380.
9. It listed: 1.The occupation of four islands at the mouth of the Danube in the autumn of 1940; 2. Daily frontier incidents involving attempts to move the frontier; 3. Attempts by Soviet vessels to enter Romanian waters by force in January 1941; 4. Incessant incursions, despite Romanian protests, into Romanian airspace amounting during April, May and June to up to seven daily over-flights; and 5. A massive concentration of Soviet military forces on the Romanian frontier

made up of 30 infantry divisions, 8 cavalry divisions, and 14 motorized brigades. *Universul*, 9 December 1941.

10. These documents are described by Gheorghe Buzatu in *Românii în arhivele Kremlinului* [The Romanians in the Kremlin Archives] (Bucharest: Univers Enciclopedic, 1996).

11. Including this author. Copies of correspondence from the Preşedinţia Consiliului de Miniştri (the Council of Ministers – Ion Antonescu's office) were held in the archive of the Romanian Foreign Ministry and in the State Archives. Orders issued by this office to the Ministry of the Interior were held in the state security archives, and copies of orders issued to the army were held in the archive of the Ministry of National Defence.

12. Examples of the Soviet view are Artem Markovich Lazarev, *Moldavskaya sovetskaya gosudarstvennost' i bessarabskiy vopros* [The Soviet Moldavian Government and the Bessarabian Question] (Kishinev: Cartea Moldovenească., 1974); and Iziaslav Elikovich, *Krakh politiki agressi diktatury Antonesku: 19.IX.42–23.VIII.1944* [The Failure of the Aggressive Policy of the Dictator Antonescu] (Kishinev: Shtiiintsa, 1983); see also Wim van Meurs, *The Bessarabian Question in Communist Historiography* (New York: East European Monographs. Distributed by Columbia University Press, 1994), p. 344.

13. van Meurs, *The Bessarabian Question*, p. 344.

14. I accept that a 'division' is not necessarily a safe basis for comparison, and much depends on its fire power, but the emphasis in the quotation is on 'mobilized men'.

15. Elisabeth Barker, *British Policy in South-East Europe in the Second World War* (London: Macmillan, 1976), p. 226.

16. Ioanid, *The Holocaust in Romania*, p. 289: 'In 1930, Romania had been home to 756,000 Jews. At the end of World War II about 375,000 of them had survived.'

17. Some Romanian historians take an overtly critical view of the Antonescu regime, in particular his policy towards the Jews and Romas; see Andrei Pippidi, 'Miturile trecutului-Răspântia prezentului', *Xenopoliana*, vol. 1, nos 1–4 (1993), p. 24; and Şerban Papacostea, 'Captive Clio: Romanian Historiography under Communist Rule', *European History Quarterly*, vol. 26 (1996), pp. 203–6.

18. *Fantasies of Salvation. Democracy, Nationalism and Myth in Post-Communist Europe* (Princeton, NJ: Princeton University Press, 1998), pp. 92, 95.

19. In the archive of the Center for Advanced Holocaust Studies I had access to hundreds of thousands of pages of documentation on the Holocaust in Romania which the museum has gathered since 1993 from Romania and Ukraine under the guidance of Radu Ioanid and Paul Shapiro.

20. Axworthy, Scafeş and Craciunoiu, *Third Axis, Fourth Ally*.

21. A fuller discussion can be found in Michael Shafir, 'Memory, Memorials, and Membership: Romanian Utilitarian Anti-Semitism and Marshal Antonescu', *Romania since 1989. Politics, Economics and Society*, ed. Henry F. Carey (Lanham, MD: Lexington Books, 2004), pp. 67–96.

22. I have borrowed this phrasing from Pippidi, 'Miturile trecutului-Răspântia prezentului', p. 24.

23. To judge from some of his comments during the 2000 election campaign Vadim Tudor evidently saw himself as a second Antonescu, offering an 'iron fist' to get Romania out of the deep political and economic crisis in which, he argued, it found itself. For a detailed analysis of Antonescu's rehabilitation, see Michael Shafir, 'Marshal Antonescu's Postcommunist Rehabilitation: *Cui Bono?*', in *The Destruction of Romanian and Ukrainian Jews during the Antonescu Era*,

ed. Randolph L. Braham (New York: Columbia University Press, 1997), pp. 349–410; see pp. 393ff. for Tudor's adoption of Antonescu as a role model.

24. The motives behind Antonescu's rehabilitation and his treatment by Romanian and Western historians are discussed by Paul E. Michelson, 'In Search of the 20th Century: Marshal Antonescu and Romanian History – A Review Essay', *Romanian Civilization*, vol. III, no. 2 (Fall–Winter 1994), pp. 72–103.

25. In a letter addressed to Eyal Arad, his Israeli political campaign adviser; I am grateful to Radu Ioanid at the United States Holocaust Memorial Museum for this information.

26. Gabriel Andreescu, 'Raportul Comisiei Internaţionale pentru Studierea Holocaustului în România', *Ziua* (18 November 2004).

27. Conclusions of the report of the Internaţional Commission on the Holocaust in Romania; at www.presidency.ro 'Raportul Comisiei internaţionale privind studierea Holocaustului în România' [The Report of the International Commission on the Study of the Holocaust in Romania]. The report is also available on the website of the United States Holocaust Memorial Museum under the title 'Romania, facing the Past' (www.ushmm.org/research/center).

28. Cristian Oprea, 'Iliescu, palmuit moral de un laureat Nobel' [Iliescu, a Moral Slap in the Face from a Nobel Laureate], *Evenimentul Zilei* (16 December 2004).

Chapter 1

1. Although Romanians represented less than 30 per cent of the inhabitants in the province.

2. This point is made by Mark Axworthy, Cornel Scafeş and Cristian Craciunoiu, *Third Axis, Fourth Ally. Romanian Armed Forces in the European War, 1941–1945* (London: Arms and Armour, 1995), p. 38.

3. Carol's discussions with the British and Germans are analysed in Rebecca Haynes, *Romanian Policy Towards Germany, 1936–40* (London: Macmillan, 2000), pp. 57–8; see also Dov B. Lungu, *Romania and the Great Powers 1933–1940* (Durham, NC and London: Duke University Press, 1989), pp. 142–4.

4. Haynes, *Romanian Policy Towards Germany*, p. 68.

5. Lungu, *Romania and the Great Powers*, p. 153.

6. For a discussion of this so-called 'ultimatum' see Haynes, *Romanian Policy Towards Germany*, pp. 77–8.

7. A. Chanady and J. Jensen, 'Germany, Rumania and the British Guarantees of March–April 1939', *Australian Journal of Politics and History*, vol. 6, no. 2 (August 1970), pp. 201–17.

8. Haynes, *Romanian Policy Towards Germany*, pp. 78–9. The guarantee was also the result of French pressure on Britain to guarantee Romania as the price of France's willingness to help guarantee Greece: D. Cameron Watt, 'Misinformation, Misconception, Mistrust: Episodes in British Policy and the Approach of War, 1938–1939', in Michael Bentley and John Stevenson (eds), *High and Low Politics in Modern Britain: Ten Studies* (Oxford: Oxford University Press, 1983), pp. 247–9. I am grateful to Rebecca Haynes for this reference.

9. Henry Roberts, *Rumania. Political Problems of an Agrarian State* (New Haven, CT: Yale University Press, 1951), pp. 215–16 where he analyses the terms.

10. G. Gafencu, *Prelude to the Russian Campaign* (London: Frederick Muller, 1945), p. 237.

11. The Romanian government allowed 70 tons of gold belonging to the Bank of Poland to reach Constanţa, where it was loaded into a ship and transferred to France via Syria; see R. Westerby and R. M. Low, *The Polish Gold* (London: Methuen, 1940).

12. On 14 October 1939, Smigly-Ridz was moved to a village called Dragoslavele. He eventually escaped from his place of internment, at the third attempt, during the night of 15–16 December 1940 and crossed into Hungary, before making his way back clandestinely to Poland. Details from Stanley S. Seidner, 'Reflections from Rumania and beyond: Marshal Smigly-Rydz in Exile', *The Polish Review*, vol. 22, no. 2 (1977), pp. 29–51.

13. Colonel Zygmunt Wenda, the former Chief of Staff of the OZN (Camp of National Unity), who also went into exile. In an unpublished manuscript *The Times* correspondent in Romania, Archibald Gibson, claimed that the Romanian government permitted '16,000 of the 24,000 Polish soldiers she had interned to 'escape' from various camps in the country'.

14. These were later to provide the model and precedent advanced by the Soviets for the establishment of the joint Soviet-Romanian companies provided for in the Soviet–Romanian Armistice of September 1944.

15. Lungu, *Romania and the Great Powers*, p. 222.

16. M. Pearton, British Policy towards Romania 1938–1941', *Anuarul Institutului de Istorie 'A.D. Xenopol'*, vol. 23, no. 2 (1986), pp. 539–47.

17. Lungu, *Romania and the Great Powers*, p. 223.

18. Haynes, *Romanian Policy Towards Germany*, p. 130.

19. Killinger recounted this meeting with Moruzov to Gheorghe Barbul, a Romanian diplomat, on 22 March 1943; see Arhivele Nationale Istorice Centrale [The Central Historical National Archives, Bucharest], henceforth ANIC, Ministerul Afacerilor Interne [Ministry of Internal Affairs]. Trial of Ion Antonescu, file 40010, vol. 28, p. 293.

20. Ibid., pp. 293–7.

21. Valeriu Pop, *Bătălia pentru Ardeal* [The Battle for Transylvania] (Bucharest: Editura Enciclopedică, 1992), p. 253.

22. Ibid.

23. Ibid., p. 255; see also Lungu, *Romania and the Great Powers*, pp. 229–30.

24. *Documents on German Foreign Policy, 1918–1945, Series D (1937–1945)* (henceforth cited as *DGFP*), vol. VII (Washington, DC: Government Printing Office, 1956), doc. no. 229, p. 247.

25. M. G. Hitchens, *Germany, Russia and the Balkans. Prelude to the Nazi–Soviet Non-Aggression Pact* (Boulder, CO: East European Monographs, 1983), p. 221.

26. Unpublished MS of Archibald Gibson, *The Times* correspondent in Romania 1928–40, in possession of this author.

27. *Al doilea război mondial. Situaţia evreilor din România* [The Second World War. The Situation of the Jews in Romania], vol. 1 (1939–1941), part 1, ed. A. Duţu and C. Botoran (Cluj-Napoca: Centrul de Studii Transilvane, Fundaţia Culturală Română, 1994), no. 8, pp. 64, 67.

28. Ibid., no. 8, p. 70.

29. Ibid., no. 8, p. 55.

30. Ibid., pp. 101–2.

31. Alex Mihai Stoenescu, *Armata, Mareşalul şi Evreii* [The Army, the Marshal and the Jews] (Bucharest: RAO, 1998), p. 114.

32. Ibid., p. 115.

33. Ibid.
34. See Larry Watts, *Romanian Cassandra. Ion Antonescu and the Struggle for Reform, 1916–1941* (Boulder, CO: East European Monographs, 1993), p. 234.
35. Ibid., p. 235.
36. *Evreii din România între anii 1940–1944* [The Jews in Romania between the Years 1940–1944]. Vol. III, Part 1, *1940–1942: Perioada unei mari restriști* [The Period of a Great Sadness], ed. Ion Șerbănescu (Bucharest: Hasefer, 1997), doc. 22, p. 36.
37. These incidents were reported to the Ministry of Justice on 3 July by the local prosecutor; see *Martiriul Evreilor din România, 1940–1944. Documente și Mărturii* [The Martyrdom of the Jews in Romania, 1940–1944. Documents and Other Evidence] (Bucharest: Editura Hasefer, 1991), no. 10, pp. 33–4.
38. *Al doilea război mondial. Situația evreilor din România* [The Second World War. The Situation of the Jews in Romania]. Vol. 1, *1939–1941*, part 1, ed. A. Dutu and C. Botoran (Cluj-Napoca: Centrul de Studii Transilvane, Fundația Culturală Română, 1994), no. 26, p. 96.
39. *Curierul israelit*, no. 22 (10 July 1940), p. 1, quoted from Alex Mihai Stoenescu, *Armata, Mareșalul și Evreii* (Bucharest: RAO, 1998), p. 106.
40. Ibid., p. 107.
41. Ibid.
42. W. W. Kulski, 'Soviet Comments on International Law and International Relations', *The American Journal of International Law*, vol. 45 (July 1951), pp. 558–9.
43. M. W. Graham, 'The Legal Status of the Bukovina and Bessarabia', *The American Journal of International Law*, vol. 38 (1944) p. 671.
44. Based on language affiliation, the figures gave the numbers of Romanians as 920,919 (47.6 per cent), of Ukrainians as 382,169 (19.7 per cent), and of Russians as 155,774 (8.05 per cent). *Pervaia vseobshchaia perepis' naseleniia Rossiskoi Imperii 1897g.*, vol. 3 (St Petersburg, 1905). By 1930, the population breakdown, according to the Romanian census, was as follows: Romanians 1,610,752 (56.2 per cent), Russians 351,912 (12.3 per cent), Ukrainians 314,211 (11 per cent), Jews 204,858 (7.2 per cent) and Bulgarians 163,726 (5.7 per cent). *Anuarul statistic al României 1939 și 1940* [The Statistical Yearbook of Romania 1939 and 1940] (Bucharest: Institutul Central de Statistică, 1940), p. 60.
45. 853,009 of whom 379,691 (44.5 per cent) were Romanians, 236,130 (27.6 per cent) were Ukrainians, 92,492 Jews (10.8 per cent), 75,533 Germans (8.8 per cent) and 30,580 Poles (3.5 per cent). In his analysis of the population of the areas annexed by the Soviet Union in June 1940 Anton Golopenția shows that in eight districts of the counties of Rădăuți, Storojineț, Cernăuți and Hotin, which constituted most of the area of northern Bukovina and the northern part of Bessarabia lost by Romania, Ukrainians represented an absolute majority of 67 per cent of the population. The population by nationality of the eight districts, based on the 1930 census, is given as Ukrainians 301,271, Romanians 53,115, Russians 37,635, Jews 31,595. Anton Golopenția, 'Populația teritoriilor românești desprinse în 1940', *Geopolitica și geoistoria*, no. 1 (Bucharest: Societatea Română de Statistică, 1941), p. 10. In the two southern Bessarabian counties of Cetatea Alba and Ismail (the greater part of which were added to the Ukrainian SSR) the Ukrainians, however, represented only 14 per cent compared with 24 per cent for Romanians, 22 per cent for Russians and 20 per cent for Bulgarians. If the figures for the other two southern Bessarabian counties of Tighina and Cahul are entered into the calculation (and parts of them were incorporated into the Ukrainian SSR) the Ukrainian percentage drops to a mere 8 per cent compared with the figure for

Romanians of 37 per cent, for Russians 17 per cent, for Bulgarians 15 per cent, for Gagauz 9 per cent and for Jews 3 per cent The figures are: Cetatea Albă 341,000 (Romanians 63,000, Ukrainians 70,000, Bulgarians 71,000, Russians 59,000, Jews 11,000, Gagauz 8,000), Cahul 197,000 (Romanians 101,000, Ukrainians 619, Bulgarians 29,000, Russians 15,000, Jews 4,000, Gagauz 35,000), Ismail 225,000 (Romanians 72,000, Ukrainians 11,000, Bulgarians 43,000, Russians 67,000, Jews 6,000, Gagauz 16,000), Tighina 307,000 (Romanians 164,000, Ukrainians 9,000, Bulgarians 20,000 Russians 45,000, Jews 17,000, Gagauz 39,000) (*Anuarul statistic al României 1939 şi 1940* (Bucharest: Institutul Central de Statistică, 1940), p. 60.

46. The breakdown of county population figures for Bukovina, based on the 1930 Romanian census, was: Câmpulung 94,816; Cernăuţi 306,194; Rădăuţi 160,778; Storojineţ 169,894; Suceava 121,327. *Anuarul statistic al României 1939 şi 1940* (Bucharest: Institutul Central de Statistică, 1940), p. 60.
47. Golopenţia, 'Populaţia teritoriilor româneşti desprinse în 1940', pp. 37–8.
48. The National Archives (PRO), War Office 208/1745, 'Balkan Invasion: Russian Invasion of Roumania', 30 July 1940. 'Of 7 Infantry and 3 Cavalry Divisions located on territory now occupied by Russians, 3 Infantry and 1 Cavalry Division lost everything; 2 Infantry and 1 Cavalry Division [lost] 50 to 70 per cent of all war materiel, remainder no loss. These losses include literally everything since units concerned were composed of Bessarabian troops who made off home leaving weapons behind and taking horses and carts with them. Casualties: Officers (?16) dead, 23 missing; Warrant Officers 49 dead, 416 missing; Other Ranks unknown, but since in addition to deserters all men of Bessarabian origin are allowed to return home, I estimate loss to army at least 150,000 men'. I am grateful to the late Brigadier-General Geoffrey Macnab for these details; see also Watts, *Romanian Cassandra*, p. 233.
49. Dorel Bancoş, *Social şi national în politica guvernului Ion Antonescu* [The Social and National in the Politics of the Ion Antonescu Government] (Bucharest: Editura Eminescu, 2000), p. 322.
50. Ibid.
51. Rebecca Haynes, 'Germany and the Establishment of the Romanian National Legionary State, September 1940', *The Slavonic and East European Review*, vol. 77 (October 1999), p. 702.
52. Ibid.
53. *DGFP*, vol. IX (Washington, DC: Government Printing Office, 1956), doc. no. 67, p. 69.
54. C. A. Macartney, *October Fifteenth. A History of Modern Hungary, 1929–1945* (Edinburgh: Edinburgh University Press, 1956), vol. 1, pp. 336–87.
55. Ottmar Traşcă, 'URSS şi diferendul româno-maghiar din vara anului 1940', *România şi relaţiile internaţionale în secolul XX in honorem Profesorului Universitar Doctor Vasile Vesa* ['The USSR and the Romanian-Hungarian Dispute in Summer 1940', Romania and International Relations in the 20th Century in Honour of Professor Vasile Vesa], eds. Liviu Ţîrău and Virgiliu Ţârău (Cluj-Napoca: Biblioteca Centrală Universitară, 2000), p. 192.
56. Arhiva Ministerului Afacerilor Externe [Archive for the Ministry of Foreign Affairs], Bucharest, Fond 71/Germania, vol. 80, pp. 129–34. I am grateful to Rebecca Haynes for providing this citation and reference.
57. Haynes, *Romanian Policy Towards Germany*, p. 158.
58. Galeazzo Ciano, *The Ciano Diaries 1939–1943*, transl. and ed. Hugh Gibson (Garden City, NY: Doubleday, 1946), p. 289.

59. One Romanian source gave the area ceded as 43,591 sq. km and the break-down of population in northern Transylvania at the time of the award as 1,305,000 Romanians, 968,000 Hungarians, 149,000 Jews and 72,000 Germans. Silviu Dragomir, *La Transylvanie avant et après l'Arbitrage de Vienne* (Sibiu, 1943), p. 43. Another put the area at 42,610 sq. km in which there were 1,315,500 Romanians and 969,000 Hungarians as well as other nationalities. Golopenţia, 'Populaţia teritoriilor româneşti desprinse în 1940', pp. 39–40. Compare this with the Hungarian of census of 1941, taken after an exodus of Romanians to southern Transylvania, which put the population of northern Transylvania *by language* at 2,577,000, of whom 1,347,000 were listed as Hungarians, 1,066,000 as Romanians, 47,500 as German speakers, and 45,600 as Yiddish speakers. Of the total Jewish population of about 200,000 of the province before the partition, 164,000 lived in the area ceded to Hungary. *Genocide and Retribution: The Holocaust in Hungarian-ruled Transylvania*, ed. Randolph L. Braham (Boston and The Hague: Nijhoff, 1983), p. 10.

60. Bancoş, *Social şi naţional în politica guvernului Ion Antonescu*, p. 329.

61. Figures prepared by the Romanian General Staff in spring 1944 for the German–Italian Commission that monitored the situation in Northern Transylvania gave the following breakdown of population by county:

County	Total Population	Romanians	Hungarians	Others (including Jews)	Refugees (to 31.1.1944)
Bihor	332,917	150,083	138,102	44,732	35,876
Ciuc	158,918	23,520	128,215	7,183	5,609
Cluj	274,401	154,968	91,179	28,254	55,659
Maramureş	176,147	103,816	11,871	60,460	6,709
Mureş	294,471	129,492	128,832	36,147	22,693
Năsăud	157,150	114,936	7,942	34,272	10,610
Odorhei	131,852	6,200	119,446	6,206	2,193
Sălaj	375,245	215,104	114,451	45,690	29,734
Satu-Mare	321,393	198,516	78,865	44,012	18,170
Someş	239,152	188,390	35,887	14,875	25,456
Trei Scaune	138,250	19,442	111,393	7,415	7,335
Târnava Mare	1,149	322	63	764	322
Târnava Mică	2,623	188	2,125	310	188

(Arhivele Naţionale. Direcţia judeţeană Bistriţa-Năsăud, Fond 'Dumitru Nacu', dosar 2. I am grateful to Ion Bolovan at Cluj University for this reference).

62. Bancoş, *Social şi naţional în politica guvernului Ion Antonescu*, p. 330.

63. The area represented almost 7 per cent of the total area of Romania and had a population of 378,000 according to the 1930 census. Of these 143,000 (37.5 per cent) were Bulgarian, 129,000 (34.1 per cent) were Turkish-speaking Tatars, and 78,000 (20.5 per cent) Romanian. However, under the terms of the Romanian–Turkish Convention of 4 September 1936, some 14,500 Romanians and almost 7,000 Macedo-Romanians were settled from Turkey on the land of 70,000 Turks in Dobrogea who opted to go to Turkey. This settlement brought

the number of persons registered as Romanian in 1940 to 98,619. To this figure must be added the natural growth in population over the decade since 1930. Golopenția, 'Populația teritoriilor românești desprinse în 1940', p. 39. The transfer of population of population began on 5 November 1940 and was largely completed by 14 December.

64. Bancoș, *Social și național în politica guvernului Ion Antonescu*, pp. 93–5. In a selfish act, which provided eloquent testimony to his priorities, Carol, in the knowledge that Romania would cede southern Dobrudja to Bulgaria, was reported to have 'sold the Balcic castle [located there] to the Bucharest City Council in order to avoid a personal loss'. Quoted Watts, *Romanian Cassandra*, p. 228.

65. By contrast, Hungary's population grew from about 9 millions in 1939 to an estimated 14.7 millions in 1941, including almost one million Romanians. Axworthy, Scafeș and Craciunoiu, *Third Axis, Fourth Ally. Romanian Armed Forces in the European War, 1941–1945*, p. 17.

66. Henry Roberts, *Rumania. Political Problems of an Agrarian State* (New Haven, CT: Yale University Press, 1951), pp. 219–20.

67. *DGFP*, vol. XI (Washington, DC: Government Printing Office, 1960), doc. no. 17, p. 22.

68. Haynes, 'Germany and the Establishment of the Romanian National Legionary State, September 1940', p. 711; see also chapter 2.

69. The standard work on the Romanian oil industry until nationalization in 1948 is Maurice Pearton, *Oil and the Romanian State, 1895–1948* (Oxford: Clarendon Press, 1971); see also Philippe Marguerat, *Le IIIe Reich et le pétrole roumain, 1938–1940: contribution à l'étude de la pénétration économique allemande dans les Balkans à la veille et au début de la Seconde Guerre mondiale* (Leiden and Geneva: A. W. Sijthoff: Institut universitaire de hautes études internationales, 1977).

70. For the figures see Roberts, *Rumania*, p. 214, fn. 13. Romanian oil exports to Germany in the mid-1930s represented some 25 per cent of total exports to that country. Călin-Radu Ancuța, 'Die deutsch–rumänischen Wirtschaftsbeziehungen während der Kriegsjahre 1940–1944', *Modernisierung auf Raten in Rumänien. Anspruch, Umsetzung, Wirkung*, ed. Krista Zach and Cornelius R. Zach (Munich: IKGS Verlag, 2004), p. 335.

71. Roberts, *Rumania*, pp. 214–15.

72. Axworthy, Scafeș and Craciunoiu, *Third Axis, Fourth Ally. Romanian Armed Forces in the European War, 1941–1945*, p. 21.

73. Maurice Pearton, 'British Intelligence in Romania, 1938–1941', *Romanian and British Historians on the Contemporary History of Romania*, ed. George Cipaiănu and Virgiliu Țârău (Cluj-Napoca: Cluj-Napoca University Press, 2000), p. 190.

74. For the effect of British purchases of Romanian oil on deliveries to Germany see Axworthy, Scafeș and Craciunoiu, *Third Axis, Fourth Ally. Romanian Armed Forces in the European War, 1941–1945*, p. 18.

75. Romanian oil production and supply figures to Germany can be found in Ancuța, 'Die deutsch–rumänischen Wirtschaftsbeziehungen während der Kriegsjahre 1940–1944', pp. 364–5. This affirmation perhaps overstates the case since there were 1. increased extraction rates of oil in Austria and Hungary; 2. synthetic fuels derived by Germany from coal and oil plants; imports to Germany from Mexico and the US via Switzerland and Sweden until December1941; 4. captured French stocks of petrol which the Panzers used to get from Northern France to the Pyrenees (I am grateful to Maurice Pearton for these observations).

288 Hitler's Forgotten Ally

76. On the other hand, the costs of maintaining the German troops sent later to Romania was borne by the German Government. Andreas Hillgruber, *Hitler, König Carol und Marschall Antonescu. Die Deutsch-Rumänischen Beziehungen, 1938–1944* (Wiesbaden: Franz Steiner Verlag, 1965), p. 159.
77. Ibid., p. 161.
78. Ibid. According to Hillgruber 1,270,000 tons of petroleum products were exported by Romania to Germany in 1939, and 1,170,000 tons in 1940 (p. 161). Axworthy, Scafeş and Craciunoiu, *Third Axis, Fourth Ally. Romanian Armed Forces in the European War, 1941–1945*, p. 190 give higher figures: 1,556,000 tons for 1939, 1,304,800 for 1940, and 3,173,700 for 1941.
79. Ancuţa gives a figure of 2.4 million tons for Romanian oil exports to Germany in 1943. 'Die deutsch–rumänischen Wirtschaftsbeziehungen während der Kriegsjahre 1940–1944', p. 355.
80. Ibid., p. 20. Ion Antonescu submitted a memorandum to Hitler dated 9/10 January 1943 in which he pointed out that Romania had exported to the Axis 8,285,185 tons of oil between 1940 and 1942 of which Germany had received 6,315,252 tons. ANIC, Ministry of Internal Affairs, trial of Ion Antonescu, file 40010, vol. 8, p. 141.
81. *Anuarul Statistic al României, 1939 şi 1940* (Bucureşti: Institutul de statistică, 1940), p. 41.
82. Armin Heinen, *Legiunea 'Arhanghelul Mihail'. O contribuţie la problema fascismului internaţional* [The Legion of the Archangel Michael. A Contribution to the Problem of International Fascism] (Bucureşti: Humanitas, 1999), p. 32, n. 5.
83. Ibid., p. 39.
84. *Anuarul Statistic al României, 1939 şi 1940*, p. 362.
85. Heinen, *Legiunea 'Arhanghelul Mihail'*, p. 40, n. 48.
86. *Anuarul Statistic al României, 1939 şi 1940*, p. 92.
87. H. Seton-Watson, *Eastern Europe between the Wars 1918–1941*, 3rd edn (New York, London: Harper & Row, 1962), pp. 203–4.
88. For an outstanding study of the Iron Guard, see Constantin Iordachi, *Charisma, Politics and Violence: The Legion of the 'Archangel Michael' in Inter-war Romania* (Trondheim Studies on East European Cultures and Societies, no. 15. Trondheim, Norway, 2004).
89. The Iron Guard (*Garda de Fier*) was the military wing of the League of the Archangel Michael (*Legiunea Arhanghelului Mihail*), a messianic ultra-nationalist movement founded in 1927 by Codreanu. Some anglophone scholars use 'the Legion', 'Legionary Movement' and 'legionary' when referring to the movement and its members, others prefer the looser terms 'Iron Guard' and 'Guardists'. I am among the latter.
90. Nicholas Nagy-Talavera, *The Green Shirts and Others. A History of Fascism in Hungary and Rumania* (Stanford, CA: Hoover Institution Press, 1970), p. 247.
91. *Liga Apărării Naţional-Creştine*.
92. I am grateful to Maurice Pearton for this assessment.
93. Eugen Weber, 'Romania', *The European Right. A Historical Profile*, ed. H. Rogger and E. Weber (London: Weidenfeld and Nicolson, 1965), p. 541.
94. The two basic studies on the Iron Guard are Francisco Veiga, *La Mistica del Ultranacionalismo. Historia de la Guardia de Hierro* (Barcelona: Universitat Autonoma de Barcelona, Bellaterra, 1989), translated into Romanian as *Istoria Gărzii de Fier, 1919–1941. Mistica Ultranaţionalismului* [The History of the Iron Guard, 1919–1941. The Mystique of Ultranationalism] (Bucharest: Humanitas,

1993); and Armin Heinen, *Die Legion 'Erzengel Michael' in Rumänien Soziale Bewegung und Politische Organisation* (Munich: R. Oldenbourg Verlag, 1986).

95. *Totul Pentru Țară* is often translated by anglophone scholars as 'All for the Fatherland', but strictly speaking, this is inaccurate; *patrie* is the preferred term for 'fatherland' in Romanian and is often used with this meaning in political parlance.

96. Weber, 'Romania', p. 549.

97. *Pentru legionari* [For the Legionaries] (Sibiu: Totul pentru Țară, 1936), p. 413.

98. *Universul*, 11 February, p. 10 and 15 February 1937, p. 9.

99. *Din Luptele Tineretului Român, 1919–1939* [From amongst the Struggle of Romanian Youth, 1919–1939] (no place of publication, Editura Fundației Bunavestire, 1993), p. 120.

100. The Pact was invoked by the Communist prosecutors during Maniu's trial in autumn 1947 as evidence of his complicity with the Extreme Right.

101. I am indebted here to Keith Hitchins, *Rumania 1866–1947* (Oxford: Oxford University Press, 1994), p. 419.

102. *Rumania. Political Problems of an Agrarian State* (New Haven, CT: Yale University Press, 1951), p. 191.

103. Ibid.

104. *Universul*, 1 January 1938.

105. Carol Iancu, *Evreii din România de la emancipare la marginalizare, 1919–1938* [The Jews in Romania from Emancipation to Marginalization, 1919–1938] (Bucharest: Editura Hasefer, 2000), p. 257.

106. These anti-Semitic measures are discussed by Paul Shapiro, 'Prelude to Dictatorship in Romania: the National Christian Party in Power, December 1937–February 1938', *Canadian-American Slavic Studies*, vol. 8, no. 1 (1974), pp. 45–88. The situation under Goga was described in a report of January 1938 from the Board of Directors of British Jewry and the Anglo-Jewish Association to the British Foreign Secretary: 'You will be aware that year by year the position of the Jews of Roumania has worsened from every aspect – political, economic, moral. Conspicuous and distressing examples of this trend have been the Law for the Protection of National Labour of July 1934; the decrees of September and October 1937 issued by the former Ministry of Industry and Commerce, Monsieur Pop, to all individual and community establishments, strongly recommending that 50 per cent of the administrative personnel and 75 per cent of unskilled labourers employed in all undertakings should be of Romanian ethnic origin; and the decree issued by the Ministry of Justice, dated October 3rd 1936, to all public prosecutors, in accordance with which the citizenship of Jews and all other minorities in certain provinces will be reviewed'. Watts, *Romanian Cassandra*, p. 160.

107. Dov B. Lungu, 'The French and British Attitudes towards the Goga-Cuza Government in Romania: December 1937–February 1938', *Canadian Slavonic Papers*, vol. 30, no. 3 [1989], p. 335.

108. Carol Iancu, *Evreii din România de la emancipare la marginalizare, 1919–1938* (Bucharest: Editura Hasefer, 2000), p. 263.

109. 'It cannot be denied that there is a strong anti-Semitic feeling in the country. That is an old question in our history. The measures to be taken to deal with it are on the principle of revision of Rumanian citizenship for those Jews who entered the country after the war. What happened was something in the nature

of an invasion of Galician and Russian Jews who came in illegally. Their number has been exaggerated; some say as many as 800,000, but the maximum was about 250,000 who invaded villages and are not a good element.... Those Jews who have lived in Rumania before the war will remain untouched. But those who came after the war are without legal rights, except as refugees. About them we shall consider what we must do.' Watts, *Romanian Cassandra*, p. 161.
110. Bela Vago, *The Shadow of the Swastika. The Rise of Fascism and Antisemitism in the Danube Basin, 1936–1939* (London: Saxon House, 1975), p. 267.
111. Watts, *Romanian Cassandra*, p. 162.
112. Sima was born on 6 July 1906 in Bucharest. As a secondary school teacher in Lugoj and Caransebeş, he joined the Iron Guard and became its local leader in 1933.
113. Watts, *Romanian Cassandra*, p. 176.
114. Hitchins, *Rumania: 1846–1947*, p. 422.
115. Sima returned secretly to Romania on 2 September 1939 – according to police reports, to plot a *coup* against Carol – but returned to Berlin at the end of the month. ANIC, Ministerul Afacerilor Interne (Ministry of Internal Affairs), trial of Ion Antonescu, file 40010, vol. 22, p. 2.
116. Watts, *Romanian Cassandra*, p. 177.
117. Public Record Office, FO 371/24988, Document 59107. 'Memorandum: Mission to Roumania in May 1940'. Hall was the author of a sensitive travelogue of Romania entitled *Romanian Furrow* (London: Harrap, 1939).
118. Hitchins, *Rumania: 1846–1947*, pp. 424–5.

Chapter 2

1. For these and biographical details that follow I am indebted to Valeriu Florin Dobrinescu and Gheorghe Nicolescu, *Plata şi răsplata istoriei. Ion Antonescu, militar şi diplomat (1914–1940)* [The Payment and Reward of History. Ion Antonescu, soldier and diplomat (1914–1940)] (Iaşi: Institutul European, 1994).
2. Expressed in a memorandum to the Minister of War on 1 December 1917; see ibid., p. 22.
3. Ibid., p. 23.
4. Valeriu Florin Dobrinescu, 'Documente şi mărturii: Ion Antonescu văzut de contemporani' [Documents and Other Evidence], *Dosarele istoriei*, vol. 7, no. 6 (2002), p. 16.
5. Ibid., p. 18.
6. Ibid., p. 36.
7. Dobrinescu and Nicolescu, *Plata şi răsplata istoriei. Ion Antonescu, militar şi diplomat*, pp. 151–70.
8. Ion Antonescu was Maria's third husband. Her first marriage was to a policeman called Cimbru by whom she had a son, and her second to a French Jew, from whom she was divorced in France. Her son by her first marriage, Gheorghe, died on 10 September 1944. ANIC, Ministerul Afacerilor Interne [Ministry of Internal Affairs], Trial of Ion Antonescu, file 40010, vol. 34, p. 29; vol. 37, p. 117.
9. Larry Watts, *Romanian Cassandra. Ion Antonescu and the Struggle for Reform, 1916–1941* (Boulder, CO: East European Monographs, 1993), pp. 87–94.

10. Quoted ibid., p. 144.
11. Ibid., p. 145.
12. *Pe marginea prăpastiei* [On the Edge of the Abyss], vol. 1 (Bucharest: Preşedinţia Consiliului de Miniştri, 1942), p. 31. The two volumes provide a documentary account of Iron Guard excesses and atrocities during the period of Antonescu's joint rule with the Guard between September 1940 and January 1941. They were first published after the suppression of the Iron Guard rebellion on Antonescu's orders, withdrawn after German complaints, and reissued in 1942 when Antonescu discovered fresh evidence of Iron Guard conspiracies against him.
13. The nickname for Codreanu. Dobrinescu and Nicolescu, *Plata şi răsplata istoriei. Ion Antonescu, militar şi diplomat*, p. 59.
14. Watts, *Romanian Cassandra*, p. 163.
15. Ibid.
16. Ibid., p. 164.
17. Ibid., p. 165.
18. Argetoianu noted in his diary for 25 March 1937 that the Ministry had given Malaxa 'an advance of 150 million lei for the construction of an hermetic pipe factory which both the railway and municipal plants would need in the future, the first for the construction of new pipe-line from Prahova [the oil region] to Constanţa [Romania's principal port], and the second for the delivery of natural gas from the oil region to Bucharest. But the essence of this business and its charm lay not in the fact that it allowed Malaxa to build himself a factory with public money. Its true essence and charm lay in the fact that at the same time, it raised the customs tax on piping imported from abroad and therefore gave Malaxa a veritable monopoly over the supply of the entire petroleum industry: a question of hundreds of millions'. Quoted ibid., p. 165.
19. One historian considers that the *lancieri* 'were responsible before 1940 for more anti-Semitic brutality and hooliganism than the Iron Guard, especially in the years 1935–1937'. N. Nagy-Talavera, *The Green Shirts and Others. A History of Fascism in Hungary and Romania* (Stanford, CA: Hoover Institution Press, 1970), p. 289.
20. The constitution allowed the proclamation of martial law in 'case of danger'. This article was invoked in 1924 in the wake of the Communist-driven revolt in the town of Tatar Bunar in Bessarabia and the proclamation of the Moldavian Soviet Socialist Republic on the left bank of the Dniester, when the Liberal government of the day passed laws on public order contraventions known collectively as the Mârzescu Law. In 1926, these were widened to legalize official censorship – in contravention of the 1923 constitution – and in the following year extended further to include 'infractions against state security'. In May 1933, the Mârzescu Law was broadened yet again to allow preventative arrest without specific charges, postal surveillance and unrestricted search and seizure. The Tătărescu government (1934–37) frequently applied official censorship. Watts, *Romanian Cassandra*, p. 166.
21. Carol had never forgiven Maniu for his opposition to Elena Lupescu's return to Romania in 1930.
22. A British report stated that one Guardist was killed in the village of Maia and a second, according to Codreanu, in Afumaţi; see Watts, *Romanian Cassandra*, p. 170.
23. Ibid., p. 170.

24. *DGFP*, Series D (1937–1945), 14 vols (Washington, DC, London and Arlington VA, 1949–76), vol. V, Washington, DC: Government Printing Office, 1953, doc. 169, pp. 235–6.
25. Watts, *Romanian Cassandra*, p. 188.
26. Ibid., p. 189.
27. Ibid., p. 172.
28. Ibid., p. 173.
29. Ioan Scurtu, *Viaţa politică din România, 1918–1940* [Political Life in Romania, 1918–1940] (Bucharest: Editura Litera, 1982), p. 216.
30. His letter of resignation is reproduced in Ion Ardeleanu and Vasile Arimia, *Ion Antonescu. Citiţi, judecaţi, cutremuraţi-vă* [Ion Antonescu. Read, Judge, be Thunderstruck] (Bucharest: Tinerama, 1991), pp. 39–50. Călinescu claimed to have recommended Antonescu's appointment as military attaché in Paris to Carol, but the king rejected the idea. Armand Călinescu, *Insemnări politice, 1916–1939* [Political Notes, 1916–1939] (Bucharest: Humanitas, 1990), p. 381.
31. Telegram sent by Fabricius to the German Foreign Ministry, 17 May 1938. *DGFP*, Series D, vol. V, doc. 203, p. 280.
32. *Căpitanul*, 'the Captain', is the literary form in Romanian; it was the nickname for Codreanu's supporters used.
33. R. G. Waldeck, *Athene Palace Bucharest* (London: Constable, 1943), p. 86. Note the use of the third person by Antonescu when referring to himself (see chapter 3). According to Hoare, Maniu testified 'that although there was a great difference between his own political conceptions and those of Codreanu he was of the opinion that a nation could not exist without a solid basis of Christian morality, and this he had found in Codreanu . . . that in all the conversations which he had had with the accused the latter had never suggested that he was in a hurry to assume office; that he would never have negotiated with a man who was planning revolt and that in his opinion the Iron Guard was neither secret nor clandestine' (quoted Watts, *Romanian Cassandra*, p. 175).
34. ANIC, Ministerul Afacerilor Interne [Ministry of Internal Affairs], Trial of Ion Antonescu, file 40010, vol. 3, p. 96.
35. Watts, *Romanian Cassandra*, p. 176.
36. Mihai Antonescu was not related to Ion Antonescu, a fact revealed by the Marshal to Hitler himself at their meeting at Castle Klessheim near Salzburg on 13 April 1943: 'although the similarity in their names is striking, they are nonetheless not related'. 'Note on the meeting between the Führer and Marshal Antonescu at Castle Klessheim', *Antonescu Hitler. Corespondentă şi întîlniri inedite (1940–1944)*, vol. II, ed. Vasile Arimia, Ion Ardeleanu and Ştefan Lache (Bucharest: Cozia, 1991), p. 78.
37. Ibid., p. 190.
38. 'From the political and military points of view, Romania is supported by her close allies and by the two great powers of the West: England and France. The recent events have greatly undermined the value of these alliances. Germany has manifested its firm desire to realize quickly its entire plan of expansion in Central Europe, even at the risk of an armed conflict. France and England could not oppose it, while the Little Entente took a passive attitude. The Little Entente, although formally in existence, has today in fact dissolved through the amputation of Czechoslovakia.' Quoted Watts, *Romanian Cassandra*, p. 190.
39. *DGFP*, Series D, vol. V, doc. 239, p. 324.

40. Ibid., doc. 264, pp. 352–3.
41. The National Archives, formerly Public Record Office (hereafter PRO), FO 371/ 24988, Document 59107. 'Memorandum: Mission to Roumania in May 1940'.
42. Watts, *Romanian Cassandra*, p. 217.
43. The National Archives (PRO), FO 371/24992. Document R6698, telegram 649, 4 July 1940.
44. Neubacher had been posted to Bucharest in January 1940.
45. Watts, *Romanian Cassandra*, pp. 220–1.
46. Ibid., p. 221. Ion Antonescu's sympathy for the Guard in spring 1940 is acknowledged by Mihai Antonescu in a declaration made in preparation for his trial in May 1946: 'In 1940 [Ion] Antonescu was given command of the army in Chişinău but was replaced by King Carol because he had taken the side of the Guardists imprisoned in Chişinău'. ANIC, Ministerul Afacerilor Interne [Ministry of Internal Affairs], file 40010. *Trial of Ion Antonescu*, vol. 3, p. 21.
47. A charge that fitted both Carol and Moruzov since they were in constant touch with Horia Sima, the Guard leader, after his return from Germany in May. Sima served briefly as Minister of Cults and the Arts in the Gigurtu government from 4 to 10 July.
48. See the official biography of Antonescu in Gheorghe Buzatu, *Mareşalul Antonescu în faţa istoriei* [Marshal Antonescu in the Face of History], vol. 1 (Iaşi, 1990), p. 52.
49. See the minutes of the cabinet meeting of 7 February 1941 where Antonescu admitted: 'From the time of my imprisonment I discussed my entire programme of government with the Germans and all the basic principles of the future Romanian state, especially those in the economic sector . . . . The discussions were carried on through the intermediary of Mihai Antonescu, who came to Bistriţa every Sunday. *Stenogramele Şedinţelor Consiliului de Miniştri. Guvernarea Ion Antonescu* [Minutes of the Meetings of the Council of Ministers. The Ion Antonescu Government]. Vol. II, *January March 1941*, ed. Marcel-Dumitru Ciucă, Aurelian Teodorescu and Bogdan Florin Popovici (Bucharest: Arhivele Naţionale ale României, 1998), p. 182.
50. 'Cable from the Polish Embassy in Bucharest to the Ministry of Foreign Affairs of the Polish Government-in-Exile in London, 4 September 1940', in Vladimir Socor and Yeshayahu Jelinek, 'Polish Diplomatic Reports on the Political Crisis in Romania, September 1940', *Southeastern Europe/L'Europe du Sud-Est*, vol. 6, part 1 (1979), p. 100.
51. *DGFP*, vol. XI (Washington, DC: Government Printing Office, 1960), doc. 9, p. 11.
52. Rebecca Haynes, 'Germany and the Establishment of the Romanian National Legionary State, September 1940', *The Slavonic and East European Review*, vol. 77 (October 1999), p. 711.
53. Ibid., p. 712.
54. *DGFP*, vol. XI (Washington, DC: Government Printing Office, 1960), doc. 17, p. 22.
55. As shown by Haynes, 'Germany and the Establishment of the Romanian National Legionary State, September 1940', pp. 712–13.
56. On 5 September, Fabricius told Pop that chaos could be avoided only if Antonescu chose 'one course: dictatorship'. *DGFP*, vol. XI, doc. 19, p. 24.
57. Ibid., p. 25.
58. Carol's decree appointed Antonescu president of the Council of Ministers 'with complete power to lead the Romanian state'. *Monitorul Oficial* (5 September 1940), part 1, no. 205, p. 5058.

59. Mircea Agapie and Jipa Rotaru, *Ion Antonescu. Cariera militară. Scrisori inedite* (Bucharest: Editura Academiei de Înalte Studii Militare, 1993), p. 163.
60. 'Cable from the Polish Embassy in Bucharest to the Ministry of Foreign Affairs of the Polish Government-in-Exile in London, 14 September 1940', in Socor and Jelinek, 'Polish Diplomatic Reports on the Political Crisis in Romania, September 1940', p. 103.
61. Haynes, 'Germany and the Establishment of the Romanian National Legionary State, September 1940', p. 718.
62. Ibid., p. 714.
63. Watts, *Romanian Cassandra*, p. 247. Michael, after taking the oath as sovereign before Antonescu and Patriarch Nicodim of the Orthodox Church, reappointed Antonescu on the same terms as his father had done the previous day. *Monitorul Oficial* (6 September 1940), part 1, no. 206, p. 5275.
64. Nagy-Talavera, *The Green Shirts and Others*, p. 308.
65. A. Simion, *Regimul Politic din România în perioada sept. 1940 ian. 1941* [The Political Regime in Romania in the Period September 1940–January 1941] (Cluj-Napoca: Dacia, 1976), pp. 9–34.
66. Haynes, 'Germany and the Establishment of the Romanian National Legionary State, September 1940', p. 704.
67. Ibid., p. 703.
68. Ibid., p. 714.
69. Ibid., p. 703.
70. Armin Heinen, *Die Legion 'Erzengel Michael' in Rumänien: Soziale Bewegung und politische Organisation* (Munich, 1986), pp. 322–45.
71. Haynes, 'Germany and the Establishment of the Romanian National Legionary State, September 1940', p. 705.
72. Ibid., p. 707.
73. Ibid., p. 708. Moruzov had been visited by Baron Manfred von Killinger, Hitler's special envoy to Bucharest, only two days earlier; for details see chapter 1.
74. Ibid., p. 709.
75. *Procesul Mareşalului Antonescu. Documente* [The Trial of Marshal Antonescu. Documents], vol. II, ed. Marcel-Dumitru Ciuca (Bucharest: Editura Saeculum, 1995), p. 162.
76. Ibid., p. 164.
77. Ibid. See also Haynes, who reports Horia Sima's contention that Antonescu did not demand Carol's abdication until he discovered Carol's plot to murder him, because he feared that if Carol fell from power, the Germans would occupy Bucharest by parachute. 'Germany and the Establishment of the Romanian National Legionary State, September 1940', p. 717.
78. Dated 18 December 1940, 14 February and 21 February 1941.
79. Dinu C. Giurescu, *România în cel de-al doilea război mondial* [Romania in the Second World War] (Bucharest: All, 1999), p. 80.

Chapter 3

1. Letter to Constantin Brătianu in *Mareşalul Ion Antonescu. Epistolarul Infernului* [Marshal Ion Antonescu: Correspondence from Hell], ed. Mihai Pelin (Bucharest: Editura Viitorul Românesc, 1993), pp. 100, 102. The letter was probably written after Yugoslavia was forced to join the Tripartite Pact on 25 March 1941.

2. I am grateful to Maurice Pearton for the phrasing of this paragraph.

3. Polish diplomatic reports claim that Antonescu was not particularly popular in the army; see 'Cable from the Polish Embassy in Bucharest to the Ministry of Foreign Affairs of the Polish Government-in-Exile in London, 23 September 1940', in Vladimir Socor and Yeshayahu Jelinek, 'Polish Diplomatic Reports on the Political Crisis in Romania, September 1940', *Southeastern Europe/L'Europe du Sud-Est*, vol. 6, part 1 (1979), pp. 108–10.

4. Rebecca Haynes, 'Germany and the Establishment of the Romanian National Legionary State, September 1940', *The Slavonic and East European Review*, vol. 77 (October 1999), p. 719.

5. 'Cable from the Polish Embassy in Bucharest to the Ministry of Foreign Affairs of the Polish Government-in-Exile in London, 14 September 1940', and 'Cable from the Polish Embassy in Bucharest to the Ministry of Foreign Affairs of the Polish Government-in-Exile in London, 23 September 1940', in Socor and Jelinek, 'Polish Diplomatic Reports on the Political Crisis in Romania, September 1940'.

6. Haynes, 'Germany and the Establishment of the Romanian National Legionary State, September 1940', p. 720.

7. Keith Hitchins makes the point that this new decree differed in one important respect from that signed by Carol on the previous day: the king *appointed* the leader; he did not, as Carol had done, grant him unlimited powers. Four years later, Michael was to appeal to this provision to justify his arrest of Antonescu on 23 August 1944. *Rumania 1866–1947* (Oxford: Oxford University Press, 1994), p. 455. King Michael did retain powers emanating from the 1923 constitution. When the National Legionary State was declared on 14 September 1940, it was done so by royal decree, as was Antonescu's promotion to Army Corps General.

8. Ibid., p. 476.

9. *Timpul*, 8 September 1940.

10. *Universul*, 8 September 1940.

11. *Timpul*, 16 September 1940.

12. See King Michael's views about Antonescu in annex 1.

13. 'Cable from the Polish Embassy in Bucharest to the Ministry of Foreign Affairs of the Polish Government-in-Exile in London, 14 September 1940', in Socor and Yeshayahu Jelinek, 'Polish Diplomatic Reports on the Political Crisis in Romania, September 1940', p. 104. The remarks on the Transylvanian leaders do not chime with an earlier appreciation of 4 September from Racynski that Maniu – a Transylvanian by birth – 'refrained from taking the lead in a resistance action, sensing lack of support for it in the army and the absence of a determined will to resist among the frightened population. Ibid., p. 100.

14. Mircea Agapie and Jipa Rotaru, *Ion Antonescu. Cariera militară. Scrisori inedite* [Ion Antonescu. Military Career. Unpublished Letters] (Bucharest: Editura Academiei de înalte Studii Militare, 1993), p. 161.

15. Antonescu's pragmatism was noted by Franklin Mott Gunther, the American Minister in Bucharest. See Introduction, n. 8, above.

16. The pro-Nazi Bucharest daily.

17. *Stenogramele Ședințelor Consiliului de Miniștri. Guvernarea Ion Antonescu.* Vol. I, *September–October 1940*, ed. Marcel-Dumitru Ciucă, Aurelian Teodorescu and Bogdan Florin Popovici (Bucharest: Arhivele Naționale ale României, 1997), p. 71.

18. *Procesul Marei Trădări Naționale* [The Trial of the Great National Betrayal] (Bucharest, 1946), p. 227. See also Antonescu's letter to the National Liberal Party leader Constantin (Dinu) Brătianu of 29 October 1942: 'In September 1940, whilst warning me that "I was doing wrong by bring the Guardists to power", you advised me, in the manner of "helping me out", to form a government with persons proposed by you and Mr Maniu. For reasons either good or bad, and on which it is not appropriate for me to dwell, I turned down your advice and I offered you and Mr Maniu the leadership of the state. Both of you refused on the pretext that, in view of the position of the army, only I could, at that particular moment, take charge of the situation. I assured you of the army's support for a sound government but still you refused . . . I had no pretension to govern this country. I offered the country to you the moment that I delivered it from the storm which was carrying it to the grave. My role should have ceased on 7 September 1940. I stayed on, however, since you all divested yourself of any responsibility and hid in the face of danger and difficulty.' *Mareşalul Ion Antonescu*, pp. 333, 348.

19. Watts, *Romanian Cassandra*, p. 249.

20. This is evident from his reply to a letter from Dinu Brătianu criticizing his conduct of the war: 'Well, Mr Brătianu, when someone has been the head of a party which from top to bottom, from the village council to the minister's office, is responsible for administrative chaos, moral turpitude, the deliverance of the country into the hands of Jews and freemasons, venality, compromising the country's future and for bringing catastrophe to the country's frontiers, he no longer has the right to speak in the name of the Romanian community.' *Mareşalul Ion Antonescu*, p. 353.

21. *Procesul Maresalului Antonescu. Documente*, vol. II, ed. Marcel-Dumitru Ciuca (Bucharest: Editura Saeculum, 1995), p. 162, and vol. I, p. 188.

22. 'Cable from the Polish Embassy in Bucharest to the Ministry of Foreign Affairs of the Polish Government-in-Exile in London, 16 September 1940', in Socor and Jelinek, 'Polish Diplomatic Reports on the Political Crisis in Romania, September 1940', p. 106.

23. Rebecca Haynes makes these points in *Romanian Policy Towards Germany, 1936–40* (London: Macmillan, 2000), p. 159.

24. PRO, FO 371/37379, document R5111, 10 June 1943. *Foreign Office Research Department Handbook*, 'Constitution and Politics of Romania', 20 April 1943, Foreign and Press Service, Balliol College, Oxford, Royal Institute of International Affairs, directed by Arnold Toynbee, pp. 3–4, quoted Watts, *Romanian Cassandra*, pp. 249–50.

25. Cable from the Polish Embassy in Bucharest to the Ministry of Foreign Affairs of the Polish Government-in-Exile in London, 15 September 1940', in Socor and Jelinek, 'Polish Diplomatic Reports on the Political Crisis in Romania, September 1940', p. 105.

26. Ibid.

27. Agapie and Rotaru, *Ion Antonescu. Cariera militară. Scrisori inedite*, p. 160.

28. *DGFP*, vol. XI, doc. 19, p. 24, 'Telegram of 5 September 1940, Minister in Romania to Foreign Ministry'.

29. See photographs of Antonescu in *Pe Marginea Prăpastiei, 21–23 ianuarie 1941* (Bucharest: Preşedinţia Consiliului de Miniştri, 1941), pp. 195–207.

30. Haynes, 'Germany and the Establishment of the Romanian National Legionary State, September 1940', p. 721.

31. '2.Mişcarea legionară este singura mişcare recunoscută în noul stat, având ca ţel ridicarea morală şi materială a poporului român şi dezvoltarea puterilor lui creatoare. 3.Domnul General Ion Antonescu este conducătorul statului legionar şi şeful regimului legionar. Domnul Horia Sima este Conducătorul Mişcării Legionare'. *Monitorul Oficial*, part 1), no. 214 (14 September 1940), p. 5414.

32. *DGFP*, vol. XI (1 September 1940–31 January 1941), doc. 381, pp. 662–70.

33. 'Cable from the Polish Embassy in Bucharest to the Ministry of Foreign Affairs of the Polish Government-in-Exile in London, 23 September 1940', in Socor and Jelinek, 'Polish Diplomatic Reports on the Political Crisis in Romania, September 1940', p. 108.

34. Mouthpiece of the anti-Semitic National Christian Party of A. C. Cuza; it was edited and published by Ilie Rădulescu.

35. *Evreii din România între anii 1940–1944*. Vol. 1, *Legislaţia anti-evreieiască* [Anti-Semitic Legislation], ed. Lya Benjamin (Bucharest: Hasefer, 1993), pp. 58–9. Some of the religious associations obtained permission to operate as non-profit private bodies and continued to do so until the Minister of Cults and the Minister of Justice persuaded Ion Antonescu to outlaw them by decree on 28 June 1943. In the ministers' view 'the religious associations' undermined the state's authority, endangered public order and threatened the unity of the state by 'diffusing religious doctrines of foreign origin'. Under the provisions of the decree, the assets of these associations were nationalized without compensation.

36. *Foreign Relations of the United States, 1940*. Vol. II, *General and Europe*, pp. 772–3, 1 October 1940, Gunther to the Secretary of State. I am grateful to Larry Watts for this reference.

37. Alex Mihai Stoenescu, *Armata, Mareşalul şi Evreii* (Bucharest: RAO, 1998), p. 108. The message was signed by Wilhelm Filderman, the Chief Rabbi Dr Alexandru Şafran and the secretary of the Jewish Federation, Dr Ion Brucăr.

38. Ibid., pp. 108–9. The signatories were Sigmund Birman and Horia Carp.

39. ANIC, Ministerul Afacerilor Interne [Ministry of Internal Affairs], trial of Ion Antonescu, file 40010, vol. 8, pp. 72–3.

40. Maurice Pearton, *Oil and the Romanian State* (Oxford: Oxford University Press, 1971), p. 233.

41. Paul D. Quinlan, *Clash over Romania. British and American Policies towards Romania: 1938–1947* (Los Angeles: American Romanian Academy, 1977), p. 66. One of the managers, Alexander Millar, wrote up his experience; see PRO (The National Archives), FO 371/29992. I thank Maurice Pearton for this reference.

42. Haynes, 'Germany and the Establishment of the Romanian National Legionary State, September 1940', p. 723.

43. Ibid.

44. *DGFP*, vol. XI, doc. 360, p. 628, 19 November 1940, Bucharest, from the Special Representative for Economic Questions, Neubacher.

45. Haynes, 'Germany and the Establishment of the Romanian National Legionary State, September 1940', p. 723.

46. Nicholas Nagy-Talavera, *The Green Shirts and Others. A History of Fascism in Hungary and Romania* (Stanford, CA: Hoover Institution Press, 1970), p. 318.

47. The victims included Mihail Moruzov, General Gheorghe Argeşanu, Prime Minister between 21 and 28 September 1939, General Gabriel Marinescu,

Minister of the Interior under Argeşanu, Victor Iamandi, a former Minister of Justice, and General Ion Bengliu, former head of the gendarmerie.
48. R. G. Waldeck, *Athene Palace*, with an introduction by Ernest H. Latham, Jr. (Iaşi, Oxford and Portland: The Center for Romanian Studies, 1998), p. 227.
49. Andreas Hillgruber, *Hitler, König Carol und Marschall Antonescu. Die Deutsch–Rumänischen Beziehungen, 1938–1944* (Wiesbaden: Franz Steiner Verlag, 1965), p. 99. The convention governing the mission's presence stipulated a figure of 19,000 German troops. The head of the mission was General Erik Hansen, who also headed the Army mission in 1940–41. On 22 June 1941, his chief of staff, General Arthur Hauffe, took over as head of the Army mission when the Romanian army joined the attack on the Soviet Union, but the post reverted to Hansen after the defeat at Stalingrad. General Wilhelm Speidel was the initial commander of the Luftwaffe mission, but in May 1942, Lt.-Gen. Alfred Gerstenberg, formerly air attaché at the German legation, took over the post for the rest of the war. Admiral Werner Tillesen was head of the Naval mission from 1940 to 1944. Mark Axworthy, Cornel Scafeş and Cristian Craciunoiu, *Third Axis, Fourth Ally. Romanian Armed Forces in the European War, 1941–1945* (London: Arms and Armour, 1995), p. 26.
50. The RAF had no aircraft which could get to Ploieşti fully loaded and back at this time.
51. Ibid., pp. 112–13.
52. During his talks with Hitler on 22 November Antonescu 'declared that he would join the Pact the following day; however, he would not be satisfied with the simple act of joining, but he would be also ready to fight with a gun in his hand together with the Axis for the victory of civilization'. *Antonescu–Hitler. Corespondenţă şi întîlniri inedite (1940–1944)* [Antonescu-Hitler. Correspondence and Unpublished Meetings (1940–1944)], vol. 1, ed. V. Arimia, I. Ardeleanu and Şt. Lache (Bucharest: Cozia, 1991), p. 39.
53. Andreas Hillgruber, *Les Entretiens secrets de Hitler, septembre 1939–decembre 1940* (Paris: Fayard, 1969), pp. 372–3; *Antonescu–Hitler. Corespondenţă şi întîlniri inedite (1940–1944)* vol. 1, p. 53.
54. This point is made by Andreas Hillgruber, *Hitler, König Carol und Marschall Antonescu. Die Deutsch-Rumänischen Beziehungen, 1938–1944* (Wiesbaden: Franz Steiner Verlag, 1965), p. 113.
55. Henry L. Roberts, *Rumania. Political Problems of an Agrarian State* (New Haven, CT: Yale University Press, 1951), p. 233, n. 13.
56. I thank Maurice Pearton for insisting on these points.
57. Hillgruber, *Hitler, König Carol und Marschall Antonescu*, p. 116.
58. *Evreii din România între anii 1940–1944*. Vol. III, Part 1, *1940–1942: Perioada unei mari restrişti*, ed. Ion Şerbănescu (Bucharest: Hasefer, 1997), doc. 105, pp. 154–5.
59. Ibid., doc. 104, pp. 152–3.
60. Hillgruber, *Hitler, König Carol und Marschall Antonescu*, p. 117.
61. Killinger, who had served in the German navy, was an old friend of Hitler and had been appointed Minister in Slovakia in July 1940.
62. Haynes, 'Germany and the Establishment of the Romanian National Legionary State, September 1940', p. 724.
63. Hillgruber, *Hitler, König Carol und Marschall Antonescu.*, p. 308, n. 39.
64. Ibid., p. 118.

65. Sima had tried to compromise Antonescu by sending Hitler a letter in which he quoted Antonescu's farewell speech on leaving his post as military attaché in London in the 1920s, a speech in which he stated that Britain must always be victorious because 'civilization must always triumph over barbarity'. Hitler dismissed Sima's letter as 'undignified and stupid'. Ottmar Traşca and Ana-Maria Stan, *Rebeliune legionară în documente străine* (Bucharest: Albatros, 2002), p. 56, n. 135.

66. Paul Schmidt, *Statist auf diplomatischer Bühne, 1923–45: Erlebnisse des Chefdolmetschers im Auswärtigen Amt mit den Staatsmännern Europas* (Bonn: Athenäum-Verlag, 1949), pp. 511–12. One must bear in mind that Antonescu spoke through an interpreter, which drew out the length of Antonescu's tirade.

67. *DGFP*, vol. IX, doc. 652, p. 1087.

68. *DGFP*, D, vol. XI, doc. 652; see also Hillgruber, *Les Entretiens Secrets de Hitler*, pp. 432–41.

69. The phrase 'a free hand to deal with the Iron Guard' was used by the British Minister Sir Reginald Hoare with reference to the meeting in a memorandum to the Foreign Office of 15 January 1941; see PRO FO 317 29990 R384/79/37, quoted R. Haynes, 'Germany and the National Legionary State, 1940–1941', MA dissertation SSEES, University of London, 13 September 1992, p. 30. Today's Iron Guard sympathizers are strongly critical of Hitler's position at the 14 January meeting. Typical is the following: '[This meeting] will be considered one of the major political errors, both tactically and strategically, of the leader of the Reich in the struggle against the Soviet colossus and of his accomplices, "the short-sighted" Western powers. We go as far as to claim that there and then, the destiny of a Bolshevized Europe was decided for several decades ahead.' V. Blănaru-Flamură, *Generalul Antonescu în cămaşa verde legionară* [General Antonescu in the Green Shirts of the Legionaries] (Bucharest: Sepco, 1995), p. 88.

70. Various allegations were made about his murderer, Dimitrie Sarandos, a Turkish subject of Greek nationality; some claimed that he was a British Secret Service agent, others that he was in the pay of the SSI, the Romanian Secret Service, and had been ordered by Antonescu to carry out the deed to discredit the Guardist Minister of the Interior General Constantin Petrovicescu. A police report into Doering's murder established that Sarandos had entered the country from Yugoslavia at the Stamora-Moraviţa frontier crossing on 30 July 1940. Sarandos was having a late meal in the 'Bucureşti' restaurant in the centre of the capital when two German officers sat down to dine. Sarandos waited for them to finish and then followed them out, at about midnight. He pulled out a Browning pistol and shot Doering several times in the stomach. Sarandos ran off, casting the gun into the snow, but was caught by Doering's chaffeur and brought to the Hotel Ambasador. United States Holocaust Memorial Museum (henceforth USHMM), RG 25.004M, reel 57, file 9039, vol. 27, ff.7–9.

71. Aurel Simion, *Regimul Politic din România în perioada sept. 1940–ian. 1941* (Cluj-Napoca: Dacia, 1976), p. 247; see also Hillgruber, *Hitler, König Carol und Marschall Antonescu*, p. 119.

72. *Evreii din România între anii 1940–1944*. Vol. III, Part 1, doc. 113, p. 167. Born in 1915, Trifa graduated in theology at the University of Chişinău and joined the Iron Guard. In 1938, he took refuge in Germany after Carol launched his campaign against the Guard. He returned in autumn 1940 and became head of the Romanian Christian Students' Union. After the Iron Guard rebellion, he fled once more to Germany. At the end of the war he went to Italy, and in

1950 emigrated first to Canada and then settled in the United States, gaining entry on the basis of a false declaration that he had never been the member of a Fascist organization. In 1951, Trifa was elected head of the Romanian Orthodox Episcopate of America which had broken with the mother church, now under Communist control. In 1962, Moses Rozen, Chief Rabbi of Romania, denounced Trifa as a member of the Guard at a press conference in Israel, but it was only on 25 August 1980 that in face of a clamour of accusation from the American media, Congressional leaders and the Special Investigative Unit of the Department of Justice that he was 'a Romanian Nazi' and 'a war criminal', he surrendered his certificate of US naturalization. He himself thus brought to an end his struggle to retain US citizenship. He was expelled from the US in 1984 on the grounds of his false declaration on entry and was given refuge in Portugal, where he died on 24 January 1987. His body was taken back to his former bishopric and buried in Grass Lake, Michigan.

73. Simion, *Regimul Politic din România în perioada sept. 1940–ian. 1941*, p. 251.
74. Hillgruber, *Hitler, König Carol und Marschall Antonescu*, p. 120.
75. *DGFP*, vol. XI, doc. 709, pp. 1194–8.
76. Generaloberst Halder, *Kriegstagebuch*. Vol. II, *Von der Geplanten Landung in England bis zum Beginn des Ostfeldzuges (1.7.1940–21.6.1941)* (Stuttgart: Kohlhammer Verlag, 1963), p. 250.
77. Simion, *Regimul Politic din România în perioada sept. 1940–ian 1941*, p. 257.
78. Matatias Carp, *Cartea Neagră. Suferinţele Evreilor din România, 1940–1944* [The Black Book. The Sufferings of the Jews in Romania, 1940–1944], vol. 1 (Bucharest: Socec, 1946), pp. 319–23. A report of the gendarmerie in Bucharest states that 98 Jews were picked up by legionaries from the streets and their homes, and taken down the highway from Bucharest to Giurgiu, south of the capital. Thirty of them were shot at kilometre 13, and 68 at kilometre 14. An official coroner's report puts the number of Jews killed during the rebellion at 120. *Evreii din România între anii 1940–1944*. Vol. III. Part 1, doc. b114, pp. 168–71. The daily *Universul* published the following national tally of victims of the rebellion: 21 army officers and men dead, and 53 wounded; civilian casualties were put at 236 dead (of whom 118 were Jews murdered by the legionaries) and 254 wounded in Bucharest, and in the provinces 117 dead and 17 wounded (ibid., n. 1).
79. Hillgruber, *Hitler, König Carol und Marschall Antonescu*, p. 121.
80. Simion, *Regimul Politic din România în perioada sept. 1940–ian 1941*, p. 272. Sima knew that he would be held responsible for the rebellion, even though it appears that Petrovicescu had given the order for the Guardists barricaded at the *Siguranţa* headquarters to open fire.
81. The complexities of the German positions on Antonescu and the Iron Guard during the January rebellion are examined by Haynes, 'German Historians and the National Legionary State, 1940–41', pp. 676–83.
82. Socor and Jelinek, 'Polish Diplomatic Reports on the Political Crisis in Romania, September 1940', p. 96.
83. *Stenogramele Şedinţelor Consiliului de Miniştri. Guvernarea Ion Antonescu* [The Minutes of the Meetings of the Council of Ministers]. Vol. V, *Octombrie 1941–ianuarie 1942*, ed. Marcel-Dumitru Ciucă and Maria Ignat (Bucharest: Arhivele Naţionale ale României, 2001), p. 425.
84. Haynes, 'German Historians and the National Legionary State, 1940–41'.

85. Simion, *Regimul Politic din România în perioada sept. 1940–ian 1941*, p. 273. Von Killinger was formally appointed German minister to Romania by Hitler on 12 January 1941. Letter from Hitler to Antonescu, Ministerul Afacerilor Interne, file 40010, vol. 8, p. 78.

86. In the transcript of his trial in May 1946 Antonescu is recorded as stating: 'After the rebellion I wanted to form a government of national union and I appealed to the party heads. They told me that I should form a military government. . . . All of the members of the parties were for the formation of a military government.' *Procesul Marei Trădări Naționale* (Bucharest, 1946), p. 50.

87. *DGFP*, vol. IX, doc. 62, p. 1087.

Chapter 4

1. After the removal of the Guardist Foreign Minister Mihail Sturdza in mid-December 1940 (see chapter 2), Antonescu assumed this portfolio until 29 June 1941, when it was given to Mihai Antonescu who remained Foreign Minister until 23 August 1944.

2. Quoted Larry Watts, *Romanian Cassandra. Ion Antonescu and the Struggle for Reform, 1916–1941* (Boulder, CO: East European Monographs, 1993), p. 338.

3. See also the minutes of his cabinet meetings throughout the period from September 1940 to August 1944 where Antonescu would regularly refer to himself in the third person; e.g. the meeting of 21 September 1940: 'Let me point out to you that General Antonescu has yet to address the country's major problems'. *Stenogramele Ședințelor Consiliului de Miniștri. Guvernarea Ion Antonescu.* Vol. I, *Septembrie–octombrie 1940*, ed. Marcel-Dumitru Ciucă, Aurelian Teodorescu and Bogdan Florin Popovici (Bucharest: Arhivele Naționale ale României, 1997), p. 69.

4. Dorel Bancoș, *Social și național în politica guvernului Ion Antonescu* (Bucharest: Editura Eminescu, 2000), p. 16, n. 9.

5. See chapter 7, and Ernest H. Latham Jr., 'Signs of Human Feeling and Attitude: The American Legation and American Jews in Romania in 1941', paper presented at a symposium on US–Romanian Relations at the Department of Contemporary History, 'Babeș-Bolyai' University, Cluj-Napoca, June 2001.

6. *Stenogramele Ședințelor Consiliului de Miniștri*, vol. I, p. 191.

7. Ibid., p. 228.

8. A balanced appraisal of the Antonescu regime is given by Keith Hitchins in his *Rumania 1866–1947* (Oxford: Oxford University Press, 1994), pp. 469–500.

9. 'Minute of the meeting between General Ion Antonescu and the German Chancellor Adolf Hitler on 12 June 1941', in Andreas Hillgruber, *Staatsmänner und Diplomaten bei Hitler. Vertrauliche Aufzeichnungen über die Unterredunger mit Vertreten des Auslandes 1939–1941* (Munich: Deutscher Taschenbuchverlag, 1969), pp. 276–91; *Antonescu–Hitler. Corespondență și întîlniri inedite (1940–1944)*, vol. 2, ed. V. Arimia, I. Ardeleanu and Șt. Lache (Bucharest: Cozia, 1991), p. 95.

10. Florin Constantiniu, *O istorie sinceră a poporului român [A Sincere History of the Romanian People* (Bucharest: Univers Enciclopedic, 1997), p. 394.

11. Ibid. In a declaration made in preparation for his trial in May 1946 Mihai stated that he had first met Ion Antonescu in 1923 in the house of a relative, Eftimie Antonescu, a former counsellor in the Court of Appeal. Mihai met Ion again on

several occasions after that. In 1935, Ion asked him to act for him in a case of bigamy brought against Ion and his wife. ANIC, Ministerul Afacerilor Interne (Ministry of Internal Affairs). Trial of Ion Antonescu, file 40010, vol. 3, p. 21. On Hitler's request for Mihai's dismissal, see chapter 10.

12. I follow Abbot Gleason in his definition of 'totalitarianism': 'there...is a core of meaning to the term *totalitarian* that was discovered early on and has never been completely lost: the idea of a radically intrusive state run by people who do not merely control their citizens from the outside, preventing them from challenging the elite or doing things that it does not like, but also attempt to reach into the most intimate regions of their lives. These totalitarian elites ceaselessly tried to make their subjects into beings who would be constitutionally incapable of challenging the rule of the state and those who control it'. *Totalitarianism. The Inner History of the Cold War* (Oxford: Oxford University Press, 1995), p. 10.

13. 'Religious associations' – the term for neo-Protestant and other sects – were banned under a decree of 9 September 1940 and some members of neo-Protestant sects were deported in 1941 to Transnistria; see below.

14. See chapter 5.

15. Henry Roberts, *Rumania. Political Problems of an Agrarian State* (New Haven, CT: Yale University Press, 1951), p. 225.

16. See chapter 4.

17. Aurel Simion, *Preliminarii politico-diplomatice ale insurecției armate din august 1944* [Political and Diplomatic Preliminaries to the Armed Uprising of August 1944] (Cluj-Napoca: Dacia, 1979), pp. 59–61.

18. A. Simion, *Regimul Politic din România în perioada sept. 1940-ian. 1941* (Cluj-Napoca: Dacia, 1976), p. 281.

19. At a meeting of the Council for Schools and the Church of 10 December 1941 Ion Sandu, the Under-Secretary for Cultural and Religious Affairs told Antonescu that 422 priests and 19 cantors had been sent before military tribunals for their part in the rebellion and that 'verdicts had been pronounced for 262'. *Stenogramele Ședințelor Consiliului de Miniștri. Guvernarea Ion Antonescu*. Vol. V, *Octombrie 1941–ianuarie 1942*, ed. Marcel-Dumitru Ciucă and Maria Ignat (Bucharest: Arhivele Naționale ale României, 2001), p. 421.

20. Dorin Dobrincu, 'Legionarii și guvernarea Ion Antonescu (1941–1944)', *Romania: A Crossroads of Europe*, ed. Kurt W. Treptow (Iași: The Centre for Romanian Studies, 2002), p. 203, n. 18.

21. Keith Hitchins, *Rumania 1866–1947* (Oxford: Oxford University Press, 1994), p. 469.

22. *Universul*, 17 April 1941.

23. Of the 38 Guardists accused of the Jilava murders in November 1940, 20 were sentenced to death – some in their absence – and seven were executed. Simion, *Regimul Politic din România în perioada sept. 1940–ian. 1941*, p. 285. General Petrovicescu, the former Iron Guard Minister of the Interior, was sentenced to seven years' imprisonment. Antonescu approved his release from jail and confinement in obligatory residence in Sibiu on 2 March 1943. Petrovicescu was sent back to prison – to Alba Iulia – after 23 August 1944, and transferred to Sibiu jail at the beginning of December 1944. ANIC, Ministerul Afacerilor Interne [Ministry of Internal Affairs]. Trial of Ion Antonescu, file 40010, vol. 29, pp. 59, 74, 96.

24. First, on 2–5 March 1941 to confirm public approval of Antonescu's measures against the Iron Guard (2,960,298 for, 2,996 against), and then, on 9 November

1941, to acclaim the Romanian army's campaign in the East (3,446,889 for, 68 against) (ibid.).

25. In Antonescu's absence the meetings were chaired by Mihai Antonescu, appointed on 21 June 1941 Vice-President of the Council of Ministers, and on 29 June Minister of Foreign Affairs.

26. Dinu Giurescu, *România în al doilea război mondial* (Bucharest: All, 1999), p. 69. As Giurescu advises, this figure, taken from the archives of the Romanian Communist Party, refers to numbers 'arrested and sentenced for anti-Fascist activity' and needs to be treated with caution since those who compiled the figure had every interest in inflating the number. On 16 December 1942, there were 1,905 Communists interned, of whom 1,211 were in the camp at Târgu-Jiu and 694 in camps and ghettos in Transnistria. Simion, *Preliminarii politico-diplomatice ale insurecției armate din august 1944*, p. 73. Florin Constantiniu writes that '10,566 persons were interrogated, arrested and sentenced for political activity, of whom 5,463 were Communists or their associates'. *O istorie sinceră a poporului român*, p. 395.

27. Ibid.

28. Meeting of the Council of Ministers, 27 November 1941. *Stenogramele Ședințelor Consiliului de Miniştri. Guvernarea Ion Antonescu*, vol. V, p. 236.

29. Ibid., pp. 416–17.

30. Ibid., p.430.

31. One of the neo-Protestant sects proscribed by the Antonescu regime.

32. *Stenogramele Ședințelor Consiliului de Miniştri. Guvernarea Ion Antonescu*, vol. V, p. 502.

33. *Procesul Mareşalului Antonescu. Documente*, vol. 1, ed. Marcel-Dumitru Ciucă (Bucharest: Editura Saeculum, Editura Europa Nova, 1995), pp. 245–6. Antonescu's order to the head of the gendarmerie authorizing the deportation can be found in Ministerul Afacerilor Interne, trial of Ion Antonescu, file 40010, vol. 11, p. 101.

34. Dated 18 December 1940, 14 February and 21 February 1941.

35. Dinu C. Giurescu, *România în cel de-al doilea război mondial* (Bucharest: All, 1999), p. 80.

36. *Mareşalul Ion Antonescu. Epistolarul Infernului*, ed. Mihai Pelin (Bucharest: Editura Viitorul Românesc, 1993), pp. 100, 102. The letter was probably written after Yugoslavia was forced to join the Tripartite Pact on 25 March 1941.

37. Ibid., p. 139.

38. Watts, *Romanian Cassandra*, p. 337.

39. Ibid., p. 339. Watts states that Ribbentrop was present at the meeting of 12 April, but the record confirms only his presence at the meeting between the two leaders on the following day; see *Antonescu–Hitler*, p. 78.

40. Ibid., p.82.

41. See chapter 10.

42. Andreas Hillgruber, *Hitler, König Carol und Marschall Antonescu. Die Deutsch–Rumänischen Beziehungen, 1938–1944* (Wiesbaden: Franz Steiner Verlag, 1965), p. 123.

43. V. V. Tilea, *Envoy Extraordinary. Memoirs of a Romanian Diplomat*, ed. Ileana Tilea (London: Haggerston Press, 1998), p. 279. Tilea did not return to Romania, but spent the rest of his life in England.

44. Hillgruber, *Hitler, König Carol und Marschall Antonescu*, p. 124.

45. Ibid.

46. Ibid., p. 125.
47. The construction of the power station was eventually begun jointly by Yugoslavia and Romania in 1964 and completed in 1971. Although the German 41ˢᵗ army corps entered Yugoslavia from Romanian territory, and German warplanes took off from Romanian airbases to attack Belgrade, the Yugoslav government in exile did not break off diplomatic relations with Romania until the beginning of May. Consequently, Romania was the last of Hitler's European allies to recognize 'The Independent Croat State', on 6 May 1941. Hillgruber, *Hitler, König Carol und Marschall Antonescu*, p. 126.
48. *DGFP*, D, vol.12, no. 330, the Foreign Ministry to the legation in Romania, 13 April 1941. I am grateful to Rebecca Haynes for this reference.
49. Hillgruber, *Hitler, König Carol und Marschall Antonescu*, p. 127.
50. Ibid.
51. Ibid., p. 129.
52. Ibid.
53. Ibid., p. 130.
54. *Antonescu–Hitler. Corespondenţă şi întîlniri inedite (1940–1944)*, vol. 1, ed. V. Arimia, I. Ardeleanu and Şt. Lache (Bucharest: Cozia, 1991), pp. 86–7.
55. Hillgruber, *Hitler, König Carol und Marschall Antonescu*, p. 131.
56. Ibid., p. 132.
57. Constantiniu, *O istorie sinceră a poporului român*, p. 406.
58. 'Minute of the meeting between General Ion Antonescu and the German Chancellor Adolf Hitler on 12 June 1941', in Andreas Hillgruber, *Staatsmänner und Diplomaten bei Hitler. Vertrauliche Aufzeichnungen über die Unterredunger mit Vertreten des Auslandes 1939–1941* (Munich: Deutscher Taschenbuchverlag, 1969), pp. 276–91; *Antonescu–Hitler*, vol. 1, pp. 93–105.
59. Ministerul Afacerilor Interne (Ministry of Internal Affairs), file 40010, vol. 8, p. 91.
60. Under the command of Field Marshal Gerd von Rundstedt.
61. *Antonescu–Hitler*, vol. 1, p. 103.
62. General von Schobert was charged with 'the defence of the whole area of Romania, saving that he could hand over the defence of Romania as a separate duty to the head of the German Military Mission in Romania once the 11ᵗʰ Army leaves Romanian territory'. *Antonescu–Hitler*, vol. 1, p. 87.
63. Ibid., p. 108.
64. *România în anii celui de-al doilea război mondial* [Romania in the Years of the Second World War], vol. 1 (Bucharest: Editura Militara, 1989), p. 365; *Antonescu–Hitler*, vol. 1, p. 108.
65. Grigore Gafencu, *Prelude to the Russian Campaign* (London: Frederick Muller, 1945), pp. 309–10.
66. Basarab I (*c.* 1310–52) was the founder of a dynasty that gave several princes of Wallachia between the fourteenth and sixteenth centuries.
67. Mircea Agapie and Jipa Rotaru, *Ion Antonescu. Cariera militară. Scrisori inedite* (Bucharest: Editura Academiei de Înalte Studii Militare, 1993), pp. 169–70.
68. A reference to the cession of Bessarabia and northern Bukovina in the previous summer.
69. Agapie and Rotaru, *Ion Antonescu*, pp. 167–8.
70. Timpul, 24 June 1941. Mihai was appointed Vice-President of the Council of Ministers and Foreign Minister on 29 June 1941 and held both positions until 23 August 1944. The sense of crusade found particular favour with the

Orthodox and Greek Catholic press. In an article in the weekly Greek-Catholic *Unirea* which appeared at Blaj, the war against the Soviet Union was defended as 'the reacquisition of what belongs to us' and a contribution to the defeat of Bolshevism which was nothing more than 'Lucifer's Empire'. 'Razboi sfant', in *Unirea* (28 June 1941), p. 1. Antonescu was portrayed as fulfilling 'a messianic destiny' in conducting his campaign against Communism, described as 'the most abject degradation of human dignity'. 'Destin mesianic', *Unirea* (12 July 1941), p. 2. My thanks to Dr Marius Bucur of the Department of Contemporary History, 'Babes-Bolyai' University, Cluj-Napoca for these quotes.

71. Ibid. See also Agapie and Rotaru, *Ion Antonescu*, p. 164.
72. Gheorghe Barbul, *Al Treilea Om al Axei* [The Third Man of the Axis] (Iaşi: Institutul European, 1992), p. 58.
73. Ibid., p. 59.
74. Alex Mihai Stoenescu, *Armata, Mareşalul şi Evrei. Cazurile Dorohoi, Bucureşti, Iaşi, Odessa* (Bucharest: RAO, 1998), p. 226.
75. Ibid.
76. Mark Axworthy, Cornel Scafeş and Cristian Craciunoiu, *Third Axis, Fourth Ally. Romanian Armed Forces in the European War, 1941–1945* (London: Arms and Armour, 1995), p. 47.
77. In Romanian, 'împuternicit al Generalului Antonescu pentru administrarea Basarabiei'. Anatol Petrencu, *Basarabia în al doilea război mondial 1940–1944* [Anatol Petrencu, Bessarabia in the Second World War, 1940–1944] (Chişinău: Lyceum, 1997), pp. 100–1; see also Ministerul Afacerilor Interne (ANIC, Ministry of Internal Affairs), trial of Ion Antonescu, file 40010, vol. 8, p. 470. The posts of governor respectively of Bessarabia and Bukovina were established on 5 September 1941 under decree 790 by Antonescu, who appointed Voiculescu Governor of Bessarabia and General Corneliu Calotescu – formerly plenipotentiary – Governor of Bukovina. *Monitorul Oficial*, part 1, no. 211 (5 September 1941), p. 5241. Calotescu was among a group of 29 officers sentenced to death for war crimes on 22 May 1945. The sentence was commuted to life imprisonment but he was released in an amnesty in 1955. Voiculescu was tried and sentenced to life for war crimes on 28 February 1946. ANIC, Ministerul Afacerilor Interne [Ministry of Internal Affairs], trial of Ion Antonescu, file 40010, vol. 8, p. 491.
78. The citation reads in part: 'For completely exceptional merits in the command of the Romanian and German armies during the great battles between the Dniester and the Bug – for the pursuance of the holy war which has lead to the crushing of the Bolshevik troops and the liberation of the population of Transnistria from Soviet tyranny...'. Agapie and Rotaru, *Ion Antonescu*, pp. 170–1. Many Romanians regarded this as a self-promotion and consequently Antonescu received the nickname 'Auto-Marshal'.
79. No. 790. Bukovina comprised the counties of Câmpulung, Cernăuţi, Hotin, Rădăuţi, Storojineţ and Suceava, Bessarabia those of Bălţi, Cahul, Cetatea Albă, Chilia, Ismail, Lăpuşna, Orhei, Soroca and Tighina. *Monitorul Oficial*, part 1, no. 209 (4 September 1941), p. 5193.
80. Agapie and Rotaru, *Ion Antonescu*, p.172.
81. Watts, *Romanian Cassandra*, p. 330.
82. Simion, *Preliminarii politico-diplomatice ale insurecţiei române din august 1944*, p. 208.
83. The syntax is Maniu's; see *Mareşalul Ion Antonescu. Epistolarul Infernului*, ed. Mihai Pelin (Bucharest: Editura Viitorul Românesc, 1993), pp. 194–5; also Giurescu, *România în cel de-al doilea război mondial*, p. 98.

84. *Antonescu–Hitler*, vol. 1, p. 118.
85. Ibid.
86. Axworthy, *Third Axis, Fourth Ally*, p. 49.
87. Instructions of the Foreign Minister to Romanian Minister in Berlin, Raoul Bossy, 13 October 1941, cited Larry L. Watts, 'Incompatible Alliances: Small States of Central Europe during World War II', *Romania and World War II*, ed. Kurt Treptow (Iaşi: The Centre for Romanian Studies, 1996), p. 101.
88. Ibid.
89. Ibid., pp. 101–2.
90. Axworthy, *Third Axis, Fourth Ally*, p. 49.
91. *Stenogramele Şedinţelor Consiliului de Miniştri. Guvernarea Ion Antonescu.* Vol. IV, *Iulie–septembrie 1941*, ed. Marcel-Dumitru Ciucă and Maria Ignat (Bucharest: Arhivele Naţionale ale României, 2000), pp. 568–9.
92. ANIC, Ministerul Afacerilor Interne, trial of Ion Antonescu, file 40010, vol. 17, pp. 92–3.
93. Axworthy, *Third Axis, Fourth Ally*, pp. 51–6.
94. *Stenogramele Şedinţelor Consiliului de Miniştri*, vol. IV, pp. 446–7.
95. Ibid., pp. 442–3.
96. Council meeting, 5 January 1942; ibid., p. 567.
97. Paul D. Quinlan, *Clash over Romania. British and American Policies Towards Romania: 1938–1947* (Los Angeles: American Romanian Academy, 1977), p. 71.
98. *Universul*, 9 December 1941.
99. This seizure of Romanian territory had been followed by other acts of provocation which signalled a continuation of the Soviet policy of expansion and conquest. These acts were listed as follows:

   1. The occupation of four islands at the mouth of the Danube in the autumn of 1940.
   2. Daily frontier incidents involving attempts to move the frontier.
   3. Attempts by Soviet vessels to enter Romanian waters by force in January 1941.
   4. Incessant incursions, despite Romanian protests, into Romanian airspace amounting during April, May and June to up to seven daily overflights.
   5. A massive concentration of Soviet military forces on the Romanian frontier made up of 30 infantry divisions, 8 cavalry divisions, and 14 motorized brigades.
   6. The imposition of a regime of systematic repression in Bessarabia and Northern Bukovina involving the deportation of hundreds of thousands of Romanians to Siberia (*Universul*, 9 December 1941).

100. Ibid.
101. Gunther (1885–1941) was appointed Envoy Extraordinary and Minister Plenipotentiary to Bucharest on 31 July 1937. His mission ended when Romania declared war on the United States on 12 December 1941. He died just ten days later in Bucharest of leukaemia and was buried there.
102. ANIC, Ministerul Afacerilor Interne, Trial of Ion Antonescu, file 40010, vol. 8, p. 100.
103. Agapie and Rotaru, *Ion Antonescu*, p. 177.
104. Ministerul Afacerilor Interne, Trial of Ion Antonescu, file 40010, vol. 8, p. 101.
105. Vlad Georgescu, *The Romanians: A History* (Columbus, OH: Ohio State University Press, 1991), p. 217.

106. *The Foreign Office and the Kremlin. British Documents on Anglo-Soviet Relations, 1941–45*, ed. G. Ross (Cambridge: Cambridge University Press, 1984), p. 82.

107. *România în anii celui de-al doilea război mondial*, vol. 1 (Bucharest: Editura Militară, 1989), p. 556.

108. 'On 20 January 1942, when I became Chief of the General Staff, the Romanian army had 33 divisions: 15 east of the Dniester and 18 in Romania. On 25 February 1942 I became aware of the promise given to the Führer by Marshal Antonescu to also send to the front the divisions in Romania: namely a first echelon of 10 divisions in the spring of 1942, followed by a second echelon of 5–6 divisions, therefore almost all the divisions in the country. There would have remained in Romania only one division in the oil-fields, and a division each to protect the Black Sea coast and Bessarabia.... I succeeded in delaying the despatch of the first echelon by six months and then sent them under-strength, keeping much of their artillery in the country.... By claiming that that these under-strength divisions needed to be augmented by men and equipment from the division which were due to be sent in the second echelon, I was able to keep in Romania all the divisions which should have formed the second echelon. In this way, by sending the first echelon to the front at only half strength I was able to keep 120,000 soldiers in reserve, and by keeping the second echelon in Romania I was able to save 100,000. Marshal Antonescu only learned of these measures in the spring of 1943 when, in presenting to him the plan to reorganize the army after the Stalingrad disaster, I had also to present to him the means of implementing it. The men and materials remaining in the country enabled us to re-form the decimated regiments after the Stalingrad disaster.... At the beginning of August 1944, the Romanian army was incomparably stronger than on 20 January 1942. When I became Chief of the General Staff' (Memorandum of General Ilie Şteflea dated October 1944, Fond Casa Regală, vol. IV, dosar 22/1944, National Archives, Bucharest, pp. 6–8).

109. Putna monastery, the foundation and burial place of Stephen the Great, Prince of Moldavia.

110. Dealu monastery, where the remains of Michael the Brave were laid to rest.

111. Curtea de Argeş, the burial place of King Carol I and King Ferdinand. Agapie and Rotaru, *Ion Antonescu*, pp. 179–80.

112. Résumé of the talks between Hitler and Antonescu on 11 February 1942 in *Antonescu–Hitler*, vol. 1, p. 184.

113. Ibid., p. 153. Mussolini had the same view; see C. A. Macartney, *A History of Hungary*, vol. 1 (New York: Praeger, 1956), p. 444.

114. *Mareşalul Ion Antonescu. Epistolarul Infernului*, ed. Mihai Pelin (Bucharest: Editura Viitorul Românesc, 1993), pp. 260–1.

115. Ibid., pp. 347, 353.

116. 'Your proposal that I should take your place at the helm of the state when, under foreign occupation declarations are made that "Romania is Marshal Antonescu" is, of course, a joke on your part'. Ibid., p. 359.

117. Axworthy, *Third Axis, Fourth Ally*, p. 30.

118. Ibid., p. 39.

119. Ibid., p. 61.

120. Notes of Field Marshal Friedrich Paulus, in Walter Goerlitz, *Paulus and Stalingrad* (London: Methuen, 1963), pp. 156–9.

121. Antony Beevor, *Stalingrad* (London: Penguin, 1999), p. 81.

122. Quoted ibid., pp. 183–4.

123. Ibid., p. 229.
124. Ibid., pp. 249–50.
125. *România în anii celui de-al doilea război mondial*, vol. 1 (Bucharest: Editura Militară, 1989), p. 489. According to Mark Axworthy, 'the current best estimate of Romanian losses on the Stalingrad axis is about 140,000'. *Third Axis, Fourth Ally*, p. 114.
126. Ibid.
127. Simion, *Preliminarii politico-diplomatice ale insurecţiei armate din august 1944*, p. 226.
128. Agapie and Rotaru, *Ion Antonescu*, pp. 183–4.
129. Hillgruber, *Hitler, König Carol und Marschall Antonescu*, p. 152.
130. Ibid., p. 153.
131. Ibid.
132. Bernd Wenger, 'The Ideology of Self-Destruction. Hitler and the Choreography of Defeat', *Bulletin of the German Historical Institute, London*, vol. 26, no. 2 (November 2004), p. 19.
133. Constantiniu, *O istorie sinceră a poporului român*, p. 417.
134. Whether the letters, which were filed by the Romanian Intelligence Service (SSI), ever reached Antonescu's desk is unclear; see ANIC, Ministerul Afacerilor Interne. Trial of Ion Antonescu, vols 35 and 37.
135. *Evreii din România între anii 1940–1944*. Vol. II, *Problema Evreiască în stenogramele Consiliuliu de Miniştri*, ed. Lya Benjamin (Bucharest: Hasefer, 1996), doc. 160, p. 501.
136. Mareş had been Minister of Agriculture between 15 September 1940 and 23 January 1941.
137. ANIC, Ministerul Afacerilor Interne, trial of Ion Antonescu, file 40010, vol. 13, p. 59.
138. Axworthy, *Third Axis, Fourth Ally*, p. 128.
139. Gheorghe Buzatu, *Mareşalul Antonescu în faţa istoriei*, vol. 1 (Iaşi, 1990), p. 389.
140. Laurence A. Steinhardt, US ambassador to Turkey.
141. *Evreii din România între anii 1940–1944*. Vol. IV, *1943–1944: Bilanţul Tragediei – Renaşterea Speranţei*, ed. Ion Şerbănescu (Bucharest: Hasefer, 1998), doc. 346, pp. 383–4.
142. Agapie and Rotaru, *Ion Antonescu*, p. 195.

Chapter 5

1. The most exhaustive collection of sources concerning the Jews in the Middle Ages in the Principalities was published by Victor Eskenasy, *Izvoare şi mărturii referitoare la evreii din România* [Sources and Evidence Referring to the Jews in Romania] (Bucharest: Federaţia Comunităţilor Evreieşti din România, 1986).
2. Şerban Papacostea, 'Jews in the Romanian Principalities during the Middle Ages', *Shvut*, vol. 16 (1993), p. 61 (published by Tel Aviv University).
3. Eskenasy, *Izvoare şi mărturii referitoare la evreii din România*, pp. 30–1.
4. Raphael Vago, 'Romanian Jewry during the Interwar Period', *The Tragedy of Romanian Jewry*, ed. Randolph L. Braham (New York: Columbia University Press, 1994), p. 33.
5. Jews were defined under the decree as: a) those of the Mosaic faith; b) those born of parents of the Mosaic faith; c) Christians born of parents of the Mosaic

faith who had not been baptized; d) Christians born of a Christian mother and an unbaptized father of the Mosaic faith; e) children born out of wedlock of a mother of the Mosaic faith; and f) women in the former categories married to Christians, if they adopted Christianity at least a year before the founding of the Party of the Nation. Atheist, blood Jews are considered Jews in the sense of this decree. The adoption of Christianity by those of the Mosaic faith after the application of this decree does not affect their status as Jews. Those belonging to Jewish religious communities at the time of the publication of this decree are considered to be of the Mosaic faith. *Monitorul Oficial*, part 1, no. 183 (9 August 1940), pp. 4079–81.

6. Dorel Bancoş, *Social şi naţional în politica guvernului Ion Antonescu* (Bucharest: Editura Eminescu, 2000), p. 136.

7. King Carol founded the *Straja Ţării* (Guardian of the Country) in October 1937 as a united Romanian Youth Movement, based on the same ideas and system as those followed by the Boy Scout Movement. The *Straja Ţării* coordinated all the youth organizations in the country, including the Boy Scouts; but, while acknowledging its debt of gratitude to the Chief Scout, Robert Baden-Powell, it felt in 1938 unable to remain as a registered Association of the Boy Scouts' International Bureau.

8. Letter signed by Alex Miller and addressed to J. B. Aug. Kessler.

9. USHMM, RG 25.004M, reel 9, file 2704/27.

10. Bancoş, *Social şi naţional în politica guvernului Ion Antonescu*, p. 137. On 1 March 1941, the Jewish theatre 'Baraşeum' was opened in Bucharest and staged performances throughout the war, including symphony concerts and jazz recitals.

11. Maurice Pearton, *Oil and the Romanian State* (Oxford: Oxford University Press, 1971), p. 233.

12. As a result of these measures 975 Jewish pharmacists were forced to work in 182 Jewish-owned pharmacies. According to one source not a single pharmacy was rented to Jews in 1943. Bancoş, *Social şi naţional în politica guvernului Ion Antonescu*, p. 138, fn 16.

13. Ibid., p. 139.

14. Radu Lecca, *Eu i-am salvat pe evreii din România* [I Saved the Jews in Romania] (Bucharest: Editura Roza Vânturilor, 1994), p. 183.

15. Bancoş, *Social şi naţional în politica guvernului Ion Antonescu*, p. 147.

16. Maria Bucur, *Eugenics and Modernization in interwar Romania* (Pittsburgh: University of Pittsburgh Press, 2002), p. 147.

17. Bancoş, *Social şi naţional în politica guvernului Ion Antonescu*, p. 142.

18. *Evreii din România între anii 1940–1944* [The Jews in Romania between 1940 and 1944]. Vol. III, Part 1, *1940–1942: Perioada unei mari restrişti* [The Period of Great Tribulation], ed. Ion Şerbănescu (Bucharest: Hasefer, 1997), doc. 128, p. 189.

19. Ibid., doc. 136, pp. 197–9.

20. Exempt from the law were Jews naturalized before 15 August 1916, Jews wounded or decorated under Romanian arms, the descendants of Jews fallen in war, baptized Jews of 20 years standing married to Romanians, Jews married to Romanians for at least ten years and who had children baptized for at least 30 years and their offspring. Bancoş, *Social şi naţional în politica guvernului Ion Antonescu*, p. 140.

21. In a telegram to Alexandru Cretzianu, the Romanian Minister in Ankara of 14 March. Ibid., p. 144.

22. Ibid.
23. Council of Ministers' Meeting, 7 March 1941. *Stenogramele Şedinţelor Consiliului de Miniştri. Guvernarea Ion Antonescu*. Vol. II, *Ianuarie martie 1941*, ed. Marcel-Dumitru Ciucă, Aurelian Teodorescu and Bogdan Florin Popovici (Bucharest: Arhivele Naţionale ale României, 1998), pp. 548–9.
24. Bancoş, *Social şi naţional în politica guvernului Ion Antonescu*, p. 140.
25. Further details in ibid., p. 141.
26. Ibid., p. 146.
27. Keith Hitchins, *Rumania 1866–1947* (Oxford: Oxford University Press, 1994), p. 484.
28. Bancoş, *Social şi naţional în politica guvernului Ion Antonescu*, p. 148.
29. It also warrants a note of caution over accepting official figures at face value. Corroboration from an alternative source, wherever possible, is desirable.
30. Bancoş, *Social şi naţional în politica guvernului Ion Antonescu*, p. 148.
31. Hitchins, *Rumania 1866–1947*, p. 484.
32. *Monitorul Oficial*, part 1, no. 113 (15 May 1941), pp. 2608–9.
33. *Monitorul Oficial*, part 1, no. 164 (14 July 1941), pp. 4039–42.
34. Its obligatory character was recognized in the replacement of the term 'community labour' (*munca de interes obştesc*) in official use by that of 'forced labour' (*munca obligatorie*) in July 1942. Bancoş, *Social şi naţional în politica guvernului Ion Antonescu*, p. 153.
35. The Bucharest police were instructed to send 9,650 Jews for work on the railways.
36. The number of able-bodied Jews between the ages of 18 and 50 in Bucharest and in each county was as follows: Bucharest, between 25,000–30,000; Buzău, 367; Ialomiţa, 671, of whom 663 had been interned; Caraş, 99; Turda, 450; Dolj, 546, of whom 235 were interned; Braşov, 825; Olt, 145; Alba, 424; Argeş, 114; Râmnicu Sărat, 216; Vâlcea, 38; Gorj, 1,069, of whom 1,048 were interned in Târgu-Jiu (788 of the latter had been assigned labour duties in various areas); Severin, 269; Damboviţa, 851, of whom 827 were interned; Hunedoara, 850; Ilfov, 12; Brăila, 1,295; Timiş-Torontal, 2,650; Constanţa, 535, held in three camps; Prahova, 0 (the Jews from Ploieşti and the rest of Prahova had been interned in the camp at Teiş, Dâmboviţa; Suceava, 2,692. *Evreii din România între anii 1940–1944*, doc. 288, n. 1, p. 400.
37. Ibid., doc. 288, n. 2, p. 400.
38. Ibid., doc. 294, n. 1, p. 406.
39. Ibid., doc. 292, p. 403.
40. Ibid., doc. 287, p. 398.
41. *Consiliul de coordonare*.
42. *Stenogramele Şedinţelor Consiliului de Miniştri. Guvernarea Ion Antonescu*. Vol. V, *Octombrie 1941 ianuarie 1942*, ed. Marcel-Dumitru Ciucă and Maria Ignat (Bucharest: Arhivele Naţionale ale României, 2001), pp. 173–4.
43. Bancoş, *Social şi naţional în politica guvernului Ion Antonescu*, p. 152.
44. Ibid., pp. 153–4.
45. Ibid., pp. 154–5.
46. Ibid., p. 155.
47. 251 of these were Jews from Bucharest, 11 from Chişinău (Bessarabia), 9 each from Arad (Banat) and Târgu-Neamţ (Moldavia), 8 from Sculeni (Bessarabia), 7 from Brăila (Moldavia), 4 from Galaţi (Moldavia), 2 from Cetatea Albă (Bessarabia), and 1 each from Cahul and Soroca (Bessarabia). United States Holocaust Memorial Museum. Nikolaev archive, 1996. A0340, reel 3, p. 59.

48. Research on this particular subject is being conducted by Jean Ancel.
49. *Evreii din România între anii 1940–1944*. Vol. 1, *Legislaţia antievreiască*, ed. Lya Benjamin (Bucharest: Hasefer, 1993), pp. 167–9, 183–4.
50. ANIC, Ministerul Afacerilor Interne, Trial of Ion Antonescu, file 40010, vol. 8, p. 25.
51. The Jews alone were required to contribute to a special fund to cover the costs of rebuilding the re-conquered provinces of Bessarabia and Bukovina and committees of Jews were constituted to administer the collection. Since their activity was threatened by the obligation to perform compulsory labour, the Ministry of Finance pressed the Army General Staff for exemptions for members of the Federation of Jewish Communities. At the same time, Filderman intervened with the army and, as a result, the exemptions were granted. *Evreii din România între anii 1940–1944*, doc. 295, p. 407.
52. Ibid., p. 408.
53. Larry Watts, *Romanian Cassandra. Ion Antonescu and the Struggle for Reform, 1916–1941* (Boulder, CO: East European Monographs, 1993), p. 360.
54. Filderman noted of his audience: 'The Marshal seemed very agreeable and in good humour. 1. The Star of David... After a short discussion, the Marshal turned to Mihai Antonescu and said: "All right, please issue an order suppressing the sign throughout the country." I had come with a new memorandum, no. 1065, which I had drawn up during the day in order to counter the possible argument that the sign had already been introduced in Germany. Obviously, I did not present it'. *DCFRJH*, vol. 3, p. 131; *Evreii din România între anii 1940–1944*, docs 231, 317, pp. 319, 429.
55. Under point 1 of these regulations, issued by the Governor of Bukovina General Corneliu Calotescu on 11 October 1941, it was stipulated: 'All the Jews in the ghetto are obliged to comply fully with the instructions, orders and summons of the military authorities. The wearing of the Star of David is obligatory in the ghetto.' *Documents Concerning the Fate of Romanian Jewry during the Holocaust*, selected and edited Jean Ancel (New York: The Beate Klarsfeld Foundation, 1986) (henceforth *DCFRJH*, vol. 5, p. 100).
56. *Evreii din România între anii 1940–1944*, doc. 425, p. 123.
57. Watts, *Romanian Cassandra*, p. 361.
58. *Evreii din România între anii 1940–1944*, doc. 285, p. 396. The number of internees in this camp on 23 July 1941 was 1,302, of whom 1,190 were Jews, 28 suspected legionaries, and 84 Communists. Ibid., doc. 198, p. 301.
59. *Evreii din România între anii 1940–1944*, doc. 199, pp. 302–3.
60. Ibid., docs 200, 201, pp. 304–5.
61. Ibid., doc. 286, p. 397.
62. Ibid., doc. 222, p. 326.
63. Ibid., doc. 227, p. 332.
64. ANIC, Ministerul Afacerilor Interne, trial of Ion Antonescu, file 40010, vol. 11, p. 93.
65. Watts, *Romanian Cassandra*, p. 376.
66. ANIC, fond Preşedinţia Consiliului de Miniştri – Cabinet, file 167/1941, pp. 64–5. I am grateful to Viorel Achim for this source; see also the text of the directive in Jean Ancel, *Transnistria* (Bucharest: Editura Atlas, 1998), vol. 1, pp. 317–18; and Lya Benjamin, 'The Jews' Image in Antonescu's Political Texts', *The Holocaust in Romania. History and Contemporary Significance* (Bucharest: Institute for Political Studies of Defence and Military History, 'Goldstein Goren' Diaspora

Research Centre, Tel Aviv University, 'Goldstein Goren' Centre for Hebrew Studies of Bucharest University, 2003), p.126.

67. ANIC, fond Preşedinţia Consiliului de Miniştri – Cabinet, file 167/1941, pp. 64–5. I am grateful to Viorel Achim for this source; see also the text of the directive in Ancel, *Transnistria*, vol. 1, pp. 317–18; and Benjamin, 'The Jews' Image in Antonescu's Political Texts', p. 126.

68. Romanian *jidan* is a pejorative term corresponding to English 'Yid' or 'kike'; *evreu* is a non-racist word.

69. *Mareşalul Ion Antonescu. Epistolarul Infernului*, ed. Mihai Pelin (Bucharest: Editura Viitorul Românesc, 1993), p. 268. This is probably a reference to one of the broadcasters of the wartime BBC Romanian Service. In a sad corollary to this remark I was told in 1991 by a director of the BBC World Service that a senior member of the National Salvation Front had complained on a visit to the BBC's headquarters in Bush House of what he regarded as 'anti-NSF bias' in the Romanian Service's news programmes which he ascribed to the 'Jews' on the staff of the Romanian Service. The director's reaction was a mixture of disgust and bemusement.

70. Ibid., p. 275.

71. Ibid., p. 295.

72. Ibid., p. 315.

73. Ibid., pp. 327–8.

74. *Evreii din România între anii 1940–1944*. Vol. II, *Problema Evreiască în stenogramele Consiliuliu de Miniştri* [The Jewish Problem in the Minutes of the Council of Ministers], ed. Lya Benjamin (Bucharest: Hasefer, 1996), doc. 160, pp. 501–2.

75. Ibid., doc. 166, p. 511.

76. *Evreii din Romania intre anii 1940–1944*. Vol. IV, *1943–1944: Bilantul Tragediei – Renasterea Sperantei* [The Balance of the Tragedy – The Rebirth of Hope], ed. Ion Şerbănescu (Bucharest: Hasefer, 1998), p. XXIII.

77. Dr Ion Costinescu, head of the Romanian Red Cross.

78. *Evreii din România între anii 1940–1944*. Vol. II, doc. 186, pp. 551–5. *Evreii din Romania intre anii 1940–1944*. Vol. IV, doc. 155, p. 178.

79. *Evreii din Romania intre anii 1940–1944*. Vol. II, doc. 187, p. 557.

80. Jean Ancel, *DCFRJH*, vol. X, p. 802.

81. Alex Mihai Stoenescu, *Armata, Mareşalul şi Evrei. Cazurile Dorohoi, Bucureşti, Iaşi, Odessa* (Bucharest: RAO, 1998), p. 318. *Evreii din România între anii 1940–1944*. Vol. II, doc. 123, p. 348.

82. For details of the relevant decrees see *Activitatea Centralei Evreilor din România* [The Activity of the Jewish Central Office in Romania] (Bucharest: Editura Alma Tip, 1998), pp. 12–13. This edition is a reprint of the original published in 1944. See also Bela Vago, 'The Ambiguity of Collaborationism: The Center of the Jews in Romania (1942–1944)', *Patterns of Jewish Leadership in Nazi Europe, 1933–1945: Proceedings of the Third Yad Vashem International Historical Conference, Jerusalem, 4–7 April 1977*, ed. Yisrael Gutman and Cynthia J. Haft (Jerusalem, 1979), pp. 287–309 to whom I am indebted for the details about the Central Jewish Office and its activity.

83. One of those who intervened was the Marshal's doctor, Dr Costescu. Bela Vago, 'The Ambiguity of Collaborationism', p. 290.

84. In September 1943 Lecca was restyled 'Commissioner General for Jewish Problems' within a new department called the State Secretariat for Labour. Radu Lecca was born in Leca in Bacău county on 15 February 1890 into a landowning

family. He was educated in Vienna and Paris and called up for war service in Romania in 1915. After the war he held a succession of commercial posts which brought him to Paris once more in 1930. He appears to have obtained sensitive information about French loans given to prominent Romanian politicians which he passed on to King Carol. On his return to France in 1931 he was arrested and sentenced to two years' jail for espionage. In 1933, he went to Berlin where he gained the confidence of Alfred Rosenberg and became a correspondent of the Nazi paper *Völkischer Beobachter*. He was given the mission of promoting Nazi interests in Romania; on his return to the country he was contacted by the Romanian secret service (SSI) with which he agreed to work. His position on the Nazi newspaper gave him excellent contacts in the German legation in Bucharest and he used these to inform Ion Antonescu of the support the Iron Guard was receiving from the Nazi Party. Antonescu told him to pass this information on to von Killinger, the German minister in Bucharest. Despite his reservations, Lecca did so, thereby forging a close friendship with von Killinger. As a consequence Lecca enjoyed the consistent support of the German legation; see the introduction by Alexandru Diță to Radu Lecca's memoir, written between 1965 and 1970, entitled *Eu i-am salvat pe evrei din România* (Bucharest: Roza Vânturilor, 1994), pp. 35–7.

85. Vago, 'The Ambiguity of Collaborationism', p. 309.
86. Ibid., p. 291.
87. Ibid., p. 292.
88. Ibid., p. 295.
89. Ibid., p. 296.
90. Ibid., p. 297.
91. Lecca, *Eu i-am salvat pe evreii din România*, p. 239. This was not the first time that the CJO had donated money to the Patronage Council (Consiliul de Patronaj al Operelor Sociale). In February 1942, Gingold had collected 100 million lei for the hospital for war-wounded run by the Council. The total sum paid by the CJO to the Patronage Council between 1 October 1940 and 15 September 1944 was 780, 615, 827 lei (Ministerul Afacerilor Interne. Trial of Ion Antonescu, file 40010, vol. 32, p. 281). After the war charges of embezzlement of some of the donations were brought against Maria Antonescu. She was found guilty for her part in 'bringing disaster to the country' and sentenced to a long prison term.
92. *Evreii din România între anii 1940–1944*. Vol. IV, p. 41.
93. Ibid., p. 249.
94. At the beginning of June 1943 Dr Nicolae Lupu, a leading member of the National Peasants, floated the idea among his party of a common approach with the Liberals to get Filderman brought back from Transnistria. Maniu agreed to the move and together with Dr Constantin Angelescu, a joint intervention was made to the Marshal.
95. *Evreii din România între anii 1940–1944*. Vol. IV, p. 273.
96. Its official name was *Comisiunea de Ajutorare de pe lângă Secțiunea de Asistență a Centralei Evreilor din România* (The Aid Committee attached to the Aid Section of the Central Jewish Office).
97. USHMM. Romanian Ministry of Foreign Affairs, RG.25.006M, reel 10, vol. 21, p. 245.
98. Among the recommendations in a report by two delegates of the Central Jewish Office, dated 22 December 1943, compiled on completion of an inspection of conditions in several Transnistrian ghettos, was 'the replacement of ghetto

heads who, through perversity or weakness, carry out a veritable embezzlement of clothing, medicines or monies which are sent.' Jean Ancel, *DCFRJH*
(New York: Beate Klarsfeld Foundation, 1986), vol. 5, p. 535.

99. Şaraga's report can be found in USHMM. Archive of the Romanian Security
Service, RG. 25.004M, reel no. 9, file 2710/33, pp. 106–63.
100. *Evreii din România între anii 1940–1944*. Vol. IV, p. 273.

Chapter 6

1. By holocaust I mean the systematic mass murder of Jews.
2. Radu Ioanid, *The Holocaust in Romania. The Destruction of Jews and Gypsies under
   Antonescu Regime, 1940–1944* (Chicago: Ivan R. Dee, 2000, published in association with the United States Holocaust Memorial Museum), p. 108. In his
   Evreii sub regimul Antonescu (Bucharest: Hasefer, 1998), pp. 124–47, Ioanid estimates the number of Jews murdered by Romanian and German (*Einsatzgruppe D*)
   units in the first weeks of the war as 23,513. Of these 6,348 were victims of the
   Einsatzgruppe D. Dinu Giurescu, in an analysis of Ioanid's figures, argues that of
   the number of victims attributed to the Romanian army (i.e. 16,805), 5,841
   were murdered by soldiers from identified units of the Romanian army whose
   deeds are documented in archives or memoir literature, and 10,964 are 'persons
   murdered without supporting documentary evidence'. D. Giurescu, *România în al
   doilea război mondial* (Bucharest: All, 1999), p. 156.
3. These figures are based on the reports sent to Antonescu by the governors of
   Bessarabia, Bukovina and Transnistria. They are the numbers of Jews deported
   and surviving in Transnistria on 15 November 1943; see USHMM. Archive of
   the Romanian Ministry of Foreign Affairs, RG 25.006m, reel 10, file 21, 133–5;
   reel 11, file 21, 589. Ioanid estimates a similar death toll in *The Holocaust in
   Romania*, p. 174. D. Bancoş in his *Social şi national în politica guvernului Ion
   Atones* (Bucharest: Editura Eminescu, 2000), p. 173, gives a similar figure of
   149,000 for the number of Jews deported to Transnistria and puts the total
   number of victims among the Jewish community in Romania at the hands of the
   Antonescu regime at 119,000. If we add the estimate of between 130,000 and
   170,000 local Ukrainian Jews who perished in Transnistria under Romanian
   administration, we have a total figure of between 250,000 and 290,000 Jewish
   dead. In a report to Antonescu dated 9 December 1941, General Constantin
   Z. Vasiliu, Inspector-General of the Gendarmerie, stated that 'the evacuation
   [*sic*] of Jews from Bukovina and Bessarabia has finished. The evacuated Jews
   have been settled in the areas shown on the attached sketch. Their total
   numbers are 108,002. ANIC, Ministerul Afacerilor Interne, Trial of Ion
   Antonescu, file 40010, vol. 8, p. 104.
4. A reflection of the callousness of the Romanian authorities in Transnistria
   towards the local Ukrainian Jews is the often cavalier attitude with which names
   and numbers were recorded. This makes an accurate calculation of the numbers
   of Ukrainian Jews who perished difficult. Furthermore, there is no reliable figure
   of the numbers of Ukrainian Jews who left Transnistria with the Soviet forces in
   the summer and autumn of 1941. Consequently, the researcher is thrown back
   on an educated estimate. Of the 300,000 Jews recorded in the 1939 Soviet
   census of the region it is estimated that between 100,000 and 150,000 stayed
   behind in the territory when the Soviet forces withdrew. (Ioanid, *The Holocaust*

in Romania, p. 177. Estimates of Ukrainian Jewish victims in the period from September 1941–November 1943 range from 130,000 (Ioanid, *The Holocaust in Romania*, p. 289) to 'at least 170,000 Ukrainian Jews were killed – the majority by the Romanians – or were handed over to the local German settlers, who butchered them (especially in the county of Berezovka)'. Jean Ancel, *Transnistria*, vol. III (Bucharest: Atlas, 1998), pp. 300–1. As regards the provinces of Bessarabia and Bukovina, Ioanid (*The Holocaust in Romania*, p. 172) concludes that a total of 124,000 Jews – 81,000 from Bessarabia and 43,000 from Bukovina – withdrew from these provinces with the Soviets in July 1941, leaving approximately 190,000 to face the Romanian and German advance.

5. Jewish victims of the Holocaust in Hungary numbered 564,000, of whom 63,000 were murdered before German occupation. The 501,000 murdered afterwards included 132,000 Jews from Hungarian-annexed northern Transylvania; see Randolph L. Braham, 'Northern Transylvania', *Encyclopedia of the Holocaust*, vol. 4 (New York and London: Macmillan, 1990), pp. 1476–8; and *Martiriul Evreilor din România, 1940–1944. Documente şi Mărturii* (Bucharest: Editura Hasefer, 1991), doc. 143, p. 264, where a report (undated) of the Federation of Jewish Communities in Romania gives the number of Jews in northern Transylvania before deportation in May 1944 as 165,061, the number deported: 151,180, the number in compulsory labour brigades between 1942 and 1944: 14,881, the number of survivors returning to Transylvania in September 1945: 15,769 (9.4 per cent), the number of survivors in other countries: 10,000 (6.1 per cent) and the number murdered in the death camps: 130,000. In a separate report by the Romanian section of the World Jewish Congress, published in Bucharest in 1945, the following details were presented about the fate of the Jews from northern Transylvania under Hungarian occupation: the Jewish population of northern Transylvania according to the Hungarian census of 31 January 1941 totalled 151,125. The numbers surviving at 1 September 1945 were put at 29,405. Between May and June 1944, 137,486 Jews were deported from the region by the Hungarian and German authorities to labour and death camps in Poland and Germany. Of these 15,769 had been repatriated to northern Transylvania by 1 September 1945. 13,636 Jews from northern Transylvania escaped deportation, either by working for the auxiliary services of the Hungarian army or by hiding. *La population juivre de la Transylvanie du Nord*, Section de Roumanie du Congrès Juif Mondial, Bucharest, 1945.

6. For a discussion of these, see Viorel Achim, 'The Romanian Population Exchange Project Elaborated by Sabin Manuilă in October 1941', *Annali dell'Instituto storico italo-germanico in Trento/Jahrbuch des italienisch-deutschen historischen Instituts in Trient*, vol. XXVII (2001), pp. 597–8.

7. The term *Ost-Juden* was used by German Jews to indicate Jews from Poland and Russia who had not emancipated themselves from the *shtetl*. It often had the connotation of cultural inferiority.

8. *Documents of International Affairs, 1939–1946*. Vol. II, *Hitler's Europe*, ed. Margaret Carlyle (Oxford: Oxford University Press, 1954), doc. no. 207, pp. 318–19, quoted Jean Ancel, 'The Jassy Syndrome (1)', *Romanian Jewish Studies*, vol. 1, no. 1 (Spring 1987), p. 38.

9. See also Andrej Angrick, 'The Escalation of German-Rumanian Anti-Jewish Policy after the Attack on the Soviet Union', *Yad Vashem Studies*, vol. 26 (1998), p. 220, fn 43.

10. *Evreii din România între anii 1940–1944*. Vol. III, Part 1, *1940–1942: Perioada unei mari restrişti*, ed. Ion Şerbănescu (Bucharest: Hasefer, 1997), doc. 122, p. 183.

11. Ibid.,, doc. 147, p. 214.
12. Titus Flavius Vespasianus, Roman Emperor (79–81 BC). During the reign of his father, Vespasian, he was commander of the Roman armies in Judea, where he put down the rebellion of the Jews in 70 BC and destroyed Jerusalem.
13. *Stenogramele şedinţelor Consiliului de Miniştri. Guvernarea Ion Antonescu*. Vol. III, *Aprilie–iunie 1941*, ed. Marcel-Dumitru Ciucă, Maria Ignat and Aurelian Teodorescu (Bucureşti: Arhivele Naţionale ale României, 1999), p. 570.
14. Ibid., p. 618.
15. Jean Ancel, *Preludiu la asasinat. Pogromul de la Iaşi, 29 iunie 1941* [Prelude to Assassination. The Iaşi Pogrom, 29 June 1941] (Bucharest: Polirom, 2005), p. 18.
16. *Al Doilea Război Mondial. Situatia evreilor din România*. Vol. 1, *1939–1941*, part 1, ed. Alesandru Duţu and Constantin Botoran (Cluj-Napoca: Centrul de Studii Transilvane, Fundaţia Culturală Română, 1994), pp. 231–2.
17. While the number of victims on the two trains has been assessed with relative accuracy, the death toll of those murdered in the city can only be estimated. Ioanid cites two sources which put the figure of the latter at about 1,000. Other sources give estimates ranging from 8,000 to 12,000 for the total number of victims in the town and on the trains. Radu Ioanid, 'The Antonescu Era', in *The Tragedy of Romanian Jewry*, ed. Randolph L. Braham (New York: Columbia University Press, 1994), pp. 136, 144. Ancel, *Preludiu la asasinat. Pogromul de la Iasi, 29 iunie 1941*, p. 11, put the figure of Jews murdered at 'around a third of the Jews in the city, more than 14,000'.
18. Ancel, 'The Jassy Syndrome (1)', p. 37.
19. Alex Mihai Stoenescu, *Armata, Mareşalul şi Evreii. Cazurile Dorohoi, Bucureşti, Iaşi, Odessa* [The Army, the Marshal and the Jews. The Cases of Dorohoi, Bucharest, Iaşi, and Odessa] (Bucharest: RAO, 1998), p. 229.
20. Ioanid, 'The Antonescu Era', p. 131.
21. Stoenescu, *Armata, Mareşalul şi Evreii*, p. 231.
22. Bancoş, *Social şi national în politica guvernului Ion Atones*, p. 156, n. 101.
23. Alex Mihai Stoenescu, *Armata, Mareşalul şi Evreii. Cazurile Dorohoi, Bucureşti, Iaşi, Odessa*, p. 234, assumes that they were.
24. Ioanid, 'The Antonescu Era', p. 131.
25. *Martiriul Evreilor din România, 1940–1944. Documente şi Mărturii* (Bucharest: Editura Hasefer, 1991), p. 89.
26. These searches, involving 140 police and 677 gendarmes, netted 317 Jews who were taken to police headquartes (the *chestura*) where 207 were detained because they owned torches or objects made of red cloth. Ioanid, 'The Antonescu Era', p. 132.
27. Matatias Carp, *Cartea Neagră. Suferinţele Evreilor din România, 1940–1944*. Vol. 2, *Pogromul de la Iaşi*, ed. Lya Benjamin (Bucharest: Editura Diogene, 1996), no. 21, p. 72.
28. Ibid., p. 28.
29. Stoenescu, *Armata, Mareşalul şi Evreii. Cazurile Dorohoi, Bucureşti, Iaşi, Odessa*, p. 245; see also Ioanid, 'The Antonescu Era', p. 133.
30. Ioanid, 'The Antonescu Era', p. 134.
31. The declaration of Gheorghe Leahu, a senior Iasi police officer, dated 2 July 1941, states that 'there were about 3,500 Jews in the courtyard when the Germans began to massacre them . . . and 2,500 left when formed into columns to be marched to the railway station'. Carp, *Cartea Neagră. Suferinţele Evreilor din România, 1940–1944*, vol. 2, p. 117. The figure of 1,000 seems credible, unlike that of 300 proposed by Stoenescu, *Armata, Mareşalul şi Evreii. Cazurile Dorohoi, Bucureşti, Iaşi, Odessa*, p. 252, which appears to be unsubstantiated. These figures do not take into account

those Jews murdered en route to the police HQ; their number has been estimated by one source as about 250 (ibid.), and by 400. Ioanid, 'The Antonescu Era',
p. 136.
32. Carp, *Cartea Neagră. Suferinţele Evreilor din România, 1940–1944*, vol. 2, p. 116.
33. All the reports by Romanian police and army officers state that the Germans were
responsible for the massacre; see ibid., passim. Ioanid, 'The Antonescu Era', p. 135,
apportions the guilt jointly between Romanian and German soldiers.
34. See Leahu's declaration, cited above, pp. 116–17: 'Lt.-Col. Chirilovici, who had
been summoned to the [14th] division, told me by telephone that a decision had
been taken to evacuate the Jews from the courtyard of the police-station. To this
end 50 wagons had been provided and steps are being taken to send them to the
station so that they should not be at the police-station when night falls for fear of
a fresh massacre which the Germans might perpetrate.'
35. One of the policemen was identified as Leon Cristiniuc. Ibid., p. 138.
36. The following account is based on Ioanid, 'The Antonescu Era', pp. 138–43.
37. According to testimony given to the Munich State Prosecutor's Office after the
war by a German officer, when the trains were 'emptied', the survivors were shot
in the open field by Romanian troops. Andrej Angrick, 'The Escalation of
German–Rumanian Anti-Jewish Policy after the Attack on the Soviet Union', *Yad
Vashem Studies*, vol. 26 (1998), 209.
38. Statement of Aurel Totoiescu to public prosecutor A. Schreiber, 16 August 1945,
Carp, *Cartea Neagră. Suferinţele Evreilor din România, 1940–1944*, vol. 2, p. 130.
39. Ernest H. Latham Jr., 'Signs of Human Feeling and Attitude: The American Legation
and American Jews in Romania in 1941', paper presented at a symposium on US–
Romanian Relations at the Department of Contemporary History, 'Babeş-Bolyai'
University, Cluj-Napoca, June 2001, p. 6.
40. Ioanid, 'The Antonescu Era', p. 143.
41. Ibid., p. 144. Stoenescu, in an infelicitous phrasing, considers 'the figures used by
some Jewish historians of 12,000, 13,000 or 15,000 as exaggerated'. *Armata, Mareşalul şi Evreii. Cazurile Dorohoi, Bucureşti, Iaşi, Odessa*, p. 253.
42. Carp, *Cartea Neagră. Suferinţele Evreilor din România, 1940–1944*, vol. 2, p. 117.
43. Ibid. In a statement to a prosecutor before his trial for war crimes in May 1946,
Eugen Cristescu, head of the Romanian Intelligence Service (SSI), declared: 'As
regards the action of the head of the SSI in connection with the incidents at Iaşi,
I wish to state that I personally gave no orders and that I had no connection with
the assembling or transport of those Jews; that a preventive measure by the
service [of this nature] could not be taken since Major Tulbure, head of the Intelligence section of the SSI in Iaşi, together with his entire staff, had crossed into
Bessarabia with the German forces; that, at this time, the squadron's headquarters were near Roman, while at Iaşi there was only a team for quartering tasked
with finding accommodation for the squadron which was due to arrive in Iaşi.
Ministerul de Interne, file 40010, vol. 10, p. 11.
44. Ioanid., 'The Antonescu Era', p. 157.
45. Stoenescu, *Armata, Mareşalul şi Evreii. Cazurile Dorohoi, Bucureşti, Iaşi, Odessa*, p. 255.
46. Stoenescu, *Armata, Mareşalul şi Evreii. Cazurile Dorohoi, Bucureşti, Iaşi, Odessa*, p. 257,
makes these points.
47. See Gunther's report to the State Department dated 3 October 1941. Watts, *Romanian
Cassandra*, p. 359.
48. In a memorandum prepared by Filderman on 22 August 1942 against the
proposed deportation of Romanian Jews to Poland, he wrote: 'Marshal Antonescu

justified the deportation of Jews from Bessarabia and Bukovina as punishment for the acts of hostility that the latter allegedly carried out against the army, and from the need to remove an important number of uncertain elements in the war-zone.' *DCFRJH*, vol. IV, p. 126.

49. *Evreii din România între anii 1940–1944*. Vol. III, Part 1, *1940–1942: Perioada unei mari restrişti*, ed. Ion Şerbănescu (Bucharest: Hasefer, 1997), doc. 174, pp. 256–7.

50. In November 1940.

51. *DCFRJH*, vol. III, pp. 32–7.

52. In a memorandum prepared by Filderman on 22 August 1942 against the proposed deportation of Romanian Jews to Poland, he wrote: 'Marshal Antonescu justified the deportation of Jews from Bessarabia and Bukovina as punishment for the acts of hostility that the latter allegedly carried out against the army, and from the need to remove an important number of uncertain elements in the war-zone.' *DCFRJH*, selected and edited Jean Ancel (New York: The Beate Klarsfeld Foundation, 1986), vol. 3, pp. 259–62, vol. IV, p. 126.

53. In his letter to Antonescu of 11 October 1941, Filderman wrote: 'Today I received a desperate appeal from the leadership of the ghetto in Chişinău. On the morning of 8 October 1,500 people set out on the road, most of them on foot, taking with them only what they could carry. Almost all, therefore, are likely to perish, since it is cold outside and they are naked, without food and without the slightest possibility of getting supplies on a journey of at least eight days in the cold and snow. Only the sick, old and children have left in carts. Thus not even the sick were spared; thus the women too left on foot. It means death, death, death of the innocents, without any other guilt than that of being Jews. I beg of you, Marshal, not to let such a tremendous tragedy take place. Please accept, Marshal, the assurance of my profound respect. Matatias Carp, *Cartea Neagră. Suferinţele Evreilor din România, 1940–1944*. Vol. 3, *Transnistria*, ed. Lya Benjamin (Bucharest: Editura Diogene, 1996), no. 101, pp. 189–90.

54. *DCFRJH*, vol. 3, pp. 259–62. In a postscript added by hand to the original text which did not appear in the published text, Antonescu added: 'A wounded soldier from Piatra Neamt was buried alive on the orders and under the eyes of the Yid Soviet commissars despite the poor man's pleas that he had four children'. Carp, *Cartea Neagră. Suferinţele Evreilor din România, 1940–1944*, vol. 3, p. 192. Antonescu gave an explicit explanation of his reasons for deporting the Jews – he preferred the term 'evacuation' – in a letter dated 4 February 1944 to the Jewish architect Herman Clejan: 'As I have declared to you verbally, I was forced to evacuate the Jews from Bessarabia and Bukovina because, due to their horrible behaviour during the occupation of those territories by the Russians, the population was so strongly incensed against them that without this security measure even more terrible pogroms would have taken place. Given all of this I decided to evacuate all of the Jews of Bessarabia and Bukovina but, through various interventions, I was impeded from doing so. Today, I regret that I did not do this because it has been established that among the Jews that remained there, dishonourable elements were recruited by the adversary of the country. There has not been a single communist or terrorist organization discovered by our police in which Jews have not been members and frequently they are constituted only of Jews...'. Watts, *Romanian Cassandra*, p. 372.

55. See USHMM, RG 25.003, reel 116, file 941.

56. Dorohoi became part of Bukovina for administrative purposes under article 15 of Decree Law 2506 which was published on 15 October 1941 in the official bulletin

Monitorul Oficial. This decree stipulated that Bukovina comprised the counties of Câmpulung, Cernăuți, Hotin, Rădăuți, Storojineț, Suceava and Dorohoi.

57. Carp, *Cartea Neagră. Suferințele Evreilor din România, 1940–1944*, vol. 3, p. 95. These 'places' were ghettos or concentration camps.

58. *Stenogramele ședințelor Consiliului de Miniștri. Guvernarea Ion Antonescu*. Vol. IV, *Iulie–septembrie 1941*, ed. Marcel-Dumitru Ciucă și Maria Ignat (Bucharest, Arhivele Naționale ale României, 2000), p. 57.

59. 'Minutes of the meeting of the Council of Ministers, 6 September 1941', in *Evreii din România între anii 1940–1944*. Vol. II, doc. 108, pp. 302, 303. See also Meeting of the Council of Ministers, 6 September, 1941, *Stenogramele Ședințelor Consiliului de Miniștri. Guvernarea Ion Antonescu*, vol. IV, p. 597.

60. For most Romanians, crossing into Bessarabia and northern Bukovina did not constitute an 'invasion' of the Soviet Union since both territories had been wrested from Romania under threat of war by the Soviet Union in June 1940.

61. It has been estimated that up to 100,000 of the approximately 285,000 Jews in the two provinces had left, having either been sent into internal exile by the Soviets following their annexation of the provinces in June 1940, or fled with the Red Army after the Romanian re-annexation in July 1941. In December 1940, thousands of families of various nationalities were deported from Akkerman by the Soviet authorities to western Siberia and to Kazakhstan – the numbers have yet to be ascertained from the relevant Soviet documents. The Soviet regime also targeted its class enemies in the two provinces; the bourgeois, the capitalists and landowners, and its political opponents – the nationalists, Zionists, priests and pastors.

62. The phrase in Romanian was *curățirea terenului*; see Paul A. Shapiro, 'The Jews of Chișinău (Kishinev): Romanian Reoccupation, Ghettoization, Deportation', in *The Destruction of Romanian and Ukrainian Jews during the Antonescu Era*, ed. Randolph L. Braham (New York: The Rosenthal Institute for Holocaust Studies, City University of New York, Columbia University Press, 1997), p. 140.

63. Ibid., p. 140.

64. Archive of the Romanian Security Service (Serviciul Român de Informații) held at the Archive of the United States Holocaust Memorial Museum, RG 25.004M, reel 24, file 20725, vol. 5, order of Vasiliu no. 37.519/1941, annex 00022; see also Shapiro, 'The Jews of Chișinău', p. 140.

65. Andrej Angrick, 'The Escalation of German–Rumanian Anti-Jewish Policy after the Attack on the Soviet Union', *Yad Vashem Studies*, vol. 26 (1998), p. 207.

66. Radu Ioanid, *Evreii sub regimul Antonescu* (Bucharest: Hasefer, 1998), pp. 129–30.

67. Ibid.

68. In September 1945, the bodies buried at Stânca Roznoveanu were exhumed in the presence of a coroner and a delegation from the Jewish community in Iași; 311 bodies were found in three common graves. According to a witness there was a fourth grave, but it could not be found since it had been dug next to a road which had since been moved. The graves revealed 33 children between the ages of 1 and 12, of whom 7 were 1-year olds and 14 aged around 6. Many of the women were merely in their nightclothes. Ioanid, *Evreii sub regimul Antonescu*, pp. 131–2.

69. *Evreii din România între anii 1940–1944*. Vol. III, Part 1, doc. 206, pp. 309–10.

70. Ioanid., *Evreii sub regimul Antonescu*, p. 135.

71. Carp, *Cartea Neagră. Suferintele Evreilor din România, 1940–1944*, vol. 3, p. 37.

72. Ibid.

73. Details in Ioanid, *Evreii sub regimul Antonescu*, pp. 134–9; and Carp, *Cartea Neagră. Suferințele Evreilor din România, 1940–1944*, vol. 3, pp. 31–5.

74. Andrej Angrick, 'Die Einsatzgruppe D', *Die Einsatzgruppen in der besetzten Sowjetunion 1941/42*, ed. Peter Klein, Gedenk-und Bildungsstatte Haus der Wansee-Konferenz (Berlin: Hentrich, 1997), pp. 88–110.
75. Ioanid, *Evreii sub regimul Antonescu*, p. 140.
76. Ibid., p. 141. There is evidence to indicate that an *Eşalon Operativ* of the Romanian Secret Service, a unit of 100–160 men, participated with *Einsatzgruppe D* in the killings of Jews during the Romanian–German advance into the Bessarabian capital Chişinău; see Shapiro, 'The Jews of Chişinău', p. 140. Documents point to the involvement of the Romanian Secret Service alongside units of the Romanian and German armies in the Iaşi pogrom of June 1941. In testimony given to the public prosecutor on 12 November 1945, Traian Borcescu, the former head of the SSI administrative office, stated: 'As regards the preparation and staging of the massacres in Iaşi, I suspect that they were the work of the First Operative Echelon [of the SSI] since Eugen Cristescu [head of the SSI] said to me on his return from Moldavia to Bucharest: 'The great deeds which I carried out in Moldavia I carried out in concert with the section II of the General Headquarters, and namely with Colonel Radu Dinulescu and Lt.-Col. Gheorghe Petrescu. In addition, I know from [SSI agent] Grigore Petrovici that a major role in the preparation of the pogrom was played by Junius Lecca, SSI head of counter-espionage in Iaşi who provided all the information on the Jewish quarters and congregations in the city and who passed this information on to Eugen Cristescu, who together with section II of the General Headquarters and the German command worked out the plans for the massacre in Iaşi. Carp, *Carteă Neagră. Suferinţele Evreilor din România, 1940–1944*, vol. 2, p. 117. From Borcescu's testimony it may appear that the SSI played only a preparatory role in the pogrom, but he went on to declare: 'In respect of the massacre, although the echelon did not receive orders to participate, nevertheless the following teams drawn from the echelon did take part: a team led by Grigore Petrovici and Captain Gheorghe Balotescu, another one led by Major Tulbure, another under the command of Gheorghe Cristescu-Gică, Eugen Cristescu's brother. I only know of these, but there may have been others. These teams worked under the command of Florin Becescu-Georgescu' (ibid.).
77. Henry Monneroi, *La Persécution des Juifs dans les Pays de l'Est* (Paris: Editions du Centre, 1949), no. 2651, 31 July 1941, p. 291. Quoted Ioanid, *Evreii sub regimul Antonescu*, p. 151.
78. 'Der I.c. ersuchte noch die Möglichkeit zu erwaegen, ob gegen die von den Rumänen durchgefürhrten unsachgemaessen und sadistischen Exekutionen von den Sonderkommandos in geeigneter Form eingeschritten und diese verhindert werden könnten. Die Sicherung von Objekten und Warenlagern gegen Plünderungen wurde seitens des I.c. besonders begruesst.gez. Sturmbannfuehrer SS (maior) Gmeiner.' 'Niederschrift über die Besprechung mit dem I.c. 11 Armee vom 16.7.1941', *Bundesarchiv Militär Freiburg im Breisgau*. Dosar RH 20-11/488, Armeeoberkommando 11, p. 18. I am grateful to Ottmar Traşca of the Institute of History in Cluj-Napoca for showing me this report.
79. A catalogue of other massacres is given by Ioanid, *Evreii sub regimul Antonescu*, pp. 141–7.
80. Shapiro, 'The Jews of Chişinău', p. 141.
81. Teodor Meculescu was born on 4 April 1889 in Piteşti. Highly decorated for his valour during the First World War as an artillery officer, he transferred to the gendarmerie in 1919. He was appointed head of the gendarmerie in

Dobrogea in 1936 and, in 1941 head of the Chişinău gendarmerie. Arrested in 1945 for his role in the deportation of Jews to Transnistria, he was tried and sentenced to 15 years' forced labour but acquitted on appeal. He was rearrested in 1957 for 'crimes against the working class', notably his part in the arrest of the Communist activist Filimon Sârbu in 1941. Found guilty in 1960, he received a sentence of 14 years and was sent to Gherla prison on 17 June 1962. His sentence was commuted under a general amnesty and he was released on 23 June 1964. He died in Bucharest in 1982. I am grateful to Ion Ciupea of the Museum of National History in Cluj-Napoca for these details.

82. Shapiro, 'The Jews of Chişinău', p. 141.
83. Ibid., p. 143. The ghetto was a demarcated area cordoned off by the army.
84. Ibid., p. 145.
85. They were not, however, subject to total confinement; some were allowed out under guard to retrieve personal items from their homes.
86. Ibid., p. 149.
87. Ibid., p. 150.
88. Ibid., p.150.
89. Ibid., p. 159.
90. Ibid., p. 160.
91. Ibid.
92. The ghetto in Chişinău is said by one scholar to have been set up by *Einsatz-gruppe D* 'at the end of July after consultations with the Romanian local commandant'. Angrick, 'The Escalation of German–Rumanian Anti-Jewish Policy after the Attack on the Soviet Union', *Yad Vashem Studies*, vol. 26 (1998), p. 210.
93. Ibid.
94. Shapiro, 'The Jews of Chişinău', pp. 151–2. The order for the shooting was given by Lt-Col Nicolae Deleanu, battalion commander, but the nature of the 'rebellion' was never established at the trial. One witness said that the massacre was prompted by a scuffle when a Romanian soldier claimed to have recognized one of the Jews as the person responsible for his beating during the Romanian withdrawal from Bessarabia in summer 1940.
95. Ioanid, *Evreii sub regimul Antonescu*, pp. 106–7.
96. Carp, *Cartea Neagră. Suferinţele Evreilor din România, 1940–1944*, vol. 3, p. 75.
97. Ibid., p.76.

Chapter 7

1. For the German reaction to the expulsions of Jews by the Romanian authorities, see Andrej Angrick, 'The Escalation of German–Rumanian Anti-Jewish Policy after the Attack on the Soviet Union', *Yad Vashem Studies*, vol. 26 (1998), pp. 203–38.
2. Ibid., p. 217.
3. Ibid., p. 218.
4. Matatias Carp, *Cartea Neagră. Suferinţele Evreilor din România, 1940–1944*. Vol. 3, *Transnistria*, ed. Lya Benjamin (Bucharest: Editura Diogene, 1996), no. 41, p. 101.
5. Ibid.
6. Alexander Dallin, *Odessa, 1941–1944: A Case Study of Soviet Territory under Foreign Rule* (Iaşi, Oxford and Portland: The Centre for Romanian Studies, 1998), pp. 198–206. This study was originally prepared as a RAND Corporation Report

(RM-1875): Alexander Dallin, 'Odessa, 1941–1944: A Case Study of Soviet Territory under Foreign Rule,' Santa Monica, CA: RAND, 1957.

7. Angrick, 'The Escalation of German-Rumanian Anti-Jewish Policy after the Attack on the Soviet Union', p. 220.

8. Quoted Jean Ancel, 'The Jassy Syndrome (1)', *Romanian Jewish Studies*, vol. 1, no.1 (Spring 1987), p. 38, citing *Documents of International Affairs, 1939–1946*. Vol. II, *Hitler's Europe*, ed. Margaret Carlyle (Oxford University Press, 1954), doc. 332; see also Angrick, 'The Escalation of German-Rumanian Anti-Jewish Policy after the Attack on the Soviet Union', p. 221.

9. Angrick, 'The Escalation of German-Rumanian Anti-Jewish Policy after the Attack on the Soviet Union', pp. 226–7.

10. Ibid., p. 229.

11. Between 9 and 23 August 1941 the average number of Jews in Edineţ was 10,000, in Secureni 21,000 and in Vertujeni 22,000. Radu Ioanid, 'The Antonescu Era', in *The Tragedy of Romanian Jewry*, ed. Randolph L. Braham (New York: The Rosenthal Institute for Holocaust Studies, 1994), p. 148.

12. Anatol Petrencu, *Basarabia în al doilea război mondial 1940–1944* (Chişinău: Lyceum, 1997), p. 325.

13. Carp, *Cartea Neagră. Suferinţele Evreilor din România, 1940–1944*, vol. 3, p. 124.

14. Paul A. Shapiro, 'The Jews of Chişinău (Kishinev): Romanian Reoccupation, Ghettoization, Deportation', in *The Destruction of Romanian and Ukrainian Jews during the Antonescu Era*, ed. Randolph L. Braham (New York: The Rosenthal Institute for Holocaust Studies, City University of New York, Columbia University Press, 1997), p. 160.

15. 'The evacuation of the Jews beyond the Bug cannot be accomplished at this time. Therefore, they should be concentrated in work camps and used in [forced] labour until the moment when, after the conclusion of operations, their evacuation to the East will be possible.' Ibid.

16. Council of Ministers' Meeting, 16 December 1941. *Stenogramele Şedinţelor Consiliului de Miniştri. Guvernarea Ion Antonescu*. Vol. V, *Octombrie 1941 ianuarie 1942*, ed. Marcel-Dumitru Ciucă and Maria Ignat (Bucharest: Arhivele Naţionale ale României, 2001), p. 492.

17. At the time these officials were termed 'plenipotentiaries', being appointed governors, in the case of Bukovina and Bessarabia, by Antonescu on 5 September 1941.

18. According to Mihai Antonescu, the Romanian prime minister, the decision to deport the Jews from Bessarabia and northern Bukovina was not taken at any cabinet meeting, but 'was taken by the Marshal when he was in Moldavia, near the front'. Under questioning on 17 April 1946 before his trial, Mihai Antonescu declared that Ion Antonescu had taken the decision 'to begin the deportation of Jews from Cernăuţi and from Chişinău' while he was in Iaşi in early July 1941. This was done because 'it seemed to him that there were too many Jews in Bessarabia and Bukovina, and because in 1940 they showed an inappropriate attitude, and because of the atmosphere that the Marshal claimed existed in Bessarabia and Bukovina, that he made the hasty decision to evacuate the Jews'. Interrogation of Mihai Antonescu, 17 April 1946, USHMM, RG 25.004M, Archive of the Romanian Information Service, reel 31, file no. 40010, vol. 43, pp. 14, 16, 19; see also Jean Ancel, 'Antonescu and the Jews', *Yad Vashem Studies*, vol. 23 (1993), p. 243; Jean Ancel, 'The Romanian Campaigns of Mass Murder in Transnistria, 1941–1942', *The Destruction of Romanian and Ukrainian Jews During the Antonescu Era*, ed. Randolph L. Braham

(New York, The Rosenthal Institute for Holocaust Studies, City University of New York, Boulder: Social Science Monographs, 1997), p. 129, n. 49.

19. 'Memorandum of General Gheorghe Voiculescu, Governor of Bessarabia, regarding the situation in the Chişinău ghetto', addressed to Ion Antonescu. From textual references the document can be dated to late December 1941; see *Evreii din România între anii 1940–1944*. Vol. III, Part 1, *1940–1942: Perioada unei mari restrişti*, ed. Ion Şerbănescu (Bucharest: Hasefer, 1997), doc. 373, p. 48; see also Ancel, 'Antonescu and the Jews', p. 241.

20. *Stenogramele Şedinţelor Consiliului de Miniştri. Guvernarea Ion Antonescu*, vol. V, p. 323. The deportations began on 16 September 1941, not in November.

21. Shapiro, 'The Jews of Chişinău', p. 161. Ancel, 'Antonescu and the Jews', p. 243; Ancel, 'The Romanian Campaigns of Mass Murder in Transnistria, 1941–1942', p. 129, n. 49.

22. Carp, *Cartea Neagră. Suferinţele Evreilor din România, 1940–1944*, vol. 3, p. 128. Figures compiled for Antonescu on the numbers of Jews in Bessarabia 'as of 25 September 1941', shows that there were 53,800, including those in the ghetto of Chişinău. Ancel, 'Antonescu and the Jews', p. 243.

23. Shapiro, 'The Jews of Chişinău', p. 161.

24. Carp, *Cartea Neagră. Suferinţele Evreilor din România, 1940–1944*, vol. 3, p. 123. In the instructions issued by Colonel Meculescu, head of the gendarmerie in Bessarabia, to the commandant of Vertujeni, Colonel Vasile Agapie, the number of Jews in the camp was 22,150. Ibid., p. 128.

25. Ibid., p. 30.

26. Shapiro, 'The Jews of Chişinău', p. 188, n. 85.

27. Alex Mihai Stoenescu, *Armata, Mareşalul şi Evreii* (Bucharest: RAO, 1998), pp. 332–3.

28. Carp, *Cartea Neagră. Suferinţele Evreilor din România, 1940–1944*, vol. 3, p. 130.

29. Ibid., p. 131.

30. Cabinet meeting of 13 November 1941. *Stenogramele Şedinţelor Consiliului de Miniştri. Guvernarea Ion Antonescu*, vol. V, p. 126.

31. Ibid., pp. 4–5.

32. Ibid., p. 8.

33. *Evreii din România între anii 1940–1944*. Vol. III, doc. 356, pp. 21–2.

34. Ibid., doc. 367, p. 39.

35. Ibid.

36. Dated 22 November 1941. *Evreii din România între anii 1940–1944*. Vol. III, doc. 399, pp. 88–92.

37. Dated 30 December 1941. Ibid., doc. 406, pp. 98–100.

38. See the memorandum of 12 October 1943, sent by Mihai Antonescu to General C. Z. Vasiliu, state secretary at the Ministry of the Interior, on the abuses committed during the deportations of 1941 and 1942. USHMM, RG.25.004M Records of the Romanian Information Service, reel 13, file 2757/82, p. 38.

39. This was recognized in the memorandum of 12 October 1943: 'War widows and war orphans, descendants of veterans of the War of Independence [1877–78], women and children whose husbands were and still are doing compulsory labour in Romania, had all been victims. There were also Jews who, at the outbreak of war, had been sent to Wallachia from the area of the front in Bukovina and Dorohoi but who, on the intervention of the Ministry of Finance, had been sent back to their homes in the autumn of 1941 in order to subscribe to the war loan to which Jews were required to do by law. After subscribing, the order for deportation came and they were deported. Had they remained in Wallachia they would have been safe.'

40. *Evreii din România între anii 1940–1944*. Vol. III, doc. 406, p. 99.
41. Ibid., doc. 399, p. 90.
42. Ibid., doc. 406, p. 99.
43. Ibid.
44. Ibid.
45. Muşat's report. Ibid., doc. 399, p. 90.
46. Ibid., p. 91.
47. Ibid.
48. H. Appelfeld, 'Buried Homeland', transl. Jeffrey M. Green, *The New Yorker* (23 November 1998), p. 60.
49. Bărcan's report. *Evreii din România între anii 1940–1944*. Vol. III, doc. 406, p. 100.
50. Dorohoi district had been transferred in 1938 in an administrative reform from Bukovina to Moldavia; after the reconstitution of Bukovina in the wake of the re-conquest in August 1941 of the northern part of the province, Calotescu persuaded the Marshal, largely on economic grounds, that Dorohoi should be restored to Bukovina.
51. After numerous petitions from Filderman and consultations between Mihai Antonescu, Vasiliu and the Marshal, the repatriation of the Jews from Dorohoi and a small group of Jews deported for political reasons was ordered on 8 December 1943. Between 20 and 25 December, 6,107 Jews, mostly from Dorohoi, were moved from Transnistria to Moldavia.
52. Ernest H. Latham Jr, 'Signs of Human Feeling and Attitude: The American Lega-tion and American Jews in Romania in 1941', paper presented at a symposium on US–Romanian Relations at the Department of Contemporary History, 'Babeş-Bolyai' University, Cluj-Napoca, June 2001, p. 4. I am grateful to Dr Latham for permission to quote from his paper.
53. Ibid., pp. 8–9.
54. Latham, ibid., p. 14.
55. Ibid.
56. *Evreii din România între anii 1940–1944*. Vol. III, doc. 370, p. 43. On 9 December 1941, General Constantin Vasiliu, Inspector-General of Gendarmes, reported to Marshal Antonescu that the evacuation of Jews from these two provinces had been completed, and that 108,002 persons had been resettled in Transnistria. This was the figure mentioned in the trial of Antonescu in May 1946. General Vasiliu declared on 12 November 1943 that the number of Jews deported to Transnistria was 110,033, of whom 10,368 were from Dorohoi (northern Moldavia), 55,867 from Bessarabia and 43,793 from northern Bukovina. Carp, *Cartea Neagră*, vol. 3, p. 447. The information bulletin of the Inspectorate of Gendarmes in Transnistria (15 December 1941–12 January 1942) states that up to that date 118,847 Jews had been deported to Transnistria through the following transit points: Iampol, 35,276; Moghilev, 55,913; Tiraspol, 872; Râbniţa, 24,570; and Iaska, 2,216. Ioanid, 'The Antonescu Era', p. 149. This contrasts with the figures submitted by the governors of Bessarabia, Bukovina and Transnistria to Mihai Antonescu in November 1943, which stated that 90,334 Jews had been deported from Bukovina and 56,089 from Bessarabia, a total of 146,423. Ibid., p. 174.
57. *Evreii din România între anii 1940–1944*. Vol. III, doc. 404, pp. 96–7.
58. D. Bancoş, *Social şi naţional în politica guvernului Ion Antonescu* (Bucharest: Editura Eminescu, 2000), p. 162.
59. *Evreii din România între anii 1940–1944*. Vol. III, doc. 513, p. 228. Confusingly, the Inspectorate of Gendarmes reported that on 1 January 1942 that there were only 401 Jews left in Bessarabia; ibid., doc. 476, p. 182.

60. Arhiva Ministerului Afacerilor Externe (Romanian Ministry of Foreign Affairs Archive), Fond Central, Problema 33 (Chestiuni privitoare la evrei), vol. 20, pp. 198, 206. Among the Jews deported from Cernăuţi on 7/8 June were Arnold and Anna Corn (pseudo. Daghani). They were eventually taken to the forced labour camp of Mihailovka in German-controlled Ukraine where they were used for forced labour by the Todt organization. In July 1943, they escaped and lived clandestinely in Berşad in Transnistria until 31 December when, with the help of the Red Cross, they left for Romania. They reached Bucharest in March 1944. Corn, under the name of Daghani, began to paint, but was unable to adapt to the artistic strictures of the Communist regime and he and his wife emigrated to Israel in 1958. Three years later they left for Europe and, after spells in several countries, settled in England in 1977. Daghani died in Hove, Sussex on 6 April 1985, a year after his wife. See Arnold Daghani, *Groapa e în livada cu vişini*, ed. Lya Benjamin (Bucharest, 2004).
61. *Evreii din România între anii 1940–1944*. Vol. III, doc. 534, p. 248.
62. Ibid., doc. 538, p. 252.
63. Ibid., doc. 339, p. 461.
64. Jean Ancel, *DCFRJH*, vol. V, pp. 278–87.
65. Popovici (1892–1946) was a lawyer. In 1989, he was recognized by the Yad Vashem Institute as a Righteous Gentile Among Nations. For details of Popovici's life, see Marius Mincu, *Ce s-a întâmplat cu evreii în şi din România* (What Happened to the Jews in and from Romania), vol. 3 (Bucharest: Editura Glob, Editura Papyrus, 1997).

Chapter 8

1. The military operations are admirably covered in Mark Axworthy, Cornel Scafeş and Cristian Craciunoiu, *Third Axis, Fourth Ally. Romanian Armed Forces in the European War, 1941–1945* (London: Arms and Armour, 1995); and the administration in Alexander Dallin, *Odessa, 1941–1944: A Case Study of Soviet Territory under Foreign Rule* (Iaşi, Oxford and Portland: The Centre for Romanian Studies, 1998).
2. *Antonescu–Hitler. Corespondenţă şi întîlniri inedite (1940–1944)*, vol. 1 (Bucharest: Coresi, 1991), pp. 116, 119–22.
3. Olivian Verenca, *Administraţia civilă română în Transnistria, 1941–1944* [Romanian Civil Administration in Transnistria, 1941–1944], ed. Şerban Alexianu (Bucharest: Editura Vremea, 2000), p. 57.
4. Dallin, *Odessa, 1941–1944*, p. 59. The area beyond the Bug was later to be known as the Reich Commissariat of the Ukraine.
5. Jipa Rotaru, Octavian Burcin, Vladimir Zodian and Leonida Moise, *Mareşalul Antonescu la Odessa. Grandoarea şi amărăciunea unei victorii* [Marshal Antonescu at Odessa. The Grandeur and Bitterness of a Victory] (Bucharest: Editura Paideia, 1999), p. 224.
6. Antonescu's *Transnistria* should be distinguished from *Transdnestria* (in Russian, *Pridnestrove*, in Romanian, *Transnistria*), the name adopted by the Russian-supported authorities in the breakaway region of the Republic of Moldova who declared a republic in 1990.
7. This did not stop some Romanian historians from seeking to justify Romania's 'historical right' to Transnistria during Antonescu's occupation of the area. Diaconescu claimed a continuous Romanian-speaking presence in the territory from

antiquity until the conquest of Transnistria and argued that the Dacian ruler Burebista's kingdom extended even beyond the Bug; see Emil Diaconescu, *Românii din Răsărit: Transnistria* (Iaşi, 1942), pp. 13–14; see also Rebecca Haynes, 'Introduction', *Occasional Papers in Romanian Studies. No. 3: Moldova, Bessarabia, Transnistria*, ed. Rebecca Haynes (SSEES, University College London, 2003), p. 115.

8. The figure of 300,000 Jews was confirmed by the census of 1939, which recorded the Jewish population by district as follows:

Odessa 233,155
Autonomous Moldovan Soviet Socialist Republic: 37,035
Mogilev 8,703
Tulchin 5,607
Yampol 1,753
Vapniarka 711
Bersad 4,271
Zhmerinka 4,630
Bar 3,869

Distribution of the Jewish population of the USSR, 1939, ed. Mordechai Altshuler (Jerusalem: The Hebrew University of Jerusalem, 1993), Tables 1–5.

9. The argument that Antonescu, in rejecting Hitler's request that he should annex Transnistria, was being consistent with established Romanian policy of not accepting from the Germans or claiming territory that did not have a significant Romanian element in the population overlooks the memorandum sent by Antonescu on 23 April 1941 to Hitler and Mussolini in which he stated that although Romania was not seeking territorial expansion at the expense of Yugoslavia, the territorial concessions made to Hungary and Bulgaria had created a new situation. He therefore requested a general revision of frontiers in south-eastern Europe and the annexation by Romania of the Yugoslav Banat, as well as the creation of a free Macedonia and autonomy for the Romanians living in the Timok and Vardar valleys. Andreas Hillgruber, *Hitler, König Carol und Marschall Antonescu. Die Deutsch–Rumanischen Beziehungen, 1938–1944* (Wiesbaden: Franz Steiner Verlag, 1965), p. 126.

10. Résumé of the talks between Hitler and Antonescu on 11 February 1942 in *Antonescu–Hitler*, vol. 1, p. 184.

11. This is one of several illuminating points argued by Larry Watts in his introduction to Dallin, *Odessa, 1941–1944*, p. 17. Hitler wanted to persuade his ally to accept Transnistria as compensation for northern Transylvania whose transfer to Hungary Germany had supervised in the Vienna Agreement of August 1940 but by the very same token Antonescu wanted to use Transnistria as a bargaining counter for the return of northern Transylvania. In Antonescu's vision Transnistria could be returned to the Ukraine or its successor regime, and Hungary could be compensated for its loss by receiving the Galician districts of Stanislav and Kolomea. Ibid., pp. 59–60.

12. It was perhaps under the influence of the term *Generalgouvernement*, applied by the Nazis to the eastern part of German-occupied Poland, and of its placement under the direct authority of a German governor, Hans Frank, that the word *guvernământ* ('government') was coined by the Antonescu regime for the authority in Transnistria and the position of governor established.

13. According to papers compiled for Alexianu's trial in May 1946, he was appointed governor of Transnistria on 19 August 1941. ANIC, Ministerul Afacerilor Interne, Trial of Ion Antonescu, file 40010, vol. 4, p. 211.

14. ANIC, Ministerul Afacerilor Interne, Trial of Ion Antonescu, file 40010, vol. 28, p. 7.
15. Dallin, *Odessa, 1941–1944*, p. 76. Alexianu had been appointed royal resident (i.e. Carol's representative) of Bukovina in 1938 and oversaw the repression of the Iron Guard there. As a result, he was sentenced to death by a clandestine Iron Guard court in November 1938, a sentence reported in Bucharest newspapers of the time. When the Iron Guard came to power in association with Antonescu in September 1940, Alexianu was suspended from his chair at Cernăuţi University. On 30 November 1940, he was summoned to the Iron Guard headquarters to be tried. Preferring to take his own life, he shot himself in the chest but the bullet lodged in his lung and he recovered. ANIC, Ministerul Afacerilor Interne, Trial of Ion Antonescu, file 40010, vol. 4, pp. 211–12.
16. Alexianu's close personal relationship with Irina Burnaia, the wife of a Romanian official, drew criticism from his staff, since she not only attended government meetings but constantly interrupted meetings with her unsolicited comments. Romanian intelligence (SSI) reported on 28 September 1942 that the governor 'was beginning to lose his moral authority' as a result of Mrs Burnaia's behaviour. USHMM, RG 25004M, file 108233, vol. 130, p. 42. It is not clear how long this liaison endured.
17. According to one Romanian army intelligence report, public officials working for the Transnistrian government received a salary 'three or four times' that for an equivalent post in Romania. Arhiva Ministerului Apărării Naţionale, Piteşti, Fond Armata a 4-a, file 752, report dated 2 December 1941. I am grateful to Ottmar Traşca for this document.
18. Ibid.
19. Radu Ioanid, *The Holocaust in Romania. The Destruction of Jews and Gypsies under the Antonescu Regime, 1940–1944* (Chicago: Ivan R. Dee, 2000), p. 188. Hoffmeyer was born in Posen on 29 May 1903 and promoted to *Brigadeführer* (Brigadier General) on 9 November 1943. His SS number was 314948, and party number 5480793; see USHMM, 'List of SS Officers compiled from files at Berlin Document Center'.
20. Its mandate was expressed thus: 'to reorganize the churches and the spiritual instruction of the population in the area between the Dniester and the Bug'. Dumitru Stavrache and Elena Istrăţescu, 'Mitropolitul Visarion Puiu la sfârşit de mandat în Transnistria' [Metropolitan Bishop Visarion Puiu at the End of his Appointment in Transnistria], *Revista de Istorie Militară*, no. 6(58) (1999), p. 22.
21. Ibid., p. 23, n. 3. Scriban was succeeded on 16 November 1942 by the former Metropolitan of Bukovina Visarion Puiu, who relinquished the office on 14 December 1943, his place being taken by Archimandrite Antim Nica.
22. Antim Nica, *Viaţa religioasă în Transnistria* [Religious Life in Transnistria] (Chişinău, 1943), pp. 5–17; see also Haynes, 'Introduction', p. 116.
23. Stavrache and Istrăţescu, 'Mitropolitul Visarion Puiu la sfârşit de mandat în Transnistria', p. 25.
24. On 21 February 1946, Metropolitan Puiu was sentenced to death *in absentia* for 'actions of terror in Bessarabia and Transnistria' by the People's Tribunal in Bucharest.
25. Dallin, *Odessa, 1941–1944*, pp. 139–40. Some 7,000 Soviet citizens are said to have accompanied the Romanian forces when they withdrew from Transnistria in April 1944 in the face of the Red Army.
26. Initially, the local Ukrainian population refused in some areas to respect the working hours drawn up by the local mayors in the cooperative farms and the Romanian army had to be used to 'encourage' compliance. Arhiva Ministerului

Apărării Naţionale, Piteşti, Fond Armata a 4-a, file 752, report dated 2 December 1941. I am grateful to Ottmar Traşca for this document.

27. Council of Ministers' meeting, 16 December 1941. *Stenogramele Şedinţelor Consiliului de Miniştri. Guvernarea Ion Antonescu.* Vol. V, *Octombrie 1941–ianuarie 1942,* ed. Marcel-Dumitru Ciucă and Maria Ignat (Bucharest: Arhivele Naţionale ale României, 2001), pp. 490–1.

28. At his trial at Nuremburg, Ohlendorf admitted that he had murdered about 90,000 Jews between June 1941 and June 1942. These included Jews from the Crimea and from regions as far away as the River Don. Jean Ancel, *Transnistria,* vol. 1 (Bucharest: Editura Atlas, 1998), p. 64.

29. Jean Ancel, 'The Romanian Campaigns of Mass Murder in Transnistria, 1941–1942', *The Destruction of Romanian and Ukrainian Jews during the Antonescu Era,* ed. Randolph L. Braham (Boulder, CO: Social Science Monographs, 1997), p. 98.

30. See chapter 6.

31. Arhiva Ministerului Apărării Naţionale [The Archive of the Ministry of National Defence], Piteşti, Fond Divizia 10 Infanterie, file 830, p. 444.

32. Ibid., p. 540.

33. Alesandru Duţu and Mihai Retegan, *Război şi societate. România, 1941–1945* [War and Society. Romania, 1941–1945]. Vol. 1, *De la Prut în Crimeea* (22 June–8 Noember 1941) (Bucharest: RAO, 1999), pp. 416–20. King Michael protested about the massacre of Jewish hostages. See Ivor Porter, *Michael of Romania. The King and the Country* (London: Sutton, 2005), p. 75.

34. A report of the 38th Infantry Regiment dated 25 October 1941. Arhiva Ministerului Apărării Naţionale, Piteşti, Fond Divizia 10 Infanterie, file 830, p. 487.

35. A handwritten note, issued under the codename 'Gorun' of General Constantin Trestioreanu, deputy commander of Odessa, stated that 'in retaliation, several Jews and proven Communists were executed by hanging and by shooting. Arhiva Ministerului Apărării Naţionale, Piteşti, Fond Divizia 10 Infanterie, file 830, dated 23 October 1941. Colonel C. Iordăchescu, commander of the 33 Dorobanţi Regiment based in the the city, reported on 23 October that '72 Jews and Communists had been shot according to orders from above following the explosion at the military headquarters' (ibid.). The bodies were thrown into the sea. I am grateful to Ottmar Traşca for these documents.

36. Dallin, *Odessa, 1941–1944,* p. 74; report of Colonel Rodler dated 4 November 1941 from Bucharest. Bericht über Wahrnehmungen in Odessa', *Bundersarchiv-Militararchiv Freiburg im Breisgau,* RH31-I, v. 108, Abwehrstelle Rumaenien nr, 11035/41 g Leiter, p. 4. I am grateful to Ottmar Traşca for showing me this document.

37. See the résumés of trial statements made by Iacobici, Macici and Trestioreanu in USHMM, RG 25.004M. reel 20, file 40011, vol. 8, pp. 56–8, 174–8.

38. *Cotidianul. Arhiva,* vol. 5, no. 3 (22 March 1996), p. 3. The list included General Cornel Calotescu, the former Governor of Bukovina. The death sentences were commuted to life imprisonment on 5 June (*Universul,* 6 June 1945). Macici died in Aiud prison on 15 June 1950 of heart failure. Death certificate issued by mayor's office in Aiud, no. 102/1950. See also *Cotidianul. Arhiva,* vol. 5, no. 3 (22 March 1996), p. 7.

39. *Stenogramele Şedinţelor Consiliului de Miniştri. Guvernarea Ion Antonescu,* vol. V, p. 120.

40. ANIC, Ministerul Afacerilor Interne, Trial of Ion Antonescu, file 40010, vol. 28, p. 7.

41. ANIC, Ministerul Afacerilor Interne, Trial of Ion Antonescu, file 40010, vol. 3, pp. 17–18. The transcript of the pre-trial examination bears the signature of Ion Antonescu at the bottom of each page and bears the date 26 April 1946. In his

indictment against Antonescu the public prosecutor claimed that the number of victims in Odessa was 20,000. Antonescu referred to this in a memorandum which he submitted and dated 16 May 1946: 'The public prosecutor has alleged in court that 20,000 were murdered, adding that they were marched in columns to four sheds – 25 metres by 16 – on the road to Dalnyk. Dalnyk is four to five kilometres from Odessa. 20,000 soldiers, in marching formation, would stretch twenty kilometres down a major road. Four sheds, measuring 25 metres by 16, represent an area of 1,200 square metres. If we calculate two, even three people per square metre – which is impossible – we would not exceed the figure of 3,000'. Marcel-Dumitru Ciucă (ed.), *Procesul Mareşalului Antonescu. Documente*, vol. 2 (Bucharest: Editura Saeculum, Editura Europa Nova, 1995), p. 170. Antonescu's arithmetic – as recorded here – is faulty. The four blockhouses would each have had an area of 400 sq. m, giving a total area of 1,600 sq. m.

42. Ordinance no. 23; see *Evreii din România între anii 1940–1944*. Vol. III, pp. 84–5; see also the annex of this book.
43. Ancel, 'The Romanian Campaigns of Mass Murder in Transnistria, 1941–1942', p. 114.
44. Sabin Manuilă was head of the census office, which was directly subordinated to Antonescu.
45. Meeting with the Governors of the Liberated Provinces, 13 November 1941. ANIC, Ministerul Afacerilor Interne. Trial of Ion Antonescu, file 40010, vol. 28, p.30a.
46. *Stenogramele Şedinţelor Consiliului de Miniştri. Guvernarea Ion Antonescu*, vol. V, p. 159.
47. Ibid., pp. 462–3.
48. Ioanid, *The Holocaust in Romania*, p. 208.
49. The report was signed by Colonel M. Stănescu. Arhiva Ministerului Apărării Naţionale, Piteşti, Fond Armata a 4-a, file 752. I am grateful to Ottmar Traşca for this document.
50. An intelligence report of 16 February 1942 of the Romanian 4th Army stated that 31,340 Jews had been deported from Odessa by the evening of 13 February (Arhiva Ministerului Apărării Naţionale, Piteşti, Fond Armata a 4-a, file 752). A further bulletin of 20 March 1942 gave the figure of 33,000. For details of the daily transports see Ioanid, *The Holocaust in Romania*, pp. 209–10; and *DCFRJH*, vol. 5, pp. 202–15, 222, 231–3.
51. Dallin, *Odessa, 1941–1944*, pp. 208–9.
52. Some of the Jews deported from Cernăuti and Dorohoi were concentrated in Pechora and Tulcin. The 'ghetto' in the former was a former mental asylum.
53. Ancel, *Transnistria*, vol. 1, pp. 155–6.
54. Ibid., p. 174.
55. Jean Ancel, 'Antonescu and the Jews', *Yad Vashem Studies*, vol. 23 (1993), p. 258.
56. Ancel, *Transnistria*, vol. 1, p. 169.
57. Ibid., p. 171.
58. Padure was born in the country of Vaslui and was in May 1945, according to trial documents, 31 years old; Bobei was from Podul Turcului in the county of Tecuci and aged 37, and Melinescu from Bucharest, and aged 32; see USHMM. RG.25.004M, reel 20, file 40011, vol. 6.
59. Padure gave a receipt for valuables, dated 17 January 1942, to Second Lieutenant Harold Fletcher, the German agricultural counsellor to the prefect of Golta county. The valuables – items of gold jewellery and 'ten gold teeth' – came from 'two civilian policemen in Domanevka, who robbed the Jews in Bogdanovka camp'. USHMM. RG.25.004M, reel 20, file 40011, vol. 7.
60. Ioanid, *The Holocaust in Romania*, p. 183.

61. Mănescu, according to May 1945 trial records, was a lawyer by training, was 34, and hailed from the village of Ghelmegioaia in Mehedinti county. USHMM. RG.25.004M. reel 20, file 40011, vol. 6.
62. Ancel, *Transnistria*, vol. 1, pp. 181–2.
63. USHMM, RG.25.004M, reels 19, 20, file 40011, vol. 6.
64. Ioanid, *The Holocaust in Romania*, p. 184.
65. A detailed description of the massacre, taken from survivors' statements presented at the postwar trial, can be found in ibid., pp. 183–4; and Ancel, *Transnistria*, vol. 1, pp. 185–90.
66. Ancel, *Transnistria*, p. 208.
67. Ioanid, *The Holocaust in Romania*, pp. 185–6.
68. ANIC, Ministerul Afacerilor Interne. Trial of Ion Antonescu, file 40010, vol. 25, pp. 82–8.
69. Ibid., vol. 28, p. 72.
70. Andrej Angrick, 'The Escalation of German–Rumanian Anti-Jewish Policy after the Attack on the Soviet Union', *Yad Vashem Studies*, vol. 26 (1998), p. 232.
71. Ibid., p. 234.
72. Ibid.
73. USHMM, Records of the Romanian Information Service, RG 25.004M, reel 27, vol. 3.
74. Quoted Raul Hilberg, *The Destruction of the European Jews*, vol. 1 (New York: Holmes and Meier, 1985), p. 374.
75. *Evreii din Romania intre anii 1940–1944*. Vol. III, doc. 532, p. 245.
76. George Tomaziu, *Jurnalul unui figurant* (Bucharest: Editura Univers, 1995), pp. 64–70.
77. For an English translation of the account, together with a brief biography of Tomaziu, including details of his fate under the Communist regime in Romania, see Dennis Deletant, 'Transnistria 1942: A Memoir of George Tomaziu. An Eyewitness Account of the Shooting of a Column of Jews near the Rov River in 1942', *Romania: A Crossroads of Europe*, ed. Kurt Treptow (Iaşi: The Centre for Romanian Studies, 2002), pp. 231–44.
78. For a fuller description of life in one Transnistrian ghetto, see Dennis Deletant, 'Ghetto experience in Golta, Transnistria, 1942–1944', *Holocaust and Genocide Studies*, vol. 18, no. 1 (Spring 2004), pp. 1–26.
79. A facsimile of the order can be found in Ancel, *Transnistria*, p. 315.
80. Ibid. p. 68.
81. Ancel, *Transnistria*, pp. 66–7. Schwab's order was periodically renewed in the three languages, hence the reference to 'marks' in this version from 1943 (personal communication, Jean Ancel).
82. Ibid.
83. Ibid., p. 69.
84. See the annex.
85. USHMM, RG.25.004M Records of the Romanian Information Service, reel 14, file 2869/208, p. 45.
86. Dalia Ofer, 'Life in the Ghettos of Transnistria', *Yad Vashem Studies*, vol. 25 (1996), pp. 236–7. 'In the Balta region, populated by 12,477 Jews, there were twenty-one ghettos and camps. Four ghettos housed between 800 and 1,400 deportees each; the exception was the town of Bersad, in which 5,261 deportees lived in September 1943. Five ghettos numbered between 200 and 500 persons each, whereas the remainder held a few dozen Jews each' (ibid.).

87. Dalia Ofer, 'The Holocaust in Transnistria. A Special Case of Genocide', in *The Holocaust in the Soviet Union. Studies and Sources on the Destruction of the Jews in the Nazi-Occupied Territories of the USSR, 1941–1945*, ed. Lucian Dobroszycki and Jeffrey S. Gurock (New York, London: M. E. Sharpe, 1993), p. 143.
88. One of the most graphic is given about Berşad ghetto in Ruth Glasberg Gold, *Ruth's Journey. A Survivor's Memoir* (Tallahassee: University of Florida Press, 1996).
89. The estimate came from the Central Institute of Statistics, which was subordinated to the Presidency of the Council of Ministers, i.e. to Ion Antonescu. The Institute's director was Sabin Manuilă (see below).
90. Much of what follows about the deportation of the Romas draws on the published research of Viorel Achim, to whom I acknowledge my indebtedness.
91. Viorel Achim, 'Deportarea ţiganilor în Transnistria' [The Deportation of the Gypsies to Transnistria]', *Anuarul IRIR 2002*, Bucharest (2003), p. 129.
92. I am grateful to Maria Bucur for this phrasing; see her *Eugenics and Modernization in Interwar Romania* (Pittsburgh: University of Pittsburgh Press, 2002), p. 147.
93. Ibid.
94. Quoted ibid., p. 148.
95. Council of Ministers' meeting, 7 February 1941. *Stenogramele Şedinţelor Consiliului de Miniştri. Guvernarea Ion Antonescu. Vol II, Ianuarie–martie 1941*, ed. Marcel-Dumitru Ciucă, Aurelian Teodorescu and Bogdan Florin Popovici (Bucharest: Arhivele Naţionale ale României, 1998), p. 181.
96. Achim, 'Deportarea ţiganilor în Transnistria', p.130.
97. Ibid.
98. *Procesul Mareşalului Antonescu. Documente*, vol. 1, ed. Marcel-Dumitru Ciucă (Bucharest: Editura Saeculum, Editura Europa Nova, 1995), p. 246.
99. These points are made by Achim, 'Deportarea ţiganilor în Transnistria', p. 130.
100. Similar racist sentiments against the Romas are to be found in Ion Chelcea, *Ţiganii din România. Monografia etnografică* (Bucharest, 1944), pp. 100–1; see also V. Achim, *Ţiganii în istoria României* (Bucharest: Editura Enciclopedică, 1998), pp. 133–6.
101. Achim, 'Deportarea ţiganilor în Transnistria', p. 132.
102. Ibid.
103. Ibid.
104. The National Centre for Romanianization (*Centrul Naţional de Românizare*) had been created on 3 May 1941 for the purpose of administering Jewish property nationalized by law on 28 March 1941. Much of the property confiscated from Jews was rented out to Romanians.
105. Achim, 'Deportarea ţiganilor în Transnistria', p. 133.
106. Ibid.
107. Ibid., p.134.
108. By burning whatever was combustible.
109. Achim, 'Deportarea ţiganilor în Transnistria', p. 136.
110. Ibid.
111. I am grateful for this information to Dr Wendy Lower of the Center for Advanced Holocaust Studies of the United States Holocaust Memorial Museum, Washington, DC.
112. Ibid., p. 137.
113. See above.
114. USHMM Nikolaev archive, RG 31008M, Microfiche fond 2178, opis 1, delo 67.

115. Ibid., delo 57.
116. Achim, 'Deportarea ţiganilor în Transnistria', p. 138.
117. Ibid., p. 139.
118. Ibid., p. 140.
119. In his own memorandum submitted to the court during his trial in 15 May 1946, Antonescu gave a figure of 1120 Jewish Communists deported. *Procesul Mareşalului Antonescu. Documente*, vol. 2, ed. Marcel-Dumitru Ciucă (Bucharest: Editura Saeculum, Editura Europa Nova, 1995), p. 176.
120. *Evreii din România între anii 1940–1944*. Vol. II, p. 463, n 2.
121. Interned Communists who were not Jews, among them the head of the so-called 'prison faction' Gheorghe Gheorgiu-Dej, leader of Romania's first Communist regime, were kept behind in Târgu-Jiu. An exception to those Jewish Communists deported was Iosif Chişinevski who remained in Caransebeş. Born in 1905 in Bessarabia, Iosif Chişinevski is believed to have studied at the Communist Party school in Moscow during the late 1920s. He was arrested in 1941 as the head of a Bucharest Communist cell and sent to Caransebeş jail. He was spared deportation to Transnistria because only Jewish Communists with sentences of less than ten years were sent to the province. Those with heavier sentences, like Chişinevski, Simion Zeiger and Radu Mănescu, stayed in Caransebeş until their release on 23 August 1944. See Pavel Câmpeanu, 'Pe marginea unei recenzii. Mistere şi pseudo-mistere din istoria PCR [In the Margin of a Review. Mysteries and Pseudo-Mysteries of the History of the Romanian Communist Party]', vol. *22*, no. 34 (23–30 August 1995), p. 12.
122. *Evreii din România între anii 1940–1944*. Vol. II, doc. 179, p. 536.
123. Ibid., p. 463, n. 6. By 4 November 1942, 777 Jews had been deported from the counties of Iaşi and Timişoară, including 182 who wanted to go to the Soviet Union, 132 for infringements of the compulsory labour law, 452 for Communist activity and 11 for converting to Christianity. D. Bancoş, *Social şi national în politica guvernului Ion Atones* (Bucharest: Editura Eminescu, 2000), p. 164.
124. A further 523 Jews who had requested repatriation to the Soviet Union after the loss of Bessarabia and northern Bukovina in June 1940 and whose names had been found in Soviet legation in Bucharest after the withdrawal of Soviet representation in June 1941, were deported on the same date. The latter were sent to Slivina camp in Oceacov county. See Matatias Carp, *Cartea Neagră. Suferinţele Evreilor din România, 1940–1944*. Vol. III, *Transnistria* (Bucharest: Doigene, 1996), p. 449.
124. ANIC, Arhive of the Romanian Ministry of the Interior, packet 91, file 569, p. 445.
125. USHMM. RG 25.004M, reel 21, file 40011, vol. 18, p. 96.
126. Ibid., p. 94.
127. Ibid., p. 97.
128. Ibid., p. 105.
129. The number of persons held in Vapniarka on 5 May 1943 was 1,312, of whom 1,092 were Jews and 198 Christians. The remaining 22 were classified as criminals and were Christians. Of the Jews, 835 were males, 136 females and 5 children. In November 1943, the number of Communists in the camp was recorded as 619, of a total of 1,312 internees. ANIC, Arhive of the Romanian Ministry of the Interior, packet 91, file 569, p. 445.
130. See the court testimony dated 10 March 1945 of one of the prisoners, Walter Isac. USHMM, RG.25.004M, reel 30, file 40013, vol. 6, p. 379. The Grosulovo internees – 563 in number – were sent under escort to Târgu-Jiu in March 1944

and were released after the overthrow of Antonescu on 23 August. Carp, *Cartea Neagră. Suferinţelor evreilor din România, 1940–1944*, vol. III, p. 412. A number of these Communists, including Simion Bughici and Aurel Rottenberg (Stefan Voicu), went on to occupy ministerial positions in the Communist government.

131. See chapter 6.

132. *Evreii din România între anii 1940–1944*. Vol. II, doc. 179, p. 540, n. 3.

133. Antoine Wenger, *La persecuzione dei cattolici in Russia, 1920–1960* (Milan: Edizioni San Paolo, 1999), pp. 198–9; details received from Dr Marius Bucur of the Department of Contemporary History, 'Babes-Bolyai' University, Cluj-Napoca.

134. Cassulo's interventions are described in Pierre Blet, *Pio XII e la Seconda Guerra mondiale negli Archivi Vaticani* (Milan: Edizioni San Paolo, 1999), pp. 241–50. For a more general view of the Vatican's position over the Jews in Romania, see A. Martini, 'La S. Sede e gli ebrei della Romania durante la seconda Guerra mondiale', *Civilta cattolica*, vol. 112, no. 3 (1961), pp. 449–63. I am grateful to Marius Bucur for this reference.

135. *Actes et Documents du Saint Siège Relatifs à la Seconde Guerre Mondiale. 8. Le Saint Siège et les Victimes de la Guerre. Janvier 1941-Decembre 1942* (The Vatican: Libreria Editrice Vaticana, 1974), p. 73.

136. Ibid., p. 108.

137. Ibid., p. 106.

138. *Evreii din România între anii 1940–1944*. Vol. III, doc. 138, p. 202.

139. *Actes et Documents du Saint Siège Relatifs à la Seconde Guerre Mondiale. 8*, p. 371.

140. Pierre Blet, *Pio XII e la Seconda Guerra mondiale negli Archivi Vaticani* (Milan: Edizioni San Paolo, 1999), p. 242.

141. *Actes et Documents du Saint Siège Relatifs à la Seconde Guerre Mondiale. 8. Le Saint Siège et les Victimes de la Guerre. Janvier 1941–Decembre 1942* (The Vatican: Libreria Editrice Vaticana, 1974), p. 510.

142. Ibid., p. 245.

143. Blet, *Pio XII e la Seconda Guerra mondiale negli Archivi Vaticani*, p. 243.

144. Ibid.

145. *Evreii din România între anii 1940–1944*. Vol. II, doc.179, p. 539.

146. *Actes et Documents du Saint Siège Relatifs à la Seconde Guerre Mondiale. 8*, p. 659.

147. Cassulo had visited Russian prisoners in Romanian hands early in 1942 and sent a detailed report to the Vatican on 10 May 1942. *Actes et Documents du Saint Siège Relatifs à la Seconde Guerre Mondiale. 9. Le Saint Siege et les Victimes de la Guerre. Janvier–Decembre 1943* (The Vatican: Libreria Editrice Vaticana, 1975), p. 153.

148. Ibid., p. 29.

149. *Actes et Documents du Saint Siège Relatifs à la Seconde Guerre Mondiale. 9*, pp. 474–5.

150. Ibid., p. 411.

151. *Actes et Documents du Saint Siege Relatifs a la Seconde Guerre Mondiale. 8*, pp. 31–2.

152. Ibid., p. 30.

153. Ibid., p. 31.

154. *Actes et Documents du Saint Siège Relatifs à la Seconde Guerre Mondiale. 10. Le Saint Siege et les Victimes de la Guerre. Janvier 1944–Juillet 1945* (The Vatican: Libreria Editrice Vaticana, 1980), p. 141.

155. Ibid., p. 354.

156. *DCFRJH*, ed. Ancel, vol. VII, p. 674.

157. The orphans were distributed as follows: 2,672 in Moghilev county, 793 in Balta, 276 in Jugastru, 95 in Golta, 111 in Tulcin, and 100 in Rabnita. 220

334 Hitler's Forgotten Ally

orphans had been repatriated to Dorohoi (*Actes et Documents du Saint Siège Relatifs à la Seconde Guerre Mondiale. 10*, p. 85.

158. Ibid., p. 86.
159. Ibid., p. 96.
160. Another document, unsigned, but perhaps written by Wilhelm Filderman, identified the author of this plea as Samuel Mosner, a lawyer from Cernăuți. Already, rumours had reached Bucharest that a group of 4,000 Romanian Jews supplied to the Todt organization by the prefect of Tulcin had been massacred once their labour was no longer needed. There was only one survivor, Dr Zippenstein, from Cernăuți. *Actes et Documents du Saint Siège Relatifs à la Seconde Guerre Mondiale. 10*, pp. 107–8.
161. Ibid., p. 43.
162. Ibid.

Chapter 9

1. Larry Watts, *Romanian Cassandra. Ion Antonescu and the Struggle for Reform, 1916–1941* (Boulder, CO: East European Monographs, 1993), p. 362. Richter (born 19 November 1912) was a lawyer. After joining the SS he served in the RHSA (Reich Security Chief Office) and was sent to Romania in April 1941 as an adviser to the Romanian government in the formulation of Anti-Semitic legislation. He became a close friend of Radu Lecca, the head of Romanian affairs in the Romanian prime minister's office, and was a major influence on him. On 23 August 1944, Richter was seized by the Romanian authorities and handed over to the Soviet army. After spending ten years in prisoner-of-war camps in the Soviet Union, he was sent back to West Germany following the visit to Moscow of Chancellor Konrad Adenauer. He was tried in January 1982 in LG Frankenthal for 'passing on instructions [to the Romanian government] on 8 August 1942 for deportations to Auschwitz' and sentenced to four years' imprisonment. Record of trials of German war criminals, USHMM, ref. 141 Js92-131/76.
2. *DCFRJH*, vol. 4, p. 120.
3. 'Transylvania' meant southern Transylvania since the northern part had been ceded to Hungary in August 1940.
4. Victor Neumann, *Istoria Evreilor din Banat* (Bucharest: Atlas, 1999), p. 155. Neumann puts the Jewish population of southern Transylvania and Banat at 40,000.
5. *Evreii din România între anii 1940–1944. Vol. II. Problema evreiască în stenogramele Consiliului de Miniştri*, ed. Lya Benjamin (Bucharest: Hasefer, 1996), doc. 179, p. 537.
6. Radu Ioanid, 'The Antonescu Era', in *The Tragedy of Romanian Jewry*, ed. Randolph L. Braham (Boulder, CO: Social Science Monographs, 1994), p. 162.
7. *DCFRJH*, vol. X, p. 215.
8. USHMM, RG.25.004M Records of the Romanian Information Service, reel 14, file 2869/208, p. 272. See also Dennis Deletant, 'Memoriul unor intelectuali români, înaintat la Palat, în vara 1942' [A Memorandum by Romanian Intellectuals, Submitted to King Michael in Summer 1942], *Sfera Politicii*, no. 107 (2004), pp. 49–53.
9. USHMM, RG.25.004M Records of the Romanian Information Service, reel 14, file 2869/208, pp. 263–70; see also Deletant, 'Memoriul unor intelectuali români, înaintat la Palat, în vara 1942'.

10. *Evreii din România între anii 1940–1944.* Vol. II, doc. 179, pp. 538–9.
11. Lecca was responsible to Mihai Antonescu, Vice-President of the Council of Minister (Prime Minister).
12. *DCFRJH*, vol. 4, p. 250. *Martiriul Evreilor din România, 1940–1944. Documente şi Mărturii* (Bucharest: Editura Hasefer, 1991), no. 106, p. 218.
13. 'Evacuation' was the term in official usage for deportation.
14. *DCFRJH*, vol. 4, p. 252. *Martiriul Evreilor din România, 1940–1944*, no. 107, p. 219.
15. Watts, *Romanian Cassandra*, p. 363.
16. Ibid.
17. Christopher R. Browning, *The Final Solution and the German Foreign Office. A Study of Referat DIII of Abteilung Deutschland 1940–1943* (New York: Holmes and Meier, 1978), p. 115, quoted Watts, *Romanian Cassandra*, p. 363. Light is shed on the absence of Romanian railway officials at Eichmann's meeting by a report of the Director General of the Romanian Railway, General T. C. Orezeanu, to Antonescu of 27 October 1942: the German Railway Directorate 'Ost-Berlin' had convened a conference on 26 September 1942 to arrange special trains for Jews from Romania to be sent to German-occupied Poland. Orezeanu had no prior knowledge of this matter and approached the Ministry of the Interior and Radu Lecca, the Plenipotentiary for Jewish Affairs in Romania. Both, he wrote, were unaware of the issue. Orezeanu sent a request to the German railways to postpone the conference, but this was ignored and it went ahead without a Romanian representative. According to information received by Orezeanu, it was resolved at the conference to provide special trains for the deportation of 280,000 Jews made up of 50 goods wagons and one passenger car (for the guards) which would carry 2,000 Jews every other day. The trains would depart from Adjud in southern Transylvania for Belzec via Orăşeni and Sniatyn, the frontier station for the General Government (Poland). In view of this situation Orezeanu ended his report by asking Antonescu for instructions. Antonescu simply wrote in a handwritten note in the margin of the report that at the meeting of the Council of Ministers on 13 October 1942 he had stopped the deportations of the Jews. See also *DCFRJH*, vol. X, no. 108, 'Minutes of the Conference held in Berlin 26–28 September 1942 regarding the evacuation of the Jews from the General Government and the dispatch of Jews from Romania to the General Government', pp. 237–8.
18. Such was Richter's enthusiasm for the deportation of Romanian Jews to the death camps in Poland that he drew up his own detailed plan. See *Martiriul Evreilor din România, 1940–1944*, pp. 211–13. *DCFRJH*, vol. 4, pp. 197–202.
19. *Evreii din Romania intre anii 1940–1944.* Vol. II, doc. 145, p. 442.
20. Some claimed that he had suffered a nervous breakdown, others that he had contracted syphilis as a young officer and its effects had resurfaced. Mihai Antonescu gave a blander explanation: the problem was food poisoning. See the diary of the Swiss Minister René de Weck, *Jurnal* (Bucharest: Humanitas, 2000), p. 135.
21. Alfred Rosenberg, the principal ideologist of the Nazi Party.
22. *Evreii din România între anii 1940–1944.* Vol. II, p. 458. The word 'deportation' was avoided. The Romanian Intelligence Service noted on 9 October 1942 that deportations were still taking place: 'We are informed that at Botosani thirty more families have been arrested in order to be deported to Transnistria' (USHMM, RG.25.004M Records of the Romanian Information Service, reel 14, file 2869/208, p. 334). On 8 September 1942, the deportation began of almost all the Jews – 407 – among the Communists interned in Târgu-Jiu to Vapniarka camp in Jugastru county, Transnistria. They arrived there on 16 September. In addition,

523 Jews who had requested repatriation to the Soviet Union after the loss of Bessarabia and northern Bukovina in June 1940 and whose names had been found in Soviet legation in Bucharest after the withdrawal of Soviet representation in June 1941 were deported on the same date. The latter were sent to Slivina camp in Oceacov county. Matatias Carp, *Cartea Neagră. Suferinţele Evreilor din România, 1940–1944*. Vol. III, *Transnistria* (Bucharest: Doigene, 1996), p. 449. The number of Communists in the camp at Vapniarka totalled 619 in November 1943 out of a total of 1,312 inmates, who included Christian common law criminals.

23. *Evreii din România între anii 1940–1944*. Vol. II, doc. 147, pp. 455–9.
24. In July, there had been discussion in Jewish circles of the news that the nuncio had instructed Catholic parishes to hold a special service on Wednesdays for Jews deported to Transnistria. *Evreii din România între anii 1940–1944*. Vol. II, doc. 179, p. 539.
25. Jean Ancel, 'Plans for the Deportation of the Rumanian Jews and their Discontinuation in Light of Documentary Evidence (July–October 1942)', *Yad Vashem Studies*, XVI (1984), pp. 388–9. Filderman also prepared a memorandum on 22 August 1942 against the proposed deportation of Romanian Jews to Poland, but it is unclear for whose eyes it was intended. It casts light on Filderman's thoughts on how to attenuate the consequences of such a plan for the Jews of Romania: 'Marshal Antonescu justified the deportation of Jews from Bessarabia and Bukovina as punishment for the acts of hostility that the latter allegedly carried out against the army, and from the need to remove an important number of uncertain elements in the war-zone, while the German armies have justified the deportation of some of the Jews in the occupied countries on the grounds of the repeated attacks on the German army, etc. Not only has no such allegation similar to the one leveled against the Jews of Bessarabia and Bukovina been made to date against the Jews in Transylvania and the Banat, nor against those remaining in Bukovina, not to mention those in the Old Kingdom, but everyone recognized that both on the occasion of the cession of part of Transylvania and afterwards that both the Jews in the territories that remained – and what is even more important – and those in the ceded territories behaved irreproachably.... If, against all possibility, Romania finds herself faced by problems which forced the government to take decisions contrary to the programme announced by Marshal Antonescu, then, in the light of what precedes and what follows, it would be politic that, on the one hand, as far as possible the execution of the plan be postponed, and on the other, that the deportations apply only to those who have settled clandestinely in Romania, to those sentenced to crimes against the security of the state, and to those born in regions other than those claimed by Romania as being Romanian. Under no circumstances should children, women and old people – that is those under one year of age and those over fifty-five – be deported. Deportation could be postponed by making emigration legal and organizing the emigration of Jews earmarked for deportation through reliable agencies and giving the Jews several months notice'. *DCFRJH*, vol. IV, p. 126.
26. Declaration of Alexander Şafran, Geneva, 10 January 1961 in *DCFRJH*, vol. VIII, p. 599. Neumann suggests that the wealthy industrialist Baron Franz von Neumann (no relative), who owned a textile factory in Arad which supplied the Romanian army with uniforms, joined Şafran and Metropolitan Bălan in their approaches to Antonescu. Victor Neumann, *Istoria Evreilor din Banat* (Bucharest: Atlas, 1999), p. 158.

27. A half-century later Queen Helen was to be recognized by the Israeli authorities as a Righteous Gentile Among Nations. The memorandum of her activities during the war on which the Israeli government based its decision stated: 'Queen Helen identified herself openly with the plight of the Jews. She even threatened to leave the country if their deportation continued. The contact she made through her Jewish doctors with the underground Jewish leadership enabled her to provide vital and irreplaceable support which made it possible to save tens of thousands. By doing so (as had her son when advocating a break with the Axis in his New Year broadcast in 1942 [*sic*]) she put her life at risk. She knew that her royalty would not save her; her sister Irene had been arrested by the Germans in Italy, her cousin Princess Mafaldi had died in Buchenwald. Hitler pressed Marshal Antonescu to "eliminate Queen Helen physically". Her opposition to the barbaric treatment of Jews in Romania constituted a daily risk to her life' (*Yad Vashem*. Undated memorandum 'On Assistance to Romanian Jews Rendered by Queen Elena During World War II'). I am grateful to Ivor Porter for this information; see also his biography of King Michael, *Michael of Romania. The King and the Country* (London: Sutton, 2005), p. 75.

28. In the original German *letzen* ('last') could either be interpreted as 'final' or 'most recent'.

29. *DCFRJH*, vol. 4 (1986), pp. 314–15. On 9 October 1942, the SSI (the Romanian Intelligence Service) reported that the literary critic Eugen Lovinescu, and the poets Ion Pillat and Vasile Voiculescu had secured the release of the poet Alfred Sperber and his wife, who had been arrested by the police in order to be deported to Transnistria, by vouching for their conduct. Oscar Walter Cisek, a deputy director in the Ministry of Propaganda, had also intervened on Sperber's behalf. USHMM, RG.25.004M Records of the Romanian Information Service, reel 14, file 2869/208, p. 334.

30. Larry Watts dismisses the argument that Stalingrad and a wish to 'save his own skin' were instrumental in Antonescu's decision. Watts, *Romanian Cassandra*, pp. 364–5.

31. *Evreii din România între anii 1940–1944*. Vol. II, doc. 139, p. 419.

32. Radu Lecca, *Eu i-am salvat pe evrei din România* (Bucharest: Roza Vânturilor, 1994), pp. 252–4. Lecca was also probably present, although he does not say so.

33. Dalia Ofer, *Escaping the Holocaust* (New York: Oxford University Press, 1990), p. 187.

34. For details of this emigration, see ibid.

35. Its engine was old and faulty, there was no kitchen, inadequate food, only one toilet and primitive berths. The Bulgarian crew did not appear to have any of the professional skills of seamen. Within a few hours the engine failed and, for an entire day, it drifted slowly until a Romanian vessel responded to its distress signal. The captain, for a fee of three million lei, which the passengers paid in jewellery and cash, made temporary repairs to the engine which lasted until the *Struma* reached the Bosphorus on 14 December, where it broke down again. On the following day, it drifted towards a minefield and was taken in tow by a Turkish ship to Istanbul and placed in quarantine. At dawn on 23 February, ten weeks after it had been nursed into Istanbul, the captain of the *Struma*, a Bulgarian national, was ordered by the Turkish coastguard to set sail for the Black Sea. The captain refused, and the refugees joined his protest by hanging out bed-sheets with the letters 'S.O.S' painted on them. Over the sides of the boat they draped signs in French with the words 'Jewish immigrants' and 'Save us!' The Turkish patrol boat withdrew but came back with 150 armed police who boarded the *Struma* and forced the passengers below deck. The *Struma* was then taken

under tow and released into open waters. Just before dawn, some 10 km from land, it was torpedoed and sank. Almost 24 hours passed before Turkish boats arrived, but by they found only one survivor, David Stoliar. Stoliar was allowed to enter Palestine two months later, after recuperating in a Turkish military hospital. It was only after 1990 that access to Soviet archives confirmed that a Soviet submarine had mistakenly identified the *Struma* as an enemy vessel and fired the fateful torpedo. Questions on the fate of the *Struma* were raised in the House of Commons on 4 March 1942 by MPs Eleanor Rathbone and Sidney Silverman, and on 11 March by Mr Lipson. In reply, Harold Macmillan, the Under-Secretary of State for the Colonies, made a statement basically in line with the details above. He concluded by saying that 'HMG [His Majesty's Government] greatly deplore the tragic loss of life which occurred in this disaster'. *Parliamentary Debates. 5th series*, vol. 378. Third volume of session 1941–42 (24 February–26 March 1942), London, 1942, cols 638, 1048–49.

36. Andreas Hillgruber, *Hitler, König Carol und Marschall Antonescu. Die Deutsch–Rumanischen Beziehungen, 1938–1944* (Wiesbaden: Franz Steiner Verlag, 1965), p. 241.
37. *Evreii din România între anii 1940–1944*. Vol. IV, *1943–1944: Bilanţul Tragediei – Renaşterea Speranţei*, ed. Ion Şerbănescu (Bucharest: Editura Hasefer, 1998), p. 359.
38. Watts, *Romanian Cassandra*, p. 368.
39. Ibid. The report came from the Jewish office of the *Abteilung Deutschland*.
40. *Antonescu–Hitler. Corespondenţă şi întîlniri inedite (1940–1944)*, vol. 2, ed. Vasile Arimia, Ion Ardeleanu and Ştefan Lache (Bucharest: Cozia, 1991), p. 83.
41. Ibid., p. 91.
42. Ofer, *Escaping the Holocaust*, p. 189.
43. *Evreii din Romania intre anii 1940–1944*. Vol. IV, doc. 327, p. 366.
44. Ibid., doc. 321, p. 360.
45. Ibid., doc. 331, p. 368.
46. Mossad was originally established to assist Jewish refugees from Nazi Germany. It was formally given the task of gathering intelligence for Israel on 1 April 1951 under that name. The Institute for Intelligence and Special Tasks [ha-Mossad le-Modiin ule-Tafkidim Meyuhadim].
47. Ofer, *Escaping the Holocaust*, p. 245.
48. Literally, the Romanian Bureau, the Agency for Transports.
49. The Mossad centre of operations for rescuing Jews from Europe had moved from Paris to Geneva in November 1939.
50. Ofer, *Escaping the Holocaust*, p. 250.
51. Jean-Claude Favez, *The Red Cross and the Holocaust*, ed. and transl. John and Beryl Fletcher (Cambridge: Cambridge University Press, 1999), p. 212.
52. Ibid., pp. 212–13.
53. *Evreii din Romania intre anii 1940–1944*. Vol. IV, doc. 336, pp. 373–4, doc. 338, pp. 375–6. A lack of coordination with the emigration committee of the New Zionist Movement and a delay in obtaining Red Cross protection for the vessel meant that the *Bellacitta* did not sail until April 1944. Other problems prevented the departure of the *Milka* until mid-March and of the *Maritsa* until April. See Ofer, *Escaping the Holocaust*, pp. 250–2.
54. Ibid., doc. 344, p. 381.
55. *Evreii din Romania intre anii 1940–1944*. Vol. IV, doc. 379, p. 414.
56. Ofer, *Escaping the Holocaust*, pp. 195–7.
57. Quoted ibid., p. 265.

58. Mihai Antonescu had given this undertaken to Charles Kolb, the representative of the International Red Cross, at a meeting with him in Bucharest on 1 June 1944. See *Evreii din Romania intre anii 1940–1944*. Vol. IV, doc. 360, p. 399.

59. *Martiriul Evreilor din România, 1940–1944*, no. 105, p. 218.

60. At a meeting of the Council of Internal Administration, held on 16 April 1943 and attended by the Minister of the Interior and the chiefs of police, the decision was taken that such Jews should be 'released from labour camps and settled in the areas in Transnistria to which other Jews had been evacuated. In no case would they have the right to return to Romania'. Ministerul Afacerilor Interne, trial of Ion Antonescu, file 40010, vol. 8, p. 112.

61. On 12 October 1943, he addressed a memorandum to the Romanian government proposing that the deported Jews be brought back to their places of domicile in Romania. Carp, *Cartea Neagră*, pp. 446–7.

62. Ibid.

63. USHMM. Central Archives of the Republic of Moldavia, RG.54.001M, reel 18, file 46372. A gendarmerie register of Jews who completed their term of punishment by forced labour between 14and 19 October 1943 listed 26 Jews from Golta camp, eight from Ananiev, and one each from Balta and Berezovka. USHMM. Czernowitz Archive. RG.31.006M, reel 12. no file number. Another group of 31 Jews 'evacuated from the town of Golta' were reported to have passed through Ungheni station on 14 January 1944, some with Timişoara as their destination, others with Arad. The message, from the police chief in Bălţi, does not specify the grounds for their release USHMM. Central Archives of the Republic of Moldavia, RG. 54.001M, reel 17, file 680.1/4634.2.

64. Carp, *Cartea Neagră*, pp. 446–7 .

65. USHMM, RG.25.004M Records of the Romanian Information Service, reel 13, file 2757/82, p. 38.

66. Ibid.

67. Ibid., p. 39.

68. USHMM, RG.25.004M Records of the Romanian Information Service, reel 13, file 2757/82, p. 39.

69. USHMM, RG.25.004M Records of the Romanian Information Service, reel 14, file 2757/82, p. 40.

70. Ibid.

71. Carp, *Cartea Neagră*, p. 410. At the Council of Ministers' meeting of 13 October 1942, General Vasiliu, the Under-Secretary at the Ministry of Internal Affairs, reported that Jewish Communists and Jews who had requested repatriation to the Soviet Union following the Soviet annexation of Bessarabia and northern Bukovina numbered 2,161, Of these, 1,538 had been sent to Transnistria. *Evreii din România între anii 1940–1944*. Vol. II, doc. 147, p. 455.

72. Ibid., doc. 178, p. 535.

73. Ibid., doc. 180, p. 541.

74. Watts, *Romanian Cassandra*, p. 372.

75. *Evreii din România între anii 1940–1944*. Vol. IV, p. 296.

76. Carp, *Cartea Neagră*. p. 412.

77. *Evreii din Romania intre anii 1940–1944*. Vol. IV, doc. 346, p. 382. Antonescu's indecision over repatriation is charted by, Ioanid, 'The Antonescu Era', pp. 249–58.

78. Ibid., p. 298.

79. Ibid., doc. 198, pp. 223–4.

80. *Evreii din România între anii 1940–1944.* Vol. IV, pp. 356–7; see also USHMM, RG.25.004M, reel 30, file 40013, vol. 6, p. 431. A Ministry of Internal Affairs report of 14 March gave the number of Jews in Transnistria on 1 March 1944 as: 31,141 deported from Bukovina; 14,683 from Bessarabia; 82 from the Regat; 553 interned in Grosulovo-Tiraspol camp; 60 inmates in the Râbniţa prison. Of this total number of 46,519, 1,974 orphans under the age of 15 had been repatriated to Romania, so that the real total on 1 March was reported as 44,545. Of the numbers from Bukovina and Bessarabia, 1,778 Jews were originally from the Regat and had been caught up in the deportations from the two provinces in 1941. *Evreii din România între anii 1940–1944.* Vol. IV, p. 355. The number of internees in Grosulovo was reported by the Ministry of Internal Affairs on 14 March 1944 as being 656 persons. Ibid., p. 298, n. 1.

81. Three categories of prisoner were distinguished by the Romanian authorities in Râbniţa: 1. Communists brought from prisons in Romania; 2. Communist partisans of both sexes who were Soviet citizens, and captured Soviet parachutists; 3. common law offenders sentenced by the local court in Râbniţa. Court testimony of Major Ştefan Mihăilescu, commander of the Legion of Gendarmes in Râbniţa, given in March 1945, USHMM, RG.25.004M, reel 30, file 40013, vol. 6, p. 340.

82. USHMM, RG.25.004M, reel 30, file 40013, vol. 6, p. 428.

83. Court testimony of Walter Isac, one of the survivors of the massacre (USHMM, RG.25.004M, reel 30, file 40013, vol. 6, p. 379); see also *Evreii din România între anii 1940–1944.* Vol. IV, pp. 299–300. The leader of the Communist youth movement, Andrei Bernard, was among the victims.

84. Dora Litani, *Transnistria* (Tel Aviv, 1981, p. 77) (in Romanian); *Evreii din România între anii 1940–1944.* Vol. IV, pp. 299–300.

85. *Evreii din România între anii 1940–1944.* Vol. IV, p. 358.

86. Randolph L. Braham, *The Romanian Nationalists and the Holocaust: The Political Exploitation of Unfounded Rescue Accounts* (New York; The Rosenthal Institute for Holocaust Studies of the City University of New York, 1998), p. 29.

87. Gustav Richter informed Berlin on the introduction of the law on 6 June; see ibid., p. 29.

88. See *Evreii din România între anii 1940–1944.* Vol. IV, doc. 360, p. 399, fn.

89. Ibid., doc. 360, p. 399.

90. Braham, *The Romanian Nationalists and the Holocaust*, p. 30. The Hungarian Foreign Ministry informed the Romanian legation in Budapest on 3 May of its intention to repatriate Romanian Jews and to give them four to six weeks to prepare for their departure. Mihai Antonescu instructed the legation on 25 May to deal with the repatriation 'of those who have Romanian passports'. *Evreii din România între anii 1940–1944.* Vol. IV, doc. 421, pp. 463–4.

91. Lecca, *Eu i-am salvat pe evreii din România*, p. 289.

92. *Evreii din România între anii 1940–1944.* Vol. IV, doc. 389, p. 429, n. 1.

93. Ibid., doc. 414, p. 456, fn 2.

94. Antonescu's decision is communicated in a note to Eugen Cristescu, head of the Romanian Intelligence service, dated 6 July 1943; see ibid., doc. 389, p. 429.

95. Ibid., doc. 422, p. 464.

96. Lecca, *Eu i-am salvat pe evrei din România*, p. 289; and Braham, *The Romanian Nationalists and the Holocaust*, p. 215, n. 99.

97. Braham, *The Romanian Nationalists and the Holocaust*, p. 33.

98. From the Bucharest representative of two American-based Jewish rescue organizations, dated 28 December 1944; see Randolph L. Braham, *The Politics of Genocide.*

The Holocaust in Hungary (New York: The Rosenthal Institute for Holocaust Studies of the City University of New York, 1994), p. 1040.

99. The ghetto in Cluj was set up on 5 May and contained 18,000 Jews; a Hungarian-language newspaper stated that on 27 May there were 30,000 Jews in the Oradea ghetto; see *Evreii din România între anii 1940–1944*. Vol. IV, p. 462, n. 1. For the fate of the Jews in Oradea, see Téreza Mózes, *Evreii din Oradea* (Bucharest, 1997).

100. Socor survived the war but died shortly afterwards in Brasov; his account of this period is given in *Furtuna deasupra Ardealului* (Storm over Transylvania) (Cluj: Revista 'Tribuna', 1991). See also Moshe Carmilly-Weinberger, *Istoria evreilor din Transilvania (1623–1944)* [The History of the Jews in Transylvania (1623–1944)] (Bucharest: Editura Enciclopedică 1994), pp. 174–8.

101. See his letter to Marton of 30 July 1944 in *Evreii din România între anii 1940–1944*. Vol. IV, doc. 435, p. 477.

102. A list of those who gave assistance to Jews in northern Transylvania is given in ibid., p. 480.

103. Braham, *The Romanian Nationalists and the Holocaust*, p. 31. Braham offers the example of Moses Carmilly-Weinberger, Chief Rabbi of the Neolog community of Cluj, who was smuggled across the border into Romania with his wife on 2 May, just three days before the ghetto was set up in the town. The couple left Constanta on 7 July 1944 for Palestine on a Turkish vessel, the *Kazbek*, chartered with the help of Mossad; see Braham, *The Romanian Nationalists and the Holocaust*, pp. 95–103, 111.

104. *Evreii din România între anii 1940–1944*. Vol. IV, doc. 425, pp. 467–8.

105. Ibid., doc. 433, pp. 475–6.

106. See the case of Eva Semlyen, highlighted by Braham in *The Romanian Nationalists and the Holocaust*, chapter 5.

107. The work of the Turda committee is described in Asher Cohen, *The Halutz Resistance in Hungary, 1942–1944* (New York: The Rosenthal Institute for Holocaust Studies of the City University of New York, 1986); see also Braham, *The Romanian Nationalists and the Holocaust*, p. 32, fn 51.

108. *Evreii din România între anii 1940–1944*. Vol. IV, doc. 367, pp. 403–4.

109. Ibid., doc. 372, p. 408.

110. Quoted Ofer, *Escaping the Holocaust*, p. 265.

111. *Evreii din România între anii 1940–1944*. Vol. III, part 2, doc. 624, p. 375.

112. *Evreii din România între anii 1940–1944*. Vol. IV, p. xx.

113. Dumitru Hincu, *Un licăr în beznă* [A Flicker of Light in the Darkness] (Bucharest: Hasefer, 1987), pp. 11–12.

Chapter 10

1. *The Ciano Diaries 1939–1943*, transl. and ed. Hugh Gibson (Garden City, NY: Doubleday, 1946), p. 568.

2. Ibid., p. 572.

3. Ibid.

4. Ibid., p. 573.

5. *Evreii din Romania intre anii 1940–1944*. Vol. II. *1940–1944: Problema Evreiască în Stenogramele Consiliului de Miniştri*, ed. Lya Benjamin (Bucharest: Hasefer, 1996), doc. 160, p. 501.

6. *Antonescu Hitler. Corespondenţă şi întîlniri inedite (1940–1944)*, vol. 2, ed. Vasile Arimia, Ion Ardeleanu and Ştefan Lache (Bucharest: Cozia, 1991), pp. 68–73. See also Dinu Giurescu, *România în al doilea război mondial* (Bucharest: All, 1999), pp. 189–90.

7. *Antonescu–Hitler*, p. 80.

8. Spitzmuller joined the French legation in Bucharest as first secretary in April 1938. For several of his reports to Paris, see Ottmar Trasca and Ana-Maria Stan, *Rebeliunea legionară în documente* străine [The Iron Guard Rebellion in Foreign Documents] (Bucharest: Albatros, 2002), passim.

9. Gheorghe Buzatu, *Mareşalul Antonescu în faţa istoriei*, vol. 1 (Iaşi, 1990), pp. 388–91.

10. Antonescu gave his reasons for rejecting an armistice at his trial in May 1946: 'In the first place I was afraid of losing the benefits of the Atlantic Charter and the benefit we derived from the public declarations made in the British parliament by Mr Churchill and Mr Eden .... The Atlantic Charter stated categorically "we will not recognize at the end of the war any change of frontier which has not been freely agreed." Somewhat later – that was in August 1941 – somewhat later Mr Eden repeated the same declaration in parliament and said: "We will not recognize frontiers which have not been freely agreed." ... Then the Russian armistice comes. What we the conditions laid out in this armistice? That we should accept the cession of Bessarabia and Bukovina. Acceptance would have meant the loss of the benefits of the Atlantic Charter and of Mr Eden's declarations. And so I, Marshal Antonescu, without any political party behind me, with only two plebiscites as political authority, could not assume the historical responsibility in the face of the present generation and in the face of past ones, that I had ceded Bessarabia .... Both Mr Maniu and Mr Mihalache, and Mr Dinu Brătianu and all the other politicians asked me on several occasions to conclude an armistice and I said, "I cannot conclude an armistice because of that problem, I cannot conclude an armistice because it requires me to turn my arms against Germany and I am a soldier and a man of honour and I cannot do that .... I offered to turn over control of the state to them .... I told His Majesty the King several times .... I got a negative reply. All the time I was told that I must conclude the armistice. So I gave up [on offering to hand over power] ...' Marcel-Dumitru Ciucă (ed.), *Procesul Mareşalului Antonescu. Documente*, vol. 1 (Bucharest: Editura Saeculum, Editura Europa Nova, 1995), pp. 213–14.

11. The source of the memorandum is unclear. It is unsigned, but bears the stamp of the Romanian Intelligence Service (SSI) certifying that it had been catalogued. In parts, it seems to be a verbatim record of a conversation between Antonescu and Maniu.

12. ANIC, Ministerul Afacerilor Interne (Ministry of Internal Affairs). Trial of Ion Antonescu, file 40010, vol. 34, pp. 140–3.

13. *Antonescu Hitler*, p. 144.

14. The plan for the occupation of Hungary was codenamed 'Margarethe I' and that of Romania 'Margarethe II'; see Klaus Schönherr, 'Die Auswirkungen der militärischen Situation 1944 auf die Deutsch-Rumänischen Beziehungen', *Revue roumaine d'histoire*, vol. 38, nos 1–4 (1999), p. 176, n. 71.

15. *Evreii din Romania intre anii 1940–1944*. Vol. II, doc. 187, p. 557.

16. *Procesul Mareşalului Antonescu. Documente*, vol. 1, p. 211. Antonescu's assertion that he had never been to Germany before August 1944 on his own initiative overlooks his request to meet Hitler in January 1941 to express his concern about the Iron Guard's activities. He travelled to Obersalzburg to meet the Führer on 14 January 1941.

17. It should be emphasized that no one on the Romanian side, be it the Marshal, Mihai Antonescu or Maniu, was able to secure the joint agreement of the Americans, British and Russians to the conditional armistice proposals which it made between December 1943 and April 1944 in Stockholm (to the Russians) and in Cairo (to all three Allies). Eventually, agreement on armistice terms was reached with Britain and the US in Cairo in April 1944 and confirmed by the Russians through the Stockholm channel in June. However, no Romanian representative was empowered by Antonescu to sign them. For an analysis of the *coup*, see Dennis Deletant, *Communist Terror in Romania. Gheorghiu-Dej and the Police State, 1948–1965* (London: Hurst, 1999), chapter 3.

18. 'Report of Lt.-Col. A. G. G. de Chastelain on the 'Autonomous' Mission, dated September 1944', in *23 August 1944. Documente*, vol. II, ed. I. Ardeleanu, V. Arimia and M. Muşat (Bucharest: Editura Ştiinţifică şi Enciclopedică, 1984), p. 802.

19. Set up in July 1940 by Winston Churchill 'in order to set Europe ablaze'. A second SOE mission to Romania, codenamed 'Autonomous' and undertaken by Alfred de Chastelain, Ivor Porter and a Romanian, Silviu Metianu, was parachuted into southern Romania at 00.30 hours on 22 December 1943. De Chastelain's task was to inform Maniu personally of Stalin's apparent change of heart in agreeing to a discussion of terms of 'unconditional surrender' by the Romanians. The group was arrested shortly after landing and held in Bucharest by the Romanians until 23 August 1944. See Ivor Porter, *Operation Autonomous: With S.O.E. in Wartime Romania* (London: Chatto and Windus, 1989).

20. The National Archives of the United States, Washington, DC, General Records of the Department of State (R.G. 59), European War, 74000119, EW 1939/2057. Reproduced in *23 August 1944*, doc. 456.

21. The Soviet official in question was a man named Spitchkine whom the Special Operations Executive surmised was acting independently of his Minister, Madame Alexandra Kollontay. Elisabeth Barker, *British Policy in South-East Europe in the Second World War* (London: Macmillan, 1976), p. 229.

22. *Foreign Relations of the United States, 1944*, vol. IV (Washington, DC: US Department of State), p. 170. The terms were also passed to the Romanian minister in Stockholm by the Soviet chargé who transmitted them on the same day (13 April) to Bucharest. See Buzatu, *Mareşalul Antonescu în faţa istoriei*, pp. 418–20; and Ivor Porter, *Michael of Romania. The King and the Country* (London: Sutton, 2005), p. 94.

23. Barker, *British Policy in South-East Europe in the Second World War*, p. 233.

24. *Culegere de documente şi materiale privind Istoria României (6 septembrie 1940 23 August 1944)* [Collection of Documents and Materials Regarding the History of Romania], ed. Ion Scurtu et al. (Bucharest: University of Bucharest, 1978), pp. 219–20. I thank Viorel Achim for showing me this anthology.

25. Barker, *British Policy in South-East Europe in the Second World War*, p. 140.

26. Ibid, p. 237.

27. Ibid., p. 238.

28. Interview with Corneliu Coposu, 31 October 1991. In a paper presented at a symposium in Paris on 22 May 1994, Coposu disclosed, in his capacity as Maniu's secretary and the person responsible for enciphering and deciphering Maniu's telegrams in the British code sent via Ţurcanu to Cairo, that in response to Novikov's suggestion to Vişoianu that the Romanian opposition should involve the section of the Comintern in Romania, Novikov was told that the number of Communists in Romania identified by the SSI (Romanian Intelligence) was 845,

of whom 720 were foreigners. In reply, Maniu was told that it was common knowledge that a section of the Comintern in Romania did not exist, but that public opinion abroad had to have the impression of the existence of a homogeneous opposition embracing all social and political categories. Maniu said that, in that case, he had nothing against the enlargement of the opposition. However, none of the Communists contacted in Romania claimed to be the true representatives of the Romanian Communist Party. With some satisfaction, Maniu cabled Novikov for his direction as to who was official representative of the Comintern in Romania and Novikov replied: 'Lucreţiu Pătrăşcanu'. 'Exilul Românesc: Identitate şi Conştiinţă istorică,' *Lupta*, no. 232 (7 October 1994), p. 5. According to Communist historiography, the meeting of 4 April in Târgu-Jiu is alleged to have instructed Pătrăşcanu, Bodnăraş and Ion Gheorge Maurer to join the other political parties in an effort to extract Romania from the war with the Soviet Union. A few days later, Pătrăşcanu negotiated an agreement with Titel Petrescu, the leader of the Social Democratic Party, to set up a United Workers' Front. Bodnăraş made his first appearance at a sub-committee charged with the preparation of plans for the defence of Bucharest on 13 June although according to one account the main purpose was to discuss future relations with Moscow. Ioan Hudita, 'Pagini de Jurnal', *Magazin Istoric*, vol. 28, no. 7 (July 1994), p. 41.

29. Iosif Şraier, the Communist Party's legal representative, conducted negotiations with Iuliu Maniu and Prince Ştirbey in preparation for the 23 August *coup*. One source claims that he received full authority from Moscow in his conversations with Maniu which initially he conducted alone. Later, he acted as Lucreţiu Pătrăşcanu's liaison in the negotiations between the Communist Party and the other members of the National Democratic Bloc. Before the Groza cabinet was reorganized in January 1946 he hoped to become Minister of the Interior, but with his political ambitions frustrated, he left Romania later that year. 'List of Roumanian Personalities, 1947', Report no. 262, 3 November 1947, Public Record Office, London, FO/371/67272 B.

30. For his biography see Dennis Deletant, *Communist Terror in Romania: Gheorghiu-Dej and the Police State* (London: Hurst, 1999), pp. 41–3.

31. On 11 June 1941, the Minister of the Interior, General D. Popescu, transmitted Ion Antonescu's order to General E. Leoveanu, Director General of Police, that the gendarmerie should be prepared to arrest all Communists between 15 and 20 June. Ministerul Afacerilor Interne, file 40010, vol. 11, p. 87.

32. Porter, *Operation Autonomous*, p. 175.

33. Barker, *British Policy in South-East Europe in the Second World War*, p. 239.

34. Titus Gârbea; see Buzatu, *Mareşalul Antonescu în faţa istoriei*, p. 487.

35. *Antonescu Hitler*, p. 173.

36. On 4 April 1944, 220 B-17 Fortresses and 93 B-24 Liberators of the 15th USAAF, escorted by 120 fighters, had dropped over 860 tons of bombs on railway yards at Chitila in the north-west part of Bucharest. Unknown to the raiders, trains carrying refugees from Moldovia were waiting in the yards. One report put the death toll at over 3,000 (PRO, FO 371/44001).

37. The southern offensive was launched from Tiraspol and aimed at Izmail, Constanţa and Bulgaria.

38. Baron Ion de Mocsonyi-Styrcea was born at Cernăuţi on 16 May 1909. He graduated from Cambridge with a degree in modern languages in 1932 and joined the Romanian Foreign Ministry two years later. Between 1 April and 11 August 1942 he was private secretary to King Michael and head of the royal

chancery, and from the latter date until 1 April 1944 served as acting Marshal of the royal court. On 23 August 1944 he was made Marshal of the court, a position from which he resigned on 4 November 1944 for health reasons, but he remained on the roll of the Foreign Ministry until the purge of non-Communist employees on 6 March 1946. He spent much of the period between September 1947 and November 1962 in prison on charges fabricated by the Communists. He was allowed to leave Romania on 4 September 1964 and settled in Switzerland (letter from Mocsonyi-Styrcea to this author, 4 August 1984).

39. Porter, *Michael of Romania*, pp. 192–3.
40. Letter from Mocsonyi-Styrcea to this author, 4 August 1984; see also Porter, *Michael of Romania*, p. 104.
41. See Nicholas Baciu, *Sell-Out to Stalin. The Tragic Errors of Churchill and Roosevelt* (New York: Vantage Press, 1984), p. 147. The courier in question, Neagu Djuvara, made it quite clear to his audience at the fiftieth anniversary symposium on '23 August 1944 in the history of Romania', held in Bucharest on 8–9 October 1994 (to which King Michael had accepted an invitation but was refused entry to Romania by the authorities), that Mihai Antonescu, with the Marshal's approval, had merely told Nanu to approach Madame Kollontay to ask whether the earlier conditions given by the Russians were still valid or would have to be negotiated. At the same time, Djuvara revealed, Mihai Antonescu instructed Nanu not to tell the British and Americans of this approach to the Soviets. Mihai Antonescu did not, as Nanu later claimed, tell him that the Marshal was ready to withdraw from the war and had given Mihai a free hand to sign the armistice. F. C. Nano, 'The First Soviet Double-Cross: A Chapter in the Secret History of World War II', *Journal of Central European Affairs*, vol. 12, no. 3 (October 1952), pp. 236–58. As Djuvara remarked, the events in the three-month period since the issue of the Russian conditions had rendered many of them irrelevant and the mere raising of the question as to whether they were still valid showed how out of touch with reality the two Antonescus were.
42. At his trial in May 1946 the Marshal recalled his meeting with Brătianu: 'And I said then, to Mr Gheorghe Brătianu: "Look here, Mr Brătianu, I have abandoned the idea of not concluding an armistice, I shall conclude it, but I need these letters of guarantee because I cannot assume the historical responsibility for destroying the Romanian people.... So, commit yourselves, accept your responsibility in writing, not verbally in words which are forgotten and which can be denied tomorrow." And then Mr Brătianu replied: "I'll go and bring you the letters, both of them, from Mr [Dinu] Brătianu as well, at 3pm." He did not come at 3 pm, I went to the palace...'. Ciucă (ed.), *Procesul Mareşalului Antonescu*, p. 215.
43. This account of events on 23 August is taken from M. Ionniţiu, '23 August 1944. Amintiri şi reflecţiuni', *Revista istorică*, vol. 2, nos 9–10 (1991), pp. 557–75; and Porter, *Operation Autonomous*, pp. 198–202.
44. Porter, *Michael of Romania*, p. 109.
45. Ionniţiu, '23 August 1944', p. 570.
46. This is the view of Ionniţiu.
47. On Strada Sighişoara. Among this group of armed civilians was Ştefan Mladin, who for a period after 23 August was one of those responsible for the bodyguard of Gheorghiu-Dej.
48. General Dumitru Popescu, Minister of the Interior, Eugen Cristescu and Radu Lecca were also arrested later.

49. The order was transmitted by General (later Marshal) Rodion Malinovski, Commander of the Second Ukrainian Front and therefore of Soviet operations in Romania, to his deputy Lt.-Gen. Ivan Susaikov.
50. Details taken from a report addressed to Stalin by Malinovski and Susaikov on 2 September 1944; see Ciucă (ed.), *Procesul Mareşalului Antonescu*, pp. 18–19. In an unsigned, handwritten note in the Romanian Intelligence Service files, an eyewitness reported that 'on 31 August 1944, around 5 pm, as I was walking along Vatra Luminoasă Street to catch the no. 26 tram, I was overtaken by a convoy of five vehicles. The first was an open-topped car and carried two civilians wearing the Romanian tricolor armband, and a Soviet officer. The second car had its roof up and had a Soviet soldier seated next to the driver. In the back sat Ion Antonescu and Mihai Antonescu. The third car carried General Pantazi, General Vasiliu and Colonel Elefterescu. The fourth car was open and had three Soviet officers. The fifth vehicle was a large lorry with Soviet troops armed with machine-guns. The convoy went off on Iancului Street in the direction of Pantelimon.' ANIC, Ministerul Afacerilor Interne. Trial of Ion Antonescu, file 40010, vol. 34, pp. 219–20.
51. Ion Pantazi, 'O mărturie indirectă despre 23 august', *Apoziţia* (1980–81), Munich, pp. 20–30; see also the same author's *Am trecut prin iad* (I Passed through Hell) (Sibiu: Constant, 1992), pp. 307–10.

Chapter 11

1. *Conditions of an Armistice with Roumania*, Miscellaneous No. 1 (1945) (London: HMSO, 1945) (Cmd. 6585).
2. Maurice Pearton and Dennis Deletant, 'The Soviet Takeover in Romania, 1944–1948', in *Romania Observed* (Bucharest: Editura Enciclopedică, 1998), p. 145.
3. Maurice Pearton, *Oil and the Romanian State* (London: Oxford University Press, 1971), pp. 265–7.
4. P. Quinlan, *Clash over Romania. British and American Policies Towards Romania: 1938–1947* (Los Angeles: American-Romanian Academy of Arts and Sciences, 1977), p. 109.
5. Hansard, 5th series, vol. 403, col. 488.
6. Winston. S. Churchill, *The Second World War*. Vol. VI, *Triumph and Tragedy* (London: Penguin, 1985), p. 202. See also Elisabeth Barker, *British Policy in South-East Europe in the Second World War* (London: Macmillan, 1976), p. 145.
7. Pearton, *Oil and the Romanian State*, p. 265. For the wider pressures on Churchill at the time, see M. Pearton, 'Puzzles about Percentages', *Occasional Papers in Romanian Studies*, ed. Dennis Deletant (London: SSEES, 1995), no. 1, pp. 7–13.
8. Marcel-Dumitru Ciucă (ed.), *Procesul Mareşalului Antonescu. Documente*, vol. 2 (Bucharest: Editura Saeculum, Editura Europa Nova, 1995), p. 170.
9. These declarations have yet to be published in full.
10. ANIC, Ministerul Afacerilor Interne. Trial of Ion Antonescu, file 40010, vol. 34, p. 251.
11. *Convenţie de armistiţiu* (Bucharest: Ministerul Afacerilor Externe, 1944), p. 9.
12. Quoted John Screen, *Mannerheim: The Finnish Years* (London: Hurst, 2000), p. 227.
13. Law 312 introduced *crima de dezastrul ţarii* (the crime of [bringing] disaster on the country) and *crima de război* (war crime).
14. Others who entered under the incidence of article 2 included prison directors and guards, police and gendarmerie officers, war profiteers, and persons responsible for

ordering the establishment of ghettos or internment camps. See Ciucă (ed.), *Procesul Mareşalului Antonescu. Documente*, vol. 1, p. 55.

15. The drafting of the list of charges against Antonescu began in February 1945.
16. The tribunals were composed of two judges appointed from the legal profession by the Ministry of Justice, and seven 'people's judges', chosen respectively from members of the seven political parties that made up the government.
17. Ciucă (ed.), *Procesul Mareşalului Antonescu. Documente*, vol. 1, p. 26.
18. *Cotidianul. Arhiva*, vol. 5, no. 3 (22 March 1996), p. 3. The list included General Cornel Calotescu, the former Governor of Bucovina. The death sentences were commuted to life imprisonment on 5 June (*Universul*, 6 June 1945). Macici died in Aiud prison on 15 June 1950 of heart failure. Death certificate issued by mayor's office in Aiud, no. 102/1950. See also *Cotidianul. Arhiva*, vol. 5, no. 3 (22 March 1996), p. 7.
19. *România. Viaţa politică în documente. 1946*, ed. Ioan Scurtu (Bucharest: Arhivele Statului, 1996), p. 156, doc. 33.
20. Ciucă (ed.), *Procesul Mareşalului Antonescu. Documente*, vol. 2 (Bucharest: Editura Saeculum, Editura Europa Nova, 1995), pp. 120–1.
21. ANIC, Ministerul de Interne. Trial of Ion Antonescu, file 40010, vol. 36, p. 1.
22. Ciucă (ed.), *Procesul Mareşalului Antonescu. Documente*, vol. 1, p. 184.
23. Ibid., p. 186.
24. The others were Mihai Antonescu (Minister of Justice from 6 June 1940–7 January 1941; Foreign Minister, 21 June 1941–23 August 1944; Minister of Propaganda, 1 April 1941–23 August 1944; Vice-President of the Council of Ministers, 21 June 1941–23 August 1944); Horia Sima (former head of the Legionary Movement; Vice-President of the Council of Ministers, 6 September 1940–24 January 1941) who fled to Germany after the Iron Guard rebellion in January 1941; Constantin Pantazi (Minister of Defence, 22 January 1942–23 August 1944); Constantin Vasiliu (Head of the Gendarmerie, 6 September 1940–23 August 1944); Titus Dragoş (Under-Secretary in the Ministry of Romanianization 6 December 1941–5 November 1943); Gheorghe Dobre (Under-Secretary for army procurement, 6 September 1940–16 November 1942, then Minister of the National Economy, 19 February 1943–23 August 1944); Ion Marinescu (Minister of the National Economy, 20 May 1941–14 August 1942, Minister of Justice, 14 August 1942–23 August 1944)); Traian Brăileanu (Minister of Education, 14 September 1940–27 January 1941); Dumitru Popescu (Minister of Internal Affairs, 20 January 1941–23 August 1944); Constantin Petrovicescu (Minister of Internal Affairs, 6 September 1940–21 January 1941); Constantin Dănulescu (Under-Secretary in the Ministry of Labour, 9 July 1941–24 June 1943); Constantin Buşilă (Ministry of Public Works, 9 July 1941–6 October 1943); Nicolae Mareş (Minister of Agriculture, 15 September 1940–23 January 1941); Petre Tomescu (Minister of Labour and Health, 27 January 1941–23 August 1944); Vasile Dimitriuc (Under-Secretary in the Ministry of National Economy, 14 September 1940–26 May 1941); Mihail Sturdza (Foreign Minister, 14 September 1940–27 January 1941); Ion Protopopescu (Minister of Communications, 24 October 1940–27 January 1941); Corneliu Georgescu (Minister, 14 September 1940–27 January 1941); Constantin Papanace (Under-Secretary in the Ministry of Finance, 14 September 1940–24 January 1941); Vasile Iaşinschi (Minister of Health, 14 September 1940–27 January 1941); Gheorghe Alexianu (Governor of Transnistria, 19 August 1941–February 1944);

Radu Lecca (Plenipotentiary for Jewish Affairs); Eugen Cristescu (Head of the Security Intelligence Police, 15 November 1940–23 August 1944).

25. Reuben H. Markham, *Rumania under the Soviet Yoke* (Boston: Meador, 1949), p. 156.

26. The Control Commission officers were Lt.-Col. Kushmin, Major Smirnov (Soviet mission), Major Hann (US mission), and Captain Key (British mission). Representatives of the foreign press included Leonard Kirschen of Associated Press, Reuben Markham of the Christian Science Monitor, and I. Lubo of TASS. Markham was expelled from the country later that year.

27. 'Ion Antonescu e un militar mistic', *Dosarele Historia*, vol. 1, no. 3 (May 2002), p. 24. Reuben Markham gave this description of Antonescu's deportment: 'Antonescu conducted himself calmly and with dignity; he looked Russia straight in the eye and refused to apologize for fighting against her. He even repeated that he had fought to win. Many Romanians felt his bearing symbolized their self-respect, and were grateful for such a symbol. They couldn't help but rejoice when they saw a Rumanian stand under a Russian gallows and calmly defy Russia'. *Rumania under the Soviet Yoke*, p. 156.

28. Ciucă (ed.), *Procesul Mareşalului Antonescu. Documente*, vol. 1, pp. 192–3.

29. This is the original incomplete syntax.

30. Ciucă (ed.), *Procesul Mareşalului Antonescu. Documente*, vol. 1, pp. 240–1.

31. Romania minus the provinces of Bessarabia and Bukovina. Antonescu used the term 'Ţara Românească' (Romanian land).

32. Antonescu is probably referring to his decree no. 2786 of 19 September 1942, which introduced the death penalty for Jews over 15 deported to Transnistria who returned in a fraudulent manner to Romania. ANIC, Ministerul Afacerilor Interne, Trial of Ion Antonescu, file 40010, vol. 8, p. 317.

33. Ciucă (ed.), *Procesul Mareşalului Antonescu. Documente*, vol. 1 (Bucharest: Editura Saeculum, Editura Europa Nova, 1995), pp. 206–8.

34. Ciucă (ed.), *Procesul Mareşalului Antonescu. Documente*, vol. 1, pp. 210–11.

35. Ibid., pp. 204–5.

36. ANIC, Ministerul Afacerilor Interne, Trial of Ion Antonescu, file 40010, vol. 7.

37. Ibid., vol. 2, p. 309. Another power of attorney, signed by Antonescu, was issued in favour of lawyers named as Constantin Simionescu Iaşi and Constantin Stroe. ANIC, Ministerul Afacerilor Interne, Trial of Ion Antonescu, file 40010, vol. 6, p. 8.

38. The text of its decision can be found in Ciucă (ed.), *Procesul Mareşalului Antonescu. Documente*, vol. 2, pp. 312–419.

39. At the end of his evidence on behalf of Antonescu, Maniu went over to the accused and shook his hand. The Communist press reacted vehemently in condemnation of this gesture.

40. Telegram of 15 May 1946 to State Department. Quoted Ciucă (ed.), *Procesul Mareşalului Antonescu. Documente*, vol. 2, pp. 188–9.

41. Telegrams no. 56 of 11 June 1946 from Jean-Paul Boncour, French representative in Romania, to French Foreign Ministry, *Lupta*, no. 67, p. 5. Quoted Claudiu Secaşiu, 'Regele Mihai şi executarea Mareşalului Antonescu. Adevăr şi Legendă [King Michael and Marshal Antonescu's Execution. Truth and Legend]', *Cotidianul. Supliment Cultural* (8 July 1991), p. 5.

42. Ibid.

43. Telegram of 28 May 1946 to State Department. Quoted Ciucă (ed.), *Procesul Mareşalului Antonescu. Documente*, vol. 2, pp. 367–8.

44. Secaşiu, 'Regele Mihai şi executarea Mareşalului Antonescu', p. 5.

45. Among those arrested was General Aurel Aldea, the Defence Minister after the 23 August *coup*; Constantin Brătianu, the leader of the National Liberals, was placed under house arrest.
46. His mother's appeal was simple and moving: 'Your Majesty, the undersigned Lița col. Baranga, aged 88, appeal with tears in my eyes to Your Majesty's magnanimity to be kind enough to grant the supreme clemency of commuting the death penalty given by the People's Tribunal on 17 May to my only son, Ion Antonescu. With firm hope in the boundless concern of Your Majesty and in the understanding of the misfortune which has befallen me, I remain Your Majesty's most humble servant Lița col. Baranga'. Ciucă (ed.), *Procesul Mareşalului Antonescu. Documente*, vol. 2, p. 421.
47. Secaşiu, 'Regele Mihai şi executarea Mareşalului Antonescu', p. 5.
48. Arthur Gould Lee, *Crown against Sickle. The Story of King Michael of Rumania* (London: Hutchinson, 1950), p. 139.
49. Telegram no. 480–81 of 8 June from J. P. Boncour to French Foreign Ministry, quoted Secaşiu, 'Regele Mihai şi executarea Mareşalului Antonescu', p. 5.
50. Ibid.
51. Ibid.
52. Ciucă (ed.), *Procesul Mareşalului Antonescu. Documente*, vol. 2, p. 423.
53. The reason why Cristescu's sentence was commuted was explained by Pătrăşcanu during his own interrogation after his arrest in 1948 as an alleged 'Anglo-American spy'. Pătrăşcanu stated that after the death sentences had been passed, a close friend of Cristescu's wife came to see him and told him that Cristescu was ready to reveal all the names of the British Intelligence agents active in Romania. He therefore commuted Cristescu's death sentence to life imprisonment and went to the Palace with only four names. He showed the list of those whose sentences had been commuted and those who were to be executed to two persons on the Control Commission, where he went first of all, and then to one of the Communist Party leaders. Cristian Popişteanu, '23 August. Mărturii inedite din procesul Lucreţiu Pătrăşcanu', *Magazin Istoric*, no. 8 (1991), p. 52. Lecca was released from prison on 15 April 1963 after his initial sentence was reduced to 18 years and six months; see *Eu i-am salvat pe evrei din România* (Bucharest: Roza Vânturilor, 1994), p. 40.
54. Ciucă (ed.), *Procesul Mareşalului Antonescu. Documente*, vol. 2, p. 427. In fact, it was the Groza government which rejected the pleas for clemency; commutation of the sentence was in its gift only. A list of the names of the seven persons sentenced to death has respectively the handwritten notation of 'execution' and 'commutation' alongside them and is signed by Petru Groza (ibid.). In an interview granted to Mircea Ciobanu in 1991 King Michael confirmed that the Marshal had refused to ask for clemency and that his lawyer had done so on his behalf: '*King Michael*: I tried everything I could to deliver him [the Marshal] and Mihai Antonescu from the hands of the Communists. *Ciobanu*: Who did you talk to about clemency? *King Michael*: To Pătrăşcanu and Groza. My entreaties were to no avail. They were under the influence of the Soviets, they had to implement a decision. They were not persuaded by any argument. I have the heartfelt conviction that it was with a heavy heart that Pătrăşcanu opposed clemency. The decision had been taken before the Marshal had been brought to Bucharest. And now some people are trying to say that I killed him. That the Marshal requested clemency. He did not! Even had he known that he would receive it, he still would not have asked for it. And had it been

granted to him, he would have refused it.' Mircea Ciobanu, *Convorbiri cu Mihai I al României* (Bucharest: Humanitas, 1991), pp. 159–60.

55. He instructed the chief procurator of Ilfov county – the location of Jilava jail – to carry out the executions. See Ciucă (ed.), *Procesul Mareşalului Antonescu. Documente*, vol. 2, p. 28.

56. Their names were Alfred Petrescu and Gheorghe Săndulescu (procurators), Gheorghe Colac (stenographer), Colonel Dumitru Pristavu (commandant), Mihail Gavrilovici (Ministry of Internal Affairs) and Teodor Totolici (prison chaplain); see *Dosarele Historia*, vol. 1, no. 3 (May 2002), p. 33.

57. Markham, *Rumania under the Soviet Yoke*, pp. 156–7.

58. This author heard it regularly in private circles in the 1970s and 1980s. For a recent expression in Romania see *Dosarele Historia*, vol. 1, no. 3 (May 2002), p. 35: 'Antonescu survived the first volley of shots, got to his feet, and then shouted: "Fire again, you wretches, for I am still alive. You cannot kill me that easily."'

59. Constitutionally, the king was commander-in-chief of the army.

60. *Dosarele Historia*, vol. 1, no. 3 (May 2002), p. 35; *Romania libera, Aldine*, no. 318 (1 June 2002), p. 4.

61. Archive of the Romanian Information Service (ASRI), fond D, file 8200, vol. 35, pp. 15–16; Ciucă (ed.), *Procesul Mareşalului Antonescu. Documente*, vol. 2, p. 453. Antonescu's wish that his wife 'withdraw to a monastery' had an ironic twist. On 14 September 1944, Maria Antonescu (1892–1964) was arrested in a village where she had been given shelter by a friend of her personal secretary. She was taken to Moscow on 18 March 1945 and interrogated only once by the Soviet authorities. She was returned to Romania in April 1946 at the same time as her husband, but allowed her liberty, living off the charity of relatives and friends. In 1950, she was re-arrested and interned alongside other women political prisoners in the nunnery of Mislea north of Bucharest where she spent the following five years. She was released into 'obligatory domicile' in a village to the east of Bucharest. Plagued by heart problems, she died of a heart attack in a Bucharest hospital on 18 October 1964.

62. Decree no. 455 of 22 June 1946.

Chapter 12

1. I have borrowed this term and the definitions of the strategies from Wim P. van Meurs, 'Romanian Expansion beyond the Dniester', *Romania and World War II. România şi cel de-al doilea război mondial* (Iaşi: The Centre for Romanian Studies, 1996), p. 140.

2. Ibid.

3. Marcel Fontaine, *La République populaire roumaine contre la culture française*, (Paris: Fundaţia Regală Universitară Carol 1, 1962), p. 31.

4. *Publicaţiile interzise* [Forbidden Publications] (Bucharest, 1948), p. 15.

5. For these points see van Meurs, 'Romanian Expansion beyond the Dniester', p. 142.

6. *Istoria RPR* [The History of the Romanian People's Republic], ed. M. Roller (Bucharest: Editura de Stat Didactică şi Pedagogică, 1952), pp. 638–68.

7. Ibid., p. 656; see also Michael J. Rura, *Reinterpretation of History As a Method of Furthering Communism in Rumania. A Study in Comparative Historiography*, (Washington: Georgetown University Press, 1961), p. 55.

8. van Meurs, 'Romanian Expansion beyond the Dniester', p. 142.

9. Ibid.

10. Ştefan Muşat, 'Coloana a V-a hitleristă în România [The Nazi Fifth Column in Romania]', *Anale de istorie*, no. 6 (1970), pp. 128–44.

11. van Meurs, 'Romanian Expansion beyond the Dniester', p. 145.

12. Dinu C. Giurescu, *Illustrated History of the Romanian People* (Bucharest: Editura Sport-Turism, 1981), p. 559.

13. van Meurs, 'Romanian Expansion beyond the Dniester', p. 145.

14. These included A. G. Lee, *Crown against Sickle* (London: Hutchinson, 1950); R. H. Markham, *Rumania under the Soviet Yoke* (Boston: Meador Publishing, 1949); R. Bishop and E. S. Crayfield, *Russia astride the Balkans* (London: Evans, 1949). The historiography of the *coup* is presented in R. R. King, *A History of the Romanian Communist Party* (Stanford, CA: Hoover Institution Press, 1980), pp. 40–3, in M. Shafir, *Romania. Politics, Economics and Society* (London: Frances Pinter, 1985), pp. 30–7, and in H-Ch. Maner, 'Zeitgeschichte Rumäniens als Politikum. Eine Studie über die rumänische Literatur zum 23. August 1944', *Südosteuropa*, 41, no. 6 (1992), pp. 388–412.

15. These points are made by van Meurs, 'Romanian Expansion beyond the Dniester', p. 146.

16. Ilie Ceauşescu, Florin Constantiniu and Mihail E. Ionescu, *Romania. 23 August 1944. 200 Days Spared from World War II* (Bucharest: Editura Ştiinţifică şi Enciclopedică, 1984).

17. N. Ceauşescu, *Romania on the Way of Completing Socialist Construction: Reports, Speeches, Articles*, vol. 1 (Bucharest: Meridiane, 1969), p. 345.

18. Ibid.

19. Ceauşescu, Constantiniu and Ionescu, *Romania. 23 August 1944*, p. 58.

20. Aurel Simion, *Preliminarii politico-diplomatice ale insurecţiei române din august 1944* [The Political and Diplomatic Preliminaries of the Romanian Insurrection of August 1944] (Cluj-Napoca: Editura Dacia, 1979), p. 208.

21. The reasons for that success have been stimulatingly analysed by Katherine Verdery in her profoundly original study of identity and cultural politics entitled *National Ideology under Socialism* (Berkeley: University of California Press, 1991).

22. Bucharest: Editura Albatros, 1975.

23. This observation is made by Adrian Cioroianu in his article 'Antonescu între Hitler şi . . . Ceauşescu', *Dosarele Istoriei*, no. 6 (2002), p. 58.

24. His first novel *Moromeţii* [The Morometes Family], published in 1955 (Bucharest: Editura pentru literatură], had broken the clichés of Socialist Realism, the artistic creed of the Communist Party, and charted the break-up of a peasant family and the loss of parental authority of its domineering head on the eve of the Second World War. A decade later, *Intrusul* (the Intruder) gave an exceptionally realistic portrayal of a young man unable to adapt to the new morality of contemporary urban society, in which the novelist saw a corruption of traditional values (Bucharest: Editura pentru literatură, 1968).

25. Two senior Party figures of the time, Ştefan Andrei and Cornel Burtică, told Adrian Cioroianu that Preda had probably received official backing for his research. Cioroianu, 'Antonescu între Hitler şi . . . Ceauşescu', p. 57.

26. Bucharest: Editura Albatros, 1975.

27. Bucharest: Editura Albatros, 1975.

28. Michael Shafir, 'The Men of the Archangel Revisited: Anti-Semitic Formations among Communist Romania's Intellectuals', *Studies in Comparative Communism*, vol. XVI, no. 3 (Autumn 1983), p. 229.

29. Cioroianu, 'Antonescu între Hitler şi ... Ceauşescu', p. 57.
30. *Delirul*, pp. 152–3.
31. Bucharest: Cartea Românească, 1975, 2nd revised and enlarged edition. The first edition had a print-run of 35,000, the second, 100,000.
32. Cioroianu, 'Antonescu între Hitler şi ... Ceauşescu', p. 58.
33. Mircea Musat and Ion Ardeleanu, *România după Marea Unire* [Romania after the Great Union] (Bucharest: Editura Ştiinţifică şi Enciclopedică, 1988), pp. 1082–1141, 1532–43; see also van Meurs, 'Romanian Expansion beyond the Dniester', pp. 149–50.
34. Gheorghe Romanescu, *Marile Bătălii ale Românilor* [Great Battles of the Romanians] (Bucharest: Editura Sport-Turism, 1982).
35. This is also the case of the maps in the historical atlas *Atlas pentru Istoria României* [An Atlas of Romanian History] (Bucharest: Editura Didactică şi Pedagogică, 1983).
36. *Antonescu. Mareşalul României şi războaiele de reîntregire* [Antonescu. Marshal of Romania ad the Wars of Reunion] (Venice: Nagard, 1986–90).
37. This is amply demonstrated by Michael Shafir, 'Memory, Memorials, and Membership: Romanian Utilitarian Anti-Semitism and Marshal Antonescu', *Romania since 1989. Politics, Economics and Society*, ed. Henry F. Carey (Lanham, MD: Lexington Books, 2004), pp. 67–96.
38. I use the term 'ultra-nationalism' to refer to extreme nationalism, that is, nationalism which is exclusive and rejects anything compatible with liberal institutions. See Roger Griffin, *The Nature of Fascism* (London and New York: Routledge, 1993), p.37; see also Şerban Papacostea, 'Captive Clio: Romanian Historiography under Communist Rule', *European History Quarterly*, vol. 26 (1996), pp. 203–6.
39. John Lukacs, *The Hitler of History* (New York: Alfred A. Knopf, 1998), pp. 50, 124 and 127.
40. Cioroianu, 'Antonescu între Hitler şi ... Ceauşescu', p. 59.
41. As demonstrated by Randolph L. Braham, *Romanian Nationalists and the Holocaust: The Political Exploitation of Unfounded Rescue Accounts* (The Rosenthal Institute for Holocaust Studies, Graduate School of the City University of New York. Distributed by Columbia University Press, 1998).
42. See the examples given by Victor Eskenasy in 'The Holocaust and Romanian Historiography', *The Tragedy of Romanian Jewry*, ed. Randolph L. Braham (The Rosenthal Institute for Holocaust Studies, Graduate Center/City University of New York and Social Science Monographs, Boulder. Distributed by Columbia University Press, 1994), p. 201.
43. Ibid., pp. 209–11.
44. Bucharest: Editura Alma, 1996.
45. Bucharest: Editura Alma Tip, 1997.
46. My parenthesis.
47. Theodoru, *România ca o pradă*, p. 5. At the same time, the word 'Holocaust' was appropriated by some nationalist historians to describe the fate of the peoples in Central and Eastern Europe under Soviet domination. Thus Gheorghe Buzatu, in his *Aşa a început holocaustul împotriva poporului român* [This is How the Holocaust against the Romanian People Began] (Bucharest: Majadahonda, 1995), differentiates the 'Brown Holocaust, unleashed and brutally perpetrated by Adolf Hitler's Germany against the Jews, from the Red Holocaust, initiated and carried out – with the same brutality, if not with a greater one, bearing mind the methods, number of victims and the period concerned – by the Soviet Communist system against the peoples of the countries occupied by the Soviet Union, both during the Second World War as well as, in particular, after

1945, practically throughout the whole of the maintenance of the Communist regimes in East-Central Europe, including Romania' (p. 5).

48. Michael Shafir, 'Memory, Memorials, and Membership: Romanian Utilitarian Anti-Semitism and Marshal Antonescu', *Romania since 1989. Politics, Economics and Society*, ed. Henry F. Carey (Lanham, MD: Lexington Books, 2004), p. 73.

49. *Istoria Românilor de la 1821 până în 1989. Manual pentru clasa a XII-a* (Bucharest: Editura didactică și pedagogică, 1995).

50. 'Alternative' was the label given to textbooks approved by the Ministry of Education but not written according to Ministry precepts.

51. *Istorie. Manual pentru clasa a XII-a* (Bucharest: Editura Sigma, 1999), p. 105.

52. Bucharest: Hasefer, 2001; see also Benjamin's invaluable collections of documents on this same topic, *Evreii din România între anii 1940–1944*. Vol. 1, *Legislația antievreiască* (Bucharest: Hasefer, 1993), and *Evreii din România între anii 1940–1944*. Vol. II, *Problema evreiască în stenogramele Consiliului de Miniștri* (Bucharest: Hasefer, 1996).

53. Bucharest: Editura All, 1999, pp. 94–184.

54. Giurescu, *Illustrated History of the Romanian People*, p. 166.

55. *Cotidianul*, 26 July 2003.

56. *Evenimentul Zilei*, 17 June 2003.

57. See above.

58. *Evenimentul Zilei*, 17 June 2003.

59. See his three-volume work *Transnistria* (Bucharest: Atlas, 1998), and his *Contribuții la Istoria României. Problema Evreiască, 1933–1944* [Contributions to the History of Romania. The Jewish Problem, 1933–1944], 4 vols (Bucharest: Editura Hasefer, 2001, 2003).

60. Bucharest: RAO, 1998.

61. Bucharest, 1946–48. An English translation appeared in Budapest in 1994 under the title *Holocaust in Rumania: Facts and Documents on the Annihilation of Rumania's Jews, 1940–1944*.

62. Alexander Dallin, *Odessa, 1941–1944: A Case Study of Soviet Territory under Foreign Rule* (Iași, Oxford and Portland: *The Centre for Romanian Studies*, 1998), p. 59.

63. Chicago: Ivan R. Dee, 2000.

64. For example, Matatias Carp, *Cartea Neagră. Suferințele Evreilor din România, 1940–1944* [The Black Book. The Sufferings of the Jews in Romania, 1940–1944], 3 vols, ed. Lya Benjamin (Bucharest: Editura Diogene, 1996); *The Tragedy of Romanian Jewry*, ed. Randolph L. Braham (New York: Columbia University Press, 1994); Paul A. Shapiro, 'The Jews of Chișinău (Kishinev): Romanian Reoccupation, Ghettoization, Deportation', in *The Destruction of Romanian and Ukrainian Jews during the Antonescu Era*, ed. Randolph L. Braham (New York: The Rosenthal Institute for Holocaust Studies, City University of New York, Columbia University Press, 1997), p. 141.

65. L. Watts, *Romanian Cassandra. Ion Antonescu and the Struggle for Reform, 1916–1941* (Boulder, CO: East European Monographs, 1993).

66. The strengths and weaknesses of Watts' study are subjected to an intensive and incisive analysis by Paul E. Michelson in a lengthy review article 'In Search of the 20th Century: Marshal Antonescu and Romanian History – A Review Essay', *Romanian Civilization*, vol. III, no. 2 (Fall–Winter 1994).

67. Watts, *Romanian Cassandra*, pp. 378–9.

68. Ibid.

69. Ibid., p. 379.

70. Ibid., p. 377.
71. For example, John Screen, *Mannerheim: The Finnish Years* (London: Hurst, 2000); see his bibliography for other monographs in English.
72. Thomas L. Sakmyster, *Hungary's Admiral on Horseback: Miklos Horthy 1918–1944* (Boulder, CO: East European Monographs. Distributed by Columbia University Press, 1994).
73. Larry Watts, 'Incompatible Alliances: Small States of Central Europe during World War II', *Romania and World War II*, ed. Kurt W. Treptow (Iaşi: The Center for Romanian Studies, 1996), p. 105.
74. I borrow this phrasing from William Oldson, *A Providential Antisemitism: Nationalism and Polity in Nineteenth Century Romania* (Canton, MA: American Philosophical Society, 1991).
75. Watts, *Romanian Cassandra*, pp. 372–3.
76. Radu Ioanid, *The Holocaust in Romania. The Destruction of Jews and Gypsies under Antonescu Regime, 1940–1944* (Chicago: Ivan R. Dee, 2000. Published in association with the United States Holocaust Memorial Museum), p. 157.
77. 'Răspunderea o am eu în faţa istoriei', *Stenogramele Şedinţelor Consiliului de Miniştri. Guvernarea Ion Antonescu.* Vol. IV, *July–September 1941* (Bucharest: Arhivele Naţionale ale României, 2000), p. 587.
78. Mark Axworthy, Cornel Scafeş and Cristian Craciunoiu, *Third Axis, Fourth Ally. Romanian Armed Forces in the European War, 1941–1945* (London: Arms and Armour, 1995), p. 217.
79. Joseph Rothschild, *East-Central Europe between the Two World Wars* (Washington: Washington University Press, 1975), p. 318. Romanian casualties (dead, wounded and missing) for the period 21 June 1941–23 August 1944 were 624,740, and for 23 August 1944 to May 1945, 169,822, giving a total for the whole period of 794,562. Axworthy, Scafeş and Craciunoiu, *Third Axis, Fourth Ally*, p. 217.

Annex

1. Jean Ancel, *Transnistria* (Bucharest: Atlas, 1998), vol. 1, pp. 389–93.

Bibliography

Unpublished primary sources

Archives of the United States Holocaust Memorial Museum
Microfilm collections

Record Group – 25.004M Romanian Information Service (SRI) records.
Fonds 9221, 8958, 8978, 9224, 9311, 9689, 9001, 9684, 9030, 9738, 10528, 10523, 9800, 9705, 9705, 9735, 9738, 10478, 7636, 7633, 7632, 7638, 7642, 7635, 7441, 7642, 10551, 10482, 10611, 10626, 10551, 7374, 10572, 76421, 10585, 10632, 10598, 4087, 4012, 1059810, 7643, 7635, 7635, 7637, 7632, 7633, 7893, 7910, 2686, 2690, 2708, 2748, 2755, 2759, 2789, 2808, 2814, 2801, 7644, 2678, 2687, 2689, 2694, 2699, 2705, 2711, 2713, 2714, 2716, 2740, 2750, 2752, 2753, 2754, 2756, 2757, 2758, 2778, 2790, 2793, 2717, 2718, 2846, 2848, 2841, 2844, 2934, 2983, 3031, 3039, 3022, 2692, 3001, 2960, 3041, 3051, 10362, 2849, 2912, 2869, 8180, 2919, 9721, 1241, 7197, 9614, 8209, 22539, 100399, 40010, rolls 33–35, 40011 (rolls 19–22), 20521, (rolls 23–24), 22725 (roll 24), 20725 (roll 25).

Record Group – 25.006M Romanian Ministry for Foreign Affairs records.
'Problem 33' (Deportation of the Jews)
vols 5–6 (roll 1), vols 6–7 (roll 2), vols 10–11 (roll 3), vols 11–12 (roll 4), vols 13–14 (roll 5), vols 14–15 (roll 6), vol. 16 (roll 7), vol. 17 (roll 8), vols 18–19 (roll 9), vols 20–1 (roll 10), vols 21–22 (roll 11), vol. 23 (roll 12), vol. 24 (roll 13), vols 25–6 (roll 14), vols 26, 28 (roll 15), vols 28, 31 (roll 16), vol. 32 (roll 17).

Record Group-31.004M Selected records from the Odessa Oblast Archives, Ukraine 25 rolls

Record Group-31.006M Selected records from the Czernovitz Oblast Archives, Ukraine

Record Group – 31.008M Selected records from the Nikolaev Oblast Archives, Ukraine
Microfiche 1028/1/86
Microfiche 1432/1/1
Microfiche 2177/3/23
Microfiche 1594/3/10
Microfiche 1594/3/31
Microfiche 2033/2/4
Microfiche 2084/1/220
Microfiche 2084/2/728
Microfiche 2178/1/2–2178/1/67
Microfiche 2418/1/92–2418/1/96

Record Group – 31.011M Selected records from the Vinnitsa Oblast Archive records, Ukraine
34 rolls
Accession A0093. General Inspectorate of the Romanian Gendarmerie
29 rolls

356   *Hitler's Forgotten Ally*

Arhiva Ministerului Afacerilor Externe (Archive of the Ministry for Foreign Affairs, Bucharest)

Fond 71/Germania: vol. 97

Arhiva Ministerului Apărării Naționale (Archive of the Ministry of National Defence, Pitești)

Fond Divizia 10 Infanterie

Arhivele Naționale Istorice Centrale (The Central Historical National Archives, Bucharest)

Fond Președinția Consiliului de Miniştri (Presidency of the Council of Ministers)
Fond Ministerul de Interne (Ministry of the Interior). File 40010: Trial of Ion Antonescu, 44 vols

Consiliul National pentru Studierea Arhivelor fostei Securități (National Council for the Study of the Archives of the former *Securitate* (CNSAS)

Archive of the Romanian Information Service (ASRI), fond D

The National Archives (Public Record Office), London

Foreign Office Records
FO 371: Political correspondence of the Foreign Office

Newspapers

Timpul (1940–44)
Universul (1940–44)

Published collections of documents

23 August 1944. Documente, 4 vols, Bucharest: Editura Ştiinţifică şi Enciclopedică, 1984.
Achim, Viorel (ed.), *Documente privind deportarea Ţiganilor în Transnistria*, 2 vols, Bucharest: Editura Enciclopedică , 2004.
Actes et Documents du Saint Siège Relatifs à la Seconde Guerre Mondiale. 8. Le Saint Siège et les Victimes de la Guerre. Janvier 1941–Decembre 1942, The Vatican: Libreria Editrice Vaticana, 1974.
Arimia, Vasile, Ardeleanu, Ion and Lache, Ştefan, *Antonescu–Hitler. Corespondenţă şi întîlniri inedite (1940–1944)*, 2 vols, Bucharest: Cozia, 1991.
Benjamin Lya (ed.), *Evreii din România între anii 1940–1944*, vol. 1, *Legislaţia antievreiască*, vol. 2, *Problema evreiască în stenogramele Consiliului de Miniştri*, Bucharest: Hasefer, 1993, 1996.
Boberach, Heinz (ed.), *Meldungen aus dem Reich. Die geheimen Lageberichte des Sicherheitsdienstes der SS 1938–1945*, 18 vols, Pawlak, Herrshing, 1984.
Carp, Matatias, *Cartea Neagră* , ed. Lya Benjamin, 3 vols, Bucharest: Diogene, 1996.
Ciucă, Marcel-Dumitru (ed.), *Procesul Mareşalului Antonescu. Documente*, 3 vols, Bucharest: Editura Saeculum, Editura Europa Nova, 1995–98.

Ciucă, Marcel-Dumitru, Teodorescu, Aurelian, Popovici, Bogdan Florin and Ignat Maria (eds), *Stenogramele Şedinţelor Consiliului de Miniştri. Guvernarea Ion Antonescu*, 7 vols, Bucharest: Arhivele Naţionale ale României, 1997–2004.

Conditions of an Armistice with Roumania, Miscellaneous No. 1 (1945), London: HMSO, 1945 (Cmd. 6585).

Documents on British Foreign Policy, 1919–1939, Third Series: 1938–39, 9 vols, London, 1949–55.

Documents on German Foreign Policy, Series D: 1937–1945, 14 vols, Washington, DC, London, and Arlington, Virginia, 1949–76.

Drăgan, Iosif Constantin, *Antonescu. Mareşalul României şi Răsboaiele de Reîntregire*, 4 vols, Venice: Nagard, 1986–90.

Duţu, Alesandru and Botoran, Constantin (eds), *Al Doilea Război Mondial. Situaţia evreilor din România, vol. 1 (1939–1941)* part 1, Cluj-Napoca: Centrul de Studii Transilvane, Fundaţia Culturală Română, 1994.

Duţu, Alesandru, and Retegan, Mihai (eds), *Eliberarea Basarabiei şi a Nordului Bucovinei (22 iunie–26 iulie 1941)*, Bucharest: Editura Fundaţiei Culturale Române, 1999.

Eskenasy, Victor (ed.), *Izvoare şi mărturii referitoare la evreii din România*, Bucharest: Federaţia Comunităţilor Evreieşti din România, 1986.

The Holocaust in Romania. History and Contemporary Significance (no eds), Bucharest: Institute for Political Studies of Defence and Military History, 'Goldstein Goren' Diaspora Research Centre, Tel Aviv University, 'Goldstein Goren' Centre for Hebrew Studies of Bucharest University, 2003.

Michalka, Wolfgang (ed.), *Das Dritte Reich. Dokumente zur Innen-und Aussenpolitik*, 2 vols, Munich, 1985.

Pe Marginea Prăpastiei, 21–23 ianuarie 1941, 2 vols (no ed.), Bucharest: Preşedenţia Consiliului de Miniştri, 1941.

Pelin, Mihai (ed.), *Mareşalul Ion Antonescu. Epistolarul Infernului*, Bucharest: Viitorul Românesc, 1993.

La population juivre de la Transylvanie du Nord, (no ed.), Section de Roumanie du Congrès Juif Mondial, Bucharest, 1945.

România în anii celui de-al doilea război mondial, 3 vols, Bucharest: Editura Militara, 1989.

Duţu, Alesandru et al., *România. Viaţa Politică în Documente*, ed. by Alesandru Duţu et al., Bucharest: Arhivele Naţionale ale României, 2002.

Ross, G. (ed.), *The Foreign Office and the Kremlin. British Documents on Anglo-Soviet Relations, 1941–45*, Cambridge: Cambridge University Press, 1984.

Scurtu, Ion, et al. (eds), *Culegere de documente şi materiale privind Istoria României (6 septembrie 1940–23 August 1944)*, Bucharest: University of Bucharest, 1978.

Scurtu, Ion, *România. Viaţa politică în documente. 1946*, Bucharest: Arhivele Statului, 1996.

Şerbănescu, Ion (ed.), *Evreii din România între anii 1940–1944. Vol. IV. 1943–1944: Bilanţul Tragediei – Renaşterea Speranţei*, Bucharest: Hasefer, 1998.

Trial of the Major War Criminals before the International Military Tribunal, 42 vols, Nuremberg, 1947–49.

Studies

Achim, Viorel, *Ţiganii în istoria României*, Bucharest: Editura Enciclopedică, 1998.

Achim, Viorel and Iordachi, Constantin, *România şi Transnistria: Problema Holocaustului*, Bucharest: Curtea veche, 2004.

Agapie, Mircea, Rotaru, Jipa (eds), *Ion Antonescu. Cariera militară. Scrisori inedite*, Bucharest: Editura Academiei de înalte Studii Militare, 1993.

Ancel, Jean, *Transnistria*, 3 vols, Bucharest: Atlas, 1998.

Ancel, Jean, *Contribuții la Istoria României. Problema Evreiască, 1933–1944*, 4 vols, Bucharest: Hasefer, 2001, 2003.

Ancel, Jean, *Preludiu la asasinat. Pogromul de la Iași, 29 iunie 1941*, Iași: Polirom, 2005.

Angrick, Andrej, *Besatzungspolitik und Massenmord. Die Einsatzgruppe D in der südlichen Sowjetunion, 1941–1943*, Hamburg, 2003.

Axworthy, Mark, Cornel Scafeș and Cristian Craciunoiu, *Third Axis, Fourth Ally. Romanian Armed Forces in the European War, 1941–1945*, London: Arms and Armour, 1995.

Baciu, Nicholas, *Sell-out to Stalin. The Tragic Errors of Churchill and Roosevelt*, New York: Vantage Press, 1984.

Bancoș, Dorel, *Social și național în politica guvernului Ion Antonescu*, Bucharest: Eminescu, 2000.

Barbul, Gheorghe, *Memorial Antonescu, Le IIIe Homme de l'Axe*, Paris: Editions de la Couronne, 1950.

Barker, Elisabeth, *British Policy in South-East Europe in the Second World War*, London: Macmillan, 1976.

Basch, Antonin, *The Danube Basin and the German Economic Sphere*, New York: Columbia University Press, 1943.

Beevor, Antony, *Stalingrad*, London: Penguin, 1998.

Benjamin, Lya (ed.), *Martiriul Evreilor din România, 1940–1944. Documente și Mărturii*, Bucharest: Editura Hasefer, 1991.

Benjamin Lya, *Prigoana și rezistență în istoria everilor din România, 1940–1944*, Bucharest: Hasefer, 2001.

Beza, Gheorghe, *Misiune de război. Al doilea război mondial*, Bucharest: Niculescu, 1994.

Binder, Hermann, *Aufzeichnungen aus Transnistrien 1942*, Munich: Südostdeutsches Kulturwerk, 1998.

Bishop, Robert and Crayfield, E. S., *Russia astride the Balkans*, London: Evans, 1949.

Blet, Pierre, *Pio XII e la Seconda Guerra mondiale negli Archivi Vaticani*, Milan: Edizioni San Paolo, 1999.

Bodea, Gheorghe I., *Tragedia evreilor din nordul Transilvaniei, 1944*, Cluj-Napoca: Hiparion, 2001.

Boia, Eugene, *Romania's Diplomatic Relations with Yugoslavia, 1919–1941*, Boulder, CO: Westview, 1993.

Braham, Randolph L. (ed.), *Genocide and Retribution: The Holocaust in Hungarian-ruled Transylvania*, Boston, The Hague, Dordrecht and Lancaster: Nijhoff, 1983.

Braham, Randolph L. (ed.), *The Tragedy of Romanian Jewry*, The Rosenthal Institute for Holocaust Studies, Graduate Center/City University of New York and Social Science Monographs, Boulder. Distributed by Columbia University Press, 1994.

Braham, Randolph L., *The Politics of Genocide. The Holocaust in Hungary*, New York: The Rosenthal Institute for Holocaust Studies of the City University of New York, 1994.

Braham, Randolph L. (ed.), *The Destruction of Romanian and Ukrainian Jews during the Antonescu Era*, New York: The Rosenthal Institute for Holocaust Studies, City University of New York, Columbia University Press, 1997.

Braham, Randolph L., *Romanian Nationalists and the Holocaust: The Political Exploitation of Unfounded Rescue Accounts*, The Rosenthal Institute for Holocaust Studies, Graduate School of the City University of New York. Distributed by Columbia University Press, 1998.

Brătianu, Dan M. *Martor dintr-o țară încătușată*, Bucharest: Fundația Academia Civică, 1996.

Browning, Christopher R., *The Final Solution and the German Foreign Office. A Study of Referat DIII of Abteilung Deutschland 1940–1943*, New York: Holmes and Meier, 1978.

Bucur, Maria, *Eugenics and Modernization in Interwar Romania*, University of Pittsburgh Press, 2002.

Buzatu, Gheorghe, *Mareșalul Antonescu în fața istoriei*, 2 vols, Iași, 1990.

Buzatu, Gheorghe, *Așa a început Holocaustul împotriva poporului român*, Bucharest: Editura Majadahonda, 1995.

Calafeteanu, Ion, *Români la Hitler*, Bucharest: Univers Enciclopedic, 1999.

Carmilly-Weinberger, Moshe, *Istoria evreilor din Transilvania (1623–1944)*, Bucharest: Editura Enciclopedică 1994.

Ceaușescu, Ilie, Constantiniu, Florin and Ionescu, Mihail E., *Romania. 23 August 1944. 200 Days Spared from World War II*, Bucharest: Editura Științifică și Enciclopedică, 1984.

Chirnoagă, Platon, *Istoria politică și militară a războiului României contra Rusiei sovietice, 22 iunie 1941–23 august 1944*, Iași: Fides, 1998.

Ciobanu, Mircea, *Convorbiri cu Mihai I al României*, Bucharest: Humanitas, 1991.

Cohen, Asher, *The Halutz Resistance in Hungary, 1942–1944*, New York: The Rosenthal Institute for Holocaust Studies of the City University of New York, 1986.

Conclusions of the Report of the International Commission on the Holocaust in Romania at *www.presidency.ro* 'Raportul Comisiei internaționale privind studierea Holocaustului în România' [The Report of the International Commission on the Study of the Holocaust in Romania]. The report is also available on the website of the United States Holocaust Memorial Museum under the title 'Romania, facing the Past' (*www.ushmm.org/research/center*).

Constantiniu, Florin, *O istorie sinceră a poporului român*, Bucharest: Univers Enciclopedic, 1997.

Constantiniu, Florin, *1941. Hitler, Stalin și România*, Bucharest: Univers Enciclopedic, 2002.

Coposu, Corneliu, *Armistițiul din 1944 și implicațiile lui*, Bucharest: Editura Gândirea românească, 1990.

Daghani, Arnold, *Groapa e în livada cu vișini*, ed. Lya Benjamin, Bucharest: Hasefer, 2004.

Dallin, Alexander, *Odessa, 1941–1944: A Case Study of Soviet Territory under Foreign Rule*, Iași, Oxford and Portland: The Centre for Romanian Studies, 1998.

Dan, Ioan, *Procesul Mareșalului Antonescu*, Bucharest: Lucman, 2005.

Deakin, F. W., Barker, E. and Chadwick, J. (eds), *British Political and Military Strategy in Central, Eastern and Southern Europe in 1944*, London: Macmillan, 1988.

Deakin, F. W., *The Brutal Friendship. Mussolini, Hitler and the Fall of Italian Fascism*, London: Phoenix Press, 2000.

Deletant, Dennis and Pearton, Maurice, *Romania Observed*, Bucharest: Editura Enciclopedică, 1998.

Diaconescu, Emil, *Românii din Răsărit: Transnistria*, Iași, 1942.

Drăgan, Iosif Constantin, *Antonescu. Mareșalul României și războaiele de reîntregire*, Milan: Nagard, 1986–90.

Duca, Ion Gheorghe, *Amintiri Politice*, 3 vols, Munich: Ion Dumitru Verlag, 1981.

Dugan, James and Stewart, Carroll, *Ploiești: The Great Ground–Air Battle of 1 August 1943*, New York: Randon House, 1962.

Dumitrache, Ion, *Divizia de cremene. Memorii din campania 1941–1944*, Braşov: Muzeul Judeţean de Istorie, 1997.

Duţu, Alesandru, *Între Wehrmacht şi Armata Roşie*, Bucharest: Editura Enciclopedică, 2000.

Duţu, Alesandru (ed.), *Romania in World War II. 1941–1945*, Bucharest: Sylvi, 1997.

Duţu, Alesandru, and Retegan, Mihai (eds), *Război şi societate. România, 1941–1945*, vol. 1. *De la Prut în Crimeea (22 iunie–8 noiembrie 1941)*, Bucharest: RAO, 1999.

Duţu, Alesandru, and Retegan, Mihai (eds), *Pe Ţărmul Nord Pontic (17 iulie 1941–4 iulie 1942)*, Bucharest: Editura Fundaţiei Culturale Române, 1999.

Faranga, Dumitru, *Jurnal de soldat, 1942–1944*, Bucharest: Editura Militară, 2001.

Furet, François and Nolte, Ernst, *Fascisme et Communisme*, Paris: Plon, 1998.

Georgescu, Vlad, *The Romanians: A History*, Columbus, OH: Ohio State University Press, 1991.

Gheorghe, Ion, *Rümaniens Weg Zum Satellitenstaat*, Heidelburg: Kurt Wonickel Verlag, 1952.

Gibson, Hugh (ed. and transl.), *The Ciano Diaries 1939–1943*, Garden City, NY: Doubleday, 1946.

Giurescu, Dinu, *România în al doilea război mondial*, Bucharest: All, 1999.

Goerlitz, Walter, *Paulus and Stalingrad*, London: Methuen, 1963.

Goma, Paul, *Săptămâna Roşie, 28 iunie–3 iulie 1940*, Chişinău: Museum, 2003.

Halder, Franz, *Kriegstagebuch*, 3 vols, Stuttgart: Kohlhammer Verlag, 1962–64.

Hausleitner, Mariana, *Die Rumänisierung der Bukowina 1918–1944. Die Durchsetzung des nationalstaatlichen Anspruchs Grossrumäniens*, Munich: Oldenbourg, 2001.

Hausleitner, Mariana, *Deutsche und Juden in Bessarabien 1814–1941*, Munich: IKGS Verlag, 2005.

Haynes, Rebecca, *Romanian Policy towards Germany, 1936–40*, London: Macmillan, in association with School of Slavonic and East European Studies, University College, London, 2000.

Heinen, Armin, *Die Legion 'Erzengel Michael' in Rumänien Soziale Bewegung unde Politische Organisation*, Munich: R. Oldenbourg Verlag, 1986.

Hilberg, Raul, *The Destruction of the European Jews*, vol. 1, New York: Holmes and Meier, 1985.

Hillgruber, Andreas, *Hitler, König Carol und Marschall Antonescu. Die Deutsch–Rumänischen Beziehungen, 1938–1944*, Wiesbaden: Franz Steiner Verlag, 1965.

Hillgruber, Andreas, *Staatsmänner und Diplomaten bei Hitler. Vertrauliche Aufzeichnungen über die Unterredunger mit Vertreten des Auslandes 1939–1941*, Munich: Deutscher Taschenbuchverlag, 1969.

Hitchins, Keith, *Rumania 1866–1947*, Oxford: Oxford University Press, 1994.

Holocaustul evreilor români. Din mărturiile supravieţuitorilor, no. ed., Institutul Român de Istorie Recentă, Iaşi: Polirom, 2004.

The Holocaust and Romania. History and Contemporary Significance, no ed., Institute for Political Studies of Defence and Military History, Bucharest, 'Goldstein Goren' Diaspora Research Center, Tel Aviv University, 'Goldstein Goren' Center for Hebrew Studies of Bucharest University, Bucharest, 2003.

Ioanid, Radu, *The Holocaust in Romania. The Destruction of Jews and Gypsies under the Antonescu Regime, 1940–1944*, Chicago: Ivan R. Dee. Published in association with the United States Holocaust Memorial Museum, 2000.

Iordachi, Constantin, *Charisma, Politics and Violence: The Legion of the 'Archangel Michael' in Inter-War Romania*, Trondheim: Trondheim Studies on East European Cultures and Societies, no. 15, 2004.

Jagendorf, Siegfried, *Jagendorf's Foundry: Memoir of the Romanian Holocaust, 1941–1944*, ed. Aron Hirt-Manheimer, New York: HarperCollins, 1991.

Laeuen, Harald, *Marschall Antonescu*, Essen: Essener Verlagsanstalt, 1943.

Lazarev, Artem Markovich, *Moldavskaya sovetskaya gosudarstvennost'* i *bessarabskiy vopros*, Kishinev: Cartea Moldovenească, 1974.

Lecca, Radu, *Eu i-am salvat pe evreii din România*, Bucharest: Editura Roza Vânturilor, 1994.

Lee, Arthur Gould, *Crown against Sickle*, London: Hutchinson, 1950.

Litani, Dora, *Transnistria*, Tel Aviv, 1981 (in Romanian).

Livezeanu, Irina, *Cultural Politics in Greater Romania. Regionalism, Nation Building, and Ethnic Struggle, 1918–1930*, Ithaca, NY and London: Cornell University Press, 1995.

Lukacs, John, *The Hitler of History*, New York: Alfred A. Knopf, 1998.

Macartney, C. A., *A History of Hungary*, vol. 1, New York: Praeger, 1956.

Macdonald, Patrick, *Through Darkness to Light. The Night Bomber Offensive against Romanian Oil, 1944*. Edinburgh: The Pentland Press, 1990.

Marguerat, Philippe, *Le IIIe Reich et le pétrole roumain, 1938–1940: contribution à l'étude de la pénétration économique allemande dans les Balkans à la veille et au début de la Seconde Guerre mondiale*. Leiden and Geneva: A. W. Sijthoff and Institut universitaire de hautes études internationales, 1977.

Markham, Reuben H., *Rumania under the Soviet Yoke*, Boston: Meador Publishing, 1949.

Manuilă, Sabin and Filderman, Wilhelm, *The Jewish Population in Romania during World War II*, Iaşi: The Romanian Cultural Foundation, 1994.

Mózes, Téreza, *Evreii din Oradea*, Bucharest, 1997.

Neubacher, Hermann, *Sonderauftrag Südost, 1940–1945. Bericht ein fliegenden Diplomaten*, Göttingen, 1957.

Neumann, Victor, *Istoria evreilor din România*, Bucharest: Amarcord, 1996.

Nica, Antim, *Viaţa religioasă în Transnistria*, Chişinău, 1943.

Ofer, Dalia, *Escaping the Holocaust*, New York: Oxford University Press, 1990.

Ogorreck, Ralf, *Die Einsatzgruppen und die 'Genesis der Endlösung'*, Berlin: Metropol, 1996.

Oldson, William O., *A Providential Antisemitism: Nationalism and Polity in Nineteenth-Century Romania*, Canton, MA: American Philosophical Society, 1991.

Pantazi, Constantin, *Cu Mareşalul până la moarte*, Bucharest: Publiferom, 1999.

Paxton, Robert O., *The Anatomy of Fascism*, New York: Alfred A. Knopf, 2004.

Payne, Stanley G., *A History of Fascism, 1914–1945*, Madison: University of Wisconsin Press, 1995.

Pearton, Maurice, *Oil and the Romanian State*, Oxford: Oxford University Press, 1971.

Petrencu, Anatol, *Basarabia în al doilea război mondial 1940–1944*, Chişinău: Lyceum, 1997.

Petin, Victor, *Le Drame Roumain 1916–1918*, Paris: Payot, 1932.

Porter, Ivor, *Operation Autonomous: With S.O.E. in Wartime Romania*, London: Chatto and Windus, 1989.

Porter, Ivor, *Michael of Romania. The King and the Country*, London: Sutton, 2005.

Quinlan, Paul D., *Clash over Romania. British and American Policies towards Romania: 1938–1947*, Los Angeles: American Romanian Academy, 1977.

Roberts, Henry L., *Rumania: Political Problems of an Agrarian State*, Oxford: Oxford University Press, 1951.

Rootham, Jasper, *Miss Fire*, London: Chatto and Windus, 1946.

Rotaru, Jipa, Moise, Leonida, Zodian, Vladimir and Oroian, Teofil, *Antonescu–Hitler, Caucazul şi Crimeea*, Bucharest: Paideia, 1999.

Rotaru, Jipa, Burcin, Octavian, Zodian, Vladimir and Moise, Leonida, *Mareşalul Antonescu la Odessa, Grandoarea şi amărăciunea unei victorii*, Bucharest: Paideia, 1999.

Rotaru, Jipa and Damaschin, Ioan, *Glorie şi dramă. Marina Regală Română, 1940–1945*, Bucharest: Editura Ion Cristoiu, 2000.

Rozen, Marcu, *Holocaust sub guvernarea Antonescu*, Bucharest: Asociaţia Evreilor Români Victime ale Holocaustului, 2004.

Safran, Alexandre, *Resisting the Storm: Romania, 1940–1947. Memoirs*, ed. Jean Ancel, Jerusalem: Yad Vashem, 1987.

Sakmyster, Thomas L., *Hungary's Admiral on Horseback: Miklos Horthy 1918–1944*, Boulder, CO: East European Monographs. Distributed by Columbia University Press, 1994.

Schmidt, Paul, *Statist auf diplomatischer Bühne, 1923–45: Erlebnisse des Chefdolmetschers im Auswärtigen Amt mit den Staatsmännern Europas*, Bonn: Athenäum-Verlag, 1949.

Screen, John, *Mannerheim: The Finnish Years*, London: Hurst, 2000.

Seton-Watson, R. W., *A History of the Roumanians*, Cambridge: Cambridge University Press, 1934.

Simion, Aurel, *Preliminarii politico-diplomatice ale insurecţiei române din august 1944*, Cluj-Napoca: Editura Dacia, 1979.

Stafford, David, *Britain and European Resistance, 1940–1945*. Toronto and Buffalo: University of Toronto Press, 1983.

Stoenescu, Alex, Mihai, *Armata, Mareşalul şi Evreii*, Bucharest: RAO, 1998.

Şiperco, Andrei, *Crucea Roşie internaţională şi România, 1939–1944*, Bucharest: Editura Enciclopedică, 1997.

Teodorescu, Eugen, *Plutonul 2 Mitraliere*, Bucharest: Editura Contemporană, n.d.

Tilea, V. V., *Envoy Extraordinary. Memoirs of a Romanian Diplomat*, ed. Ileana Tilea, London: Haggerston Press, 1998.

Tomaziu, George, *Jurnalul unui figurant*, Bucharest: Editura Univers, 1995.

Traşcă, Ottmar, Stan, Ana-Maria, *Rebeliune legionară în documente străine*, Bucharest: Albatros, 2002.

Treptow, Kurt (ed.), *Romania and World War II*, Iaşi: The Center for Romanian Studies, 1996.

Troncotă, Cristian, *Glorie şi tragedie. Momente din istoria Serviciilor de informaţii şi contrainformaţii române pe Frontul de Est (1941–1944)*, Bucharest: Nemira, 2003.

Udrea, Traian, *23 August 1944. Controverse Istorico-Politice*, Bucharest: Editura Alex-Alex, 2004.

Vago, Bela, *The Shadow of the Swastika. The Rise of Fascism and Antisemitism in the Danube Basin, 1936–1939*, London: Saxon House for the Institute of Jewish Affairs, 1975.

van Meurs, Wim *The Bessarabian Question in Communist Historiography*. East European Monographs. Distributed by Columbia University Press, New York, 1994.

Verenca, Olivian, *Administraţia civilă română în Transnistria 1941–1944*, ed. Şerban Alexianu, Bucharest: Editura Vremea, 2000.

Völkl, Ekkehard, *Der Westbanat 1941–1944. Die Deutsche, Die Ungarische und andere Volksgruppen*, Munich,1991.

Völkl, Ekkehard, *Transnistrien und Odessa (1941–1944)*, Schriftenreihe des Osteuropainstituts Regensburg-Passau, vol. 14, Regensburg, 1996.

Waldeck, R. G., *Athene Palace*, with an introduction by Ernest H. Latham, Jr., Iaşi, Oxford and Portland: The Center for Romanian Studies, 1998.

Watts, Larry, *Romanian Cassandra. Ion Antonescu and the Struggle for Reform, 1916–1941*, Boulder: East European Monographs, 1993.

De Weck, René, *Jurnal. Jurnalul unui diplomat elveţian în România: 1939–1945*, ed. Viorel Grecu and Claudia Chinezu, Bucharest: Editura Fundaţiei Culturale Române, 2000.

West, Nigel, *MI6. British Secret Intelligence Operations, 1909–45*, London: Weidenfeld and Nicolson, 1983.

Wilkinson, Peter, Astley, Joan Bright, *Gubbins and SOE*, London: Pen and Sword, 1997.

Contributions to books

Ancuţa, Călin-Radu, 'Die deutsch- rumänischen Wirtschaftsbeziehungen während der Kriegsjahre 1940–1944', *Modernisierung auf Raten in Rumänien. Anspruch, Umsetyung, Wirkung*, ed. Krista Zach and Cornelius R. Zach, Munich: IKGS Verlag, 2004, pp. 333–70.

Angrick, Andrej, 'Die Einsatzgruppe D', *Die Einsatzgruppen in der besetzten Sowjetunion 1941/42*, ed. Peter Klein, Gedenk-und Bildungsstatte Haus der Wansee-Konferenz, Berlin: Hentrich, 1997, pp. 88–110.

Benjamin, Lya, 'Bazele doctrinare ale antisemitismului antonescian', *România şi Transnistria: Problema Holocaustului*, ed. Viorel Achim and Constantin Iordachi, Bucharest: Curtea veche, 2004, pp. 237–51.

Deletant, Dennis, 'Transnistria 1942: A Memoir of George Tomaziu. An Eyewitness Account of the Shooting of a Column of Jews near the Rov River in 1942', *Romania: A Crossroads of Europe*, ed. Kurt Treptow, Iaşi: The Center for Romanian Studies, 2002, pp. 231–44.

Dobrincu, Dorin, 'Legionarii şi guvernarea Ion Antonescu (1941–1944)', *Romania: A Crossroads of Europe*, ed. Kurt W. Treptow, Iaşi, Oxford and Portland: The Center for Romanian Studies, 2002, pp. 199–230.

Hausleitner, Mariana, 'De la românizarea Bucovinei la Holocaust, 1918–1944', *România şi Transnistria: Problema Holocaustului*, ed. Viorel Achim and Constantin Iordachi, Bucharest: Curtea veche, 2004, pp. 127–44.

Heinen, Armin, 'Ethnische Säuberung. Rumänien, der Holocaust und die Regierung Antonescu' in *Rumänien im Brennpunkt. Sprache und Politik, Identität und Ideologie im Wandel*, ed. Krista Zach, Munich: Südostdeutsches Kulturwerk, 1998.

Iordachi, Constantin, 'Problema Holocaustului în România şi Transnistria–Dezbateri istoriografice', *România şi Transnistria: Problema Holocaustului*, ed. Viorel Achim and Constantin Iordachi, Bucharest: Curtea veche, 2004, pp. 23–77.

Neumann, Victor, 'Evreii din Banat şi Transilvania de Sud în anii celui de-al doilea război mondial', *România şi Transnistria: Problema Holocaustului*, ed. Viorel Achim and Constantin Iordachi, Bucharest: Curtea veche, 2004, pp. 145–61.

Ofer, Dalia, 'The Holocaust in Transnistria. A Special Case of Genocide', *The Holocaust in the Soviet Union. Studies and Sources on the Destruction of the Jews in the Nazi-Occupied Territories of the USSR, 1941–1945*, ed. Lucian Dobroszycki and Jeffrey S. Gurock, New York and London: M. E. Sharpe, 1993.

Pearton, Maurice, 'Puzzles about Percentages', *Occasional Papers in Romanian Studies*, ed. Debnnis Deletant, no. 1, 1995, pp. 7–13.

Pearton, Maurice, 'British Policy Towards Romania: 1939–1941', Dennis Deletant and Maurice Pearton, *Romania Observed*, Bucharest: Editura Enciclopedică, 1998.

Pearton, Maurice,'British Intelligence in Romania, 1938–1941', *Romanian and British Historians on the Contemporary History of Romania*, ed. George Cipăianu and Virgiliu Ţârău, Cluj-Napoca: Cluj-Napoca University Press, 2000.

Shafir, Michael, 'Marshal Antonescu's Postcommunist Rehabilitation: *Cui Bono?*', *The Destruction of Romanian and Ukrainian Jews during the Antonescu Era*, ed. Randolph L. Braham, New York: Columbia University Press, 1997, pp. 349–410.

Shafir, Michael, 'Memory, Memorials, and Membership: Romanian Utilitarian Anti-Semitism and Marshal Antonescu', *Romania since 1989. Politics, Economics and Society*, ed. Henry F. Carey, Lanham, MD: Lexington Books, 2004, pp. 67–96.

Shapiro, Paul A., 'The Jews of Chişinău (Kishinev): Romanian Reoccupation, Ghettoization, Deportation', in *The Destruction of Romanian and Ukrainian Jews during the Antonescu Era*, ed. Randolph L. Braham, New York: The Rosenthal Institute for Holocaust Studies, City University of New York, Columbia University Press, 1997, pp. 135–94.

Traşcă, Ottmar, 'Relaţiile româno-germane şi chestiunea evreiască: august 1940–iunie 1941, *România şi Transnistria: Problema Holocaustului*, ed. Viorel Achim and Constantin Iordachi, Bucharest: Curtea veche, 2004, pp. 252–328.

Vago, Bela, 'The Ambiguity of Collaborationism: The Center of the Jews in Romania (1942–1944), *Patterns of Jewish Leadership in Nazi Europe, 1933–1945: Proceedings of the Third Yad Vashem International Historical Conference, Jerusalem, 4–7 April 1977*, ed. Yisrael Gutman and Cynthia J. Haft, Jerusalem, 1979, pp. 287–309.

van Meurs, Wim P., 'Romanian Expansion beyond the Dniester', *Romania and World War II. România şi cel de-al doilea război mondial*, ed. Kurt W. Treptow, Iaşi: The Centre for Romanian Studies, 1996, pp. 139–52.

Watts, Larry L., 'Incompatible Alliances: Small States of Central Europe during World War II', *Romania and World War II*, ed. Kurt Treptow, Iaşi: The Center for Romanian Studies, 1996.

Journal articles

Angrick, Andrej, 'The Escalation of German–Rumanian Anti-Jewish Policy after the Attack on the Soviet Union', *Yad Vashem Studies*, vol. 26 (1998), pp. 203–38.

Câmpeanu, Pavel, 'Pe marginea unei recenzii. Mistere şi pseudo-mistere din istoria PCR', *22*, no. 34 (23–30 August 1995), p. 12.

Cioroianu, Adrian, 'Antonescu între Hitler şi . . . Ceauşescu', *Dosarele Istoriei*, no. 6 (2002), pp. 55–60.

Deletant, Dennis, 'The Molotov–Ribbentrop Pact and its Consequences for Bessarabia: Some Considerations on the Human Rights Implications', *Revue Roumaine d'Histoire*, vol. XXX, nos 3–4 (1991), pp. 221–2.

Deletant, Dennis, 'Ghetto experience in Golta, Transnistria, 1942–1944', *Holocaust and Genocide Studies*, vol. 18, no. 1 (Spring 2004), pp. 1–26.

Dennis Deletant, 'Memoriul unor intelectuali români, înaintat la Palat, în vara 1942', *Sfera Politicii*, no. 107 (2004), pp. 49–53.

Ionniţiu, Mircea, '23 August 1944. Amintiri şi reflecţiuni', *Revista istorică*, vol. 2, nos 9–10 (1991), pp. 557–75.

Maner, H-C.,'Zeitgeschichte Rumäniens als Politikum. Eine Studie über die rumänische Literatur zum 23. August 1944', *Südosteuropa*, 41, no. 6 (1992), pp. 388–412.

Martini, A., 'La S.Sede e gli ebrei della Romania durante la seconda Guerra mondiale', *Civilta cattolica*, vol. 112, no. 3 (1961), pp. 449–63.

Michelson, Paul E., 'In Search of the 20th Century: Marshal Antonescu and Romanian History – A Review Essay', *Romanian Civilization*, vol. III, no. 2 (Fall–Winter 1994), pp. 72–103.

Pearton, Maurice, 'British Policy towards Romania 1931–1941', *Anuarul Institutului de Istorie 'A. D. Xenopol'*, vol. 23, no. 2 (1986), pp. 527–52.

Papacostea, Şerban, 'Captive Clio: Romanian Historiography under Communist Rule', *European History Quarterly*, vol. 26 (1996), pp. 203–6.

Pavlowitch, K. Stevan, 'Yugoslavia and Rumania, 1941', *Journal of Central European Affairs*, vol. 23, no. 4 (January 1964), pp. 451–72.

Pelin, Mihai, 'Misiune în România', *Almanah Flacăra* (1986), p. 297.

Presseisen, Ernst L., 'Prelude to Barbarossa': Germany and the Balkans, 1940–1941', *Journal of Modern History*, vol. 32 (March–December 1960), pp. 359–70.

Secaşiu, Claudiu, 'Regele Mihai şi executarea Mareşalului Antonescu. Adevăr şi Legendă', *Cotidianul. Supliment Cultural* (8 July 1991), p. 5.

Memoirs

Sebastian, Mihail, *Journal. 1935–1944*, transl. Patrick Camiller; Introduction and notes Radu Ioanid, Chicago: Ivan R. Dee in association with the United States Holocaust Memorial Museum, 2000.

Unpublished papers

Latham Jr., Ernest H., 'Signs of Human Feeling and Attitude: The American Legation and American Jews in Romania in 1941', paper presented at a symposium on US–Romanian Relations at the Department of Contemporary History, 'Babeş-Bolyai' University, Cluj-Napoca, June 2001.

Index